# BORIS YELTSIN
## THE DECADE THAT SHOOK THE WORLD

BORIS MINAEV

Glagoslav Publications

# BORIS YELTSIN
## THE DECADE THAT SHOOK THE WORLD

by Boris Minaev

Translated by Svetlana Payne

© 2014, Boris Minaev

Published with support of
The Foundation of the First Russian President B.N.Yeltsin

© 2015, Glagoslav Publications, United Kingdom

Glagoslav Publications Ltd
88-90 Hatton Garden
EC1N 8PN London
United Kingdom

www.glagoslav.com

Published with support of The Foundation
of the First Russian President B.N.Yeltsin

ISBN: 978-1-78437-922-3

This book is in copyright. No part of this publication may be reproduced, stored in a retrieval system or transmitted in any form or by any means without the prior permission in writing of the publisher, nor be otherwise circulated in any form of binding or cover other than that in which it is published without a similar condition, including this condition, being imposed on the subsequent purchaser.

# CONTENTS

Author's Foreword . . . . . . . . . . . . . . . . . . . . . . . . . . . . . . . . . . . . . . . . . . . 5
The Early Years (1930-1980) . . . . . . . . . . . . . . . . . . . . . . . . . . . . . . . . . 6
Dear Mikhail Sergeyevich… (1985-1987) . . . . . . . . . . . . . . . . . . . . . 46
Exoneration (1988) . . . . . . . . . . . . . . . . . . . . . . . . . . . . . . . . . . . . . . . 97
The Last Utopia . . . . . . . . . . . . . . . . . . . . . . . . . . . . . . . . . . . . . . . . 127
Project 'Russia' (1990) . . . . . . . . . . . . . . . . . . . . . . . . . . . . . . . . . . . 164
Details of a Skirmish (January to August 1991) . . . . . . . . . . . . . . . 191
The Lion Gets Ready to Spring (1992) . . . . . . . . . . . . . . . . . . . . . . 262
Ten Blanks (1993) . . . . . . . . . . . . . . . . . . . . . . . . . . . . . . . . . . . . . . 291
'We Believe in You…' (1994) . . . . . . . . . . . . . . . . . . . . . . . . . . . . . . 321
Journey into the Whirlwind (1995) . . . . . . . . . . . . . . . . . . . . . . . . . 343
'With Him, We Feel Safe' (January-July of 1996) . . . . . . . . . . . . . . 377
The Second Term (1996-1999) . . . . . . . . . . . . . . . . . . . . . . . . . . . 439
Six Peaceful Years . . . . . . . . . . . . . . . . . . . . . . . . . . . . . . . . . . . . . . 515
Epilogue . . . . . . . . . . . . . . . . . . . . . . . . . . . . . . . . . . . . . . . . . . . . . 520

Photographs . . . . . . . . . . . . . . . . . . . . . . . . . . . . . . . . . . . . . . . . . . 525
Timeline of Boris Nikolayevich Yeltsin's Life . . . . . . . . . . . . . . . . . . 565
Bibliography . . . . . . . . . . . . . . . . . . . . . . . . . . . . . . . . . . . . . . . . . . 567

# Author's Foreword

The literature on Yeltsin is vast. Memoirs have been produced not only by politicians — first-hand participants in the events, Yeltsin himself penned three volumes of recollections — but also assistants, press secretaries, political analysts, journalists, MPs, retired members of Gorbachev's Politburo, public figures now long forgotten, generals of special services and security service staff. I started working on Boris Yeltsin's biography when he was still alive. I hoped he would read my manuscript but I did not make it in time. In my work I have used not only publicly accessible documents that have been printed or made otherwise accessible but also interviews that are published for the first time. I have received huge help and support from my friends, my journalist colleagues and Boris Yeltsin's family, particularly the series of interviews with his wife Naina and daughter Tatiana, for which I am deeply grateful.

8 December 2008

# The Early Years
# (1930-1980)

There is no question of a direct legacy of religious traditions in the Yeltsin family, even though Yeltsin's grandfather, Ignaty, had been a parishioner, along with everybody else in his neighbourhood, of a regular Orthodox church, the one in which Boris Yeltsin was later baptised. It is more a question of inheritance received indirectly, as a persistent theme in Russian life.

Yeltsin's family tree had one particular characteristic, however — his forefathers *had never been serfs*. Or to be more precise, they were never *manorial property*, and had never been owned by any individual. In the Urals, including the areas that the Yeltsins had come from originally, peasants had been mostly *state-owned*, which means they did have a master but it was not a lord of the manor but a clerk. The clerk's responsibilities included collecting taxes or dues to the state, in the form of peasant labour. Another important characteristic was that such peasants had an option of buying their manumission and they could do so of their own free will.

At the same time this world had its own periphery, too: husbandmen, labourers and craftsmen. All of this was completely interdependent, guided by its own internal unwritten laws, and — most importantly — by a shared destiny, a common existence from which it was inconceivable and impossible to escape.

However, a state-owned peasant existed outside this self-contained world. He was, of course, also expected, on seeing a landowner, to bow and take his hat off but with him it was different: he did not believe passionately in the sacred nature of the established order of things, he was simply doing what was required. He was independent but equally he couldn't rely on anybody else, only himself. His immediate owner, the state, was too far away.

The history of Yeltsin's family is a graphic example of how the Soviet era dealt with those who were independent by nature and inclined to rely not on the 'society', and thus swim in the allotted stream, but to be self-reliant. Both of Yeltsin's grandfathers — Ignaty Yeltsin, on his father Nicolai's side, and Vasily Starygin, the father of Klavdia Starygina, his mother — were middle-ranking peasants in the Urals. Their farms would have been relatively substantial. The collectivisation in the 30s was designed to target just such farmsteads.

Ignaty Yeltsin, along with his four sons owned a mill. Ignaty's sons modernised the tiny village mill and increased its capacity with additional millstones bringing their number to a total of seven. Each son had a horse as well as some cows, sheep and other livestock. At harvest time, the Yeltsins were hiring additional help in the village.

Vasily Yegorovich Starygin, Yeltsin's other grandfather, was a skilled wood worker, a carpenter and a cabinet-maker. He built houses, in the traditional Russian fashion. His wife, Afanasia Starygina, was the best-known dress-maker in the village that was sewing clothes for the entire neighbourhood.

However, back in the thirties, Vasily Starygin wasn't as wealthy as Ignaty Yeltsin. His sin before the Soviet power lay elsewhere; when building houses, he would hire seasonal workers and thus, according to Marx, Engels and Lenin, he was an exploiter.

Both grandfathers had to pay the price after 1930.

Cattle, the mill and the threshing machine — all this was confiscated, taxes charged and paid in arrears and Grandfather Ignaty was deported to Nadezhdinsk (now Serov) in the north of the Urals. The 'new people' who had had a hand in their *dekulakisation** would later go round sporting their confiscated clothes. The chairman of the village Soviet lived in their house. And what were the charges? It was being owners of the mill that had been servicing the entire village!'

---

* The Soviet campaign of repressions, including arrests, deportations, executions and property confiscation of millions of the better-off peasants and their families in 1929-1932.

In the summer, the dispossessed Yeltsin brothers, who had stayed on in the family home in Basmanovo, were forced to repair the machinery that previously had been theirs: the mill and the thresher, although now it all belonged to the *kolkhoz("collective farm")*.

Ignaty and his wife Anna lived in a dug-out hut, on short commons, in Nadezhdinsk for Ignaty no longer could work at the lumber-mill; he had been stripped of all his worldly possessions and started losing his eyesight. At 61 years of age, former miller Ignaty Yeltsin, Boris Yeltsin's grandfather, died — defeated, blind and exhausted. The year was 1936 and his grandson was five years old.

Meanwhile, two of Ignaty's sons, brothers Nicolai and Andrian Yeltsin, came to realise that for them, branded with the anathema of having been dispossessed as *kulaks*, there was no life in Basmanovo, at least not in the nearest future with no way of providing for their families. In 1932, both brothers, having obtained the permission from the chairman of the *kolkhoz*, left for a construction project in Kazan

It was the *Aviastroi* — a huge aircraft plant that would become the pride of the Tatar capital city and the flagship of its industry. It would be the first to manufacture military aircraft and the famous Tupolev jetliners, TU-104. At this point, however, *Aviastroi* was just a huge greenfield site, a construction pit teeming with workers' wheeling barrows and where they lived in ramshackle huts.

Construction, however, spelled rescue, being at the same time both hard labour, as ever in Russia, and their only solution. All through the 20th century, the territory of the former Russian Empire had been a scene of transmigration with the titanic shuffling around of huge and diverse groups of the population. Even in the more humane years of the Khrushchev era, when the long-awaited exonerations suddenly became a reality and crowds of released convicts headed homewards from the camps, even then huge numbers of people would move from their native towns and cities to Kazakhstan, to develop the 'virgin lands' of *tselina*. Later millions would move to the construction sites of BAM (the Baikal-Amour Railway Thoroughfare), to Tiumen, to Urengoi and other *Komsomol (Young Communist League)*-sponsored construction projects mushrooming across the country with every year. Those people would populate out-of-the-way places and develop them, some motivated by high patriotic sentiments, some by the promise of rich pickings whilst others because they had been ordered, convinced, forced or indoctrinated.

The construction of a formidable superpower was underway. However, be it the later time of the 'thaw' or the ostensibly quiet, almost lethargic epoch of the BAM railway project and the Olympic teddy bear mascot, this superpower could never do without dugout huts, the shacks, the train carriages used for habitation in the tundra, without the horrendous daily life of the migrants, without the life on scant food rations and unrelenting work, without innumerable people frost-bitten and crippled, without diseases and generally without widespread sacrifice.

It had always been thus, even in the earlier years when the residents of entire villages would be forced into railway wagons, barely fit for carrying humans, by the progressively-minded Stolypin* (under Stalin those very carriages would be carrying millions of convicts) and sent to 'vacant' territories. Then came the revolution, the civil war, and the people were uprooted yet again and would flee, resettle, head away — this became a way of life. After 1917 hundreds of thousands of armed folk would roam the countryside, involved in mutual extermination; millions of Russians escaped from the civil war to Europe; the remaining millions would go on to build Stalin's plants and factories, to produce timber and procure ore, to 'forge victory' in the WWII — only to die from scurvy or starve to death.

Against this background, the escape of Nicolai and Andrian to the construction project in Kazan was only one of many stories, of which there were scores and hundreds across the country. The entire country was one torrent of enforced migration. While at Aviastroi, the family was struck with yet another misfortune. Nicolai and Andrian were arrested on a tip-off from an informer. They had been brought in for questioning to the local OGPU**.

---

* Pyotr Arkadyevich Stolypin (1862-1911) served as Prime Minister. His tenure was marked by efforts to counter revolutionary groups and by the implementation of noteworthy agrarian reforms.

** Joint State Political Directorate was the security service of the Russian Soviet Federative Socialist Republic (RSFSR) and the Soviet Union from 1922 until 1934, formed from the Cheka, the original Russian state security organization. Its first chief was the Cheka's former chairman, Felix Dzerzhinsky.

With regard to the charges, the interrogation records mention a Nicolai Otletayev, a carpenter, whose evidence provided the whole basis for the case. Otletayev testified that during the working hours Nicolai Yeltsin 'forbade the workers to read newspapers' and complained of the poor quality of the food.

A hunger riot at a Stalinist construction site was even more dangerous than a political one. People raised on the peasants' work ethic could, in principle, survive on rations of lean soups, or soups cooked from rancid meat but the cost of such soup was deducted from their hard-earned wages so it was a very sensitive issue; hence the situation that the brothers found themselves in.

It is hard to discover what saved the brothers. Most likely, the investigating officers were rushed and bored of dealing with those 'country yokels'. Equally possible was a quota that dictated the transfer of a certain number of workers to a different construction site. The result was that they were sentenced to three years in the camps.

Nicolai served his time at the construction of the Moscow-Volga canal (another project of the century*, another case of epic importance). He was released seven months ahead of time for exemplary work performance. How his wife, Klavdia Yeltsina survived during that time, her young son in tow, was a separate story. She would never have managed on her own — with no work or accommodation. She did try to find employment as a seamstress, she went even for petty jobs, but as an alien peasant from the Urals, and a wife of the 'enemy of the people', her chances were nil. There was no home for her to return to — her father, Vasily Starygin, along with his entire family, had been living by then in the sub-Polar Urals, sent into a distant exile. True, he had managed to build a house there and survived — unlike his in-law; Vasily Starygin died eventually in 1968, in Butka**. Klavdia was saved by pure chance. While in prison, Nicolai Yeltsin had met a doctor Petrov, a native of Kazan, who took pity on the toddler

---

\* Clichéd political and newspaper jargon of the day.

\*\* Butka is situated several kilometres away from Basmanovo. Both villages were part of the same collective farm but the 'maternity hospital', that is to say, the village hospital, was in Butka. That is why many biographies call Butka the 'native' village of the Yeltsins. In reality, Yeltsin's father bought a house in Butka, in Korotky Projezd Street, when already retired, in the 1960s.

and his Mum. For two years, Klavdia and the young Boris lived as part of the family of the political convict, Dr Petrov.

In 1937, Nicolai returned from Kazan. Soon after the arrival of their second son, Misha, Nicolai and Klavdia, along with the children, moved to Berezniki in the Perm Oblast, the place where Nicolai's brothers worked. They wanted to reunite the family. There, Nicolai Yeltsin took part in the third great construction project of his life, a huge chemical plant under construction in Berezniki, where he finally found a reasonably stable position: firstly as a carpenter, then as a foreman. Their mother Anna, Boris's grandmother, also joined them from Serov where she had buried her husband. She lived in the family of Nicolai's eldest brother, Ivan, and died five years later, at the beginning of the Second World War. In Berezniki the horrendous and senseless deprivation of the Yeltsins during the thirties finally came to an end.

Boris Yeltsin, the eldest son, started school. For the next six years the family lived in a hutment, although they did have running water — albeit outside. Despite the fact that in winter they all slept cheek by jowl to stay warm; the walls were no more than thin partitions; that long communal corridors were always full of other people; that this human anthill was everywhere; that life boiled down to survival and a hand-to-mouth existence — nevertheless, here, in Berezniki, a new, more optimistic note first sounded. The children were growing up, they were like everybody else, not deportees, not disenfranchised, and even a humble household of sorts started taking shape. Yeltsin's fate was undeniably shaped by the terrible years, the era of hutments — dark, murky times when life itself was hanging by a slender thread. And the lasting legacy from this era was the Yeltsins' will to survive.

'My father,' writes Yeltsin in his President's Journal, 'never spoke to me about his arrest and imprisonment. Talking about it was forbidden in our family.'

In his later interviews Yeltsin would say the following about his father:

'He had never been close to the Communists, and had never been one himself. This was reflected in his conviction that Communism was the wrong path for Russia. Generally, it was not the done thing in our family to discuss the Soviet regime and Communism and when we did we spoke very reservedly.'

Even so, Boris Yeltsin was a Soviet man, the product of the fifties and sixties, when his personality was formed. The Yeltsins were not anti-Soviet but neither were they Soviet. The mindset of the family was that of the ordinary Russian people the very group who would set the scene for the deepest rifts of the nineties.

The first detailed account of his father's arrest only appears in the book, President's Journal of 1994. In response to questions to Naina Yeltsin on whether Boris Yeltsin ever spoke about it with her, or the daughters, or in the intimate family circle she replied, 'No, he said nothing. Boris Nikolayevich only found out the full details of his father's arrest in 1992, when he was already President of Russia. The case file was delivered to him from the KGB (then called the FSK), it was all there — his father's denunciation, the interrogation protocol, the sentence, and so on. Before then he had known nothing — only that his father had worked on a building site in Kazan, then on Moscow-Volga canal, and that was it... It seems that Nicolai Ignatievich had strictly forbidden his mother to mention any of this to the children. Otherwise, Boris would have had to state this in the application form for the university or when joining the Party. His father foresaw it, which is why he did things this way..... He didn't want to impede his son's future career.....He was ashamed of having been a zek*'?

The town of Berezniki, where Boris Yeltsin spent his childhood (from 1937 to 1948), was far from a 'god-forsaken corner', and hardly a mere settlement as often alleged. Berezniki had enormous factories the most notable the chemical plant producing potassium, and could hardly be called a 'backwater'. The Yeltsins lived in the workers' barracks, a roughly built wooden communal structure, on the outskirts of Berezniki from 1938 until 1943 when the state gave a room** in an apartment block. By 1944, when their third child Valentina was born, he had already built his own house. 'The house by the pond' is how it is referred to by the family until today. By this time undoubtedly, these people belonged to the Soviet 'middle' class.

---

* A colloquial acronym from the Russian word *zakliuchenny* — an inmate, a convict or a prisoner.

** Accommodation was provided only by the state.

## THE EARLY YEARS (1930-1980)

Boris Yeltsin was a kind, hard-working and an excellent pupil, the head boy of his school form. Never the less, in his own memoirs Yeltsin remembers, 'we used to engage in punch-ups — district against a district. Some sixty or a hundred people, with sticks, clubs or just bare fists would join in the fight. I always took part in those scuffles, although I did get my share of thumpings.

Then again: 'It was wartime, all our lads were striving to be at the front but we were, naturally, not allowed. We were making pistols, rifles, even cannons. We decided to get hold of some hand grenades and take them apart so as to work out what was inside. I undertook to slip inside a church that was used as an ammunitions depot. At night, I crawled underneath three rows of barbed wire and while the sentry was on the other side of the building, sawed through the bars of the window grate, grabbed two RGD-33 grenades and... made my way out. We went some 60 km away, into the forest, and decided to disassemble the grenades. I did have the good sense to convince my pals to get at least a hundred metres away. I squatted on my haunches, put the grenade on a stone and went at it with a hammer. As for the fuse — I didn't know it existed, so I never took it out. Boom... and my fingers were gone. On my way back to the city I kept losing consciousness. In the hospital they asked my father's consent, then they removed those fingers and next time I showed up in school I was sporting a white bandage on my hand.'

After another episode exploring one of the rivers across the taiga Yeltsin became very ill with typhoid and consequently missed a critical part of his schooling. Rather than retaking the year he studies on his own and, with some difficulty, secured himself a permit to sit the exams without attending classes and managed not to waste a year.

Yeltsin also fell afoul of one of his teachers when he complained about the brutal and unfair treatment on behalf of his class. The teacher would force the children to run their housekeeping errands, in a practice not uncommon in rural Russia, in a traditional set-up which entitled a provincial teacher to some recompense from the students — after all, the teacher laboured for them too: marking their work, securing a different, better future which Yeltsin would have none of. The denouement of this story was that the school Teachers' Council issued him, in lieu of the matriculation certificate, with a so-called wolf ticket* (thus, pre-empting Gorbachev's Politburo**). However, Boris went off to the Municipal Party Committee to retaliate. The teacher was punished, Boris became reinstated and successfully finished his secondary education. Even then, he knew where to turn. He already worked out the mechanics of the system, the design of the corridors of power.

Yeltsin passed his entrance exams and became a student of the Urals Polytechnic. At the Polytechnic, Yeltsin lived in the halls of residence, in a room shared with seven other students. Having spent his childhood in the workers' barracks, for him these conditions were nothing new. Then there was Komsomol***. Like everybody else, he attended meetings, votes and elections but avoided 'politics'. That said, he rapidly advanced to the forefront of everyone's attention, practically in the course of just one term. 'He never sought to be high profile, it just happened,' says Naina Yeltsin.

Sports form a major constituent in the Soviet university curriculum, and soon Yeltsin participated in a range of sporting events in his department: cross-country runs, skiing and swimming competitions, relay races and, especially, volleyball. At first he was rejected by the volleyball club — after all, he was missing two fingers on his left hand. But he practised fanatically and in the end made his way into his year's team, then the team of his department and, eventually, the team of the Urals Polytechnic to become a noted player in the institute.

With his team he toured in the Baltic republics****, the Volga region, Moscow, Leningrad, Georgia and Azerbaijan. There were national competitions, training camps, matches — even after graduation he still played and trained for a whole year representing the local club Lokomotive.

---

* A colloquial expression to denote a version of a document with restrictive clauses in comparison to the full document. Figuratively, the term remains in use in many of the countries of the former communist bloc usually to denote any kind of document that negatively affects one's career.

** Political Bureau, the top executive body of the entire Communist Party and its Central Committee.

*** *Komsomol* — the acronym for the Young Communist League, an organisation uniting young people from the age of 14 to 28 and mandatory for career advancement.

**** Countries known today as the Baltic States formed three republics within the Soviet Union: Lithuania, Latvia and Estonia.

## THE EARLY YEARS (1930-1980)

One of the reasons volleyball became so important was that it was in the programme of the Olympic Games and in 1952 the USSR joined the movement.

Playing volleyball at the national level provided a certain degree of freedom even in the Soviet Union and it was an important feature in Yeltsin's student life. One could travel extensively, live by special rules and be exempt from the general regime. These trips always followed the same routine; off the train — into a hotel — over to the sports hall — back to the hotel. Naturally, there was never time to look around and understand how all those towns and cities lived. Never the less, these short forays would whet his appetite for real travel.

True, one had to pay for this with back breaking work when preparing for sessions and exams, when getting credits for technical subjects. One had to be not only bright but to do some plain old-fashioned cramming. Yeltsin did admit himself that his student years taught him how to survive on only four hours of sleep and, what's even more remarkable, helped him develop a special memorising technique, a photographic memory with total recall enabling him to commit entire pages to memory. This quality would prove very useful in his future life.

'Before I started my studies in the institute I had never really seen my country, hardly ever been anywhere. That is why I decided to set off on this trip during the summer holidays… Without a kopeck in my pocket, a minimum of clothes, in plimsolls, a shirt and a straw hat — that was my exotic attire when I was leaving Sverdlovsk…I was travelling mostly on the carriage roof, sometimes in the tiny vestibule of the carriage, sometimes on the footboard, sometimes by lorry. I was, of course, more than once detained by militia: where, they would ask, are you off to? I would say something like, "to Simferopol, to visit my granny". "And in which street does she live?" I knew that in each city there must have been a Lenin Street…'

'I sent letters from each new city to my mates at the institute. My route ended up taking in Sverdlovsk–Kazan–Moscow–Leningrad–back to Moscow–Minsk–Kiev–Zaporozhe–Simferopol–Yevpatoria–Yalta–Novorossiysk–Sochi–Sukhumi–Batumi–Rostov-upon-Don–Volgograd–Saratov–Kuibyshev–Zlatoust–Chelyabinsk–Sverdlovsk.'

The country had just thrown off the yoke of the war. Along the way he met all sorts of people including ex-zeks who were also travelling on the roofs of railway carriages as well as the soldiers and evacuees who travelled inside. Along the way were towns and cities, semi-starved but already bustling as people were coming back and striving to restore their way of life; all over there were construction sites, coal pits, workers' barracks and shanty living quarters.

What were the late forties and early fifties like? It was the time of combating cosmopolitism* and the launch of the 'cold war'. It was not yet entirely clear whether peace would last; the newspapers were full of alarming news: a crisis in the Middle East, a conflict in Korea, tests of nuclear weapons, numerous empires crumbling. It was the time of food still rationed, of endless queues and the monetary reform of 1947. People's clothes — viewed with today's eyes — were those of paupers and beggars: men in badly patched trousers and jackets, women in home-made dresses produced from the most basic fabrics. It was a piece of very good luck to lay hands on some cloth brought back from the West as war trophies.

In his first year at the institute he had to go through yet another ordeal: a very serious bout of tonsillitis. As per usual, he was too impatient to recover completely and so abandoned the regime of 'rest and keeping to his bed'. He plunged full tilt into his volleyball training and ended up in hospital with complications involving his heart. This was a first incident and proved to be an omen of what was to happen to his heart in future. He was forced to take a year out and thus, Naina, who had been in the year below, became his contemporary.

Anastasia Guirina — Naina — came from Orenburg with her family, where her father worked on the railways, having moved there from their native village of Titovka in the Sharlyksky District of the Orenburg Oblast. Some evenings she would go to a dance, invited by cadets from the pilots' college resident in town. 'Cosmonaut Number One' Yuri Gagarin was amongst them and Naina remembers his face.

Then again, books in those days were hard to come by, the waiting lists in the libraries were huge. But the thirst for reading was so strong that

---

* One of the last ideological witch-hunting campaigns unleashed by Stalin. Under the pretext of combating 'rootless cosmopolites' and enhancing the loyalty to Russia, the campaign very quickly took on a flagrantly anti-Semitic character and led to yet another round of persecutions and arrests.

sometimes a favourite book would be carefully dissected into 'portions' — so as not to wait for too long — and then Naina and her classmates would read it in bits passing their portions from hand to hand (the school was for girls only, boys studied separately after their fifth year). That was how, for instance, the entire class read *The Count of Monte Christo*. When they were finished with it, they simply sewed the book back together again and returned it to the library.

The relationship with Boris started as a friendship. What were they talking about? Certainly, not love. 'Yes', says he in his own memoires, 'the relations were nothing more than a friendship to start with'. Yet once they did kiss in front of the door leading into the assembly hall, before the beginning of some student party. The kiss was modest and naive but it did open a new page. Gradually, he came to realise that he couldn't live without those meetings and this relationship, and that this quiet and considerate girl had become an essential part of his life. As for her, any type of relationship that was not *lofty* was a complete taboo. She was not tempted by student marriages and, 'Yes, we did say that we should get married but I don't think either of us believed it ….. when at the end of the fifth year we both got our degrees and he insisted that we should get married, I answered that I wasn't sure. I did not want to get married at such a young age. After graduation he stayed in Sverdlovsk and I left for Orenburg. We decided to wait a year and then meet again to see if our feelings remained strong enough. Of course we were writing letters to each other, I still keep a pile of his, whereas I did not write back all too frequently, I just did not like writing'.

'Then, a year later, I suddenly receive this telegram from Kuibyshev from our mutual friend Seryozha Palgov saying: "Come urgently, Borya's heart's acting up". Well, this gave me a fright, I rushed down to Kuibyshev. I arrived at his hotel on the banks of the Volga and was standing their wondering, 'How is he? Where is he? Is he in the hotel or in a hospital? And suddenly there he was! He was walking out of the hotel door and heading towards her. He was, plainly, in very good health and in good spirits, a smile on his face. I was not put out by this devious ploy, simply overjoyed'.

A month later he came over to Orenburg to ask for her hand in marriage.

How significant were those years in the Urals Polytechnic in the department of industrial and civil construction, what was it like? The earliest impression to shape the views of that generation was the country around them lay in ruins. 'Many our senior students were seconded to the west of the country', continues Naina , 'to the Ukraine, Byelorussia and the western Russian oblasts: there was nothing but devastation over there, things had to be built up from scratch. Our friends would work for various construction projects and help develop designs for new districts and new facilities, and then return to Sverdlovsk. We had not been given those assignments just yet but we knew that it was always on the cards.'

Generally speaking, an institute (or, for that matter, a university or any establishment for higher education) had many implications in the Soviet life, especially in the fifties and sixties. Unlike analogous institutions in the West, or in contemporary Russia, it assimilated a huge mass of very disparate people. Confident city kids rubbed shoulders with those who came from remote villages in the sticks. Children of party functionaries, members of the *CheKa**, favourites of fortune and the elite of the time studied alongside the offspring of former political prisoners and social outcasts; austere war veterans alongside bright young things; young boys wet behind the ears alongside those who came from the *rabfak* (**) who'd been around the block a couple of times and came through a school of hard knocks either in the army, at some industrial works or in the militia.

It was a formidable social melting pot that wore off sharp edges, blurred distinctions, and removed superstitions inherent in one's family, class, ethnic group or estate, forced people into working out one shared language of the generation.

Graduates of the Soviet higher educational establishments had access to huge and evolving industrial resources. Thus, in a laboratory, especially if it worked for defence, the graduates dealt with the most advanced technologies and provided worthy competition for R&D developments from elsewhere in the world. And finally, as managers and foremen, these

---

\* *CheKa* (Russian acronym) — the Extraordinary Commission, internal security service, precursor of the KGB.

\*\* *Rabfak* — *Rabochy fakultet*, a special unit enlisting those who came to a university from factories and farms. It acted as a kind of a buffer zone before its contingent could catch up on missing knowledge and join the normal classes.

## THE EARLY YEARS (1930-1980)

students could end up working at some major industrial facilities or design and construct plants and installations on a huge scale, managing thousands and tens of thousands of people. This was the route the young graduate Yeltsin took.

It was these people that ensured gigantic post-war progress in all spheres. It was a nascent class of the new intelligentsia, the backbone of the new country that rapidly covered the distance from extreme poverty to meteoric and brilliant careers all over Russia.

For example, the *Virgin Land Project* of the Khrushchev's era covered the vast expanse of the Kazakh and Altai steppes to be ploughed and cultivated for the production of grain. Yet the term could easily be applied to the entire country which itself was like a virgin land. It could also be used to describe its industry and science.

Yeltsin chose as his sphere of professional interest a sector that proved to be a particularly apt example of the emerging times. In the conditions of rapid progress in the post-war USSR, construction was a sector of permanent growth. The country was being rebuilt at a phenomenal rate across the board. Already under Stalin they started erecting in Moscow edifices that later came to be known as *high rises* and *Stalin Buildings* (the project was completed after Stalin's demise). They were an outstanding architectural achievement at the time, even if the contemporaries considered them ugly and 'superfluous' and the fashion turned to concrete and glass. From the fifties and through to the seventies, Moscow lived in the conditions of a permanent construction boom that spread to the residential and cultural sectors alike. The most prominent and best-known projects in 1950s-1970s were the sporting complex in Luzhniki, Young Pioneer's Palace in the Sparrow Hills, cinema houses *Rossiya* and *October*, the Olympic Stadium, the hotel *Rossiya*, the building of the USSR Telegraphic Agency (TASS) in Nikitsky Gate square, the new building of the Moscow Art Theatre, a new residential district of the Olympic village, the Moscow Palace of Youth and many more. These, however, are only milestones from Moscow alone. They only demonstrate the scope of the entire phenomenon: a mass-scale construction that permeated all areas of people's lives.

Despite being somewhat unprepossessing to look at, all these buildings of that era typified for a long time a kind of Moscow's signature image and it is impossible to imagine the city without them. 'Stalin's' style (turrets, towers, columns and lavish façades) would be reinstated in Moscow concurrently with the 'Luzhkov's baroque' when skyscrapers and luxury, yet again, became fashionable. However, Yeltsin came into the construction industry when building designs tolerated nothing apart from the austere rectangular stumps.

At the same time practically everything had to be built anew! Huge facilities for plants and factories, intricate power stations, institutes and libraries, schools and kindergartens, stadiums, community centres ( called Palaces of Culture), shops, residential blocks, animal production units, garages, bridges, roads and so on. The 'glass and concrete' architecture may be cursed *ad nauseam* today, tumbledown and derelict, it does look obsolete and depressing. Having said all this, it is impossible to overestimate the social significance of that construction boom. In effect, the construction sites were a visual illustration of the processes underway in the country at the time.

And of course the issue of accommodation — the notorious Khrushchev's slums — five-storey housing blocks referred to by professionals as Lagutenko houses after the name of the project's chief designer. The houses were (and still are) amazingly cheap to build — with their flimsy partitions and crammed individual flats. Endless quarters of these white-and-grey boxes were being erected everywhere and at a very rapid rate. These were houses for a new life, the life without squabbles in a communal kitchen or the savage camaraderie of the workers' huts: the one enormous barrack that was life under Stalin. Now ever family had its privacy. These were the houses that Yeltsin had to build and these industrial premises and houses would become his professional life. The houses would soon be improved, altered, they would have more stories and a somewhat better interior planning, yet the essence remained unchanged: these were mass-scale residence blocks, the scale multiplied by millions of square metres.

After they were married the Yeltsins moved to Sverdlovsk, however Naina decided to give birth to their elder daughter, Lena, over in Berezniki where she moved in with her mother-in-law for a month to learn from her various maternal skills. All in all, this route between Sverdlovsk and Berezniki became an integral part of their family life. The young parents were working, with Boris Yeltsin, at first, virtually living on his site.

## THE EARLY YEARS (1930-1980)

Work on the construction sites were dire years when he could find himself a foreman to a team of convicts. It is often said that, at first, he refused to work as a foreman and, instead, mastered within the space of one year a range of worker's professions: from a bricklayer to the crane operator. However, an entry in your employment records to the effect that you have been employed as 'working class' — for at least three months or half a year — was a huge plus in those years: it improved your chances of making it into university or becoming a Communist Party member. Professional classes were on a waiting list that could last years, while industrial workers were accepted right away. However, in Yeltsin's case it not a stratagem for improving career chances. At this point, however, Yeltsin had no interest in politics.

However, it did prove to be an invaluable experience for a future top manager was this acquired understanding of a construction project as a whole wherein each detail, each cubic metre and each stage of works were interlinked. 'To know the essence of work in a way that is not inferior but better than that of your subordinates.' This was his creed and he adhered to it all his life.

The familiarisation with all aspects of construction enabled him to confront one of the more pernicious scandals of this sector of the Soviet economy. 'Falsification of worksheets' especially presentation of accounting documents for non-existent outputs was endemic. 'When I started taking precise measurements of the brickwork,' Yeltsin goes on to say in his *Confessions*, 'how much concrete had been utilised, how much of this or of that, things got tough', as he collided with the system.

'One morning, soon after yet another facility had been certified as completed, Yeltsin discovered that neither the workforce nor the equipment were in place,' says Yeltsin's American biographer Leon Aron in his book. 'It transpired that the superintendant sent them over to build a garage for a manager of the united construction enterprises. It was standard practice at the Soviet construction projects that materials and workers would be permanently used for the personal needs of their bosses. Consequently the employees were stunned when an irate Yeltsin pitched up on the spot allocated for the future garage and ordered them to return to their official work site.'

Yet gradually he prevailed but the reality of a Soviet construction site was creating resistance at every step of his career. One such example of him dealing with this was in dealing with the embezzlement of materials needed for decorating new flats. He inaugurated a scheme whereby those who would live in the newly-built flats would be invited to visit. Thus, for the first time ever, the workers had to deal with live people face to face and to meet the actual people who would have to move into these skeleton apartments. He also gave impromptu incentives to those who made key contributions to a project by making a gift of the 'watch off his hand' to those of his subordinates who had distinguished themselves which became a feature of his personal style

Houses often had to be completed by the 7th of November, the anniversary of the Revolution, or the 1st of January (New Year). If a house had not been completed by this target date the allocations to the new projects would be cut down as a trade-off. A case like this would be a catastrophe, a production emergency. Yeltsin became adept at convincing managers of various plants to provide the full allocation of workers therby preventing the 'all hands on deck' last minute desperate efforts to meet the deadline.

At the age of twenty-nine, only four years after he came to work in the industry as a foreman, Yeltsin was appointed the chief engineer in the huge Construction Administration (called SU-13) where he was manger of thousands of people.

Apart from his natural inclination to keep his distance from subordinates and bosses alike, Yeltsin always displayed this uncommon, impressive and overarching ability to perform. Today he would be called a workaholic. Work wasn't just a job for him, it was his life. He was a natural 'lark'\*, he rose early. He would leave home on foot at six in the morning (in those days, they lived in the Chemical Plant District on the outskirts of Sverdlovsk). He calculated personally that the distance to work was 12 km and it took him two hours to get there, covering those kilometres in big strides. This was physically demanding in its own right. He would start his working day at eight, sometimes seven. 'To go to his work by public transport meant changing buses in the centre, travelling in an overcrowded bus for an hour and a half or even two hours. Boris

---

\* Russians divide people into 'larks' — early risers and 'owls' — people who get up late and are more productive in the evening.

preferred walking,' Naina explains. His subordinates were often irritated by his incredible punctuality. Just as he could not stand the 'books being cooked' or accounts falsified, he was completely intolerant of people being late. If an employee was late for the morning briefing by one minute, he or she was not admitted.

Yet even those who made it there in time were equally agitated when waiting for their turn for a conversation with him. Yeltsin was completely averse to turgid explanations. Never raising his voice, never resorting to obscenities and never using the familiar '*ty*' in address, he would simply cut ramblings with a stern: 'Get to the point!'

Yeltsin never used obscene language. In Russia, there is practically not a single person, at least male, who would not resort to such ornaments in their speech. Besides, Yeltsin grew up in a very humble peasant family in the Urals — in the town of Berezniki, home to a huge chemical plant where convict labour is almost a fixture. And convicts are people who would not only use expletives but make them their *lingua franca*.

Moreover, in the later years of Yeltsin's life, when this peculiarity of his was known sufficiently widely, his colleagues would stop using offensive words in his presence. All this might be easier to understand if Yeltsin himself had been a soft-spoken and invariably tactful person with a reluctance to hurt people's sensibilities. Far from it! Practically at all the posts he occupied in his lifetime, in dealing with his subordinates he could be brusque, sometimes extremely harsh, and even inclined to hectoring. His daughter Tatiana recollects, 'Dad could speak very politely but his politeness was SUCH that sometimes it could plunge people into something like a catatonic state'.

Whilst this could have been a way simply of disconcerting people, a rather different explanation has been suggested by Timothy Colton in his biography of Yeltsin. Yeltsin was born in the Urals. It is perfectly possible that the ancestors of Yeltsin's family, like those of many other residents of the Urals and Siberia, could have been 'adherents to the Old Catechism', or to put it in Russian, 'Old Believers' or *starovers* *.

---

* Adherents to the Old Catechism during the schism in the Russian Orthodox Church following the liturgical reforms of Patriarch Nikon in the second half of XVII century. They were persecuted and many fled to remote places (Siberia, and further east) to set up their own communes and continue their traditional way of life.

Ever since the religious schism in the XVII century they have been considered heretics, and as punishment for heresy had been sent into exile to the Urals and beyond. The Old Believers never smoked. Nor did Yeltsin — he couldn't stand the smell of tobacco — and most of his subordinates were also non-smokers. Old-Believers never used foul language, generally adhered to puritanical morals, especially in their family lives and were zealous workers rather like Yeltsin, in his best years — he would be driving his subordinates into the ground with his work schedule, his exacting standards and his durability. Ironically, in this phase of his career, Yeltsin was surrounded by old believers, 'Old Believers' in the ossified Soviet system, the Communist faith, which ultimately would prove to be his ultimate challenge.

In the day to day things, other habits that Yeltsin never countenanced were undue familiarity, sloppy appearances, that is the absence of a jacket and tie and the telephoning of subordinates at home. He was perfectly aware that they should let be, at least when off work.

Many of 'tabloid-style' biographies assert that it was the construction sphere with its incessant emergencies that first made Yeltsin, an athletic young man who continued practising volleyball even during his first year of employment, turn to the bottle. It would not be surprising in those harsh circumstances. But this is not true.

Yeltsin first started taking part in the long dreary formal parties only when he came to work for the Party *Obkom* — and there, it was a must. 'Those who make these assertions simply do not understand what a construction site is really like,' confirms Naina Iosifovna. 'In all 14 years that he worked on the site, Boris Nikolayevich never drank with his staff — neither before, nor during working time, not even when a facility got the certificate of completion.'

And it is true that overcoming emergencies or exigencies, setting records for which he was renown would have been impossible had he backtracked by as much as an inch from his own rules.

A further most important trait of Yeltsin's style was fearlessness in terms of making enemies. It is not so courageous to be a demanding hardliner with those who report to you (although any manager will confirm that this, too, requires courage). It is much more dangerous to keep your integrity when dealing with your bosses. Anyone who has had this experience will confirm that people united in power can always reach an agreement behind the back of a stroppy newcomer and then strike from the rear.

When Boris Nikolayevich worked for the SU-13 that belonged to the regional construction trust *Yuzhgorstroi*\* his boss was called Sitnikov. He was an experienced specialist and had a temper as strong and uncompromising as Yeltsin's. B.N.'s methods incensed him, so altercations were frequent. In the space of only one year Sitnikov gave him a couple of dozen official reprimands and warnings. Yet when Sitnikov left Yeltsin got a promotion — on the recommendation of none other than Sitnikov himself!

Yet Yeltsin was putting himself on the line much more dangerously when arguing with Party bodies. On a demand from the First Secretary of the *Raikom*\*\* that Yeltsin should present himself at the meeting of the *Raikom* Bureau, Yeltsin did not show up. He refused once and for all to attend meetings at the *Raikom*.

When Yeltsin was first appointed the DSK (integrated house-building factory) top manager, a newly-built five-storey building collapsed in Sverdlovsk. Yeltsin himself had taken no part in that project, he had not been appointed yet but it fell to him to bear responsibility for the accident. The Bureau of the Sverdlovsk *Gorkom* moved for Yeltsin's expulsion from the Party but that was when the Second Secretary Ryabov got involved and vouched for the young specialist. Yeltsin got off with a severe reprimand.

As Ryabov says himself in his memoirs, 'I gave birth to Yeltsin five times' — referring to Yeltsin's transfer to Moscow in 1985 to be appointed head of the construction department in the CPSU Central Committee. It was also Ryabov who recommended Yeltsin for the post of the DSK boss, and also invited him to work for the *Obkom* — first as the section head and then the Construction Secretary, and finally, advocated promoting Yeltsin to the First Secretary of the *Obkom* after Ryabov himself was transferred from Sverdlovsk to Moscow.

It goes without saying that in his generation Yeltsin was not unique. There appeared an entire cohort of young 'chief engineers' who were, up to a

---

\* Southern Municipal House-Building Trust.

\*\* District Party Committee.

point, the product of Kosygin's economic reforms. Unlike those at the top of the production sector in the forties or fifties, they did not grovel in front of the *Gorkom*, *Raikom* or *Obkom* because they were not so totally dependent. Industry and manufacturing were viewed by those young specialists not as an integral part of the 'Party activities' but the sphere of their personal responsibility and calling. The times called such people forward, and then buried them by dissolving them in Brezhnev's system of power.

Yeltsin's American biographer T.J. Colton says, 'He used to express himself briefly and categorically. To indicate that a speech was rambling or irritating, he would just raise an eyebrow or slide a pencil between his fingers and start drumming on his desk. If the source of irritation persisted he would deliberately break the pencil into two. According to a Sverdlovsk physician, there was a special ward in Hospital No 2 kept vacant on the days of the *Obkom* sessions — in case, following the scathing proceedings, some of the *Obkom* members would 'be taken poorly'.

Yeltsin grew up in the era when a leader or a boss could only operate by constantly resorting to damning criticism, yelling, swearing and verbose speeches. The reverse side of this style was a so-called 'heart-to-heart' conversation or the moment of truth when the boss would open-heartedly appeal to the people for help. Yeltsin's style excluded both. All he required was that the work should be done well and on time and he perceived everybody only as professionals. The concept of *work* in Russia includes an entire stratum of human relations, subtle, unobtrusive and even invisible. The 'boss-subordinate' axis is forever compounded by the whole range of factors: attraction and revulsion, traditions and rites, family ties and connections. In short, 'work' comprises an entire world wherein a person does not just earn his livelihood but lives and expresses him- or herself in all sorts of ways, including love and friendship. That is why Yeltsin's uncompromising, single-minded approach was at first given a hostile reception.

The rank-and-file workers might put in pitiable performances, drink, even steal, just generally can't be bothered and ignore the work ethic — but when the time is right, if the boss asks them from the bottom of his heart, they can work miracles. Their sheer work heroism will be second to none. This is the norm. It is not stipulated or recorded anywhere, not in fiction, not in the CPSU Programme, not in the employment contract. But everyone is aware that this is how things are done.

The boss may be exceptionally highly placed and beyond reach of common workers as far as the production hierarchy goes. They depend on him lock, stock and barrel. Yet, according to those unwritten rules, he turns out to be dependent on them as well. Or to be more precise, not on them as such but on this collective public opinion formed around him: vertically and horizontally. He may talk about meeting targets and the work discipline but the subordinates know that what is of real importance is the role played by this person within this entire hierarchy, this comprehensive system of reciprocal obligations and ties. What is really important is how this person can justify this credit of confidence.

Non-transparency is at the basis of this Russian world. One thing is said and another meant. The main things are never mentioned. Everybody understands everybody else without having to even finish the sentence. Everyone is aware what is 'right' and what is 'wrong'; moreover, everybody knows it not from books or accounting documents. Any deviation from those norms gets punished. It entails what used to be called in those days 'operational consequences' — this precarious balance, this unstable stability. It was in this world that Yeltsin was operating and encountering resistance.

After Yeltsin was appointed the chief engineer of the SU-13 he assembled senior managers and instructed them to prepare the financial report: what resources they had available, what salaries were being paid, what was the cost of power and materials. Somebody said defiantly, 'But we are builders, not some goddamn book-keepers!' However, eventually, they had no choice become immersed in the labyrinths of the 'socialist accounting' and to see how things really were. This 'transparency campaign' continued also in the DSK.

In 1963 Yeltsin left the SU-13 having worked there for two years, and in 1966 he became head of the DSK. In the space between these two events, in 1964, Khrushchev was demoted at the October plenary session of the CC CPSU. The night before the session in question Brezhnev had summoned the KGB Head Semichastny, and bluntly asked 'How are you going to ensure my security?' Semichastny was as blunt. 'What do you mean?' he asked. 'Can you place some submachine gunners in the entrance to my house so that I could get some sleep?' replied Brezhnev.

After Khrushchev, the country ended up with three 'leaders': the General Secretary of the Communist Party of the Soviet Union (CPSU) Leonid Brezhnev, the Chairman of the Council of Ministers Alexey Kosygin and the Chairman of the USSR Supreme Council, Nikolay Podgorny. It was clear that Brezhnev was the most influential but rank-and-file Party members could only guess how much independence he enjoyed within this *'troika* structure'. The quiet taciturn Kosygin appealed to many: an industrialist, a renowned plant director, an intelligent and self-contained man. People liked the idea of being led by him, they had confidence in his economic reforms. However, Brezhnev managed, between 1966 and 1968, to stealthily fold up the programme of reform and remove from power those who had at least a theoretical claim to it. In 1968 he sent the Soviet tanks to Czechoslovakia. The country would start feeling the full weight of Brezhnev's autocracy several years hence.

In 1972, Yeltsin's father suffered a severe stroke. He eventually died in 1977. Father's illness and death hit Yeltsin hard. In 1965, when Nikolay Yeltsin retired they had bought a house in Butka, the same village where Boris was born. The Yeltsins returned to their native place. From now on, till the very end of their school years, Lena and Tanya would spend all their summer vacations at their grandparents', in the country. The parents would visit them regularly: Naina would come for the weekends by train, or sometimes they would come down together with Boris in his car to which he was entitled by his post. On vacations they visited Bulgaria and Romania a couple of times but spent most free time in their favourite Kislovodsk. For all the variety, their vacations did have some fixtures: Lena and Tanya would set off to Butka, and the Yeltsins would set one vacation week aside for rafting down the Chusovaya River. It didn't work out every summer but the tradition survived for many years, "We would hire a flat-bottomed boat from the sports centre, go down by day, then stop for the night and build a fire. We once had an *Obkom* agricultural secretary with us. So he brought along, just imagine, a cage full of live chickens! Of course, I never took part in the slaughtering and plucking of those poor things, but for several evenings I was making the Tsars' *Oukha*\* with chicken meat!". The only

---

\* A fish soup which becomes 'Tsars" when cooked on the basis of several changes of stock — starting with the tiny fish one eventually adds the more valuable fish.

## THE EARLY YEARS (1930-1980)

time when they went down a different river, the Belaya, they were delivered to the starting point not by a car but by helicopter.

During this period, Yeltsin was either the chief engineer or the head of the DSK. They lived in a two-room flat*. On one occasion he was very ill, so a colleague came along to have him sign some documents. Yeltsin was playing with the girls and when the lady entered the room she saw that he was sitting with them under the table. 'I will never forget the expression on her face', says Naina. "She was simply stupefied. This... over there... is Boris Nikolayevich?" — was all she ever managed to utter.'

From time to time his health would play up. There was the first heart attack in 1968, an acute otitis in 1973, a stomach ulcer in 1980 — in short, there were reasons for concern although, on the whole, his strong body was coping successfully. There were no worries about 'harmful habits' — but then again, why should there be? Boris Nikolayevich was always convivial at parties, sparkling with good humour and laughter. At the same time he could not stand drunkenness, no one ever saw him 'worse for wear', according to Naina, he never even 'smelt of alcohol'.

In 1960, the Second Secretary of the Sverdlovsk *Gorkom*, Fyodor Morshchakov, had talked Yeltsin into joining the Communist Party. In 1968, Yakov Ryabov offered him a post in the *Obkom*. He would spend nearly eight years working for the Sverdlovsk CPSU *Obkom* as head of the Construction Section and later as Secretary in charge of Construction (1968-1976). Then, for about nine years (1976-1984) he was the *Obkom* First Secretary, the chief of the oblast, and then followed the 'Gorbachev period', with its ups and downs (1985-1991), and subsequently, for eight and a half years he was the first president of a completely new country, the Russian Federation (1991-1999) and for seven years Pensioner Number One (2000-2007).

Very little is known about the initial *Obkom* period and according to some sources, Yeltsin found it hard: the ex-chief engineer, head of SU-13 and DSK, he realised he wasn't used to subordination whereas bosses here abounded and he ended up in the heavy shadow of well heeled, thick-set

---

* In the Soviet Union, like in Russia today, one counts ALL rooms in a flat, not just bedrooms.

Party boyars from the old days, first Konstantin Nikolayev and then Yakov Ryabov.

During those years he was receiving repeated offers: to move to Moscow and work within the Construction Committee (*Gosstroi*) administration; to become the Second Secretary of the Kostroma *Obkom*. He was reluctant to move but every time would seek Ryabov's advice on the issue and the latter would invariably tell him: do not rush.

Once in *Obkom*, Yeltsin found himself in a completely new framework, with a new level of responsibility with a new level of targets — a link in the huge and comprehensive system that was managing the entire country. Coming to terms with it and learning its workings took years. Working for the SU-13 and the DSK Yeltsin was building houses, even the whole districts of five-storey houses; social and cultural facilities — schools, shops, laundrettes; he was building industrial and manufacturing faculties. However, when he became 'head of section' within *Obkom* he came face to face with the actual scope of the Soviet construction and the Soviet economy.

The Sverdlovsk Oblast was a veritable industrial giant. It covers the area that equals four fifths of Great Britain and exceeds many erstwhile republics in terms of the territory and the size of its population. Within its confines, there were 740 plants and factories. Most of those moved to the oblast during the Second World War, and some stayed on afterwards. The Mid- Urals were producing steel — millions of tonnes of it; pipes, carriages; it gave the country its coal, ore and machine tools; but most importantly — it produced tanks, nuclear warheads, engines for the military equipment; it was enriching uranium and even manufacturing biological weapons.

The sheer size of the defence industry can be illustrated by the fact that (quoted by Yegor Gaidar in his book *Collapse of an Empire*) by the time Gorbachev ushered in his *perestroika*, the USSR had three times as many tanks as the armies of the US and Western Europe put together. And production was still growing...

It was here in the Urals that major production facilities were situated: in Nizhny Tagil at the Ural Carriage-Building Plant, at the Chelyabinsk Tractor Plant and in Sverdlovsk. All these enormous facilities were needed for defence although they did manufacture some civilian goods as well. The iron ore mines, non-ferrous and chemical plants and rolling mills — all were constantly improved, enlarged and expanded while new and new factories were being built in the Sverdlovsk Oblast. Construction and refurbishments were financed by the central ministries but implementation was performed by the workers of the Urals. It was Yeltsin's duty in his role of the chief supervisor to manage this gigantic industrial conglomerate invisible to the rest of the world since the oblast was closed to visits by foreigners.

Naturally, he had nothing to do with the financing side of things and was not responsible for the projects. Yet the final responsibility was his. Having come in contact with the construction site of such enormous proportions Yeltsin felt confused: he had never experienced anything so absurd at his previous posts.

In his days as SU-13 chief engineer or head of the DSK he insisted that his subordinates should understand accounting, whilst keeping a close eye on salaries and the performance targets, not to mention accounting for the cost of power and building materials. A foreman or a supervisor was accountable for the most fragile ceramic item. Yet here, on the national projects, trainloads of timber, tonnes of iron and concrete, millions of roubles would simply disappear, just sink without trace. The director of one Sverdlovsk joint construction administration would 'lend' to another manager, such as the head of a defence plant, an entire trainload of cement — a high-deficit commodity — and the latter could just as easily never give it back. Telegrams to the ministry, appeals to the Central Committee were no use. The debtor was brought to justice only after the *Obkom, by this time* Yeltsin, became involved. He just could not grasp how can you legally steal a trainload of cement! The scope of industrial construction dwarfed all those 'planned' losses.

Engineering projects and industrial construction were 'absorbing' billions of national expenditure, that is, they were forever increasing their output, launching more and more new facilities and installations — in order to increase output even further. It was a boundless process without any meaningful confines, with no terminus or transit stations, and without any thought given to the dynamics of development.

Evidently, Yeltsin was aware of where the money for these formidable investments was coming from: it was exactly then that the gigantic new oil fields were first developed in Western Siberia, and the Sverdlovsk *Obkom* was responsible for putting in new 'strands' of oil and gas pipelines which enabled the rivers of gold to ebb away, depleting the country's reserves of natural resources.

Yet this colossus baffled belief for it was directed not from some central point of planning but by its own elemental laws of extensive development: to produce more and more steel, more and more tanks, more and more enriched uranium, chemical and machine-tools, build new and new plants.

And for what purpose?

Anyone, especially a trained civil engineer with the attendant mindset, would have been flummoxed by the image that this Soviet industrial tornado thus revealed. Yet baffling were not only its dimensions but the contents, too. Now he had access to all relevant information and was working with all the enterprises in the Sverdlovsk Oblast and all ministries involved in production and manufacture within it, he could be absolutely positive: *this country was preparing itself for war.*

There was no other intelligent explanation for this frantic manufacture of tanks, missiles, bombs and war planes. No explanation of 'peaceful deterrence' seemed adequate. Yet this discovery was running counter to the official propaganda and the daily rhetoric in the newspapers. No one was telling the Soviet people that they should ready themselves for war. On the contrary, all official efforts of the Soviet leaders were aimed at the achievement of lasting peace; the word 'peace' had a key presence in the official doctrine.

Moreover, the very people who built those tanks and engines, made steel for tanks and engines, filled warheads with enriched uranium often lived in very demanding conditions. Up until mid-seventies, the Ural Mechanical Engineering Plant (*Uralmash*) was encircled by an entire quarter consisting of workers' barracks dating from pre-war times, flimsy sheds built of planks, draughty, designed around a so-called 'corridor system' — one long corridor being flanked with rooms, toilets at both ends. More often than not, one kitchen and one toilet would be shared by tens of families, or at times even this was too much to ask for — the 'conveniences' were outside.

The people who manufactured the most sophisticated tanks and filled them with most advanced devices, produced the steel, the carriages and lorries were spending their time after work queuing for soap and detergent, to say nothing about meat and butter. Their clothes were shabby and sometimes they really had to go without most essential things.

As an engineer, Yeltsin was perfectly aware of how long these people would have to wait till they got their individual flats. He knew something else he couldn't avoid knowing in those years: the Soviet power was economising on its population — their quality of life, its light industry, culture and medicine — but where defence was concerned, no cost was too high. Huge means were spent or even wasted on the heavy industry and engineering.

Why?

Such preparations for war were indeed flawed. To be more specific, they were preparations for the previous war. It was a fiction, a bluff needed for justifying those investments, for ensuring that this huge mechanism was self-perpetuating. War served as a silent symbol, a substantiation of the extravagant money-losing giant of an economy.

The scale of Soviet construction sites with foundation trenches stretching to the horizon, causeways several kilometres long, cranes rising to the sky line, fleets of lorries as long as a convoy of tanks with the human anthill consistently reforming and reshaping vacuous voids was stupendous. Never the less, a factory shop or plant on a brownfield could easily be left to rot for years. When building an apartment block the workers would economise on toilets and bricks, but they would use tonnes of timber or equipment and never give a thought to whether it was justified. This was the essence of the process of socialist chaos. It was as powerful as the market forces that Yeltsin had to come to grips when he eventually moved to Moscow. Yeltsin dedicated an entire stage of his life, the first eight years in the *Obkom*, to studies of its principal mechanism, its power transmission, the language used for managing all these chaotically planned processes. The name for this mechanism was simple — 'Party work'.

The role of transmission was performed by the 'Party apparatus': Party meetings, Party Committees, District Committees, conferences and assemblies held to approve reports and elect new officials, meetings of the Oblast Committee bureau and its plenary sessions, and, finally, the Central

Committee. The language was the language of the Party functionaries. Of course Yeltsin was a Soviet person and a boss into the bargain, and all those nuances, in theory, were an open book to him. Yet it was one thing to know, but another to speak like this himself. To master the remarkable mechanics of the Party speak, to learn how to express yourself in formulae and phrases that to us, today, feel not just incomprehensible but even unpronounceable.

Yet in those days nothing whatsoever took place without this language, those Party hieroglyphics. The entire mystery of life fitted within this set of coded signs. As a person used to getting right to the point in his speech and thoughts, Yeltsin found it rather difficult to master this new language.

The most rigid protocol prevails with unswerving attention to every detail and procedural rule: a separate room for Politburo members, the order of procession to the stage, assignment of seats in strict correspondence to a place in the hierarchy. Viktor Maniukhin, the former First Secretary of the Sverdlovsk Party *Gorkom*, appointed in early 80s the deputy speaker of Russian Supreme Soviet, recalls:

'Tradition dictated that a representative of the Communist Party was seated on the left from the Chairman at the first presidium table, and members of the Politburo and ministers were in their assigned seats behind. The Chairman and we, his deputies, would get together backstage, in the presidium quarters, and a somewhat bigger room next door was used by the Politburo members. There was a big oval table there onto which drinks, mineral water and fruit were served. At precisely two minutes to ten our Chairman would appear on the doorstep of this neighbouring room and invite the Politburo members to take their seats and the session would start its work. According to the accepted protocol all the Politbureau members (in those days headed by the General Secretary Leonid Brezhnev) would enter our room and shake hands with all deputies. The procession was headed by Leonid Brezhnev, followed by Mikhail Suslov\*, Andrei Kirilenko\*\*, Andrei Gromyko and others. When Leonid Illich stepped

---

\* Mikhail Andreyevich Suslov (1902-1982), a Soviet statesman. He served as a de-facto Second Secretary of the CPSU from 1965 and was the chief ideologist of the Party until his death in 1982.

\*\* Andrei Pavlovich Kirilenko (1906-1990), a Soviet statesman.

back and let the others through I was shaking hands all round but felt all the time somebody's heavy stare. I looked round and realised that it was Brezhnev: his gaze was direct and unblinking, and from time to time he would make a smacking sound with his lips. He was said to have a little suction irrigator in his mouth for moisturising his throat. Well, I thought, here we go, a scrutiny like this does not promise anything nice. But nothing happened to my relief.'

'After this the Chairman, followed by his deputies, would climb the steps, take their seats and only then would the Politburo appear in the presidium. The audience would rise and applaud. When it first happened we thought that the audience applauded us, the deputies, but then we looked round and joined the ovation. We directed it somewhat aside. I happened to be just over a metre away from Brezhnev's chair. Since Brezhnev spoke in a loud, tuneless bass I was often an involuntary eavesdropper to his exchanges with Kosygin. They would chat about all sorts of things: from the price for a *Moskvich* car and its petrol to the national production of meat'. Maniukhin recalled that Brezhnev and Kosygin were chatting about totally mundane things and used the perfectly normal language understandable for everyone.

Then Leonid Brezhnev would take the floor:

'Our Party does its utmost for strengthening the Communist movement in the entire world. We have always been proceeding from the premise that the current international situation, escalation of the class struggle in the global arena are insistently calling for mobilisation of all reserves available to anti-imperialist revolutionary forces. It is thus clear that only the Communist movement is called upon to speak out in favour of uniting efforts of all revolutionary fighters, all supporters of peace, national independence, democracy and socialism' (Brezhnev, Leonid, *The Speech at the XX Party Conference of the Leningrad Oblast*, 16 February 1968). Not a single word there is used by chance or is superfluous. The arena is always global, the forces — anti-imperialist and the movement is that of Communism.

Of course speeches have the right to exist: official ones, ceremonial ones, those to mark an occasion. Of course there was the in-house Party vernacular. But one was inseparable from the other. These very rigid formulae and set phrases, the gobbledegook of the Party documents amounted to the protoplasm of the mechanics of power, its principal mystery successfully mastered by Yeltsin, the young *Obkom* member.

'Present-day problems', 'progressive experience', 'Communist movement of workers', 'escalation of the class struggle at the current stage', and most especially — 'the role played by Leonid Illich' in all of this. It must not simply be at the tip of one's tongue but become an integral part of your existence and your mentality, whether asleep or awake. However, committing it all to memory was not enough. He who does not know how to write and then make such a speech is worthless here. He who cannot dissect the profound speaker's *message*, his *principled stand* from the flow of adjectives and nouns should just not bother. The pomp, ritualistic nature and perpetuity of sacred symbols and gestures made up the basis for this 'zombification' through which this caste kept the country in check.

His teacher of this tricky political science was Ryabov who had singled out the young engineer as far back as in the *Gorkom* days. But Yeltsin himself, now the young *Obkom* member, was striving to grasp the essence of this political art — the art of exerting political will. Even so, Yeltsin somehow managed to preserve his own individual way of expression which was important to his future.

It was Ryabov's promotion that played an important role in Yeltsin's destiny following a chain of events: the USSR Defence Minister Grechko died to be replaced by Dmitry Ustinov, who had been the head of the Soviet defence industry since the Second World war. After that Ryabov, the former First Secretary of Sverdlovsk, was promoted to be a Secretary of the Central Committee of the Communist Party of the Soviet Union (CC CPSU), probably, as a counterbalance to the omnipotent Ustinov — Brezhnev did not like strong personalities in his immediate circle.

At the end of this chain, at Ryabov's prompting, Yeltsin became the First Secretary of the Sverdlovsk *Obkom* in 1976. There had been a more obvious candidate, Gennady Kolbin, a real *apparatchik*, but he had been sent to Georgia to try to manage the new ambitious head of the Georgian branch of the CPSU, Eduard Shevardnadze, who was making uncomfortable waves. However, the appointment still had to be justified in front of Brezhnev.

Ryabov recalled: 'I had a chat with Boris and explained how to behave.

The following day I introduced Yeltsin to Brezhnev; what followed was a normal constructive conversation. Brezhnev pointed out that I was recommending not the Second Secretary but him, a mere secretary. Although this did happen when selecting people for the Party work, still, it meant additional responsibility. Boris Nikolayevich thanked Leonid Illich, the Bureau and the Central Committee secretaries and promised to apply every effort to justify the trust thus vested in him. The date for the Oblast Committee's plenary session was also fixed there. On 2 November 1976 the plenary session of the CPSU *Obkom* elected Yeltsin the First Secretary.'

There were a number of long-standing problems in the oblast. The oblast experienced shortages of meat and he was working himself flat out to set up direct deliveries of chicken meat from the south of the country whilst also building a battery farm. Under him, municipal shops started offering even such delicacies as live fish — so *kolkhozes* urgently had to dig ponds for the production of this ridiculous trout.

The densely populated city, home to numerous plants, was experiencing chronic shortages of accommodation. Yeltsin created the 'youth construction movement': after work, men would be building houses for their families in the hope of getting a flat not in 10 or 15 years (the Soviet average) but in three or four years. The oblast had been waiting, for a long time, for the new premises for its celebrated musical theatre and Yeltsin built it. However, a new, intrinsically different *style* was soon to emerge in the First Secretary's *modus operandi*. It was the style that went straight over his patron Ryabov's head.

This style was revealed with full force in his very first speech as the *Obkom's* First Secretary. Yeltsin started with ritualistic pro forma pronouncements and, in his opening paragraphs, listed the Party's achievements. He went on to sing praises to the 'Leninist Central Committee' and 'personally to Leonid Illich' — only to veer over to a consistent, uncompromising and comprehensive analysis of problems, bottlenecks, failures and gaping holes in the society of 'developed socialism'*. He would do the same before a huge audience at the 26th CPSU Congress with the senior Party chiefs

---

* Brezhnev asserted that whilst the Soviet Union had not yet quite attained the stage of Communism yet, it was already at the level of developed socialism, thus having progressed in comparison to the early years of the Soviet power.

(Brezhnev, Suslov, Kirilenko) seated right behind him — he would do the same, with the same passion and even abandon. He would bring problems to the forefront of everyone's attention.

Insufficient iron ore production, poor figures of growth in the power industry, poor mechanisation, failure to meet production targets for consumer goods, sub-optimal efficiency of capital investments, extensive use of manual labour, and catastrophic shortages of accommodation. Workers' barracks and semi-basement dwellings were being removed far too slowly. Cities did not receive anything resembling the adequate supplies of meat, milk and eggs; cowsheds were in a hazardous state, new mechanised farms were rarely built whilst road construction in the country was in a deplorable state. Generally, it demonstrated the eternal Russian *inability to stick to a plan*, work efficiently and with good results.

The results counted. Yeltsin became a member of the CPSU Central Committee, and then a deputy to the USSR Supreme Soviet. He led the SPCU delegation to the Federal Republic of Germany.

Meanwhile, following a visit to his native Nizhny Tagil where he seems to have committed something of a faux pas in Party circles by referring to Brezhnev's ill-health, a closely guarded secret, Ryabov was moved, gently and gracefully, to a different position, aside and downwards: he became Deputy Chairman of the USSR *Gosplan*\*. According to the Soviet Party hierarchy of the time, this was a serious demotion.

Brezhnev's unique system was, as ever, operating smoothly. The General Secretary would personally telephone each First Secretary — be it at level of an *Obkom* or a republic, indeed every influential person in the country — to congratulate on all achievements and ask about all developments. He was aware of all personal matters — health and family, and of course was totally cognisant of what the 'VIPs' ever said about him personally. At the time, Brezhnev was heading fast towards complete senility, his brain was in a semi-ruined state, he was becoming visibly infirm, his speech was failing — in two years' time he would be dead. Yet the system he created was functioning without a glitch!

After the demotion of, the now *persona non grata*, Ryabov, he found himself without support in Moscow. His 'friendship' with another son of

---

\* The State Planning Committee, the senior body for all state planning.

Sverdlovsk, Politburo Member Kirilenko, was of little help: Kirilenko had been in the Kremlin far too long; he did not know Yeltsin well.

Yeltsin could talk as much as he pleased about workers' initiatives and transferrable red banners stationed in his oblast but in this new situation he had to choose a new strategy in the corridors of power.

As ever calmly and ritualistically, he bowed to Brezhnev in all his speeches and reports. In the early years he was always quoting Brezhnev in his speeches — but only three years later he instructed his aides to mention Brezhnev only at the beginning and at the end of a speech. Others, of course, mentioned him eight, eleven, thirteen times, dedicated verbose passages to dear comrade Brezhnev, and unearthed rare publications and little known facts from his biography. Yeltsin was amongst the first to realise that this era was gradually sinking into the past.

Gradually, step by step Yeltsin started channelling his mastery of the Party-speak in a different direction completely, carefully feeling his way. The first clear example was his 'potato speech' of 1978. Instead of doing the usual and distributing the quota among companies and enterprises, Yeltsin spoke on local TV and addressed his fellow Sverdlovsk residents directly, thus bypassing administrative levers. He was asking for help in harvesting vegetables and potatoes, he was reserved and quiet but very convincing*. Nearly 90,000 Sverdlovsk residents took heed and joined the 'potato battle', as Yeltsin later phrased it in his brochure, *The Middle Urals* — 'their hearts dictated their decision'. He wanted to address the people directly, bypassing Party Committees and the usual channels.

Naina always shopped for food herself, waited in queues, listening to how shoppers grumble about the lack of this or that product. Anything could become an item of deficit in the Soviet days —meat, milk, butter, detergent, cereals and even salt. It is perfectly possible that those complaints were voiced with particular feeling when she was around to bring the message home to her. On the question of whether she discussed of these messages with her husband she says:

'Of course we did. But I did see that he was working himself into the ground in his efforts to make people's lives better. Under him, supplies

---

* Standard Soviet practice of sending workforce from all institutes, plants and schools to help the failing Soviet agriculture with collecting the harvest.

improved somewhat: one could easily buy chicken, eggs, even live fish — they started up production of some trout from the ponds nearby... And then I heard those late night discussions when, for example, there would be only two days' worth of flour supplies remaining in the city and how he was extorting those supplies from the central agencies, urgently sorting things out. I was not surprised; everybody's life back then was hard.'

Yeltsin's salary at the time — that of the First Secretary of the *Obkom* — was six hundred roubles, and Naina Iosifovna, as a senior design engineer, was making around three hundred. This was quite a comfortable sum in the Soviet economy. Naina says they had no savings and spent the money like everybody else, on food, clothes and everyday items, and when something significant was needed, we would borrow.' They maintained they never bought deficit goods, as Naina puts it, 'I felt embarrassed, ashamed of laying my hands on *deficit* goods.'

On 18 December 1982 Yeltsin appeared again on local TV, this time to answer questions sent in by TV viewers. After the Sverdlovsk studio announced this epic event, about one thousand people wrote in. Yeltsin spent two hours and twenty minutes answering those written questions. Warming to his theme, Yeltsin continued his meeting with the Sverdlovsk residents — now without the camera crews. He entered into discussions with a mixture of teachers, journalists, students, school principals and workers. The more questions were submitted, the more passionate and the more heated the atmosphere in the auditorium became. His answers took the public aback with their honesty. He discovered in himself a gift for public speaking. But most importantly, he set the boundaries for the 'bitter truth' (his own expression) himself, without reference to the Central Committee. 'It was at this conference that I first heard the truth about the USSR. It could have been not the whole truth, maybe, just a small portion of it. But what I heard was a revelation,' Andrei Goriun, Sverdlovsk researcher of Yeltsin's life is recollecting his experiences.

When Yeltsin was to meet students at the Sverdlovsk Palace of Youth, post boxes were erected in prominent places in sixteen higher educational establishments, and for an entire month everybody could drop in a letter or a question. Yeltsin was inundated with questions and answered all of them. The meeting lasted for five hours. It was unprecedented.

When visiting a bauxite mine in the northern Urals, he was receiving packs of notes right there on the stage; people would simply hurl them from the audience. According to eyewitness accounts, Yeltsin grabbed those notes and rushed with them to the presidium, where the various company bosses were seated, to solve the problems. His answers during a session with Sverdlovsk school principals were a prime example of Yeltsin's style. He reads notes from the audience, 'The bank director refuses to allocate funds needed for construction and refurbishment works in my school'. He pauses. Back comes his answer, 'He is already busy allocating those funds. Talk to him after the meeting.' The district committee for catering refused to open a cafeteria in a small school because it was seen as extravagance. 'They are not opposed any more,' is Yeltsin's reply. His public pronouncements took everyone aback with their degree of openness.

Never the less, one couldn't hope that every family should have a separate flat by 1990. Rationing of food (meat and butter against ration cards) would continue. One kilogramme of meat per person — on festive occasions, that was all he could promise his audience, all that students could count on, just like everybody else in the Sverdlovsk Oblast.

He spoke about the latent inflation, 'Book prices are going up because there is an increase in the prices for paper, printing equipment and materials'. He revealed the classified instruction by the Central Committee and the Council of Ministers to suspend temporarily the construction of all cultural, sporting and administrative facilities if they had been less than half-completed. Naturally, such decisions were never published in a newspaper. All of this really meant just one thing: the country's economy was gradually succumbing to a crisis and the country was really tightening its belt. He was saying things that a Party leader was simply not allowed to mention to such an audience. His public answers to such questions meant he was taking risks, and quite major ones at that.

After Yeltsin paved the way, local bosses started putting in regular appearances on local TV to attend Q&A sessions. Yeltsin made them perform live on air. The programme was first called *Leaders Answering People's Questions* but later was renamed the more neutral, *Face to Face*.

When he was talking to people, he enjoyed the support of an entire team stationed backstage: aides, assistants, typists who typed up questions right away who were forwarding enquiries to local bodies, trying to get a response and solve the problem. This was not just populism; it was serious political action. Yet Yeltsin, when practising his style, was no stranger to dramatic effects. 'Is this true,' heckled a student in the audience, 'that you wear Italian-made shoes?' He edged forward from behind the stand and lifted his foot up to reveal 'Made by Sverdlovsk Shoe Factory!'

Yeltsin was a person to do things with a flourish. Or to be more precise, he had a knack for effective gestures but, like all Party bosses of the period, he still had to retreat into the carapace of ready-made definitions and protocol when necessary. Yet, first and foremost, he was a public politician probably, at this point, the only one in the country.

Yeltsin's neighbours, First Secretaries in the Perm, Tyumen and other oblasts, heard on the grapevine about Yeltsin's 'audiences' and registered their disapproval.

The Central Committee representative in charge of overseeing the Sverdlovsk Oblast was, however, turning a blind eye to what amounted, pure and simple, to sedition. After all, Yeltsin's authority was huge, both with the Central Committee and within his own oblast. A cautious inclination to 'look the other way' in response to his 'populism' (what if it all had been authorised?) also characterised the Party press. It goes without saying that *Pravda* did not run verbatim accounts of his many-hour-long meetings with the common people, instead it published short and snappy replies provided by comrade Yeltsin to 'letters from the working populace'. Then again, he himself hardly regarded those public meetings a break-through although this public approach would have a huge bearing on Yeltsin's future.

Of course, Yeltsin never was anything like opposition in disguise, nothing like Lech Wałęsa clad in the unswerving Party uniform — a suit. His main line of activity, just like that of any other First Secretary, was the duty to claw out allocations of supplies and resources for their oblasts, from Moscow and various central agencies. He had to ensure the allocation, to procure the august signature, 'to obtain a positive resolution for the issue'. Thus, for example, having received the infinite number of required approvals he finally managed to launch the Sverdlovsk metro project. He also managed to manipulate the system to solve the long standing problem of the run-down workers barracks so that all that was left of the erstwhile shanty towns was a distant memory.

In the late seventies the Party adopted its Food Programme. The Soviet state allocated considerable resources to 'giving a boost' to agriculture and

## THE EARLY YEARS (1930-1980)

finally setting up proper supplies of food to the country. With considerable administrative effort Yeltsin managed to divert some investments from the Central Non-Black Earth area* to his Middle Urals. The problem of food security was one of his principal scourges until the very end of his leadership in the oblast. He could occasionally wheedle tonnes of meat and butter for the November celebrations or the festivities on the May Day but this was nothing like a proper solution. His efforts to turn the things around by building a battery farm, arranging direct deliveries of fruit and vegetables from the south, or introducing hydroponics or better fertilisers — proved futile.

In the Urals, sometimes, in order to meet the targets for 'creating meat resources', they would slaughter lean animals not yet fattened or even young calves. Meat shortage in shops was a chronic disease and Yeltsin, of course, couldn't find a cure. Yet there was some progress even in this sphere, the trickiest one for him. Thanks to the introduction of several battery factories meat, albeit chicken meat, now found its way to shop counters and fruit and vegetables, whilst somewhat frost-bitten, became available too. The *kolkhozes* and *sovkhozes* in the Urals noticed signs of support from their Party boss who had opened up for them a significant credit line.

At the same time, there were other worries to top the list of the First Secretary's activities, those that could only be dealt with behind closed doors. The first such calamity was the accident at the Beloyarsk Atomic Power Station. Luckily, it proved possible to avert the tragedy to the extent that there were no casualties and no radioactive discharge in what could have been a major incident to rival Chernobyl. However, tragedy did strike at a closed, maximum security, plant in Sverdlovsk — one that was dealing with deadly micro-organisms in the manufacture biological weapons. About a hundred people were struck down by a disease which proved ultimately fatal. A subsequent enquiry revealed the symptoms of the victims to be similar to those brought about by anthrax.

There was finally the celebrated case of the demolition of the Ipatyev's house, the historic mansion in downtown Sverdlovsk where the last

---

* It is a huge territory in European Russia that stretches from Arctic Ocean to the black soil steppes in the south and from the Baltic Sea to the Western Siberia. It comprises 29 oblasts and autonomous republics that are further integrated into four huge economic districts.

43

Russian tsar had been executed together with his family and close servants. This order was in response to a classified decree from the Politburo and a command from the KGB and its head, Andropov, to which Yeltsin was forced to 'find a positive resolution to the issue'. As a result, virtually overnight, only a vacant site remained where Ipatyev's house had been.

Naina Iosifovna, when asked I there was there some unrest among Sverdlovsk population in connection with the destruction of Ipatyev's house replied, 'You know, none....... everybody was aware that the demolition was inevitable. What do you think he should have done? Surrender his Party card?'

On wider issues on his responsibilities, Naina continued, 'he would often bring Muscovites to our place. What's more, it always happened impromptu. Usually, he would give me a ring from his car: "Naina, get ready for action". Sometimes he would bring five or six people. I remember, for example, that this is how we were visited by Petrovsky, the USSR Minister for Public Health, as well as other members of the Central Committee.'

Not a very easy task to throw an impromptu party for five or six people:

'What of it? One can always fry some potatoes. He was, by the way, totally undemanding food-wise. His favourite dish was potatoes with tinned meat. He often asked me to prepare it for him even here, in Moscow. We often had *pelmeni*\*. Together with Klavdia Vasilievna, Boris Nikolayevich's mother, we used to make them in huge numbers, for weeks ahead.

The Soviet *Realpolitik* meant, primarily, the art of cultivating unofficial contacts, the ability to be indispensible and to belong and the ability to become a good and reliable partner for an important person or a group of 'big shots'. It meant an ability to turn up at the right time at the right place. When people talk about things like 'a leg up', 'such and such bringing so and so along', 'such and such being personally devoted to so and so, which did wonders for his career' — normally, these phrases have a derogatory connotation and reveal a shade of condemnation. In reality, no career is ever conceivable without these intricate interdependencies. Mikhail Gorbachev's star was on the rise from the moment he began his heart-to-heart conversations with Andropov during the summer vacations near

---

\* A Russian (mostly, Siberian) national dish — a type of small ravioli filled with meat.

Stavropol. Likewise, Chernenko's career was launched when Leonid Illich was the First Secretary of sunny Moldova: these examples are endless — and not only in Russian history.

A 'long-standing acquaintance' has always been invaluable when it comes to getting most significant state posts — be it in the eighteenth, nineteenth or twentieth century. To trust somebody, you have to *know* this person. To appoint this person to a position of high importance, you have to trust him.

Yeltsin's entire career consisted exclusively of unexpected upturns. A thirty-year-old engineer, until quite recently merely a foreman and then head of section that should, by all rights, just plod along for years and years before even dreaming of any promotion — suddenly he bursts into the construction industry elite of one of the most industrialised oblasts in the country. Then again an industry executive — and not even the most prominent one at that — with a lack of experience of operating within the Party system, becomes the First Secretary of the oblast. A barely known provincial with only a tangential acquaintance to Gorbachev then becomes elevated to candidature for the Politburo membership. Finally, expelled from big-time politics and having no recourse to resources in power — he is elected the first President of Russia. He seems to have surfed the tide of the times.

An iconoclast, he was successful in safeguarding and strengthening the fundamental Soviet principles. Yet had achieved a goal paramount for a man of his position: he acquired total self-confidence and he knew how to operate.

# Dear
# Mikhail Sergeyevich...
## (1985-1987)

In early 1984, a newly-minted member of the Politburo, formerly the First Secretary of the Tomsk Oblast, came to attend the oblast conference of the Sverdlovsk Party organisation. The memoirs by the Sverdlovsk *Gorkom's* Secretary Viktor Maniukhin describe this visit as follows.

'... A new Politburo member, Yegor Kuzmich Ligachev[*] was expected to pay a visit. Once, at lunch — and *Obkom* secretaries used to have their lunch on the same floor as the office of the First Secretary — Boris Nikolayevich said, "I have just telephoned Tomsk to find out from my opposite number what we should prepare for Ligachev's menu. I was told he does not drink alcohol and prefers his buckwheat porridge with milk. So kasha[**] it is, then. He is going to be with us for a total of five days. We shall assign a secretary for each of those days to be at his disposal. I shall keep him company only at the conference."

Members of his staff were astonished — in theory, he should have escorted him personally...

---

[*] Yegor Kuzmich Ligachev, (b. 1920) is a Soviet politician who was a high-ranking official in the Communist Party of the Soviet Union (CPSU). Originally a protégé of Mikhail Gorbachev, Ligachev became a challenger to his leadership and was one of the participants in the failed putsch of 1991.

[**] The Russian for 'porridge'.

New members — Gorbachev and Ligachev — were protégés of Yuri Andropov's. It was common knowledge that these two, Gorbachev in particular, were his young successors. On his deathbed, Andropov summoned both of them and then spent a long time discussing things. Following his demise, despite all the sly resistance of the Politburo octogenarians, Mikhail Gorbachev quickly advanced to the post of the Second Secretary in charge of ideology and was chairing the Politburo sessions in the absence of the perpetually ailing Chernenko. Despite the muffled jiggery-pokery from the side of the ancient Brezhnevites eager to elbow him away from the throne, it gradually became clear to all that he was, indeed, the true heir.

From the very beginning, Ligachev and Gorbachev formed an inseparable tandem. They both were from the same generation as Yeltsin, both had worked as heads of their respective oblasts but — most importantly — their oblasts were less significant in terms of scale and industrial potential. For quite some time now he felt piqued and jealous of their sweeping and inexplicable rise.

'Mineral secretary' (a snide moniker slapped on him by some venomous colleagues), Gorbachev had been organising vacations for the influential Central Committee (CC) secretaries and ministers: lunches, dinner parties, walks and fishing expeditions — when they would come down to Kislovodsk and Pyatigorsk to overhaul their fatigued gastric tracts. That was how he had met Andropov.

Ligachev, who arrived in Sverdlovsk to attend the Party conference in the beginning of 1984, struck Yeltsin as somewhat weird. This beloved buckwheat kasha of his — that had to be cooked in advance, his carefully advertised teetotalism (whereas in reality he never said no to a brandy), the affected patriotism towards Tomsk, proclivity for waxing lyrical and contrived sternness — all of it, to him, felt like a desire to show off.

Yeltsin considered his own businesslike speech at this Party conference and the follow-up Q&A session totally routine for *this* Party organisation, but it plunged Ligachev into a state of somewhat eccentric agitation.

He grew restless and kept going on and on about how this should be a new way for tackling problems: through analysis that's principled, businesslike and substantiated. This is what we need 'in our times', 'in our era'. And only a deaf man would miss the implied assertion that it was none other but Ligachev himself who should sit in judgement of all that.

Yeltsin felt that Ligachev had some hidden agenda — what with his tireless folksy wisecracks, weasel words and a state of unremitting excitement. The First Secretary was hugely relieved when the guest said his goodbyes and left.

… The experience, nonetheless, proved significant: Ligachev remembered Yeltsin's speech at the conference and his direct rapport with the audience, and immediately mentioned Yeltsin to Gorbachev. Gorbachev had his own experience of Yeltsin to fall back on, and it was far from pleasant.

This is how Yeltsin himself describes their first meeting with Mikhail Sergeyevich in 1983.

'Yet another inspection from the Central Committee came over to Sverdlovsk. They were quite frequent back then. This one was inspecting the agricultural matters.' ('They had planted something inadequate, or they had been planting it all wrong, and were repeatedly reprimanded because of that — I do not remember the details all that clearly,' was Naina Iosifovna's comment when I asked her to describe that first *disagreeable* encounter.)

Yeltsin saw the CC Secretariat's pronouncement on the situation in the Sverdlovsk Oblast agricultural sector as unfair and challenged it directly at the *Obkom* bureau before approaching the CC representative, Kapustian, with his comments. The latter responded by addressing a memo to the CC Secretariat in which he complained about Yeltsin's conduct: allegedly, Yeltsin had been breaking the party discipline. Following which, Yeltsin was summoned to Moscow for an audience with the Politburo member in charge of agricultural affairs — Gorbachev.

'… He welcomed me like nothing happened, we chatted and when I was about to take my leave he asked, "Are you familiar with the contents of that memo?" — all this with a kind of intrinsic disapproval. I answered that yes, I had read it. Then Gorbachev goes, forcibly and coldly, "You must learn your lesson!" And I said, "Lessons must be learned from the resolution, we are taking it all on board. As for the biased comments presented in the memo, I have no time for any of this." "Still, you must give it a thought," he always used familiar '*ty*' with everybody, absolutely everybody. I haven't met a single person that he would address politely, using '*vy*': no matter that a person could be much older than him — Gromyko, Shcherbitsky, Vorotnikov — the lot. Whether it was lack of manners or a habit, hard to say, but when he was thus '*ty*'-ing you it felt uncomfortable and I was instinctively resisting it, though I never mentioned it to him.'

Naturally, Gorbachev kept in mind the Sverdlovsk secretary's 'instinctive resistance', so when Ligachev started singing him exalted praise, his response, to begin with, was reserved. However, presently the circumstances changed dramatically.

The year 1984 was a special milestone in our country's history. It wasn't just that the Brezhnev cohort, the ancient Party leaders, started gradually losing ground. The crisis had started much earlier: economic problems and the Afghan war, Brezhnev's eternal ailments, anxiety in the air...

The top manager of the defence industry, Ustinov and Andropov, who quit the KGB to become the second person in the Party — their tandem, bizarre though it may sound, was a real indication of the profound crisis within the system. The crisis that proved fatal for the USSR.

The complex of defence industries, the army and state security came to form a tightened fist and emerged as a force by far overpowering Brezhnev's system of 'checks and balances' and his personal control over the Party.

Brezhnev had never enjoyed the reputation of an intellectual but his acute intuition and common sense ensured a balance of power badly needed in this enormous country, both within and without. The breaking point came in 1979 when the *troika* (Brezhnev–Andropov–Ustinov) made a decision to invade Afghanistan.

Had Brezhnev retained his power and influence, he would never have allowed this reckless piece of military opportunism. No matter how many geopolitical arguments in favour of the whole thing were quoted in hindsight, the Afghan war sapped the economic foundations of the country and brought about the international isolation and the boycott of the Moscow Olympic Games.

... Viewed from the point of view of a common Soviet citizen, the Olympics were the apex of global recognition. The usual blurb in the sports history books was about confirming our sporting achievements in the years after the Second World War. At the same time the Olympics were an instrument of assessing our country and working out how it fitted with the rest of the world.

Regrettably, in this *celebratory* Olympic year so essential for the USSR's international prestige, the Soviet troops entered Afghanistan. This was a huge political mistake.

As a result, half the countries renowned for their sporting excellence — the Olympic powers — declined to send their official delegations. The level of sporting challenge collapsed, the value of Moscow medals plummeted. The broadcasting around the world was curtailed. The *raison d'être* of the Moscow Olympics — political, as well as sporting — was half-wasted.

... Still, from a common Soviet citizen's point of view, things were going according to plan: galas, races, athletes under starter's orders, medals and the magnificent closing show, complete with the Moscow Olympic mascot — Mishka (Teddy Bear) floating in the evening sky above Moscow. Compared to all of this, some of the habitual American scheming paled into insignificance.

Yet in reality a painful blow was delivered to the Soviet prestige.

The final years of Brezhnev's rule are a somewhat mysterious page in our history. The suicide of a Brezhnev's intimate circle member, General Tsvigun\*, and the stand-off between the KGB and the MVD\*\* (right after Brezhnev's death, General Shchelokov, head of the Soviet militia shot himself, and Brezhnev's son-in-law Yuri Churbanov, Shchelokov's senior deputy, received a long prison sentence) gave rise to conspiracy theories and wild guesses — but bits of the puzzle never did fall into place.

At the same time the Procurator's Office launched scores, even hundreds full-scale criminal inquires into the activities of the upper echelons. The driving force behind it all was Andropov.

The campaign to enhance 'socialist legality' and combat corruption was invariably targeted those close to Brezhnev: members of his family, friends and those near and dear to him.

---

\* General Semyon Kuzmich Tsvigun (1918-1982), deputy head of the KGB, the Soviet intelligence and internal security agency.

\*\* Ministry of the Interior.

The clichéd narrative in history books describes the fight of 'honest' Andropov against the legacy of 'dishonest' Brezhnev. But a logical question suggests itself: why was it that Brezhnev, who had been so watchful in ensuring the total loyalty of the higher echelons in the Party, who had never allowed even a disguised hint at his worsening state of health and had kept meticulous count of how often he got mentioned in press — why was it that he let Andropov deliver those ghastly backstage punches?

In all likelihood, it was his strategy of mobilisation.

Be it the much talked-about 'fight against corruption' or Gorbachev's 'anti-alcohol' campaign (a perfect extension of the Andropov's concept of 'harsh rule'), be it the drive 'to enhance labour discipline' — launched in the brief months of Yuri Vladimirovich's * stay in high office — all these were but fragments of the whole. Meanwhile, the 'sum total' was this: to plunge the society into a state of pre-war confrontation. Andropov was implementing a philosophy of imminent war to justify a much more inflexible external policy (as opposed to Brezhnev's *detente*). The milestones of this approach were aggression in Afghanistan, a newly spiralling arms race and the campaign to impose a very harsh order within the country.

Brezhnev's USSR was perceived by the West as an integral part of the global system. Yet as soon as Andropov firmly consolidated his power, the East-West relations entered the stage of crisis, which ushered in Gorbachev's *perestroika*, pushed the country into a dead end and eventually buried the USSR.

In Brezhnev's times, volumes of trade had been increasing; oil was exchanged for grain, machinery and other products. Now the USSR started its catastrophic fall into the economic precipice.

So when and how did the comprehensive systemic crisis first hit the Soviet state?

The year was 1984.

Now it was the socialist countries' turn to boycott the Olympics in Los Angeles. The disaster of the South Korean passenger Boeing, shot down by a Soviet fighter plane, was the final straw in our relations with the West. At the same time, in the mid-eighties, oil prices hit rock bottom,

---

* Andropov's.

which coincided with a decline in the oil production within the USSR. Meanwhile, US President Reagan encroached upon yet another 'sanctuary' of the Soviet international politics — the parity in the arms sphere. In the absence of petro-dollars, keeping abreast of the American space weapons programme proved excruciating. The Soviet defence industry had already been devouring one third of the budget.

The country took its place in never-ending queues for 'deficits' — from cut-crystal tableware and gold, to toilet paper, meat, cheese and sausage.

And then the country's top leaders started dying — one after another. Up there, in the spheres of power, things were not right, that much was clear to all. Suddenly it transpired that no mechanism was in place for passing this very power on.

Meanwhile, the Soviet people were inundated with an ever increasing torrent of ideological gobbledygook. It is inconceivable today, but back in 1984, a sentence of several years in prison for watching a home video was nothing remarkable. Performing of and listening to rock music was outlawed (some rock musicians and their managers found themselves either brought in for questioning, on the verge of arrest, or already behind bars). Another law decreed that dacha plots* had to be downsized (once more in the post-war history); a ban was issued on charging 'speculative' prices when selling home-grown strawberries at farmers' markets.

The same was happening in ideology: thing formerly quite acceptable in print were now banned; artists whose names, only yesterday, were synonymous with the pride of Soviet culture become pariahs — Aksyonov**, Liubimov*** and Konchalovsky****. The crackdown on 'dissidents,' was gaining momentum. Relatively lax rules of Brezhnev's era were now a thing of the past.

---

\* Dacha — summer house, often a source of additional food supplies from the adjacent plots; in the Soviet days, it was needed to countermand deficit, today — to get access to cheap produce.

\*\* Vasilii Aksyonov (1932–2009), a popular Soviet and Russian author, in 1980 emigrated to the U.S. and stripped of the Soviet citizenship.

\*\*\* Yuri Liubimov (b. 1917) — artistic director of the legendary Taganka theatre.

\*\*\*\* Andrei Mikhalkov-Konchalovsky (b. 1937) is a Soviet and Russian film director, film producer and screenwriter. Emigrated to the USA and after *perestroika* returned to Russia.

And still, the early eighties were not an era of unequivocal *gloom*. Politics and daily life kept diverging, and by now there was a yawning gap between the two. The best remembered film premieres in 1984 were *A Cruel Romance* by Eldar Riazanov and Vladimir Menshov's *Love and Pigeons*. Both are films about love and focus on personal feelings and simple household joys, asserting uniqueness of private life. In that year of shared anxiety such films proved *memorable*.

The main legacy of Brezhnev's era — a nebulous sense of tranquillity, the stillness of public life — was about to sink without trace, but for now, common Soviet people were unaware of the fact that tectonic shifts were imminent. Meanwhile, the First Secretary of the Sverdlovsk *Obkom* was about to make his crucial choice. A point of no return — both in his career and in the life of the country — was drawing closer.

... Early in the winter of 1977 Naina Iosifovna chanced on a friend from the institute days.

Her friend was teaching at the Urals Pedagogical Institute in where Yeltsin's elder daughter had been a student from the year before. The friend wasted no time in bringing a message of joy: her daughter was such a gifted girl! Lena was solving problems ahead of the class, and even helped the others with their assignments on perspective geometry! The entire group was poring over her notes!

However, the praise felt affected. And Naina Iosifovna ventured cautiously: what's the big deal? Lena had never brought home anything but '*fives*' and already in her second year rejected parental help with her homework... 'You really are not getting it!' her friend persisted. 'Everybody in our department is convinced that the daughter of the First Secretary would only be accepted because of her father's position! Allegedly, it never happens otherwise.'

'Now you see for yourself that it does.'

In the evening she described this conversation to both Lena and Tanya.

Tanya, who had spent the entire winter choosing a university, suddenly announced that she would never ever study in Sverdlovsk. 'I don't want to be on public display.'

For Naina Iosifovna it was a real blow.

'So where do you intend to study, then?'

'Not in Sverdlovsk!'

A couple of months later, having gone through the School-Leavers Guide with a fine-tooth comb, Tanya chose Moscow State, the Department of Computational Mathematics and Cybernetics, a degree not on offer from either the Urals Polytechnic or the Urals University. Cybernetics was a totally new subject, only recently made legal in the USSR*.

'But you will never get the grades!'**

'So then I'll have to return,' Tanya was *sang-froid* personified.

Naina Iosifovna started asking around, approaching friends whose children were studying in Moscow. She just couldn't picture a quiet domestic Tanya living a life of her own, in a strange city, without friends or family. The very thought was intolerable.

Yet the father unexpectedly defended his younger daughter's decision.

'If she is sure, let her go!' was his contribution to the domestic council. Tanya was overjoyed.

For her first entrance paper (mathematics) she got a *'three'*. But after this first exam the number of applicants was halved. Within the remaining half, only several people got a mark above Tanya's: a *'three'* was not bad at all.

Naina Iosifovna wasn't sure whether to be happy or miserable. In all honesty, she was rather pleased: she so did not want her girl to stay in Moscow! But she underestimated Tanya who went on to get a *'five'* at the oral exam on mathematics, despite some excruciating additional probing by the examiner. Physics — also *'five'*. Literary essay — *'four'*. She made it!

Tanya's academic brilliance, forbearance and willpower should have made her parents proud. However, the imminent separation felt bitter and this precluded jubilation.

True, the first year in Moscow proved tough, especially for a child used to quiet domestic joys and pastimes. 'I just couldn't get used to Moscow', Tanya is recollecting. 'First off, people were so hard to accept: I saw them

---

* In the Soviet Union research in several fields was suppressed, mostly for ideological reasons. Cybernetics was one such field, viewed for a long time as a bourgeois pseudo-science.

** Until recently, to be accepted into a higher educational establishment (institute or university) school graduates had to sit entrance exams (separate from graduation exams in school).

as withdrawn, beaten down and, truth be told, haughty. At least as regards our year at the uni, Muscovites kept themselves to themselves and never mixed with us, students from outside the capital city.'

In Moscow, too, Tanya stubbornly stuck to her guns: when asked about her father she would reply that he was 'in construction'.

All these efforts notwithstanding, in her second year the smoke-screen had to be lifted. Boris Nikolayevich, aware that his daughter lived in the halls of residence and managed her tiny household herself, decided to make her a royal gift: a set of non-stick Teflon-coated pans manufactured by a defence plant in Sverdlovsk. Hard to say whether owning those pans gave Tanya much joy but when Boris Nikolayevich, a huge package in his hands, showed up at the entrance to Tanya's lodgings he had to show the warden on duty his ID. The ID read 'First Secretary of the Sverdlovsk CPSU *Obkom*'. The student on an entrance control rota was from the same year as Tanya. The news flew around the dormitory and soon Tanya had some explaining to do.

'But you said that your father was a common construction worker?'

'Turns out he isn't that common.'

This will prove to be her scourge in later life: how do you know if a person wants to be friends with you, and not with your father's status?

The only form of *blat* Tanya used with relish was access to the theatre box-office in the *Oktyabrskaya Hotel* — the hotel was used exclusively by the Party elite, and access to its premises was closed to outsiders. Boris Nikolayevich, when in Moscow on business, always stayed there. 'Following Dad's sojourns in this hotel I would go on a veritable "theatrical spree": Taganka, Sovremennik, Lenkom, the Bolshoi\*...'

Naina Iosifovna hoped she would be able to convince Tanya to get a transfer to either the Urals Polytechnic or the Urals Pedagogical. The arguments were quite weighty: at the time, the Sverdlovsk Polytechnic was justly considered to be among the best establishments in the country. 'Tuition here is just as good!' Naina Iosifovna was adamant, 'whereas you are there on your own, without parents or friends!'

---

\* Famous Moscow theatres the tickets for which, in the Soviet days, were rarer than gold dust.

In spring, when in Sverdlovsk, Tanya popped over to a couple of lectures at the Ural State.

'The teachers here are good,' she said calmly. 'But Mum, you know, over there we are taught by the people who *wrote* those manuals, whereas here I will just use their books. Do you think it makes a difference?'

Naina Iosifovna realised that resistance was indeed useless.

The next important development: Tanya married a fellow-student, a handsome and bright boy in the same year as her — Vilen*. The modest reception held in the restaurant of a Moscow hotel. The only guests were the young couple's parents, the best man and the bridesmaid plus several Yeltsin's colleagues from Sverdlovsk. The party, the spread, the toasts, the yells of '*Bitter*\*\*!', the music... Tanya, meanwhile, did not look all that glowing. She admitted to her mother that she didn't like 'all this officialdom'.

Many years before Naya Guirina had promised herself that she wouldn't marry while still a student. Tanya, her daughter, chose a different path but the marriage lasted only two years. Tanya got custody of their son — Borya Yeltsin-junior.

The big apartment on the Rabochaya Molodezh\*\*\* Embankment felt somewhat deserted: Lena and her family also moved out. In 1979 she had her first child — a daughter, Katya, followed, in 1983, by another girl, Masha. Lena and her husband Valery Okulov lived in a small two-room flat in the outer reaches of Sverdlovsk, next to the Koltsovo Airport where Valery worked as a navigator for a civil airline.

... One morning Naina Iosifovna woke up in tears. 'Boris asked me why I was sobbing like this. Did I have a bad dream? And I answered that I dreamt that we were to move to Moscow.'

---

\* A little aside — the name is the initials and the first three letters of Lenin's name: Vladimir Illich Lenin. Used to be popular in the early years of the Soviet state's existence.

\*\* The tradition at Russian weddings: the guests spontaneously start chanting *bitter* (alluding to their drinks) so as to urge the bride and the groom to kiss and 'sweeten' their drinks.

\*\*\* Working Youth.

She did believe against all evidence that they would continue to live in Sverdlovsk, and was clinging desperately to this hope. Yet gradually she was coming to understand that the frightening dream was probably going to come true. Her husband was invited, more than once, to move to Moscow for his work and the invitations were becoming ever more insistent. So far he had declined but it was sure to happen — sooner or later.

On 3 April 1985 Yeltsin was on his way to the *Obkom*. There and then, directly in his car, he received a telephone call through the governmental exchange. The caller was Vladimir Dolgikh, a Politburo member and the CC secretary for the affairs of industry. He suggested that Yeltsin should become head of the construction and engineering department, in short — his direct subordinate.

Without much ado, Yeltsin declined.

Another couple of weeks later he was telephoned by Yegor Ligachev, Persona Number Two in the Party. His arguments were nowhere near as cold and emotionless as those put forward by Dolgikh. He reminded Yeltsin about the party discipline, insisted that 'our time', 'our era' was beckoning. All of this was happening during the initial months in office of the new General Secretary of the CPSU Mikhail Gorbachev.

Biographers have unearthed a tiny detail — according to the bureau members of the Sverdlovsk *Obkom:* in 1985, when announcing his transfer to Moscow — to head the CC CPSU construction and engineering department, comrade Yeltsin was fiddling with a pencil. He snapped it in two. With him, it probably didn't even register but they all remembered the incident.

Yeltsin was hardly happy with this advancement since it was against the unwritten rule: previously, First Secretaries went straight to the posts of the CC CPSU Secretaries.

Readers nowadays readers might be hard put to explain the difference between the Secretariat of the Central Committee and its Bureau, and the subtle nuances inherent in these two facets of power. Thus, it is time to make a detour into the Party hierarchy, however brief.

CC Secretaries — with the General Secretary being at the top of the pyramid — supervised respective departments: from culture to engineering. They controlled ALL Party bodies and cells.

At the same time the Politburo was made up — in addition to the most prominent and deserving CC secretaries — of the Chairman of the USSR Council of Ministers, Ministers for the Foreign Affairs and Defence, the KGB Chairman, First Secretaries of the two capital cities — Moscow and Leningrad, the most respected and famous secretaries of the 'fraternal republics' (under Brezhnev it meant Ukraine, Byelorussia, Kazakhstan and Azerbaijan).

This entity embodied a 3D manifestation of power: it was bringing together the supreme Party elite and representatives of the administrative 'vertical' (security and foreign politics), ensuring the horizontal (that is to say, across-the-country) geographic representation.

The upwards trajectory from the post of the CC secretary for construction and engineering was not exactly short, but it was not unrealistic. However, not every CC secretary made it into the Politburo. These two bodies shared a lot of ground in their work: in terms of membership and decision-making. At the same time, the country knew at least the names of its Politburo members whilst secretaries were often relatively anonymous.

Once admitted into this power system, a person (if he could avoid grievous political transgressions) became a life-long member of the ruling Olympus, one among fifteen or twenty rulers of the USSR.

... For the first two months the Yeltsins stayed in the new block of the *Oktyabrskaya Hotel* in Bolshaya Yakimanka Street, nowadays the *President Hotel*.

All their possessions and books, packed in crates, were left in Sverdlovsk, in the empty flat on the Rabochaya Molodezh Embankment.

'I followed him right away, you could say, not even bothering to change my clothes.' Naina Iosifovna casts her mind back. 'My sister did all the packing. I believed that I shouldn't leave Boris alone, not for a day. I went back to Sverdlovsk for a couple of days, resigned from my job, and then started looking for a vacancy in a Moscow Design Bureau. Then it dawned on me: no! I had worked at my previous place for so many years, among my own people. And I realised that I would simply not be able to do the same in Moscow.

In the morning Boris would leave for work and I would be left on my own. I had no idea what to do with myself in this huge and strange city. I had never enjoyed my business trips to Moscow and always tried to conclude whatever business I had in one day and fly back on the same evening. So here I was, in Moscow, and possibly, for ever... One evening, on my way back to the hotel, I suddenly burst into tears — couldn't move, everything was a blur... I made it to my hotel room and telephoned my friend in Sverdlovsk. I never mentioned any of this to her, of course, simply asked how they were, what was happening. And then I ordered myself to stop. It was impossible to continue in the same vein. I had to start a new life.'

Two months later Yeltsin was promoted to Central Committee's Secretary for construction and engineering. It happened much sooner than he expected. His mood improved overnight.

When in Moscow, the Yeltsins were assigned a flat in a new house in the Second Tverskaya-Yamskaya Street, next door to the Belorussky railway station.

'It was a very good apartment, nicely appointed,' says Naina Iosifovna. 'A quiet courtyard, Gorky Street within a stone's throw, shops. But the district itself was quite depressing for both of us: noisy traffic, a tramline right underneath our windows, pollution. I would open the windows in the summer and discover a layer of soot on the sill.'

In Moscow, the new CC secretary was provided with not just one but two flats: to accommodate two families. They had to decide: which of their two daughters would live separately. Since Lena's family at the time was bigger — there were already two girls growing up there — it was concluded that Tanya and the little four-year-old Borya would move in with the parents.

'Little Borya had this tiny room — a box-room with a window, some three of four square metres. There was only space there for a bed and a bedside table. But this way he did have a room of his own,' reminisces Tanya. 'We left the big living room and Dad's study alone. Thus, there were two more rooms: mine, and the one for my parents.' The Yeltsins' bedroom and study were overlooking the street. The trams kept the inhabitants awake at night, just like in Sverdlovsk — in the 'house for the secretaries'.

The first summer was spent at the dacha in Uspenskoye village where they shared a small wooden house with the family of the prominent CC employee, Anatoly Lukianov. The atmosphere was family-like and warm: Tanya and Lena were friends with his daughter Lena.

Life was gradually falling into a pattern.

In the morning, Naina Iosifovna would see little Borya off to the kindergarten, then would pop over to Lena's. Over there, Naina Iosifovna would help her daughter look after her little girls: Katya and Masha. Then, having done some shopping in the neighbourhood shops, she would return home. Following her Sverdlovsk routine, she did her shopping herself. She worked out rather quickly where it was better to shop for milk, or vegetables, or frankfurters. Now her husband was a candidate member at the Politburo and the First Secretary of the *Gorkom*, but her habits stayed the same. She would also take her family laundry to the laundrette and clothes to the dry cleaners', and queue for 'deficit' products.

Meanwhile, those products were becoming more and more difficult to find and the queues were getting longer and longer. 'Once, I was in a queue for chickens, at a shop at the corner of Gorky Street. It must have been a whole year since we had moved to Moscow. The chickens were somewhat underwhelming, blue and thin. I asked the sales assistant to look for a better one* in the pile, but she retorted venomously, "We are picky today, aren't we?" As I was mumbling something in my defence, there was this sarcastic voice from behind, "If only the assistant were aware that she is serving the *Gorkom* First Secretary's wife, she would probably find it in herself to speak softer..."

It was their neighbour whom Naina Iosifovna already knew by sight. Some old acquaintances from Sverdlovsk — the Petrovs and the Zhitenevs — also lived in the same building. Still, most of the residents were high-ranking officials from the Central Committee, Stroyev and Ziuganov** among them, and somehow, in Moscow, it was not customary to share some quality after-work time with your colleagues' families. The Central Committee was simply too *big* a body.

---

* Supermarkets and self-service shops appeared later, in the nineties, so prior to that the queue would be served over the counter by a sales person.

** Gennady Andreyevich Ziuganov (b. 1944) is a Russian politician, First Secretary of the Communist Party of the Russian Federation (since 1993).

Thus, during the first half of 1985 Yeltsin worked as head of department, and later CC secretary for construction and engineering. His new remit offered vast possibilities for a person who knew his industry 'like the back of his hand' (his favourite phrase). But unpredictable things did happen too. When Yeltsin (who travelled more than all other secretaries put together) arrived in Tashkent to attend the plenary session of the republican Central Committee, he suddenly found himself besieged by crowds of people. They assembled around his hotel, demanding that they should be allowed to see him and discuss things: corruption of the new Uzbek leader Usmankhodzhayev. Yeltsin was provided with a pile of compromising materials. Having amassed a dossier of facts upon his return to Moscow he passed it on to Gorbachev. Gorbachev's response was vehement rejection: Usmankhodzhayev is an honest communist; these are simply attempts to slander his name. Moreover, the second person in the Party hierarchy — Ligachev — is ready to vouch for him.

Yeltsin remembered this incident well.

On 23 December 1985 Yeltsin was summoned to the Politburo and told that he was to head the Moscow municipal Party organisation. The appointment of course was a final step in a long chain of approvals.

Yet Yeltsin was aware of the fact that the speed with which the issue had been settled was somewhat extraordinary: Mikhail Gorbachev was engaged in rearguard skirmishes with members of the Brezhnev team, the 'Old Guard' he resented so much (the ranks, by the way, did not include Foreign Minister Gromyko who was the first to voice resolute support to the nomination of the new General Secretary at the fateful session of the Politburo). Gorbachev remembered well being the target of office politics, when attempts were made to 'hold him back', to prevent him from chairing Politburo sessions.

Former First Secretaries of Moscow and Leningrad, Grishin and Romanov, had to retire, the sooner the better. Then Tikhonov and Ponomarev* followed suit. The 80-year-old Gromyko could be left in peace, he presented no danger.

---

* Nikolai Alexandrovich Tikhonov (1905-1997) was a Soviet Russian-Ukrainian statesman. Boris Nikolayevich Ponomarev (1905-1995) was a Soviet politician, ideologist and historian, and a member of the Secretariat of the CPSU.

The First Secretary of the Moscow *Gorkom* Viktor Grishin had a personal meeting with Chernenko, the then General Secretary, shortly before the latter's death. The ailing Konstantin Ustinovich* was casting his vote at the Supreme Soviet elections. The TV coverage of the meeting, with a fragile Chernenko fighting to keep his balance and a confused Grishin muttering something into his ear, did Grishin, the Moscow ruler, a bad turn. The gossipmongers immediately branded him the 'heir'. Later, Gorbachev vehemently denied that 'at the top' Grishin could ever be perceived as Chernenko's successor. Anatoly Lukianov** named a different candidate — Grigory Romanov. Be it what may, a mere several months after Gorbachev's enthronement, Grishin and Romanov were forced into immediate retirement. The rumours of Grishin living out his last weeks in power spread around Moscow like fire.

Yeltsin started attending to the city's affairs as early as the autumn of 1985. Vladimir Resin, who had served for many years under Luzhkov*** as the boss of Moscow construction industry, in his memoirs describes, in some detail, the mechanism whereby Gorbachev replaced the 'city ruler' of Moscow.

'The paper *Sovetskaya Rossiya* (the official press organ of the CPSU Central Committee) published an invective that went off like a bomb. The article alleged that Moscow construction sites were in shambles. Following the tip-off from the press, the Central Committee passed a decision and thus the USSR People's Control Committee got involved. Committee members stockpiled compromising materials: distorted accounts, "window-dressing", and procedural violations when completing housing projects... It triggered a much trumpeted-about campaign against falsifications, malfeasance and poor quality. That was a signal for Viktor Vasilievich Grishin to leave the stage.

---

\* Chernenko.

\*\* Anatoly Ivanovich Lukianov (b. 1930) is a Russian Communist politician who was the Chairman of the Supreme Soviet of the USSR between 15 March 1990 and 22 August 1991. One of the founders of the Communist Party of the Russian Federation (CPRF) in 1993, he is described by its leader Gennady Ziuganov as the 'Deng Xiaoping' of the party.

\*\*\* Yuri Mikhailovich Luzhkov (b. 1936) is a Russian politician who was the Mayor of Moscow from 1992 to 2010. He was also vice-chairman and one of the founders of the ruling United Russia party.

...The *Gorkom* plenary session voted unanimously in favour of electing Boris Yeltsin the First Secretary. I heard him address the audience in the Pillar Hall in the House of the Unions*, reporting on the performance of the body that he had just come to lead.

Like no one before him, Yeltsin focused on his plans to reconstruct the capital city. He admitted that no one had ever answered this paramount question: how and in what direction should the city develop? Thus, everybody in that hall worked out why the First Secretary of the Sverdlovsk *Obkom* had been transferred to the second-rank position of heading the CC Construction Department...'

When leaving Sverdlovsk, did Yeltsin know that he would be made boss of Moscow? No, he did not, and Naina Iosifovna confirms this surmise. The position of the construction secretary within the Central Committee suited him just fine. Resin's version of events only goes to prove that Yeltsin's transformation into the First Secretary of the Moscow *Gorkom* was completely unexpected; many saw it as illogical and sensational.

In February of 1986, the XXVII Congress of the CPSU elected Boris Yeltsin a candidate member of the Politburo.

... Whatever his place of work, it was his wont to start with an in-depth research of the scene of action. In this instance, the scene was huge, poorly sign-posted and very much like a gigantic maze.

The city centre, beautiful but unkempt, highways overloaded with transport, filthy streets, cloned 'dormitory boroughs', irregularly scattered factory blocks sticking out against the skyline — a real eyesore, wastelands, endless crooked wooden fences and everywhere a seal of some fussy neglect.

'Exploratory attacks', similar to the one shared with Vladimir Resin (from eight in the morning till ten at night), became regular. Once he climbed out of the comfortable *ZIL* and took a Moscow trolleybus — during the rush hour. Dumbfounded security guards were trying to cordon him off from 'rank-and-file Muscovites' storming the trolleybus doors. They failed.

---

* A historical building in Moscow.

Yeltsin, tall and imposing, squeezed by the frenzied throng, rode for several stops and then fought his way towards the exit.

His first discovery was that Moscow was overcrowded. Transport, shops, schools, kindergartens and hospitals operated at overcapacity, the waiting lists for municipal accommodation were endless.

The reason — the ever-increasing influx of *limitchiks*, recruited not only by the construction projects but by all major works and factories, bus depots, house management committees and militia. *Limitchiks* as people with temporary residence permits in Moscow were normally put up in dormitories, derelict and unkempt beyond description.

People lived there, cooped up, for years, often in appalling conditions of hygiene, having long since forsaken dreams of passable accommodation. The existing housing stock, too, was in a deplorable state. This is what his engineer's eye spotted right away.

Yeltsin's first undertaking in his capacity of the city's master was to create the master plan for the city's development. This plan, started in Yeltsin's days, was amply utilised by subsequent city fathers.

The plans aside, he was eager to curtail the influx of workforce into Moscow immediately. In the First Secretary's opinion, this ever-increasing torrent allowed the Moscow bosses to disguise the low labour efficiency and poor quality of investments.

The issue of the inefficiency of production was nothing new for Moscow managers. Year in year out, they were listening to the same old mantra delivered from high podiums. But for the first time the message was driven home so sternly and with such conviction. Yeltsin worked out that *limitchiks*, stripped of many civic rights, browbeaten and existing in a semi-legal limbo, had been tacitly perceived as a price of the metropolis's expansion.

Official records alone showed that between 1964 and 1985, over 700,000 individuals moved into Moscow. Yeltsin branded them 'slaves of the developed socialism* in the late XX century'. He went even further and said, 'They quickly became chained to their enterprises by their temporary Moscow residence permit, their place in the dormitory and a cherished

---

\* A favourite idea of Brezhnev's — according to him, by the late sixties the Soviet Union entered the phase of *developed socialism*.

dream of permanent residence. One could abuse them the way one pleased: they would never complain. The tiniest conflict — and they would get kicked out, stripped of their temporary registration...'

This torrent of *limitchiks* was a way of 'corrupting' (Yeltsin's term) management of the companies. Bosses saw no need to modernise production and mechanise manual procedures. One third of the employable municipal population was involved in hard physical labour!

So what did this audacious newcomer from Sverdlovsk offer to Moscow's wise men? Despite the meagre 2.8% that constituted planned annual production growth in Moscow, Yeltsin promised that in the nearest five years it would go up 'at least' 125-175%. This would be a result of tremendous improvements in labour productivity (20% annually), industrial modernisation and cutting down the share of manual labour (by 20%).

His way of dealing with it was completely hands on. He was particularly fond of unannounced flying visits to Moscow plants — about the time the first shift was due in\*. 'You should have seen how irate the people are', Yeltsin was telling the plenary session of the Moscow *Gorkom*. This is what Yeltsin told Mr Olbik, a Latvian journalist, in the interview in August of 1988. 'If I was planning a visit to a plant I would research how the workmen would get there. At six in the morning I would take a bus, get to the metro station, take another bus on arrival, and by seven would make it to the company's gatehouse. And not wait till the top manager showed up, just go to the production floor, drop into the canteen. So if, say, the conversation turned to "hellish" problems of transport I would have a very good idea of what the people were talking about'.

Soon after Yeltsin accepted his position of power, the new plan stipulated that the hazardous enterprises should be moved to beyond the city's confines and no new plants, factories and administrative buildings should be built within the city limits.

Yet another new initiative of Yeltsin's was a prohibition on pulling down historical edifices. He launched restoration of historical monuments and

---

\* About six or seven in the morning. — *Author's comment.*

cultural landmarks. He brought in a decree whereby offices, headquarters and institutes situated on the ground floor of historical buildings had to relocate and give way to cafes, restaurants and shops. Yeltsin was the first to start celebrating the Day of the City — the tradition still alive and popular even now, twenty years later.

To demonstrate that he meant business, that he did care about public welfare, Yeltsin launched an attack on the 'sacred shrine' of the Moscow authorities — the Moscow Party elite.

'Out of 33 First Secretaries of district committees,' says Yeltsin in his *Confessions*, 'I had to replace 23. Not everybody was demoted for reasons of poor performance, some were actually advanced. Most admitted they could not work in a new way. Some had to be persuaded. In short, it was a hard and painful process.'

The echo of 'open and very harsh' collisions with Moscow leadership stayed with him for years. He was accused of cruelty, of ruining people's lives. He would retort, 'I was badly affected by the tragic case of the former Kievsky\**Raikom* First Secretary. He committed suicide by throwing himself off the seventh floor. By then, it was already half a year since he'd left *Raikom* and moved to the Ministry of Non-Ferrous Metallurgy. The situation seemed normal. And then out of the blue, such a turn of events. Later, when a campaign of persecution was unleashed against me, some were trying to suit this accident to their purposes and accuse me of being the cause of this person's death, since it looked like he'd killed himself after I removed him from his post. A legend appeared: allegedly, he made his way out of the session room and then jumped to his death. What really got me was that somebody could be capable of using even a person's death as a trump card...'

'To start with, Gorbachev was pleased with the new Moscow secretary's ardour and approved of his attempts to air out the *Gorkom* corridors; he did not consider Yeltsin to be an important piece on his chessboard. According to Gorbachev's daughter, the name of the new *Gorkom*'s Secretary was hardly ever mentioned during his nightly debriefing sessions at home,'

---

\* A Moscow district.

says Andrei Grachev, press secretary of the first and only President of the USSR.

But Gorbachev was getting more and more annoyed by Yeltsin's 'public performances'.

Approximately at the end of 1986 Gorbachev stopped receiving Yeltsin privately.

This vacuum was immediately filled with the CC Second Secretary Yegor Ligachev who made it his business, mostly likely both on instruction and his own initiative, to interfere — aggressively — in all Moscow affairs, criticise, make frequent and often clueless telephone calls, and generally drive Yeltsin to distraction.

Gorbachev was playing a complicated game. He was spinning a fine yarn to the conservatives whilst persistently pushing through his own ideas, he was restraining some mysterious radicals and democrats, he was politely 'doffing his hat' to Brezhnev's dinosaurs: the First Secretary of the Ukrainian Central Committee Vladimir Shcherbitsky and Andrei Gromyko. He was shooting his arrows in all directions simultaneously, while keeping the 'balance of powers' understandable to him alone.

Yeltsin was incapable of playing a yes-man and was positively failing to grasp his own role within a multi-faceted political structure created by Gorbachev.

The first open collision between Gorbachev and Yeltsin occurred at the Politburo meeting on 19 January 1987, during debates on the draft report on staffing policy, prepared for the attention of the Central Committee plenary session.

One after another, attendees were taking the floor. Yeltsin's 'speech… was harsh and categorical,' recollects Vitaly Vorotnikov, a member of Gorbachev's Politburo.

So what was Yeltsin saying on that day?

'*Yeltsin*. I would ask you to understand my proposals correctly. I shall present them openly.

Firstly, *perestroika's* success is somewhat overestimated. The situation with personnel is such that being over-optimistic is dangerous. Some are simply not ready for revolutionary change.

Secondly, our analysis of the past 70 years*. It is eagerly awaited. We must have the courage to admit that jamming on the brakes is the fault of both the previous Politburo and the Central Committee.

Thirdly, guarantees of success. Routinely mentioned are socialism, the Soviet people and the Party, yet they have been in existence all those 70 years! Therefore, by no means do they guarantee that we have reached a point of no return. At the same time, the guarantees are formulated in the final chapters of the report. The most prominent among them is democratisation of all spheres of life.

Fourthly, it is worth mentioning the entire workforce sustained a profound shock. Yet the higher echelons of power there is no renovation, no restructuring. The criticism in the report is only directed downwards.

… Sixth. The list of particularly badly affected territories. The ones that are named are Uzbekistan, Kazakhstan and Moscow. I would add Rostov and Kirghizia.

*Gorbachev.* This instruction of yours shall be incorporated.'

The General Secretary is trying to cautiously pull Yeltsin in: 'This *instruction* of yours shall be incorporated'. Irony, even sarcasm, is palpable: instead of putting forward observations, like other colleagues, the First Secretary of the Moscow *Gorkom* is performing an appraisal. And some appraisal it is, too: he is accusing the Politburo of self-satisfaction — 'the criticism in the report is only directed downwards'. He is revising not just some provisions but the very spirit of Gorbachev's report!

Even in terms of form, Yeltsin's speech is dramatically different compared to other speakers' interventions. He is essentially making a *co-report*: the first, the second, the third — that is, he is talking twice, three times, four times longer than is expected… He is apparently unaware of his own role and the rules, stipulated in advance. Listening to Yeltsin, Gorbachev starts to seethe with anger.

Yeltsin carries on.

'…The protracted stay of the same person in office devalues both his attitude to duty and his relations with others. It leads to self-satisfaction.

*Gorbachev.* Do finish off, though you are making valid criticisms.'

---

* Of the Soviet power.

Having taken the floor at the end of the debate, Gorbachev lamented the fact that Yeltsin *had not paid sufficient attention to the report* and even read out loud passages in his text that Yeltsin, in his opinion, *overlooked*. That was a veritable arrow shot at the candidate member of the Politburo who had grown too big for his boots.

'None of it went beyond the usual scope of discussions held at the Politburo,' recollects yet another former Politburo member Medvedev. 'But Boris Nikolayevich felt offended. When people dispersed he stayed in his chair. His face was contorted with rage... He was banging on the table with his fists.' In his memoirs, Medvedev includes notes that he and his colleague Yakovlev were writing to each other at the same Politburo session in connection with Yeltsin's speech.

*Medvedev to Yakovlev.* Turns out there is somebody more leftist than us. Good.

*Yakovlev to Medvedev.* Good but seems to me he is showing off somewhat. I don't like it.

*Medvedev to Yakovlev.* This is as may be, but this is the role.

*Yakovlev to Medvedev.* Lagging behind is terrible but running a few steps ahead is destructive. (Medvedev, V. A., *On Gorbachev's Team: Insights*).

The next day Gorbachev telephoned Vorotnikov and told him that Yeltsin's speech had left 'a bad taste in the mouth'. 'Yeltsin's methods: flirting with the masses, promises, shake-ups of personnel, lots of words, little tangible work. Moscow economy and trade, despite the huge amount of help from other republics, has not improved. All he does is quote previous drawbacks'.

It was Vorotnikov's birthday, so on the evening of the same day Yeltsin also gave him a call. This is how Vorotnikov recollects this conversation.

"'I got carried away. Do you believe that I laid it on a bit too thick?"

"Others do argue sometimes, too. One should simply be a bit calmer. You are always a procurator. Your words are harsh. It shouldn't be like this."

"I do agree, but such is my temper.'" (Vorotnikov, V., *And This Is How It Happened...*).

Despite all this, he carried on 'laying it on too thick'. During one of the Politburo sessions, Gorbachev's assistant made this record:

*'24 March 1987.*

*Chebrikov*\*. *Glasnost*\*\* is already used against *perestroika*. It is used in such a way as to distract from real problems, channel energy into the protection of monuments, kick up a fuss about unrelated issues, promote, beyond any measure, the non-governmental groups and invoke ungrounded expectations.

Plurality is unbridled. The press are printing anything they please and offer no apologies over lies or slander… Censorship has been abolished but at the same time the state guidance over the country's spiritual life has also been totally removed. Such are facts.

*Yeltsin.* This morning I come up to a kiosk. The salesman says, "I have nothing to offer, neither newspapers, nor magazines. It all sold out within half an hour." This is how avidly people are interested in the current news. At the same time the middle-level managers and middle-ranking party official are impenetrable, either from below or from above. They are hiding away in their offices. They are a spanner in the works, all a-quiver with fear of losing their posts. One should not be afraid of replacing them, although everybody is grumpy. Such are our times. Over a million and a half live in communal apartments in Moscow. A native Muscovite has no hope of getting a flat if within a family the per capita ratio of living space is 5 square metres\*\*\*.

*Gorbachev.* We should reform the accommodation standards in Moscow. Generally speaking, I believe that your first priority should be accommodation, after that — public health.'

Yet again, Gorbachev is throwing some water on the fire built by Yeltsin. To his taste, the latter is too uncompromising. Listening to him, the 'oldies' get annoyed. This is not what Gorbachev needs.

Once at a Politburo session Yeltsin complained that in Moscow there

---

\* Chairman of the KGB. — *Author's note.*

\*\* Openness, transparency — one of the key elements of Gorbachev's reforms.

\*\*\* Flats were provided by municipal authorities on the basis of assessing one's situation. To get accommodation, one normally had to wait for several years. It could, therefore, happen that the person would get married, have children and end up squeezed in one or two rooms but if the rooms were big, or the kitchen was somewhat more spacious than usual (assessments were run on the basis of the total floor space) he could fall short of qualifying by, say, some square centimetres per head.

is a shortage of bakers. Gromyko retorted irascibly, 'Do you need the Politburo's sanction to teach you, instead of your grandmother, how to suck eggs?' The audience burst out in raucous laughter. Within Gorbachev's Politburo, Yeltsin was an outsider.

Gorbachev's press secretary Andrei Grachev recollects.

'Gorbachev was clearly inspired when theorising on the subject of Lenin's true bequests, while the need to eradicate vestiges of Stalin's legacy left him cold. With obvious pleasure he would drag Politburo members into many-hour-long discussions of the subject. Firstly, he viewed these debates as a means of personal development, and secondly, while rereading a little volume of Lenin's works* he was beginning, unbeknownst to himself, to "role-play it" in order to create, within the post-Brezhnev's Politburo he inherited, the atmosphere of passionate ideological battles...

The US Secretary of State George Shultz recalled that once, having started with Gorbachev the planned negotiations on missiles and warheads, they slid onto global subjects and a discourse of global developments in the 15 or 20 years to come. As a result, the 'boring' issue of counting the warheads was quickly brushed aside and delegated to the experts, while the high contracting parties immersed themselves, for two hours, into futuristic discussions, thus warping the General Secretary's schedule of meetings.

Yeltsin had very vivid recollections of this General Secretary's reluctance to attend to tedious routine matters. His reading of it all was somewhat different — what he saw there was not grandiose plans and strategic thinking but an elementary lack of a normal workable mechanism for decision-making.

'Politburo was in session on Thursdays,' Naina Iosifovna recollects. 'Boris Nikolayevich would return home virtually ill. It was a frightful sight. Once he said, "I do not want to belong to this gang that is busy destroying the country."'

Let us try to look at Moscow of that time through his eyes.

---

* Mikhail Sergeyevich always kept a volume from Lenin's collected works on his desk, close to hand. — *Author's comment.*

He started with what ostensibly was the easiest — the shops. Strange though it might seem, he believed that this was the most grievous problem. He knew that Moscow was supposed to enjoy the best standard of supplies in the country. But what was there in reality? A dull range of products, queues, a suspicious flurry of activity in the auxiliary rooms*, grumpy sales personnel. Any type of meat, even chicken, butter, mayonnaise, cereals, cheese and sausage — everything in short supply. Queues for any staple.

Once, on his usual 'walk' he popped into a food shop and — like he used to do in Sverdlovsk — started asking the salesgirl on what was available, what wasn't and why. In response she yelled blue murder: 'Who the hell do you think you are, to impose your own rules here? Are you from the OBKHSS**?'

He summoned the frightened director, gave him a good talking-to, and made a note of all data: the shop number, director's name, unavailability of these and those products — and left, hoping that this would spur them into at least some semblance of action.

There was another overwhelming incident: once, on his way out towards his car, he heard somebody's quick footfalls. A young girl was running after him. 'Comrade Yeltsin,' she whispered with fervour, 'may I have a word?'

And she told him everything: how she was hired to work on the shop floor, how she was made to rig the scales, to deceive shoppers, employ a bag of tricks in order to generate some clandestine income and then share it, shelling out to everybody — the department head, the shop director. She insisted that it was common practice: everybody was chiselling, all the way along the line — up to the district trade committee, to the headquarters; everybody had a finger in the pie with one hand washing the other, and you just couldn't break away, and she had nowhere to go if she got fired, because she had a small child, you see, and cry into her pillow at night and avoid the shoppers' eyes, so do something, do something...

There was a follow-up to this story. He summoned the girl to the *Gorkom* and set the investigative agency on the case, waited for

---

* A hint at the staff hoarding merchandise in high demand and reselling it privately at inflated prices.

** Department to Fight Embezzlement of Socialist Property.

developments and, finally, new heads rolled, new scandalous dismissals took place — even though he had already fired an impressive number of high-ranking executives. Yet his intuition was telling him that the system could not be dismantled rapidly.

And then again, should it be dismantled? That was the principal question.

Yeltsin realised that what he was confronting was not just a smooth mechanism for theft, not just the 'trade mafia'; he ran into the entrenched *habit*, the popular mentality, a way of life. It was impossible to make accounting in retail transparent and thus work out how the huge (in terms of the USSR) resources of Moscow food supplies were distributed in reality. The reason for this was simple: the shadow system of distribution suited everybody just fine.

Yeltsin fired the top manager of *Mostorg*\*, the senior investigating officer of the municipal Procurator's Office (exposed in connection with bribes from retailers), directors of vegetable warehouses — not to mention heads of district departments. In 1986, a boss of *raitorg*\*\* (an incredibly high position in Moscow terms, for the incumbent had a sacred right of access to any retail depot, any deficit product) could be kicked out of his office over such a trifle as 'insufficient supplies of cold drinks to residents of Moscow in the seasonally hot months'. The retail caste that held even the formidable OBKHSS in contempt were now showered with penalties, even if they saw pretexts as ludicrous. Still, comatose girls offering sparkling water and juices did appear at every street corner.

Yeltsin tried to change tack: if one could combat clandestine packages and bundles, he could at least reduce prices for fruit and vegetables available at the farmers' markets, organise direct deliveries from *kolkhozes* and *sovkhozes*, set up weekend fairs (that still exist in Moscow).

He was ardently pushing this idea through and did organise a triumphantly successful first-ever food fair: amateur performers were

---

\* Headquarters of the entire network of Moscow retail shops.
\*\* City district retail headquarters.

singing and dancing, overjoyed shoppers carried away their 'green vitamins'...

For all the success of this undertaking, for all the coverage on TV and in press, pretty soon things reverted to familiar drabness: vegetables, and especially fruit, became scarce, there were queues in front of each counter and even outside, quality products disappeared completely, premises grew unkempt and filthy, the holiday finished and satisfaction waned.

Young people born in the eighties or nineties do not remember the atmosphere of a Soviet retail shop, with its specific odours (say, smelly wood shavings on the dirty floor in the winter); they never had to elbow their way towards a counter piled high with nothing but frozen chickens and filets of oceanic cod, wrapped up in fragments of frayed cellophane. They did not have to scrape frost-bitten potatoes out of a soggy paper bag or wait in frenzied vodka queues. They do not even know what a *talon** is — and there were talons for everything: sugar, tobacco, meat, vodka and detergents... They picture the life in the USSR from the newsreels featuring imposing parades of ballistic missiles in Red Square and the mascot of the Moscow Olympics... I used to be glad that our children know nothing of the kind. Now I sometimes think it's a shame.

Even back in Sverdlovsk, Yeltsin had to tackle problems that were similar across the entire huge country. But in Sverdlovsk he understood it all clearly: the very pattern of life, the system of power, social context, profundity and composition of those separate problems. Here, in the capital city of the empire, the lack of transparency was overwhelming.

In Sverdlovsk only one GP surgery (the so-called *spetspoliklinika*) — the famous Hospital No 2 serviced all privileged groups: from *Obkom* secretaries to Party veterans. In Moscow there were about seven hundred of similar sectoral establishments. The writers had a hospital of their own, the railway staff — the one that belonged to their ministry, whilst academics could use several. These were not isolated privileges but a system of life, a self-contained comfortable universe existing within one city, carefree and smug, with a sublime infrastructure of social handouts, benefits, privileges and perks. This universe was resolutely opposed to change.

---

* A coupon entitling one to purchase a limited and prescribed number of items or goods.

So how was it possible to annihilate the system of perks in the retail trade and leave the others, say, public health or education, intact?

On the surface, a full-front cavalry charge launched by comrade Yeltsin against MGIMO* and the Foreign Ministry's Diplomatic Academy — two most upscale links of the Moscow educational network where children of diplomats and high-ranking party officials were getting their degrees — proved a success. There were inspections, reprimands and articles in press, a campaign against the unfair distribution of vacancies (the very same *blat*), corruption and nepotism. But it wasn't enough to dismiss a couple of staff members; but to ensure lasting results meant creating public support, and this is precisely what did not happen.

Yeltsin tackled the system of social inequality in education from below, starting with the network of secondary schools. He just could not grasp why in Moscow a child from a common family had no chance of ever getting a place in any of the numerous elite schools offering a more advanced curriculum in foreign languages. And rank-and-file establishments had classes filled to overcapacity, teachers who could resign in the middle of a school year, high rates of juvenile delinquency and at times no elementary conveniences...

An important question: why was 'social fairness' gradually becoming topmost on Yeltsin's agenda?

Afterwards he would be accused of populism: allegedly, his defence of the miserable and the wronged was nothing but a trump card that in politics. But it's possible that Yeltsin, a Soviet man through and through, was genuinely shaken by the depth of the social abyss that he witnessed in Moscow. He, 'an alien from Sverdlovsk', was not like that. Their family was not like that. In their parochial view, this 'luxury' available to bosses was excessive. Within this context, Naina Iosifovna's custom of doing her own shopping and collecting her laundry from a laundrette looked completely ridiculous. Yet she was obstinately sticking to the familiar routine.

In placing the Moscow party organisation and the life of this huge metropolis in Yeltsin's care, Gorbachev did not expect that within a year

---

* Moscow State Institute of International Relations.

and a half Yeltsin would dispose of a goodly number of district secretaries and deliver a painful blow to the caste directly connected to the hub of power in the country. Then again, Gorbachev probably did not perceive the deeper meaning of this fight.

The harmony (if harmony meant stability of the whole structure) was based on the division between the pole of privilege and the pole of *limitchiks*. One ensured the existence of the other through their interdependence.

He did not want to accept this system. And in retaliation the system rejected him.

Boris Nikolayevich once found himself in a 'dormitory borough'. He arrived there to debate the issue of upgrading public amenities. This visit of his was thoroughly documented by Moscow and Western correspondents. The venue was an ordinary Khrushchev five-storey slum house, a building erected from pre-fabricated concrete panels.

'When Yeltsin showed up he was immediately surrounded by hundreds of people, some were shouting while the others were looking on from their balconies. "Get down to our basement!" their indignation was palpable. "The stinking mud is knee-deep there! The sewerage pipe has long since rotted away! The roof is leaking and no one gives a damn!"

Yeltsin climbed down into the basement, then had a good look at piles of rubbish in the courtyard. The throng around the First Secretary was getting tighter. "Our children are playing among mounds of refuse that crawl with rats!"', reported a Moscow correspondent of an American newspaper.

He saw it all in Sverdlovsk, even worse, but over there people felt protected by the stability of life, its continuity. Meagre existence, filth, shortages, absence of staples — all this was dealt with thanks to the shared feeling of popular stoicism, patience and fatalism — 'it used to be much worse right after the war', 'life is gradually getting better', 'what can you change?', 'one should live and hope for the better'. But here in Moscow the penny dropped: he realised that their patience was wearing thin. He realised that what he was facing was subdued despair and barely controlled fury, 'Pass the message on to Gorbachev! Boris Nikolayevich, we are with you!'

Yes, the patience came to an end. And it was none other but Gorbachev himself who provoked this rupture. Every unusual, tantalising, *new* word published in a daily or in a magazine, every article and disclosure was whipping up impatient and avid expectations, bordering on hysteria, and an awareness that things couldn't go on as before. The patience was no more, these were different people, not like before, and they were capable of many things. To call a spade a spade, they were capable of mutiny.

He was trying to alert the others, to explain that the cauldron was about to boil and overflow, that the volcano was about to erupt. He did it in the dry emotionless language of his speeches, for example, at the Politburo sessions or plenary sessions of the Central Committee.

Today Yeltsin's speeches from those days feel somewhat bizarre. The wheels of history were getting into motion, yet he was expressing himself in the old customary language of administrative instructions and decrees.

Here is a characteristic excerpt from one of such speeches.

'I would like to openly express my worry in relation to some issues. Many "why's" suggest themselves. Why do we keep discussing, congress after congress, the same old problems? Why has our party vocabulary adopted the alien word *stagnation*? Why, in the course of so many years, we have failed to eradicate bureaucracy, social unfairness and abuses of power? Why is the demand for radical change swamped, even now, in this inert layer of smooth operators carrying the party card?'

And here is probably the key point.

'...*We mustn't lose momentum lulled by a continuing political stability in the country.*'

What Yeltsin probably meant here was that the external facade, of the Soviet stability was a disguise for the constantly increasing pressure, an impending disaster.

At the plenary session of the CPSU Central Committee in January of 1987, Gorbachev mentioned the word *democracy* for the first time. He used it in a new, non-Soviet, context. 'We need democracy at all levels,' he said. That was the watershed, the borderline. What prompted the General Secretary to make this step and face the jeopardy of democratic elections?

It probably makes most sense to look for the answer not in the politics but in the economy.

This is what the Prime Minister at the time, Nikolai Ryzhkov, wrote somewhat later, in the nineties.

'In 1986, the global oil and gas prices plummeted while the fuels had traditionally accounted for a high percentage in our exports. What was to be done? The most logical thing was to revise the composition of exports. Unfortunately, only the most economically advanced countries could do it fast enough. Our industrial products could not compete in the global market. Let's take, for example, machine-building. The volume of exports, as compared to 1986, stayed practically the same — but those goods were primarily exported to the Comecon* countries! Capitalists were buying only some 6% of the total volume! That was why we were exporting mostly raw materials.'

Let us complete Ryzhkov's thought. Exports of machinery output were a very poor source of hard currency for the treasury. Hard currency was generated only by exports of oil and gas, so when the prices dropped (down to $19.9 per barrel) the budget of the country got twisted badly out of shape.

The problem, though, was this: the availability of hard currency defined the most important thing — whether the USSR leaders would be capable of feeding their own people and avoid a food crisis. This threat was looming in earnest.

'By mid-eighties, every third tonne of bread and bakery products had been produced out of imported grain. Animal production was dependent on the grain imports... The impossibility of cutting down the cost of grain imports**, coupled with the uncompetitive nature of the processing industry and the unpredictable prices for raw materials used for paying for food imports, had become, by mid-eighties, the Achilles' heel of the Soviet economy' (Gaidar, Yegor, *Collapse of an Empire*).

When Gorbachev first came to power, this Achilles' heel could still be plastered over, though it did require some radical measures. What was needed, for example, was a considerable reduction of investments in the processing industries and exports of raw materials (say, non-ferrous metals)

---

\* The Council for Mutual Economic Assistance was an economic organisation under the leadership of the Soviet Union that comprised the countries of the Eastern Bloc.

\*\* The USSR had to buy grain even in the years of good harvest since it normally operated on the basis of long-term contracts with the exporting countries — the USA, Canada, Argentina and China. — *Author's comment*.

directly to the world markets. Another option: cutting down the volume of state purchases from the manufacturing industries working on defence-related contracts, bringing down the number of tanks, missiles and other armaments continuously manufactured in the USSR at the levels suitable for a country on the threshold of a war, not on the brink of an economic disaster. Yeltsin recognised the scope of this impending catastrophe much earlier than his colleagues at the Politburo.

And finally, year in, year out, the budget deficit was increasing. This is what Ryzhkov was saying on this subject at the plenary session of the CC CPSU: 'The country has started its Twelfth Five-Year Plan carrying the grievous financial legacy. For a long time now we haven't been able to make ends meet, we live on credit. The spiralling imbalance is becoming a chronic phenomenon which brought the system of finance and credit to the brink of complete disarray.'

All of it prompted a gradual increase of prices for staple goods and products –to prevent the 'goods famine' and withdrawal of money from the trade transactions. Neither the first, nor the second or third measures had been carried out in good time.

To extricate themselves from the grain and oil pitfall, from the clutches of a financial catastrophe, in essence, Gorbachev's government had to make one very unpopular decision: TO CUT DOWN SPENDING.

Yet in political terms such a decision equalled suicide.

From the USSR State Bank archives: 'By the end of 1989, the worth of construction projects that were never completed amounted to 180.9 billion roubles, out of which 39 billion were in excess of industry norms…' These dry figures disguise the terrible truth. While the shortages of foodstuffs and consumer goods were becoming ever more significant (Gorbachev's government curtailed the volume of purchases from abroad), the construction of new factories and plants was still going ahead.

Gorbachev was afraid of his own elite. He was wary of disturbing the economic system that had been formed before. Gorbachev's press secretary Andrei Grachev reminisces, 'It became clear that neither the slogan of *acceleration** nor the appeal to all citizens of the country *to step up their working*

---

* Keywords in Gorbachev's programme of reforms.

*efforts* were capable of altering existing practices, to say nothing of the overall order of things. At the same time the concept of reforms launched by the new leadership lacked integrity. Attention was becoming diffused as one initiative replaced another. Mostly, what was adapted were old boilerplates, the ones dating back to the days when Gorbachev, together with Ryzhkov, were sifting through hundreds of reports submitted by experts and academic institutions to prepare memos on the required scientific and technological advances and a possible economic reform. In the event, these materials had never proved useful to either Andropov or Chernenko.'

As a result, only one, the most unsuccessful of Gorbachev's initiatives — the anti-alcohol campaign — survived in public consciousness. Vineyards were cut down, ancient wine cellars were boarded up, sales of vodka were rationed, and distilleries were closed down. The budget sustained colossal losses.

To make people work better by such initiatives and appeals was as much of a utopia as to make the party apparatus believe in *perestroika* and *acceleration*. Thus, Gorbachev tried to shift accents: it proved impossible to reform economics, let's reform the political system.

The plenary session of the Central Committee in January defined the task: managers at all levels, including party committees, must be elected by direct and secret vote. All spheres of life must be democratised.

'"We should not be afraid of chaos" — this mysterious quote from Lenin's oeuvres Gorbachev favoured particularly', Andrei Grachev recollects. 'The quote had an optimistic ring to it, Lenin's authority was also supposed to help him maintain self-control. Yet there was a very important nuance: Lenin called upon his comrades to refrain from panic *vis-á-vis* the profound cataclysm that broke out in Russia mostly against the will of the *Bolsheviks"*... As for Gorbachev, his good intentions of emancipating the society were objectively creating "chaos" which he was going to control and regulate exclusively through democratic methods.'

---

* Lenin's faction in the Russian Socialist Democratic Labour Party (precursor of the Communist Party). The name stems from the result of the strategic vote taken in 1903 (Lenin's vision got the majority, *bolshinstvo*) whereupon the Party split into those who advocated more liberal and pluralistic methods (*Mensheviks*) and those who, like Lenin, were in favour of a mono-party arrangement and hegemony of proletariat (*Bolsheviks*).

Incapable of producing a positive programme of economic reforms, Gorbachev decided to consolidate the society in a different way: through *searches for an internal enemy*: bureaucrats, self-important and arrogant officials — 'a spanner in the works of perestroika' and the ones to blame for everything.

Did Gorbachev realise what a genie he was letting out of the bottle when he ordered the country, where the power of authorities was absolute and where the market economy was not even mentioned out loud yet, to become democratic? Of course he did not.

In his new scheme of things there was simply no place for 'heavy Ural-made tanks' like Moscow's First Secretary. Yeltsin's example and his stand-off with the Moscow apparatus had taught Gorbachev that a direct onslaught on the party routine was simply not realistic. It caused muffled protest — heightened irritation — which was dangerous.

Most significantly, comrade Yeltsin was definitely going too far in his clash with the Moscow administration. He was playing with fire. Advocacy of 'social justice' was all very well but from the political point of view it could bring about unforeseen consequences.

With hindsight, Yeltsin's fight with 'privileges' — all those black *Volgas* stopped by traffic police on entry into the city to check the driver's waybill so that no wives or daughters could thus be given a free lift from the dacha; an attempt to democratise elite schools and universities; the movement for 'honest trade'; the efforts to eliminate 'hard manual labour' at enterprises — all of it, in the context of today's social divergence, looks historically doomed. Privileges of the Moscow elite were peanuts compared to today's fortunes but the characteristic trait of that world of party masters and their servants was a peculiar stench of lies and hypocrisy.

The luxuries inherent in the party life and tucked away behind the tall fences caused a more morbid irritation than the open eye-catching luxury of today. It was repugnant for a different reason: because of its make-up of lofty words about honesty, principles, class approach and care for 'working people'. And this is what Yeltsin was attacking in 1986 with the full force of his temperament. He was simply applying party principles that he understood too literally.

Gorbachev — flexible, fluid, adaptable, who had lived in Moscow since 1978 as a Politburo member — managed to grasp and accept the rules of this game.

But from the very start, Yeltsin had no intention of accepting those rules. He could have played on the same team as Gorbachev, stay tuned in to impulses generated by the General Secretary, try and grow into the Gorbachev's system of power and then, having solidified his position, get down to the reforms of Moscow and the comprehensive restructuring of its life. Yet something within him made these traditional tactics impossible. Yeltsin *took to heart* the pronounced principles of Gorbachev's *perestroika* and believed that changes for the better must occur not some other time but here and now and spread to all cells of the public organism, however small. He believed in Gorbachev's reforms too deeply, passionately, in a way that believers adhere to a new religion. In his attempt to use the chance and change things Yeltsin went too far.

As early as the spring of 1987 he was seeking a personal meeting with Gorbachev. Although they did meet regularly at the Politburo, Yeltsin was looking for an opportunity to meet in private — in order to discuss his problems in a meaningful and substantive way. But Gorbachev procrastinated and several times changed the timing of this rendezvous.

Possibly, he was aware of Yeltsin's difficulties in dealing with the Second Secretary Yegor Ligachev; he could suspect something else, unpleasant, leading to a lengthy and painful heart-to-heart — and simply was reluctant to get involved. Most likely, he waited for the problem to go away, and then there would be no need to look into it. It is equally possible that Gorbachev was simply annoyed and displeased with Yeltsin's behaviour, but did not want his personal feelings to colour his business relations.

Whatever the case, the palaver dragged into the summer. So when the summer was over, on September 12th, having returned from his annual leave, Yeltsin sent Gorbachev a long letter. Here it is.

'Dear Mikhail Sergeyevich,

My decision to write this letter has been a difficult one and has taken a long time to make. It has been one year and nine months since you and the Politburo made an offer, which I accepted, to come to the head of the Moscow party organisation. Reasons for either accepting or rejecting it were, of course, of little importance. I realised that it would be incredibly hard, that the experience I have, including the work experience, would have to be expanded considerably.

None of it bothered me. I felt your support and got to work with confidence, unexpected even for me. I worked with the new team with a selfless ardour, sticking to principles of collective responsibility and camaraderie.

The first milestones have been passed. What has been done is unquestionably little. Yet the most crucial result, I think (not to go into details), is that the very ethos, the spirit of Muscovites have changed. It is, of course, a spinoff of the general situation in the country. Yet, strange though it may seem, I am feeling increasingly dissatisfied.

Now, in the actions and words of some high-ranking officials I started noticing things I never noticed before. Humane attitudes and support are giving way, in case of some Politburo members and CC secretaries, to indifference to events in Moscow and coldness towards me.

Generally speaking, I have always tried to make my views known, even if it ran counter to the opinions of others. The result was an ever-growing number of undesirable situations. To be more precise, given my style, my directness and my biography, I have found myself unprepared for work in the Politburo.

I cannot but mention several matters of principle.

As regards Yegor Ligachev's style. In my view (and the view of some others), it is inacceptable, especially now, although I would hate to belittle his positive qualities. And his style is influencing the style in which the CC Secretariat operates. Some "provincial" secretaries are emulating him uncritically. But primarily — the entire party stands to lose from it. To "decode" it all — the party will be harmed (if it were done publicly). It is only you, personally, who can change anything in the interests of the party.

The party organisations have ended up in the tail-end of all grandiose events. Nothing here, with the exception of global politics, has been affected by *perestroika*, which creates a veritable chain of causes and effects. And eventually we wonder why perestroika gets stuck at the level of primary party cells.

The concept and the language are revolutionary. As for execution, especially within the party itself — there is nothing apart from the same old story: a parochially opportunistic, petty, bureaucratic, apparently high-sounding approach. This is where they start diverging: the revolutionary word and the deeds in the party that are at odds with a political approach.

Abundance of paperwork; the need to count, every day, tomatoes, tea, railway carriages... and no significant break-through\*, briefings on petty pretexts, chicanery, unearthing of negative facts for the material. Questions to "big himself up".

I am not even speaking about attempts at criticism stemming from below. I am very concerned by the fact that others think like me but are afraid of speaking up. I believe this is the most dangerous thing for our party. On the whole, I think, in his work Yegor Kuzmich\*\* is lacking a systematic approach and subtlety. His constant referrals to his "Tomsk experiences" are embarrassing.

As for me personally, his constant carping at me, ever since the June plenary session of the Central Committee and the session of the Politburo on September 9th , cannot be seen as anything other than consistent persecution. I cannot work out the role of the newly-created commission and I ask you to rectify the situation. It appears he is not in tune with the party mechanism but is working to create discord. I am reluctant to discuss his attitude to Moscow affairs. I am amazed at how it is possible to fail to ask, at least once, in the course of two years, about the situation in 1,150 party cells. Party committees are losing their independence although it has already been granted to *kolkhozes* and enterprises.

I have always defended exactitude and demanded control. But the performance should not be motivated by fear as is the case now with many party committees and their First Secretaries. I hold Yegor Ligachev responsible for the fact that relations between the Central Committee and local organisations lack integrity and a spirit of camaraderie, as befits members of the same party, for only such an atmosphere stimulates creativity, confidence and even self-sacrifice at work.

This is where the "broken mechanism" manifests itself. The apparatus

---

\* Sic! It is a verbatim report.

\*\* Ligachev.

must be considerably reduced by up to 50% and its structure revamped significantly. The experience of Moscow *Raikoms*, be it limited, still proves the point.

I am depressed because of the attitude of some comrades from the Politburo. They are smart, that is why they have changed colours quickly. But can one really trust them? They are convenient and I am sorry, Mikhail Sergeyevich, but I feel they are becoming convenient for you, too. I am finding myself seeking refuge in silence even when I do not agree, just like some are feigning consent.

I realise that I am inconvenient. I also am fully aware of the fact that to settle the issue of me cannot be easy. But it is better to acknowledge mistakes now. Given the current personnel issues, problems associated with me shall only multiply and impede your work. I sincerely do not wish this to be the case.

Also, I do not wish it for yet another reason, for despite your incredible efforts, this fight for stability will lead to stagnation, same as before. This is unacceptable. These are some reasons and explanations that have prompted this request addressed to you. It is not weakness and not cowardice.

*I request to be relieved of the post of the First Secretary of the Moscow City Committee of the CPSU and responsibilities of the candidate member of the Politburo of the CC CPSU. I ask of you to treat this letter as an official letter of resignation.*

*I hope it will not be necessary for me to address the CC CPSU plenary session directly.*

Yours sincerely,

*Boris Yeltsin'*

... Compared to 1990 when it was first made public in Yeltsin's *Confessions*, nowadays this letter puzzles. And for increasingly numerous readers under 30 years of age, it is rife with riddles and nebulous details.

Comrade Ligachev, CC plenary session, plenary session of the Central Committee, Politburo — how to make head or tails of it all?

Why is the author of the letter so concerned with the fate of some 'party committees' and 'party organisations' — is it the same or are they different after all? What does it mean — 'negative facts for a material' and why does Yeltsin despise it so? What sort of a commission was created unbeknownst to him? Who is making him count, on a daily basis, tomatoes, tea and railway carriages — totally disparate things?

Even more important are contradictions in meaning. What does the author want: to be dismissed himself or to have Ligachev punished? Is he trying to warn the General Secretary of the approaching perils or does he say the bitter truth about him directly to his face? In a nutshell, what is his purpose? Not even mention the clumsiness of style where the author says, for example that 'reasons for either accepting or rejecting it were, of course, of little importance'.

At the same time one can say the history of contemporary Russia started from this letter. It can be viewed as the first document of our revolution. A revolution never chooses its leaders, sources and documents. Ours was born of *this* letter.

Yeltsin's actual message is rather straightforward: he wanted to work in Moscow in the same way as he did in Sverdlovsk, following transparent rules that were clear to him, to have his hands untied, be independent of the political games in the Kremlin and shoulder the full weight of responsibility. It was utopian but he believed it to be a realistic approach. In short, there was ground for thought. And Gorbachev did think it over. Let us see what happened next.

'Gorbachev would later say', writes Yeltsin's American biographer Leon Aron, 'that he decided to avoid haste and ponder the issue thoroughly. He told no one of Yeltsin's missive. Upon his return from vacation he telephoned Yeltsin and suggested that they should meet and talk — a bit later. To Gorbachev "later" meant after the next plenary session and the festivities in connection with the anniversary of the October Revolution...'

However, it is not true that 'Gorbachev told no one' about Yeltsin's letter. Says Anatoly Cherniayev, Gorbachev's assistant:

'When on holiday, at the dacha in the Crimea, at the appointed hour I stepped into Gorbachev's study. He was saying something heatedly into the telephone receiver. As I was making my way in the conversation was coming to an end. I sat down and he held out some sheets to me. "Here, have a read." "What is it?" "Do have a read." It was Yeltsin's letter in which he was saying that he couldn't continue in "this" way. Allegedly, he had given it his best shot and in return, instead of help, was bumping into constant hindrances. And it is none other but the CC Secretariat and Ligachev personally who were throwing sand in his wheels. He was applying for a permission to resign.

"What shall I do with this?" asked M.S.*

I recalled that Gorbachev had been repeatedly praising Yeltsin — at the Politburo and on some other occasions, and had been saying that Yeltsin had received a complex and neglected posting... A day or two later I was again a witness to their "couple of minutes" on the telephone. Gorbachev was paying compliments and was very solicitous. "Wait, Boris, cool down, we'll sort it all out. We are on the eve of the 70th anniversary of the October**. Moscow is the flagship city here. We should prepare ourselves properly and have a worthy celebration. Important things must be done and said in connection with this occasion. Get down to work; let us manage this event the right way. Then we'll attend to things. I am asking you not to raise this issue (about resignation)". After he put the phone in its cradle M.S. told me, "I did manage to persuade him — with great difficulty. We agreed that he would take it easy before the celebrations and would create no fuss."

'Yeltsin insisted that he had taken a different message. "Later", he thought, meant a couple of days, a week at most. But a week passed by, then another. Gorbachev kept his silence.' (Leon Aron).

At the CC CPSU plenary session that was held on 21 October 1987 Gorbachev made a presentation on the occasion of the 70th anniversary of the October.

It was the only item on the agenda. Yeltsin raised his hand.

'*Comrade Ligachev, the chair*. Dear comrades, the presentation is thus concluded. Perhaps there are some questions? Do ask. No questions? If not, let us confer on this.

*Gorbachev*. Comrade Yeltsin has a question.

---

\* Mikhail Sergeyevich.

\*\* Revolution of 1917.

*Chair.* In which case let us decide — is there a need to open debate?
*Gorbachev.* Comrade Yeltsin would like to make a statement.
*Chair.* The floor is given to comrade Yeltsin, Boris Nikolayevich, the First Secretary of the Moscow CPSU *Gorkom*, candidate member of the Politburo. Boris Nikolayevich, if you please.'

Why was Gorbachev so clearly insisting on giving Yeltsin the floor (Ligachev was equally clearly against it)? He could stay silent or personally ask Yeltsin to postpone his speech till after the session. But it must have suddenly occurred to Gorbachev that this question would have to be settled — sooner or later. His tactics of procrastinating and dodging the situation brought no results. Yeltsin did not heed the signal and his administrative mutiny was inevitable. Well, if this was the case, Gorbachev decided to provide him with the opportunity. If Yeltsin wanted it so badly — let him get it off his chest. Let there be p*erestroika*. Let there be g*lasnost*.

His many months' long annoyance against the person who had created this grievous, uncomfortable and totally unnecessary situation in the Politburo erupted at the most unexpected moment. Gorbachev *allowed* Yeltsin to speak.

Equally, Gorbachev could be adversely impressed by a muffled threat at the very end of Yeltsin's letter: 'I hope it will not be necessary for me to address the CC CPSU plenary session directly'. It was a challenge. So in the instant when Yeltsin raised his hand Gorbachev decided to abandon pity, stop protecting this bizarre person and fight back.

Back to Yeltsin.

'... The lessons of 70 years are hard ones, mainly grievous cases of defeat. The power within the Politburo, just like in any party committee, was in the hands of one person. And this one person was above any criticism. The situation in our Politburo now is different but what is taking place is forever more voluble glorification of the General Secretary by some Politburo members. Nowadays when the new democratic forms of association are being created, this is inadmissible. We are being carried in this direction.'

Declaring the floor open to Yeltsin, Gorbachev was still hopeful that the atmosphere in the assembly would bring him to his senses. It was one thing to write a personal letter, and something totally different to address the session. The mere interior of the Kremlin hall should have produced a sobering effect on Yeltsin and help him formulate his criticisms in a more palatable fashion, smooth things over a bit, adopt a more civilised line of behaviour — one gentleman, albeit a hot-headed and passionate but still a gentleman, had decided to voice his disagreements to another one. We shall give both a slap on the wrist, issue instructions, come to think of it — even set up a committee! After all, there is always a way out!

Instead, Yeltsin delivered a slap in Gorbachev's own face — as if there were no tomorrow.

Gorbachev declared the debate open.

'Twenty five people voiced their condemnation of Yeltsin. Among them — Eduard Shevardnadze, Alexander Yakovlev (leading democrats in the Politburo!), his fellow Sverdlovsk native Kolbin, head of government Ryzhkov (also a native of Sverdlovsk), Chairman of the Moscow Council Saikin (who actually tried to defend Yeltsin but ever so timidly), Chairman of the KGB Chebrikov, Chairman of the Supreme Soviet Gromyko, academician Arbatov, his former boss and protector in Sverdlovsk Ryabov — the list would have been longer had Gorbachev given them all free rein!

'*Ye. Ligachev.* As regards voluble glorification within the Politburo. I have no part in it and I have never been seen singing inordinate praise. Comrade Gorbachev and I are, like all of you, on good and honest terms, as befits party members... As for popular enthusiasm being now on the wane, I believe this is not true in principle. This is casting doubts on our policy as a whole... In my capacity of the Central Committee member I feel from the bottom of my heart that we have the support of our people, and this is what inspires confidence that the cause to which we dedicate our lives shall be carried out and translated into reality... If we do not drown our *perestroika* in talk we shall not bury it, we are not grave-diggers but pioneers. And it is my sincere belief that the party shall be victorious. (*Applause*).

'*G. Arbatov, CC CPSU member, Director of the Institute for the USA and Canadian Studies of the USSR Academy of Sciences.* I believe comrade Yeltsin caused significant damage to the cause. It is probably too late to rectify it because the ripples produced by his speech will spread…

*N. Ryzhkov, member of the CC CPSU Politburo, Chairman of the Council of Ministers of the USSR.* As regards the General Secretary. Well, I don't know. It seems to me — how does comrade Yeltsin even dare to be so brazen as to touch on this subject? Yes. We all respect him*. To be quite frank, I am happy that I work with him. In my opinion, as soon as he** moved to the Moscow party organisation he started developing political nihilism. He got the taste for being quoted from abroad by various radio stations…

*A. Yakovlev, member of the CC CPSU Politburo, Secretary of the CC CPSU.* In my view Boris Nikolayevich has confused the big events happening in the country now with his petty slants and urges… This is exaltation over the pseudo-revolutionary phrases, a case of self-adoration.

*Ed. Shevardnadze, member of the CC CPSU Politburo, Foreign Minister of the USSR.* I wanted to refrain from using this word, maybe my speech is somewhat too emotional but to a certain extent this is a betrayal of the party… *(Applause).* Who in this audience harbours any doubts that comrade Ligachev is a crystal-pure man of integrity? I don't believe there is anybody like this among us. I don't know… *(Applause).* I would characterise this statement by Boris Nikolayevich as totally irresponsible… *(Applause).*

*A. Gromyko, member of the CC CPSU Politburo, Chairman of the Presidium of the USSR Supreme Council.* I think we shall act correctly if we demonstrate one more time that the party shall not tolerate that its ranks should be thrown into disarray… It is Lenin's behest to us. *(Applause).*'

That was the debate. And this is what Gorbachev had to say.

'Comrade Yeltsin believes that he cannot continue working within the Politburo although, according to him, the issue of him being the First Secretary of the party *Gorkom* shall be settled not by the Central Committee but the municipal committee. This is something of a novelty. Maybe what is under discussion here is the secession of the Moscow party organisation?'

Gorbachev was equally piqued by the accusation of creating a new

---

\* Gorbachev — *Authors' comment.*

\*\* Yeltsin — *Author's comment.*

cult of personality: 'Boris Nikolayevich, we all know what cult means. It is a system, the system of power. You do not know the difference between chalk and cheese. Shall I run a course on the basics of politics for you?'

Yeltsin answered, 'By now there is no need.'

'*Gorbachev*. Democracy, personal commitment, independence is all very well. But... The plenary session has been presented with a crucially important report. But because of you, of your ambitious persona, we are dealing with you. Really, to go so far and drag the CC into a debate of this kind!

*Yeltsin*. It was an outburst...

*Gorbachev*. What is your attitude to your comrades' comments?

*Yeltsin*. Apart from some expressions, I agree with the assessments. In speaking today I let down the CC, the Moscow organisation. It was a mistake.

*Gorbachev*. Shall you find enough strength in yourself to carry on?

*Yeltsin*. Judging by the appraisal of the speakers the opinion is rather unanimous. I am repeating what I said before: I am asking to be relieved of the candidacy into the Politburo members and the post of the MGK\* secretary.

*Gorbachev*. In essence, the approach demonstrated to us by Yeltsin should be rejected as a very grievous blunder that casts aspersions on the atmosphere within the Politburo. It is inadmissible. At the party conference we shall develop mechanisms for replacing both Politburo members and the General Secretary when they have outlived their use. No one shall be clinging to their high offices. What is the purpose of such a speech? Was it to discredit Ligachev? But he is totally open to the public eye. Yes, there are all sorts of murmurs; the radio is bursting with gossip. Take Arbatov, he says that in the West they are trying to drive a wedge between Gorbachev and Ligachev while a conflict between Ligachev and Ryzhkov is kept in reserve, etc.

I also find it hard to work in the Politburo. The Politburo must be a collegiate political body dealing with matters of principle. And you go on pulling the wool over my eyes.

There is nothing constructive in your speech. And you give it at a time

---

\* Moscow Municipal Committee.

when we need constructive ideas, when everybody should make a good effort. You have simply showed us your true colours. I also wanted to say something else: why is this happening?

A person in such a high office is proved to be politically weak and to have poor knowledge of theory. Clearly, he finds it hard. If he wanted to he could manage. But what's the use of talking now! I, personally, am in a difficult situation.

I would like to conclude thus: let us make no decision in the heat of the argument. I suggest the following:

1. The session shall recognise Yeltsin's speech as politically fraught.
2. The Politburo and the MGK shall be instructed to consider Yeltsin's letter

of resignation from the posts of the First Secretary of the MGK of the CPSU taking account of the exchange of opinions that has taken place at the plenary session of the Central Committee.'

Gorbachev went on and on and spent quite some time speaking.

But by then Yeltsin didn't care. He had crossed the line and became an apostate. His die was cast.

In the summer of 1987, prior to writing a letter to Gorbachev requesting his permission to resign (or possibly having already penned it) Boris Nikolayevich convened the family: Lena, Tanya and Naina Iosifovna — for a serious discussion.

'He was calling us one by one into his study and asking us all the same question,' Tanya recollects. 'Major changes are possibly going to happen in our life, I may lose my position, lose everything — the flat, the dacha, we may be forced to leave Moscow. Are ready for such a turn? I answered, of course we are, Dad. We are always with you, it's OK, we'll manage. But I sensed very strongly that Dad believed, for some reason, that having left the Politburo he may continue as the First Secretary in Moscow. He still was harbouring some hope in this respect.'

The future was of course the subject of discussion with Naina Iosifovna.

'"Well, if nothing else, I should be taken on by some construction trust," said he. I asked, "Where? In Sverdlovsk?" He thought it over and answered, "Well, why not?" "But you must realise", I added, "that there is a First Secretary of the *Obkom* in Sverdlovsk, too. He will be carrying out the CC decrees and no one will leave you in peace and allow work quietly." "In which case we shall go to somewhere in the North*," said Boris Nikolayevich. "Look here," I was suddenly enraged. "Why must you think about this? How to provide for us? We do have adult children after all: they will care for us somehow. And listen, I am ready to scrub floors, to work as a cleaner but I do promise we will not starve." "Aha, it was just a dare!" he was triumphant. "It was my test for you; I WANTED TO HEAR what you were going to say…'"

The days after the plenary session were grim. After October 21st he kept going to work for nearly three more weeks: like a robot, like a live corpse — all the time being aware that his destiny had already been decided. For him it was torture.

On November 7th together with other Soviet leaders he climbed Lenin's Mausoleum** and there the vacuum manifested itself physically: only two people shook hands with him — the Polish leader Wojciech Jaruzelski and the Cuban Fidel Castro. The rest made believe they did not notice his presence.

He was standing bare-headed and watched festive columns passing by. The marchers were cheering.

'On November 9th,' tells Naina Iosifovna, 'he came to the *Gorkom* and succumbed to a heart seizure. It was a seizure, nothing more. He ended up in the resuscitation department of the Kremlin hospital in Michurinsky Prospect. I would come over to see him at seven in the morning and leave late in the evening; sometimes I stayed overnight, simply to be close by. I noticed immediately that he was being pumped with medications that produced an adverse reaction in him: Seduxen and Valium. He couldn't even speak, was barely able to lift himself off his bed. The doctors were insistent that all of it was necessary. But I felt increasingly overcome with

---

\* Many of Soviet construction projects below the North Pole were recruiting workforce on a contract basis.

\** The platform on top of Lenin's Tomb in Red Square has always been the place from which the leaders and dignitaries watch and welcome parades and manifestations.

worry. Two days later they gave him a stimulant instead, I think it was Nootropil, he unexpectedly regained his speech. The phone went off: it was Gorbachev on the government line. I sat close to him and heard it all. Gorbachev was saying that Boris should "pop over" to the *Gorkom* plenary session. "Mikhail Sergeyevich," answered Boris, his speech laboured, "I cannot even make it to the toilet." Gorbachev answered sternly, "It's OK, the doctors shall help." I nearly cried out — over my dead body! It is impossible! Boris said that if he failed to show up they may clamp down on the entire organisation. That it would be a new "Leningrad affair*", like in the fifties, when everybody was first arrested and then shot. For some reason he was convinced that the *Gorkom* bureau would be defending him and the only way to save his colleagues was to shoulder all the blame. But I kept resisting his arguments.'

This was when the doctors interfered: raised him off his bed and helped him dress. Yeltsin was tottering. Naina Iosifovna cried in despair, 'Where is your Hippocratic Oath?' 'I have my own set of hippocrats', came the harsh reply from the Kremlin physician. Another doctor told her, 'Don't worry — he will be given injections that last about an hour.' But the plenary session lasted several hours. Yeltsin's condition upon his return to the hospital was critical.

Generally speaking, this tradition of acting in a pack when trampling somebody underfoot, the verbal flogging and forcing someone to run the gauntlet stems from the very old Soviet rites, the Party assemblies in the twenties and the thirties, show trials and the ethos of Stalin's state.

Boris Pasternak, a poet of genius, died after such a public lashing at the Union of Writers in 1960.

When people, with whom you chatted amicably, are now throwing stones — it is a unique experience. The only person who silently shook his hand after the plenary session was CC member Viktor Chernomyrdin.

However, a different degree of public ostracism was in store for him at the *Gorkom*.

---

* The Leningrad affair, or Leningrad case, was a series of criminal cases fabricated in the late forties — early fifties in order to accuse a number of prominent members of the Communist Party of the Soviet Union of treason and intention to create an anti-Soviet organisation out of the Leningrad Party cell.

Over there he would learn all there was to know about a pack of bloodhounds let off their chain.

Moscow Party bosses spent several hours crucifying him on every charge imaginable. They recalled his rudeness, his staffing policy (he dismissed one too many), his populism, his hauteur. Worn out and barely aware of what he was doing, Yeltsin made a muddled and confused speech expressing his penitence. That was precisely what Gorbachev was after. That was why Yeltsin had been pumped with powerful drugs.

When the vote was over the participants started filing out of the audience. Yeltsin stayed on the podium, in the presidium, he could not stand up.

In the wings, the doctors were waiting.

He was taken to the same clinic, the one in Michurinsky Prospect. Naina Iosifovna recollects, 'When he was brought back I started screaming my head off and telling them that only fascists in concentration camps could do such things, that with them it was even worse, that Gorbachev was an executioner. I do not know if the head of security passed these words on to him…'

The 'treatment' continued. He remained semi-conscious because of the drugs.

'Once they convened a board of doctors and, as was their wont, over a cup of coffee, in a nice and relaxed atmosphere they came round to discussing the state of Yeltsin's health. That was when Gorbachev called. Boris Nikolayevich was talking with great effort and as I could work it out they were discussing his retirement,' says Naina Iosifovna. 'This was when I cut across the doctors' discussion and said that it would be only possible to discuss his retirement when he was capable of responding adequately, when he was *compos mentis* again. If you can't be bothered with the hassle, send him to a regular municipal hospital but do not discuss his pension with him now. Several days later Gorbachev called again and said, "Boris, you shall work for *Gosstroi* as a deputy head. Your status shall be equal to that of a minister." I remember I was approached by an emergency physician who told me under his breath, "If you do not want him to become disabled if you want him alive, get him out of here and quick." It gave me a terrible fright. And we discharged him from there having signed a letter whereby all responsibility for his health stayed with us.

…We put him up in a vacation lodge in Barvikha*. There he was soon on the mend. The first snow fell and we even brought him skis.'

He did not die. He did not become a cripple. He was breathing. He could walk.

He made his first step on his new ski track…

---

* A holiday home in a village nearby Moscow.

# Exoneration
*(1988)*

On 9 November 1987, Mikhail Gorbachev was told that Boris Yeltsin, the former First Secretary of the said *Gorkom*, had made an attempt on his life.

'On November 9th,' writes his American biographer T. Colton, 'they found him in the vacation centre… covered in blood, and immediately whisked him off to the Kremlin hospital in an ambulance. He had stabbed the left side of his chest… with scissors. The choice of implement and the wound surface indicated that it was pure desperation, a cry for help, not suicide as such. Yeltsin never referred to his stay in hospital openly, he only mentioned that he had had a "breakdown", a severe headache and chest pains…'

'I remember that right after the plenary session he had a terrible pain in the region of his heart. When I saw him in the evening he constantly kept his hand on the left side of the breast. Generally speaking, he was in a terrible state; after all, he had become a pariah in the blink of an eye. It's hard to say how Dad managed to hurt himself with scissors but I am sure it was a nervous breakdown and not an attempt to kill himself. Had he really meant it, he would have used his pistol. We never discussed it with him — not then, not later. It was too difficult for him,' recalls Tatyana, his daughter.

It is true that afterwards Yeltsin never mentioned this, not once, not in a single book or an interview of his. It was Gorbachev who first explained it all in his memoirs fifteen years later.

Gorbachev should never have believed the rumours but he did.

All in all, between October 21st (the date of Yeltsin's speech at the plenary session) and November 11th (the date when a semi-conscious Yeltsin was delivered to the Moscow *Gorkom* assembly) quite a few things happened.

For example, Gorbachev's assistant Anatoly Cherniayev wrote to his boss to the effect that Yeltsin should be forgiven. It is a different era nowadays and such issues should be settled in a different way.

Several days later, on November 3rd-4th, Saikin, chairman of the Moscow Council executive committee and bureau member of the Moscow *Gorkom*, wrote to Gorbachev suggesting a compromise: dismiss Yeltsin from the Politburo but leave him head of the Moscow Party cell.

Gorbachev was extremely annoyed at this initiative. The Muscovites obstinately stuck to their guns, he decided to teach them a long-overdue lesson. He decided to convene the Moscow *Gorkom* plenary session at once.

Another worrying development: rallies in Moscow and Sverdlovsk. Several under- and postgraduate students of the Moscow State University presented a petition in support of Yeltsin to their rector's office. Gorbachev decreed that the guilty party should be suitably punished but no one should be expelled. The last thing he needed was to attract public attention to the incident. Several hundred people got together in front of the *Gorkom* in Sverdlovsk and submitted an appeal to the Politburo. The rally spent several hours in the pouring rain and then dispelled.

Those were, alas, very unpleasant facts. At the same time Gorbachev was suddenly piqued and amazed. He never expected students to show interest. Somebody must have incited them. But who?

The 70th anniversary of the Great October Revolution was celebrated with galas and conferences all over the country. A ceremonial meeting took place in Moscow, too. On November 6th, Yeltsin, the First Secretary of the CPSU Moscow *Gorkom* made a speech addressing the Moscow Party activists. His voice was flat. He had spent many a sleepless night by then. Naina Iosifovna always by the side of his bed, was trying to make him feel better with herbal infusions and sleeping pills he always disliked (one is always woozy the next day).

... Gorbachev was sitting there, tense. In the course of an hour and a half that it took to deliver the speech he must have been mentally scrolling, over and over, the details and nuances of the October plenary. After all, he did ask Yeltsin whether he would be capable of carrying on. But the latter rejected the proffered hand! He publicly turned down the offer of working for the Politburo! What was he counting on? Support from the Moscow cell? Here they are, comrades Muscovites, assembled in the audience and mentally taking stock of pros and cons. We shall see...

... While still in hospital, Yeltsin was offered a post of the first deputy to the Chairman of the USSR's *Gosstroi*. Had he been offered a post of an ambassador to somewhere (Gorbachev did discuss this option, too, with his assistants) or something else of an equally humiliating nature, he probably would have returned to Sverdlovsk. But the last thing Gorbachev wanted was a string of demonstrations — as a result.

Yeltsin first came along to *Gosstroi* still a candidate member of the Politburo.

'First it was security guards who made their way into the reception,' recollects Lev Sukhanov, the then assistant to the Gosstroi Chairman, 'and then — Yeltsin himself. He looked athletic, clad in an elegant navy suit, a snow-white shirt and a stylish tie.'

Yeltsin was trying to 'keep to his standards' but doctors from the Fourth Administration* insisted that a first-aid box be installed on the wall in the office adjacent to Yeltsin's — the so-called room for repose. Alarm buttons were fitted on his desk and in the conference room. In the next-door office, they fitted a sofa, too.

For medical reasons, he was not allowed to work for longer than four hours a day. He who used to start his working day at 6 or 7 A.M. and wind down, sometimes, at midnight! Routinely, he slept for four hours — and found it sufficient! 'During the night hours,' Yeltsin wrote in his *President's Journal*, 'those hard, probably the hardest days of my life often come back to me... Not many are aware of the nature of this torture: to sit in a

---

* The Fourth Main Administration in the Ministry of Public Health of the USSR provided medical services especially for the high level Communist party and government officials.

dead silence of your office, in a complete vacuum, subconsciously waiting for something... For example, that the phone would ring — or that it wouldn't.'

In February the CC plenary released him from his position within the Politburo.

Although this was quite a technical matter he still took it very hard, his health deteriorated, so yet again there were doctors, injections, medications...

He was clearly going through post-traumatic stress disorder, endlessly churning in his mind the same phrases and fragments of his speech. At the same time: he was *waiting* for something, he says so himself.

When offering him a post in the *Gosstroi* Gorbachev literally told him this, 'Be aware, I shall never let you back into politics.'

By old Soviet yardsticks, the punishment was lenient. He remained a minister, a member of the CPSU Central Committee, as if to say: we are giving you a decent job but do not believe that you got away scot-free. But this ambiguity failed to pacify Yeltsin.

He made repeated attempts to become 'one of ours' in the *Gosstroi*. This is what Lev Sukhanov has to say about his first months there.

'Yeltsin spent nearly the entire year of 1988 in a condition of psychological stress which did not deter him from his routine obligations. It was as difficult to push a third-rate project 'through Yeltsin' as it was to reverse the flow of the Siberian rivers. Meanwhile this crazy idea had already been discussed at the *Gosstroi* — along with placing some manufacturing facilities along Lake Baikal. Yeltsin was emphatically opposed to both projects; he was submitting memoranda, made constant calls to fellow ministers, got in touch with Ryzhkov himself. To the latter's credit, he heard Yeltsin out and promised help.'

Incidentally, Lev Yevgeniyevich Sukhanov, his new assistant in the *Gosstroi*, stayed with Yeltsin for a long time and eventually became a member of his team.

So, it was probably Sukhanov who told his boss that a Xerox of his classified speech at the October plenary was on sale by the metro station!

'How do you mean, on sale?' asked the stupefied Yeltsin. 'Go on, get me a copy!'

It turned out that Yeltsin's 'speech', passed from hand to hand as *samizdat*\* and already offered by some enterprising citizens by the metro stations, had nothing in common with what he actually did say at the memorable plenary. Moreover, somewhat later it transpired that about eight (!) versions of this 'speech' were in clandestine circulation. It was a kind of a peculiar literary monument, a new popular mythology. But Yeltsin realised right away that hundreds and thousands of his 'speeches', reproduced in a 'do-it-yourself' way, now diffused all over the country would all end up, among other subversive documents, on the desks of Soviet leaders and the KGB.

According to false speeches Yeltsin had being saying this:

'We must withdraw our troops from Afghanistan. I believe comrade Shevardnadze should give it his best shot. At the moment he is busying himself with other issues, less urgent, and is spending months abroad at a stretch… I am forced to ask the Politburo to shield me from being patronised by Raisa Maksimovna\*\*, from her almost daily phone calls and lectures.'

'Yes, comrades, I am finding it difficult to explain to working people why seventy years after the power had been transferred to workers and farmers they still have to queue for sausage that contains more starch than meat, while our tables are groaning with sturgeon, caviar and other treats, effortlessly obtainable from sources from which the working people are safely barred…'

Reading these passages reminiscent of revolutionary poetry and ascribed to the folk hero and protector comrade Yeltsin was puzzling. But there were also letters. It was the letters that finally convinced him that counterfeited speeches were not a frame-up but genuine mythology.

In their letters, people were expressing their support, compassion, admiration, excitement and love. There were hundreds of them. Naina Iosifovna was storing them in a large box but gradually the stream started dwindling, obviously channelled into other agencies. In Sverdlovsk, for

---

\* Virtually means *self-published*, an activity entailing criminal charges in the Soviet days.
\*\* Gorbachev's wife.

example, notices appeared on post boxes — 'Letters addressed to comrade Yeltsin in *Gosstroi* shall not be accepted for posting'.

Some visitors would seek his audience in person. For example, Ilya Ivanovich Malashenko, a lawyer and retired lieutenant-colonel, came along to *Gosstroi* and requested to be shown into Yeltsin's office 'simply to shake his hand'. Sukhanov immediately ushered him into the office — for Yeltsin, it was the best medication imaginable. During the May Day demonstration, again, he was approached and people were shaking his hand and expressing their gratitude.

It all meant just one thing: Yeltsin, as a public figure, had not become invisible. So to erase his name completely and forever, from the pages of the press and public consciousness, Gorbachev needed to possess the same degree of cruelty as Stalin. But this was running counter to his pronouncements and his own nature. Most importantly, however, the times had changed.

'Didn't you fear that his resignation would be followed by something else, much more frightening?' I ask of Yeltsin's daughter.

'Frankly speaking, we didn't. We realised that the times had changed and no genuine reprisals would ensue. The worst that could have happened — he would have been sent back to Sverdlovsk. What we did fear was the state of his health, his moods.'

A question to Naina Iosifovna, 'After all that had happened, what did you think of his attempt to exonerate himself, to return to politics? Did you have any suspicions that things may get worse? Did you try to stop him?'

She thought it over and answered with a question, 'How could I have stopped him? He couldn't just surrender. It was against his nature.'

Unquestionably, Boris Nikolayevich's family played a huge part in his exoneration. 'All of us,' says his younger daughter Tanya, 'were trying to spoil him a bit, to cook something tasty, to buy something interesting, to distract his attention, to spur him into being active again. And it did take an effort to buy something then — such was that life. I remember I learnt that Czech beer, his favourite, was available in a particular shop. I rushed headlong over there. The anti-alcohol campaign was at its peak, the shop floor was a veritable brawl, shoppers drunk and swearing. It was probably the only time in my life when I waited in such a crowd, among drunken thugs, for several hours. I did make it, though, and bought two crates. They had to be taken out of the shop somehow, towards a taxi rank. I remember, I was carrying one in my hands and kicking the second one forward but I felt exalted that I would give Dad a present.'

It should be mentioned that just then, in 1988, Tanya married an engineer Leonid Dyachenko. They worked together in the Design Bureau *Salut*. The programmer-mathematician Tanya worked for the ballistics department and was developing the programme for remote docking of spacecraft (intended for use on unmanned cargo vessels making deliveries to the *Mir* station). It is quite possible that it was her husband who gave Tanya a lift in his car when she wanted to carry home the two crates of coveted imported beer.

A new stage in Yeltsin's exoneration was his public speeches, primarily interviews. He gave several, but not all of them saw the light of day in the Soviet Union.

At the same time the Western media had a heyday. Though unforthcoming during his first encounter with an American TV crew, in his interview (May of 1988) to an American journalist Peter Snow Yeltsin spoke much more definitively. Asked 'Would you like to see Ligachev demoted and removed from the centre of power — since in your view he is opposed to reforms?' Yeltsin's answered with a flat, 'Yes, I would.'

And then, as he was spending his summer vacations in Latvia, the first interview made its way into a Soviet newspaper. It was published by a tiny local *Jūrmala* and the republican daily *Soviet Youth*. Subsequently, this interview was carried by scores of newspapers at the district and oblasts level, as well as by some industry-sponsored titles. Despite the resistance of Party authorities, the progressively-minded editors were already breathing the air of *glasnost* and sensing the advent of 'new times'.

So what did Yeltsin say to the Latvian journalists?

'We have subdued the human spirit. People find themselves squashed under the weight of questionable moral standards, decrees and instructions that cannot be challenged. We have taught people to unite for the purpose of putting a consorted stranglehold on discord rather than for seeking concord with each other.'

Everybody realised that this shot was aimed at Gorbachev. This was the old Yeltsin speaking: unbroken, unsubdued, as point blank and vehement as ever.

By the way, it was also in Jūrmala*that Yeltsin first watched a game of tennis. This is how it happened.

'I met Boris Nikolayevich Yeltsin,' writes Shamil Tarpischev** in his book *The First Set*, 'in August of 1988 when the USSR national team played in Jūrmala against the Dutch team in the Davis Cup tournament.' Yeltsin, along with Naina Iosifovna, came along to the stadium to support "our own". The next day I played doubles with republican bosses in the "Riga Seashore" vacation home. I spotted Yeltsin who was walking by, together with his wife. They must have been staying there too. I said hello, shook hands and noticed that Yeltsin's hand was very cold. Then again, he did not look all too well — he was clearly surviving on medications.

A year later on the same beach I was playing football with my tennis mates. The ball rolled over towards the water edge. I ran off to retrieve it and saw Yeltsin. "Oh, Boris Nikolayevich, you are here again? Are you on vacation?" "Hi Shamil!" Turns out he remembered my name. Unexpectedly for myself, I suggested a game of tennis to him. He tried to make excuses, "I am a very poor player!" "Still, let's try doubles!" "I have never even played doubles before!" Somehow I did manage to talk him into it. He enjoyed the experience.'

On 13 March 1988 Gorbachev left on an official visit to Yugoslavia. He knew it perfectly well, had known for quite some time — it was the ABC of politics — that the supreme leader who leaves his country is taking risks but was pushing presentiments to the back of his mind — it was only a short visit.

The incident with Yeltsin, however disagreeable, had just been resolved. Also, it was an important lesson for anyone who sought to split the unity among the country's leaders.

---

\* A seaside resort in Latvia — much frequented in the Soviet days by the artistic and sports elite.

\** President of the Russian Tennis Federation, member of the International Olympic Committee.

## EXONERATION (1988)

So what could possibly go wrong? Will they hold an extraordinary plenary session? Hastily knock together a group of Politburo members antagonistic to *perestroika*?

But at least half of the Politburo members were his staunch, sincere and dedicated supporters. The rest inspired no fear, they had no views and were incapable of aggression — he could always spot it in others.

The punch was packed unexpectedly and hit hard: there was a publication in *The Sovetskaya Rossiya* daily. A social sciences* lecturer from Leningrad, one Nina Andreyeva, penned a controversial article — 'I Cannot Relinquish My Principles'.

Ideologically speaking, the article contained nothing new. The same laboured arguments to be expected from the worm-eaten Party dogmatists, those who had spent decades of carefree, well-sated, affluent and senseless existence ensconced in their managerial offices. Indeed, hands off Stalin — the banner of our triumphs; we used to go on an offensive with his name on our lips; even Churchill respected him (never mind that he was a bourgeois nit himself); hands off our moral values (Stalin being one of them); leave our socialism alone; you are the fifth column sent by the West, turncoats, hirelings, outside our country...

The novelty was in the delivery: the typesetting of the article itself, the place assigned to it on the newspaper page, the thorough editing obviously performed by the old-school Party writers. Each phrase was sharp, brought to the level of Jesuit scholasticism, perfected like Brezhnev's reports — one could sense, one could read between the lines: *it was no accident*! More than that: it was the viewpoint of the taciturn majority, of the Party, or — let's raise stakes — the attitude of the people itself!

Relatively soon it became known that Ligachev had read the article and, what's more, *prior to publication*.

... No, he would strike back and retaliate with the very weapons they had used. It shall be an article in *Pravda* that would cross all the t's and dot all the i's.

He summoned Yakovlev and instructed him accordingly. However, before it was all resolved in his favour, Gorbachev did have a very grievous

---

* In the Soviet context, it meant history of the Communist Party of the Soviet Union, Marxist-Leninist philosophy and political economy of socialism. — *Author's comment*.

experience at the Politburo. This is what happened according to the minutes kept by Medvedev* and Gorbachev's assistants Cherniayev and Shakhnazarov.

'On March 23rd, the following conversation took place in the presidium quarters during the break in proceedings at the congress of collective farmers.

*Ligachev.* The press started kicking all those new ones in the teeth... They say there was this article in *The Sovetskaya Rossiya* — a very good one, true to our Party line.

*Gromyko.* Yes, I believe the article is very good. It calls a spade a spade.

*Gorbachev.* I scanned it before going to Yugoslavia.'

He gets interrupted... told that it is a very worthy article. Do pay attention...

'*Gorbachev.* I did read it properly upon my return.'

Again, they are outdoing each other singing the article praise

'*Gorbachev.* I happen to be of a different opinion.

*Vorotnikov.* Well I never!

*Gorbachev.* You "never" what?'

Awkward silence, looking at each other.

'*Gorbachev.* So that's the way it is, isn't it? Let's have a conversation at the Politburo. I can see that things are going somewhat off kilter. I smell a schism. What do you mean, "Well I never"? The article is opposed to *perestroika*, to the February plenary session**. I have never been against a free exchange of opinions: be it in press, by letter or in an article. But I have learnt that this article has been converted into a Party directive. The objections to the article were banned from being printed... This is a different matter altogether.

As for the February plenary, it wasn't "my" report that I presented.

---

\* Vadim Medvedev, the secretary of the Central Committee of the Communist Party of the Soviet Union (CPSU), chief party ideologist in late 1980s.

\*\* A primary issue for the opposition was the repeal of Article 6 of the Constitution, which prescribed the supremacy of the CPSU over all the institutions in society. Faced with opposition's pressure for the repeal of Article 6 and needing allies against hard-liners in the CPSU, Gorbachev obtained the repeal of Article 6 by the February 1990 Central Committee plenum.

We all discussed it and then approved it. It was the Politburo report. And now it turns out that there is a different direction put forward... I am not holding fast to my post but for as long as I am here and I am boss, I shall defend the ideas of *perestroika*. No, that's not the way it works. We shall debate it at the Politburo.'

Each member of the Politburo and the Secretariat was expected to explain where he stood in respect of the 'manifesto of anti-*perestroika* forces' (that was how the article in question was officially branded in *Pravda's* editorial of April 5th...). Some, primarily Ligachev, had to justify themselves and provide evidence of their non-involvement in preparing the ill-fated article. Others, like Vorotnikov, who imprudently referred to the article as a 'benchmark' — had to beat their breast explaining that they had not read it carefully enough and failed to spot the anti-*perestroika* rhetoric. Although the exhausting many-hour-long marathon of a session did produce the unanimity coveted by the General Secretary, no one had any illusions about the nature of such a forcibly imposed concord.

... He had spent a long time and put in a lot of effort in establishing a balance of power within the Politburo, the proper and diligently maintained equilibrium. It was common knowledge that Yegor Ligachev was a faithful and passionately devoted Communist — so he provided a counterbalance for a Westerner such as Yakovlev. All this created a foundation, a *terra firma* on which Mikhail Sergeyevich felt safe and at ease... Also, everyone knew how he valued this balance, this potential for manoeuvre, this flexibility.

And all of a sudden it all changed. It all went awry.

The balance got distorted and the throne started wobbling. He detested those monarchist metaphors reeking of Régime Ancien — but there was no escaping them.

All of them *must* be afraid of him. They must *shake* with fear. Yet this was something he did not like, it wasn't in him, he didn't know how to go about it. He resented those rulers who rule through terror.

Even so, he believed that a country, even the one like the USSR, can be ruled in the absence of fear, by assigning people to their jobs correctly, by explaining things to them correctly, and above all — by acting as a role model. All it took was deft navigation around challenges, among political wings and.

And now, lo and behold — a breach opened up in the hull.

During his ten year at the Politburo Gorbachev had never seen or experienced anything like it. But now it all looked a fomented plot, a creeping coup d'état.

In his place, Brezhnev would have started a gradual and meticulous removal of potential adversaries from power. Khrushchev would have openly excommunicated them. Stalin would have just eliminated them in one fell swoop. But Gorbachev embarked on a different route, the one best suited to his nature. He took to more political manoeuvring.

Mikhail Sergeyevich was a wholeheartedly devout Communist. Words and phrases like 'a socialist choice', 'the Great October victory', 'Revolution' and 'Lenin' were sacred to him.

'For him, Lenin, whose works he did read and reread constantly, was a mesmerising character — not only by virtue of the latter's intellectual might but also... his ability to make an expedient about-face in views. Lenin's only God was political reality to whom he would willingly sacrifice any theories, dogmas and paradigms, including his own.' (Arkady Grachev).

Gorbachev decided not to wait till the next Party congress which, under the CPSU Statute, should have provided the venue for raising the issues of principled importance. Time was running out...

Thus, the XIX Party Conference was a kind of a half-way house between two congresses.

Yeltsin was elected to take part in the conference on behalf of the Karelian* delegation, seated in the balcony, at the greatest distance from the podium. But his nomination had been a subject of a fierce tussle. The pressure from 'below' was meeting with staunch resistance from 'above', Gorbachev himself included. (Several companies from Sverdlovsk, with several thousand employees each, were eager to put him down as their nominee but in all vain).

At the conference, Gorbachev unveiled, for the first time, his plan for 'democratisation', or to be more precise — Sovietisation of the USSR.

---

* *Karelia* — the land of the Karelian peoples, an area in Northern Europe of historical significance for Finland, Russia, and Sweden. It is currently divided between the Russian Republic of Karelia, the Russian Leningrad Oblast, and Finland. Whichever way you look at it, it is very far from both Sverdlovsk and Moscow.

# EXONERATION (1988)

He had been hatching this plan, for a whole year, in deliberations and comprehensive consultations with a think-tank of experts and his personal aides. The pivotal element was the idea of reverting to electivity of the bodies of power. On the one hand, it was supposed to strengthen Gorbachev's hand in fighting 'conservatives and bureaucrats', low-lying 'Brezhnevites', still of danger to him. On the other hand, his plan was intended to solidify his position against radicals like Yeltsin and unruly crowds... It was a powerful insurance, a shock-absorber and a new stabilising tool.

Technically speaking, all agents of power in the USSR — be it the Party authorities or Soviets — were supposed to be elected. The Central Committee of the USSR's Communist Party was elected by the Party congress, once in five years. The delegates to the congress itself were elected by the local Party cells. The composition of the Politburo was approved and altered at the plenary session of the Central Committee.

Similarly, *Obkoms* were elected at the Party conferences at the oblast level; the *Obkom* would elect the bureau. Re-elections to the Soviets of People's deputies of all types were also taking place once in five years, the Supreme Soviet of the USSR and the RSFSR included. In the Soviets, representatives of authorities were conferring side by side with 'reliable' non-Party members: famous workmen and collective farmers, academics and artists. It was a comprehensive multi-layered structure of governance, and an intricate mechanism of appointments, approvals and votes was there, in place, at all every step.

Yet, everyone in the USSR was perfectly aware of the fact that in reality no elections ever took place. To end up on the ballot paper or in the draft decision on elections to a Party cell, the nominee must have been first approved from 'above'. And Gorbachev decided to change the *modus operandi* of this mechanism.

From now on, a secretary of the Party committee had to wear two hats: his own and that of a head of the local Soviet. At the same time, those leaders had to be elected by direct vote and by secret ballot, and what's more: for both (!) positions, there had to be several nominations.

Some specialists on the history of *perestroika* (Leon Aron among them) viewed these developments as a genuine revolution from 'above'. But in view of the burgeoning democratic opposition, Gorbachev was avoiding the paramount question — that of the Party's monopoly on power. Besides, Gorbachev's amendments did not contain any clarifications for an eventuality if, say, the local Party big-wig failed to win the vote. It was precisely this half-cooked nature of Gorbachev's concept of electivity that Yeltsin subjected to criticism, although ostensibly the concept made perfect sense.

...At first, the delegates to the Party conference did not even grasp the gist of what was being debated. After all, at one stage Leonid Illich Brezhnev used to 'combine' the two supreme posts in the country: he was concurrently the General Secretary in the Party and the Chairman of the Presidium of the USSR Supreme Soviet. Did it mean that Party secretaries also had a duty to 'sit on two chairs'?

Being aware of how the brains of his comrades worked, the General Secretary, speaking from the podium of the Kremlin Palace of Congresses, a huge portrait of Lenin directly above his head, explained in words of not too many syllables that no, they had no such duty. They now had to be elected by direct general vote and on a competitive basis standing for posts against other possible candidates. Moreover, Gorbachev continued, since the overall power should gradually be transferred to the Soviets, the Party secretaries *not elected* would have to vacate their posts.

The delegates of the XIX All-Union Party conference expressed their well-grounded doubts to Mikhail Sergeyevich.

Is it necessary? Is it worth doing it so abruptly? Won't some comrades fail to understand it fully?

Mikhail Sergeyevich's reply was unequivocal: this resolution of the Party conference shall not be even put to vote.

After some ado, the conference calmed down and voted. As the delegates were already getting to their feet in order to mark the closing of the conference with the Party anthem (*Internationale* that goes 'Arise, you prisoners of starvation! Arise, you wretched of the earth! For justice thunders condemnation: A better world is in birth!"), Gorbachev raised his hand, asked for the floor and climbed the podium.

Out of his pocket, he produced a piece of paper folded in four, spread it open and, eyes to the text, asked the delegates of the conference to carry yet another, urgent resolution: on holding next year the All-Union congress

---

\* English lyrics by Charles H. Kerr.

of the USSR People's Deputies, on a procedure for its organisation, on its decision-making bodies and so forth.

Stunned, the delegates raised their hands. It should be noted that votes were taken not simply with a show of hands: delegates were to raise their Party conference mandates (unlike a Party congress when votes were taken with a show of Party membership cards — in reality, a tiny hardback logbook, with the portrait of Lenin on the red cover and records of dues paid within). According to the old Soviet tradition, those books had to be raised high above one's head.

Generally speaking, they couldn't wait to get out of there and go home.

Technically speaking, the delegates voted (albeit without being aware) in favour of abolishing the Party monopoly on power.

That power had been established as a result of the Civil War, firing squads, prison camps, a deadly struggle against other revolutionary parties and political movements still in existence in 1917. The power that rested on dictatorship, blood, an unremitting threat of war and unmitigated suffering of the people, this power had started disintegrating a long time ago — gradually and imperceptibly. And now, in response to the impact of the very logic of the process of history, it started mutating.

No one grasped the real meaning of it all — not the delegates to the conference who had voted for this decision with their mandates, nor Gorbachev himself, nor his followers in the Politburo. Nobody realised or foresaw where this 'overlapping of positions' and these elections would really lead to.

For now it was seen as a way of attracting attention to the conference and stepping up the media frenzy. Yet the broader public was scandalised at the attempts to fix a public flogging for *Ogonyok's* Editor-in-Chief Vitaly Korotich. Over a decade later Vitaly Alexeevich was telling the author of this book, 'I nearly collapsed with fear as I was climbing the podium of this conference. It was simply appalling!'

The story went thus. Shortly before the conference, *Ogonyok* had carried the article by two investigating officers of the General Procurator's Office: Gdlyan and Ivanov. The article immediately caused a furore. It said, in black and white, for the first time ever in the history of the country that numerous Party functionaries, sometimes of the highest rank, wallowed in corruption and took bribes. Facts and clear evidence were quoted to back this allegation.

A delegate, speaking at the conference, read this excerpt out loud from *Ogonyok's* article and demanded that the Party member Korotich should take the floor and be answerable to the Party conference for this dirty slander.

As Korotich was walking down the aisle towards the podium, the catcalls followed his progress, 'Disgrace! Scoundrel! Turncoat!' The only thing that supported Korotich at this moment was Gorbachev's presence in the presidium. Gorbachev's eyes glared irately in harmony with the mood in the audience but Korotich somehow sensed that he would not let him be crucified by this madding crowd. Every time when a Party plenary session or a congress was foaming at the mouth, eager to castigate yet another opportunist or apostate, be it Yeltsin, Korotich or, a year later, academician Sakharov, Gorbachev was gripped by a fit of fear. In his mind's eye he could picture how one day he would be similarly trampled underfoot.

Thus, the public lashing was botched and cut short. On this issue Gorbachev did not go along with the incriminatory frenzy shown by the audience.

Although the XIX Party Conference resembled strongly Brezhnev's congresses, it still became the venue for some unaccustomed bravery.

Primarily, it was the speech delivered by Yeltsin.

He had spent the entire month of June drafting this presentation.

'Dad was on edge,' says Yeltsin's elder daughter, Yelena, 'when working on this speech. We lived at the dacha in Uspenskoye\* at the time. Every day, he would show us a new version of bullet points, read them aloud. All in all, there were nine versions. We were discussing them, giving some advice. Then we found an old typewriter somewhere, I think it was an Underwood, and set to typing it all up... He did not want the text of his speech falling into someone else's hands.'

This speech had to focus on a central idea — and Yeltsin unexpectedly was coached in this by none other but an old crony of Brezhnev's, Chairman

---

\* A village near Moscow.

of the Party Control Committee, and member of the Politburo comrade Solomentsev.

After Yeltsin granted an interview to the American journalists, Solomentsev summoned him to Old Square\* and sternly admonished him to the effect that a CC member had no right to speak about Politburo members in similar terms; he\*\* must have all his interviews and public statements cleared by superior authorities in advance. 'This is what Party discipline is all about, Boris Nikolayevich. Or, perhaps, it is something you have just learnt about?'

This clash that provided him with a key point for his speech, a code which helped him build the entire system of arguments.

'His idea,' says the younger daughter, Tatyana, 'turned out to be *exoneration*. The concept came into fashion during *perestroika*. It provided an angle for reconsidering the opinions about people, words, concepts, entire peoples. Dad had voiced this idea some time before: he wanted to be exonerated in his lifetime, not posthumously.'

… All that was very well, but he still had to get to the podium somehow. How? Yeltsin was seated at the balcony, along with the Karelian Party delegation. He sent a note to the presidium on the very first day of proceedings and asked for the floor. There was no answer. On the fourth day of the conference he warned his colleagues that he intended to speak. They were supportive.

Gorbachev announced the list of speakers before taking a vote on the resolution of the conference. Yeltsin was not on it.

So he proceeded to descend into the stalls. He climbed three steps and asked for the permission to speak. Gorbachev and Solomentsev started conferring with each other. A staff member of the CC general secretariat came up to Yeltsin and suggested that he should proceed to the presidium behind the scenes to discuss the situation 'together with Mikhail Sergeyevich'. Yeltsin realised that he should not exit the audience. He would never be allowed back in. Journalists were also whispering to him, 'Boris Nikolayevich, do not go out!'

---

\* Address of the CPSU Central Committee headquarters.

\*\* There were no women in the Politburo and practically none in the Central Committee.

He declined to leave the hall and waited. Another responsible comrade made his way to him and passed Mikhail Sergeyevich's message — he would speak by all means but now he must make his way back to the balcony and rejoin the Karelian delegation. Yeltsin shook his head again in refusal and took the vacant seat in the front row, directly in front of Gorbachev.

At length, Solomentsev got up and announced that the floor was given to comrade Yeltsin, member of the Central Committee, first deputy to the USSR *Gosstroi's* Chairman.

Yeltsin started with comments on some previous incidents.

He said that his 'inarticulate' presentation at the plenary of the Moscow *Gorkom* was the result of a grievous state of his health at the time. Once again, in the presence of four thousand stunned delegates he repeated the question of whether or not he believed that comrade Ligachev ought to be 'removed' from the Politburo and repeated his reply: yes, that was his considered opinion!

Then he went on to the problems and bottlenecks — as was proper.

The first point — whether or not there were areas within the Party that were 'out of bounds for criticism'. The General Secretary in his presentation had stated that there were no such areas yet this was patently not true.

Secondly — privileges of the Party aristocracy, all those mansions, dachas, 'vacation homes' of such splendour that one feels ashamed'. There was a suggestion of the introduction of a mechanism that would ensure the impossibility of creating a 'new cult of personality'.

'Quite a few countries', Yeltsin was going on, 'view it as a norm that when the leader quits, his team follows suit. We are used to leaving the blame at the door of those deceased. It looks now as if it was just Brezhnev who had been the guilty party for our stagnation*. So where were all those who had been sitting on the Politburo for ten, fifteen or twenty years — then as now? They used to vote in favour of various programmes. Why did they promote the sickly Chernenko? Why has the Party Control Committee been penalising members for relatively insignificant

---

* Brezhnev's era was subsequently branded in the common political speech as the time of *stagnation*, thus necessitating Gorbachev's *acceleration* and *glasnost*.

## EXONERATION (1988)

transgressions against the Party provisions but is full of fear when it comes to dishing out punishment to republican bosses — on charges of bribes, or of causing millions of damage to the state, and suchlike? I believe that some Politburo members, since they belong to a collegiate body and enjoy the trust of the Central Committee and the Party, must explain why the country and the Party have been reduced to this state? After which they should be expelled from the Politburo. (*Applause*). It is more humane than to criticise posthumously and then shift to a new burial place!'

And finally the point for the sake of which he decided to speak — political *exoneration*.

Within the context, it was a totally unexpected use of the word. Exoneration should apply to those who were prisoners under Stalin, the innocent victims, those who were executed in the GULAG.

But the word was very powerful — the entire country and the full body of the press were discussing exoneration of those convicted and eventually proved to be innocent: Bukharin, Kamenev, Zinovyev and thousands of others. So the word made a mark. It hit its target.

The audience fell silent and listened even closer.

'Comrades delegates, I have a very sensitive issue to discuss. (*Pause, noise in the audience*). I would like to raise the issue of exonerating me personally after the October plenary session of the Central Committee. If you believe that the time has already come for that, then I have exhausted my agenda.'

He did it deliberately — so that Gorbachev would not be able to interrupt this, the most important part of his speech, and drive him off the platform.

He pretended to be assembling his papers, cast a gloomy glance into the presidium. The noise in the audience was increasing and then Gorbachev interjected, 'Boris Nikolayevich, do speak, the audience are waiting. (*Applause*). I believe, comrades, that we should dispel the aura of secrecy from Yeltsin's case. Let Boris Nikolayevich say everything he deems necessary. And afterwards, if we feel it imperative to say something we can also say it then. Off you go, Boris Nikolayevich!'

Yeltsin said,

'... You are aware that my speech at the October plenary session of the CC CPSU was deemed "politically erroneous" by the decision of the plenary session. Yet the questions I raised there have been repeatedly discussed in the press and put forward by Communists. These days all these questions have been practically offered for discussion from this very podium, offered in reports and presentations. I believe that my only mistake was bad timing — on the eve of the 70th anniversary of the October Revolution... I am badly shaken by the events and I appeal to the conference to annul the decision passed by the plenary session on my account. If you consider it possible to repeal that decision you will thus exonerate me in the eyes of the rank-and-file Party members. This is not just a personal plea, it would be in the spirit of *perestroika* and my view is that it will help matters along since it will boost people's confidence...'

Gorbachev was, yet again, faced with the necessity to fight the defector.

To lose to Yeltsin, just like that, with the entire country watching, was something that he simply couldn't do.

So this time Gorbachev was completely determined to take his stand above the fray. Let Yeltsin be punished by somebody else. Let the comrades speak...

And speak they did. The First Secretary of the Central Committee of Estonia, Vaino Vialias, mounted the platform: you know, comrades, when he was an ambassador to Nicaragua, comrade Yeltsin came over with a delegation and on a visit to the textile factory spotted a practically naked child. It was an extremely poor child, comrades. 'What's up, you don't want to work? Why don't you wear trousers?' comrade Yeltsin allegedly said to the child. The Estonian secretary could hardly contain his indignation over comrade Yeltsin's tactless escapade in Nicaragua, and the Palace of Congresses was somewhat taken aback.

Eventually the floor was taken by a rattled Yegor Ligachev who, as Yeltsin suggested for the second time, now in front of TV crews and journalists, should be dismissed from the Politburo.

Ligachev was talking for a long time but there was just one phrase that made his name go down in history: 'Boris, you are wrong!' said Yegor Ligachev.

Posters and badges 'Boris, you are right!' became ubiquitous in the capital city within just a few weeks. They were proudly sported on lapels and hats. Moscow's opinion clearly differed to that upheld by the Politburo members.

## EXONERATION (1988)

Gorbachev tried to respond to Yeltsin. One would have thought that he would deliver a new crushing blow. But the mere progress of the conference altered the atmosphere in the audience and the blow was absorbed — the debates proved too heated, the situation too dramatic for the negative pathos of a speech to be channelled into just one direction. Gorbachev was highly critical of Yeltsin but at the same time remembered his services to the Moscow Party cell, quoted from the hitherto secret report on the October plenary session whereby it was recorded that Yeltsin did apply for resignation *himself*.

The first several hours after the discussion of his speech were very hard for Yeltsin. Members of the Karelian delegation were avoiding eye contact. This was the hardest. He made his way out of the audience, found the first aid station set up for the delegates and asked for an injection. The nurses started fussing... The cardiac palpitations gradually subsided. He returned to his seat, head dropped. The vote on the main points of the agenda was announced.

Despite the fact that six out of eleven speakers were criticising Yeltsin and one, Volkov, invoked mixed feelings in the audience, it soon became clear that he would not be exonerated but won't stand condemned either. The presidium lost to Yeltsin on points. In essence, it was exoneration after all.

Overall, this forum had a resounding public resonance. As a matter of fact, the very idea of democracy re-appeared there — albeit in an embryonic and typically Soviet form.

This is what Andrei Grachev wrote in his diary:

'In terms of flying passions, escalated emotions, reversed rituals and violated taboos, the conference was an astonishing event, indeed, a thriller.

The most significant, though, was the fact that it did away with a myth of the CPSU monolithic unity and revealed a genuine plurality and, unexpectedly, the multi-partite nature of the Soviet Party elite, hereto pent up in a constrictive tin of a space created by a single party regime. "The conference unpicked it all," Mikhail Sergeyevich is still emphatic when recalling those events. "For ten days I was at the helm during this squall and thought we were about to capsize. Also, many delegates were much more radical than me".'

'What sort of a *perestroika* is this?' a metallurgy plant worker from the Urals was asking from the high podium. 'The shops are as poorly supplied with foodstuffs as before. There was no meat and there still is none. Consumer goods have disappeared.'

This 'conservative' speech must have been received much more sympathetically than many liberal pronouncements. The conference raised many issues that simply could not have been put in words before: the budget deficit, inflation and ethnic relations. That was precisely what the leadership of the CPSU had feared.

'Whether this is recognised or not, it changes nothing,' Valentin Falin, head of the CC International department, wrote to Gorbachev in a private note during the proceedings. 'The fact remains, even if two factions speak ostensibly a similar language and if delegations are happy to applaud whomsoever — this only serves to exacerbate the situation, for one *unfair* morning they will go after the strong one... Why do you procrastinate, what do you need consensus with your opponents for — with those who are prepared to waste *perestroika* retail and wholesale?'

This note by Valentin Falin is a remarkable document. It mirrors the intensity of fermentation, ideological schism, the strength of subterranean shocks shaking the Party and its leadership during those ten disturbing days. Each word seemed to be pushing Gorbachev, and the Politburo, and the entire CPSU into a precipice. The thing was that now totally different f people were mounting the platform too, and they were in majority. More excerpts from the 'testimonial evidence' by Andrei Grachev.

'... Yegor Ligachev, in his speech, unequivocally stated that it* could have had a different start and, accordingly, a different continuation. He let it be known that it was him, along with some other members of Brezhnev's team, who "had created Gorbachev" and brought him to power. It was an open challenge to the General Secretary and many were waiting for his reaction. The fact that he avoided direct collision, did not remove from his post the Editor-in-Chief of *The Sovetskaya Rossiya* paper and did not publicly rebuff Ligachev, to say nothing about his reluctance to distance himself from the conservatives, was perceived by many as yet another proof of his weakness of will, indecisiveness, fateful proclivity to administrative compromises at whatever cost.'

---

* *Perestroika — Author's comment.*

Yet, one could never brand Gorbachev's decisions on the staff issues made after the XIX Conference 'soft' and 'toothless'.

According to Grachev, he initiated '... the voluntary resignation of more than 100 (!) individuals in the Central Committee'. Nearly half of the Politburo was also replaced.

He appointed Vadim Medvedev to the post of his deputy (secretary of the Central Committee in charge of ideology) — thus attempting to put a decisive end to the conflict between two irreconcilable opponents: Yakovlev and Ligachev. Most significantly, he practically eliminated the sacrosanct element of the CC — its Secretariat that used to be headed by Ligachev. From then on, the country and the Party had only *one* leader.

Initially, the regular Party members were sanguine about these changes; they viewed it all as a return to Brezhnev's times with the fullness of power gradually concentrating in the hands of one man. Not everyone worked out why Gorbachev set about introducing a comprehensive reform of the Party apparatus. Only those closest to him knew that the reform of power should go much further than the majority of the CPSU members imagined. Gorbachev, as ever fearful of the Party coup, was methodically removing power from under the old Party faculties and concentrating it all in his own hands.

Today, memoirs by Gorbachev's erstwhile aides and supporters — Boldin, Cherniayev, Grachev and Shakhnazarov — make for quite interesting reading.

They all put a variety of questions to Gorbachev: why, during the Party conference, when a split within the Party became a reality, hadn't he created within the CPSU a new, 'healthy' party, a party of the democratically-minded? Why hadn't he removed Ligachev and other conservatives from the Politburo (as Yeltsin urged him to do)? Why, on the other hand, hadn't he got rid of Yeltsin himself — by dispatching him as an ambassador to some prestigious country?

This last rebuke is something Gorbachev could really do without, especially when coming from his former friends.

For it wasn't about Yeltsin. It was about the last General Secretary's personal qualities. The bizarre proportions of his nature, his ambiguities, zigzags and reflections of his perceptions bear witness to the scope and profundity of his soul, which was, nonetheless, that of a timid individual.

Vitaly Korotich, the legendary Editor-in-Chief of the *Ogonyok* magazine, describes in his memoirs several most important meetings with Gorbachev that opened his eyes to many aspects of the latter's character.

'The "country's leader" was becoming more and more dependent on his trusted aides and staff. He nearly always flared up when somebody from his "inner circle" felt offended; he was afraid of his own coterie and was emphatic that he would not let them be hurt. As for adversaries, he cracked down on them the best he could (he told me to plan a series of articles to destroy Yeltsin)... Forever unsure of himself, the General Secretary was devious and always groping for points of support that, in truth, simply did not exist in nature... He never understood Sakharov and was chasing him off the platform even though, prior to that, he had saved him from exile. Overpowered by his own reflexes of a bureaucrat, he was eager to put everyone in a firmly subordinate position while being more dependent on the others than most.'

At a meeting with the magazine readers in Leningrad, Korotich was forthright, 'Deliberately choosing my words and not naming names, I said that some leaders surround themselves with fools. "However, I hope," I said, "that this will not be for long. Disarmament is underway and so I believe that the biggest among the missiles and fools will be removed as a matter of priority".' Consequently a session of castigation by Gorbachev was awaiting him in Moscow.

'Until now, the thing that stunned me most at that meeting was how the then leader of the Soviet working masses greeted me with a stream of choice obscenities... Having mentioned my mother and all her relatives*, Gorbachev made a pause and showed me a pile of papers in front of him. Then he started screaming again, "This describes everything you blabbered about yesterday in Leningrad! This shows how you insulted decent people! Don't I know myself who to work with? Who is the leader of *perestroika*, you or me?" "You", I assured Gorbachev forcibly. "Of course, it is you and nobody else!" "So there," said the General Secretary, suddenly placated, and offered me a salami sandwich.

"Ligachev has been in the Central Committee for seventeen years — do you really believe he is not prepared for his post?" Mikhail Sergeyevich

---

* Taboo slang and a very strong swear language.

## EXONERATION (1988)

was booming and sputtering the breadcrumbs. "Now, you equally can't stand the *Siloviki* *like Yazov whereas we had all been licking Brezhnev's ass, every single one of us! This is water under the bridge now, and today we should be uniting people instead of hurling insults in their faces!"

As a limping Alexander Yakovlev was seeing me out of Gorbachev's office, he lowered himself down in the doorway (must have known the spot) and said, "Do you realise that Gorbachev has just saved you? Later today the Politburo will convene for a session, and the ministers for state security and defence will be demanding your resignation…" Until today I remember the feeling that overcame me at this moment. I realised that… the country's top leader was screaming his lungs out for the sake of microphones installed by his clerks in his office.'

A question from the students of the Higher School of *Komsomol* at their meeting with Yeltsin on 12 November 1988, after the XIX Party conference: 'You are as popular among the people as Gorbachev. Could you lead the Party and the state?' His answer was reserved, 'When we have elections with several candidates I can stand for office like anyone else.' However, at the same meeting, he mentioned Gorbachev respectfully, referred to him as an unquestionable leader, a 'like-minded' colleague. Yet he was unremitting in his criticism of Gorbachev's reforms: he attacked 'the areas closed to criticism', and 'amendments to the Constitution', and the very principle of 'holding two concurrent posts' that Gorbachev considered a revolutionary breakthrough.

A curious detail: several days earlier, on November 7th, he sent Gorbachev a telegram with a message of greetings on the occasion of the October anniversary**. Gorbachev was happy to quote this telegram in his book but interpreted it as yet another sign of Yeltsin's weakness whereas in

---

* The term is commonly applied when referring to enforcement ministers and their agencies: the FSB (formerly — KGB), the Defence Ministry, the Ministry of the Interior, etc.

** The actual events of the 1917 Revolution took place on 25th of October of the Old Style (before the revolution, Russia lived by the ecclesiastically approved Julian calendar). The rest of the world had Gregorian calendar, the difference between the two being, by 1917, 13 days. Thus, ever since the new chronology was introduced, all dates predating the calendar reform are shown in two formats: Old Style and New Style. Thus, in the new system, the October revolution, whilst keeping its name, was celebrated on November 7th.

reality its message was polysemantic: Yeltsin was returning to high politics despite Gorbachev's intention to keep him perpetually out in the cold.

Elections — this is the new word that filled him with hope. He decided to stand.

The elections formed the main contents of Gorbachev's political struggle, too. He was also expecting a lot from this development. Vapid mediocrities among bureaucrats would be forced to clean up their act. *Perestroika* adversaries would have to watch their step. Extremists and populists would have to enter a fair competition to win people's confidence. Whereas he would be victorious without fail! He had a head start on all points, advantage on all chessboards! This move in his game was sophisticated and deliberate, and the game itself was fair and full of exquisite harmony.

There was just one slim shadow cast on this global and serious decision of his: he realised that Yeltsin would be taking part too. Well — let him try.

... The year 1988 brought the society a vague sense of hope. It was discernible everywhere. The exhausting war in Afghanistan was drawing to a close. The press was publishing the first tentative articles about the Chernobyl disaster of 1986. At the time, the authorities had simply hushed up the disaster at the atomic reactor that caused a monstrous ecological catastrophe and tried to cover it up.

The newspapers articles became much more vivid, fresh and dynamic. New words and phrases were in the air and had not become trite yet. 'Common human values' was one. It wasn't quite clear what they really meant in the context but then again, they portended no evil either. TV programmes were creating new celebrities, for example genuine Russian intelligentsia like academicians Likhachev* and Panchenko**; academician

---

* *Dmitry Sergeyevich Likhachev* (1906-1999), Russian intellectual, literary historian, and author of more than 1,000 scholarly works who devoted his life to defending his country's Christian and cultural heritage; having survived four years (1928–32) in Soviet forced-labour camps, Likhachev was rehabilitated (1936) and appointed (1938) to the staff of the Institute of Russian Literature in Leningrad (St. Petersburg), where he became known as the doyen of Russian medieval literature.

** *Alexander Mikhailovich Panchenko* (1937-2002), historian, specialised in Russian literature and culture, Member of the Russian Academy of Sciences, Professor, member of the Union of Writers.

# EXONERATION (1988)

Sakharov and his wife Elena Bonner set up the public organisation *Memorial*\* (Yeltsin was among the founders).

*Glasnost* and *perestroika* came to be habitually used in the same context as *moral criteria* and *culture*. The children of the sixties\*\* started carefully advocating the return of the great names and ideas into our life. People started talking about inviting back those who had had to emigrate to the West: Solzhenitsyn, Liubimov, Aksyonov and Voinovich.

Hope was brimming even in the sports programmes: our athletes put in a successful performance at the Seoul Olympics and won more gold medals than expected; the national football team, managed by the great Lobanovsky, played in the finals of the European Cup. Theatres gladdened hearts with new premiers; magazines were offering fantastic publications unimaginable in the olden days. The film *Assa* went on general release, featuring a new generation hungry for change. Now it was clear that they would see their hopes borne out.

There appeared the first private cafes, restaurants, shops, middle-men, first cooperatives.

The USSR's international politics showed all signs of a firm choice to follow the course that rejected the 'cold war' principles. Gorbachev started regular meetings with foreign leaders and Mitterrand, Reagan and Thatcher (later — Bush and Major) became his regular interlocutors. The Soviet leader and his ministers began taking part in G-7 meetings albeit as an associated member (the Soviet papers called G-7 'the club of most developed capitalist countries').

A major European event was the unification of Germany. When the wall fell in Berlin everybody perceived it as the dawn of a new era.

The word *perestroika* entered all languages on earth. The Western world was cautiously allowing itself a better look at the details of our life. For the first time in ages the number of tourists into our country and the number of our people travelling abroad multiplied which meant that Western news

---

\* *Memorial* is an international historical and civil rights organisation that operates in a number of post-Soviet states. It focuses on recording and publicising the Soviet Union's totalitarian past, but also monitors human rights in Russia and other post-Soviet states.

\*\* Inspired by the denunciation of Stalin's cult and initial liberalisation of Khrushchev's era, the generation whose youth fell on the sixties was the first ever generation of the Soviet young people publicly espousing and promoting liberal and democratic values.

and novelties, films, fashions, magazines, books, names, technologies, and ideas could now travel to us much faster.

Gradually, the outflow of those who had long been dreaming of leaving the country for good started gaining momentum. The word *refusnik* was disappearing from speech. Those who had been expecting permission to leave for 10 or 15 years and very nearly abandoned all hope started packing their cases. Local Jewish emigration was gradually transforming itself into the 'fourth' or even 'fifth' wave*.

Yet the dull subterranean tremors were unsettling this fragile and indistinct expectation of renewal that was barely starting to strike root.

The year 1988 was the first year when awful pogroms swept through the USSR. In Fergana, Novy Uzen** and later Sumgait people were slaughtered on a mass scale for reasons of ethnicity.

Information on these events was classified and only some muffled snippets of news were making it through to Moscow. The Soviet censorship was still in place. However, it was already clear that things were wrong in the Soviet Union. Its breath was already laboured.

There emerged the first rich people (albeit rich by the Soviet yardstick). They were rapidly amassing great fortunes.

For the first time, too, there appeared people who publicly announced that they belonged to a separate subculture and had no intention of following common rules. The word was adopted to describe them — *informals*. They were of all colours and persuasions: from street rebels and teenagers (metal rock fans, punks and hippies) to the first entities with a political agenda — the *Pamyat* society, environmentalists and the association *Memorial*.

For the first time ever discussion was opened on the subjects of drug abuse and prostitution since it turned out these phenomena did exist in the USSR too — and how. The people were stunned when the message first

---

* Traditionally, the 'first wave' is considered to be the emigration that left immediately after the October Revolution, the 'second' — related to the WWII, the 'third' — scandalous expulsions of Brezhnev's times, newly allowed by fiercely controlled Jewish emigration and the defectors.

** The town within the Fergana Valley.

hit home: they had been living in different worlds, almost like different countries — albeit within the same borders.

One country, ostensibly the same for everyone who went to bed and got up in the morning to the radio broadcast of the Soviet national anthem, this very country, completely identifiable with each cell of it, in every distant nook, was becoming, bit by bit, more diverse.

And as the country was awakened from its social slumber by Gorbachev's *glasnost*, sinister apathy and disbelief, as it found its own voice and started speaking out, it became clear that he patience of a Soviet citizen had finally run out.

Thus, the social transformation that started in 1988 was probably the most significant outcome of that year. It got somewhat overshadowed by other, more dramatic and impressive events. The authorities sensed that something of this nature was underway but they failed to appreciate fully the scope of this new phenomenon and the rapidity with which it was expanding.

In 1988, some very important but rather subtle changes were occurring in Yeltsin's life. His exoneration, in essence, was happening without any decrees or instructions from the Party bosses.

He was no more a 'man of the system', a Soviet high-ranking boss (his 'consolatory' posting in the *Gosstroi* only served to emphasise his status of a pariah). From now on he was 'separate' from the éclat of his position; in a league of his own, an ordinary *person* who walks the streets, meets people and chats to them...

Yet he was a special person who was rapidly becoming a hero of his people, the first ever public politician in his country. From the summer of 1988 the new *status quo* was firmly established.

More and more volunteers were coming to his side, more and more like-minded people were offering help and support. In the beginning he couldn't quite see the point of it and was somewhat wary of this new cohort. Yet, bit by bit, the roles crystallised: under the new law, 'authorised agents' had a right to represent his interests in various regions of the Soviet Union. They were suggesting that he should stand as a candidate from Sakhalin, Kamchatka, Kiev, Odessa, Khabarovsk Territory, Krasnoyarsk, Leningrad Oblast, Murmansk, Moscow, etc., etc., etc...

At the meeting with the students of the Higher *Komsomol* School at the end of 1988, when asked about elections Yeltsin was quite reserved: 'he had not decided yet' where to stand as a candidate. He did not mention, though, that he would have to choose among fifty regions of the country. Everywhere they wanted Yeltsin as 'their' deputy.

# The Last Utopia

Once, when in Spain, Yeltsin was involved in a plane accident. Prior to the take-off, the local airline had replaced the aircraft twice, but when already airborne, something went wrong with the engine and the plane started losing altitude…

Although his behaviour looked bizarre, Yeltsin *flatly refused to fasten his seatbelt.*\*

Someone cried out, 'Boris Nikolayevich, what are doing, belt in!'

But he just sat there, silent and pale, glued to the window. Yeltsin's mood proved infectious: his aide Lev Sukhanov, seated next to him, did not dare fasten his seatbelt, having decided to share his boss's destiny, come what may. The plane did land after all — although their landing was very rough. 'It was a horrendous jolt', wrote Yeltsin in his book. Sukhanov got away lightly but Yeltsin had to undergo an urgent and risky spine surgery performed at the local hospital.

There was also a road accident in the centre of Moscow. In broad daylight, in Tverskaya Street, an over-enthusiastic *Lada* materialised out of thin air and rammed into the side of his black office *Volga*, on its speedy way towards the city centre.

For three days Moscow was abuzz, with journalists, sympathisers, voluntary aides, investigating officers and regular citizens, all trying to work out:

---

\* When trying to verify this fact I asked Naina Iosifovna. Her answer was curious, 'He never belted in, not in a car, not on the plane, never'. — *Author's comment.*

whose *Lada* had it been? Had comrade Yeltsin's car been undercut on purpose? Had it been an agent of some hostile forces, an ex-veteran of the enforcement agencies, for example, or even a red-brown shirt*? Why this ramming attack?

And no one wanted to believe the car owner, a humble pensioner who kept apologising, feebly: sorry, I just didn't look! Whereas the explanation was simple —comrade Yeltsin's car, while going at the speed allowable for government vehicles had no flashing beacon or siren. Because comrade Yeltsin firmly forbade his driver to exercise this privilege.

And then the famous episode on the bridge near Rublevo-Uspenskoye Schosse — when on 28 September 1989 he tumbled down from a considerable height, semi-unconscious from the impact and ended up, for rather a long time, in icy water. He remembered only this: somebody had thrown a sack over his head, he managed to free himself in the water, but the sack had never been found. He also remembered that a car had pulled up from behind — but militiamen on the beat, the ones who pulled him out of water, did not confirm the existence of any strange cars in the vicinity.

Sharp tongues mentioned a drunken rampage, an amorous escapade, or even a self-publicising stunt. Yeltsin was expected to respond, at least run his own investigation and offer his version of events — but he stayed stubbornly silent, the only comment being 'I have no claims to make, no one is to blame. I am sorry.'

It wasn't clear, though: where was the real threat stemming from?

Gorbachev, investigators, Minister of the Interior Bakatin, Korzhakov** (subsequently — head of Yeltsin's security) and generally everybody involved spoke with one voice: if he had received a hit to the head, where

---

\* Red-brown shirts — an ideological cliché used to denote association of communists and extreme right (fascist, Nazi, etc.) forces and/or ideologies.

\*\* Alexander Vasilyevich Korzhakov (b. 1950) was a security service general who served as Boris Yeltsin's bodyguard, confidant and adviser for 11 years.

was the wound? Also, how did he manage to get off so lightly, almost scot-free!

Gorbachev was foaming at the mouth and demanding explanations. He was asking logical questions, of course — the country demanded answers and conspiracy theories among the democratically-minded public were rife.

But Yeltsin kept mum. At the Supreme Soviet session he *refused point blank* to talk on this subject. The consensus was that he was holding something back.

However, if one considered the chain of similar events in his life in its entirety, this was his normal reaction.

So, had there been an attempt on his life or not? Since no new facts have come to light in the twenty years that passed I shall venture my own theory...

Flash-like assaults of this type was the KGB's area of expertise if someone had to be intimidated. The scenarios differed: from regular telephone calls to hit-and-run accidents involving members of the family and severe beating by the entrance to your residential building.

It is curious that the theory advocated now, many years hence, by his former head of security Korzhakov, totally coincides with the version of events vehemently defended by Gorbachev and Bakatin: nothing had ever happened.

'For a long time', says Naina Iosifovna, 'I was trying to work out the role played by Alexander Korzhakov in our lives. For a long time I felt that he had emerged by Boris Nikolayevich's side for a reason, not at his own initiative. I have no proof of course, but I just couldn't brush aside the thought that the KGB had assigned him to Boris Nikolayevich — to keep an eye on him. I felt that his resignation from the KGB and "voluntary protection" offered to Boris Nikolayevich were details of some big game. After 1991 these fears dispelled, but not completely... Boris Nikolayevich's granddaughter, Katya, never took to him at all. We were trying to convince her, "Look, Alexander Vasilievich is a kindly man, look how much he helps granddad!" And she would retort, "And you look at his wicked tiny eyes!"'

Afterwards, after 1991 no irksome mishaps would be capable of tarnishing his fame. Quite on the contrary, all these 'incidents' would make it grow exponentially, so much so that should Yeltsin happen to trip in the street it would make national news. His fame was expanding independently from his own efforts and was mythical, incomprehensible and enormous.

He attempted to explain this phenomenon himself, even tried to laugh it off. 'It is not that I am particularly attractive. It is just that when the anti-*perestroika* forces, some top leaders among them, have spent an entire year making Yeltsin's name taboo and causing me all sorts of harm they only managed to generate a powerful pressure into the opposite direction,' he said in an interview.

He was right of course. The Yeltsin myth was born in spite of the officialdom and all attempts to push him out of politics.

The public demand for a leader was simply too strong: the need to see a character from legends to appear, a warrior in shining armour, the one who did not burn in fire and did not sink in water.

On 11 February 1989, less than two weeks before the official deadline for nominating candidates for the First Congress of People's Deputies of the USSR, Yeltsin was flying to Perm by military aircraft.

He first left for Leningrad, however, to 'throw them off the scent'. He was met there by 'certain comrades' who took him to a military airfield and dispatched him to Perm onboard an army plane — 'clinging onto something that was either a cruise missile or an artillery shell' was how he remembered it in his memoirs. Such was the reality of his election campaign: all meetings were subject to tight control from the centre and the local Party cells, thus, he had to be ingenious.

As for the missile, it was not a joke.

He was flying inside a military 'truck with wings', holding fast onto the cold metal body of a huge shell to the accompaniment of the deafening noise from the engines (soundproofing, like any such comforts, were not part of the design).

It should be said that he was flying in order to stand for the position of a people's deputy, to a location none other but Berezniki, the town of his childhood. The Berezniki authorities were unprepared for his arrival and had no time to convene a district assembly while his fellow residents welcomed him with a standing ovation. He was standing in this modest provincial audience, against the backdrop of red banners and Lenin's portraits, and felt stunned and moved.

The task was formulated briefly and to the point: Yeltsin must not come through. How was it implemented? In his *Confessions*, Boris Nikolayevich is quoting from one of many 'rule books', back in the day guiding practical actions of every Party functionary.

'It feels counterintuitive but whilst being an advocate of pressure and authoritarian methods in dealing with his own staff, he still deems it possible to sit on the public board of the *Memorial*. Isn't it the type of flexibility that in reality proves to be just a lack of principles?'

'What are his motives? Supporting the interests of the common people? In which case why can't he support these in his current capacity — that of an incumbent minister? He is most likely motivated by his injured vanity and frenzied ambitions. Why should any voters become pawns in his hands?'

'He is not a political figure — he is some kind of a political *limitchik*.'

All this pretentious hogwash was making reading matter in Moscow Party *Raikoms*! They would convene esteemed people: university lecturers, plant managers, leaders of district agencies and pontificate to them about 'Yeltsin's love of pressure'.

Meanwhile by that time regular folk couldn't care less who he had been meeting and which personnel management methods he advocated. They could have been told that Yeltsin was personally in the pay of the American imperialists, that he was regularly drinking blood of Christian infants, owned a harem and a villa in the Canary Islands — none of it would have been believed. Yeltsin in 1989 was a hero. *Raikom* meant nothing...

Attempts to block Yeltsin's nomination as a candidate to become a USSR People's Deputy were undertaken not only by individual staff members of specific *Raikoms* or *Obkoms* — all local authorities were drafted into the project. He was refused the rent of the premises for his election campaign meetings, the dates were shifted back and forth, 'politically unreliable' individuals were forbidden access, 'anti-assemblies' and 'anti-rallies' were organised. This Soviet-style system operated was cruel but unbelievably awkward... Yeltsin, by now, was protected by a powerful force — the thrust of popular support, ungovernable, formidable and completely selfless.

Most significantly, in all of this Yeltsin felt completely in his element. He was the first and practically the only politician within the entire USSR who was completely ready for operating publicly.

His 'authorised agents' were speaking at the meetings in more than ten Russian regions that nominated him as a candidate. They were carrying Yeltsin's letters in which he was expressing gratitude for support. But not a single letter contained as much as a hint as to where exactly he was going to stand. He was reluctant to open his hand.

'Muscovites have not taken to you, Boris,' Gorbachev had once told him.

Have they not? Now was the time to see.

In Kuntsevo\*, by a cinema house, about 100 of his supporters had been waiting for him, for several hours, in the cold October wind. They were carrying slogans 'Boris Yeltsin is the choice of the people!', 'If not Yeltsin, then who?' The assembly was in session for nine hours and Yeltsin ended up on the list of candidates.

And this is how he was nominated in Cheremushki — as described by a British journalist.

'A tightly packed hall in the district House of Culture\*\* and a disappointed crowd waiting in the falling snow in the hope of catching a glimpse of him, crying out a couple of words or touching their idol. As Yeltsin started speaking many took out their notepads and pens — some out of habit and others — from suspicion that the press would never cover Yeltsin's words or deeds truthfully. They were lucky to end up in this hall and they saw it as their duty to report the truth to those who were not there.'

Indeed, nothing of what was happening in the country in January and February of 1989 caused more furore than those election meetings. People were virtually gaining access by storm; militia and voluntary security were driving visitors off, pushing and dragging them away, demanding 'invites'

---

\* Here and subsequently the author is quoting names of Moscow districts.

\*\* Community Centre, venue for functions, concerts and other events.

issued by Party *Raikoms*. There were general scrums. The proceeding would last for nine, or even twelve hours. Each candidate had to climb the platform and give detailed answers to questions from the electorate.

Yeltsin was asked hundreds of those, he would choose the angriest or the nastiest ones and answer in his habitual style, ironic and prickly. The country had not seen or heard anything like it for many decades. It felt sublime — to realise that things pronounced from the podium were not cribs drummed into the speaker but real answers to whatever questions. It was intoxicating.

So what did candidate Yeltsin have to say?

His speech in the aforementioned constituency called for 'the control of the people over the Party, social justice, revival of the spirit of compassion'.

The Fourth Department of the Public Health Ministry (the so-called Kremlin health facilities) should be given over to pensioners, orphans and Afghan veterans. Special distribution depots must be closed. Elections at all levels must be competitive and held on the basis of a secret ballot.

The power should be transferred to elected entities (congresses). The Party should cede its governing role and obey decisions of a congress (the same should go for the government and all political and public organisations — 'without exception' insisted Yeltsin having kept his famously long pause). Politics, economics and culture must be decentralised. Mass media must also report to the society as a whole, not just 'a group of individuals'. The new Soviet parliament should provide a facility for its deputies to run a national referendum 'on the most significant political issues'.

However, the cornerstone of all his election speeches, like before, was the demand of social fairness: 'to expand the supplies of foodstuffs and consumer goods, services and accommodation', 'to curtail defence and space programmes in favour of a strong social policy', 'to eliminate food chains and warehouses exclusively servicing the elite', to establish parity between an 'apparatus' rouble and a rouble 'of the people'.

Yeltsin was operating with the words from Gorbachev's glossary: plurality and *perestroika*, but his speech couldn't have been more dissimilar to the 'Address of the Central Committee to the Party, to All Soviet people' carried by *Pravda* on January 13th as part of 'preparations for the elections'.

Fine-tuned to the mood in the audience, he was ahead of his opponents by several strides. He was saying, albeit cautiously and with reservations, the things that they were still afraid of saying. He was setting targets that for many were still a distant glow in the future.

Let us take for example the phrase 'individual' ownership of land. The expression 'private property' was still a taboo even for him, a champion of social justice and the iconoclast. 'I refrained from using this term. One should take popular psychology into account,' said Yeltsin in his commentary on the land reform in Estonia where they had already (!) reinstated the rights of heirs to land plots.

'On the other hand, call it what you will. The most important thing is to bring back to people and their children the feeling of being a master of the land.'

Yeltsin's behaviour and analysis of his actions gave ground for conclusions that he was oversimplifying issues, that he a politician eager to come to power — through elections, public opinion, public methods of campaigning. It was so unimaginable from the standpoint of our political tradition, so unprecedented and bizarre that the elite (including the brightest commentators) experienced natural repulsion. In a country where power could only be yours as a result of a deadly scramble behind the scenes, it felt like a daring defiance. It even seemed immoral.

Yeltsin's 'populism', that is to say, messages of his political programme that felt unrealistic and unachievable at the time — would be slapped on him as a political label for quite some time to come. But two or three years later his slogans were translated into reality: market, private property (on land, among other things), multiplicity of parties, privatisation of companies and enterprises.

At the January plenary of the CC CPSU in 1989 where the Communist Party had to select 100 delegates to the forthcoming Congress of People's Deputies Yeltsin suffered yet another public flogging. However, by now, in the opinion of the public, he was an unquestionable leader. That is why the "flogging' backfired.

The new campaign was launched by a CC member, 'an eminent worker' Tikhomirov. In his speech Tikhomirov was asking such rhetorical questions as to why did comrade Yeltsin speak of a multi-party system?

Who vested him with this authority? Why did he appeal to create a '20-30% of opposition' in the new legislative body? How did he know what percentage of opposition the Soviet people needed? And finally, why, when he, an ordinary worker, Tikhomirov, had brought along his friend, an inventor and a development enthusiast to the *Gosstroi*, Yeltsin made them wait in his reception for four hours?

'This lathe turner was not only perfectly *au courant* with the details of Yeltsin's political platform,' a Moscow correspondent of some Western paper expressed his amazement, 'he was equally cognizant with the details of his private life.' Salt-of-the-earth, Tikhomirov explained to the session that Yeltsin's daughter resided in a flat of 100 square metres and drove the *Gosstroi* office car, Yeltsin himself had been given his flat by the ministry, his family members were still using services of the Fourth Department of the Ministry of Public Health and he himself recently used a health resort voucher! Comrade Yeltsin had the nerve to pontificate about social justice! Democratisation, was Tikhomirov's conclusion, had enabled all kinds of demagogues to slander the Party and the Soviet power! Communists should never allow this happen!

Tikhomirov was seconded by a construction foreman from Moscow, a collective farmer from the Leningrad Oblast, a shoemaker from Kishinev, all quoting their own arguments and facts to illustrate the same statement: 'not good enough, comrade Yeltsin!' An *ad hoc* commission was promptly set up to investigate Yeltsin's activities.

For the sake of fairness it must be added towards 1989 Yeltsin's membership in the Central Committee did look somewhat bizarre. This is his interview with a BBC correspondent.

'Many see you as an alternative, a founder of a new party, a new system within the Soviet Union.'

Yeltsin replied, 'I have given no grounds for such thoughts. It is another thing entirely that my programme does contain a veritable series of revolutionary... measures. But I am neither the founder of a new political opposition nor a leader of an opposition party.'

'But people want you to be!'

'Don't say that I am calling on them to create a party in opposition. No! The conditions are not ready yet.'

So was he with the system or against it? Was he within or without? In 1989 Yeltsin probably did not have an answer himself.

However, Tikhomirov's assault increased the momentum of his election campaign. Moscow exploded in indignation. The day after Tikhomirov's letter was published by *Moskovskaya Pravda,* a rally of seven thousand people assembled in the centre of Moscow. Several days after the plenary session — another rally, attended by ten thousand. One of the best known took place in the Urals Polytechnic where he was well remembered.

In Moscow, in Gorky Street, the monument to the founder of the city Prince Yuri Dolgoruki was plastered all over with leaflets and placards 'Yeltsin is the deputy of the people!', 'Hands off Yeltsin!' Somebody's voice, full of emotion, was booming through the loudspeaker: 'People sense deceit and lies... It is now clear that the vanguard of the Party, its Central Committee, has taken a stand against the people...'

'Yeltsin! Hands off Yeltsin! Yes to Yeltsin! No to mafia!' the crowd was chanting. Militia blocked the square.

Just ponder these facts. Still, why did militia allow these rallies? Why weren't people afraid of putting those rallies on?

The answer is simple: the system couldn't operate as before. It was already impossible to completely subvert the freedom of election. Yeltsin was one of those 'rams' who was pushing those 'innovations' forward and making the impossible possible.

At the same plenary session where Yeltsin was so violently denounced by workmen, collective farmers and shoemakers, he was the only one to vote 'no' to Ligachev.

A hundred nominations, each one approved unanimously. Gorbachev was scanning the audience from under the celebrated Kremlin chandelier, through his famous gold-rimmed glasses. He feigned misunderstanding, 'Unanimously? What? You, Boris Nikolayevich? One abstained...' Yeltsin did not argue — so be it, he abstained.

Yet later, behind the scenes, Yeltsin was approached by a gray-haired dignified marshal who silently shook his hand and, in answer to an amazed gaze, whispered quietly, 'I also wanted to vote against Ligachev...'

'So why didn't you?' 'I closed my eyes already, and was about to shoot up my arm... And then I just got cold feet...'

A battle commander, a marshal got cold feet?

So someone had to explain the new rules of the game, to be a pioneer. It had to be someone with sufficient courage.

A pre-election meeting took place at the district HQ — the Pillared Hall of the House of Unions, this being the second most prestigious venue after the Kremlin. The last step before the actual election took place. The audience consisted of the self-satisfied but frightened Moscow elite: Party committee secretaries, bosses of enterprises, leading specialists, municipal functionaries.

He would never make it through this ring-fence! They trusted the election law invented by Gorbachev. They had faith in things being under control.

'Everyone knew,' writes Yeltsin, 'what the outcome of the district meeting was going to be. The apparatus was promoting two nominations: Brakov[*] and Grechko, the latter being a well-known cosmonaut. My only hope was that I would still manage somehow to reverse the mood in the audience and make them enter all nominees into voting register. Then I would be in with a chance[**]. At the same time I sensed that it was a no-go and that this audience had only two surnames drummed into everybody's head...'

Right before the opening of the session, cosmonaut Grechko came up to Yeltsin and told him that he intended to withdraw his candidature. Yeltsin kept himself in check. 'No, come on, think it over...' he said to Grechko quietly, barely moving his lips. 'I have thought it all over, Boris Nikolayevich,' Grechko's voice was as quiet, and he returned to his seat.

When the cosmonaut painstakingly answered all his questions and announced his resignation from the race, the audience was in shock but voted for Yeltsin. Grechko announced his decision at two in the morning,

---

[*] Top manager of the ZIL automobile manufacturer. — *Author's Comment*.

[**] The election law provided for a loophole: a district assembly could either place on the ballot paper only the two candidates who scored the highest or it could include everyone. — *Author's comment*.

just before the final vote took place. According to the rules, two names now went on record: Brakov had 577 votes, and Yeltsin — 532.

Yet when millions of Muscovites made their way to the election booths, the picture was entirely different.

Yeltsin won the Moscow election with something like a landslide result: he received 91.53% of the total number of people taking part (at the same time, nearly 90% did vote on that day). His supporters counted 5,238,206 votes. Five million!

Brakov was voted for by something like 400,000 of Moscow residents. It was nothing short of a miracle — this total support of an opposition candidate, the one with an extremely radical programme, a dangerous person who was going to usher in instability and change. Were the people in the USSR that dissatisfied with their life? It was nothing short of a miracle.

Even candidates of the Soviet era, with only one candidate nominated at all stages, couldn't necessarily boast of such a success. Voters had always supported those nominations — obediently — for just that reason: they believed that *miracles never happen*. Now complete aloofness gave way to complete faith.

But Yeltsin's biggest shock was still ahead of him. It came at the very First Congress of People's Deputies that opened on 25 May 1989 in the Kremlin Palace.

The country was all ears. People were thronging everywhere where one could listen to the proceedings or watch them live: shops, radio posts, shop windows. TV sets and radios were on full blast in cars (the weather was hot and the drivers would roll down their windows, so that the sound was travelling down the city streets). The coverage could be heard in offices, flats, onboard ships and trains, and those who had to attend to work or any other business felt severely deprived.

'Those ten days when nearly the entire country was avidly following the fervent debates at the congress gave the people, politically, more than the preceding seventy years…' Yeltsin was referring, of course, to the seventy years of the Soviet power. 'It was one country that started watching the proceedings on the day of the opening of the congress, and a different one on the day when it closed.' His view was shared by many.

*Ten Days that Shook the World* was a typical headline in the Soviet press in 1989.

The First Congress of the USSR People's Deputies was different primarily in terms of the ambience, the tonality of speeches. It must have been similar to the Constituent Assembly in 1917* — the one that was supposed to map out Russia's destiny and decide the future of its Constitution but was never allowed to achieve any of it. The underlying message of every speech and contribution was the very *air of the times* that was physically palpable in the audience.

There were 2,250 People's Deputies of the USSR in that hall. From that number, 750 represented 'public organisations' (the Communist Party of the Soviet Union was considered to be one of them, therefore its quota was 100 seats).

The remaining 1,500 vacancies were distributed among territorial entities.

By the way, the Supreme Soviet of the USSR, first elected in 1936, was much more scantily represented. Accordingly, it wasn't only representatives of union republics, entitled ethnic groups, territories and oblasts that had made it into the Kremlin Palace of Congresses. Also present were those with a mandate from specific rural communities, which more or less meant villages and tiny towns. It was almost like a Zemsky Sobor** of the Soviet era.

Members of the Politburo were seated in the audience, along with the rest of the CPSU delegation. When the TV coverage commenced, the huge stage of the palace was deserted. The gigantic portrait of lonely Lenin above it only emphasised the impression of a gaping void. Today it

---

* The All-Russian Constituent Assembly was a constitutional body convened after the October Revolution of 1917. It is generally recognised as the first democratically legislative body of any kind in Russian history, elected despite resistance from the side of the ruling Bolshevik party who had failed to obtain a majority of seats. It met for 13 hours, from 4 P.M. to 5 A.M., 18–19 January [Old Style, 5–6 January] 1918, whereupon it was dissolved by the Bolshevik-Left Socialist Revolutionaries coalition government.

** The Zemsky Sobor was the first Russian parliament of the feudal estates in the XVI and XVII centuries. The term roughly means *assembly of the land*. It could be summoned either by tsar, or patriarch, or the Boyar Duma.

looks insignificant. On the day it caused a furore. There was no 'presidium' in the first minutes of the congress! What's more, the presidium had to be elected (although of course the names of the people who would take place there had been known in advance).

Incidentally, the 'miracles of democracy' had started even earlier. This is an excerpt from the memoirs by Anatoly Sobchak who came to Moscow from Leningrad several days prior to the opening of the congress.

'In Moscow it turned out that preparations were already underway. We were told that Deputies from Russia would first meet the leadership of the Party and the Russian government.'

Politburo member Vitaly Vorotnikov was to act as a mediator. '… <But> it <soon> turned out that this seasoned *apparatchik* of the old school, who had chaired hundreds of state-level events, had no ability for controlling a dissenting forum. He was used to dealing with walking machines, so he just withered and looked completely at a loss.'

Thus, Gorbachev chaired the meeting.

In answer to Sobchak's question of whether speeches and decisions would be censored in advance, Gorbachev said, 'None of us in the congress has any intention, comrades, to make decisions instead of you, to say nothing of applying pressure.'

'That was when I physically sensed Gorbachev's charisma and the scope of his personality,' adds Sobchak. Still, being an insistent lawyer from Leningrad, he had no business being mollified by the 'charisma and scope'.

'We were familiarised with results of the CC plenary session (which had taken place a day earlier) and recommendations for appointing top state officials. I was taken aback and indignant with nominees for the Chairman of the Supreme Court and the Committee for Constitutional Supervision… The supreme judicial post in the country was to be filled by an individual totally unknown in professional circles — he had worked for only several months as the chair of the Moscow municipal court and before that — as a people's judge.' Sobchak made a speech and *all* candidates bar one (Chairman of the Council of Ministers) were rejected. The Politburo convened a new plenary session and offered different nominations to the congress.

Against this background, Yeltsin's speech* where he listed the main points of his election programme became just one of many events. True, he never was grandiloquent, and the beauty of style was not his forte. He was, as ever, brief and reserved, presenting bullet points in a somewhat toneless voice.

But there were others, and we never thought that it could be so interesting to discuss politics. Yuri Afanasiev, rector of the Moscow History and Archives Institute; Professor of the Leningrad University and a brilliant lawyer, Anatoly Sobchak; Academician Dmitry Likhachev; one of the best known economists of his time Gavriil Popov — along with Yuri Vlasov, an Olympic weight-lifting champion whose speech at the congress was among the most memorable and irate. He focused on the eerie role played by the KGB in the life of the Soviet society: the audience was listening with bated breath.

Academician Sakharov was also among the delegates at the congress. A dissident, only two years previously he was in permanent exile in Gorky.

Gorbachev was addressing him in full (first name and patronymic) since the word 'comrade' was self-evidently ill-suited in this case. Sakharov started with saying that the congress must be the supreme body of power in the country. He then suggested recording it in a special resolution (which was not done).

However, soon it became clear that the country still lived very much in conditions of the Soviet power. On June 2nd, a Ukrainian delegate Sergey Chervonopisky climbed the podium — a veteran of the Afghan war, a young man on prosthetic limbs.

Sobchak was writing that 'leaflets started circulating in the Kremlin palace foyer already in the morning. They informed of Sakharov's interview to a Canadian paper *Ottawa Citizen* wherein he insisted that during the

---

* He was saying, among other things, this, 'Esteemed comrades deputies, voters from Moscow and other parts of the country, this congress is called to make a decision on the fundamental issue which will shape the future of our country. It is the question of power that must rightfully belong to the people in the face of the supreme legislative body... At the plenary session of the Central Committee of the CPSU that took place yesterday my motion on something like a practical transfer here, at the first congress, got no support. The decision was made to recommend for the leadership posts the same individuals who failed to steer the society away from crises in politics, economics, finances and living standards.'

Afghan war Soviet helicopters had been executing their own soldiers who got encircled by the enemy — to prevent their surrender.'

Sergey Chervonopisky was outraged. 'We feel most indignant at this irresponsible and seditious knavery by our famous scientist, and consider this impersonal accusation a malicious attack on the Soviet Armed Forces. We view it as libel, as yet another attempt to sever the sacred unity between the army, the people and the Party...'

The deputy from Ukraine, on his prostheses, had a great difficulty in getting off the platform. The audience gave the young veteran very nearly a standing ovation. When Sakharov asked for the floor he was met with hooting and whistles, the audience kept him from speaking and was drowning his words with clapping. Sakharov tried to defend himself, 'I only wanted to say...' But the rest of his speech was submerged in the pandemonium. He left the floor stooped and shaken*.

Despite the initial impression, Sakharov was not destroyed by this incident. He was internally ready for such a response. Say historians Geller and Nekrich: 'Speaking at the congress on the last day of its proceedings, Sakharov proposed to remove Article 6 from the text of the Constitution — the article whereby total control over the country was granted to the Party. He insisted that Mikhail Gorbachev had consolidated nearly absolute power in his hands. The latter being in the chair, he was repeatedly trying to interrupt delegate Sakharov's speech but Sakharov simply quietly went on speaking. Then the mike was switched off. The country could see the speaker but not hear him. In his closing address Gorbachev deemed it necessary "to discard insinuations of me having accumulated all power in my hands". The General Secretary was most insistent that "it runs counter to my views, my outlook and even my nature".'

In September of 1989, in an interview to *Le Monde*, when asked about his opinion of Mikhail Gorbachev Sakharov answered, 'On the one hand, I realise that *perestroika* was his initiative, although it was a historical necessity. On the other hand, I can see that he is very indecisive in his

---

* Sakharov tried to justify himself, he was quoting from the foreign press, and the facts mentioned there proved his words; he spoke about crimes against humanity that the Soviet Army had been committing in Afghanistan, that this very war was a crime. For the first time ever in our country he announced the number of Afghan casualties — a million of locals killed — but no one wanted to listen. — *Author's comment.*

actions... So you end up feeling that that the only real change, so far, has been his advent to power. I may be exaggerating a bit but generally it is true.'

Meanwhile the congress and its national TV coverage went ahead.

In a way, television was helping bring ideas of the First Congress home to the mass audience. So what ideas were those?

Was it that one of the richest countries in the world was still rationing its food in days of peace (Yuri Vlasov)? Was it that the role of the CPSU should be curtailed through '*ad hoc* legislation' (Yeltsin)? Was it that the economy needed profound and radical reforms (Popov)?

No, the amazing novelty lay elsewhere: in the openness of its democratic procedures, in the freedom to ask for the floor without having to notify the presidium in advance and get a 'go ahead' on the text of your speech. It was a school of parliamentary life for the entire country: open, dramatic, packed with action and clear to all.

In his *Confessions* Yeltsin wrote, 'After my convincing victory at the elections hints were dropped that, allegedly, at the congress, I was going to enter a scramble for power with Gorbachev and contest the position of a chairman... I do not know who started it: whether it was my supporters, jubilant because of this victory, or the other way round — my adversaries, scared by Muscovites' passionate reaction. Yet the rumours continued to spread.'

About a week before the congress Gorbachev phoned Yeltsin and suggested that they should meet. They met at the Kremlin.

'The meeting lasted about an hour.' Yeltsin writes in his book, 'We were seated face to face for the first time in a very long time. The conversation was tense, exhausting, I said to his face many things that I had on my mind.'

They had trouble understanding one another. Eventually Gorbachev realised that the conversation was going nowhere. He softened his tonality and asked Yeltsin about his most immediate plans. 'I said at once: the congress would decide on all of this. Gorbachev didn't like what he heard; he still wanted some guarantees and so carried on: what was my attitude to working in economic management? Maybe, I was interested in a job in the Council of Ministers? But I was sticking to my guns: the congress would provide all the answers.'

Which guarantees is Yeltsin talking about?

Electing Gorbachev the Chairman of the Supreme Soviet was one of the most dramatic points of the congress. Should there be one candidate or several? This simple question sent the country in a veritable frenzy. People just couldn't imagine that such a question could be asked in such a matter-of-fact way.

The idea that the head of state should be elected, even if it is a safe bet and the outcome was nearly hundred percent clear, still felt like a sacrilege. It was like a request to prove that God exists. He does. Why bother proving?

The deputies were so exercised that they would spend several hours discussing the motion. For some, inebriated with the new freedom of speech, it was a deeply principled issue: an unknown Deputy Obolensky demanded to be included in the voting lists. An alternative candidate to the Chairman of the Supreme Soviet: a blasphemy! For Yeltsin, the nature of Gorbachev's fears and doubts was now clear.

That audience of nearly three thousand people, out of whom about seventy percent were elite and bureaucrats, was far from loyal to the General Secretary. The audience were murmuring under their breath, annoyed, now aware of their power and Gorbachev, most likely, simply feared that Yeltsin would be at the head of this conservative wave of protest against the '*perestroika's* chief architect'.

Another procedural issue that caused a storm in the audience was the elections of Supreme Soviet members, that is deputies who would work there on a permanent basis and sit on committees and commissions, developing laws and acts — in a word, the future political elite. The list had been put together in advance and agreed at the Politburo. The Soviet machine was still in operation.

Yeltsin's name was not among those future prime political leaders. The conversation in the Kremlin had not been forgotten. There was no place for him at the Supreme Soviet.

And then another miracle occurred. A Deputy Kazannik, professor of law from Omsk, yielded his place in the Supreme Soviet and requested that Yeltsin be included in the voting list. Gorbachev realised that it became dangerous to openly challenge Yeltsin. The last thing he needed was a schism or a squabble at the congress.

'Gorbachev was aware,' Popov reminisces, 'that if the Supreme Soviet to which neither Sakharov, nor Afanasiev or me were elected ended up having no opposition deputies at all, it would never work as an instrument of pressure on the Central Committee — the way Gorbachev conceived it. I spoke to Gorbachev. He said, "I see no way out." "And if we find this way out ourselves will you support us?" "Yes", he answered. And he kept his word. The rest is well known. I had a conversation with Siberian Deputy Alexei Kazannik and he decided to reject his place in the Supreme Soviet. Yeltsin came after him in terms of votes collected. That was how he made it into the Supreme Soviet.

By the way, why didn't Yeltsin nominate himself for the Chairman of the Supreme Soviet and didn't want to compete with Gorbachev? Was he afraid of losing? After all, the 'aggressively obedient majority' was unlikely to vote in his favour. Still, he must have had other reasons.

Most probably Yeltsin's goal had never been fighting Gorbachev personally. He was aware of his importance and role in history. At least he was then, in 1989.

So what was the essence of events in May of 1989? I think was this: two and a half years later, in December of 1991, it would not be the great USSR, a country of reinforced concrete, of peoples and territories tied to each other with manacles and irons, bristling with missiles and guarded by submarines and aircraft carriers in all its seas — it was not this country that was going to disintegrate. A different entity, quite dissimilar to the USSR was born in May of 1989 — a special, unique, *Gorbachev's own country*.

Everything in this country was at odds with everything else. There, unimaginable things co-existed peacefully with some other, equally impossible, phenomena: the Communist Party that was voluntarily giving up its total power; an empire that was watching benevolently as 'democratic separatism' was emerging on its outskirts; the leader of this state and the head of this party trying to do a balancing act on a razor's edge so that nobody's feelings were hurt — instead of creating a new party and a new state.

The Congress of People's Deputies was a distilled essence of this country of Gorbachev's. But was it viable, this country?

... Yet another important consequence of the congress was the creation of *ad hoc commissions* — a special page in our history. There were three of those set up at the time: one — in relation to the Molotov-Ribbentrop Pact; another one — to analyse findings of the team of investigators headed by Gdlyan and Ivanov; and a commission to investigate events in Tbilisi*.

That is why the congress had to listen to General Rodionov as he tried to explain how it could have happened that in April of 1989, in Tbilisi, when dispersing a crowd in front of the House of Government, his troopers had used trenching spades and as a result 19 people got killed**. Explaining didn't come easy: the question of who had issued the order to use the troops remained a mystery. Gorbachev was abroad, the Second Secretary Ligachev, who was 'house-sitting' in his absence, denied responsibility. On the other hand Ligachev simply couldn't but tell Gorbachev about events in Tbilisi, he had no right to hold such information back.

That was also why the congress was forced to listen to mutual accusations, nearly insults, hurled at each other by the deputies from Armenia and Azerbaijan who dumped the blood-soaked problem of Karabakh, in all its gory details, onto the podium for all to see.

And then the audience, up to seventy percent consisting of rank-and-file stone-hearted Soviet functionaries, was watching, in grim amazement, as the deputy from Lithuania, musicologist (!) Landsbergis climbed the podium and crisply explained the congress's decisions were not legitimate in the Baltic republics since those could not henceforth be considered Soviet.

Finally, there was the subject of repressions and crimes committed by Stalinism, and of exoneration in history. But the topic of Stalin led the

---

\* The events are explained below.

\*\* 'Demands to disband autonomous entities within Georgia, particularly where it concerned the status of Abkhazia, and for Georgia to secede from the USSR were put forward by nationalist movements headed by Gamsakhurdia, Tsereteli and Chanturia and caused mass riots in Georgia. Georgia's Party leadership with the First Secretary Patiashvili at the head made a decision (with Moscow's accord — Gorbachev was abroad, visiting Cuba and England) to bring in troops to disperse the demonstrations. On the night of April 8$^{th}$, 19 people died, hundreds were wounded or poisoned by gases.' (R. Pikhoya, *Moscow. Kremlin. Power*, Moscow, 2007).

need to talk about repressed peoples, which meant — *redistribution of land,* return of the Meskhetian Turks to Meskhetia and of the Crimean Tatars to the Crimea*. It meant the conflict in the Prigorodny** District and so on — the list was huge...

Yet another commission, chaired by Alexander Yakovlev, was charged with a mission to prove or disprove the existence of the so-called 'Molotov-Ribbentrop protocols'.

For historians in the XX century, the *secret protocols* of 1939 — on the division of Europe between Stalin and Hitler — were a great mystery that motivated tireless research. In the West they knew that these protocols had to be kept either in the Kremlin or at the Foreign Ministry HQ in Smolenskaya Square (unless they had been destroyed). Western historians regarded available copies as a genuine source for quotations. Our scientists were vehemently denouncing the copies as forgery.

The Party propaganda was proceeding from the premise that even if the originals had survived there was no way on earth they would ever be made public.

This huge responsibility had to be shouldered by Gorbachev. He discussed it with Boldin, his aide of many years, the new head of the General Administration Department in the CC CPSU***.

---

* Today, the Meskhetian Turks are widely dispersed throughout the former Soviet Union (as well as in Turkey and the United States) due to forced deportations during World War II. At the time, the Soviet Union was preparing to launch a pressure campaign against Turkey and Stalin wanted to deport the strategic Turkish population from Meskheti since they were likely to be hostile to Soviet intentions. In 1944, the Meskhetian Turks were accused of smuggling, banditry and espionage in collaboration with their kin across the Turkish border; nationalistic policies at the time encouraged the slogan: 'Georgia for Georgians' and that the Meskhetian Turks should be sent to Turkey 'where they belong'. Approximately 115,000 Meskhetian Turks were deported to Central Asia and only a few hundred have been able to return to Georgia ever since.

** The East Prigorodny conflict was an inter-ethnic conflict in the eastern part of the Prigorodny district in the Republic of North Ossetia-Alania, which started in 1989 and developed, in 1992, into a brief ethnic war between local Ingush and Ossetian paramilitary forces.

*** To avoid duplication of names with the Secretariat of the Central Committee, this department, effectively performing the functions of a chancery was still called General Administration Department (Obshchy otdel) although all it was involved in was managing documents and the keeping of current files.

Thus, officially, only three people knew of the existence of those protocols: the owner of the safe Gorbachev, his ex-aide Lukianov and Boldin. Unofficially, the circle was somewhat wider, for example, there was Andrei Gromyko, the great Soviet diplomat, who, in his day, had handed them over to Stalin, fully aware that the protocols must never end up in the Foreign Ministry. But Gromyko was old and, besides, he knew too many Soviet secrets — the existence of the protocols was just one more. But what a secret it was!

'When I took up my position as the boss of the Administration Department in the Central Committee,' Boldin writes, 'I read a report alleging that the protocols were kept in the archive. What's more, they were not enclosed in an envelope, carried no special stamps or labels, and thus could be available to many employees.' Boldin immediately asked for an audience with Gorbachev.

'If memory serves me right, the secret protocols consisted of two pages of text signed by Ribbentrop and Molotov and a rather large map showing the western areas of the USSR and adjacent countries, signed by Ribbentrop and Stalin. Molotov's signature on the document was in Latin script... I do not believe it was by chance. Most likely, he hoped it would help challenge the authenticity of the document. Stalin, on the other hand, used no subterfuges, and the three letters of his name and surname ('J. St.') were conclusive proof that dotted all the i's.

'Mikhail Gorbachev,' Boldin continues, 'read the protocol very carefully and then unfolded, on his desk, the map showing the old and the new borders in the west. It was a large-scale map, on it there were cities, towns, settlements, railways and motorways, rivers, elevations and lowlands. All inscriptions were in German. The General Secretary was examining the line of agreed frontiers that half a century earlier had served as a demarcation line between the two powerful states. He was making his observations and from time to time asking questions. He was not surprised that the documents existed; his voice rather betrayed his annoyance at having to deal with the past. "Put it all in the deepest end of the drawer," he said by way of concluding.'

The hunt for the protocols was going on not only abroad where the interest, for evident reasons, was huge. The search was joined by CC secretary

Yakovlev and head of the International Department Falin. Boldin alerted Gorbachev, who snapped, 'Do not show anything to anyone. I shall tell those who should know.'

And thus the following incident took place at the First Congress of People's Deputies of the USSR which shook Boldin profoundly, the latter being head of Gorbachev's office and, generally speaking, a devoted Communist.

'… When the questions of the Soviet-German protocols came up at the congress, leading to a discussion of the situation in the Baltic republics, Mikhail Sergeyevich announced, to my complete amazement, that all attempts to discover the originals of the secret treaty proved futile.' Boldin was dumbfounded; he did not expect that his boss could lie so unblinkingly, while looking the audience 'in the face'.

Yet the story did not finish there. 'Some time after he addressed the congress Gorbachev asked me, nonchalantly, whether I had destroyed the protocols. I answered that I was not authorised to do it in the absence of explicit instructions.

"You do realise what these documents really amount to?"'

Gorbachev wanted Boldin to get rid of the documents *of his own accord*, without a direct order. But Boldin did not get the hint. And the General Secretary felt outraged.

Why was Gorbachev so afraid of the map annotated by Stalin and Ribbentrop? Why was he eager to destroy this evidence — if Boldin is to be believed? Why was he ready to deceive his closest colleagues and friends, Alexander Yakovlev, for example? It does not take a genius to understand that by publishing the 'protocols' he would provide a powerful trump card to the movement advocating the Baltic republics' cessation from the USSR.

Annexation of them in 1940 could thus be equated with the annexation of Czechoslovakia. Gorbachev was terrified at the prospect that the USSR could break up. But who knows: had he mustered the courage and made this sinister secret public in good time, maybe the issue would have been resolved differently?

Let us give credit to Boldin's intellectual honesty — he never did destroy the documents. Boris Yeltsin found them in the General Secretary's safe after the August of 1991 and put them in public domain.

... But let us return to 1989, back to the congress.

'I do not know from which point the General Secretary started using favours from secret services and having telephones tapped,' Valery Boldin goes on to say. 'Most likely, it coincided with his ascent to the political Olympus. But I had my first experience of it all when the team of investigators from the General Procurator's Office of the USSR, with Gdlyan and Ivan at its head, had the audacity to refer to his Stavropol past...

'With time, Gorbachev developed a real taste for decoding records of his opponents' conversations. With time he authorised me[*] to do it, excepting the most secret documents. That went on until the First Congress of the People's Deputies.

'Election of several of Gorbachev's opponents as deputies to the congress confounded the KGB Chairman, Vladimir Alexandrovich Kriuchkov[**]. I witnessed a conversation... between Gorbachev and Kriuchkov, who announced that the secret services could not continue tapping deputies' conversations.

'"Mikhail Sergeyevich, my people refuse to do it and I have no right to insist. It is against the law." Kriuchkov was saying.

'"What are you saying, Volodia? The political struggle is intensifying but all of you want to do is continue sitting on the fence. Think it over and find a solution."

... It goes without saying that at the time the principal focus of interest was Yeltsin. But after he was elected a member of the Supreme Soviet of the USSR and later — President of Russia, Kriuchkov raised the same issue with Gorbachev again, and received an angry response, 'Do you really want me to teach the KGB its duties?'

Little by little, Gorbachev's fear of a coup d'état grew into a real mania. His pet fear was Yeltsin's union with conservatives — in the Politburo and at the congress, that's why it was so important for him that Yeltsin was a radical, an 'unbridled democrat'.

---

[*] Boldin.

[**] At the time, Head of the KGB.

At the congress, Yeltsin was appointed head of the Committee for Construction and Architecture. From now on his presence in the country's supreme legislative body, the Supreme Soviet of the USSR, was totally legitimate.

In the autumn of the same year, KGB put another portion of most interesting documents on Gorbachev's desk.

Between 9 and 17 of September 1989, Yeltsin visited the USA on an invitation issued by the Foundation for the Social Inventions. His visit was hosted by the Esalen Institute in San Francisco. Yeltsin couldn't really go as a statesman, on a state visit — and was reluctant to go on a lecture circuit as a private individual. The Foundation for Social Inventions managed to find a solution.

The terrible incurable disease of AIDS had just started making headlines; and as a result of *glasnost* and *perestroika* the new made it into our newspapers. Soviet manufacturers of medical supplies produced no disposable syringes while in the West they cost pennies.

Yeltsin's advisors suggested to Yeltsin that the fee from public speeches in the USA may be used for buying disposable syringes. In Moscow Yeltsin explained the idea to the US Ambassador, Jack Matlock. In his turn Matlock scanned the programme of visits and pointed out that in the course of eight days Yeltsin would have to speak to at least 20-30 audiences. 'It is a hectic programme and I hope your work will be remunerated,' said ambassador politely. 'My plan is to buy disposable syringes for hospitals here,' answered Yeltsin.

He flew into New York. At 7.15 A.M. he gave an interview to the programme *Good morning America* broadcast on the ABC television network. Then a visit to the Stock Exchange was followed by other meetings and interviews. At midday, over lunch, he delivered a lecture in the Council on Foreign Relations. After that he recorded an interview for *MacNeil/Lehrer News Hour*, spoke at the Columbia University and set off for dinner at the River Club organised by David Rockefeller. Shortly before midnight he boarded the plane to go to Baltimore.

And that just the first day of the visit!

He was offered vodka at all receptions but invariably asked for water instead. 'I shall collapse after the first sip,' was his polite explanation to generous hosts referring to his extreme fatigue.

Yeltsin saw all the principal landmarks of New York but the strongest impression was left by a regular roadside supermarket in Houston.

'It happened on the way to the airport, following a brief visit to Lyndon B. Johnson Space Centre: Yeltsin visited, for the first and only time during his trip, an American supermarket — "Randall".' (Leon Aron).

Yeltsin wanted to drop in unannounced, 'so that the owners would have no time to dress the windows'. He expected that on so huge a trade floor there would be many shoppers. He wanted to chat to 'regular folk', find out about 'their problems'. But at this time of day the shop was nearly empty and to him, this was one of many amazing things. Abundant lights, a kaleidoscope of colours, clean counters glowing softly — all of it dazzled the person who was used to unsightly Soviet food shops.

'Yeltsin asked a staff member how many lines they were carrying. The answer was — about thirty thousand. They examining cheeses and ham, started counting types of salami and lost count,' his assistant Sukhanov was writing.

After that Yeltsin stopped a lady shopper and asked, having apologised in advance, about her family's income and what proportion of it they spent on food. "Three thousand six hundred dollars a month, out of which 170 dollars is our weekly food shop". Those were mind-boggling figures. A Soviet family would spend a lion's share of its monthly expenditure on food (nearly 60%). What's more — the food that looked and smelled quite different to the range in "Randall".

This 'culture shock' experienced by Yeltsin (he would be repeating later — imagine, it was an ordinary shop, by the roadside, in some tiny place, not even in New York!) would define many things in the destiny of our country. He viewed this discovery as nothing less than a *national humiliation*.

On board the plane, according to Sukhanov, he was sitting 'with his head in his hands' and asking the same question over and over, 'What have they done to our miserable people?'

… Yeltsin generally wanted to meet as many 'rank-and-file Americans' as possible. But some shocking discoveries were still in store for him even there: a 'common farmer' had two computers on his desk and was using them for keeping on top of prices, dynamics of the demand and so on.

Yeltsin was bowled over and kept reiterating, 'Ligachev should see this!' At the time Ligachev was in charge of agriculture and was foaming at mouth defending collective farms. 'How many people would *our* pig farm of this type employ?' he was asking his companions. And then would answer his question himself, 'While they only have two!'

Back in Moscow Yeltsin mentioned to Ambassador Matlock that he would like to have a chat with President Bush and deliver to him a 'message' extremely important for the future of *perestroika*.

The Kremlin was watchful of the American reaction to this.

A huge wave of publications, interviews, sensational pronouncements made by Yeltsin played their role, and the American administration decided to receive Yeltsin in the White House but in such a way as to preclude any hurt feelings on the part of Gorbachev.

Condoleezza Rice, at the time a special aide to George H.W. Bush, met him by the Western wing of the White House. In the car, it was announced that the official meeting with the President was not possible but, of course, a representative of the new Soviet parliament would be given a warm welcome by National Security Advisor Brent Scowcroft. Yeltsin felt slighted...

'Cold rules of etiquette adopted at the White House under Bush Sr. did not provide for a hitherto unknown individual pitching up at the hot kitchen of history, especially not this rough Siberian giant: a tall and awkward guy in an ill-fitting suit and a cheap tie.' (Leon Aron).

The issue, of course, was neither his suit nor his tie (Yeltsin looked resplendent in all his suits, anyone who saw him in person may confirm it). Yeltsin presented a strong opposition to Gorbachev — and the White House did not have a clue about what to make of it. But for Yeltsin, the meeting with the President of the United States was a matter of principle.

'They made it to the site for visitors' parking,' the American biographer continues his story, 'and Yeltsin refused to get out of the car. They cajoled him out and showed him to the lower corridor of the western wing. "Those who are to meet the President use a different entrance," he said to Condoleezza Rice. She answered that his meeting was not with the President but with General Scowcroft. This caused a storm of protestations...'

Condoleezza Rice was making a huge effort to steer him to the relevant floor. Yeltsin announced that he was going nowhere without his assistant Sukhanov. This was against the agreement but the Americans obliged. The guests were issued visitor's tags.

'I am Yeltsin and not a visitor,' he grumbled.

General Scowcroft spent several minutes talking to him and then President Bush popped into the office — 'by chance', smiling and shaking hands. He greeted the guest from Moscow standing.

The Moscow guest rose to his feet and suddenly discovered that Bush was as tall as himself. 'We are worth each other,' said Yeltsin.

According to Scowcroft's records, the meeting lasted 16 minutes.

Bush asked Yeltsin about Gorbachev — what should one make of him? Yeltsin responded that along with many others, he was admiring the latter's efforts but it was important to move further and further forward...

It was a victory, clear and unequivocal.

Several hours prior to his meeting with President Bush in Washington, D.C., Yeltsin had flown to Baltimore. Despite the fact that David Rockefeller's private jet landed at one in the morning, a dinner table groaning with drinks and snacks was waiting for them in the hotel room. The next day's schedule included a ceremonial breakfast at 7:45 A.M.; after that — a lecture and a meeting with prominent university professors and politicians. Excited and bursting with impressions, Yeltsin and his aides stayed up, talking, until 4 A.M. That night, Yeltsin did not manage to get any sleep.

Despite the fact that Yeltsin was close to fainting, at five o'clock his aide Yaroshenko took him on a stroll across the park. Then Yeltsin used the last resort: he took two sleeping pills and went out like a light.

Two hours later the event organiser Muller came over to pick him up and escort him to the meeting with the 'Baltimore *beau monde*'. Yeltsin was pleading that all events be cancelled. 'Boris Nikolayevich, they say that they will not survive such disappointment,' the interpreter was droning on. 'Tell them it is me who will not survive this day,' said Yeltsin.

Soon Yeltsin was shown, on the arm of his escort, into an overcrowded hall.

As soon as he made his entrance there, his eyes went alight — 'as if someone pressed a button,' recollected one of his aides. Yet it took him about an hour in the armchair to come to. After that he started gathering momentum and spoke with a renewed confidence. But these several hours during which he was fighting the influence of the sleeping pills, taken two hours before the meeting, cost him a lot.

… Dishonest correspondents exist not only in our country. Yeltsin's 'inadequate behaviour' was the subject of a tiny article by Paul Hendrickson in *Washington Post*. The article was entitled 'A Style'. The correspondent had even spoken with the cleaner in the hotel. She disclosed the fact that she discovered an empty whisky bottle there. All that was required now was a logical conclusion: Yeltsin drank the entire bottle on his own.

At the same time not a single person he met that day (including General Scowcroft and President Bush) mentioned anything about Yeltsin's lack of sobriety. His public lecture was recorded on video and later broadcast by the Soviet TV. It showed the lecturer as nothing more but a totally exhausted man who was, nonetheless, extremely excited under strain; he was finding it very hard to speak but still ploughed on with growing energy and drive.

Yet the malicious article started its long journey to Moscow. First, it was reprinted by Italian *La Repubblica*. Then the translation was taken on by the Soviet paper *Pravda*.

'Boris Yeltsin, a folk hero of Moscow, Gorbachev's Cassandra… is a source of endless prophecies of a catastrophe, insane spending of money, interviews and especially the smell of famous whiskey from Kentucky.' Neither *Washington Post* nor *La Repubblica* breathed a word about what Yeltsin had been saying, who he had been meeting with and what the Americans' impressions were.

Very few among the readers worked it out that the Kremlin was vexed by the fact that Yeltsin had been received at the White House.

The article reprinted by *Pravda* from the Italian *La Repubblica* made no mistake when referring to his 'grim prophesies'. He did prophesy, constantly insisting that 'people were tired of waiting', that 'if we did not change the situation profoundly, within the nearest future the country should have a social explosion'. He was saying to the Americans, 'You simply do not know the reality of how people live in the Soviet Union'.

Yeltsin was very often accused of 'whipping up tensions'. But in July of 1989 he received a serious argument in support of his social alarmism.

The miners went on strike.

Miners were considered one of the best-paid professions in the USSR. Their wages were two or three times higher than the average; they had longer holidays, their ministry had special recreation centres in all of the Soviet Union's spa areas.

What the miners demanded wasn't something extraordinary. These are some of the bullet points put forward by Kuzbass* miners. 'We demand that protective clothing should be issued on demand and in accordance with approved schedules. All workers should be issued towels and soap, based on the quota of 800 grams per person in the shower**. Arrangements should be in place for water aeration (by hand or by machines). All miners, engineers and technical personnel should be provided with quilted jackets, because a powerful current of cold air at the lift stops causes numerous illnesses in winter. Arrangements should be made for organising controlled supplies, against a signature in the ledger, of a range of meats and sausages. Reports of this should be presented monthly to workers' assembly'.

On July 16th, representatives of 100,000 miners from nine Kuzbass mines met to set up the regional strike committee. The sessions of this meeting were broadcast around the oblast through loudspeakers erected on all pillars and posts in municipal squares, and in miners' settlements near the mines. On the same day, Gorbachev and Prime Minister Nikolai Ryzhkov appealed to the strikers, urging them to return to work, and promised to send down a high-profile commission. The miners decided it was too little too late. The number of people who had stopped work now exceeded 140,000.

The miners' strike overturned all concepts of what could and could not be done in the USSR, especially since it spread to practically all mines in Kuzbass and Vorkuta. Instead of using all possible means of bringing the strikers under control: threats, bribery, deployment

---

\* Kuzbass, or Kuznetsky Basin, lies in south-western Siberia in Russia and is one of the largest coal deposits in the country.

\*\* Monthly. — *Author's comment.*

of troops and militia, attracting the free labour of convicts, making attempts to reach a tacit agreement, splitting the unified front into several parts, imposing an informational veto (as had been the case with all preceding governments) — Gorbachev's government went down a different route.

An *ad hoc* commission headed up by Politburo member Nikolai Sliunkovmet with the miners and arrived at somewhat paradoxical conclusions: miners' demands were announced to be fair, but the blame for what happened was placed squarely at the door of local authorities.

Thus, Gorbachev, from the Kremlin, supported the miners. Their strike was seen as 'wide-spread democracy' in action. Most importantly, the diehard enemies of *perestroika* were identified too: bureaucrats, functionaries, *apparatchicks* and the local elite. Whereas as far as miners themselves were concerned, Yeltsin became the person they wanted to see and with whom they agreed to enter into a dialogue.

This was duly noted, both in Moscow and in the West. It now looked that Gorbachev was prepared to sacrifice the local Party bosses if only it would help him prevent Yeltsin from gaining extra political points. The Kuzbass situation demonstrated to local elites, very clearly, the intentions of the Kremlin: to throw the local barons to the wolves.

... That year, yet another important event was the setting up of the first *legal political organisation* in the USSR: the so-called Interregional Group of Deputies (IRGD).

Its nucleus was formed in the early days of the First Congress of the People's Deputies of the USSR and centred around the democratic wing of the Moscow delegation, although it also involved deputies from Leningrad and many other areas. On 29-30 July 1989, the group ran its first conference and adopted the 'Keynotes for the action plan to enhance and implement *perestroika*' and elected the Steering Committee. The group (including those who could not attend in person) counted 388 members.

Twenty-five people were elected into the Steering Committee, among them Academician Andrei Sakharov, Boris Yeltsin, Yuri Afanasiev[*],

---

[*] Doctor of Historical Sciences, professor, founder of the Russian State University of Humanities.

Gavriil Popov, Anatoly Sobchak, Gennady Burbulis\*, Mikhail Poltoranin\*\* et al. Yeltsin, Afanasiev, Popov, Victor Palm\*\*\* (Estonia) and Sakharov were elected co-chairs.

Several of the IRGD members were practically involved in independent political movements: say, a leader of the Popular Front of Karelia Sergei Belozertsev or a member of the Steering Group of the Moscow Popular Front Sergei Stankevich. However, the majority of members were prominent members of the Soviet intelligentsia with far from radical views. Only 49% participants in the first conference were unequivocally in favour of a multi-party system, and 5% believed it advisable to keep a system with just one party in it. Most of them viewed Sakharov as an extreme radical and he received the least votes among co-chairs — 69 (Yeltsin got 144).

Yet for their time they all were unquestionably progressive and courageous people.

Gorbachev was shocked to learn about the group's existence since it undermined a coherent plan by Anatoly Lukianov: to control the congress by way of forming the so-called 'territorial groups' headed by trusted Party comrades. But the IRGD was an association of deputies according to their *political* views. From the very beginning it became a 'faction of non-content', an opposition — something that Gorbachev feared and was eager to prevent.

At the point when Yuri Afanasiev climbed the podium and announced the launch of the IRGD Gorbachev demanded that the television coverage be stopped.

Moreover, practically not one of the IRGD members made it into the Supreme Soviet. It was then that Yuri Afanasiev gave his famous definition for the congress: 'an aggressively obedient majority'.

That was the thing — the 'majority' at the congress viewed democrats as dangerous upstarts, windbags, political vagabonds and outsiders, and thus a peril to the entire system.

This 'majority' acted of their own free will and didn't need encouragement from above to start clapping their hands in order to drown

---

\* A Soviet, later Russian politician.

\*\* A professional journalist and a statesman.

\*\*\* Estonian and Soviet scientist, academician of the Estonian Academy of Sciences.

the words spoken by Sakharov or Afanasiev, Sobchak or Popov; they froze in grim suspense at the sight of Yeltsin, murmured contemptuously at Galina Starovoitova*and Evdokia Gayer** (Gayer represented interests of small ethnic groups in the Russian North, and Starovoitova — in the Caucasus).

Gorbachev's response to the IRGD was, up to a point, a resonance of this collective sentiment but his attitude to the left-wing deputies (as he saw them) was full of contradictions. (It must be added that the terms 'left' and 'right' are used here as Mikhail Sergeyevich was interpreting them *then*. To him, the 'left wing' was not communists but the democratic opposition. The 'right flank' consisted of Politburo conservatives and the Party on the whole.)

Strange though it may seem but the deputies forming the IRGD were far from hostile to Gorbachev. On the contrary, some of them managed to define in their speeches the programme of Gorbachev's *perestroika* in such transparent and specific terms that it was finally taken on board by all viewers glued to their TV sets. Nearly all members of the Interregional Group of Deputies respected Mikhail Sergeyevich personally; some were even awe-struck.

Nonetheless, this 'opposition' was unacceptable to Gorbachev for a number of complicated reasons; it did not sit right with his plans and felt dangerous. At times things were bordering on the absurd. IRGD members were on good terms with Gorbachev; he was warm and friendly with them, exchanging greetings at the congress; he would listen to them very attentively and some of them could telephone him directly without much ceremony. Yet — they all were under the surveillance of the KGB, their telephones were all bugged (according to Boldin's memoirs), and each step was shadowed by agents.

---

\* *Galina Vasilyevna Starovoitova* (1946-1998) was a Russian politician and ethnographer known for her work to protect ethnic minorities and promote democratic reforms in Russia. Murdered by a contract killer in 1998 in St Petersburg.

\*\* *Dr. Evdokia Alexandrovna Gaye*r (b. 1934) member of the Supreme Soviet of the USSR (1989-1991) and Parliament of Russia (in the middle 1990s), deputy head of the State Committee on the North (1991-1993), and one of the public leaders of indigenous minorities of the North, Siberia, and the Far East.

The KGB regarded those who spoke at democratic rallies, even if they were People's Deputies, not as political allies but provocateurs and dangerous elements. Huge rallies in Moscow in 1989 and 1990 were organised with the direct involvement of the group leaders: Yeltsin, Afanasiev, Starovoitova, Sakharov, Gdlyan, Burbulis and Stankevich. Thus, they were automatically classified as 'extremists' despite their personal attempts to prevent clashes and provocations. Should it prove expedient, the KGB was ready to arrest them and even 'shoot to kill'.

Things were far from simple in this *Gorbachev's land*. On the one hand — there were friends. On the other — there were enemies. Here — real candidates for a serious role in parliamentary politics. There — targets for close surveillance.

There was no unity among the opposition either. It was a diverse group of people with diverging views and different tempers.

Within the IRGD it was 'professors', representatives of the academic elite who called the tune. All of them were Party members, extremely cautious and unswervingly moderate. All of them (with the exception of Sakharov, Starovoitova and some democrats of the younger generation) found themselves in politics by chance, and the prospect of leading the 'masses', speaking at rallies and engaging in a stand-off with the official authorities (they were in opposition after all!) filled them with unease. They were much better suited to the role of experts, judges or teachers.

It was not a coincidence that in the autumn Gorbachev's envoy — Yevgeny Maksimovich Primakov* — started attending the IRGD sessions. He knew many of those in the 'professorial wing' personally, they spoke the same language. He started acting as a bridge between the authorities and the newly-minted opposition.

The only genuinely big political player there was Yeltsin — already a leader of huge numbers of people who combined both organisational and managerial skills. He knew how power worked.

---

* Yevgeny Maksimovich Primakov (b. 1929) is a Russian politician and academic. During his long career, he served as the Russian Foreign Minister, Prime Minister of Russia, Speaker of the Soviet of the Union of the Supreme Soviet of the Soviet Union, and chief of the Foreign Intelligence Service(SVR). Primakov is an academician and a member of the Presidium of the Russian Academy of Sciences.

But it was precisely this clear advantage of Yeltsin's that left the IRGD leaders feeling uncomfortable. Some were put off by his overly tough stand towards Gorbachev, others — like Sakharov and Starovoitova — by his recent candidacy for Politburo membership and a place in the highest Party *nomenklatura*. Some others were afraid of leader-mania and feared that Yeltsin's name would overshadow everybody else and push them to the margins.

That is why a decision was taken to manage the group collectively.

Gavriil Popov later believed that Yeltsin's pride was 'mortally wounded' by this decision. That he never forgave them. But this is simply not true: under Yeltsin, Popov himself became Mayor of Moscow. During the August putsch of 1991 he was among those in the White House, and had always enjoyed cordial relations with Russia's President.

'Did you attend the IRGD sessions?' I ask of Naina Iosifovna.

'I did several times.'

'What was Boris Nikolayevich's attitude to those proceedings? What was he saying afterwards?'

'He treated them very seriously; it was part of his political fight. It is just that when the Russian congress elected him Chairman of the Supreme Soviet of Russia his interests shifted elsewhere. But I saw the IRGD members not only at their meeting in the House of Cinema. They used to come by: Popov, Sobchak, many others. Sometimes there would be ten or fifteen people dropping in… Popov would sometimes bring his wife along; we would visit them, too. We were in constant contact by phone, arranging things. Sometimes the phone would ring at night. Boris Nikolayevich spoke on the telephone with Sakharov and Bonner but they had never been over.'

Despite the fact that Gorbachev did like some group members personally, he was repelled by their political views. The only venue they could use was the House of Cinema. They were banned from publishing their own informational leaflet. Their activities were dropped from the official reports of the congress. Gorbachev was denying the group any official recognition — he didn't want to see them as a fully-fledged faction of the new USSR parliament.

They had no status — not a single legislative initiative put forward by the group could be taken up for consideration at the congress. In a word, the inter-regional group created with a view to perform constructive legislative work was going nowhere. Its activities were at a dead end and this was influencing the atmosphere within the group accordingly.

The conflict among the group members reached its logical pinnacle in the late autumn of 1989. Sakharov, Starovoitova and the young democrats demanded that they should proclaim themselves a 'political opposition', form a party — in order to be able to push through amendments to the Constitution and, if need be, 'fight the existing system' not only through the parliament but also through mass disobedience (strikes, rallies and demonstrations).

The professorial wing explained its opinion most exhaustively through the lips of Anatoly Sobchak. He made a fair point that the real opposition to Gorbachev was not them but the 'aggressively obedient majority', the Party apparatus, pro-Communist deputies. And if they opposed Mikhail Sergeyevich, they would be objectively strengthening this majority's hand.

Yeltsin found it hard to listen to all of this or to take part in debates. The atmosphere at the sessions was high-strung. Frustrated with their inability to find a common platform, the people who respected one another and admired academician Sakharov started resorting to personal remarks; civility was giving way to annoyance. Gradually, the ranks of the IRGD started dwindling. Deputies who announced their intention to join started leaving.

... On 14 December 1989 Andrei Dmitrievich Sakharov died. He was lying in state in the Academy of Sciences on Leninsky Prospect. It had been the Academy that nominated as a deputy to the Congress. Huge crowds came to say a final farewell to the great scientist and a great dissident.

The cause of his death might have been utter exhaustion caused by the complex and unpredictable situation at the congress, or the stress brought on by a bitter conflict between his belief in the reality of change and the dire nature of practical events. And, of course, his death had been brought forward by his exile in the city of Gorky — the place where he had gone on numerous hunger strikes, written countless letters to the authorities and never got a reply, the place of suffering and incarceration.

Politburo members put in a brief appearance and stood as guards of honour by Sakharov's coffin. Gorbachev was there too, so was Yeltsin. It was as if Sakharov, even after death, was pleading with them to come to an understanding and to join efforts. But it was no use.

# Project 'Russia'
## (1990)

It was summer of 1990. Naina Yeltsin recollects:

'One day he came home from the congress, pale and completely washed out. Suddenly he turned round and said, "It's time to save Russia!"

'Frankly speaking, I understood nothing and even got scared. What Russia? The Soviet Union was still in existence and no one was even thinking in those terms. So I asked, "Borya, what are you talking about? What Russia?"

'"Our Russia!"

'I made him put his feet up, gave him some medications, herbal extracts, felt his forehead — maybe he had a fever? Then I called Tanya and we held council: I explained to her that her father was off his head, I thought he was delirious.

'Tanya asked why I was scared. I answered, "He is banging on about the need to save Russia." "So what of it?" Tanya said. But I just wasn't getting it... What was all this about?

'I couldn't conceive then of Russia as a separate state. But he saw what was coming and thought in different terms,' Naina Iosifovna sums it up.

... These 'different terms' were an oddity even for his wife. But he saw the big picture and realised that the country called USSR was gradually spiralling out of control.

In January of 1990 Yeltsin went on a visit to Japan. He was there at the invitation of the TV Company TBS and some business circles.

## PROJECT 'RUSSIA' (1990)

Like in the USA, a lot was expected of him. His hosts were looking for was a clear, transparent and above all — new approach to some issues of concern: the Kuril Islands, destiny of the burial sites of the WWII Japanese POWs, an opinion on the status of the Baltic republics within the Soviet Union and on prospects for *perestroika* in general... Yeltsin addressed these issues while speaking on a popular primetime TV talk show which went on air at 11 P.M. The official circle of Yeltsin's communication consisted of Prime Minister Kaifu, Foreign Minister Nakayama and Construction Minister Harada, but he also met, privately, with numerous businessmen and journalists.

It was apparent that in Japan Yeltsin was perceived as a politician of a very special status, someone who had had a meeting with President Bush in the White House and had an aura of an opposition politician. Similarly to the US, his hosts were eager to show Yeltsin their country: Hokkaido Island, an ancient temple, 'a robot-manufacturing plant', a small family-run restaurant, a fish market in Tokyo...

Everywhere he went he saw this incredible abundance of everything, superfluity of colours and smells, a sense of stability and reliability of life — just like on his recent trip to the USA.

Again and again, the same question was coming to torment him: why was it that *between* those two great powers — on in the East and one in the West — there lied such a huge country with such insurmountable problems?

The heart of the matter was not technologies (he saw some formidable construction projects in Russia too). It was not cultural traditions or industriousness of the Japanese or the Americans. Yeltsin knew full well that Russians knew how to work, too — both rapidly and with creative abandon.

But where did the secret of this excessive material strength, this stability of the Western and Eastern worlds lay? Why was it that his own country knew nothing but material poverty bordering on destitution? Why was lit that shanty towns and semi-military barracks formed an inalienable characteristic of Russian existence? He was not the only Russian abroad to asking the same question. But Yeltsin tried to find a new answer.

Starting from 1989 his life was dominated by a new project that transcended the pattern of his previous existence in politics but, simultaneously, was its logical evolution.

Russia and the Soviet Union — what sort of a hierarchy was that? Gradually this dichotomy, so familiar and taken for granted from the earliest childhood, started feeling wrong and precarious, offering more riddles than solutions.

... Elections of deputies to the congress of Russia were scheduled for March 1990. Some Gorbachev's associates later blamed him for agreeing to set up two parallel and similar political entities: the congresses of the USSR and of Russia. But having set the things in motion, Gorbachev was no longer in a position to tighten the reins. The elections to and the very ethos of the Russian congress were radically different to the situation with the All-Union event.

No 'lists' were to be put forward by Communists or any other associations and organisations. It wasn't that Gorbachev was after a more democratic election –those entities simply were not there. For example, Russia did not have its own Communist Party or the Academy of Sciences, there were no Russian national trade unions (they existed only by sector of the industry).

So whose capital was Moscow? Was it the leading city of Russia or of the entire empire that spread across practically half the globe?

Say, the Japanese raised, yet again, the issue of the Kuril Islands. To the USSR, with its complicated geopolitical interests and the superpower status, economic interests came second — but Russia could benefit from the joint use of those: keep them Soviet but convert them into a free economic zone...

While at the head of the Sverdlovsk Oblast Yeltsin saw with his own eyes the inexhaustible resources of the Urals: oil and gas pipelines transporting fuels to the West, metals, and metallurgical plants. But the people indefatigably creating the military and economic might of the entire country didn't even have enough to eat! Prior to every public holiday, each successive First Secretary's had been racking his brain as to where to source several tonnes of meat or butter, in order to 'feed the oblast'. It had been a titanic effort even to demolish the workers' barracks and move their residents to some bearable dwellings, to build a metro system, to put in a single road leading north — a lifeline for the oblast. Moscow had been constantly building up administrative pressure, reluctant to okay these initiatives and allocate resources. Yet it had been very happy to pump those resources out of the region. So whose capital was Moscow? Did it belong to Russia or to the USSR?

Yeltsin decided to stand for the office of Russian People's Deputy in his native Sverdlovsk.

For two weeks he was holding countless meetings, sometimes speaking several times a day. By the way, it was during his election campaign in Sverdlovsk that he acquired a group of his voluntary assistants who helped him prepare his presentations and answer questions. Those were Gennady Burbulis, Alexander Urmanov, Gennady Kharin, Liudmila Pikhoya and Alexander Ilyin, all of them from Sverdlovsk, all social scientists from the Ural University. They first suggested recording Yeltsin's public repartees and the most successful answers to notes, thereby creating ready-to-use templates. This was how he first got his speechwriters.

Unexpectedly, the Sverdlovsk *Obkom* of the CPSU acted benevolently towards Yeltsin's election campaign. There were no bans, no one was trying to throw a spanner in his works, and the few condemnatory articles in the Party press read formalistic and stilted. He was even invited to use the city's best hotel, also owned by the *Obkom*, as his election headquarters. Yeltsin, however, declined the gift. He moved, 'along with the others', in the local *Urals Hotel* that turned out to be proved noisy and filthy. In the end his assistants persuaded him to relocate to a furnished flat that belonged to a local plant and was used for putting up visiting 'consultants'.

His victory in Sverdlovsk was a landslide — 85% of the votes.

From now on his trademark style became direct address to the people, and even his 'weak spots' — physical massiveness, a proclivity for unrestrained verbal improvisations, extreme openness and a naive belief in his own words — all became part and parcel of his image and a point of strength. The word 'Russia' foremost in his vocabulary, he became a simple 'Russian' who ended up in power.

... It should be noted that Yeltsin never was a remarkable speaker. He couldn't enunciate for hours like, say, Gorbachev or Fidel Castro. Still, answering notes from the audience, his favourite genre, could go on for many hours. He knew how to keep the audience in suspense — but not with the help of a monologue. He would read his speeches clearly and unemotionally, from his notes, never taking more than 25, 30 or 40 minutes at the most.

The election campaign of the future Russian Deputy already contained messages about his new political project: a multi-party system and the expedience of introducing private ownership of 'the means of production and land'. He was uttering words unacceptable to Gorbachev, to the Party, to the official authorities. But most importantly, he spoke about a totally new Russia.

'The new Constitution brought in through a public referendum was to ascribe priority… to essential rights and freedoms of citizens: freedom of assembly, freedom of political association and freedom of conscience and faith,' writes Yeltsin's biographer Leon Aron. It is not a coincidence that Yeltsin's emphasis was on the fundamental values of Western democracy.

But let return to Yeltsin's programme of 1990. It was proposed that adherence to democratic rights and liberties should be overseen by the Constitutional Court. Russia was to become a presidential republic, its president elected every five years out of several candidates in the course of direct, general and equal elections through a secret ballot. No president may stay in office for longer than two terms. An incumbent president must suspend his membership in any political parties or organisations.

The new Constitution of Russia should abolish the guiding role of the Party — from now on Russia was to be a 'de-ideologised state'. Perhaps it was not the most beautiful word in Russian but it was perfectly understandable in 1990: Russia should be a country without Communists at its helm. But Yeltsin went even further: cells and committees of *any* party shall be acceptable at enterprises, *kolkhozes* and *sovkhozes* and any other public sector organisations only if *allowed* by the staff. Today it looks self-evident but at the time it was a revolutionary measure, an unheard-of insolence.

Yet the pivotal concept of Yeltsin's programme, his project 'Russia' went far beyond any anti-Gorbachev or anti-Party mottos. To be fair, the idea had been formulated before him. For example, this is what the famous writer Valentin Rasputin was saying at the Congress of the USSR People's Deputies:

'We, the Russian people, respect and understand national sentiments and problems of all peoples and ethnic groups of our country without exception. But we want to be understood, too... Here, at the congress, there are very conspicuous initiatives put forward by the Baltic deputies who are using parliamentary measures to incorporate some amendments into the Constitution whereby they would be able to say goodbye to *this country*... But... maybe Russia should secede from the Union too, since you are blaming her for all your grievances and believe that your progressive intentions are thwarted by her low level of development and clumsiness? ... It would, by the way, help us, too, to resolve many of our problems, be it now or in the future.'

In the same year of 1990 *Komsomolskaya Pravda* published an article by Alexander Solzhenitsyn entitled *How Shall We Organise Russia?* Here is a quote from this text.

'In the course of three quarters of a century, while incessantly brainwashing us on the subject of "the socialist friendship of peoples", the Communist power has been so neglectful, it has... befouled so many aspects in relations between these very peoples that one cannot even see a way that could bring us back to the peaceful cohabitation of nations... very nearly achieved in the last decades of the prerevolutionary Russia... Centrifugal forces in many peripheral republics have already acquired such a momentum that without violence and blood they cannot be stopped... All we can do is become more adroit in preventing too much misery, so that the split shall occur without unnecessary human suffering and only where it is inevitable... Three Baltic republics, three Trans-Caucasian republics, four republics in Central Asia, perhaps Moldavia, too, since it is rather drawn towards Romania, these eleven republics — yes! — will unavoidably and irrevocably break away.'

However, it is important to point out that Yeltsin's programme resonated not only with the 'public opinion' and views of 'democratically-minded intelligentsia' (in other words, neither the most numerous nor the most influential part of the society) but with the general public. The 'resurrection' of Russia became a highly topical subject practically for all classes, strata and political movements. Yeltsin supplied this idea with dry pragmatic features.

Russia was a donor for the entire USSR, producing 60% of the Soviet gross domestic product. At the same time, its living standards were close to being the lowest in the country. Russia had been helping other republics with raw materials and other resources — depleting those severely. Why was it that the Ukraine and Byelorussia were members of the UN, and Russia wasn't? Why didn't it have an Academy of Sciences, television, radio and informational agencies? Why was it a Cinderella?

The USSR, as a voluntary association, should only keep the minimal central apparatus — for 'strategic planning'; the rest should be delegated to the republics themselves.

In 1990 it sounded like a political utopia, at best — a very distant prospect. But as an alternative to Gorbachev's policy it did make sense.

January of 1990. Bloody events are taking place in the capital of Azerbaijan — Baku. The Popular Front organises rallies to demand independence but those lead to street pogroms against Armenians. Atrocities unheard of in this peaceful city leave people dead. The pogroms are stopped but the rallies continue. The Popular Front demands resignation of the 'pro-Moscow' government. The army is brought in and another 125 people die in the crackdown on protesters. Who were those 'extremists'? Experts believe that the swing towards nationalism was a result of Gorbachev pinching the interests of well-established local elites. Suddenly stripped of power, they responded in their own way: in the language of roaring crowds. 'It wasn't a coincidence that the initial explosions happened in those places where Gorbachev had replaced republican leaders: in Almaty, Yerevan and Baku', is the conclusion made by historians Geller and Nekrich.

To reconcile the hostile parties and to pacify nations called for measure transcending the use of military force, since it only served to 'freeze' those national volcanoes of passions temporarily. It called for an integrated political plan, a common project — things that the Soviet leadership simply did not have.

One month prior to the events in Baku, in December of 1989, the Lithuanian Communist Party announced its departure from the CPSU. The Lithuanian Seim was preparing the Declaration of Independence. Gorbachev rushed over to Vilnius, in order to talk sense into the 'Lithuanian comrades'. It was no use. He was greeted by street demonstrations, and Lithuanian leaders were prepared to stick to their guns.

This is what Grachev has to say.

'Mikhail Sergeyevich went to Lithuania together with Raisa Maksimovna\* feeling energetic, even cheerful. Gorbachev anticipated how he would untangle the "Lithuanian knot" and thus teach a lesson not only to the confused locals but his own aggressive critics in Moscow too, those who accused him of a laissez-faire attitude to nationalists and a weakness of political steering.

When preparing for the trip Gorbachev told his aide G. Shakhnazarov, "You see — I simply cannot give in."

… When the trip was drawing to a close, a grim Gorbachev had to plead with the local Party boss Brazauskas that they should wait with their decision to leave the Union "until the relevant law has been worked out." Mikhail Sergeyevich was downcast for two reasons: not only did he not achieve his primary target, he also discovered that he had forgotten how to work political miracles.'

Brazauskas recollected that when Gorbachev first learnt about the decisions passed by the XX congress of the Communist Party of Lithuania, he got to him on the phone. "What have you done, Algirdas?" — asked Gorbachev icily. But during the General Secretary's trip to Lithuania (by the way, the first visit to Vilnius paid by any CPSU leader), his offensive attitude started changing. At the very beginning he still hoped to be able to persuade, to out-talk, even to scare his… Thus, Gorbachev was speaking to the intelligentsia and asked them, for the umpteenth time, "So do you really want to walk away?" And then he heard how the audience came back with a unanimous powerful "Yes!"'

According to Brazauskas, the psychological crisis occurred on the eve of his departure. There were three of them in the car: Gorbachev, Brazauskas and Raisa. All kept silent. Then Gorbachev said, addressing no one in particular, 'What has gotten into them?' And then, without a pause, 'I need a drink.' When saying goodbye at the airport, he uttered, 'I see, you've made your choice.'

'To tell the truth, Gorbachev never threatened us,' says Brazauskas

---

\* His wife.

in his memoirs. He goes on to say, full of evident compassion to the former Soviet leader: 'He found it hard, of course, to resolve the chief contradiction: to keep the state intact and to grant republics new rights. He had no levers or tools to achieve this.'

Harsh economic sanctions were adopted against Lithuania: increased prices for oil and gas, and practically an embargo on some vital supplies — down to medications.

At the February plenary session of the CC CPSU (1990) Gorbachev managed to convince the top party bosses to agree to have Article 6 of the Constitution repealed and to introduce the institution of presidency.

Revocation of Article 6, hitherto providing legal guarantees for the power of the CPSU, was the opposition's main slogan. Hundreds of thousands attended rallies in the centre of Moscow, carrying posters 'Away with Article Six!' Yeltsin intended to abolish the CPSU omnipotence within Russia through new legal acts of the Russian parliament but had no hopes about the All-Union congress agreeing. Yet it happened with amazing speed, practically in a flash.

But only with the benefit of hindsight and thanks to what we know today about the particulars of Gorbachev's visit to Vilnius can we be sufficiently confident about the motives — his and those of the Central Committee — in agreeing to such a revolutionary step. The main factor was the threat of the Soviet Union disintegrating. The events in Vilnius proved with abundant clarity that the Party was no longer a deterrent. The Lithuanian scenario was soon to be followed by all others: first remove your Party from the CPSU, then adopt a declaration of independence. The February plenary session realised the need for some response. The alarming course of events required a new legitimacy and a new legislative base. Only the President of the USSR could oppose separatist movements in republics. So in vesting Gorbachev with additional powers the CC members were not endorsing Gorbachev's democratic reforms but voting in favour of the hard line approach towards the republics in the Baltic area and Trans-Caucasus.

The Politburo got together on the 7th of March. Gorbachev was insistent about the need to revoke Article 6 and introduce the institute of presidency.

'*Gorbachev.* The presidency is knocking on our door — through revocation of Article 6... We should not hesitate. We should turn towards presidency in good time. We mustn't give up our position. No party ever gives up its position if it does not self-disband. We must preserve the Party's influence in the society. By cancelling Article 6 we shall provide constitutional support for the Party.'

Politburo members had another worry to conside: what if Gorbachev did not get elected?

'*Lukianov.* Can you ever reach an agreement with those bumpkins (People's Deputies)? They will do as they please. What's the Central Committee for them? They are their own Central Committee. They shall do all they can to prevent us from amassing two thirds of the votes for electing the president.'

Politburo member Frolov, by now forgotten by everybody except historians, asked a pertinent and very correct question: 'We need a decree by the plenary session that would be binding for the deputies who are in the Communist Party. If not, why convene the plenary at all, why have the Central Committee?'

They should force Party members to vote for Gorbachev! Meanwhile, the Party members are in majority at the congress — something like 90%!

This is the background against which the Third Extraordinary Congress of the People's Deputies of the USSR opened in March of 1990. Gorbachev was elected President.

At the beginning, Gorbachev made a speech advocating the introduction of a post of the President of the USSR. Deputy Alksnis urged to have elections only on a competitive basis — a first arrow in Gorbachev's direction. The Gorbachev's supporters offered their nominations — Prime Minister Ryzhkov and the Interior Minister Bakatin, but before the vote both, as if on cue, both removed their candidacies. But the 'bumpkins' (Lukianov must have had a crystal ball) were on the alert: with no one's permission, with no say-so from 'Mummy or Daddy', a totally unknown deputy from Kemerovo Oblast with a Georgian name of Avaliani*

---

* Teimuraz Avaliani later became the deputy of the Duma of the Russian Federation. — *Author's comment.*

suddenly leapt forward and nominated himself. Transfixed at such audacity, the audience broke out in a burst of applause — in admiration for the maverick.

In the back room, Gorbachev's press secretary Andrei Grachev approached his boss Yakovlev, the latter tense and flushed because of the unforeseen volatility of the situation, 'Alexander Nikolayevich, why all this circus, wasn't it a better idea for Mikhail Sergeyevich to stand at the general election? The éclat would be greater too...'

'And are you sure he'll get elected?' snapped a grim Yakovlev gazing underfoot.

In the end Gorbachev's nomination went through: he got 59% of votes.

Yeltsin and Gorbachev were elected, respectively, Russia's People's Deputy from Sverdlovsk and President of the USSR simultaneously, in March of 1990. At the time these two events seems incorporable: to become one of many deputies — or the first ever president in the history of the country. But the subsequent events led to new conclusions.

What Gorbachev was involved in at the congress was complex and smart political manoeuvring. No longer did he have to be wary of the CC plenary sessions or the Politburo meetings. He had nothing to fear in connection with the upcoming XXVIII congress of the CPSU (a historic congress since it happened to be the last) that could or could not re-elect him as General Secretary of the Party, the party itself being only one component of the political process over which he had the full and undivided power. Now all his actions aimed at maintaining stability in the country, fighting republican separatism or introducing radical economic reforms were clad in the armour of genuine and unquestionable legitimacy. He could do whatever he desired, he was president!

Technically, it was impeccable. But in real life this new victory of Gorbachev's reeked of bitter disappointment, unwitting hypocrisy, weakness and fear.

Although the head of state was not elected by the entire nation, the election was judicially sound: he was voted for by the People's Deputies. But it had happened with a blood-curdling screech. Even here, at the congress where everything was manageable and managed, where high posts and privileges were distributed backstage and where the presidium was completely unanimous — Gorbachev had trouble being elected. It took two attempts and an appeal from Academician Dmitri Likhachev's — the latter practically pleading from the elevated position of his age and experience that the deputies should not 'split the country'.

Pale and dismayed, Gorbachev was watching the vote by roll-call. Was that the democracy he had dreamed about?

Although in spring of 1990 the Party stopped being the mainstay of the country, in other words, in essence, stopped being the state establishment, it could not remain passive. First, some well-known People's Deputies — Yeltsin, Burbulis, Sobchak, Travkin, et al. — formed the 'democratic platform' within its ranks.

Then, in March of the same year the Communist Party of the RSFSR came into being and elected Ivan Polozkov, a person of ultra-reactionary persuasions, its chairman.

Both the Russian Communist Party and Polozkov appeared on the political arena with one purpose only — to prevent Yeltsin from being elected Chairman of the RSFSR Supreme Soviet (he had made his intentions on this account public).

Polozkov had no other claim to glory — a regular Soviet functionary. But the way he spoke, the expression on his face, his entire image (vaguely reminiscent of a typecast 'bureaucrat' from the Soviet comedies) — all of it was in tune with a particular public sentiment: the rejection of change and reforms.

It is amazing that Gorbachev chose him for such an important role, although he could choose from among his Politburo colleagues or some deputies at the congress. But he selected a died-in-the-wool, orthodox figure that was to help him orchestrate his collision with Yeltsin at the Russian congress.

It was a chain reaction of wrong moves: Gorbachev wasted his chance of creating a new party — a social-democratic party of the European type although he did have all the requisite resources: a power base, the ideology, the programme and capable leaders. Such a party, *his own party*, could have saved Gorbachev.

But this didn't happen. Gorbachev's main bugbear was a schism, a plot and the emergence of chess pieces on his board that would be of equal stature to him.

Thus, at the congress Gorbachev was elected President and the Russian party of communists that he created started work, trying to influence the deputies to the new Russian parliament.

At the end of April Yeltsin visited Great Britain. It was an important trip: he met with Margaret Thatcher, attended presentation of his *Confessions*, greeted the crowds eager to meet the author and get his autograph and, as usual, gave numerous interviews.

Directly from London Yeltsin went to Cordoba in Spain, then appeared on TV in Barcelona and in transit had the memorable near-crash described above. It was then that Boris Nikolayevich first complained of an acute pain in his back.

The old sports injury (displaced vertebrae) flared up again, right in the hotel. All interviews planned for the morning had to be cancelled. 'By noon a neurosurgeon arrived and having asked the patient lots of questions pronounced the diagnosis: an inter-vertebral hernia that was pinching the nerve.'

Yeltsin's condition was rapidly worsening. He lost control of one leg and had to be rushed into the hospital. It turned out he was in unbelievable luck: Professor Joseph Llovet, the world's leading authority on neurosurgery, was a resident doctor there.

'A conclave of doctors convened at the hotel. They confirmed the original diagnosis: the chronic hernia changed its shape and was squeezing the nerve. One leg was already paralysed. It was urgently necessary to decide whether or not to agree to surgery,' writes his aide Sukhanov.

Yeltsin's first reaction was: no way. He must make it home and be treated by his own doctors. But the Spaniards were insisting on urgent surgery, otherwise it could take years to treat the condition and some important bodily functions may be lost. Professor Llovet promised that the patient would be on his feet practically the next day. The alternative was months on a hospital bed — and a collapse of all his political undertakings.

So Yeltsin went into the operating theatre.

The operation was performed on April 30th, and on the morning of May 2nd Yeltsin tried to walk. This is how he described it in his book:

'Drenched in sweat I rose to my feet, made a step. They were securing me, of course, lest I should fall from the suddenness of it. I made it to the wall. Job done. All the time the TV crew was filming. That'll do for today, they said, get back to bed. They made me walk three times. In the end I did it without fear.'

In 1990 Yeltsin himself was like a plane performing dynamic turns. He had developed an enormous speed and had no more time for safety regulations and concerns for a soft landing. The elections at the First Congress of the RSFSR People's Deputies were taking place immediately after the Barcelona imbroglio, and the level of associated stress proved much higher than in any road accident.

The congress opened on May 16th.

Vitaly Vorotnikov (about to resign from the post of the Chairman of the RSFSR Council of Ministers) opened the congress with a motion to adopt the Declaration of Sovereignty. It was Gorbachev's preventive move. The idea of sovereign Russia being in the air, he decided to introduce it through the mouthpiece of the official leadership, to overtake Yeltsin's initiative.

The concept of sovereignty proposed by Vorotnikov did not provide for loosening ties with the USSR. The new union treaty was expected to delineate how much authority Russia would voluntarily delegate to the centre. Yeltsin immediately put forward a different draft of the declaration, a more radical one. It was already impossible to seize the initiative from him. Everybody in the hall knew perfectly well that this idea and the hope for its success were firmly associated with Yeltsin's name.

Gorbachev was seated at the balcony. His aides had spent quite some time choosing the place for the USSR President and decided that he should sit next to the banner of the USSR, above the audience.

Gorbachev's speech on the sovereignty of Russia made it very clear that he mistrusted the whole idea. Comrade Yeltsin has called upon us 'to bid farewell, in one fell swoop, to the socialist choice made in 1917', said Gorbachev. But for the citizens of Russia, the 'socialist choice' and 'the power of the Soviets' are not just empty talk. These are fundamental values. And what is comrade Yeltsin offering us instead? A change of the political system? If Yeltsin's definition of federalism were analysed properly, said Gorbachev, it would transpire that it contained nothing apart from 'an appeal to break down the USSR under the banner of restoring the Russian sovereignty'.

Gorbachev's speech was long and passionate. He referred to the bloody Time of Troubles\* when Russia had been split, torn apart and worn out. He asked: maybe Boris Nikolayevich is still cherishing his old idea of setting up several republics within Russia, so as to disintegrate Russia into separate principalities?

The last statement deserves a separate comment after the congress, bizarrely, those 'separate principalities' started emerging — as if by magic!

Several weeks later the historic Declaration of Independence of Russia was adopted, and immediately 'declarations of independence' were adopted by all, even the smallest Russian autonomies, including Buriatia, Kalmykia, Chuvashia and Tuva while the so-called 'autonomous territories' promptly upgraded their status to republics. All and sundry started quoting 'the right of nations to self-regulation' and some republics even wanted to become signatories to the new union treaty — that is, to enter the new USSR as independent entities.

In the summer of this year, while travelling around Russia, Yeltsin would coin his famous phrase — 'Get as much sovereignty as you can swallow!'

The ideology of 'decentralisation' is one of the mostly important political accusations hurled at Yeltsin by his opponents. But at the same time, his counter-intuitive move in some strange way cooled off some hot heads in the RSFSR national autonomies. The Volga region, the Northern Caucasus, the areas beyond the Urals and in the Far East suddenly realised that beautiful declarations notwithstanding, the economic might of Russia was not to be trifled with. Yeltsin, who answered challenges from local elites with unexpected equanimity, eventually kept Russia whole. Let us return, however, to the congress.

---

\* The Time of Troubles was a period comprising the years of interregnum between the death in 1598 of the last Russian Tsar of the Riurik Dynasty and the establishment of the Romanov Dynasty in 1613. In 1601-1603, Russia suffered a famine that killed one third of the population, about two million. At the time, Russia was occupied by the Polish-Lithuanian Commonwealth and suffered from civil uprisings, usurpers and impostors.

The alignment of forces was totally wrong for Yeltsin. A most optimistic estimate revealed that his supporters counted for less than a third of the deputies (about 350 votes). To be elected, president needed 531, that is, more than half. Yeltsin was perfectly aware that pro-communist deputies were much more numerous than those who supported reforms.

'I realise,' said Yeltsin, 'how varied the deputies are in their attitude towards me personally. The complexity of *perestroika* taught me the expediency of a political compromise... and the ability to enter a dialogue with different political forces...' And then, 'Today all of us, the deputies, irrespective of where we stand (whether we are democrats, *apparatchiks*, centrists, within or outside of any party) are united by our shared role and responsibility...'

Yeltsin, in his speech, did not counter a single point made by Gorbachev and avoided any open polemics with his views, having opted for a purely business-like relationship. Besides, a strong argument in Yeltsin's favour was the fact that he did have a concrete programme. He came to the congress with a list of 12 laws that to be drafted as a matter of utmost urgency.

Gorbachev's conduct was totally different. Before the decisive vote he assembled 400 communist deputies in the Kremlin and demanded that they should not vote for Yeltsin since the latter's name was synonymous with a huge political risk for Russia.

The election speech of the main candidate from the communists, Ivan Polozkov, was full of striking contradictions. He was uttering the same words as Yeltsin: sovereignty, democracy, equal status of various forms of ownership — but at the same time, when hitting on key points of his creed, he would raise his voice, his spectacles sparkling irately. The 'socialist choice', he was saying, is the most important thing, it is the choice of the people and we have no intention of ever giving in to anybody over it.

Everyone understood that Polozkov was no challenge to Yeltsin as a leader of a new country — and by that time there was no doubt that a new country would emerge.

It was plain for all and sundry that the most important aim for the 'centre' was to thwart Yeltsin's election — the rest was insignificant. Incidentally, the deputies suddenly realised the weight of the mission: they were to vote for the person who would embody the future of their country! They got filled with a new sense of importance. To win meant getting more than half of the Russian Congress's votes. On May 26th, the first voting day, Yeltsin got 497 votes, Polozkov amassed 473, and the third candidate (the unknown candidate from Kazan who nominated himself) — 12.

On the evening of the same day there was the second round: Yeltsin — 503 (28 votes short of a victory) and Polozkov — 458. The tension was building up.

On May 28th, the communist deputies started demanding that both Yeltsin and Polozkov be removed from the subsequent round of voting. It felt like a dead end.

But the motion was declined. However, Polozkov quit the race voluntarily, and six more candidates followed suit. The Kremlin put forward another nomination: Alexander Vlasov, Chairman of the RSFSR Council of Ministers and before that — the USSR Minister of the Interior. That was yet another Kremlin's mistake. Polozkov was a favourite with conservative deputies and a new political party, while Vlasov was an embodiment of Gorbachev's power. Besides, his previous post (Interior Minister of the USSR) was a hint that Russia needed some 'law and order'.

Meanwhile Gorbachev left for the G-7 summit in Canada. The fact that the President of the USSR had a 'nomination up his sleeve', and that he was ready to spring it on the audience just like that made it very clear: he did not respect the deputies. All Gorbachev wanted was to get rid of a radical Yeltsin and a radical Polozkov, and select a moderate — someone who would vote obediently in favour of the supremacy of the union authorities over those of Russia. Thus, having suggested Vlasov, Gorbachev lost the election *by his own efforts*. In this specific case, his beloved tactics of compromises and manoeuvres spelled disaster.

Results of the last voting round: Yeltsin — 535, Vlasov — 467, Valentin Tsoi (a Khabarovsk deputy, head of a cooperative) — 11.

Victory!

What it had cost him was described by some eye witnesses. After Gorbachev, in his speech, launched a devastating attack on Yeltsin's views, Boris Nikolayevich went pale but stayed silent. A lady deputy in the chair next to his exclaimed, 'Boris Nikolayevich, are you all right? Do you want some heart medication?' He smiled back and replied, 'Thanks, I am OK.'

But when the results of the triumphant vote were announced, for the first time Yeltsin allowed himself a broad smile.

The tight coil within him could finally unwind...

On June 12th, the First Congress of the Russian Deputies adopted the Declaration of State Sovereignty of the Russian Federation: 907 votes 'pro', 13 — 'con' and 9 abstained.

At the very beginning, some 30 various associations of deputies — political, professional and territorial ones — officially registered their existence. In an interview Yeltsin called the Russian parliament 'democratic' — it represented various points of view. 'Nowadays it is only natural,' Yeltsin added.

'After the Barcelona accident,' Naina Iosifovna is recalling, 'he found it hard to be sitting for hours. The accident made his habitual back pains worse. He would return home totally exhausted, the shirt wet with sweat. He couldn't move and was just sitting there, deathly pale.

... Once, I virtually pleaded, "Borya, do stop thinking about what you must do! You owe nothing to anybody, you must think about your health! If you want, I'll drop to my knees..."

I was so desperate that I did kneel in front of him –I was scared stiff that he would die.'

'At this point I entered the room,' continues Tatyana, Yeltsin's younger daughter, 'and saw an amazing picture: Mum on her knees in front of Dad. I was scared, "Mum, what are you doing?" But she did not look embarrassed at all, just started saying that I should also plead with Dad to allow himself some rest, that he couldn't continue on like this... Finally, we took him to bed. I whispered to Mum that it was no use, he just could not do it any other way.'

In the summer of the same year he went on a three-week-long tour of Russia. It was a totally unusual undertaking. For the first time ever he was looking at Russia through different eyes: Vladivostok, Sakhalin, Novokuznetsk, Kamchatka...

His meetings took him all over the country. Tatar oil drillers, Sakhalin fishermen, Vladivostok dockers, workmen building an atomic power station, submarine crews and the Nivkhs — Sakhalin's indigenous people — were his audience.

In the Bashkir town Sterlitamak, as he was addressing the local authorities, Yeltsin learnt that a crowd gathered in front of the administrative building and wanted to see him and listen to what he had to say. Yeltsin left the audience, climbed on top of the roof and continued his speech from there. This story made its way to the Central TV and made an indelible impression on millions of TV viewers.

In each town and city, each god-forsaken settlement or village he heard the same old story: food supplies are abysmal, consumer goods are like gold dust. Children have nothing to wear and very little to eat. Experts calculated that in 1990 the population of the USSR kept 165 billion roubles in their 'pillowcases' and 337.7 billion roubles in their savings' accounts. These astronomical figures meant only one thing: there was nothing to buy.

Meanwhile the printing press was operating at overcapacity: the government kept printing more and more money: 18 billion roubles a year, this jeopardising the entire financial system of the USSR.

And this is what was happening in the consumer good market.

Soap. Outside Moscow, it was rationed: 130 g per capita per month. In the city of Kostroma, in order to buy baby soap one had to produce the passport showing that you had a child younger than three years of age.

Food staples. The Moscow Oblast introduced ration cards. This enabled everyone to buy, monthly, half a kilo of meat, half a kilo of flour and 300 g of pasta. In that September there was a serious shortage of bread.

Cigarettes. A wave of 'tobacco mutinies' hit Moscow, Yaroslavl, Sverdlovsk and many other places. Crowds were blocking streets and pillaging tobacco kiosks.

Alcohol. On August 22nd, in Chelyabinsk throngs of people who had spent hours queuing in front of a wine shop burst into the district Soviet and picketed the local thoroughfare. They stoned and completely vandalised several buses and trolleybuses. Clashes with militia left several people wounded.

That summer my wife and I, together with our two small children, went on a cruise down the Volga. Food in many cities en-route was available only against a passport. But the real shock was mooring in small towns, for example, the famous Ples, glorified by many Russian artists. As soon as the dock hand cast the line and erected the gangway, the crowd of local residents rushed forward, elbowing their way among the cruisers. The idea was to beat the others in a queue to the ship buffet and thus get at least something. People's faces were dreadful: a mixture of shame and despair. They were buying up virtually anything they could lay their hand on: matches, sweets, cigarettes, tins, anything at all... Those who were too late turned round and trudged home empty-handed, bitter and disappointed.

And here is another witness account.

'I remember the horrible "tobacco mutiny" in St Petersburg in 1990,' writes Anatoly Chubais* in his book *Privatization: Russian Style*. 'At the time I worked for the executive committee. Every day we were putting together consolidated communiqués: so much is left; so much can be sourced... It felt like bulletins from the war front. Anything we could procure, with immense efforts and through savage barter deals, was distributed among shops, in a more or less equal measure. Once we had nothing at all to distribute for an entire week. An enormous queue appeared in Nevsky Prospect, in front of the central tobacconist... Meanwhile the shop was empty and there was no telling when anything at all would be delivered to it. So then people found some scaffolding (a nearby block was under repairs), barricaded the prospects, built fires... Militia cordons were being swept away, one by one. It was very scary. That's what the non-performing rouble was all about. In a situation like this you may be a minister many times over but it is no use yelling at the telephones receiver or trying to sort things out. The humblest of manufacturers would retort, "I don't give a tinker's cuss about your instructions. And what can you do to me, you?"'

To start with, Moscow enjoyed a slightly privileged status. In the early nineties, Muscovites had received 'consumer matriculates'. Those ID-type documents were not borough-specific and entitled residents of the entire Moscow to certain goods. The scheme caused an outrage elsewhere in Russia, particularly indignant were next-door oblasts. The reason was that for quite some years they had been supplying themselves with sausages,

---

* *Anatoly Borisovich Chubais* (b. 1955) is a Russian politician and business manager who was responsible for privatization in Russia as an influential member of Yeltsin's administration.

cheeses, frankfurters, cereals, tinned products and others foodstuffs from the Moscow shops. 'Sausage commuter trains"* had been a common sight.

Eventually, Moscow got affected too. A well-known democratic deputy from Moscow, Ilya Zaslavsky, who represented interests of the poor and the disabled, suggested that in his borough no food or consumer goods should be made available to people residing elsewhere. Based on this initiative, one could only buy anything on the strength of either a passport (with a residence registration) or a special ID issued by the local Soviet.

... So what was happening to food supplies in 1990? Why had the 'shopping baskets' been emptied — virtually overnight, sending people into endless queues?

Firstly, rouble was rapidly devaluating because of latent inflation. Due to various political factors (including the pressure brought on the USSR government by the deputies) wages and pensions were rising constantly. This 'asset-stripped' national currency inevitably eroded availability of goods.

Secondly, the bond between central ministries and production bosses was weakening, which led to the emergence of a so-called 'barter market': producers hoarding their products in order to exchange those for goods manufactured elsewhere. Production managers could now buy outputs of their own companies at ridiculously low prices — set by the state. This done, they would sell the goods on the shadow market, which at the time was estimated as accounting for a quarter of the national income.

The problems had been building up over a long period of time.

By the end of the eighties, the oil production was plummeting and the foreign currency revenues shrank. The USSR State Bank issued this statement. 'In 1989, the increase in the available funds accumulated by the population testifies to the existence of an unsatisfied demand, which is a result of shortages of goods and services. As of the beginning of 1990, the

---

* Residents from cities and oblasts bordering on Moscow would arrive in the morning by an over-ground commuter train, stuff their bags full and then make it back home with several days' worth of supplies for the entire family or village. Since everybody was trying to get away with as much as one could physically carry, the smell, say, of salami was overbearing, hence the name.

USSR State Bank estimates the volume of underutilised money as 110 billion roubles versus 60 billion roubles early in 1986...'

In other words, this 'unutilised remainder of money' doubled in three years. Which meant just one thing: the country was sliding down into the economic abyss.

At the same time the USSR was getting ever more dependent on grain imports. The grain prices were growing whilst the hard currency reserves in the budget were undermined by the shrinkage of oil production volumes and the plummeting prices for oil.

The crisis spread to all spheres: hard currency, grain, oil, the state of the monetary system and supplies of goods. It was all one huge tangle and it all was urgent. Western banks were refusing the USSR credits quoting insolvency of the Soviet foreign trade missions.

So what was to be done?

'Against the background within which unfavourable prices for commodities dominated export markets,' writes Yegor Gaidar, 'the national government delivered three additional blows to the country's financial system. First of all, there was the anti-alcohol campaign that depleted the national budget; secondly, it was adopting the programme of accelerated rates of economic development which presupposed considerable increase of state investments; and thirdly, curtailing imports of consumer goods from abroad.'

Gorbachev was engaged in feverish negotiations with Western leaders trying to secure big credits for the USSR. Credits were slowly and very reluctantly made available. Western countries were launching programmes of charitable (they called it 'humanitarian') aid.

All of it, however, was too little too late.

What was urgently needed was a most profound reform of the Soviet economy: the pricing policy and methods to save rouble from inflation. But for all the continuous debates on the methodology of such a reform, new forms of ownership and spending cuts, no coherent programme emerged.

So it was against this rather troubled socio-economic background that the newly-elected Chairman of the Supreme Soviet of Russia Boris Yeltsin started recruiting his new government.

'... In Moscow the influence of the new centre of power was becoming gradually felt. A sign of this was a veritable pilgrimage into Yeltsin's reception of various post seekers.' (*Yeltsin's Epoch*).

Yeltsin needed an urgent answer to the question of who was going to be his Prime Minister. After a series of discussions, interviews and rejections, he selected Ivan Silayev, a heavy industry representative and an ex-minister of the USSR. He liked Silayev's pragmatism, honesty and decency.

Two key figures were supposed to act as 'buttresses' for a minister who was somewhat advanced in age: Vice-Premier Grigory Yavlinsky and another young economist, Boris Fyodorov, head of the Ministry of Finance. Both were younger than 35, both already known for their striking pronouncements and eloquent analysis of economic problems. Yavlinsky suggested that the Russian government approve of a programme for extricating the country from the crisis — it was a brainchild of Gorbachev's advisor Academician Stanislav Shatalin's, programme '500 Days'.

The programme had two radically new components. First, it proceeded from the premise of confirming the monstrous truth: the Soviet economy was disintegrating; it had to be not just reformed but rescued. Based on this, the programme offered a stage-by-stage approach: each new initiative was planned in terms of days.

Secondly, it was a market-oriented programme that called for reforming the prices-making mechanisms and the monetary system, advocated privatisation of small and middle-sized companies, sales and purchases of land and a tax reform — all this counter to the age-long norms and traditions of the Soviet centralised system.

The programme that had been developed by Yavlinsky in the course of several years and designed to alter the entire Soviet economic universe, had already been rejected by the leadership of the Union.

Still, in the summer of 1990, in the course of a joint press conference Gorbachev and Yeltsin made essentially the same point: the country badly needed an anti-crisis programme and Yavlinsky's proposal may well be it. This went down as a veritable sensation: the two leaders were now joining efforts to save the country!

But the programme, adopted by the Supreme Soviet of Russia

on September 11th (October 1st was earmarked as the first of the 500 days) ended up hanging in the balance, for it had met with an obdurate resistance from the top echelons of power within the USSR, primarily from the Prime Minister Nikolai Ryzhkov's office. Ryzhkov justifiably saw the Shatalin-Yavlinsky programme as a personal threat, but this, however, wasn't the whole story.

The programme '500 Days' unequivocally rejected the values of the 'socialist choice' that Gorbachev held so dear: the draft intended for the press opened with this passage — 'Humankind has not been able to discover anything more efficient than the market economy'. This alone was enough to fill the hearts with horror.

Ryzhkov believed that a 'precipitous soaring of prises' was the weakest point in the programme. He wasted no time in drawing Gorbachev's attention to it, prophesying a catastrophe that would be worse than the current one, since it meant unemployment, strikes and industrial actions, and the break-up of the country. But worst of all was the way the programme treated the role of the Centre, which was entirely different to the USSR President's nearest coterie. Ryzhkov put forward his own programme.

'The main divergence between the two programmes lay in the balance of power between the Centre and the republics. The economic union suggested by the Shatalin-Yavlinsky programme meant a confederation of the European Union's type. Ryzhkov, on the other hand, favoured a vaguer, milder but unmistakably more Soviet union,' (Leon Aron). He was for a unitary state.

Sensing that the ground was receding from under his feet, on August 23rd Ryzhkov requested a meeting between the government's presidium and Gorbachev. He wanted to prove that the crisis had not been a direct result of the course followed the Soviet leadership. This is an excerpt from his speech:

'While the brunt of responsibility for the situation in the country is placed squarely at its government's door, every attempt is being made for removing this government from the system of state management. The government today remains the only real force to resist intensification of destructive and destabilising factors. Resignation of this government will alter the balance and alignment of the political forces in the country.

'Just as urgent is the problem... of manageability. Its loss is extremely dangerous. It manifests itself primarily when the government's decisions are not borne out, President's decrees are ignored, republican laws are assigned priority over the union ones, declarations of complete state sovereignty are adopted, etc. At the same time the responsibility for everything, down to tobacco supplies, is expected to be shouldered by the central leadership.'

Ryzhkov was stubbornly convincing Gorbachev that the programme '500 Days' (and the Russian leadership behind it) was encroaching on the very foundations of the political system: 'Attempts are made to introduce radical changes not so much into the economic ties uniting the republics and the USSR but the very nature of the political system, ... and to abolish the existing system of government.'

Ryzhkov's programme was effectively a cover under which the Union authorities could engage in their own politics and keep the republics in their orbit.

Gorbachev instructed his economic advisor Aganbegyan to merge the two programmes: that by Ryzhkov* and that by Shatalin.

In his memoirs Nikolai Ryzhkov recalls an interesting episode: on Gorbachev's suggestion, the authors of the two competing programmes were to meet at a government's dacha — and try and 'come to an agreement'. But nothing came out of this idea. In his book Ryzhkov gives vent to his hurt feelings and remembers how 'they didn't want to listen and 'were talking down their noses'.

Given the context, Mikhail Sergeyevich had to make a choice and select one programme over the other. However, as on many previous occasions, the USSR President played both ends against the middle: in the end, neither programme was adopted!

Crumbling under pressure from all sides, Gorbachev withdrew to a deeply entrenched position. But Ryzhkov had it tough too: several weeks after the desperate polemics at the Supreme Soviet he succumbed to a heart attack.

---

* The programme developed by the governmental economists with Aganbegyan at the head provided for a so-called planned rise of prices and a very cautious minimal integration of market mechanisms into the planned economy. It was made public back in the spring at the session of the USSR Supreme Soviet and generated a wave of criticism by independent economists.

'In the first days of December', writes Ryzhkov, 'a one-to-one meeting with Gorbachev took place on my request. There I informed him of my final decision to resign from the post of the head of the country's government. He was calm, even relieved. Like me, he was ready for this difficult conversation...'

At the time it seemed that the harsh social consequences of market reforms could somehow be avoided, that one could have a 'soft' entry into the market. Few politicians realised and acknowledged the need for a painful rise in prices.

To start with, Yeltsin did not want to recognise it either. Economist Yevgeny Yasin remembered how in May of 1990, at the session of the USSR Supreme Soviet Nikolai Ryzhkov announced that he would double all food prices but the price of bread would go up three times. Yeltsin who had just been elected Chairman of Russia's Supreme Soviet said, 'We do not need managers like Ryzhkov. We, on the other hand, know how to introduce the market economy painlessly.' 'It was my first meeting with him... I was compelled to tell him, "Boris Nikolayevich, refrain from such bold statements, for you will never be able to be as good as your word. It is unavoidable."'

When forming his new government Yeltsin was in constant consultations with the most prominent economists who all spoke with one voice: liberalisation of prices could not be avoided any more; the time for a 'mild and gradual' transition to the market had now been lost.

So what happened while Ryzhkov was in hospital and why did Gorbachev take his resignation so lightly? On the surface, the 'governmental' programme won over the programme '500 days'. In reality there were no winners. On October 16th, Gorbachev tabled his own, 'revised', version of the programme for the Supreme Soviet to consider. It wasn't called '500 Days' anymore and contained no specific deadlines or plans. According to Yavlinsky and Shatalin, the first stage of privatisation of the state property was supposed to happen in the first 100 days whereas Gorbachev's programme contained a vague suggestion that this may actually require a long time. Liberalisation of prices (originally, the 250th day) was delayed till 1992 (by the way, that was when it did take place eventually, albeit in circumstances that verged on a complete catastrophe and in the absence of a 'single union of Soviet Republics'). In addition, creation of individually-owned farms was to be carried out at the discretion of *kolkhozes*.

... Meanwhile the Soviet economy continued disintegrating rapidly.

In 1990 yet another landmark event took place in Yeltsin's life: at the XXVIII congress, the last ever congress of the Communist Party of the Soviet Union, he publicly announced his resignation from the ranks of Communists. This step didn't come easy: his entire career had been associated with the Party. But abolition of the Party's supremacy was one of the mainstays his political programme, and so he told the congress: 'I believe that to combine the post of the Chairman of Russia's Supreme Soviet with my membership in the CPSU is inadmissible.'

At this Congress yet another of Gorbachev's former supporters — Alexander Yakovlev — was not elected to the Politburo. In December Foreign Minister Eduard Shevardnadze also resigned — having publicly predicted a military coup and having shut the door behind him with a load bang.

Not two full years had passed since the first signs of a split between 'conservatives' and 'liberals' in the Politburo. And now it had ceased to exist in its former shape. No erstwhile comrades-in-arms stayed by Gorbachev's side. All the 'headstrong and intractable ones' had left, along with the dangerous and the independent. Those that stayed were moderate and obedient but the 'shaking up' of the Politburo, initiated by Gorbachev, backfired: he was left on his own and to start with didn't even realise that the void around him was expanding.

At the Congress a deputy from Checheno-Ingushetia, a completely hitherto unknown Sazhi Umalatova, in her speech addressed Gorbachev and urged him to resign. Although the audience grew still with shock this passionate member of the Communist Party voiced the thoughts of nearly everybody at this Congress.

# Details of a Skirmish
(January to August 1991)

The year started with the events in Vilnius.

Early in the morning of 13 January 1991 armed troopers of the Alpha Group* and the Vilnius OMON** burst into the premises of the TV centre. They forced their way through the crowds at a rally, killing 13 and wounding more than 160 people in the process. A shudder ran through the country at the bloody news: it felt like this was just the beginning. The fences and walls of Moscow houses were covered with graffiti overnight: 'Hands off Vilnius!', 'We are with you!'

Messages were scribbled with black paint on concrete, or in white chalk over bricks, in the dead of night by the light of hand-held torches. Those who were making them were not necessarily convinced champions of the secession of the Baltics. It was simply that people were afraid of yet another dictatorship.

There was practically no official coverage of the Vilnius events. Newspaper correspondents were pestering the officials for any details in an attempt to piece together the fragments.

Procurator General Trubin told *Izvestia* newspaper, 'It is impossible to guarantee a constitutional resolution there, since the standoff in the Baltic

---

\* *Alpha Group* (also called the Alfa Group or Spetsgruppa A) was an elite counter-terrorist task force of the KGB.

\*\* Riot police.

republics continues and what we see, practically, is two militias and two Procurator's Offices.'

Minister of the Interior, Pugo: 'I am astounded and depressed at this turn of events. When blood is being shed and events develop the way they do, the situation is fraught with a possibility of more blood and even more grievous consequences*.'

*Literaturnaya Gazeta*: 'Boris Pugo, whose appointment as the Interior Minister of the USSR is yet to be confirmed, had no coherent explanation to offer to the deputies on the issue of an omnipotent "Committee for National Rescue" that is capable of bringing tanks to the streets of Vilnius; at the same time the USSR Defence Minister Yazov offered a startling explanation. Referring to his not being entirely cognizant of all the details (allegedly, he had not been there in person) and insisting that he never issued an order to launch a tank offensive, he presented his own version of the Vilnius tragedy. It is as follows. Members of the "committee for national rescue" had been assaulted near the parliament building and so approached the commander of the Vilnius garrison. The latter was so overwhelmed with their plight that he issued a command to capture the TV centre– since it had been broadcasting "anti-Soviet programmes" non-stop. Thus, according to Marshal Yazov, the massacre by the TV centre was a result of an emotional outburst by an individual general!'

... No one knew anything. No one has a valid explanation.

'On January 7th troops were urgently deployed in Vilnius. On January 8th these assault units got to work. According to a news anchor of the *Vremya*** programme, they had taken the House of Press and several other municipal facilities "under their protection". There were casualties. All communications with Lithuania had been severed. The airport had been closed, the trains stopped...' — *Kommesrant Daily* was writing on January 14th.

And here is a classified source: Vasily Mikhailov, head of the CC CPSU department for national politics, was informing the leadership of the country that 'as reported by designated officials of the CC CPSU who are currently in Lithuania, on January 11th, in Vilnius, the paratroopers

---

\* An interview to the same *Izvestia*. — *Author's comment*.

\*\* The national evening news broadcast.

established control over the House of Press and DOSAAF* (the building is also used for the HQ of the National Security Department) and in Kaunas — the officer training school. This action was carried out, on the whole, without major clashes... At 17:00 local time, the Central Committee of the Communist Party of Lithuania held a press conference, in the course of which head of the department for ideology, Yeromolavichius, informed the audience of the creation of a Committee for National Rescue of Lithuania. This committee has assumed the overall authority in the country. It uses a radio instruments plant as its headquarters. The committee has approved a message to the people of Lithuania and also presented an ultimatum to the Supreme Soviet of the Lithuanian SSR...' (Yegor Gaidar, *Collapse of an Empire*).

This document explains quite a lot. No, it wasn't a matter of one individual general overreacting. There was a plan, conceived and devised in Moscow, with no room for spontaneity. And representatives of the Central Committee who had arrived in Vilnius in advance were carrying out a part of this strategy. Yet leaders of the country who knew the truth were finding refuge in silence, getting away with generalities, and no one was in a hurry to take the responsibility for the dead.

Yegor Gaidar refers to these events in his book: 'Mr Cherniayev (aide to the USSR President Gorbachev) was later telling Mr Braithwaite (the UK ambassador) that the decision had been taken on the orders from the USSR Army Commander, General of the Army Varennikov who had not coordinated it with M. Gorbachev.' But Cherniayev's version does not stack up — the presence in Vilnius of the 'designated CC CPSU officials' was a direct indication that the Kremlin had been aware of the coup and sanctioned it. This sanction could only be issued at the top level: the Politburo and Gorbachev himself.

... Vilnius bruised even further the soul of the gentlest and the most liberal General Secretary the CC CPSU in its entire history. Events were urging him to depart from the course of gentleness and liberalism. Gorbachev made do with platitudes about 'not being informed'.

---

* DOSAAF was a paramilitary society in the Soviet Union: a *Voluntary Society for Assistance to the Army, Aviation and Navy*.

He was reluctant to assume responsibility for the bloodbath and the human sacrifice. He was simply incapable of uttering those words. This was not how he was going to resolve the country's problems.

Events in Vilnius marked a watershed for all protagonists in the historical drama. The army, security forces and the interior troops were given a fresh command to withdraw. The milieu of Gorbachev's hawks (marshals and generals: Varennikov, Akhromeyev, Yazov, et al.) started murmuring in protest.

It was a watershed for Gorbachev, too. Having brought tough executives to the Politburo and all the enforcement posts, having presented them with an action plan and very nearly a *carte blanche*, after Vilnius he retreated into himself, grew pensive and obstructed the process, already underway, of a stabilisation by force.

This is what the note from aide Cherniayev to his boss:

'The choice now is this: either you say directly that you wouldn't tolerate it if even an inch falls away from the Soviet Union and use all available means, even tanks if need be, to prevent this from happening — or you admit that a tragic development, uncontrollable from the centre, has taken place; in which case you denounce those who have applied force and caused human deaths and put them on trial.'

But no choice would be made. No attempts to identify a guilty party would ever ensue. No one would shoulder either moral or criminal responsibility (with the exception of the members of the Committee for National Rescue who after 1991 would spend a long time in the Vilnius prison because they had believed Moscow and Gorbachev). The 'system' got unruly and started functioning of its own accord.

So which decisions were taken at this time by Yeltsin?

Two hours after the tragedy he flew to Tallin\*. Riga and Vilnius had already suffered from the actions of the centre; blood had already been shed there. There remained just one capital where the central forces had not yet interfered. He went over to where he felt his help might be needed.

The interior troops of the USSR were on red alert there too. The parliament was encircled. The head of the Estonian parliamentarians

---

\* The old spelling of the Estonian capital — now it is Tallinn.

would say later: but for Yeltsin, all sorts of things could have happened to us that evening.

Luckily, Tallin avoided the bloodbath. Inside the parliament building defended by supporters of the Estonian independence — armed with only hunting rifles and kitchen knives — Yeltsin and the heads of the three Baltic republics signed the memorandum.

'The recent actions taken by the Soviet leadership against the Baltic states have created a realistic threat to their sovereignty, brought about an escalation of violence and caused the loss of human lives...

Latvia, Estonia, Lithuania and Russia declare that:

Firstly, the signatories hereby recognise each other's sovereignty;

Secondly, all power within the countries whose representatives have signed this memorandum belongs only to the legally elected bodies;

Thirdly, the signatories hereto consider it inadmissible to use the armed forces for solving internal problems with the exception of cases when such use would be demanded by the legally elected bodies...'

Having signed this document Yeltsin climbed into a car and spent the night riding by country roads to Leningrad. He was strongly advised to refrain from getting back home by air.

In supporting, decisively and unequivocally, the Baltic independence Yeltsin revealed yet another quality of his: an ability to make a choice in a situation when out of two options both are 'worse', when the choice is painful and brings no relief. In a nutshell, it means making a choice when the choice is impossible. But choose he did — the lesser of two evils.

The USSR was beyond salvation, no matter how much armed force and how many tanks were used, how many paratroopers were firing their arms. Several months later this would become evident for everybody.

Already on the next day after Tallin, on January 14th, at the press conference in the Russian Supreme Soviet Yeltsin read out the address 'To Russian Army in the Baltic States':

'You may be told that the restoration of public order requires your help. But do violations of the Constitution and the law amount to restoration of public order?'

His message was clear: Russian soldiers, do not shoot at people. It was another slap in the face to Gorbachev and the centre.

Meanwhile, the feelings of worry and impending doom were almost palpable. 'There was a more than a realistic threat that Vilnius methods would be transported to Moscow,' writes historian Rudolf Pikhoya. 'On February 1st, the RSFSR Supreme Soviet adopted the resolution. Among other things it said this: "To denounce the illegal involvement of military units and militarised formations in political conflicts... To stipulate that application of measures consistent with the state of emergency shall not be possible within the RSFSR unless approved by the RSFSR's Supreme Soviet."'

And this is the response from the Secretariat of the Central Committee of the Communist party:

'To party cells, all communists in the USSR Armed Forces, the Committee for State Security, internal troops of the Ministry of the Interior and the railway troops... The so-called "independent" mass media are systematically casting aspersions on the party, the Armed Forces, organs and troops of the KGB and the Ministry of the Interior... There is clear evidence that under the pretext of plurality of opinions pseudo-democrats are striving to sow the seeds of mistrust towards their own army, to drive a wedge between the commanders and their subordinates, between senior and junior officers, to humiliate the defenders of our Motherland. Lofty values like military duty, honour and allegiance to loyalty oath are subjected to doubt. Attempts are made to drag the army apart between ethnic quarters and to impede the conscription campaign.'

... After such an appeal to the communists, every officer had no choice but to place the unit within his command on red alert and ensure its readiness for battle.

Twenty-four hours later the KGB Chairman Kriuchkov sent a letter addressed to the USSR President Gorbachev wherein he unequivocally put his boss up against the wall.

'The policy of appeasing the aggressive wing of "democratic movements"... provides pseudo-democrats with an unimpeded ability to carry out their designs aimed at usurping power and changing the nature of the political system.' So what did Kriuchkov suggest? 'Economic repressions against shadow businessmen. Tighter control over the press — before it's too late. And finally, and most importantly: taking into account the depth of the crisis and a possible worsening of the situation, one cannot preclude the expediency of forming, at the relevant moment, of a temporary facility with a remit of carrying out emergency measures vested in the President by the USSR Supreme Soviet.'

As it happens, on the same day the RSFSR Supreme Soviet adopted a resolution of running, on March 17th, a referendum which also included this question on the referendum sheet: 'Do you consider it advisable to introduce the post of the RSFSR President to be elected by public vote?' It is just possible that it was this question that pushed Kriuchkov towards the idea of a putsch.

Yet another key event of those days — Yeltsin's speech on central TV.

The RSFSR Supreme Soviet had been demanding for some time that that the top management of *Gosteleradio*[*] should give airtime to their leader, enabling him to explain Russia's position. On 19 February 1991 this broadcast finally took place. In terms of format, it was an interview where an anchor was asking Yeltsin questions. 'One gets a feeling that there is some mistrust, dislike, maybe of a personal nature, between you and President Gorbachev. One gets a physical sense that each action taken by the President meets with a counter-move by Russia,' said the host. 'Perhaps it is the other way round?' answered Yeltsin.

By the end of the TV programme Yeltsin suddenly requested time for addressing citizens directly. The host was taken aback. He gesticulated invitingly to Yeltsin and cast a confused glance towards someone out of the frame. Both the viewers and all those in the studio felt that the live programme may be stopped abruptly.

This, however, did not happen. Yeltsin made his statement — slowly, with long pauses, as was his wont in situations of crisis.

'I shall be frank — God is my witness that I have made many attempts to start genuine cooperation, we have had several five-hour-long meetings to discuss our problems but, regrettably, the result was invariably the same[**]... I consider my excessive confidence in the President a personal mistake.

'... Having carefully considered the events of the recent months

---

[*] State Committee for Radio and Television Broadcasting equal in its status to a ministry.

[**] Yeltsin means his personal meetings with Gorbachev. — *Authors' comment.*

I declare... that I dissociate myself from the position and policies of the President and call for his immediate resignation!

I believe in Russia...'

It was a bombshell.

Demands for resignation were nothing new: be it intransigent communist deputies, miners on strike or the most passionate democrats — after the bloodshed in Tbilisi and Vilnius, after the tsunami of events that swept over the country, they all considered Gorbachev the embodiment of the evil of non-action, a symbol of political paralysis pregnant with a national catastrophe.

Now it was coming from the USSR state television, and live. From this lectern, the appeal for the General Secretary of the CPSU Central Committee and the President of the USSR to resign reeked of blasphemy. It sounded as a direct challenge to the political stability and reliability of the state.

... Rallies, elections, demonstrations, street clashes, creation of dissociated political organisations, free press, finally, the very words about the resignation of the first person — all this was last experienced in 1917. The shock reached its apogee.

Almost immediately there was a turbulent squall of responses. Communist deputies, some republican leaders (for example, Nazarbayev* and Kravchuk**), central papers and the official commentators of central television proclaimed their scathing denunciation. Russia's Supreme Soviet was also divided. On February 21st, Deputy Svetlana Goriacheva read out the statement signed by all leaders of the Russian parliament except Yeltsin and his First Deputy Khasbulatov. The statement referred to Yeltsin's 'political machinations', mentioned settling accounts with political opponents, inadmissibility of confrontation with the centre, that is the Kremlin, contempt of the Constitution, etc. On Gorbachev's initiative, Russia convened an extraordinary congress of People's Deputies.

---

\* Kazakhstan.

\*\* Ukraine.

## DETAILS OF A SKIRMISH (JANUARY TO AUGUST 1991)

On February 26th, Gorbachev answered Yeltsin personally from Minsk*.

As usual, his speech was evasive. He was talking about those who rejected legitimate forms of conflict resolution, who acted against the popular interests and bypassed their own parliament, he mentioned democrats in the 'right flank'. He insisted that most people did not attend rallies; they supported the 'socialist choice' and the CPSU. Yet there were elements who aimed to undermine the unity of the country.

Ostensibly this was declaration of war. But there was something in this speech that cast doubts on Gorbachev's determination to go all the way. He did not name Yeltsin and made no specific reference to his actions.

But in a conversation with his personal assistant Ignatenko, Mikhail Sergeyevich allowed himself to speak plainly: 'Boris Nikolayevich's number is up. He is fidgeting for he fears responsibility for what he did or didn't do to Russia.' Gorbachev ran one briefing after another; he demanded that his aides 'should launch an offensive'. And finally, the most important task — 'We must win over the Russian Congress'**.

The Russian Congress opened on March 28th.

For the first time in ages troops were brought into the capital city. Soldiers lined up along the streets, row upon row. The OMON were rapidly deployed in full combat gear. By the decree of the Ministry of the Interior, for the duration of the congress the Moscow militia was excluded from the Moscow Soviet's jurisdiction. All rallies in Moscow were banned. The Congress refused to start its proceedings — in protest. 'We are under arrest', said one of those assembled in the hall. The attention of the press was drawn to red water cannons: Muscovites had never seen such machines. The scenario was obvious: the Congress would remove

---

* Capital of Byelorussia.

** 'A new briefing took place in the CC CPSU between March 10th and 17th. Gorbachev's speech there was very short-spoken, if not downright cynical... This is the gist of what he was saying: we are approaching the dénouement; we must win at the Russian congress. We must install harsh control over the television. We must fill broadcasting space with our point of view. On March 23rd we must organise a rally in Moscow.' (R. Pikhoya, *Moscow. Kremlin. Power.*) Gorbachev was preparing for a direct attack on the Russian parliament and was pitting his colleagues against it. A stream of rude passages recorded by CC Secretary A. Girenko never made it into the historical literature — what a pity. — *Author's comment.*

Yeltsin from power, the soldiers would cut through the crowds but if some of the displeased ones still made it through — it would be the turn of water cannons and the OMON.

This is what the American researcher of Yeltsin's life, Leon Aron, says:

'Moscow intellectuals were advising Yeltsin to avoid confrontations with the regime. He should sit tight, wait out the worst, save what can be saved, bring the losses down to a minimum. The Mayor of Moscow, Gavriil Popov, suggested an "organised withdrawal of the democratic forces". Instead, Yeltsin did what he always did — and will continue doing — in a dire situation of crisis. Confident of his ability to hear Russia, he addressed the people directly over the shaking heads… of professional politicians. He was acting in accordance with his favourite Russian proverb, his political motto: "one should fight fire with fire" or "the best defence is an offensive"! Several months earlier Yeltsin had told a journalist what he always told his children and grandchildren: if someone is trying to pick a fight with you in the street and is ready to strike, make sure to strike first, if only by a second!'

Unquestionably, Yeltsin's character, his inability to sit and wait, his inner urge to escalate an already extreme situation — all these traits of his were a serious political factor in 1991.

For all this, Yeltsin's only weapon at the time was his public statements, declarations, appeals, open letters, meetings with people and presentations to the delegates. And that was it. The only time when he was allowed to speak on TV was the famous speech on February 19th. Central press practically never published his documents and interviews.

At the same time the President of the USSR Gorbachev, along with the Central Committee of the Communist Party and the authorities on the whole, had access to enormous resources of power.

It was not just the army or the militia — although they were truly important. It was, above everything, the world's strongest system of state governance, the so-called vertical of power that operated without a hitch from Moscow to Kamchatka; the Soviet press run by party cells and the *Komsomol* organisation, the TV and radio networks but most importantly — the Soviet way of life where people were accustomed to living in a state that was sluggish but confident in its own might.

## DETAILS OF A SKIRMISH (JANUARY TO AUGUST 1991)

It goes without saying that Yeltsin had nothing of the kind. Yet he had a different type of support — something that Gorbachev did not have. It was the backing of the street: unstructured, indistinct and nebulous. It scared the authorities no end. Yeltsin did not call for mass disobedience, he instigated no riots — he was simply playing in accordance with a new, different set of rules.

On February 24th, March 10th and 28th gigantic rallies took place in numerous Soviet cities. Up to half a million people spilled out into the streets of Moscow. These events were a response to the attempts to escalate violence, a reaction to Tbilisi, Vilnius and Baku\*. In this atmosphere the use of force or repressions was already unrealistic.

Yet let us return to the Extraordinary Third Congress of the RSFSR Deputies that opened on March 28th. The deputies, resentful of the presence of troops in Moscow, left the Congress premises and demanded that the central government should 'put an end to provocations'.

The following day the troops were pulled out.

But the real struggle at the Congress was yet to start. Communists counted at least half of the number of deputies and they were readying themselves for confronting the democratically-minded Chairman. The votes were split roughly down the middle. Yeltsin was following the debates tensely. He was watching a sea of human heads — nearly a thousand delegates. Some of them found it hard to control their emotions: there were shouts from the floor, some would leap to their feet, gesticulate wildly, appeal for silence or amble round the hall in an attempt to agree on a block voting... This image of a turbulent Russian congress with its endless voting, debates escalating into yelling and direct insults would become a kind of a déjà-vu. But during those March days in 1991 he realised that the worst — troops in the streets, the OMON, a crackdown on demonstrations and bans on rallies — was already behind him. Possibly, it was then that he concluded: any democratic procedure by far surpasses its alternative, an undemocratic option.

... Unexpectedly for everyone, the floor was taken by Alexander Rutskoy from the Communists of Russia faction. A colonel, a pilot and a veteran

---

\* Capital of Azerbaijan and a venue for bloody ethnic clashes.

of the Afghan war, a handsome man with a splendid moustache who would shortly become the first and the last Russian Vice-President, he announced that he believed it inadmissible to re-elect the Chairman who enjoyed such broad popular confidence. His speech was among the factors that impressed the audience at the congress.

The scenario of 1990 repeated itself. The centre's attempts to apply too much direct pressure on the Russian parliament backfired. The counter-reaction exceeded Kremlin's calculations.

Deputies voted in favour of creating the office of the presidency of Russia. It was another step towards Russia's independence and curtailment of Gorbachev's authority.

Russian presidential election was Gorbachev's last chance to arrest Yeltsin's ascent to the pinnacle of power. It was an illusory hope and a weak chance — Yeltsin was too popular, had accumulated too many public expectations, hopes and emotions. But the laws of a political fray did not allow to yield to a competitor without a fight.

Yeltsin had five contenders: a political debutante Zhirinovsky who was trying to marry anti-communism with an imperial idea and die-hard nationalism; a retired General Makashov, brainwashed with the idea of a global Zionist conspiracy; a trade union leader Aman Tuleyev — an advocate of resurrecting the Soviet system of distribution; and two Gorbachev's comrades-in-arms — ex-Premier of the Soviet government Nikolai Ryzhkov and the ex-Minister of the Interior Bakatin.

Yeltsin declined to take part in televised debates in favour a different way of fighting for votes, a trusted and habitual one — trips around the country.

Yeltsin visited Tula, Voronezh, Chelyabinsk and Leningrad where he spoke at the major Kirov machine-building plant and reissued his appeal for Gorbachev to resign. Rallies in his support were held in all major Russian cities. People were chanting, 'Yeltsin! Yeltsin!' and 'Gorbachev, resign!' They were carrying Yeltsin's portraits cut out from newspapers.

The political wrestling spilling over into the streets was gradually becoming a common phenomenon. At times half a million would turn up to a rally, and so clashes between participants and militia were unavoidable. Yet for the time being the authorities in Central Russia, fearful of destabilising the situation, were managing to avoid bloodshed, especially in main cities. The degree of militia's aggression was always defined from above.

The approved routes for processions were normally controlled by OMON in full combat gear, armed with plastic shields, bludgeons and special implements (Muscovites got their first taste of all this police know-how borrowed from the West). OMON would 'mop up' adjacent courtyards and side streets, block access to venues from which the crowds were barred. But there never were any beatings or shootings.

The crowds also displayed civility. To the democratically-minded public that consisted mostly of the Soviet middle class, people well-educated and — although it may sound strange — law-abiding, Gorbachev personally was not an enemy. He was perceived as a multi-dimensional figure, a confused politician full of contradictions but nothing more sinister than that. People were making their demands known, using the language of rallies and slogans to express their sentiments — but there was no fury. Quite the opposite, the crowds were full of joy, even exhilaration because at last, here, in the USSR, one could openly express one's opinions and be unafraid. It was the spring of the Soviet freedom and civil courage.

Alongside demonstrators marched all sorts of famous people: deputies, artists and actors, writers and journalists, their presence also a safeguard against escalation of violence. It may seem bizarre but for Gorbachev, too, these people, huge assemblies of them, people openly protesting against the power of the CPSU and his politics, weren't enemies. They were showing the 'hawks' in his circle that it was dangerous to start open warfare against them. Or, at least, it was premature…

The USSR republics, of course, were a different story.

Bloodbaths in Tbilisi, Vilnius, Riga and Baku proved that political struggle could take the shape of a tough action thriller.

Scores of victims, blood stains in the squares on the morning after the night-time clashes, horror, fury and countless 'wounds' or 'sores' that opened up on the huge flabby body of the USSR.

For the crowds in Vilnius, Tbilisi or Baku, the Kremlin (with or without Gorbachev) meant a stronghold blocking the road to national freedom. This stronghold was propping up the local political brass by force of arms. And the latter, in their turn, in the opinion of the crowd, had to be overturned and punished as a result of a 'fair' popular mutiny. The emotions and the logic of those rallies were totally different. For the Kremlin, for Gorbachev, for Moscow as the imperial centre, these crowds, albeit not that numerous, spelled a deadly threat and they had no compunction over using OMON. But what was permissible in the provinces was inconceivable in the metropolis.

In that February and March, about 3 million signatures were collected in support of Yeltsin's candidacy for the post of the President of Russia. There were many telltale details, some of them really touching: for example, an elderly couple came up to the Supreme Soviet security and asked them to pass on to Boris Nikolayevich a jar of home-made jam and a jar of pickled cucumbers.

"Cause they are really mean to him, you know,' said the lady pensioner to the soldier on guard in front of the Russian 'White House'. In a future 'Yeltsin museum' those jars (if they survived) should be assigned a place of honour. It was an amazing symbol of his attractiveness, a symbol of the Yeltsin myth of 1991 — he was a defender of the people who were rapidly falling into abject poverty as a result of Gorbachev's *perestroika*. The main weapon enabling Yeltsin to win one political struggle after another was the support of these very people who were getting poorer and poorer with each passing month.

But what is significant: despite the fact that several years later this image was replaced in the people's consciousness for its exact opposite, Yeltsin himself stayed, till the very end of his life, within the same system of coordinates. It was this personal indisputable faith of his, his belief that he was the 'President of all Russian people' that kept him afloat during all future cataclysms.

...The referendum of 17 March 1991 will forever be the turning point in Russian political history. Not just a majority but the overwhelming majority of the population voted in favour of preserving the integrity of the Soviet Union. Then in the same year, the same people spoke in favour of independence of their respective republics at their local referendums.

Gorbachev viewed the results of the vote as a paradox.

The same 70% who wanted Russia to have its own president (in other words, Yeltsin) voted for preserving the Soviet Union, with Russia being its constituent part.

So what did they want — Yeltsin or Gorbachev? Peace or war? A united state or an autonomous Russia? How was one supposed to understand these funny people?

Gorbachev was painfully contemplating the events of the recent months. If one were to enact the scenario presented by the conservative wing of the Central Committee and the generals — Interior Minister Pugo and KGB Chairman Kriuchkov, declare a full-scale war on riots, start using weapons against 'provocateurs', introduce a semi-military regime with enterprises and curtail the freedom of press and assembly — what then?

Gorbachev knew that in this case he would become a hostage, with zero options for a political manoeuvre — and this is when he failed to 'win over' the Russian congress, remove Yeltsin from his current post and 'squeeze' him off the list of candidates for the Russian presidency. The Party itself was bursting at seams.

On April 18th, Alexander Yakovlev sent Gorbachev a warning letter: 'Everything testifies to the fact that the Party is mutating towards Stalinism... For as much as I know — then again, the analysis confirms this — a coup from the right is in the making. What this will entail will be something like a neo-Nazi regime. Up till now I have been restrained only by the common cause, personal trust and loyalty to you... The escalating campaign of humiliation removes my moral and ethical responsibilities... This is why I shall seek worthy methods for combating burgeoning fascism.' Ideological nuances aside, the attempt did take place.

At the April plenary session of the CC CPSU (24-25 April 1991) the party functionaries subjected Gorbachev to scathing criticism: 'he did to the country what no enemy ever could'. They demanded to legally enshrine the status of the CPSU as the ruling party, tighten control over the mass media and introduce a state of emergency. Gorbachev announced his intention to resign from the post of the General Secretary. 'This statement... created discomfiture among the plenary session attendees... Gorbachev was requested to withdraw his statement. He refused. So the Politburo passed the following decision: "Proceeding from the supreme interests of the country, the people, the Party, to remove Mikhail Gorbachev's motion on the subject of his resignation from the agenda…" The absolute majority at the plenary of its participants didn't dare vote for Gorbachev's resignation…' (Rudolf Pikhoya).

Thus, although Gorbachev scored a tactical victory but strategically Gorbachev was in a constant retreat.

Meanwhile yet another painful problem, large as life but previously brushed aside, stared him in the face: the need to reform the political structure of the USSR, the degree of republican sovereignty. He had no other field for manoeuvre but as per usual, opted for a compromise, trying to reconcile all warring parties: democrats and believers in a strong state, Russians and 'nationals', the Kremlin elite and the local party bosses. Overnight, Yeltsin was transformed from 'Enemy No 1' into not exactly the best friend (this was inconceivable) but a partner, a rightful member of the political process (after all, he did win the first round of the presidential election — 5.7% of votes). To start with, Gorbachev had Yeltsins down as a political lightweight. He was proved wrong.

For all this, support of Yeltsin's candidature was far from universal. Yeltsin's aides recollect, 'On the eve of the election day newspapers were carrying appalling astrologic forecasts. They promised all sorts of misfortunes to those who would venture out of their homes (!) or even open their windows.'

TV journalist Nevzorov commented on Yeltsin's remark that if he was not elected he would quit politics, 'This is pure and simple evidence of the fact that this politician has no intention of doing anything for those hundreds of thousands of poor souls trudging through mud with their ballot papers. All he cares about is power, absolute and unlimited.'

But Yeltsin, with no access to television, or resources of power, or crafty PR, was emerging victorious because he was the only alternative to Gorbachev. At least, that is what the street believed. An anonymously composed limerick from the time is a colourful example of this:

*Yeltsin knows our worries,*
*Vote, all of you, for Borya!*

## DETAILS OF A SKIRMISH (JANUARY TO AUGUST 1991)

The nation elected Yeltsin.

Now Yeltsin could do a lot, for example speak freely through the press. There emerged Russia's own press organs — *Rossiyskaya Gazeta* and *Rossiya*, work had already started on creating the Russian television.

When travelling abroad he was now received as a head of a foreign state, not a common Russian bureaucrat, a new alternative leader of the country.

He won on all fronts and was the first ever president within the entire USSR elected directly by the people. Gorbachev, whom he had been urging to retire only recently, was ready for unprecedented concessions.

Yet his joy was laced with vague anxiety. Yeltsin sensed the danger that emanated from the developments behind Gorbachev's back.

On July 12th, Yeltsin took an oath on the Russian Constitution.

It was the first inauguration of its kind and his nervousness was transmitted to everyone in the audience.

Suddenly, a side door burst open and in swept Gorbachev — he came to congratulate Yeltsin!

Yeltsin calculated the number of steps he took very carefully. In order to shake hands, he wanted Gorbachev to be the one approaching him, and not the other way round. Or to be more precise, he wanted them to come to a stop simultaneously (which was hard, given the difference in their physique), for it to be a meeting of equals. A feeble smile on his lips, Gorbachev cottoned on to the game and accepted the rules. He made those steps.

Then he made a speech, his voice hoarse with emotion.

'Here we are, one more president in our country,' said he.

And another phrase from the same speech, 'The whole world follows what you and I are doing now.'

Hereafter, Gorbachev's hallmark rhetoric enveloped these initial statements but the faint bitterness in the mood of the President of the USSR was felt by all. Smiles and lofty pronouncements were little help.

Yeltsin's inauguration speech in 1991 was an adequate reflection of the way he was at this stage. There were no, as yet, precipitous escapades, long pauses and unexpected jibes, he was not trying to speak in aphorisms. Yeltsin in 1991 was extremely reserved, even stand-offish.

'Excesses' would appear later, when through sheer exertion of an excruciating dedication he, to use his own phrase, 'had placed his neck on the railway track'.

On 23 April 1991 Gorbachev opened a new round of deliberations over the Union Treaty — on the basis of the formula 'nine plus one' (leaders of nine union republics and the President of the USSR)˙. This 'Lukianov's' draft was put together in committees and sub-committees of the USSR Supreme Soviet by the USSR deputies and lawyers. It was published in the central press to comply with the habitual Soviet ideological technique that required a 'public debate'. On March 17th the referendum substantiated the legitimacy of the new Union — in a word, Moscow remained the head of everything. The draft was ready for signing.

But there was a tiny problem: republican leaders were not prepared to sign it.

... But why was it necessary at all to rework the treaty between the republics signed back in 1922?

The idea was conceived at the First Congress of the USSR Deputies. Gorbachev needed to amend the fundamental document in order to ascribe a new status to the union relations, to avert disintegration of the Soviet Union, to preserve it, if only partially. On top of that, the new treaty would secure Gorbachev's power. It was his only chance of avoiding the option of applying force, imposing a state of emergency and entering a civil war in the republics...

The verbatim records of the session of 24 May 1991 give us some idea of how the Novo-Ogaryovo˙˙ process was unfolding, how painfully slow was its progress towards Gorbachev's favourable 'consensus'.

---

* By April of 1991, the negotiations were involving only representatives of Azerbaijan, Byelorussia, Kazakhstan, Kyrgyzstan, Russia, Tajikistan, Turkmenia, Ukraine and Uzbekistan while representatives of Georgia, Armenia, Moldavia (who later acceded to the treaty on creating the CIS — Commonwealth of Independent States) and the tree Baltic republics declined to take part. — *Author's comment.*

** The preparation of this treaty was known as the Novo-Ogaryovo process named after Novo-Ogaryovo, a governmental estate where the work on the document was carried out and where Gorbachev was in talks with leaders of Union republics.

'Work in Novo-Ogaryovo', write Yeltsin's assistants, 'was organised in such a way that the participants were not to bring along any advisors or consultants. This decision had been made in order to ensure the highest degree of confidentiality. Only three or four people, seated at the little side tables, were to help Gorbachev generalise and analyse comments and proposals.'

Yeltsin took the floor.

'*Yeltsin*: 'As regards the name — I, for one, am convinced that it should be the Union of Sovereign States. It reflects the current status of republics. The people are used to it. Moreover, Mikhail Sergeyevich has already mentioned it in a speech. It was noted, of course. True, this name... gives some ground for doubt but I wouldn't insist on an alternative approach and would personally support the proposal of the Union of Sovereign Soviet States.

*Nazarbayev*. Soviet Republics or States?

*Yeltsin*. Republics. It was a slip of the tongue.

*Gorbachev*. That is to say — the USSR?

*Yeltsin*. Yes. Now about the signing of the Union Treaty, I appealed to my colleagues many times before and am appealing to them now... with a request to sign the Treaty underneath the Russian Federation\*.

I have promised, repeatedly, that we shall vest you with such powers as you are ready to take upon yourselves. If you have suggestions on your independence in the external sphere, in the international relations — you are welcome; we shall grant them to you. We suggest the same approach towards the Union.

*Gorbachev*. But there must be coordination.

*Yeltsin*. Coordination is a must.'

Significantly, Yeltsin here is speaking on behalf of the centre, the leadership of the Union, not just Russia. His support of the Union Treaty is a kind of a guarantee. The mere process of negotiations would not be possible otherwise.

Novo-Ogaryovo was the venue for an attempt to create a new state

---

\* Yeltsin means that Russia should be at the top of the list of Treaty signatories. Even this procedural issue was a subject for heated debates at the time. — *Author's comment*.

model but to conserve the union (alas, without the Baltic states who refused to take part in the Novo-Ogaryovo process). To this end Gorbachev was ready to pass on a huge portion of his powers to republics. In practical terms this model looked thus.

First of all — one currency, one army, and one economy. So naturally, central organs of power, both legislative and executive, managerial bodies and, of course, one leader of the country.

Secondly, and most importantly, every other political right was to shift from the centre to the republics: the right of limited sovereignty, the right to have their own constitution (and laws), to engage in external economic activities (and generally, identify their own economic priorities), to shape internal policies. This meant redistribution of the national budget — a sizeable portion of income would now stay with republics. In effect, it was a model similar to today's European Union.

… Quite possibly, it was a historical chance. Possibly.

Yet I would like to offer a different point of view: the idea was doomed from the very beginning. Should it this new, weak and unstable state of Gorbachev's really come into existence after the signing of the New Union Treaty, Russia and the rest of the country would have succumbed to a formidable civil war.

The republics of the Soviet Union were so infirm economically that they had no means of resolving, independently, a single task they were facing. The European countries shared one economic market which offered the prospect for growth as well as mutual assistance… The attempt made in 1991 in the Soviet Union was an attempt to bring together enfeebled economies of the former republics that by then had nothing in common.

In addition, ethnic clashes in those republics hitherto had been taking place over some ancient grievances and affronts (Karabakh, South Ossetia, Abkhazia, Fergana Valley, and Trans-Dniester area). The new conflicts would have erupted on a new basis: between the titular ethnic groups and immigrants, Russians and non-Russians. So then our troops would have had the perfectly legitimate right to enter any republic with fire and sword — to protect compatriots. The carnage in Yugoslavia would have seemed a game of tin soldiers by comparison — such was the real contents of a 'new national policy' within an empire whose centre is weakened and a lion's share of its powers had gone over to local rulers.

At the last session Gorbachev asked President of Russia Yeltsin and President of Kazakhstan Nazarbayev to stay behind — to discuss concrete nominations for the leadership posts in the rejuvenated Union. 'I offer Nursultan Abishevich Nazarbayev for the post of Prime Minister. The head of the KGB should also be replaced, I suggest Bakatin. What do you think, Boris Nikolayevich?'

They were really close to signing the new treaty and had a lot of confidence in each other — Gorbachev was associating his future with these people.

By the way, most researchers believe that this 'top secret' (!) conversation (recorded by the KGB and, naturally, circulated among the Kremlin's higher echelons) was probably one of the most tragic mistakes of Gorbachev's career. It played the role of the proverbial match that set off the keg of powder: Kriuchkov, Prime Minister Pavlov and Vice President Yanayev felt affronted by this 'treachery' and came to a final arrangement among themselves.

Of interest is yet another detail of the intrigue: Gorbachev left on vacation to his beloved Foros* — to think things over and to catch a breath of fresh air — before he achieved his main objective, before he was firmly in control. The date for signing the Union Treaty was set for August 20th...

Early in the morning on August 19th Yeltsin woke up at his dacha in Arkhangelskoye**. Tanya was gently shaking him by the shoulder in an attempt to get his attention.

'Dad, get up!' she pleaded. 'It's a coup!'

'What?'

Still half asleep and irritable, he sat up in his bed. Then he broke out in a cold sweat. It was seven in the morning, the day was Monday. The central TV was broadcasting, on all channels, some melancholic classical music.

---

* A resort in the Crimean peninsula.

** A village and a resort area in Moscow's vicinity.

In the Soviet Union of the eighties, such a broadcast signified the state of mourning. That was how the country bid a final farewell to its General Secretaries: Brezhnev in 1982, Andropov in 1984 and Chernenko in 1985. The ritual was thoroughly thought out, approved and fine-tuned, a carbon copy of the proceeding in 1953 — at Stalin's funeral.

Yeltsin was trying to figure out whether it meant that Gorbachev was dead. Some five minutes later (he was transfixed in his chair in front of the TV, they brought his tea, he only had two sips), the main programme started. The news cut into the classical music without any fade-outs. An emergency broadcast.

Presenters read out an address to the Soviet people, made on behalf of the new authorities — the State Committee for the State of Emergency. There was a phrase in this text that went thus: 'In connection with the impossibility for the president of the country to carry out his duties for reasons of poor health'.

So, has something happened to Gorbachev?

But it simply cannot be. They said goodbye in Novo-Ogaryovo, Gorbachev was in good health, cheerful and exuberant. Perhaps something happened to him while on holiday?

But if this were the case, the information would have been more specific. What's there to hide?

GKChP* (this was the official abbreviation; this was how the presenters pronounced it) called on the nation to observe law and order. The address laid out, in clear terms, the platform of the new power... These were the main points.

Chaos and anarchy have made the country ungovernable. The disintegration of the USSR must be averted. August 20th is the date set for signing the new Union Treaty that would, without doubt, spell the end to the Soviet Union. *Perestroika* has run into a blind alley. We are going through a grievous economic crisis. The normal life of millions of people is threatened by an explosion of criminality. There are centrifugal tendencies. Our production is in a steady decline. Living standards plummet, inflation

---

* The Russian acronym for the State Committee for the State of Emergency.

is on the rise. A lack of fuel and spares has placed *kolkhozes* on the brink of a catastrophe. There is a threat of starvation. Crops must be saved; foodstuffs must be stored for the winter. These are the measures we are forced to take. In the nearest future GKChP shall start regulating, freezing and bringing down prices; it will increase pensions, salaries and benefits…

All decisions by GKChP are proclaimed mandatory and shall be carried out without fail by authorities and citizens across the entire territory of the Soviet Union. All bodies of power must ensure strict adherence to the regime of emergency. Rallies, demonstrations and industrial actions are banned, along with all political parties, public organisations and mass movements that impede normalisation of the situation. If need be, a curfew shall be imposed and rigorously observed. Spreading provocative rumours and disobedience to officials shall be repressed without mercy. Publication of all periodicals in Moscow is suspended with the exception of nine newspapers…

In the preceding weeks the final draft of the Union Treaty (that GKChP promised to take to the national referendum) had been harshly criticised by the Council of Ministers and the Presidium of the Supreme Soviet in connection with curtailment of powers of the Union authorities. On the day of the coup, TASS* distributed the communiqué by the Chairman of the Supreme Soviet, Anatoly Lukianov, who would soon be named as the mastermind of the putsch.

A coup.

The word finally explained it all.

Luckily, his closest colleagues and assistants all lived nearby, in the village of Arkhangelskoye, so they could assemble promptly. If there were no jams, or tanks, a drive to the White House should take half an hour…

Meanwhile no one could quite believe what was happening. People were hectically telephoning each other, trying to get some news. The *Swan Lake* and Chopin's nocturnes were still playing in the background when a different type of music was already piping up in Moscow streets: that

---

* Telegraph Agency of the Soviet Union.

of screeching tracks, of low-pitched diesel engines resonating in the solar plexus, the scrunching sound of asphalt ripped apart.

Proceeding down the Mozhaisky and Minsky Schosse, troops were marching into Moscow: endless convoys of tanks, trucks and armoured personnel carriers. The first to pull in were units of the Tamanskaya and Kantemirovskaya Divisions, along with the 106th Guards Airborne Division and the troops of the Ministry of the Interior — Dzerzhinsky Division and Special Task Force. A full list of combat units making progress towards the centre of the city would cover an entire page.

Moscow found itself enveloped by fumes, deafened by the clanking of tank tracks and submerged in a state of complete shock.

Specific details of that morning were recounted in numerous witness accounts, books, chronicles, articles and interviews. Yeltsin also described it all in his *President's Journal*: how urgently and hastily the outline of an appeal to the peoples of Russia was put together. The document was typed against the clock by Lena (Tanya was dictating by phone). How they were trying to fax it through from the neighbouring dacha. How Anatoly Sobchak popped in for 15 minutes before leaving for Leningrad and frightened Naina Iosifovna with his parting heart-felt words: may God be with you!

During the initial minutes and hours it all still seemed a kind of a farce but shrewd Sobchak grasped immediately the drama and the peril inherent in the situation. Yeltsin's dacha was encircled by a number of 'visitors' — KGB agents and Special Task Force, some of them hiding in the nearby woods but some were openly pulling up by the entrance, parking their cars and waiting.

It meant just one thing: he could be arrested any time. Yeltsin's security, Kalashnikovs at the ready, took position in the house. They affixed additional cartridge chambers with the black tape — all was ready for combat.

Yeltsin called up Grachev — General Commanding Officer of the Airborne Forces. He did not yet know that Defence Minister Yazov had put Grachev in control of the deployment of troops in Moscow.

This is how Yeltsin described this conversation in his book.

'Shortly before the putsch I visited the exemplary Tulskaya Division*'.

---

* It was among those units that entered Moscow on that day. — *Author's comment*.

I was shown around battle units by General Commanding Officer of the Airborne Forces Pavel Grachev. I liked him...

After some hesitation I decided to ask him a difficult question, "Pavel Sergeyevich, should it so happen that our legally-elected power in Russia were to face some danger — say, some terror plot, an attempted arrest... Can one rely on you?" He answered, "Yes."

So on August 19th I gave him a call. It was one the very first calls from Arkhangelskoye. I reminded him of our previous conversation.

Grachev was taken aback, took a long pause, one could hear his laboured breathing at the other end of the telephone line. Finally he said that in his capacity of an officer he could not disobey orders. And I said something like: I do not want to pull the rug from under you...

He answered, "Wait a minute, Boris Nikolayevich, I shall send my reconnaissance company over to you in Arkhangelskoye." I thanked him and that was how we parted. My wife remembers that I replaced the receiver and said, "Grachev is ours."'

Further on in his book Yeltsin insisted that Grachev's attitude played an important role in the failure of the putsch.

So whose idea was the putsch that occurred on 19-21 August 1991?

A quote from the book *The Kremlin Plot* by the Procurator General of Russia Valentin Stepankov and the special investigator Yevgeny Lisov — they were in charge of an inquiry into the GKChP activities.

'On August 6th, the day after Gorbachev had left with his family for Foros, Kriuchkov summoned two KGB officers — Yegorov and Zhizhin — and told them to put together a strategic forecast for imposing a state of emergency in the country. The General Commanding Officer of the Airborne Forces Pavel Grachev was in the Ministry of Defence's team. It took the experts two days... to reach the conclusion that it was inadvisable to introduce the state of emergency.

"But after the Union Treaty gets signed it will be too late!" Kriuchkov protested.

"On August 14th," testifies Alexei Yegorov, "Kriuchkov summoned us again. He told us that the situation was grim. Gorbachev was incapable of assessing it adequately. He had a psychotic disorder. We should introduce the state of emergency."

Within 24 hours, they jotted down, on Kriuchkov's instruction and together with Grachev, a list of measures to support the state of emergency.

The material that was used as a basis for GKChP's Decree No 1 was on Kriuchkov's desk in the morning of August 16th.

Soon afterwards, at 11:30, Oleg Baklanov* arrived at Kriuchkov's office in the KGB headquarters. The long conversation between served as an impetus for the plot. The principal pieces of the forthcoming events were set in motion.

At 14:00 Kriuchkov issued an instruction to his deputy to form a group of communication specialists with a task of flying to Foros and severing the President's communication lines.'

The 'pressure group' convened on August 17th at a closed facility — code name *ABC* — in Varga Street (a blind concrete fence, behind it — a green park, a large grey modern building, long dinner tables, taciturn waiters). The group included various Soviet top-ranking officials, among them Vladimir Kriuchkov (KGB), Dmitri Yazov (Ministry of Defence), CC CPSU Secretaries Oleg Shenin and Oleg Baklanov; Head of Presidential Administration Valery Boldin; Prime Minister Valentin Pavlov et al. — practically, an assembly of nearly every enforcement agency in the country.

The secrecy was Kriuchkov's idea. He was the 'host' in this house and he called the shots. Their first task was to approve the action plan. Then they had to identify and brief those to fly to Foros to Gorbachev.

Apart from the persons listed above, GKChP also included Minister of the Interior Pugo, Vice President Yanayev, a 'distinguished farmer' Starodubtsev and a 'prominent industrialist', chairman of the Association of Industrialists, Tiziakov. *De facto*, the Speaker of the Supreme Soviet Anatoly Lukianov was also a member. However, 24 hours prior to the putsch none of the above individuals knew they were supposed to be involved and so were not present at Varga Street.

General Varennikov was made responsible for explaining the GKChP views in Kiev, to where he planned to go immediately after Foros.

The same Varennikov, together with Baklanov and Shenin, were

---

* In Gorbachev's CC CPSU, Oleg Baklanov was responsible for issues of defence. By the time of the above events he was in a new post of Deputy Chairman of the Defence Council and represented the military industrial complex within the GKChP.

appointed chief negotiators with Gorbachev. If possible, they were to seek the latter's tacit consent.

Still, who was the real mastermind? Who was in charge of recruiting this team of Gorbachev's *perestroika* gravediggers?

Neither investigators nor journalists managed to find out anything about the course of negotiations within the GKChP prior to August 6th. This is why: Committee members had never convened together for a plenary session or even a partial meeting. There had never been any proper planning, but most importantly — the GKChP members were not ready psychologically.

Nevertheless, GKChP did prepare a package of documents (for example, details of a temporary curfew in Moscow and some 'urgent measures' like closing down some newspapers, stepping up the work discipline, etc.) and made those public on the very first day of their official existence.

A paradox lay in the fact that all these documents (at least in their substantive aspects) were instructions from diverse Soviet ministries. For example, Mikhail Sergeyevich was perfectly familiar with the package of economic measures: it had been prepared by a team of his advisors and had to be approved by the relevant authorities (the Supreme Soviet and the government). GKChP or anything like it had nothing to do with this package. In fact, the proposed measures were totally realistic and even displayed a certain slant towards market economy. Even the rules and regulations for a state of emergency, including provisions on the imposition of a curfew, were not written specifically for the GKChP but in response to increasingly frequent bloody clashes at the USSR ethnic peripheries. These measures had been prepared by Gorbachev for the eventuality of a sharp change in the political course*.

---

\* 'The situation of emergency as such, along with the mechanism for declaring thereof, was provided for legally. The law 'On Legal Regime of the State of Emergency' was adopted by the USSR Supreme Soviet in 1990. Under this law, the state of emergency could be imposed by the Supreme Soviet but only at a request or with the approval of the Presidium of the Supreme Soviet or the supreme organ of power of a respective republic.' (R. Pikhoya, *Moscow. Kremlin. Power*) — *Author's comment.*

A legitimate question suggests itself: what stopped them from arresting Yeltsin? Once they managed to isolate Gorbachev, this arrest could have radically changed the situation. Several people did get arrested that morning, among them, for example, an activist of the *Shield*\* organisation Nikolai Proselkov. It wasn't a random act — there must have been a list of those to be isolated without delay. Yeltsin topped this list.

... From the transcript of the interrogation of General-Major Valery Vorotnikov, head of the USSR KGB's Administration for the Protection of the Constitution, as quoted in the book *The Kremlin Plot*:

'On the morning of August 19th I was handed a list of names of those to be detained — should the need arise. The names at the top were underlined. I noticed right away the names of Alexander Yakovlev and Eduard Shevardnadze — they headed the list. All in all, the list included 70 names. Together with the list I received 18 blank forms signed by the Moscow superintendent authorising the administrative arrest... Those arrested should be delivered to military unit No 54164 of the Airborne Forces located in the village of Medvezhie Ozera near Moscow. By the morning of August 19th, a spacious barracks had been prepared, ready to receive them.'

Other sources reported that some other 'die-hard extremists' (Deputies Urazhtsev, Gdlyan and Ivanov) were also arrested that morning. Yet at the last moment arrests were suspended. Why?

There are several plausible explanations. GKChP members were trying to project the putsch as a legitimate event. Another version: they were, to put it mildly, a bunch of not very bright, lacklustre people who believed that bringing tanks into Moscow streets, and imposing a state of emergency would suffice, and things would fall into place of their own accord. (The only decisive person among them, General Varennikov, was in Kiev at the time).

There are some more exotic theories:

'There were not fanatical Communists either. Plot members in their pronouncements did not mention one word about the Communist Party or socialism.' (Leon Aron).

---

\* A public organisation set up for protecting social interests of the army personnel and their families.

However, I believe that the only real reason why GKChP plotters did not resort to repressions and gunfire was *fear*.

They feared the popular revolution — resistance — Yeltsin. They feared real power that might be dumped on their shoulders.

People conferring on August 17th at ABC and on August 18th in the Kremlin couldn't stand Gorbachev (although they detested him to varying degrees) for his indecisiveness, weakness, inconsistency. They had their own understanding of their duty to the country and felt, of course, like saviours.

But they were afraid of this new country and the people coming out into the streets. They dreaded having to drown it all in blood. And in the long run they were afraid for their own sake. This fear manifested itself in various ways: through body shakes (Yanayev had had more than enough alcohol before signing the documents); a hypertensive crisis (Pavlov suffered it the day after); paranoid melancholia (Starodubtsev lured a young woman and her little daughter into his hotel room where he picked up dumbbells and set about showing off his biceps); and suicide (Pugo killed himself after the putsch).

That was why they were attempting to scare the others: with funereal music, tanks, menacing decrees, deliberately circulated rumours and the Special Task Force.

...This is what was happening in the streets while Yeltsin was making his initial decisions in Arkhangelskoye.

In the centre of Moscow crowds were stopping trolleybuses and positioning them, with the passengers' help, across thoroughfares and principal squares: Tverskaya Street, Kalininsky Prospect, the Garden Ring and Manezhnaya Square. Trucks were pulling up by those trolleybuses. Tanks and armoured personnel carriers that had reached their destination would be immediately encircled; people were climbing up onto the vehicles, striking up conversations with the crews. They were asking soldiers to explain why they had arrived in Moscow, they pleaded with them not to shoot, distributed cigarettes, food, water and ice cream. Older women were spreading their gifts of homemade food on the armour, all the time chastising the soldiers, 'Who are going to shoot? Your own mothers? Is that what we've been raising you for?' Some had homemade jam to offer. Girls were scampering up the tank turrets and distributing flowers.

Military vehicles, still on the move in the late morning of August 19th, were experiencing a much more hostile reception. People were driving crowbars into their caterpillars; their passage was blocked by line-ups of people and trolleybuses. Mostly, tanks would come to a halt. Some — for example in Manezhnaya Square — would reverse, to loud cheers from the crowd. Some were trying to cut their way across the cordons but even blank salvos from tank guns couldn't make crowds disperse.

The first rally of protest counting several hundred participants took place by the Moscow Council at 9 A.M. on August 19th. Yeltsin's address to the citizens of Russia was pinned up on the wall. Posters were saying that Yeltsin was calling for a national strike. Young people were enlisting in 'self-defence brigades'. Three blocks down Tverskaya Street*, in Manezhnaya Square, drivers were using their own cars, empty buses and a crane for blocking access to the square. A trolleybus packed with passengers and carrying a slogan 'Away with GKChP!' was wedged across the street leading up to the square. Demonstrators were waving tri-coloured flags** and portraits of Yeltsin.

Hand-written leaflets were flying from the windows of the Moskva Hotel — the place of accommodation for many Russian deputies. Those crowding the tanks were delivering lectures to the soldiers explaining the nature of democracy.

By the end of that rainy day the centre of resistance shifted from the Moscow Soviet and Manezhnaya Square to the White House. Shortly after midday, bristling crowds started accumulating on the Kalininsky Bridge over the Moskva River. By the barricade erected across the river from the White House, along the side of the Ukraine Hotel, a line-up of women was holding a long banner which read, 'Soldiers, do not shoot your mothers and sisters!' When two military trucks with their crews tried to break through the barricade in the Kalininsky Prospect, people started hurling themselves at the vehicles and smashing glass in their windows. An officer fired a shot in the air. The crowd did not even stir. The trucks turned round and left.

---

* In relation to the Moscow Soviet building.

** Russian national flag as opposed to the red flag of the USSR.

The forecourt in front of the White House was a flurry of hectic activity. A bulldozer and a crane were hauling along concrete slabs and heavy-duty pipes. One of the pipes was decorated with a graffiti slogan — 'Junta, get the f**k out!' People were dragging metal railing and reinforcement bars found at the nearby construction sites. Some were loaded up with benches pulled out from the neighbouring playground. Buses and trucks were blocking all entrances into the building.

By late morning crews of four tanks changed sides and joined the jurisdiction of the Supreme Soviet of Russia. Drivers of these tanks immediately became objects of passionate admiration. They were stuffed full of sandwiches and constantly offered hot tea. Their tanks were bedecked with flowers.

That was the picture of events put together on the basis of newspaper coverage by Yeltsin's American biographer Leon Aron.

And this is what *Ogonyok* weekly had to say during those days.

"'You just won't go through, you just won't…"

The man was repeating those words like a mantra while fiercely pressing his sinewy arms against the carriage of a grumbling tank. He looked about forty-five, prematurely balding — the thin hair on his crown plastered down by the heavy rain and drooping over his eyes in untidy strands. But his hands were busy trying to stop the tank, and there was hatred in his eyes as he was watching the metal giant, not bothering to push back the drooping strands of hair. An ordinary string bag was slung over his wrist, a pack of cheap cigarettes and a loaf of rye bread visible within. He was wearing a kind of a bluish cardigan, knitted by hand from an unpretentious pattern, a pair of well-worn trousers and sandals on his bare feet.

His face white with fear and effort, he looked as one with the body of the tank, ignoring both the ministrations of a militiaman, escorting the column, and the lieutenant colonel in command of the battalion. Presently he turned towards them, gave them a once-over and croaked hoarsely, "And you… Get lost, you trash… No way, you won't go through…"

The tank rattled, letting out a thick plume of smoke, and jerked forward, casting the guy aside with its powerful thrust. The crowd gasped but he, turning visibly even whiter, rushed again towards the tank that had sagged on its brakes, and pushed himself against the carriage again.

"All the same! All the same, you won't go through," he barked addressing none other but the tank, as if it were some live adversary.

"Step aside," a plain man in an open-necked shirt told him quietly and convincingly, and then took him by the elbow and started pulling him aside.

"And who the hell are you?" a voice from the crowd asked rhetorically.

"I am from the KGB," the person answered with a kind of a singsong tenderness.

"So slink out of here," voices from the crowd chanted in reply, in perfect unison.

All this was happening on August 19th, at about midday, on the slope towards the Krasnopresnenskaya Embankment, at the foot of the stairs of the Supreme Soviet of Russia.'

Meanwhile things were getting hot in Arkhangelskoye.

Having conferred with his comrades-in-arms (the official cliché rapidly acquiring a new meaning), Yeltsin issued an order: to go to the White House. The grim-faced security man made him put on a bullet-proof vest. The entire family was seeing him off.

'All right, but if you are stopped en route, what are you going to do, open retaliatory fire, or what?' Naina Iosifovna cried in despair.

Yeltsin himself, In his book, recollected those events thus.

'I had to say something, so I said, "We have a Russian flag on the bonnet, they won't dare stop us."'

Seventeen years later Naina Iosifovna has a different memory of the episode.

'He said, "I shall take the flag from the bonnet and shall go towards them."'

She was close to tears when parting from him, 'What sort of protection is this — a bullet-proof vest! The head is still vulnerable!'

He set off in his office ZIL. As he was going through the distant outskirts, where residents had been woken up by the din of the tanks, he noticed that people were already queuing in front of the shops, eager to start hoarding cereals, salt and matches — war had broken out!

But he did get through!

At the same time in Arkhangelskoye adults were making urgent plans to evacuate the children. Staying at home was dangerous. A staff security man offered them, for the first night, the use of his flat. It was a stone's throw away, here, in Kuntsevo.

They called a minivan, having packed hurriedly, just the most essential stuff. Little Borya asked a 'childish' question, 'When they shoot, will they aim at the head?'

Women grew pale; they all took their seats in the van. The guards commanded that the children should lie on the floor, and they made it through the gates! They drove past plain-clothed individuals in *Volga* cars, militia, numerous checkpoints at the exits from their village. Patrols would peer into the van: women, children, bags. They were waved through. They were allowed through, too!

The early morning of August 19th was sunny. It was a beautiful and luminous day — Transfiguration, the Festival of the Saviour*. The rays of sun were transecting invisible threads.

Yet it felt surreal and dreamlike: tanks, monstrous decrees by GKChP, miserable soldiers, atop their machines, lined up along clean Moscow streets, chaos, dismay and despair.

The White House.

The soldiers of the cordon, yet again, let the presidential car through, to the underground garage. Yeltsin came up to his office in the lift. At this moment he was guarded only by militiamen (not one of them left their post, either on that day or later), and the security — not numerous but resolute.

He telephoned Vice President Yanayev and demanded explanations. What was happening to Gorbachev? Where was he? What was the real state of his health? He got evasive answers from which only this was clear: the fate of the President of the USSR was still in their hands.

He gave a call to the KGB Chairman Kriuchkov and tried to convince him that their plans were unrealistic: even if they did win, the deaths of thousands of people would take the putsch outside the law and propel the country into international isolation.

He called up Defence Minister Yazov and General Grachev, other

---

* Festive occasions in the ecclesiastical calendar of the Russian Orthodox Church.

military bosses and tried to get from them the details of the situation and establish some sort of contact with the most formidable force of the moment — the military. His attempts bore fruit: on Yeltsin's instruction, Yuri Skokov, one of the leaders of the Russian government, entered into permanent contact with Grachev and even met him personally.

Yeltsin's telephone activity on the 19th and 20th was simply incredible.

The direct governmental communications channels in the White House were disconnected but landlines still worked. However, there was one white telephone, complete with the state emblem, which had recently been put in his aide's office and was still in operation. It had not been entered into the directory and therefore — simply forgotten. Thus, he was capable of placing calls and getting through!

…Meanwhile Grachev was forced to play two ends against the middle. As a boss of the GKChP military operation he simply had no right to leave his 'battle station' — he was, after all, an officer under an oath of allegiance. But as a sober-minded person he was feverishly looking for a solution.

He came up with the idea of dispatching to the White House a unit of paratroopers under the command of General Alexander Lebed. The idea was to block Yeltsin while simultaneously preventing bloodshed.

Lebed placed his people along the perimeter of the White House and made his way into Yeltsin's office. His task (on Grachev's instruction) was to persuade Yeltsin 'not to do anything silly'. Lebed was exuding as much male charisma as Yeltsin himself: a low-pitched voice, a shaved head, a powerful torso — in a word, a picture of the special task force officer.

'Look, Boris Nikolayevich,' he said, 'what are your walls panelled with? The entire building is nothing but plastic — extremely combustible. Can you imagine what's gonna happen if it's hit with just one incendiary missile? The building will go up in flames within seconds; people will start jumping out of their windows…'

Yeltsin stayed silent. It was premature to make a reciprocal move. But before parting he quietly asked, 'OK, what would you do if you were in my place?'

Two strong-willed powerful men looked into each other's eyes. Logically speaking, Lebed should have continued in the same vein: suggest surrender and offer help in taking Yeltsin out of the White House. But suddenly he realised that it was no use. He was not a democrat, not a 'republican', he was simply an honest army guy — and suddenly he said to Yeltsin, 'The army is carrying out orders. But whose orders are those? Gorbachev is temporarily dismissed, it's confirmed officially. So take over command of the Armed Forces.'

What?

'Since the Supreme Commander-in-Chief is no more — accept command yourself.'

With this Lebed made his way out of the White House. Without much ado Yeltsin issued the decree whereby he announced himself the Supreme Commander-in-Chief of the Armed Forces within the territory of Russia.

In those days — on August 19th and 20th — he was countering each GKChP decree with one of his own. His assistants and volunteers plastered the walls and fences, metro carriages and entrances to residential buildings with Yeltsin's appeals and decrees. The officially banned radio station *The Echo of Moscow* continued its broadcasts, although everyone was expecting it to be jammed at every second. The might of popular resistance demonstrated itself in those quiet ordinary people that went round the city plastering Yeltsin's leaflets on any vertical surface they came across.

Among those documents of particular prominence was the very first one, prepared back in Arkhangelskoye.

'To citizens of Russia!

On the night from August 18th to 19th, the legitimately elected president of the country was removed from power.

Whatever reasons have been given to justify this removal, we are dealing with a right-wing, reactionary and anti-constitutional coup d'état.

For all the hardship and dire ordeals experienced by our people, the democratic process in the country is gaining an ever greater momentum and is becoming irreversible...

Such a course of events has caused aggravation to the reactionary forces, and has pushed them to irresponsible opportunistic attempts to resolve most complex political and economic problems by way of force.

We have always believed that the method of force is unacceptable. It discredits the USSR before the entire world, undermines our prestige with the global community, and throws us back to the era of the Cold War...

All this compels us to proclaim the so-called committee that has come to power unlawful. We declare accordingly that all decisions and instructions of this committee are illegal.

We are convinced that local authorities shall unswervingly abide by the constitutional laws and decrees by the President of the RSFSR...

The President of the country Gorbachev shall undoubtedly be provided with an opportunity to address the nation. We demand immediate convocation of the Extraordinary Congress of the Peoples' Deputies of the USSR.

We are completely confident that our compatriots shall reject arbitrary rule and lawlessness of the participants in the putsch who have lost all vestiges of conscience and scruples. We call upon the military to display a lofty public spirit and take no part in the reactionary coup.

Until these demands are met we urge everybody to join an indefinite national walk-out.

We have no doubts that the global community will give an objective assessment to this attempt of a right-wing coup.

Signed: Boris Yeltsin; Ivan Silayev; Ruslan Khasbulatov.'

On August 19th, having read out this address at the press conference, Yeltsin came out of the building, climbed the carriage of one of the four tanks 'on guard' in front of the Supreme Soviet of Russia, shook hands with the tank driver and read the statement to those assembled. TV camera crews were also present and recorded this overwhelming moment.

Meanwhile more and more people were assembling at the White House. 'Defenders' formed units, these units were given targets, they were erecting barricades, organising shifts, listening with bated breath to Yeltsin's speech amplified by the loudspeaker — in a word, people created a kind of a huge live shield.

By nightfall the crowds in front of the White House thinned. But already the following night people were building fires and erecting tents —

in the little park and in the square. By now it was tens of thousands (if one included those keeping vigil in city streets and squares). Those people were ready to die...

And what were the GKChP up to on the same day — August 19th? They were trying to calculate their options in Foros: the GKChP with Gorbachev's support, albeit a tacit one, and the GKChP without it were two completely different scenarios and required two different tactics.

... As to the events at the Crimean residence of the President of the USSR on the eve of the putsch, there are two main accounts: one by Gorbachev and his aides, the other one by the 'guests' — GKChP participants and their sympathisers (Baklanov, Shenin, Boldin, Varennikov and Plekhanov).

According to the first version, Gorbachev rejected cooperation with the GKChP and didn't sign decrees on the state of emergency. The territory of his dacha was under strict surveillance, telephones cut off; Gorbachev, his aides and family spent several days practically under house arrest. Preparing himself for the worst, he recorded, with his household camera, an appeal to the nation (the recording exists) to leave evidence of his non-involvement in the plot.

The second version emerged several years after the events of 1991. Boldin, Shenin, Baklanov and Varennikov stated unanimously that his standpoint on the day was far from clear-cut.

This is what historian Rudolf Pikhoya writes on the subject.

'Some muted rumours about the plot had already been in circulation. On June 20th, when in Berlin, the US Secretary of State James A. Baker informed Foreign Minister of the USSR Bessmertnykh that the American intelligence services had learnt about preparations for displacing Gorbachev from power and the involvement of Pavlov, Yazov and Kriuchkov in these plans. The same information was passed on to Moscow through the US Ambassador at the time, J. Matlock.

On August 5th or 6th, Kriuchkov was meeting with Yazov and they agreed to "research the situation". According to Kriuchkov, this was as good as a direct order by Gorbachev.

...One can assert that plot participants foresaw three scenarios for the further developments.

The first and the best, envisaged that the President of the USSR Gorbachev, who would have experienced unified counteraction from the leadership of the CPSU, the state apparatus, the KGB, the army and the Interior Ministry, would be forced to sanction the imposition of the state of emergency. This action would thus acquire the air of legality which would be completely enhanced by the Supreme Soviet of the USSR. Gorbachev's fate in this case remained in the hands of the plotters who would, having used him, replace him with a new President of the USSR.

The second and a more realistic scenario (accepted as a working plan) envisaged Gorbachev taking his typical position of reticence... like in the spring of 1989 in Tbilisi and Vilnius: I didn't know, I wasn't informed. That is why the plot members would announce that Gorbachev was ill. This would enable Gorbachev to dodge responsibility. As for the plotters, they were thus receiving a facility for placing Yanayev on the scene and replacing Gorbachev with Yanayev. Gorbachev's further destiny would depend on the results of the state of emergency. He could try and reach an agreement with GKChP leaders and keep his post. He could also lose it... and could, after all, declare that he had been against the GKChP from the very start.

There existed the third prognosis. Gorbachev would resolutely protest and use the means at his disposal (personal security, appeals for help in the USSR and abroad). In this case, a group of leaders of the *Siloviki* (enforcement) agencies remaining in Moscow would have to crush his resistance... An extremely disagreeable scenario, yet obviously the one for which provisions were made too, for the rumours of Gorbachev's illness were very actively distributed. A group of Moscow psychiatrists were asked to prepare medical notes on a psychic disorder afflicting the President of the USSR.'

Let us sum it up.

It is unlikely that the GKChP were seriously counting on the first version, the version of him being 'well-disposed' towards them: after all, Gorbachev was not among the plot initiators. Conspirators pitched up in Foros unannounced, and Gorbachev was refusing to see them for quite some time.

The second scenario: a refusal to sign the documents, a taciturn Gorbachev — was, in principle, acceptable too.

Still, there were three forecasts for Gorbachev's possible actions: the third one being resistance.

Did it take place?

This Rudolf Pikhoya's comment:

'Gorbachev's refusal to cooperate with the conspirators was not final and prompted no rupture of relations between him and the delegation from the GKChP. According to Gorbachev, he was counting on their common sense while the plot participants were convinced that it was unthinkable for a politician of this stature to say "yes" publicly. They parted quite amicably, members of the delegation exchanged handshakes, and Gorbachev's security had no grounds to interfere.'

I cannot but recall Naina Yeltsin's comment during our interview: it is impossible to picture Boris Nikolayevich in Gorbachev's place. He never would have waited or obeyed any orders, worse, a command from some KGB General.

So did they exists, those commands? Had there been an arrest, isolation, and infringement of the freedom of actions of the USSR President?

Despite the fact that the head of Gorbachev's security Medvedev, in his book, sounds convincing when insisting that there had been no threat to Gorbachev's life, some other testimonies prevent us from giving his words a hundred percent credence. For example, presidential aide Cherniayev writes about being banned from leaving the premises; and when he insisted that he should telephone his wife, his every word was controlled by a KGB officer seated nearby. There are some other details that confirm that Gorbachev and his near and dear were kept in strict isolation from the outside world. So what did happen in reality?

Most likely, seeing that Gorbachev was taking no active steps, his head of security decided to take orders from his direct boss, General Plekhanov*.

---

\* 'As soon as the "gang of four" had left... I asked the security officer over to my office. The latter said that everything was now controlled by General Generalov (Plekhanov's deputy), the newly arrived from Moscow. So I asked him to come along — we had known each other for quite some time. The General gave me a polite "explanation": communications are cut off, Gorbachev is going nowhere and no Union Treaty is going to be signed. No one shall leave Gorbachev's dacha, and there are submachine gunners brought along by Plekhanov and placed by the garage where Gorbachev's cars fitted with the governmental communication devices are parked. He, Generalov, has brought along "in addition" several colleagues; the external protection of the dacha is "reinforced" by border guards... For two days even the local residents were prevented from leaving the territory of the dacha — those were gardeners, cleaners, maintenance specialists, kitchen staff, etc.' (Anatoly Cherniayev, *Six Years with Gorbachev*).

Anatoly Cherniayev recollects: 'He was lying in his bed and making notes in a pad. I perched next to him and started swearing. He gave me a sad glance. Said, "Yes, it may finish badly. But, you know, in this situation I believe in Yeltsin. He will never yield to them, never give in. So then — there will be blood. When I asked them yesterday about where Yeltsin was, one of them said, "Already under arrest," and the other specified, "Shall be arrested."'

Investigating officers of the Russian Procurator's Office made sure to ask the President of the USSR about that notorious exchange of handshakes with the GKChP. Gorbachev replied that he had hoped that his 'firm stand' would bring them to their senses.

Gorbachev's behaviour in Foros could not be branded as hypocritical play-acting. Within this system of coordinates his conduct was bordering on courage. But it was the courage of a weak person who accepted his defeat right away.

The GKChP were perfectly aware of all of this. Yet Gorbachev's 'taciturn dissent' failed to inspire them with new confidence.

Their press conference broadcast on the evening of August 19th by central TV showed clearly: the conspirators were mortified. We saw shaking hands, mumbled answers, all of them ill at ease. It became clear that it was a weird coup. It was a bizarre junta. A genuine junta would be prepared to come to power wading through rivers of blood and never tolerate brazen questions from journalists.

By the way, a significant detail: among the GKChP members there was not a single publicly known figure, no one who would have appeared, if only once, on TV or addressed a congress with a speech of high brilliance. The most 'talkative' among them, Yanayev, was remembered only by a trite joke he made when being appointed Vice President of the USSR — when asked about his health he answered, 'My wife has no complaints.'

The ignominious press conference where they all failed to come up with any coherent stories — although it was eagerly awaited — revealed their complete inability to talk to the country.

However, there was certain logic to the GKChP's actions. They were simply biding their time. Had the GKChP survived for another two or three weeks (possibly, even one would have sufficed) — the situation might have reversed completely in their favour. The old methods of governance would have kicked in, local administrative and party authorities would have recovered from shock — and then who knows? Time-tested phrases and customary responses would have conjured up the background for a mediocre faceless power.

...This hypothetic week would have provided a chance to resolve the 'problem of Gorbachev', too (either announce publicly that he was under house arrest or come to some sort of an arrangement with the 'boss'). But most importantly, it would have given time to work out who their leader was — who was making the decisions, for such an amorphous 'team leadership' had no way of surviving for long.

In this case, of course, it would have been impossible to avoid repressions, clashes and casualties but the main levers for ruling the country could have been captured by the GKChP within several days. For all this, GKChP still would have probably failed economically, since the centrally-controlled economy was bursting at the seams and the strategic resources were about to run out.

Yet this design was warped as early as August 19th when a hotbed of resistance emerged right there, by the Kremlin's side, and Yeltsin himself openly attacked the conspirators. He made GKChP members take improvised decisions, operate off the cuff. Because of this, the countdown was not in days, but hours and even minutes.

On the morning of August 20th, the plot participants reconvened in the Kremlin, this time without Pavlov, struck down with hypertension, and listened to the presentation from KGB Chairman, Kriuchkov. KGB analysts were warning that if the duality of power continued any longer, the situation would spin out of control.

Deputy Chairman of the KGB Genii Ageyev recollects: 'It became clear that one could not procrastinate anymore and delay Yeltsin's arrest. Preparations for the seizure of the Supreme Soviet of Russia started at 9 A.M.

In the morning, in a telephone conversation Kriuchkov authorised me to get in touch with the Deputy Defence Minister Achalov and start developing the operation aimed at locking in and seizing the White House. He identified the place to where the arrested Yeltsin should be delivered. Again, it was Zavidovo.' (Stepankov and Lisov, *The Kremlin Plot*).

However, what could have been achieved within a couple of hours on the morning of August 19th (for example, occupation of the Supreme Soviet premises and Yeltsin's arrest) now, on the 20th, proved incredibly hard.

Be it what may, they had no plans to retreat. The attack on the building seemed unavoidable. Rumours about the assault started spreading in Moscow: it should start in the evening, about eight or nine o'clock, then at night, then at six the following morning.

At night there was a downpour.

Defenders of the White House were showed how to operate if poisoned by tear gas: soak handkerchiefs and wrap them around the nose and the mouth. Women were commanded to leave the building but nearly none of them left. Yeltsin's closest allies stayed on, too — with the exception of Prime Minister Silayev. He came into Yeltsin's office and asked for a leave to retire from the premises, to spend the night between the 19th and the 20th with his family. At the time he was nearly 70. Like many he believed that if he stayed in the White House he would die.

Everyone was exhausted by lack of sleep and overdrive. Photographer Yuri Feklistov immortalised a vignette: a hefty guy with a submachine gun, one of the White House defenders, asleep on the shoulder of Mstislav Rostropovich, the famous cellist who, instead of a cello, is also holding a gun.

Rostropovich came to the White House on the first day of its blockade and after Yeltsin was, probably, its most celebrated defender.

Generally speaking, many curious events were taking place in the White House. Famous actors and politicians were coming and going. There were lots of journalists — both from Russia and abroad. Some of them demanded to be equipped with submachine guns, the others preferred to get their story and leave for their editorial offices — to polish it off.

Joyous news arrived that the 'international community' supported the White House: both George W. Bush and John Major (Prime Minister of the United Kingdom) telephoned Yeltsin. To be completely precise, President Bush made this call nearly 24 hours after the coup. Up to this point he had been getting away with cautious statements, expressing his worry over the state of Gorbachev's health and a hope that the new authorities should adhere to the path of democracy. Leaders of Soviet republics — Nazarbayev and Kravchuk, whose relations with Yeltsin were far from rosy, also expressed support.

Yeltsin's bodyguards were urgently developing plans for rescuing Yeltsin in case of an attack. One could exist the building through a network of underground manholes and corridors, thus getting to the opposite bank of the Moskva River, by the Ukraine Hotel: a wig and a change for clothes had already been prepared, to help Yeltsin's disguise. Also, there was an underground bunker, well-equipped against a nuclear attack and capable of providing refuge for as long as it took for 'our boys' to arrive. On the night between the 20th and the 21st Yeltsin agreed to go down there, although he realised all 'our boys' were within and around the building. There was simply no one else to come to rescue.

Finally, head of security suggested evacuating Yeltsin to the American embassy whose backyard was across the road, some 200 metres from the White House: the Americans responded with enthusiasm. Yeltsin refused point blank.

In this dire situation people were showing their mettle in different ways. Having remembered his army days, Rutskoy assumed active command over the submachine-gunners and was regularly checking the pickets. Khasbulatov, Burbulis, Shakhrai and other members of Yeltsin's 'staff office' continued working on the documents, making telephone calls, receiving and dispatching correspondence. Finally, on that last night, everyone descended into the bunker. Somebody placed a bottle of vodka on the table.

Yuri Luzhkov, then Deputy Mayor of Moscow, was sitting there, his face aloof, hand in hand with his young pregnant wife Elena. He didn't drink and said practically nothing. On the other hand, Gavriil Popov, the first Mayor of Moscow, made a passionate speech extolling democracy.

People behaved differently but practically no one left the White House.

… On the night between August 20th and August 21st, the events reached a crescendo: the long-anticipated deployment of armoured vehicles.

According to General Lebed's memoirs, number of troops moved during those days into Moscow was staggering. It was a major military operation, comparable to a large-scale exercise manoeuvre or a battle in the Second World War. More and more military units kept landing at the military airfields. However, in terms of efficiency and expediency, it was chaos. Lebed called it — 'a deliberate chaos'.

The very idea of bringing in military machines to suppress resistance of the Muscovites was insane. Several well-trained special force units would have performed this task much faster. But tanks and APCs caused fervent agitation among the crowds; people felt enraged, throwing themselves under the wheels and caterpillars, hurling anything that came to hand under the carriages, clambering on top — anything to impede their operation.

Three APCs were forging ahead in the tunnel under the Garden Ring. They needed to cross Novy Arbat and swerve towards the White House. A young White House defender climbed onto the carriage and tried to open the hatch — he wanted to talk to the crew. But the officer decided that what he saw in the guy's hands was a bottle with some flammable liquid, about to be used to incinerate the crew. So the officer opened fire. Two other young men rushed forward to drag the body away, but were squashed by the tank that reversed unexpectedly.

This tragedy claimed the lives of Dmitry Komar, Ilya Krichevsky and Vladimir Usov.

There were no more casualties on that night…

The terrible news spread around Moscow like fire. People's fury reached a degree when one could sense it physically — even if you were not among the defenders of the White House. APCs that failed to redeploy were encircled by agitated crowds, incendiary devices in the hands of many people. Thankfully, not a single vehicle was burnt — otherwise salvos at the crowds would have been unavoidable.

Officers of the Alpha group — the KGB elite subdivision, trained specifically to act as an assault team — claimed, in their memoirs, that on that night they refused to take the White House by storm. There are no grounds to disbelieve them.

On the other hand, the only way for them to gain entry (as was envisaged by the plan developed at the GKChP military headquarters) would have been along the 'corridors' in the crowd created by paratroopers and APCs. But no 'corridors' ever opened as the crowds didn't allow APCs to approach the building.

At six in the morning, when the progress of the military vehicles had already been arrested, a rumour swept around the crowds: the assault was imminent — this time there would be no combat vehicles, only infantry and the special task force. People joined hands and formed a live shield, several rows deep.

Yet no attack ever took place: a respective command was already impossible to issue. After two endless days of waiting, of receiving contradictory orders, experiencing public contempt and chaos, officers were refusing to obey orders.

A grim rainy morning was hanging over Moscow.

That morning Pavel Grachev phoned up his direct boss, Defence Minister of the USSR, GKChP member Dmitry Yazov. In essence, Grachev's question was this: what next?

'Let them go f**k themselves,' answered Yazov. 'I've had enough of this sh**'*

Grachev got the message and started the withdrawal of troops from Moscow.

Tanks by the White House revved up and set off for home, happy tank drivers saying goodbye to the girls who had provided them, in the course of those days, with a plethora of smiles and telephone numbers.

The plane carrying GKChP members urgently left for Foros, to see Gorbachev. Now they were seeking his protection.

Yeltsin himself suggested that the GKChP members should give a lift to Gorbachev. Tatyana, the President's daughter, confirms the fact, 'Dad called them up and told to go to Foros and bring Gorbachev back.'

---

\* R. Pikhoya narrates this key development — the army's refusal to support GKChP actions — in a much drier language. 'At six in the morning of August 21st, the Defence Ministry convened its board wherein most Generals spoke to the effect that the troops must be pulled out of Moscow, the red alert should be replaced with level readiness and recommended that the Defence Minister D Yazov should retire from the GKChP. Yazov agreed to all suggestions apart from one — withdraw from the GKChP. "This is my cross," he said, "I shall bear it to the very end."' — *Author's comment.*

But when the GKChP were already speeding towards the airport he realised that leaving Gorbachev alone in their company was dangerous. Gorbachev declined to talk to the conspirators and boarded the plane carrying Russia's Vice President Rutskoy who had brought along several submachine gunners.

In his very first speech when off the plane, Gorbachev expressed his gratitude to the 'leadership of Russia'.

The evening of August 21st marked the official closure of the putsch.

When I first started working on this book, unexpectedly for myself I asked my younger son, a student: what would he find interesting in a book on Yeltsin? He answered: 'Details of the skirmish.'

'What skirmish?' I was amazed.

'That one, in 1991.'

'And what do you generally know about 1991?' I was curious. 'What did they tell you about it in school?'

'I was still little then,' my son was evasive. True, he was three at the time.

'Look here, buddy,' I was suddenly struck with an idea. 'Bring me your history textbook from school.'

He rummaged on his shelves and produced *Guidelines on National History for University Entrants* (Moscow, Prostor, 1993, p. 402. Editorial board: Orlov, A.S., Polunov, A. Yu. and Shchetinov, Yu. A.).

In the chapter entitled 'Novo Ogaryovo' the putsch of 1991 was described with one (!) phrase:

'The Draft Treaty of the USSR provided for a transformation of the union state into a confederation and for elimination of the Centre's numerous powers, while keeping the system of presidency intact. On 19-21 August 1991, the central authorities undertook an attempt to avert such a development by force, however, this attempt failed. Thus was started the final stage in the disintegration of the USSR.'

And this is all that young citizens of the Russian Federation are supposed to know about the putsch a mere 15 or 20 years later — even those who have their sights trained on a university! Meanwhile 'normalisation of relations with the USA, China and other countries' covers a page and a half of dense text.

I dedicate this chapter to those who would like to tell their children a different story about the putsch of 1991.

Don't Give in to Fear (1991, August-December)

Almost immediately after the downfall of the GKChP and his return to Moscow, Gorbachev expressed his intention to sign a decree to award Boris Yeltsin the title of the Hero of the Soviet Union[*].

Yeltsin declined, saying 'heroes were those who were building the barricades,' and the Soviet television broadcast his explanation.

On August 25th Moscow was bidding farewell to Dmitry Komar, Iliya Krichevsky and Vladimir Usov. At least a million people walked from Manezhnaya Square to the White House and then to Vagankovskoye Cemetery. People lined up along the streets, holding flowers. A hundred-meter-long Russian tri-coloured flag was shimmering in the wind, unfolded above the marching crowd.

The central TV's coverage of that funeral drove the last nail in the coffin of the GKChP's and the Soviet power...

Just like another grandiose funeral procession from a hundred year before — the burial of Nikolai Bauman[**] that had been attended by tens of thousands of Muscovites and resulted in the barricades of 1905[***], this ceremony portended a storm — a new revolution.

Moscow was scorching in a heat wave.

Over the coffins of these three boys Yeltsin made a speech — paying a debt of gratitude to the heroes who had sacrificed their lives for the sake of Russia's freedom and independence. He ended up with most important words, 'Forgive me,' he said, 'for I've failed to protect your children.'

Another rally — a rally of victory — took place by the White House. It is noteworthy that Gorbachev never showed up and made no speeches: he

---

[*] The highest distinction in the Soviet Union awarded for heroic feats in service to the Soviet state and society.

[**] *Nikolai Bauman* (1873-1905) was a professional Russian revolutionary and member of the Bolshevik party.

[***] The first and failed revolution in Russia.

was profoundly depressed by the betrayal of his allies, people with whom he had communicated, cooperated and shared plans on a daily basis, people that he had undoubtedly valued and promoted to high positions. But even more significantly, he was disconcerted by a radical change that following the August of 1991 had occurred in his relationship with Yeltsin.

A person that he had subjected to moral execution, a rebel and mischief-maker whom he had made run the gauntlet and suffer painful lashes; a person persecuted by Soviet newspapers and kept back from becoming a deputy; a person whose every step was followed by the KGB; a person who was an adversary and a rival — this very person had now become his saviour! For someone used to unlimited and boundless power this was excruciating.

But Yeltsin was finding it hard too. True, he was jubilant; he had scored the ethical victory over Gorbachev, saved the country on the brink of a precipice while Gorbachev was among those to blame. Yet, he himself was also perplexed.

Their roles had been reversed so rapidly that neither had the time to stop and think. So how were they supposed to talk to each other now? Both were nervous and keen to strike the right note.

At the public signing of the Decree that suspended activities of the Communist Party in Russia, Yeltsin's powerful, full-bodied bass sounded triumphant. And Gorbachev's baritone was cutting through, 'Wait, Boris Nikolayevich, wait, this will never do...' But approximately a month later, at the plenary session of the CC CPSU Gorbachev announced his decision to resign from the post of the General Secretary. Only recently he had opposed a ban on the Party's activities, yet now he was quitting its ranks. The Party had betrayed him. Yet the Party believed that he was the traitor.

... After the putsch Gorbachev was forced to make some decisions concerning his personnel. Many of his team were behind bars in Lefortovo\*. Three of them — Interior Minister Pugo, Marshal Akhromeyev and chief administrator of CC CPSU's affairs Kruchina (the principal keeper of the Party's financial secrets), had committed suicide. Gorbachev was still unaware that he had returned to a different country. He appointed Marshal Moiseyev Defence Minister and Leonid Shebarshin — head of

---

\* One of the prisons in Moscow.

the KGB. Yeltsin immediately went over to the Kremlin to try and prevent these appointments: Moiseyev had been involved in preparing the plot, and Shebarshin was Kriuchkov's man. Thus, willy-nilly Gorbachev started making his decisions with account of Yeltsin's position. Gradually, their actions were becoming coordinated.

In August and September of 1991, during the time that seemed right for indulging in eloquence, and launching a final and decisive assault on the foundations of the Communist regime, Yeltsin suddenly went quiet. His only step in this direction was a temporary ban on CPSU's activities within Russia. All his public appearances showed restraint and a somewhat bizarre cautiousness.

Out of a hundred or so regional leaders in Russia (chairs of local Soviets and executive committees), 72 had supported the GKChP. Procurator's Office immediately brought charges against all participants and supports of the putsch but Yeltsin stopped the process, insisting that Russia shouldn't penalise honest rank-and-file members of the communist party. Most radical democrats (Starovoitova*, et al.) demanded to 'cleanse' all CPSU members from power as it had been done in Eastern Europe — but the motion hung in mid-air. The idea to make public the lists of secret KGB informants was rejected too.

Yeltsin did not disband the congress of the USSR People's Deputies and did not announce a new election of the deputies to the Russian Congress. In a word, he brought to a halt this revolutionary wave of 'gentle' repressions and political strikes aimed at the former authorities. The democratic press was full of appeals to 'purify ourselves', 'repent', and 'act decisively', but he was finding refuge in silence.

He had a first-hand experience of public repentance extracted under duress. He could imagine what it felt like to be a secretary of a local *Raikom* or a Party boss at a major plant in contemporary Russia. He didn't want these people persecuted or jeered at.

Eventually he would stand accused in connection with all of this: he failed to destroy the Party *nomenklatura* and enabled its creeping revenge;

---

* One of the leaders of the Democratic Russia movement, a Deputy of the RSFSR Congress of the People's Deputies.

he suspended but didn't ban the activities of the Communist Party; he bring in new personnel; he didn't start a crusade against Communism; he didn't bring the nation together on the basis of a lofty idea of catharsis and repentance for the sins of Stalinism... So why hadn't he done any of this?

He was aware of the dangers inherent in such a policy. It was very easy to incite a pogrom mentality in Russia, to ignite hatred and a desire to undermine the foundations completely.

As a result, it is always the scum that triumphs, and Yeltsin simply did not want to promote hatred and abhorred a situation when power could be grabbed by chancers, eager to reap the fruit of somebody else's victory.

Meanwhile in Moscow, on August 22nd, the crowds were booing and hooting as the monument to Dzerzhinsky* was hauled off its pedestal. A mobile crane hoisted the 'Iron Felix' up into the night sky. As the crowds approached the KGB HQ the officers within made sure that their individual weapons were ready for combat use. Only the involvement of the democratic leaders helped prevent the bloodshed.

On August 23rd, the crowd was ready for an assault on yet another building in the vicinity of Lubianka — the Headquarters of the CPSU Central Committee in Old Square, guarded only by some totally confused militiamen. The attackers demanded to open up 'secret archives' and 'produce GKChP documents'. There was a spontaneous outcry — 'They are busy destroying the documents of the putsch!' The crowd went berserk. It took a huge effort to thwart the assault — otherwise it meant violent riots across the entire Moscow, where each *Raikom* and militia station would have been smashed. What then? A new GKChP?

... In mid-September Yeltsin took a scheduled leave, which left many commentators bewildered, if not indignant: after all, the putsch of August 19th had shown clearly that the country and Moscow needed him there, he couldn't leave even for one day! His place was in the Kremlin!

Meanwhile that was precisely why he decided to retire from the public eye: the putsch made it abundantly clear that the old system of power was

---

* The monument to Felix Dzerzhinsky, Lenin's associate and the founder of the CheKa security service, stood in Lubianka Square in the centre of Moscow, in front of the KGB Headquarters.

crumbling, or rather it was in a free fall. Union ministries and offices were closing down in rapid succession, since they no longer had reasons to exist: their instructions and orders were simply ignored. By now it was totally unclear who ruled the country and the Union.

Yeltsin went to a resort in Sochi, where he was ostensibly spending time knocking the tennis ball, swimming far into the sea, or reading morning newspapers and news bulletins over breakfast. In reality he was reviewing his options.

Scenario number one: he supports Gorbachev. They start meeting regularly, jointly select a new team. Old Gorbachevites should be brought back: Shevardnadze and Yakovlev. Yavlinsky should also be included, and possibly, Sobchak? The first step in this direction has already been made: Bakatin as chief of the KGB, for now, suits them both. Inspire Gorbachev with a new gusto, charge him with his own energy. It is sufficient to say a word, give a glance or a hint and Gorbachev would start playing in accordance with new rules and with new people.

In this case he would end up shouldering Gorbachev's mission — darning a patchwork blanket with rotten threads. He would be responsible for a probable civil war between Russians and non-Russians in ethnic enclaves, subsidise those republics from some non-existent resources when Russia itself is close to hunger, engage in a hopeless dialogue with the Baltic republics, Georgia and Moldova who cannot get out of the Soviet Union fast enough.

His other option could be to sign a treaty that would grant Russia more independence. He will start building a different Russia, with no reference to the Union. Let the other republican leaders adjust.

Besides, the need for a radical economic programme had become dire. Yeltsin feared an economic collapse and this fear wasn't groundless.

According to the data published by *Ekonomika i Zhizn*, within just one year the GDP had fallen by 12%, while personal consumption had slumped by 17%. Retail prices had grown by 200%, with prices for staples more than tripling. Oil exports had been halved. Aeroflot was cancelling most national flights and closed down nearly half of its internal operations for lack of fuel. Rouble had sunk against the dollar by 86%. The Bank for External Trade had requested that the schedule for discharging the USSR's foreign debts should be reconsidered and announced a default for the total amount of $5.4 billion. The entire reserve of hard currency amounted to $100 million. The Russian gold has evaporated in a most bizarre fashion: it transpired that during 1989-1991 the Soviet Union had sold abroad 1,000 tonnes of gold — the greater part of its reserves, having less than 300 tonnes left.

The situation regarding bread was truly appalling. Although in 1990 the harvest was the lowest in 15 years, in 1991 it was down by a further 25%. There was no money to buy grain while imports accounted for one third of the volumes required to avoid hunger. At the same time *kolkhozes* were refusing to sell their grain at the purchasing prices set by the state, and the grain was slowly rotting away. Moreover, there was no hard currency to charter vessels that could bring imported grain into Russia.

More and more frequently, newspapers were coming out flashing the word 'hunger' in their headlines. Everyone talked about it. The task of every male was to make sure there was a sack of potatoes, better two, stored on the balcony. To survive the winter — such was the motto of the day. For now, however, one had to make it through the autumn.

Here is an excerpt from the fact sheet prepared for the Russian government.

'Archangelsk Oblast. Meat products are rationed at 0.5 kg per capita per month... Milk is sold out within an hour. Butter is available against ration cards at 200g per capita per month. Ration cards are not backed by resources... Flour is not available through retail outlets and is provided only to bakeries. Bread is available sporadically. Sugar is sold at the standard of 1 kg per capita per month but no sugar has been available since June when the Ukrainian plants cut down their supplies.

Nizhny Novgorod Oblast. Meat products are available against ration cards but there is nothing to sell in December. Bread sales are erratic. A lack of grain for bread making...'

And it was the same story everywhere.

In the latter half of September Gorbachev sent personal letters to the G7 Chairman and leaders of the European Union states. His message was desperate — he was pleading for a credit of $7 billion in order to purchase over 5 million tonnes of grain, nearly a million tonnes of meat, some sugar and 350 thousand tonnes of butter.

Gorbachev's aide Cherniayev wrote in his diary: 'Yavlinsky informs me that on November 4th, the Bank for External Trade declared itself bankrupt: they have no means to pay for maintenance of our embassies abroad, trade missions and other representative agencies — they will also have no money to pay for bringing them home. The boss instructed me to write to John Major, the G7 chair, with this message: "Dear John, come to our rescue!"'

Former Deputy Chairman of the USSR government Abalkin remembered meeting in early October of 1991 the then boss of the US Federal Reserve System Alan Greenspan, 'one of the most experienced financial specialists of our times. We have known each other for a long time; we understand each other well and practically speak the same language. He asked, "Do you realise that you have only several weeks to prevent a financial collapse?" I answered that according to our estimates, we have two months.'

Something had to be done immediately — this was Yeltsin's chief motivation in those months of worry.

The economic programme for the following year had to be identified at once. The 'crisis government', the 'rescue government' had to be appointed immediately.

Yeltsin had the '500 Days' programme. However, a whole year passed since it had been discussed at the Russian Supreme Soviet. Yeltsin believed that the country no longer had those 500 days. Besides, when creating his programme Yavlinsky was proceeding from the premises of a *Unionised* economy — yet another factor to weaken its relevance.

This was when Yegor Gaidar got introduced to Yeltsin. Gaidar was a young economist, an author of many talked-about analytical reviews, a representative of a famous St Petersburg seminar group — the one that used to assemble in remote places, out of town, to discuss problems and topics absolutely forbidden for discussion in the Soviet Union.

Why did Yeltsin summon Gaidar of all people? After all, the latter was a pure academic, with no experience of practical work in the national economy — after all, there were quite a few professionals around, highly qualified and experienced economists — for example in the *Gosplan**, in

---

\* The State Planning Committee.

the central agency for supplies (*Gossnab*), in departments, institutes and trusts.

But the problem with those hands-on specialists was that they had been performing an applied function — servicing the Soviet industry and the system of supplies, both falling apart at a catastrophic speed. That is why the need was not for those who specialised in the economics of today but in the economics of the future. Unlike many other well-known authors writing on economic subjects and enjoying huge success in Gorbachev's ear, Gaidar belonged to same cohort of specialists but was writing not for the general public but for professionals. Readers of his economic reviews were specialists and decision-makers.

Thus, Gaidar presented himself to Yeltsin's office.

He was greeted by a very tall grey-haired man. Gaidar was nearly half Yeltsin's age but, most importantly, had this unquenchable confidence that all the other candidates lacked — as if possessing some secret knowledge not accessible to those still thinking in categories of 'socialist planning'.

And another thing: Gaidar was quietly looking Yeltsin in the eye and softly saying things that no one had ever dared tell him before:

'Boris Nikolayevich, are you sure you will have sufficient political resources to undertake such a responsibility... for the unpopular decisions — to put it mildly?'

Liberalisation meant that lots of dreadful words, almost forgotten in Russia or at least not experienced for more than fifty years — since the days of Lenin's NEP, would now become everyday reality: unemployment, rising prices, free currency operations — and this was Russia where no one had even touched a real dollar for generations?

Shock therapy — later Yeltsin would say that other programmes were also considered, milder and more gradual ones. However, the consensus was that they may simply run out of time and fail to prevent the catastrophe of national bankruptcy. Alas, the country on the brink of hunger needed shock.

Yeltsin was convinced by this logic — to go through an ordeal and trials in order to recover and live a normal life. But he was convinced those would be temporary sacrifices.

'How much time will it take for the economy to start growing?' asked Yeltsin. A lot depended on this answer and Gaidar was also very aware this.

'I need a year. About a year.'
The issue was settled*.
And so it came to be that Gaidar's young team of economists (Chubais, Fyodorov, Aven, Shokhin, Nechayev and Lopukhin) were put up at the state dacha in Volynskoye and charged with a task to write their economic programme. The team included specialists on privatisation, currency markets, foreign investments and a free market of shares and bonds. There were no specialists like that in the official Soviet economic circles — it was simply not possible.

On 28 October 1991 opened the second phase of the Fifth Congress of the People's Deputies of Russia. The main issue on the agenda was approval or rejection of the course of economic reforms proposed by the President.
Yeltsin had prepared a comprehensive report, but he had also jotted down, by hand, the main provisions. His notes have survived. This is the beginning of his note:
'Not to forget:
—military reform;
—economic treaty (on a shared economic space);
—not a report but something like an address to all citizens of Russia and deputies;
—give timescale for some 'heavy-handed' measures;
—don't give in to fear (the presentation should not exceed one hour)…'

But apart from courage he needed popular support.
Newspapers, radio and TV started preparing people, explaining the gist of the forthcoming liberalisation of prices. But this was not enough —

---

* This is how this history-making conversation was remembered by Yeltsin. But while working on this book I turned to Yegor Timurovich Gaidar for the details. This is what he wrote to me. 'During our conversation in October of 1991 I never told Boris Nikolayevich that it would be possible to restore economic growth in Russia in the space of one year. It was impossible. By that time the GDP's decline in Poland who had been the first to start economic reforms after the collapse of communism had been lasting two years. We had no grounds to believe that the post-socialism recession in Russia would be briefer. Boris Nikolayevich misunderstood me. I told him that within a year we should conquer the problem of deficit in the consumer market. I never used the term "shock therapy" in that conversation. I believed then as I do now the term to be unprofessional and amateurish.'

in his interviews and, finally, in a personal TV address broadcast live on 28 December 1991, Yeltsin himself called for understanding and patience, promised assistance to low-income groups, undertook to fit the reform in the shortest timeframe possible. He urged them to realise that without the reform things would only get worse.

Among those vigorously opposed to the idea of 'shock therapy' were those who could potentially work in the government — for example, Yuri Luzhkov. Gorbachev's economists — Shatalin, Abalkin, Petrakov and Bunich — considered Gaidar's government too young and immature. And finally, members of Yeltsin's team — Khasbulatov (who was also an economist) and Vice President Rutskoy — all of them criticised Gaidar's programme, all of them mistrusted the new government.

Finally, the congress started its work. Huge powers were vested in the congress of Russian deputies. They could reject this programme right away, at the very first stage.

Do not give in to fear!

He was speaking in total silence. He was asking for additional powers — he suggested that his decrees should have the status of law for the duration of the period of reforms. In other words, he was taking up the complete political responsibility.

Yeltsin did have an alternative — to leave the development of the economic programme to the congress, to keep his political capital intact, to distance himself from painful decisions. Many of those in the audience would have acted exactly in this fashion.

Yeltsin behaved differently: mesmerised the audience with his determination to go on to the bitter end. He quoted the experience of Poland but the deputies were aware that Russia was not Poland — despite the shared frontiers. Poland was a country where the memory of the pre-war era was still alive, where half the population would love to own a shop or some small business, and for them, it was easy to see the value of setting the prices free. The picture over here would be totally different...

The same people who several months later would trample Gaidar's government underfoot, at this moment obediently voted 'pro'. The programme was adopted by a majority vote, with 12 people voting against.

The power of the Union President was suspended in mid-air and was growing into a worrisome political problem in the run-up to 1 January 1992, the day when prices were to be freed. The country that was rapidly disintegrating couldn't afford to have two presidents and two centres of power. The process of disintegration had to be arrested in the political sphere too.

This is how, within a space of several days, he conceived the idea of the Belovezha Accords for which, decades later, some would still be cursing him, while others would be grateful.

By this time, the time of signing the accords, the Soviet Union had ceased to exist in reality, with not a single republic recognising its existence. The process had been started by Gorbachev himself when in 1990 he announced that all republics should sign the new Union Treaty. In doing so he was taking a huge political risk but it had been dictated by events: the horrible massacre in Fergana Valley; events in Tbilisi, Riga and Vilnius; Armenian pogroms in Sumgait and Baku; the war in Karabakh; clashes in South Ossetia, Abkhazia and Trans-Dniester area; the huge tension around the problem of the Crimean Tatars; unrest in Grozny... Developments in Vilnius and the stand taken by Yeltsin in the beginning of 1991 sent the pendulum in one direction but then it swung back. Thus, what was perceived at the outset as a tranquil and peaceful political process proved to be a time bomb.

True, Gorbachev did his best. But the rapidly spreading economic crisis, the profundity of which ex-Premier Ryzhkov, the new Premier Pavlov and Gorbachev himself had failed to understand, made those attempts useless. There was no leverage to keep the republics of the USSR together.

On the night to August 20th, Latvia and Estonia proclaimed their independence. On August 24th, right after the downfall of the GKChP (a significant coincidence) Ukraine followed suit.

A comment in the new daily — *Kommersant* — contained a very important thought that explained the inevitability of the Novo Ogaryovo's failure in the wake of the putsch:

'While in other countries a putsch is normally undertaken by a handful of miscreants who are subsequently put in prison while life reverts to normal, the August putsch turned out to be without precedent. Practically the entire leadership of the country has made a concerted effort to break various articles of the Criminal Code: law enforcement agencies (top army commanders, higher echelons of the Ministry of the Interior and the KGB), executive power (cabinet of ministers), legislative power (Lukianov and Co.) and the Party authorities (CPSU bosses). And when the higher ranks of the state are substantially composed of either criminals or their accomplices who then suffer a crushing defeat from their own people, this state cannot survive. The entire leadership of the state collapses into a political limbo and what emerges out of this vacuum is a different. This is just what has happened — only what has emerged, is several states.'

September 2nd was the first day of the Congress of People's Deputies of the USSR. Yeltsin's aides were writing: 'By then, there were no volunteers to engage in a tug of war between the centre and the republics. It was imperative at least to start the process of agreeing on a state model suitable for new conditions…' The deputies passed the Law 'On Bodies of State Power and Management in the Union of the SSR during the Transition'. The 'transitory' nature of the period was by now common knowledge.

By September 10th, only three out of the fifteen republics that had formerly made up the union, had not proclaimed their independence: Russia, Kazakhstan and Turkmenia. A month later it was just Russia and Kazakhstan. Having regained his psychological equilibrium after the putsch, Gorbachev reopened the Novo Ogaryovo negotiations and Yeltsin attended every session. However, heads of the other republics were less amenable.

At the very first meeting in Novo Ogaryovo that was convened on November 14th to agree on the text of the new draft (Gorbachev was desperately eager to rush it through), only ten republics were represented, and out of those — only four had sent their heads of state (Yeltsin was one of those). The rest preferred to delegate officials of the second or even third rank.

Ostensibly, it looked as if the putsch had never happened. The President of the USSR Gorbachev, the leaders of the biggest republics — Yeltsin, Nazarbayev, Shushkevich and others –were assembled around the same table and in the same out-of-town residence. In front of them were the same documents. Even after August 19th, the working groups prepared five (!) drafts of the Union Treaty and the last of them, finished by November 14th, was entitled 'The Treaty of the Union of Sovereign States' and was widely discussed in press.

Yet something changed in this historic hall...

The first item on the agenda was the name of the new country.

The working draft was the Union of Sovereign Republics. The words 'socialist' and 'Soviet' were no longer adequate.

'*Yeltsin*. They'll say that we've lost one "S" on the way.

*Nazarbayev*. Can't it be the USS — the Union of Sovereign States?

*Gorbachev*. The USS it is then. We should decide on the main thing, though: shall we or shall we not create a union state?

*Nazarbayev*. I have a feeling that with or without that's what people will come to. Are we willing to do it?

*Yeltsin*. We are willing to have a union.

*Nazarbayev*. In which case, the second question: what type of a union?

*Gorbachev*. I insist most strongly — if we do not create a union state I predict disaster...

*Yeltsin*. A union of states!

*Gorbachev*. If there is no state I shall take no part in such a process. I should leave the premises right away and you'll stay behind and continue working.

*Yeltsin*. It is called being emotional.

*Gorbachev*. What are you saying, really!

Break. Gorbachev knew how far he was going to go in terms of concession — from a federal state to a confederation.' (*Yeltsin's Epoch*).

The grand finale of this drama took place on November 25th when Yeltsin and other heads of republics insisted on a confederation. The centre kept only defence, inter-state parliament and the presidency. Gorbachev agreed. Yet at some point he broke down and left the hall. Yeltsin asked a colleague to bring Gorbachev back, so that after the session they could all meet the press together. Gorbachev, having quickly progressed from despair to euphoria, came out to the journalists and, brandishing the text of the treaty, announced that they 'have agreed on everything'. Yeltsin told the journalists the truth — it all depended on the attitude of Ukraine.

Gorbachev, Yeltsin and the others returned to the conference hall. The verbatim report reads:

'*Gorbachev.* As we agreed at the previous session of the State Council, today's session must include the issue of initialling the Union Treaty.

*Yeltsin.* Not a confederate democratic state but a confederation of democratic sovereign states.

*Gorbachev.* Why should we put words in the mouth of the Supreme Soviet, let's just explain to them our opinion... I see no point in reopening debate.

*Yeltsin.* In which case when initialling I shall attach the protocol statement.

*Gorbachev.* Well, if the President of Russia makes comments and is against maintaining the state — what else is there to discuss. I don't understand how you can switch your views quite so quickly... This is, after all, our joint project!

*Yeltsin.* No, Mikhail Sergeyevich, at the time I reserved the right to withhold my final opinion. You must have forgotten.

*Gorbachev.* Let us consider the text approved by the decision of the State Council. We shall forward it to the Supreme Soviet for consideration.

*Yeltsin.* I think we can be briefer: forward the present draft to the Supreme Soviet's consideration.

*Gorbachev.* And what's the difference?

*Yeltsin.* The difference lies in the word "approved".

*Gorbachev.* And if it is not approved it cannot be forwarded. Look here, how about we do it this way: all of you, you stay behind. Come to an agreement without witnesses, we shall leave you to it. You decide what you want. But I would like to warn you, my comrades with whom we jointly came through such trials by fire. As they say, I have a gut feeling that there'll be trouble if we come out of the State Council session and don't say — there shall be a state! A new one, a different one but there will be a state! I am leaving you to talk things over.'

Twenty-four minutes later Yeltsin and Shushkevich came out, too, and joined Gorbachev. Another half an hour later they all went upstairs to the conference hall. It took another half an hour to discuss the procedure for initialling the treaty, the need for some new agreements, and in what form the treaty should be tabled in front of the Supreme Soviet. Finally, the President of Russia came to the main point.

'*Yeltsin*. Another matter of principle — it makes, of course, absolutely no sense to sign and initial the treaty without Ukraine — there will be no union. In such a case, Ukraine will immediately take decisions that will do the Union in. It should be avoided. As soon as they pass a decision on their national currency — that's it, we're finished.

*Gorbachev*. Well, I believe it should be the same over there, too. I shall be straightforward: if we fail to reach an agreement with you now, it will be a gift to all separatists.

*Yeltsin*. It will be a show of respect to Ukraine and proof that we want to be together with them.

*Gorbachev*. Heaven knows, I have already… Like someone said, "Gorbachev has already used up all he had". This is what you probably think too. In which case, how about you agree without me? But I stand firm. This is what I agree to and can work with, and beyond that — no. I don't want to be associated with the impending chaos that will be unleashed when the attitudes are so vague. It will be one big misfortune. If someone doesn't want a union, just say so. Because otherwise it is like this: the Union, the Union, but as soon as we come close to creating the union and preserving the state what happens is manoeuvres. And even Ukraine here…

*Yeltsin*. As for Ukraine, you can give no guarantees.

*Gorbachev*. No one is offering guarantees, Boris Nikolayevich; you cannot even give them for Russia.

*Yeltsin*. And what sort of a union is it — without Ukraine? I cannot even imagine. If they quote December 1st, let's wait till December 1st.'

It was still feasible to sign a new treaty, albeit an imperfect one. There was only one hitch — Ukraine flatly refused to do so.

Andrei Grachev insists: '… Gorbachev knew, most likely not even with his intellect but with an instinct of a politician, that each passing week intensified the republican elites' appetite for power while the habit of living within a union state was weakening… Most likely, that was why Gorbachev unexpectedly switched his priorities, and although it was already possible to sign economic agreements, announced, "We shall force the process of creating a political union".'

But Gorbachev's plans were not destined to become true.

So why had Ukraine, while actively supporting the USSR President in June, suddenly made an about-face and changed its attitude? In order to understand this, we must take a closer look at the personalities of Yeltsin and Kravchuk (key figures of the Belovezha Accords).

Both were prominent Party figures that had become national leaders in the course of turbulent political developments. Both were presidents, approximately of the same age.

But that was where similarities ended.

Yeltsin was a construction engineer; Kravchuk was a Secretary for Ideology specialising on Marxism-Leninism.

Yeltsin was an opposition figure kicked out of the Politburo with a scandal. Kravchuk was a functionary who had made his way, slowly but surely, to the post of a Secretary in the Ukrainian Central Committee.

Kravchuk no longer believed in the strength of the Union 'centre', or Gorbachev, or the Union government, or their ability to *contain* Yeltsin's influence.

On 1 December 1991, 80% of the adult population of Ukraine came to polling stations to answer the key question of the referendum: 'Do you support Ukraine's independence?' Ninety percent of them answered 'yes'. On December 5th, the Ukrainian Rada voted in favour of declaring the Union Treaty of 1922 null and void.

A brief personal aside. On 9 May 2007, I was watching a Victory Day programme. A famous actor — Vasily Lanovoy — was reminiscing about the early days of the war when endless columns of German troops were rolling through his village. The grandfather of the future Soviet star came up to the gate, looked at this impressive spectacle and whistled: 'A-ha, that's the end of moscals!"*

...This old man's first reaction to a historic cataclysm was, in my view, very precise — a confirmation of separateness of the fate of the Ukrainian

---

* Celebrated in connection with the victory over the Nazi Germany in May of 1945. An offensive epithet of Russians used by Ukrainians. Literally- a Moskovite.

people in this tragedy. The Ukrainians have always believed, down to the marrow of their bones, that their destiny was a separate one from Russia. That day, as I was watching the TV screen, I understood all this particularly clearly. None of it boiled down to the figures of Kravchuk, Yeltsin or Gorbachev. The enormous energy of national self-perception, dormant in the people up to a time, suddenly burst out.

Thus, Ukraine had suddenly left. What was to be done?

8 December 1991.
The scene was the Belovezha Forest: a place that had once been a royal hunting estate. Some excellent photographs still survive, showing a jubilant Emperor Nikolas II, his retinue, game wardens and their plentiful kill.

The idea to meet up in Belorussia belonged to Stanislav Shushkevich. For purely psychological reasons, a new treaty could not be signed either in Ukraine or Russia. It had to take place on 'neutral ground'.

Easy-going Shushkevich — a physicist and an academician — had come to power, like many democratically-minded intellectuals of Gorbachev's first wave, when called upon to save his country from perturbations. He understood that whatever the design of a new union, Belorussia had to be involved and stay in the thick of it.

In the evening, after the hunt, while the working groups were drafting the texts of the documents, Yeltsin conferred with Kravchuk and Shushkevich.

He emphasised that all republics were interested in the treaty, not just the three Slavic states. The rest would catch up 'afterwards'. Gorbachev had all but forced the republics into signing the treaty, assuming it was not up to them to decide whether they wanted to 'hop aboard this train' or stay behind on the platform. Yeltsin was sure that the Belovezha Accords would be joined by all except the Baltics.

The second question concerned nuclear armaments. Yeltsin proposed that nuclear warheads of all existing and future members of the Commonwealth of Independent States\* (CIS) — and by then nuclear

---

\* The organisation that came into being as the result of the Belovezha Accords described in this chapter.

weapons had been deployed not only on the territory of Russia but also in Kazakhstan, Belorussia and Ukraine — should be either destroyed or redeployed to Russia. The single command over the armed forces was a must during the period of transition (and possibly in the future).

In Shushkevich's residence the documents first had to be typed by a typist and then scanned. It turned out that the hunting lodge had no printers or Xeroxes. The working groups were in a state close to panic. Here, in the slow-moving Belorussia, to deliver drafts to the printers would have taken a whole day. It was equally silly, even humiliating, to be just sitting round waiting for a delivery of the office equipment. Somebody from the Yeltsin's team suggested: let's run each page through two fax machines, here they are, over there!

It was awkward and slightly absurd. Assistants were rushing from a room to a room, bundles of paper in their hands…

Were they committing a crime, a quiet coup? I firmly believe that what they did was prevent was on the territory of the former USSR which by then was *de facto* non-existent.

This is what participants in the Belovezha Accords were telling later.

*Stanislav Shushkevich.* The idea of this meeting belonged to me. When we first met in Novo Ogaryovo, I invited Yeltsin and he agreed… Closer to December I repeated my invitation and asked Boris Nikolayevich, in jest, if we should invite Gorbachev too. Yeltsin replied that if Gorbachev were to come he would pass up.

'On December 7th Yeltsin arrived in Minsk. We met in the office of the Chairman of the Byelorussian Council of Ministers, Viacheslav Kebich (my office as a Chairman of the Supreme Soviet was much more modest). I suggested signing a tri-partite communiqué — a sort of advice to Gorbachev, something in the vein of: "Gorbachev, you are not ruling, the danger is enormous, enough of those talks about the Union Treaty"… What we suggested in the beginning was considerably milder than the accords eventually signed in Viskuli\*. The statement of the Soviet Union having stopped to exist as a geopolitical entity was born there and then.

---

\* The official name of the residence in the Belovezha Forest. — *Author's comment.*

Kravchuk flew in, I met him at the airport and right away he said that it was not worth coming here for the sake of a communiqué and implied that we should go further.'

*Leonid Kravchuk.* 'Yeltsin brought along Gorbachev's text about the creation of a union. Gorbachev proposed that Ukraine should have a right to incorporate any amendments, to reconsider entire paragraphs or even put forward a new draft — on one condition. It had to sign this treaty. Yeltsin put the text on the table and conveyed Gorbachev's question: will you sign this document, with or without corrections? He himself was going to sign it only after me. Thus, the fate of this treaty totally depended on Ukraine. I answered "no". So immediately it became necessary to prepare a new treaty. Specialists were working on it all through the night. We signed it quickly, without any discussions or debates…'

*S. Shushkevich.* 'Why did we choose the residence in Viskuli? It had been built specifically for hosting VIP guests. It was equipped with a line for governmental communications and was next-door to an air force base. One should hand it to our government — everything was arranged at the highest level possible\*. All I had to do was to play host…

'We had no suspicions that Gorbachev might 'storm' the residence although we did discuss such an eventuality… But who would dare apply force in order to abort our efforts at finding some sort of a solution? The KGB? But after Kriuchkov's removal one didn't have to fear them…'

*L. Kravchuk.* 'We could safely rule out that Gorbachev would resort to force. As a leader of the USSR he earned international acclaim by starting democratic reforms in the USSR… His reputation was synonymous with *perestroika*. It was a serious historical consideration.'

… Yet all the necessary security measures were in place during the meetings. The Viskuli residence was guarded by the Special Task Force. Officers from Yeltsin's and Kravchuk's security services were in constant communication with Moscow, Kiev and Minsk (Shushkevich didn't have his own security service). Liaison was established with nearby military units, border guards and air defence troops.

---

\* In those days, in the Soviet Union it meant — highest standards of ceremony and hospitality. Xeroxes (that the reader may have noticed were conspicuous by their absence) as any other types of copiers, were under lock and key and generally unavailable in an attempt to stamp out sedition and prevent dissemination of self-made materials.

*S. Shushkevich.* 'In the evening there were the three of us working in the residence: Yeltsin, Kravchuk and me. But in practice, we agreed that we should be six-strong. Soon, we were joined by Prime Minister of Ukraine Fokin, Chairman of the Council of Ministers of Byelorussia Kebich and Russia's Secretary of State Burbulis. Till the work was completed that was the line-up.

Fokin and Kebich, heads of the executive power in their states, were experienced specialists who would correct our definitions and clarify practical complications. As for Boris Nikolayevich, he invited over not the head of government but the Secretary of State... Burbulis, person number two in his state, was politically proactive. As I recall, it was him who formulated the question: will you agree to sign a document declaring that the Soviet Union as an entity in the geopolitical reality (it was his phrase, the "geopolitical reality") has disintegrated or ceased to exist?

'In the evening we were close to reaching an agreement over this conceptual aspect: conscious of the danger associated with an uncontrolled break-up of the USSR, we have a right to confirm that the USSR has fallen apart and we must do our utmost to preserve the military unity. We realise that this is a nuclear power that is disintegrating, and each of the states taking part in the meeting has nuclear weapons on its territory... We concluded that this should be presented in an official document and instructed the working group that consisted of representatives of each party accordingly. We also told them it should be done overnight.'

*Boris Yeltsin.* 'From our side it clear that those accords had to be signed there, without delay.'

*S. Shushkevich.* 'The day of December 8th is instilled in my memory. After breakfast we commenced our work with the documents. First we wrote the text of the Accords. We would receive the draft of the preamble from the working group and comment: we like this, we don't like that... And the preamble would go back to the working group. Every provision was accepted only when all six of us were in agreement...

'Kravchuk was restraining us all the time. He kept filtering provisions of the Accords in the light of the referendum that had taken place in Ukraine. We could include any phrases concerning integration and cooperation. But Kravchuk's particular concern precluded anything on the subject of "fraternal unity" with Ukraine within the framework of the former Soviet Union.

'Ukrainians weren't naive: to develop normally, they needed Russia to recognise their independence. To be honest with you, we needed the same.

'Practically, the only thing we left united was the army, the strategic armed forces. When the Accords were ready we announced that it would be signed by the three of us — we felt there was no need for a gala performance.

'As for alcohol, I felt like a designated driver, the others behaved nearly the same. Only when an acceptable provision would be born out of an arduous discussion did we allow ourselves a tiny shot of good cognac.'

*Vyacheslav Kebich.* 'The topics we discussed most of all were: the destiny of President Gorbachev, what to do about those states that took no part in the conference, the formula for foreign politics and the formula for the country's defence.

We never raised the issue, for example, of severing connections between our plants. The Accords were, in our view, a political statement. We were indignant at Gorbachev's behaviour and were ready to sign anything.'

As we can see each party that had signed the new treaty followed its own logic. Yeltsin's logic at the time told him that Gorbachev had lost the historic chance of creating a new union and had wasted his potential in endless elaborations of provisions. The new treaty was giving a chance of promoting economic reforms and moving forward.

'In the beginning of the nineties,' Naina Iosifovna recollects, 'when Russia was providing huge economic assistance to the CIS countries — in the form of credits and fuel supplies, the money was just flowing out. I remember saying to Boris Nikolayevich: what are we doing? Tell me. After all, we have the same problems in our country! Pensions are not paid, and scholarships, and benefits, our medicine is dire straits, old people are living in misery, tell me, why? He once answered, "Those who live over there are our people, too." Do you see? They too were our people!'

On the same day, in the evening of December 8th, they tried to get in touch with the head of Kazakhstan Nazarbayev and invite him to Belovezha.

Nazarabayev was in the air, en route to Moscow, and it proved impossible to get a line through the onboard facilities.

Nazarabayev called back when already in Vnukovo airport, having spoken to Gorbachev first. His response to the invitation was reserved; he said that he should examine the text of the Accords.

Yet Kazakhstan was to be the first of Central Asian republics to join the CIS. It happened on December 11th of the same year.

All three leaders were aware that once the accords had been signed someone would have to telephone Gorbachev. They didn't even discuss the idea of offering him a position within a new entity. They knew perfectly well that he would decline.

It was Stanislav Shushkevich who informed Gorbachev of what had taken place in the Belovezha Forest. This was the conversation as recalled by Gorbachev himself.

'Shushkevich telephoned me and said that we had reached an agreement and I would like to read it out to you.

"What agreement?"

"Such and such."

"And why is it you who's calling?"

"As a representative of the depository state."

"Wait a minute, you have agreed already about everything? Two days ago?"

"Yes, and we spoke to Bush; he is supportive."

"You converse with the President of the United States but fail to notify the President of your own country... This is shameful! It is vile — that's the long and the short of it!" Nevertheless, I took it in my stride. Because there was the country and there were people living in it.'

Gorbachev made a public statement lashing out against the Belovezha Accords. Still, he conceded that Ukraine's joining the treaty was 'a positive development'.

...The year 1991 was drawing to an end. On December 12th, the Supreme Soviet of Russia ratified the accords. Leaders of the Central Asian countries urgently convened in Ashkhabad and also decided to accede. At the end of December a meeting took place in Alma Ata and members and founders of the CIS were publicly announced: Azerbaijan, Armenia, Byelorussia, Kazakhstan, Kirgizia, Moldavia, Russia, Tajikistan, Turkmenia and Uzbekistan. Georgia joined later.

On December 25th, Gorbachev made a last desperate attempt to turn the tables: an initiative group started preparing the Extraordinary Congress of the People's Deputies of the USSR. But the congress never managed to convene...

The USSR stopped existing.

Thus, Gorbachev had to leave — that much was clear.

But Yeltsin needed an intermediary for talking to the President of the USSR. He asked Alexander Yakovlev, a favourite and the most loyal of all Gorbachev's associates, to act in this capacity. In the recent year, Yakovlev had broken off both with the party and Gorbachev.

This is how Andrei Grachev describes this meeting.

'Immediately after Yeltsin's return they agreed on a meeting to discuss conditions of the Kremlin's "surrender". This meeting took place on December 23rd in the Walnut Room and lasted nearly ten hours. Mr Yakovlev was acting as a kind of a second in a duel. During this time the Presidents were able, in an unhurried man-to-man talk, to discuss not only the technical issues of the transfer of power from the Union to Russia — the transfer of the Politburo archives and the President's personal archive known as the archive of Stalin, as well as the transfer of nuclear codes — but once and for all to have it out with each other. They agreed on the terms of Gorbachev's resignation: presidential pension, dacha, cars, security, and premises for the Gorbachev Foundation, situated in the former Lenin's School for activists from the fraternal communist parties...

They discussed the Russian President's plans to reform the economy: the team assembled by Burbulis intended to "cross the Rubicon" at the very beginning of 1992 and set all prices free. Based on their assurances, Yeltsin was counting on the economy recovering from the first round of "shock therapy" somewhere by the autumn and asked "to withhold from criticising him at least during the first half of the year". Mikhail Sergeyevich promised his support "as long as he would be pushing forward democratic reforms". They agreed that on December 25th, right after Gorbachev announced his resignation on TV, Boris Nikolayevich would come to his office for the handover of the nuclear codes. The very next day Gorbachev had a telephone conversation with President Bush and told him, "You may have a quiet Christmas with Barbara. I resign as of tomorrow. All will be OK right with the "push-button'." He promised to vacate his Kremlin office by the New Year so that the new owner could move in. Yeltsin had no objections, especially since it wasn't long to wait.

By about ten in the evening the Presidents parted. According to Yakovlev, he found Gorbachev — who had carried out the painful procedure of handing over the keys in a 'calm and dignified fashion' — on a sofa in the lounge of his office, his eyes red. 'So you see, Sasha, that's how it is,' he said.'

On December 25th, Yeltsin spoke before the Supreme Soviet of the RSFSR and announced the resignation of the former president of the country. In his speech before the Supreme Soviet, Yeltsin noted that it was important 'to break the vicious mould' of the country's leaders leaving their posts and finding themselves excluded from life around them, after which they get reburied posthumously and dragged through the mud...

On December 26th, the Russian tri-coloured flag replaced the old Soviet one above the Kremlin.

On the same day Gorbachev handed over to Yeltsin the so-called 'nuclear case': the panel for controlling the country's strategic weapons, guarded, round the clock, by two officers. It was a legendary symbol of power, and a key to the formidable might that used to belong to the USSR.

Gorbachev, exhausted and vexed, said, 'Take it. Now it is yours.'

The transfer was completed.

The disintegration of the USSR, apart from all the other problems — international, economic and geopolitical ones, left the world with a far bigger conundrum, possibly the biggest of all: the problem of control over the nuclear forces of the former USSR. And this is what sheds some light onto the previously mentioned telephone call made by Yeltsin to Washington, D.C. out of the depths of the Belovezha Forest.

The President of Russia called President Bush to let the latter know: there was no danger! The Union had fallen apart but this was not a coup, not a conspiracy, the nuclear forces of the USSR were still under Gorbachev's control, and his departure from power would be calm and peaceful. It was not a political curtsy; it was a guarantee of nuclear safety for the USA. But for this telephone call, one can only imagine the USA's reaction to dissolution of a nuclear power.

Among the leaders of G7 the only one who considered the break-up of the USSR unavoidable was Prime Minister of Great Britain Margaret Thatcher, but she believed that one shouldn't fear this eventuality.

Everyone else, writes Thatcher, including Bush Senior who was friends with Gorbachev, were afraid of it and never wanted it to happen…

In the XX century, every single empire — the British, French, Portuguese, Austro-Hungarian and Ottoman — fell apart, while the Spanish empire had disintegrated a century earlier. Germany and Holland lost their colonies oversees, in a word — not a single empire survived.

And every time it happened, the process of disintegration unfolded against the background of an acute national feeling of shame and national catastrophe. This is what Winston Churchill was saying in 1942, 'We intend to keep what belongs to us… I haven't become His Majesty's Prime Minister to chair elimination of the British Empire.' Having lost India in a bloody war, the British were fighting fiercely for the Suez Canal. The French were waging nightmarish wars in Algeria and Indochina. When De Gaulle made a decision to end the Algerian war he very nearly plunged his nation into the state of a civil conflict; the General's enemies issued a death sentence and were within an inch of carrying it through…

… What remains is this vital question: what has been lost together with the empire?

# The Lion Gets Ready to Spring
## (1992)

By 1992, Yeltsin no longer had to move around either in a silvery *Moskvich* (his first ever personal car, bought in 1990, which he stubbornly kept using to revive his driving skills) or a black *Volga* — a black Mercedes limo with armoured windows was manufactured for him on a state order from Germany and equipped to the latest technological standards. Now he could get in touch with anyone he wanted directly from his car, be it the Minister of Defence, Clinton or Kohl, or any official in the Russian Federation, even in the remotest corner of the country.

They finally moved out of the noisy and crowded area near the Belorussky railway station, out of the flat associated with the grimmest period of his life, to Barvikha, then to the village of Gorky, to an old house with a colonnade. His residence included everything, down to an open air tennis court and a swimming pool. He examined mistrustfully numerous annexes, rooms and facilities, his study where telephones were lined up on his desk. Generally speaking, it all was great, particularly, the tennis court but...

He kept asking himself: did it mean that his fight against unearned privileges was over? He wasn't totally sure himself what to make of those visible and impressive changes in his working and living circumstances.

Practically every weekend the entire family would get together: two daughters, two sons-in-law, three grandchildren. 'To start with, Tanya and I, together with the children, would come to Barvikha from town on Fridays,' Lena reminisces. 'But all sorts of things were happening, Dad was having it harder and harder, first we would just stay on for longer but eventually we moved over there completely.'

'In the early years before the reconstruction and repairs, I really didn't like living in Barvikha,' Naina recollected. 'It is possible I was depressed by the fact that it had once been Gorbachev's home. Anyway, the house looked dark, remote and cold. Boris Nikolayevich would go to Moscow for work, as I would, too, and we would both spend the entire day in the city. Very soon the whole family realised how hard it was to be under constant surveillance. Severe limitations were imposed on the grandchildren as well. For example, the press kicked up a huge fuss when Borya was sent to study in England — whereas all we wanted was to send him away from this relentless stress and attacks. He was suffering from this separation and wearing us all down with constant letters, so a couple of years later he returned. However, when we all did get together, the entire big family, those were, of course, very happy times. All through the years of his presidency we lived together, all three of our families.'

Boris Nikolayevich was also finding it easier — to have his entire family around him. 'One could not survive any other way in those difficult times,' concluded Naina Iosifovna.

On 9 December 1992, Yeltsin returned home, to the dacha in Barvikha village, from the Seventh Congress of the People's Deputies of Russia, in a very depressed state of mind. He greeted no one, locked himself in the sauna, and stayed there for quite some time. Naina was trying to work out what was up, why he was in such a state? The family were terrified. The memories of 1987 were all too fresh.

This is how Yeltsin recalls it himself in his *President's Journal*.

'That evening, on December 9th, I came home rather early. I saw the eyes of my wife and children and rushed to the sauna. I locked myself in. Lay on my back and closed my eyes. Frankly speaking, I thought all kinds of thoughts. Not good... Not good at all... Someone from my family said — you must ask the people whether it should be you or them... I somehow latched onto these words. The political scientists and lawyers had been urging me to announce a referendum for quite some time.'

... On the evening of 12 December 1992, when a compromise seemingly had been reached at the congress, Naina Iosifovna called Yegor Gaidar. 'You are all so young and brilliant, think of something, help Boris Nikolayevich! He is not young anymore, he finds it very hard!' And she burst out sobbing into the telephone receiver.

These sobs of a normally reserved Naina Iosifovna bore clear witness to what Yeltsin was going though during the congress. That on December 12th he was, possibly, in a worse state than on December 9th. How could this be? Let's look at what preceded this conversation.

One morning on 2 January 1992, on my way to work I dropped into a food shop in Nizhniaya Maslovka Street. The shop was unusually quiet. No one was arguing with the sales assistants. There were no queues. People were standing by the counters, examining the long-forgotten products (of which there was an accustomed abundance) and eyeing the price tags. 'Alyonka' chocolate, which I had not seen for many years, amazed me with its price, something like 7.80 roubles. The price of the Brezhnev's days — 40 kopecks, or 1.2 roubles that it had cost in Gorbachev's era could be safely forgotten as a thing of the past. Now, after years of vacuum and waiting lines, the shops finally had things to offer. But people didn't dare, they first had to get used to it all.

The phrase 'the Gaidar reform' is still an invective in Russia and sometimes it's referred to as the 'predatory reform'. But it can be summed up in a different way, those two words: private ownership.

It hadn't existed in the USSR, not in any shape or form. Of course, there had been shadow entrepreneurs, running underground manufacture of various good in short supply, and selling them clandestinely. They were persecuted and given prison sentences. In Gorbachev's times there emerged cooperatives who were trying to run their business on the basis of a very vague legislation. They would be summoned to the Procurator's Office, to the Department for Fight against Embezzlement of Socialist Property (OBKhSS), prosecuted and given prison sentences, too. Finally, there were collective farmers who used to sell potatoes and mushrooms at collective farmers' markets, or residents in resort areas who would lease their flats to holidaymakers — but even these were prosecuted and sent to prison. It meant there were ways of earning but there was no private ownership. It had been banned as early as 1917*.

Thus, all that the Yeltsin-Gaidar government did in 1992 was one simple thing: they reinstated private ownership in the country. For the rest of humanity, this right is as inviolate as the right of life or the right to believe in God. But in Russia of 1992, it was unheard of. The return of this sacred right to Russia was extremely hard and resulted in considerable losses.

Gaidar was warned: how come you are introducing free prices for goods and services but haven't first privatised state assets? You will get monopolistic manufacturers calling the tune! (True enough, that day looking at the price tag on a bar of 'Alyonka' chocolate in my shop felt ghoulish). The prices only self-regulate freely if there is competition, whereas we have nothing of the kind: all these plants and factories, shops and retail outlets are owned by the state.

Gaidar was told: how come you are introducing free prices for merchandise while you are not applying it to principal resources, say, fuels?

Gaidar was cautioned: how come you are introducing capitalism and private ownership in the absence of an adequate legislation and a strong state that would enforce these laws? This is a sure way towards banditry!

And right on cue, bandits did spring into existence.

It is interesting to hear what Gaidar himself has to say in connection with all this:

'The situation was totally unique, nothing like this had ever happened anywhere in the world before. School textbooks had no ready recipes for anything of the kind. So people, no matter how highly qualified in their respective fields, had never experienced any of this before and so found it extremely hard to get their bearings. Of course, we tried to seek advice from experts whose opinion we respected but not a single one among them would have taken control of the situation that emerged in Russia in the autumn of 1991. They simply had no experience of such economies.'

---

* With the only brief interlude being Lenin's New Economic Policy (NEP) that lasted for only few years and was cracked down be Stalin in the late 1920s.

It must be added that Gaidar himself was warning that if the budget deficit continued to grow, that is, if the state didn't cut back its spending, if the credit and benefits made available to enterprises stayed the same — that is to say, if the money printing machine didn't stop (in 1991 the State Mint was operating on three shifts a day, the money was printed even during the night, and still there was a shortage of banknotes) — the country would lurch into hyperinflation. And true enough, it was as if he was looking into a crystal ball. Hyperinflation started almost right away. Instead of an expected three-fold increase of prices (in March of 1991, under Gorbachev, prices had already tripled), what happened was a ten-fold hike, and sometimes it was even higher.

...Many enterprises came to a standstill.

The state stopped its planned purchases of companies' outputs and insisted, instead, that manufacturers should 'enter the marketplace' themselves. The problem was — there was no market. It was equally unclear who, in an a real 'market', was going to buy the products made by Soviet factories and plants, such as irons or TV sets. Cash that in the context of price liberalisation instantly acquired some value started rapidly 'evaporating' from the budgets at all levels: the state, the regions, down to the budgets of tiny villages and towns. People set about accumulating interest on deposits; money was borrowed, lent and re-borrowed. What ensued were delays on paying salaries and pensions. In order to overcome the deficit of products, the president signed a decree on free trade. Now, people could sell anything they liked, and it could be from hand to hand, or off the lorry, or over the counter. One could bring into the country any products or merchandise from abroad, and there were practically no limits or duty to pay. This was yet another attempt to 'feed', 'clothe' and 'shoe' those who were in dire straits as the result of the years of the crisis.

In 1992 trade provided the only real way to earn a livelihood. Thus, the entire country started trading. People took to 'shuttling' products; in other words, you bought something in Point A where it was a bit cheaper and took it to Point B where it cost a touch more. Huge bags were carried by hand, by car and by rail — by hook or by crook, if only one could bring and sell it. It was a terrible, savage, primeval business. Still, there was no other way: the country finally had some goods and people had to make a living, otherwise it was impossible to survive.

It must be said, however, that far from everyone in our country was eager to earn money from the sweat of their brow. Some preferred simply to take it away by force from those who had earned it honestly: from those very 'shuttles', the first entrepreneurs. A veritable civil war was unleashed against private property, a real shooting war. This was something that no one had predicted and probably couldn't have predicted if they tried.

Thus, the fact that the people spontaneously declared a civil war on private property and those who owned it was probably the most unpredictable consequence of the Gaidar reform. Later, authorities and Yeltsin were named as principal culprits. But how was it the authorities' fault if man was turning against man? This war against initial owners of private property was waged not only by the Russian marginal circles — gangsters and the like; it was also actively supported by the Russian bureaucracy. Civil servants responded to the emergence of a new class of rich people with an amazing speed: they immediately felt like getting rich too, and what's more — at the expense of the entrepreneurs. Finally, the saddest of all was the reaction to private ownership in the popular mentality. The most graphic illustration of this mentality, the most vivid and striking was the appearance in the nineties of numerous, and very funny, jokes about 'new Russians'. The butt of these jokes was this thick-skulled creature, a disgusting and over-pampered character whose language and actions were always ugly and ridiculous. The folk mentality — at the level of jokes, language and thought — was rejecting the new reality and refusing to accept it as a fact.

Yet the tougher the 'undeclared war', the clearer one could see that the vehemence of this resistance was caused exactly by the fact that this new phenomenon was rapidly striking root in reality: in the 'thick of people's life', as Lenin used to phrase it, and nothing could be done to stop it.

Yet the 'war' against private ownership didn't only take some latent forms and indirect routes. There were some perfectly blatant hostilities. The first organised action against the government and the President since the launch of reforms — a rally in Manezhnaya Square — took place on 9 February 1992. It was attended by some hundred thousand people. The rally's chief organiser was the RCWP — the Russian communist party of the workers that came to replace the banned communist parties of the

USSR and RSFSR. The rally participants demanded restoration of the Soviet Union and a new government.

On February 23rd, columns of the Working Russia and RCPW members set off from the square by the Belorussky railway station, down Tverskaya Street, towards the Kremlin. At the head of the columns walked the veterans of WWII. Among the participants were militants from the Trans-Dniester area — those who had already had experience of clashes with the Moldovan police, as well as former army officers. The march was stopped only at the Minsk Hotel* where they started making their speeches on the spot. General Albert Makashov said in his address to Russia, 'Dear Motherland, do get off your knees, it is time to make the final step!'

The targets pursued by the rallies in spring of 1992 can be illustrated through a leaflet put out for distribution at the so-called *National Veche*\*\* that the opposition was intending to convene in Manezhnaya Square on March 17th, on the day of the opening of the Congress of the People's Deputies of Russia:

'CITIZENS! A year ago the first ever referendum was carried out in our country. The people said a decisive YES to the Union of the Soviet Socialist Republics. Yet the supreme officials have overridden the will of the people, transgressed against the Constitution of the country and, to curry favour with Western capitals, have declared the USSR null and void. By doing so the Gorbachev-Yeltsin clique has provoked the break-up of the state, robbery of its own people and a civil war.

The duty of honest people is to restore the legitimate power and prevent the planned genocide... We must help deputies to assemble and affirm the will of the people — the results of the referendum.

The National Veche shall be convened concurrently with the congress. Its aim:

    - To confirm the popular will expressed at the referendum;
    - To put an end to the inhuman policy and adopt a programme for leading the country out of the crisis;

---

\* Mid-point on the above route.

\*\* *Veche* ('a council' in the Old Church Slavonic, pronounced *'vie-cheh*) was a popular assembly in medieval Slavic countries.

–To appoint the Head of State and the Government of the USSR nominated by the congress.

We urge the working collectives from the shop floors and ploughshares to elect representatives from their cities, oblasts and republics and to send them to Moscow for taking part in the *National Veche*. We call on the working people of the capital city, the army personnel and militias to attend the *Veche* too.

Meet: 17:00 on March 17th in Moscow's Manezhnaya Square.

THE WILL OF THE NATIONAL VECHE IS SACROSANCT!

The Working Russia movement'

Later, the organisers were insisting that the *'veche'* was attended by over three hundred and fifty thousand people. According to the militia, the figure was closer to a hundred thousand.

One Voitsekhovsky, an ex-OMON officer from Vilnius, was saying:

'Nowadays we, the members of the Vilnius OMON, are scattered all over Russia… We all are gritting out teeth, repeating — the time shall come… The cattle cars will arrive yet. The fathers of the 'democrats' felled the trees\* and they'll be pulling up the stumps, damn it! I'm asking you to appoint me not a boss, just the head of one cattle car, and eighty percent of them will never make it, for they will be executed to prevent an attempt to escape.'

…Meanwhile, little by little, the features of a new economy and a new life started to emerge through all this smoke and the fumes of burning fires.

The year 1992 was a very interesting time.

During the summer the entire country was glued to its TVs for they were showing the Olympic Games in Barcelona. It was the last time we could watch our athletes performing in the same team, representing the CIS.

The country was equally transfixed in front of television sets when the American series *Santa Barbara* was on. A joke coined in 1992: 'You

---

\* Presumably, the reference to the number of political convicts who had been deployed in forest procurement in Siberia in Stalin's times.

are condemned to death, what is you final wish?' — 'To re-watch *Santa Barbara* from the very first episode.'

And, of course, the first American-style programmes that appeared on our TV. Entertainment diluted by advertising was fascinating to watch because it was all completely new.

Things Russian and things American merged in some whimsical and weird way, be it advertising, show business, politics or even the language. The country's move towards modernisation in 1992 was understood simply as copying Americans.

In other words, life in 1992 was much more interesting than politics. Then again, one somehow had to make ends meet, survive and gather no moss.

Huge rallies caused much less popular interest than some beauty contests, newly available imported household and office equipment and the ability to freely travel abroad. It was as if the people's interest in politics had been exhausted in 1991. Yeltsin, as finely attuned to this public sentiment as ever, was taking it all onboard.

Still, at the same time there existed as if another Russia. In August of 1991, the Institute for Socio-Political Research under the Russian Academy of Sciences marked the first anniversary of the putsch by publishing a big report: 'On Socio-Political Situation in Russia Based on Results of the First Half of 1992'. Among other things, its authors were writing: 'The President and his associates have tied their fate to the concept of fast and radical transformations; they have come to occupy an extreme position that is repellent to a considerable part of practically-minded politicians, managers, soldiers and academics' (i.e. — practically the entire country's elite!).'

'People are ready for acts of civil disobedience.' 'One fifth of the population is ready to start building barricades.''Over 30 million people are below the line ensuring physical survival'. There were numerous similarly horrifying forecasts.

In June, a round table of the unified opposition issued a statement: 'Yeltsin's regime in its present form is living its last months or even weeks. To save its skin, it starts changing the stage design and bringing to the fore new politicians whose reputation is allegedly not smeared in mud.

Boris Yeltsin cannot even resort to extreme measures since the army and law enforcement agencies do not support him. The agony of this regime has already started'.

The communists were supported by the former President of the USSR. In his interviews to Western media, he was harshly critical of the government. While on a visit to Israel in June of 1992, Gorbachev was saying that 'the growing discontent in Russia may cause a social explosion, and should this happen, it would spell not only the end of democratic reforms but, possibly, also bring in a dictatorship'. At home he was more reserved. Nonetheless, a phrase of his, uttered in a private circle, backstage, became widely known: 'When this power structure collapses my main task will be to deftly pick it up'. When speaking to *Komsomolskaya Pravda*, Gorbachev announced, 'If the President chooses the path of dissolving the parliament and the congress it will mean that he himself has decided to go down the route of dictatorship.' Gorbachev was branding Yeltsin a dictator in advance. His assessment coincided with the opinion of the communist opposition.

The presidential press service issued this statement, 'Mikhail Gorbachev who in six years of reforms never mustered the courage to embark on the reform of the economy is makings ever more patronising pronouncements against the government and the President whilst they are taking real steps towards reforming the state*... President Yeltsin shall have to undertake the required legal steps to prevent any damage to the course of reforms.'

The President authorised Interior Minister Yerin to check 'on the living standards of the people — particularly those trumpeting everywhere that they have nothing apart from the pension.' Since it was true, Gorbachev did mention his pension as his only source of income, consequently the documents at the Gorbachev Foundation were audited. Some of the Foundation's premises were taken away, specifically those rented out to various commercial companies and Gorbachev had his governmental *ZIL* replaced by a black *Volga*. That said, even after these events, the Foundation kept over 1,000 square metres of floor space while Mikhail Sergeyevich preserved his dacha, security and communications. After this episode their

---

* The word *reform* is repeated three times within the space of one phrase, which is a reflection of the nervous tonality of the statement on the whole. — *Author's comment.*

relations were severed forever and, since then, Yeltsin didn't fire a single shot at Gorbachev, no matter what the latter did or said.

Curiously enough, another acutely critical article (in *Nezavisimaya Gazeta*) was initiated by an author who was, at the time, an inmate at the Matrosskaya Tishina˙. Mr Lukianov, in prison in connection with the investigation of GKChP activities, gave an extensive interview and left no stone unturned in his criticism of the course of reforms. He appealed to the communist party to go on the offensive. It looked like even those over whom Yeltsin had ostensibly scored a decisive victory now doubted his ability to survive. They brimmed with new hatred.

At the same time Yeltsin was mercilessly harangued by the most radical democrats, too. An excerpt from a confidential analytical memo by Yeltsin's aide Sergei Stankevich stated that 'it is extremely dangerous and harmful to create a tight association between the name and reputation of the President and this or any other government.' Everybody, including the 'gentle opposition' consisting of Gorbachev's intellectuals and academics, was now urging Yeltsin to drop Gaidar. But worst of all, the Gaidar government found itself under a vehement attack from the Congress of the People's Deputies, the Supreme Soviet and its Speaker Ruslan Khasbulatov (he called the government 'irresponsible' while a less reserved Vice President Rutskoy referred to them as 'boys in children's pink shorts').

In short, the shots were fired from everywhere: right and left, front and rear. And from every street corner one word was booming: catastrophe, catastrophe, catastrophe!

The first appeals for the government to resign came already in April of 1992, at the Sixth Congress of People's Deputies of Russia. One deputy berated the President over the fact that most of the members of Gaidar's government were Jews. It turned out to be incorrect — Jews didn't make the majority at all. However, if this vignette could be put down to anti-Semitism of one individual, there were other accusations too, and they would be hurled at Yeltsin for decades to come. The government was declared responsible for the birth rate in the country falling by 30% which

---

* A prison in Moscow, literally — Seamen's Silence.

meant planting a demographic time bomb under very foundations of the nation. At the same time any specialist on demography would confirm that social policy aimed at increasing birth rates can only have so much influence. It could be confirmed by the fact that these rates were in a steady decline in European Russia during the most stable years of Brezhnev's rule. The demographic curves were creeping up or down in response to a totally different logic.

Yegor Gaidar himself wrote the following of the Sixth Congress: 'The August shock had been overcome and there had been no harsh repressions in the wake of the putsch. The imminent threat of hunger and a total economic catastrophe had receded. The opposition had pulled up their socks: now was the time to start yelling that, given the hardships experienced by the people at the initial stage of transformations, it had all been done against the will of the Congress and the Supreme Soviet, the wrong way, not the way it had been agreed. It should have been softer or harsher, slower or faster — in any way, different...'

And about Khasbulatov in 1992, Gaidar wrote at the time:

'The chairman Khasbulatov is orchestrating the congress masterfully and, by using a thousand-voice-strong polyphony, is playing his own symphony. He doesn't place the issue of confidence on the agenda but does all he could to make criticisms, even of the most demagogic nature, go on and on. In all the evidence, he is not ready yet for a direct confrontation with the President and doesn't believe that the time for bringing down the reforming government is ripe. Yet he is trying to ensure that they leave the congress extremely weakened, demoralised, obedient to the Supreme Soviet or, to be more specific, to Khasbulatov himself.'

Gaidar suggested to his government that they should start an offensive.

And so Gaidar did present the congress with an ultimatum: either the deputies support the government in their reforms or the government resigns. The congress got frightened and decided to wait it out.

'After the majority of the congress panicked and withdrew, it became clear that we had scored an unquestionable victory, albeit a temporary one.'

Of course, Yeltsin expected a public reaction to the painful reforms. He expected something even worse, for example, unrest, mutiny, mass-scale industrial actions — but the number of those suddenly fell by 600%. He was also expecting his ratings to fall. Yet the decline was not catastrophic: his ratings crept down but never plummeted. The number of those who supported reforms and associated with them their hopes was still over half of the total numbers polled.

Yeltsin remained firm and confident in his estimates. 'Gaidar has scored a bull's eye,' he said in an interview to *Komsomolskaya Pravda*. But Democratic Russia, *a* movement hitherto unswervingly supportive of the President, had now distanced itself, displeased with Gaidar. Prominent figures inherited from Gorbachev's parliament –Afanasiev, Batkin, et al. — were leaving. Their view was that Gaidar's policy was taking the country straight down the road to extremism and a vengeance from the reds and the brown-shirts.

People's confidence was waning; the coverage of reforms in mass media was full of contradictions. Gaidar's government suited no one.

Yeltsin's intuition was telling him retreat would be tantamount to suicide. Gaidar's reforms constituted the gist, the pivot, the underlying value of the new political era. To give up attempts to radically rearrange Russian life would mean admitting defeat. His victory in August did not mean that he, personally, had come to power. That victory was in the changes that were now underway and had to go forward whatever the cost. He had to preserve this government but not by way of a dictatorship or resorting to force. It was imperative to steer away from either of these two dangerous extremities. There had to be a third way and it was imperative to find it.

A significant conversation took place between Yeltsin and Gaidar sometime during these months — one of many that they conducted throughout 1992. Gaidar, completely different to him in terms of temperament, mentality and professional occupation became his constant interlocutor, a source of confidence, strength and staying power. And vice versa, Yeltsin was cheering up Gaidar who found himself in politics for the first time in his life. Gaidar brought him an unexpected proposal: to set up, within the government, a special unit responsible for explaining to general public what various steps meant, why they were undertaken, why in this sequence. It should eliminate 'economic ignorance' while making economic basics clear even to a child. An idea of this kind should have been to Yeltsin's taste — him being an ex-party functionary, yet his reaction was unexpectedly acerbic.

'Do you intend to restore the CC CPSU Agitprop Department?' he asked Gaidar head-on. 'As long as I am alive, it's not going to happen.'

In the eyes of the people, Gaidar was gradually acquiring the status of a lonely hero who, although in power, was inconvenient to all, belonged nowhere, was needed by no one but who 'at least was trying to do something'. Under the Constitution, the congress could dismiss any government at any minute. So Yeltsin started a bigger game. To gain time, he set off down the road of gradual and cautious concessions, of which there would be so many in that year of 1992, to the extent where it may be generally called 'the year of concessions and compromises'.

First, Yeltsin fired a minister from Gaidar's government –the one responsible for the Fuel & Energy Complex. After that he gave the axe to the Central Bank's director accused of being involved in the scandal with counterfeit 'Chechen letters of advice' when an immense amount of cash had been stolen from the state. The price of a compromise with the congress was that the Central Bank was now headed by Gerashchenko, a tough opponent of Gaidar's reforms who set the money-printing machine at full speed.

At the Sixth Congress of Russia's People's Deputies of April of 1992, Yeltsin had reinforced the team of 'boys in pink children's shorts' with experienced business managers and ex-bosses of major industrial complexes. Thus, the former USSR minister of gas and energy Victor Chernomyrdin became a Vice-Premier, along with two others.

The press started yelling of Yeltsin's 'defeat'. In November, he met representatives of the Civil Union. The press were barred from the event. In effect it was a process of bargaining over the fate of Gaidar's government. They tried to convince him to dismantle the cabinet of ministers. Representatives of the industrial lobby made no attempts on the destiny of the President himself but still, threatened him with the upcoming congress. In essence, the core of Gaidar's team had to be rid of. 'Under these conditions, Gaidar may stay the Premier,' finished the group's spokesman.

Yeltsin was silent. His silence lasted so long that those present started exchanging nervous glances. It was not easy bearing his famous pauses.

'Under such wholesale changes, Gaidar will leave of his own accord,' he uttered eventually. 'We shall never find a better Premier. Then again, it will be tough for me to give up Burbulis, too. Gaidar must stay.' (*Yeltsin's Epoch*).

He later wrote in his memoir that the speed with which he was changing players in his team was a result of a 'run-away' acceleration of the political time. In all those years Gaidar was the only exception from this iron rule. He didn't want to 'replace' him. Not for all the tea in China. It was because of him that he was locking himself up in the sauna and attacked the congress with the ferocity of a tank.

Let's try to understand why.

Yeltsin was convinced that a new powerful Russia was growing from within the old Soviet country. And it was this Russia, and not just some wobbly administrative construction, that was the future: a class of new owners — entrepreneurs. People who would not be prepared to give up their newly acquired right to make money or their right to private ownership.

There exists a wonderful anecdote about Brezhnev. His assistants asked him why the minimal wage incorporated into the Party's economic programme was so low: an ordinary person would never make ends meet with a salary like that. 'You know little of how ordinary people live,' Brezhnev answered and raised his eyebrows. 'Two sacks of potatoes may go to the state but one sack stays. They will unavoidably steal something in any case.' Seemingly, the anecdote illustrates the ruler's wisdom. The ruler must not interfere and let Russian life follow its own course in accordance with its specific laws and traditions. But Yeltsin was a different type of ruler. He saw it as his duty to prevent the theft of this sack of potatoes. He had to make sure that somebody planted these potatoes, somebody else would buy them, yet another person would buy the product, so that both the seller and the buyer were happy…

But for now he was under constant pressure; he read innumerable analytical memos. People were seeking his audience. Assistants, aides, representatives of movements and deputies were constantly in and out of his office. Everyone was trying to 'influence' him. The overall impression of this year was that he was losing his taste for political debates and conversations.

He was reading piles of those documents, thinking things over, keeping his silence.

But in his spare time he interacted with his new 'private circle'. He always valued a 'small team' more than a big official one.

'How open was he in this social sphere?' I ask of Yeltsin's daughter Tatyana.

'I don't know. I believe no one ever knew Dad completely.'

Yeltsin's 'private circle' in 1992 consisted of his Head of Administration, Yuri Petrov (his colleague from the Sverdlovsk *Obkom*), *Siloviki* ministers: Viktor Yerin (Minister of the Interior) and Pavel Grachev (Minister for Defence). Also, there were two more people present who belonged there not just out of duty, although they did deal with his security: Mikhail Barsukov and Alexander Korzhakov. Some new names emerged with time. Gradually, the circle was joined by his literary assistant Valentin Yumashev and a famous tennis player and coach Shamil Tarpishchev. This was understandable since there was a new passion in Yeltsin's life — tennis.

It all started in Jūrmala when, in 1988-1989, Shamil Tarpishchev first suggested to Yeltsin to pick up a racket. Upon his return to Moscow, Yeltsin started training regularly. First at the tennis court in Luzhniki* although later he discovered some other courts, somewhat more secluded and out of sight of Moscow's gaping public.

His partners in those years were a variety of people; however, most often his partner was Shamil Tarpishchev. Usually, they played against somebody from the close circle: Korzhakov, Foreign Minister Kozyrev, Secretary of State Burbulis or the abovementioned Yerin and Grachev. Tennis was a hobby for many of them.

The House of Receptions in Sparrow Hills built back in the days of Khrushchev became a 'tennis centre'. It was a beautiful private residence in the most spectacular part of Moscow, situated on the premises under surveillance and fitted out with a sports complex. Thus, starting from approximately 1992, there emerged something like an unofficial club that came to be called the 'presidential'. The most prominent figures in the new Russia would come here about once a week to play tennis and discuss

---

* A famous stadium in Moscow situated in the city district of the same name.

current affairs. The club had its rigid rules and a statute — 'the statute was prepared in jest but the code of conduct was defined there in detail,' writes Shamil Tarpishchev. 'If I want to use a tennis court I must call ahead and book it. And Korzhakov's booking was not given priority over, say, the booking made by Kozyrev. The only one for whom exceptions were made was, of course, Boris Nikolayevich... As far as I remember when I was leaving the Kremlin* the club already counted 56 members.'

As a matter of fact, in the XX century Boris Yeltsin was the first leader of Russia who had been professionally engaged in sports since his early youth. Authors of memoirs never noted that Nicholas II would have displayed any particular love for athletics. Out of all types of sportsmanship, Lenin preferred political discussions and Stalin — armed expropriation of banks. Brezhnev and Khrushchev gave all their young vim and vigour to the party work and Gorbachev... well, he didn't practise any sport either.

Everybody knows that an athlete's mentality is characterised by the unconquerable will to win, the subconscious ability to find fascination in a fight and a propensity for taking risk. At the same time, Yeltsin's main sporting trait was his total incapacity for losing — he responded to losing points like a child. Yeltsin's American biographer Leon Aron quotes an interview with his volleyball partner from the days in the Sverdlovsk *Obkom*. On that eventful evening Yeltsin formed two teams: the *Obkom* bureau versus Yeltsin's staff members.

'In the first game of this historic match the staff members wiped the floor with the bureau (Yeltsin's) team with the score of 15:2. Yeltsin got very agitated and hot-tempered. Having smashed their "bosses", the staff members came to their senses and for the second game decided to put forward a different set of players but even this team was superior to their adversaries, so they started winning again. It was only through Yeltsin's desperate efforts that his team managed to coordinate their performance and avoid losing the match in which only he and one other colleague were scoring. The captain Alekseev then ordered his team to lose and thus help the bureau save face. "We shall triumph in the third game," Yeltsin promised his team mates. However, when after the interval Alekseev

---

* In 1996. — *Author's comment.*

ordered, "First team, take your places!" they heard Yeltsin's voice, "No, this team stays!" In the heat of the contest Alekseev got carried away, so he turned to Yeltsin and asked, "Is this an order to lose?" Yeltsin didn't answer. The bureau won the third game and, thus, the match.

Yeltsin immediately came up to Alekseev, "Stop this circus!" So the teams arranged a more balanced share of talent. Some payers came over to Yeltsin and Petrov, after which a "good and fun" game started. Later, when presenting Yeltsin with the winner's pennant Alekseev couldn't keep from a barbed comment. In mock imitation of an official phrase he said, "So, Boris Nikolayevich, it was friendship that won!" Yeltsin, hot and sweaty in the face, answered sharply, "Which friendship are you talking about? It was our team's victory!" Alekseev felt as if he was "lashed with a whip". Yeltsin's information officer came up to him in the changing room, "You mustn't talk like this to the First Secretary!" "Look," Alekseev retorted, "we were both wearing shorts, we were on the sports ground and not in an office!" Fifteen years later Yeltsin's disagreeable reaction was still fresh in Alekseev's memory. But... all of it was brought on by the heat of competition. Yeltsin hated losing — whatever the game. He always fought to the bitter end. Such was his nature.'

His other passion in 1992 was Zavidovo — a hunting estate where Leonid Brezhnev had once made the US Secretary of State Henry Kissinger and his chums from the Warsaw Pact to fish and sit by the bonfire. Yeltsin loved this place. Hunting returned into his life after Sverdlovsk — as a hobby and a way of relaxing in 'the company of real men'. Yet the company in Zavidovo was something else. Yeltsin had always been the life and soul of any party, always reigning, always in the driving seat and unstoppable. A flow of his somewhat tough practical jokes, jests and goads was sometimes too much for his company. At the same time, unlike Brezhnev, he never switched to '*ty*', never was overly familiar with anyone. The only exception — apart from his university friends — was his assistant Lev Sukhanov who had provided him with moral support in the months of a heavy depression in 1988. He would even 'fraternise' with him — a barbarous boyish habit that he had carefully preserved from the times of his childhood: one is supposed to mix one's blood from a pricked finger with your 'brother's'. On the other hand, in public he said '*vy*' even to

Sukhanov. In a word, Yeltsin could open up in front of the people who made up this 'narrow circle' and to him it was vastly important.

Yet in Zavidovo it was as if his 'instinct of friendship' took on a different form. People that he addressed responded differently. Gaidar *never* came to Zavidovo. Here it was all clear: he was a different type of a person, with different habits and hobbies. Having become the Prime Minister, Chernomyrdin would come to Zavidovo all the time.

However, there were two more highly placed characters that could never put in an appearance here, on principle — Rutskoy and Khasbulatov — since from early 1992 both had become his bitter enemies.

Yeltsin writes about Ruslan Khasbulatov in his *President's Journal*:

'I remember who introduced us. It was Sergei Krasavchenko, chair of the Supreme Soviet's committee for economic reform and a member of the Interregional Group of Deputies. When Khasbulatov went out of my office Krasavchenko said, "Boris Nikolayevich, be firm with this person. You cannot leave him alone, that's the way he is. Keep an eye on him and make sure he is following, ok?" I recalled those mysterious words later but at the time, frankly speaking, they went straight out of my head. Khasbulatov seemed bright and cultured. He also seemed quiet.'

Professor in the Institute of National Economy, a Moscow Chechen Khasbulatov was, indeed, both bright and cultured. At the end of the eighties, he started actively publishing his articles wherein he talked about the disastrous state of our economy and the ways out of the crisis. Riding this wave, he was elected a deputy — in a word, it was a well-beaten path for a democrat of Gorbachev's invocation. Chechens are naturally brave and Khasbulatov, undoubtedly, acted courageously in 1991. He was intelligent and became Yeltsin's loyal associate in 1991, valued the chance given to him by Yeltsin, the chance to enter big-time politics and become a major player. In March 1991, at the most precarious, most dangerous moment, when armoured personnel carriers and troops had encircled the Supreme Soviet, Khasbulatov stayed loyal to Boris Nikolayevich. His quiet (and indeed, soft) voice worked magic with frenzied deputies. Suddenly, he became an irreplaceable figure at his post, a most valuable tamer of the congress. And finally, in the days of the August putsch, Khasbulatov was one of the most important members of Yeltsin's team. Caucasian temper, intelligence, self-control, dignity and willpower — he had it all, all those characteristics which turned out to be in great demand.

But in 1991, as many contemporaries could bear witness to, Khasbulatov expected that Yeltsin would offer him the post of Prime Minister and authorise him to form the government. In the end the government was formed by Gennady Burbulis, and Yegor Gaidar became the Prime Minister. Gaidar, who in the recent past had been head of a department in the prestigious magazine — *Communist*, used to repeatedly reject professor Khasbulatov's articles — a heinous offence.

So it really was not a good idea to 'leave him alone', tête-á-tête with his resentment and grievances. That was Yeltsin's biggest mistake in 1992. Everyone can take offence, but if you were as passionate as Ruslan Imranovich, the offence would start dominating your behaviour and become the propelling force of all your politics.

Alexander Drozdov, Khasbulatov's assistant in 1990-1992, Editor-in-Chief of the RSFSR Supreme Soviet's Presidium's paper *Rossiya*, recollects:

'Khasbulatov showed real subtlety when dealing with the Chechens. On the one hand, when I was his assistant and occupied an office across the corridor, I was told — we do not receive "relatives", especially those in a broader sense of the word, the countrymen. Still, there were those from Chechnya who were bringing some papers to sign. Mostly, the papers dealt with quotas, sales of petrol and petroleum pitch. I cannot say they were numerous but I paid attention to something else: the influence of the Chechens in the "Moscow sector" of the Russian economy grew immeasurably. It was apparent that they started feeling strong. On the other hand, I remember that Khasbulatov cut us short when we first published an article about Dudayev*. The gist was that nothing should ever be published in connection with this man. I think that Khasbulatov, with his elevated position within the new Russian leadership, had a terrific chance to put the relations with Chechnya on the right track or to find some other solution to the problem. This was probably his mission in history — to avert the later events — but what evidently came into

---

* *Dzhokhar Musayevich Dudayev* (1944-1996) was a Soviet Air Force general and a Chechen leader, the first President of the Chechen Republic of Ichkeria, a breakaway state in the North Caucasus.

play were clan (*teip*, in Chechen) relations and his implacable attitudes. Khasbulatov was our permanent author in *Komsomolskaya Pravda* where I had worked before and that was where we had first met. But generally speaking, I came to realise that we, the paper staff, had formed a wrong opinion about this charming and intelligent professor. I recall a series of his articles on Stalin and Soviet bureaucracy and how I realised that his profound interest in the subject was not coincidental.

'Initially, he wore a sweater to work and never tired of demonstrating his openness. At the time the White House was a place with unrestricted access, people worked there for the sake of ideas; it was the time of hopes and a spring of democracy. However, little by little, I started paying attention to how Khasbulatov was mediating sessions of the Supreme Soviet, what a brilliant actor he was, what a shrewd psychologist, how masterfully he combined the carrot and the stick and, most significantly, how quickly he was building himself up within the apparatus. Very rapidly, especially after the August of 1991, our jobs were redistributed and went to mature *apparatchiks* from the Central Committees of *Komsomol* and the Communist Party, the old friends from Old Square such as those from the Department for Ideology and the Department for General Administration. It was very obvious…

'Of course, he was very skilful in dealing with the Supreme Soviet. Yeltsin generally found it a burden — all those procedural issues, technical issues, time limits, and the endless coordination. Yet Khasbulatov was a natural who knew how to make his audience eat out of his hand and how to manipulate it. In a way, he was somewhat compensating for Yeltsin and so, initially, the latter treated him with respect, and what's more — not as some shadow leader but a very serious figure in the political field. Yet gradually these deeply rooted personal traits of his started coming to the fore: his hierarchical thinking and the striving for supreme control within an entity created by him. Sometimes it manifested itself quite unexpectedly, for example, in the shape of totally extraordinary loutishness and a complete lack of self-criticism. Generally speaking, he didn't see a single figure that he would believe to be his equal and moreover considered himself to be an historian, an economist, a politician as well as an analyst.

'True, Ruslan Imranovich had many gifts: an economist with a degree in law, a person who could wield a skilful pen — in short, a brilliant man of many talents. Still, he failed the trial by power and there probably came a moment when he asked himself: why Yeltsin? I can do as well myself. By then, not only did he have a powerful apparatus and a huge influence over the Supreme Soviet, he fell in love with the attributes of power that included personal bodyguards and the flat. He was first offered a flat formerly occupied by Gorbachev, then Brezhnev's flat in Shchusev Street of which he chose the latter*.

'Once, when a letter by Yeltsin was being discussed at the Presidium, he said, "If you cannot chop off the hand kiss it!" It was his understanding of folk wisdom.'

In the beginning of 1992, Khasbulatov first 'tested his vocal cords', and with a good reason: the Constitution of the RSFSR treated the congress as the country's supreme legitimate power. Russia's presidency was introduced by an amendment to the Constitution. Thus, another amendment — and the presidency in Russia would simply vanish. Should this be the case, who would be the first person in the country? He, the Chairman of the Supreme Soviet. The power at stake was so huge that it dictated a certain logic of actions.

The story with the government was even more straightforward. The congress approved the Prime Minister and the congress could annul any decree by the President or the government. The reason? Russia's fundamental law was Soviet in spirit, and in the new context it simply didn't work. Any decision required endless amendments: say, to elect a new Procurator General, or a new head of the Central Bank, and so on. At the end of 1991 the congress did make certain concessions to Yeltsin and during the period of 'transition' granted his decrees the status of laws, although even those could be vetoed, if necessary, by two thirds of the votes. Or one could make an amendment and Yeltsin's decrees would be revoked by a simple majority. An amendment to the Constitution was a simple but powerful tool introduced by Yeltsin himself in 1990. Most significantly, however, Yeltsin had no right to dissolve the congress but the congress could dismiss the President.

All this had been known before but previously Yeltsin and Khasbulatov had worked in a tandem, and the problem was how to make the congress

---

* Yeltsin declined to move in. — *Author's comment.*

agree to this or that decision. Now Yeltsin would have to *plead*— whatever the issue at hand. Whether he wanted to keep Gaidar, or set the timeframe for stabilisation projects, or adopt new laws — whatever the idea his hand was always weaker. Under the Constitution, the only master was the congress. By now Khasbulatov's grievances had accumulated into a critical mass and from the high podium he launched a personal campaign aimed at letting the society realise: both the President and the government were completely in his power.

Khasbulatov took some additional steps: the guards in the Supreme Soviet were now heavily armed and much more numerous. He lured Vice President Rutskoy and the lobbyists from the Civil Union over to his side — thus strengthening his own position. Through deputies, he increased his profile in various regions. He was clearly getting ready but for now all remained subtle and discreet. The denouement finally occurred at the Seventh Congress of People's Deputies.

As for the congress itself, by 1992 the Russian People's Deputies were, in essence, a new political class. In the days of the USSR deputies of the Supreme Soviet had acted as representatives of their regions who didn't live or work in Moscow: this 'silent majority' of political extras was there to vote, obediently, several times a year, in favour of laws and decrees developed by the Central Committee, ministries and departments. Maximum of what they could achieve was to ask a 'guy sitting next to me', perhaps some minister or member of the Central Committee, for some indulgence or additional financing for their region.

But the new times changed it all. Now the Russian deputies were working on a professional basis. Former plant managers, school and university teachers, secretaries of *Obkoms* and executive committees, provincial bosses of various calibre — now were a new and influential elite. They were driven around in chauffeured cars with governmental licence plates, received keys to state-owned flats and, most importantly, could decide on the destiny of their country.

According to social polls in 1992, this new 'political class' was even less popular then the government — for all its 'reforms of robbery'. These self-important 'upstarts' irritated more than Gaidar's incomprehensible reforms. Gaidar at least 'knew what he was doing'. The deputies clearly didn't have a clue and their only claim to fame was participation in endless voting. Their names and faces were totally unmemorable (unlike deputies of the Gorbachev's congress) but they formed the principal decision-making body in the country. And though unpopular, the deputies started slowly but surely pulling the rope in this tug-of-war over to their side. This grey political quagmire finally started worrying Yeltsin. At the same time the amorphous mass took shape and became combustible.

For all this, at the Seventh Congress in December of 1992 Yeltsin was, as ever, ready for a compromise. What he needed was not war but breathing space — to be able to bring at least the first stage of the project to fruition, to see the initial results. And Yeltsin offered the deputies a formula: a 'period for stabilisation' that would mean a moratorium on any decisions that undermined the systems of power.

However, no moratorium was on the cards. 'A hostile murmur was coming from the audience. One could physically sense ill will. Only a couple of times during the speech there was some lukewarm applause that came from the benches occupied by democratic factions,' Yeltsin's aides would write later.

Khasbulatov made a move. He made some incendiary statements: 'The complete fiasco of the economic policy', 'the economy had become uncontrollable, the process had acquired characteristics of a speedy disintegration', and finally — the country needed a new government. Khasbulatov's economic priorities were somewhat reminiscent of Brezhnev's era — 'the prices had to be regulated', for example. Finally, he responded to Yeltsin personally: 'Of course, there is an unquestionable need for a more or less lasting period of stabilisation but it is hardly right to deviate from the Constitution and the laws even during such a period.' And according to the Constitution, the government could be fired here and now!

'The President,' write his aides, 'was listening to his rival's speech with a hardened grim face.'

At the congress, Gaidar also made a speech. He was aware of the fact that for this audience he was an enemy and that it made no sense to persuade, to prove, to resort to eloquence. In a quiet and measured voice, he read his report — full of statistics and computations, and this professional academic tonality sent the deputies into a fit of rage.

One witness wrote, 'Now, when he is sitting in this aggressively-minded audience, Yeltsin faces a dilemma: either tolerate this *unbearable humiliation*\*, bob and weave in search of a compromise, or heed the advice of those who had long been trying to talk him into the dissolution of the congress.'

At this moment Yeltsin had, in his suit pocket, several pages with the text of his speech which said, among other things:

'The congress that has transformed itself exclusively into a podium of destructive criticism and is incapable of creative work, has now discarded its responsibilities for the fate of Russia and its people. The congress has outlived its usefulness. When receiving the power of the President from our people I pledged to serve the new democratic Russia. Adhering to this oath today I must resort to decisive measures.'

But these words were never pronounced.

Yeltsin was still within the paradigm of 'looking for a third way'. In a private meeting with faction coordinators he gave a promise that law enforcement ministers (*Siloviki*) should be approved (in effect — appointed) by the Supreme Soviet which, from his side, was a gigantic political concession...

Today all of this inspires complex feelings. True, the deputies and their pointless verbiage were irritating. True, Khasbulatov was getting on everyone's nerves with his intrigues and lugubrious pronouncements. True, all that endless political manoeuvring made the viewers want to cry out — oh, damn it, to hell with it all!

But there was life there. It was open politics.

He was still guided by the logic of compromise.

Yet there was no compromise to be had!

Khasbulatov was pushing for a decision on Constitutional amendments that would allow the Supreme Soviet to form (or dismiss) the government which, effectively meant that the Supreme Soviet would become the only ruler of Russia

---

\* Italics are mine. — *Author's comment.*

So when on the evening of that day, when Yeltsin returned home and locked himself up in the sauna, it was not because he was piqued or peeved — it was because he was feverishly calculating his options. His team set to work but the idea took a long time in gestation. On the tenth day of the Congress's Yeltsin, in his speech, used the phrase 'a creeping coup'. This was already serious. The memories of how Yeltsin had dealt with the previous coup were still all too fresh.

This is how he defined the real agenda of the congress — the way he saw it:

'Firstly, to create conditions... under which the President and the government would find it intolerable to operate, in effect — to demoralise them.

'Secondly, to introduce, whatever the cost, amendments to the Constitution that would vest huge authority and rights in the Supreme Soviet that has become a stronghold of conservative and reactionary forces.

'Thirdly, to block reforms and impede all positive developments, thereby preventing the situation from stabilising itself.

'Fourthly, to convene, in April, the Eighth Congress of People's Deputies whereat to lynch both the government and the President along with the reforms, and democracy...

'I blame myself for agreeing, repeatedly, to political concessions, something I did for the sake of reaching a political consensus... Working with such a congress has become impossible.

'I had no illusions,' Yeltsin continued, 'and yet I was hoping that... the deputies, particularly those who come from the provinces, would take a reasonable approach to my proposals and demonstrate common sense.

'The walls of this hall are blushing from this incessant stream of abuse, obscene language used against specific individuals, wickedness, rudeness and pushiness that are sweeping over the congress, morbid ambitions of frustrated politicians, their fistfights — what a disgrace for all to see! The Constitution, or what it has become, is turning the Supreme Soviet, its leadership and Chairman into monopolistic rulers of Russia. They have elevated themselves above all executive bodies but, as before, they hold responsibility for nothing.'

He paused. The audience could hardly believe their ears. They were petrified. He came to the crux of the matter.

'I believe it imperative to appeal directly to all citizens of Russia, to all voters. I see the way out of this deepest crisis of power only in a national referendum. I am not insisting on the dissolution of the congress but ask the citizens of the country to identify whose side they are on.'

'The deputies heard him out in deadly silence,' write Yeltsin's assistants. 'What they feared most of all was quickly becoming a reality. The situation was all the more dramatic since the President's speech was transmitted live by two central TV channels. Preparations for this live broadcast had been carried out in strict secrecy — only two TV bosses (...) and President's press secretary Kostikov knew anything about it.

'In effect, Yeltsin addressed the nation directly over the heads of the deputies. When Khasbulatov worked out that Yeltsin's speech was being broadcast live he turned pale as a sheet but couldn't change a thing.'

Yeltsin suggested that the deputies who supported the President should leave the hall and move over to the Hall of Facets* — the congress was taking place in the Grand Kremlin Palace. However, this dramatic move didn't work. At the time he was only supported by an isolated few, and many were undecided. When the buzz subsided, most deputies remained seated.

Nevertheless, it was during this congress that Yeltsin came to an important and symbolic decision: he accepted the resignation of Gennady Burbulis, the Secretary of State and the First Vice-Premier, the man who had been instrumental in recruiting Yeltsin's first government and greatly its influenced initial steps.

According to his press secretary at the time, Gennady Burbulis commented thus:

"'That's the way it should be done," he said finally. "In view of the President's position, it is even possible to draw some political benefits from his decision. This is a move rich in symbolism. However, some things are clear already. We must finally translate into reality our thoughts about a party, maybe, a presidential party, generally speaking, an entity which will work for the future, for the elections. In a nutshell, I spoke to Yeltsin half an hour ago. He called me and said that I had been appointed head of the group of presidential advisors and that the post of the Secretary of State has been eliminated..."'

---

* A famous hall in the Kremlin whose walls are decorated with mufti-faceted ornaments.

Why did her agree to accept this resignation — and similarly, that of Mikhail Poltoranin that followed shortly?

Poltoranin and Burbulis were loyal presidential associates and powerful statesmen. So when those two, just like Khasbulatov, started clashing with each other, exacerbating tensions which were already high, Yeltsin decided to make this move that he believed to be purely tactical. He was confident that sooner or later both would be back.

Yet it didn't work out quite like that. The role of closest advisors gradually moved from Burbulis and Poltoranin to the experts and genuine advisors, analysts –not independent figures and public politicians. Their work was coordinated by President's senior aide Viktor Iliushin.

It appears that the heart of the matter was this: Burbulis was, in essence, a 'party leader', that is an ideologue of a party that had never been created. Sooner or later, democrats of the Gorbachev era were leaving, for Yeltsin had no time for the 'party' logic and 'party' mentality.

Besides, it seemed to him that by sacrificing Burbulis he would save Gaidar.

There were other disagreeable episodes such as the speech made by Defence Minister Barannikov. As soon as the referendum was first mentioned, Khasbulatov summoned him and asked him severely whether he was loyal to the Constitution and the congress. A military man, Barannikov answered without a hitch, 'Glad to serve Russia! Hoorah!' Even Khasbulatov found it disagreeable.

Chairman of the Constitutional Court Valery Zorkin, yet another 'mild-mannered professor' of the early democratic era, was also present at the congress as a guest. He had just declared the ban on the communist party illegal, so the congress could count on his support. The move must have been planned by Khasbulatov: Zorkin's role was to explain to Yeltsin that his idea of a referendum was inappropriate. His voice soft and cultured, Zorkin was urging Yeltsin and Khasbulatov to make peace.

This proved to be quite possible: the Conciliatory Commission, the working group and experts jointly laboured around the clock and produced the decree for the next congress: 'On Stabilising the Constitutional System of the Russian Federation' wherein Point One stipulated that on April 11th a referendum should be held… not just on whether to give a vote of confidence to President or the congress but on 'a draft of the fundamental provisions of the new Constitution'. Thus, enactment of the amendments to the current Constitution (the ones limiting Presidential powers which provoked Yeltsin's harsh response) was suspended. To the joy of the congress, President reciprocated by agreeing to put to a vote candidatures for the post of Prime Minister. At the cost of an immense effort the compromise was reached.

Still, Yeltsin obstinately included Gaidar in the list of eighteen candidates. Right before the vote, Gaidar asked Yeltsin to have a word. He reminded him their earlier conversation — that whilst the President would most definitely have to sacrifice his first government, he should support Viktor Chernomyrdin's nomination for the post of the Premier, since the latter had had several months' experience of working within his government.

Yeltsin had a right to go for any nomination from the list since the procedure had no legal base. However, since Gaidar received only 245 votes and Chernomyrdin had twice that, he gave up...

Chernomyrdin's candidature was welcomed with enthusiasm.

Gaidar's resignation stunned not only for the political elite but the society on the whole. It looked like Yeltsin suffered his first serious political defeat. We all felt that the President held this peculiar and intensely private academic very dear and were ready to tough it out — maybe for a year, maybe longer — to the bitter end. And although both the deputies and the press were busy making Gaidar a whipping boy, now there was no one to hold responsible.

As Khasbulatov and the congress were celebrating their victory and the democrats were bemoaning their bitter loss, Yeltsin finally got it. He finally grasped to where 'the lion should leap'.

... If you remember, on the evening of Gaidar's resignation, Naina Iosifovna gave him a call. As they were talking she burst into tears. Hard to say what solace Gaidar had to offer. Most likely, he simply said, 'Come on, Naina Iosifovna, it will be all right. Just believe me.'

# Ten Blanks
*(1993)*

His mother came to visit Yeltsin in Moscow during the most turbulent period, in early 1993. By that time Klavdia Vasilievna was already 84. Yeltsin writes little about Klavdia Vasilievna in his memoirs but there are exceptions.

For example, in the first volume of his *Confessions* he recalls:

'Mum told me about how I was baptised. The little church with a priest was the only one for the entire region of several villages. Births were quite plentiful but infants were only christened one day a month that is why, on this particular day, the priest was working very hard: parents, infants and crowds were all milling around him. The baptism was arranged in a somewhat primitive fashion: there was a tub with some holy fluid — water with certain herbs. A baby would be dipped in, head and all, then pulled out, blue in the face from screaming, pronounced christened, given a name and recorded in the church ledger. As is the way in the country, parents would offer the priest a glass of spirit, some home-made brew, moonshine, vodka — whatever they could...

Taking into account that my turn only came up in the second half of the day, by then the priest could barely stand. My mother, Klavdia Vasilievna, and my father, Nikolai Ignatievich, handed me over to him and he dunked me in the tub. The problem was that he forgot to pull me back out, for he got carried away theologising about something with the congregation. My parents were apparently some distance from the font and couldn't work out what was going on immediately. When they did, Mum rushed forward screaming, dragged me up from the bottom, and yanked me out. They resuscitated me. I cannot say that this is what influenced my attitude to religion, of course it didn't. Actually, the priest wasn't too upset. "Well," he said, "once he's survived this trial he must be strong and shall be named Boris…"'

Klavdia Vasilievna believed in God. Even in 1931, when religion was all but outlawed, when crosses had been knocked off the church buildings and churches themselves were closing. At this time, the clergy were routinely executed, religion was denounced in schools and newspapers were carrying malicious satirical articles about 'the accursed clergy' — these people, along with other community members were still going to the church since it was the only way of life they knew. Without God, life made no sense. Be it as it may, Boris Yeltsin unquestionably grew up as an atheist. Indeed, as a *Komsomol* member he recalls making his Mum remove the main icons from the living room

As President of the country, Yeltsin first put in an appearance at the patriarchal service on Russian Orthodox Christmas, 7 January 1992 and again in 1993. Yeltsin was the first state leader who, following the demise of the Soviet power, openly admitted the role of the church in the spiritual life of the country. Perhaps, in some way, he was making it up to his mother after his earlier dismissal!

Sometimes he would sit together with his mother in the kitchen and have long quiet conversations. She would ask something. How is this one doing, and that one…? She was curious about things 'they don't mention on the TV'. Sometimes she would just look at him in silence. In Alexander Sokurov's[*] documentary Yeltsin would refer to these times with heartfelt words, full of love and pain. 'She would look like that, would give me those long gazes…'. And then the last, the hardest day came.

Writing about it in his *President's Journal* he says:

'Mum died at half ten in the morning. It was a Sunday. The day before, on March 20th, she had watched TV with the rest of the family. She

---

[*] *Alexander Nikolayevich Sokurov* (b. 1951) is a Russian filmmaker. His most recent significant works include a semi-documentary, Russian Ark (2002), filmed in a single unedited shot, and Faust (2011), which was honoured with the Golden Lion, the highest prize for the best film at the Venice Film Festival.

watched my statement about the imposition of the state of emergency*. She came up to me, gave me a kiss, told me, "Well done, Borya!" and retired to her room.

The previous day, Sunday, saw the opening of the extraordinary session of the Supreme Soviet, with Democratic Russia and communists rallying in Moscow squares. I was attending to all of this, preparing the next steps, researching the information for the coming session and in constant communication by phone with the enforcement ministries and Chernomyrdin. By midday I was first informed about Mum being poorly. I said, "What are you waiting for? Take her to the hospital!" They replied that doctors were attending to her, an ambulance had been called.

She died a quiet death, in her sleep, very still. That's what the doctors told me. There was a church funeral service. Mum was buried at the Kuntsevo Cemetery in Moscow.'

It so happened that that very week, starting from the day of Klavdia Vasilievna's death — March 21st, and up to March 28th — proved to be a turning point. From that week onwards, he stopped losing ground to the congress and started gaining, slowly, gradually, missing points from time to time, but surely progressing towards his goal. It could be said that Yeltsin's entire being was mobilised because of his mother's death. There is no question that Yeltsin's mother was a survivor, like much of the family, but in her case she was always sustained by her self-sacrifice for the good of her family.

Yeltsin recalled: 'I felt hungry all the time. Whether I was two, three, five, ten or fifteen — I was hungry, hungry, hungry. Just imagine. Mum was cutting up those tiny slices of bread, about as big as half a finger, ever so thin, for all members in the family, and we were five. She would give it around and keep the tiniest bit for herself, of course. This is my earliest and the strongest memory of my childhood,' he once said in an interview. His mother was an inspiration, she had overcome death and danger and survived the horror of daily existence: hunger, diseases, cold, the cruelty of people and the times.

Within the session of the Supreme Soviet of Russia on 21 March, not a word was said about Klavdia Vasilievna's demise. No official message of condolences was offered to the President, neither at the congress nor at the session. But on March 22nd, the session closed for one day. To make

---

* To be precise, the "special procedures for governance". — *Author's comment*.

amends for the absence of official condolences, Vice President Rutskoy with the Chairman of the Constitutional Court, unexpectedly turned up at the Kuntsevo Cemetery with a wreath but were quietly asked to leave. How had this dysfunctional state of affairs arisen?

To return to events at the beginning of 1993, on January 5th, the newly-appointed Prime Minister Chernomyrdin announced that the government was about to introduce regulated prices for some staple items. Market reform supporters were shocked. The new Vice-Premier for economic matters, Boris Fyodorov, took it upon himself to make clear to the head of government the ruinous effects of such a step. Yeltsin also excoriated the government. As a result, the government's decree was repudiated. In the same month, the Constitutional Court issued a resolution whereby the ban imposed by Yeltsin in 1992 on the activities of the Front for National Rescue was to be lifted. The Front, which was openly appealing to overthrow the 'the regime of fascist occupation' and unashamedly preaching the threat of a 'Judo-Masonic conspiracy', thereby became legitimate.

Russian communists also gained legality. In the same month of January they convened their united congress where they gave a standing ovation to GKChP members released from custody and Gennady Ziuganov was appointed the party leader.

Moreover, the Eighth Congress of People's Deputies that was in session from March 10th to March 13th in Moscow revoked all agreements had been reached between all branches of power on December 12th. Thus, with Gaidar's resignation, the deputies' mood was triumphant — they were eager to limit Yeltsin's power even further. Khasbulatov, the Speaker of the Congress, promised that there would be no more compromises with the Kremlin. The congress of Russia's People's Deputies stripped the President of the majority of his emergency powers. Also, the congress passed a resolution banning the call for a referendum in 1993 as had been requested by Yeltsin at the previous congress.

Quoting Article 104 of the Constitution of 1974 the parliament announced itself the supreme power in the land.

On 20 March 1993 Yeltsin appealed to the nation on TV proclaiming:

'The country cannot carry on in a situation of a perpetual crisis of power ...if we continue wasting our resources in this way we shall never extricate ourselves from abject poverty, shall never secure peace for our citizens'.

The Eighth Congress was, in effect, the ex-party *nomenklatura* taking revenge.

The congress has buried a referendum on the private ownership of land and done away with the April referendum on the fundamental precepts of a new constitution. The tragic consequence of the congress was the undermining of the power structures and the governance of Russia itself. In effect, there were two governments in the country: a constitutional one in the Kremlin and one seated in the Supreme Soviet whilst pursuing fundamentally diverging policies.'

Yeltsin had signed a decree 'On Special Procedures for Governance until the Crisis of Power is Overcome' under which April 25th was announced as the day of the vote of confidence in the President and Vice President. 'I have resorted to this for one reason only,' said the President. 'I was not elected by the Congress or the Supreme Soviet. I have been elected by the people. So it is up to them to decide whether I should continue in this capacity and who should rule the country: the President and Vice President or the congress of People's Deputies.'

Concurrently, a vote should be taken on the draft of a new constitution and the draft law on the election of the federal parliament. Under the new Constitution, there would be no congress. Both the Congress and the Supreme Soviet should continue their work until the new election, their powers should be maintained. However, under this Decree, any decisions made by governmental bodies and officials aimed at revocation or suspension of the presidential instructions and the government's resolutions should be declared null and void.

Vice President Rutskoy rushed to the Constitutional Court and urgently, even before it was officially published, submitted the text of the Decree to them. The Constitutional Court convened for an emergency meeting and declared the text of the unpublished document (i.e. the document that had not yet come into force) unlawful. Yeltsin's team was also split. The Secretary of the Security Council, Yuri Skokov, refused to endorse the decree. This was worrying since Skokov was close to the *Siloviki*. The position of the army and militia was unclear since they may not feel able to crack down on the mass riots which would undoubtedly take place.

On March 24th, the decree 'on special procedures of governance' did come out but in a much more streamlined format. The 'special procedures', that is a moratorium on the congress's decisions aimed at curtailing presidential powers, was not mentioned at all. On the day of the decree's publication Yeltsin, assisted by Chernomyrdin, met Khasbulatov and Zorkin in the Kremlin. At this meeting behind closed doors he made the last attempt 'to come to an agreement': 'he didn't want either this congress or a resolution of the acutely aggravated crisis by force, that is, by dispelling the congress.' (*Yeltsin's Epoch*).

Nevertheless, they failed to reach an understanding.

The Supreme Soviet urgently convoked the Ninth Extraordinary Congress of the People's Deputies. Once again, the country, with a heavy sigh, installed itself in front of their TVs. What was going to happen?

To start with, the events were unfolding in a fashion that was neither one thing nor the other. The Chairman of the Constitutional Court, Valery Zorkin, made a presentation, the gist of which was abundantly straightforward: a number of provisions of the President's televised appeal to the nation broadcast on March 20th run counter to the Constitution. Clearly, officials that 'had misled the President' while he was preparing his appeal to the nation 'must be held responsible and removed from their posts'. On the evening of March 25 6th, Yeltsin dismissed two more members of Gaidar's team: Minister of Economics, Andrei Nechayev, and Minister of Finance, Vasily Barchuk. Barchuk was replaced with Boris Fyodorov, an intelligent and even more progressive liberal economist. Yet when speaking at the congress the President confirmed that he was ready to make even more replacements. He was trying to compromise whilst engaging in *tactical* substitutions and had no intention of altering his course.

On March 26th Yeltsin addressed the congress. Having reminded the delegates that the national vote and referendum to be held in April would also include the issue of the confidence in the President, he suggested that the ballot papers should also include the question of confidence in the congress. On March 26th the assembly also considered the issue of placing on the agenda the question of terminating the presidential powers. This, however, did not receive quite enough votes to make it onto the agenda. The deputies did go on to decree that the results of the 'poll' should be taken in relation to the total number of eligible voters, not the number of those who would cast their votes at the ballot boxes. In other words, they were disavowing the results of the vote in advance

However, on March 27th another development sent the whole country into turmoil yet again. Late in the evening, completely unexpectedly and against all plans, Yeltsin climbed the congress podium. He was dishevelled, enraged like a wounded bull with his clothes in disarray — a virtually unprecedented occurrence. He was labouring his phrases.

'Esteemed People's Deputies, we have gathered here to come to an agreement. Shall we leave having failed to settle our differences? Neither the Russian people nor our voters will understand us. They will never forgive this. Of course, I am, just like you, maybe... no, not maybe — for sure, I am responsible, up to a high degree, for such a situation. But you were also jointly passing decisions at the previous congresses but I harbour no hard feelings! These decisions were the right ones but, unfortunately, we have failed so far to bear them out. I believe we should calm down. Let us at least create a draft resolution that will keep a quiet and balanced tonality, so that our people, the Russian people, can calm down and get to work.'

It is not what he said, not the words he used, it was the way he said it.

The deputies were discountenanced and taken aback.

In a TV interview in 2007 Shamil Tarpishchev, Yeltsin's tennis coach maintained that would say that Yeltsin conceived this idea of 'showing 'em' (the congress) after a game of tennis, on the spur of the moment.' The coach remonstrated: 'Boris Nikolayevich, but what about your appearance, your hair? And he answered: it's OK; let them see a genuine Yeltsin.'

As a result, another conference amongst a closed circle took place late at night. The President and the congress tried to work out a new agreement. Yeltsin forced the leadership of the congress to sit down at the negotiating table.

During the morning of March 28th events at the congress started developing at a precipitous rate. In the morning, a meeting took place between Yeltsin, Khasbulatov, Chernomyrdin and Zorkin. Representatives of the republics, territories and oblasts were also in attendance. An agreement was reached: instead of a referendum, there should be an early election of the President and the deputies. This agreement formed the basis of a draft resolution distributed among deputies.

The events that took place that evening, night and morning galvanised the Ninth Extraordinary Congress. The deputies flew into a rage at this new accord between the two branches of power. The major concern, of course, was the pre-term election. The issue of an impeachment rapidly made its way onto the agenda. The 'swamp', the more passive part of the congress, quickly worked out their less than glorious prospects. Yeltsin was taking a risk when he demanded early elections of both the President and the Congress but he knew what he was getting himself into: he was determined to cut the knot of this prolonged stand-off at whatever cost. Had the opposition at the congress managed to get two thirds of votes (689 out of 1,033), this would have spelled immediate defeat for Yeltsin. 'It was one of the most dangerous moments in the country's post-war history and maybe in the history of the entire humankind... At this point, there was no clarity whatsoever about who commands the Russian army, militia and border guards. The country came as close to a civil war as it had done during the attempted coup in the August of 1991,' wrote Yegor Gaidar later.

Yeltsin's supporters gathered for a rally at the Vasilievsky Spusk* nearby St Basil's cathedral. Several thousand people were anxiously awaiting news from the congress. Yeltsin made two more appearances there. The first time was before the vote. He was alone. The second time was afterwards, and as Gaidar would say in his memoirs, it was 'with a numerous and cheerful entourage'.

In the late evening an improvised podium was set up on a lorry with a side let down. The impeachment had failed! The deputies fell short by 72 votes. The President's voice amplified by speakers carried across the Red Square. Transmitted by television, it was carried over the entire country of Russia. 'I owe a debt of gratitude to you, my dear Muscovites, for your support... I shall do all I can to justify your confidence... the communists failed in their attempt to start a coup. They were overpowered by the people, the reforms, democracy and young Russia.'

His triumph was in the fact that it proved possible to prevent a civil war. For all of that, what was the price? In December, he had failed to preserve Gaidar's government. He proved unable to introduce the so-called 'period

---

* Basils Descent. A 'descent' (spusk), in Russian, refers to an established path leading down to a water body. This particular descent is running down from Red Square (St Basil's cathedral) to the Moskva River.

of stabilisation' — that is, to reach an agreement with the parliament on a truce, albeit a temporary one. The previous year he had failed to achieve financial stabilisation — this was because the Supreme Soviet appointed Gerashchenko Chairman of the Central Bank and the latter set the treasury printing machines operating at full capacity. The country was caught up in an avalanche of hyperinflation. The impeachment that very nearly took place in March showed yet again that power in Russia was hanging in the balance. The following day, the congress that had by now ended up in a complete deadlock finally approved of a referendum (not a poll) to be held on April 25th and endorsed its questions.

What would have happened had the deputies given those 72 votes needed for an impeachment on March 28th? A question many people were asking at the time. The Presidential Security Service (SBP) prepared a scenario of emergency measures to avert the congress declaring itself a supreme power, to prevent Rutskoy from being sworn in. This scenario included switching off the lights in the hall and 'neutralising' deputies through the use of sleeping gas. Each deputy had already been assigned to an SBP staff member and, under this plan, they would have been led out of the audience, carried out, evacuated. Impeachment would have been a disaster for Russia which ever outcome had prevailed — whether power had ended up in the hands of Rutskoy and Khasbulatov or if the plan prepared by the 'enforcement' agencies been carried out. Whatever the final pathway, almost certainly it would have been some general that would have ended up at the head of the country.

Indeed, there were quite a few generals that year who were eager to carry out their personal 'emergency rescue plans'. Their full-scale performance would follow in October whereas for now it was just the rehearsals. There was, for example, General Achalov, a former Commander-in-Chief of the Airborne Forces and Deputy Defence Minister. Back in 1981, naturally, on the Central Committee's orders, he very nearly introduced troops into mutinous Poland — the Polish General Jaruzelski got in the way by imposing his cosmetic 'state of emergency' and thus saving the country from invasion. In 1990, he entered Baku in order to suppress the riots. The army was too late to stop the carnage of the Armenian pogroms but by then the purpose lay elsewhere: the crushing of the 'Popular Front' and the crackdown on the Azerbaijani uprising. General Achalov was giving orders during hostilities in Vilnius, as a result of which 13 residents of the Lithuanian capital were killed. He was preparing the 'second annexation of the Baltic states'. In 1991, he was among the GKChP leaders.

Now, in 1993, he was once more ready to save the nation. In his capacity of an influential Supreme Soviet member General Achalov was building bridges between the Supreme Soviet and the Armed Forces. Being aware of political manoeuvring by his former colleague and boss, Defence Minister Grachev issued a special order: the armed forces are outside politics, the army shall not attack its own people, and the army shall stay neutral. This formula, 'the army shall stay neutral', proved of some significance. Later, in October, Yeltsin would urge Grachev to abandon this but back then, in May, the 'armed neutrality' seemed good.

The direct appeal to the nation, a hallmark of all of Yeltsin's years in power proved a great vindication. The total turnout was 64% of voters. Not only did the people say 'yes' to Yeltsin himself (53%) but the majority also voted for his socio-economic policy (58.7%). A majority had also voted for early re-election of Deputies but the congress had already 'indemnified' themselves in advance since the relevant resolution had decreed that the decision on the early election would be adopted only if the vote was related to a majority of the total number of voters.

Five days passed and then came 1 May 1993 when a rally convened near Kaluzhskaya Square where a statue of Lenin still remained. Led by irreconcilable opposition leaders, there followed a march of militant 'people's squads'*, activists of Anpilov's Working Russia and Terekhov's Officers' Union, all of them are ready for street fighting. They were armed with cobblestones and iron rods and they were well-versed in the methodology of street clashes. However, at the head of the columns, as a rule, walked old people, pensioners, and war veterans with their medals — of course the militia could not touch them. The 'red columns' intended to break through militia cordons and get to the centre: via Bolshaya Yakimanka and

---

* Voluntary People's Druzhina, variously translated as Voluntary People's Guard, People's Volunteer Squads, People's Volunteer Militia, etc. were voluntary detachments for maintaining public order in the Soviet Union — an idea similar to that of the Neighbourhood Watch.

the Big Stone Bridge, to Manezhnaya Square. Backstreets and courtyards near Kaluzhskaya Square were packed with people. Militia cordons were under pressure, crowds were surging forward; scuffles, scrambles and panic ensued. One militia man was crushed under the wheels of a stolen truck. He was the first casualty of the duality of power.

The duality of power was omnipresent and it was already dictating the rules of life. The essence of duality of power was duality of legitimacy: on the one hand, an absolutely legitimate Presidential power, now confirmed by the people. Yet the congress was also legitimate. What's more, under the Constitution its authority surpassed that of the President. Up to a point this situation was predictable. Yeltsin's legitimacy was based not on some established state institutions or the popular unity, for neither existed. Yeltsin's power was supported only by the people's personal trust in their leader, the president of the country. Yet it wasn't enough for staying in power.

It was around this time that the stance taken by the country's vice president, Alexander Rutskoy, finally became crystallised. In March of 1991, Rutskoy was heading the Communists for Democracy faction and, rather unexpectedly, supported Yeltsin in the turbulent debates at the congress. Constitutional amendments on introducing the institution of presidency also provided for the election of a Vice President. Time was passing and a suitable candidate couldn't be identified. Finally, several days prior to submitting the documents to the election committee, the speechwriters themselves suggested Rutskoy — an erstwhile military pilot, awarded the title of the Hero of the Soviet Union for his performance in Afghanistan, a handsome and charismatic man, Rutskoy was expected to attract to Yeltsin the votes of vacillating communists, army personnel and their families, and the female vote.

It transpired rather quickly that Rutskoy was very different to Yeltsin and had no intuitive rapport with him. Gradually, all of Rutskoy's programmes — the anti-corruption commission, the military reform, agricultural reform — started revealing the same discrepancy between the form and content: striking pronouncements on the outside and a total vacuum within. Little by little, Rutskoy was becoming ridiculous. However, in the situation of split powers he was growing dangerous, too. Dangerous is anybody whose vanity is injured, particularly if it is a person in a highly elevated position. Starting from 1992, Rutskoy was increasingly gravitating towards Khasbulatov on the political arena. During the crisis in March of 1993 he was completely at one with the congress, the Supreme Soviet and the Speaker himself. He had handed over the unpublished text of the presidential decree on 'emergency measures' for the period of transition to Yeltsin's adversaries. Indeed, it was Rutskoy who set the impeachment ball rolling.

Technically, still in the Kremlin and on Yeltsin's team, he was becoming, ever more clearly, a player for the opposing side. Instead of honourably resigning, he embarked on a path of direct conflict and betrayal.

With ministers, procurators and the Vice President continually defecting from one centre of power to the other — all of this was just one aspect of the deepening crisis. Of greater concern was the fact that the crisis of dual power was undermining the economy.

The Supreme Soviet approved the inflationary budget. Yeltsin incorporated his corrections. The Supreme Soviet rejected them. The privatisation programme met with vehement resistance in the provinces. In effect, each region of Russia, each town and city had two independent leaders, two bosses: one headed the Oblast Soviet and the other was the head of local administration, the governor. At times, they would cancel each other's orders, at times — their instructions would be mutually contradictory. Gradually, local executive bodies were thwarted and resorted to simply going through the motions.

In July of 1993 the Central Bank, as part of their monetary reforms, effected the exchange of banknotes — the old Soviet money was replaced with new Russian roubles. The Ministry of Finance had never been informed and they were not ready at all and the country was thrown into chaos. The amount that could be exchanged for new notes was exceptionally small and the deadlines were extremely tight. The official justification was protection of the rouble against the rouble intervention from the republics. Yet, as Gaidar says, the only common-sense way of putting paid to this was through discontinuing the shipment of gratuitous cash against CIS countries' requests. If they want to buy roubles — they are welcome to but it should be a commercial transaction. The way was open to speculation and profiteering became rife. It was totally predictable that such regulation would cause Russians to try to get rid of old money in a stampede into panic buying and hoarding staples, as well as fuelling inflation and damaging the market.

Gaidar phoned to the President and said that, to ameliorate the situation the best thing would be to increase the sums that people could exchange, push back the deadlines and, for now, keep the smaller denomination bills in circulation. The President agreed at once, he must have been ready for this decision. However, by now none of it could compensate for the political and economic damage.

By the end of the summer it became clear that the economic policy of the government was falling apart. The budgetary crisis had been further aggravated by the state's existing obligations to purchase grain at prices considerably exceeding their capacity. This crisis thus became uncontrollable.

The experience of the Yeltsin family was similar to that of all Russians at the time. His daughter Lena was leaving for Karelia that evening, and suddenly, in the morning, there was an announcement that only new money was now accepted in Russia while the old banknotes, up to the amount of 30,000 roubles, could be exchanged in savings banks, whilst all their vacation money was in the old banknotes.' (*President's Journal*). The maximum of 30,000 roubles in a country ravaged by hyperinflation was very little — all money in excess of this was so much waste paper. Ultimately, the draconian mechanism for carrying out the exchange was amended and the minimal exchangeable amounts were increased and deadlines extended. It proved possible to suppress widespread panic.

Yeltsin had brought in a model of a reform that was progressive in character. However, the Central Bank had essentially been suborned by the Supreme Soviet determined to throw a spanner in the works of reforms, and by its policies had plunged the country into hyperinflation. Then, by means of an essentially repressive measure — the money exchange –the Central Bank was then trying to curb it.

Strangely, what settled in after this was a kind of summer apathy. All the political initiative acquired in April was being lost according to the press. Yet, as became apparent during the summer, Yeltsin was repeatedly trying to come to an understanding with the congress leadership to adopt the joint action plan.

However, a familiar issue re-emerged; 'Moscow was animatedly discussing rumours of Yeltsin's grievous disease,' writes political scientist Lylia Shevtsova. 'Allegedly, that was why he was unable to control the situation. "In August of 1991 no one believed that President Gorbachev was ill. In August of 1993 many were reluctant to believe that President Yeltsin was in good health," the papers were saying. These concerns were echoed in the Western press.

Meanwhile, Yeltsin's team had been making progress and Yeltsin eventually came back to Moscow, somewhat hefty but not in "the most grievous state of health" at all.'The programme had been formulated. Yes, he would take extreme measures but essentially constructive. The Constitution would not be abolished but a new one created. Not a proroguing of the congress but the establishment of a new one a 'professional' parliament representing real parties, communists included. If the parliament refused to adopt a new Constitution it would become adopted by the people at a referendum.

In the beginning of the summer, the Constitutional Council got to work. It seemed a motley collection and commentators joked that Yeltsin had assembled 'seven pairs of every bird and clean animal along with one pair of every unclean animal'.

Russia's regions sent their representatives, so did the political factions at the congress of People's Deputies public organisations. In a word, it was the Constituent Assembly* all over again. Only sailor Zheleznyakov was missing but he was quick to appear. The work of the Council opened on its very first day with a scandal. Following Yeltsin's ceremonial speech, where he described the need of a new Constitution for the new Russia, Khasbulatov ran up to the podium and demanded, in breach of protocol, to be given the floor. Yeltsin refused, so Khasbulatov, along with his associates, left the auditorium forthwith. Even so, Yeltsin called upon Khasbulatov and his companions to return the next day. The Deputies returned but Khasbulatov didn't. However, in the end, the Council's work became stymied for a totally different reason. The leaders of the

---

* The Russian Constituent Assembly was established in the wake of the October Revolution of 1917 to form a new constitution after the overthrow of the Russian Provisional Government. It was dispelled by the *Bolsheviks* on the spurious pretext of 'the guards being tired out' as announced by the captain of the guards, sailor Zheleznyakov.

republics refused to sign the declaration on the founding principles of the Constitution because they were unhappy with provisions for their rights (the sovereignty of Tatarstan, Bashkortostan and other smaller entities). Yeltsin therefore suspended the activities of the Constitutional Assembly in July, before leaving on holiday.

It was by no means a waste of time, however. During these two months experts, lawyers, advisors and several working groups managed to merge two drafts of the Constitution: the one prepared by the group of deputies headed up by Oleg Rumiantsev and the one prepared by the President's Administration. 'Within a just over a month', write Yeltsin's aides, 'the draft Constitution was developed whereby the President became head of state with broad powers in the executive sphere.' The text of the Constitution where the principles of a presidential, and not parliamentary, republic prevailed, was finally becoming reality.

It could now be put to the vote.

So what of Khasbulatov, the Chairman of the Supreme Soviet, who seemed to be trying to undermine the work on the new Constitution, and in the process, violating decisions of his own parliament? Back in the winter and spring, Yeltsin was meeting with him continuously, speaking with him on the phone and holding negotiations, but during 1993 these contacts stopped. Khasbulatov was, as ever, a character much beloved by the political newsreels and commentators but by this time he was a controversial figure. The Supreme Soviet's Speaker made no effort to present himself in front of TV cameras in a more or less civil fashion or to court popularity.

Khasbulatov was bright and he was perfectly well aware of the fact that he had a formidable tool in his hands: the Constitution of the Russian Federation that was currently in force. He was totally aware of his own power — the power gained by this seemingly gentle professor of economics who turned out to be quarrelsome and vindictive, and disappeared from view after the events of September and October. This power stemmed from the Congress of the People's Deputies.

By the summer of 1993, all of the more or less constructively-minded deputies had resigned from leading posts in committees or had gone to work for the government. No parties or movements were represented at the congress since the congress perceived itself as the only political force. The congress wanted to rule the country without the president and even the government. And all these aspirations were nursed in the absence of any personal responsibility.

The power vested in the Chairman of the Supreme Soviet by the Congress and the Constitution was masterfully used by Khasbulatov in his political struggle. From now on, Khasbulatov was an independent figure fighting for supremacy. Later on Khasbulatov would offer a completely different explanation for the events in 1993.In his book, he would say, '… The truth lies in the fact that the Supreme Soviet was forcibly dragged into the confrontation. It is also true that the Chairman was affected by this most grievously. It is true as well that if Chairs of Chambers and members of the Presidium, instead of being engrossed in gossip and intrigues, had joined him in his attempts to actively influence the Kremlin, the tragedy would never have taken place.'

While on holiday, Yeltsin started preparing his main steps. Rutskoy, the Vice President, had completely lost his confidence and was removed from all his important posts, including the Anti-Corruption Committee and the Federal Centre for the Development of Agriculture. Yeltsin also cleared the enforcement agencies from individuals that he deemed unreliable and, finally, he brought Gaidar back into the government in September.

Among those who were the first to learn about Yeltsin's new 'offensive' were Viktor Chernomyrdin, Yegor Gaidar and Sergei Filatov and Yeltsin had identified the deadline as September 20th. However, the 'troika' was not at all happy about the plan. All three were convinced that the time for the offensive had been lost, that the congress should have been removed from the political arena back in April whereas now the timing was wrong. They were not prepared at this point to take on the hardliners. Gaidar met with Chernomyrdin and asked him to talk Yeltsin out of his plans, since at the moment such steps were extremely ill-timed. Chernomyrdin had a conversation with the President but the President flatly refused to change his plans.

Yet the most unpleasant response was awaiting Yeltsin on September 18th, at the meeting with the *Siloviki* in Novo-Ogaryovo. All enforcement ministers — defence (Grachev), internal affairs (Yerin) and security (Golushko) — were also unanimous in trying to convince him to defer the scenario to a later date. They gave as their reasons that it was 'embarrassing' to resort to the use of force in Moscow at the time when the CIS leaders had arrived for a scheduled meeting — but, most importantly, that it was no longer possible to disarm the White House without bloodshed.

The previous day, on September 17th, Khasbulatov had urgently convened an extraordinary session of the Supreme Soviet. Khasbulatov was totally *au fait* with developments.

On September 21st, Yeltsin was finally delivering his long-expected riposte.

He made another televised appeal.

'You and I, we hoped that the breakthrough would happen after the referendum in April when the Russian people supported their President and the course he is pursuing. Alas, those hopes were thwarted. The recent days have finally put paid to hopes of ever restoring constructive cooperation. Decisions made with respect to the budget, privatisation and other issues serve to aggravate the crisis and damage the country terribly. All efforts undertaken by the government to somehow alleviate the economic situation meet with a wall of stone.

One can count on the figures of one hand the number of days when the Supreme Soviet would not be twisting our arm and stymieing our efforts. Esteemed compatriots, the only way to overcome this paralysis of state power in the Russian Federation is through radical rejuvenation on the basis of grassroots democracy and constitutionality.

The Constitution that is currently in force does not provide for any of this. Neither does it provide for a procedure of adopting a new Constitution that could envisage a dignified way out of the crisis of statehood. In my capacity of the guarantor of our state's security I am obliged to offer a way out of this impasse, I must break this perilous vicious circle.'

Yeltsin made a pause and took a sip of tea from the cup sitting on the table in front of him.

'Vested with authority bestowed upon me at the national election in 1991, enjoying the confidence in me confirmed by the citizens of Russia at the referendum in 1993, I have endorsed by my decree alterations and amendments to the current Constitution of the Russian Federation.

...The Federal Assembly of the Russian Federation shall henceforth become the supreme legislative body. It shall be a bicameral parliament operating exclusively on a professional basis.

The election will take place on 11 and 12 December 1993...

I am in favour of running pre-term presidential elections after a certain period once the Federal Assembly is up and running.

It is up to you, the voters, to decide who will occupy this post in Russia for the new term.'

The gist of this famous decree of Yeltsin's boiled down to this: starting from September 21st, the Supreme Soviet and the Congress of People's Deputies were declared disbanded and their authority annulled. At the same time, the deputies were guaranteed full preservation of their privileges: they had a right to return to the place of employment they had held prior to being elected and each one of them could stand for election to the Federal Assembly. There were no plans for imposing a state of emergency and the citizens of Russia maintained all their rights and freedoms...

The presidential address was broadcast in the evening. Two hours later Khasbulatov announced that Yeltsin was no longer President. Another three hours later, deputies in the Supreme Soviet voted for removing the President from power proceeding from amendments to the Constitution previously adopted by the Congress. This time the house was made by only 146 votes — that was all it took for making this historic decision. Vice President Alexander Rutskoy was proclaimed President. He was sworn in after which he made a keynote address mostly focusing on the economic reform which was, yet again, branded criminal and anti-national. Rutskoy announced his intention to stop from all its principal initiatives: privatisation, free market, monetarised budget — and return to regulated prices and a planned economy.

The same assembly of deputies appointed new bosses of enforcement agencies: Barannikov was announced Minister of State Security, Dunayev — Minister of the Interior (both recently dismissed by Yeltsin) and Achalov — Minister of Defence. Contrary to expectations, however, the post of Prime Minister remained vacant.

Meanwhile the Kremlin was preparing its retaliation against these long-awaited acts by the Supreme Soviet. On September 21st, Premier Yegor Gaidar convened an urgent meeting of the working group and formulated, for the first time, the tactics of the presidential side towards the White House which was at the time the seat of the Supreme Soviet. He enumerated specific steps envisaged: cutting off all utilities and communications: electricity, water and telephones. To start with, Chernomyrdin refused to sign these instructions but a day later reluctantly acquiesced.

The White House was encircled with a cordon, albeit not a strict one: it was possible to come and go on the basis of any official ID — whether you were a deputy or a journalist. So the cordon was penetrated by any who aimed to join the ranks of the fighters in the Whitehouse against the 'anti-national' regime. There were hundreds of them, including members of Barkashov's group, the groups led by Terekhov and Makashov, Anpilov's* militants as well as some Cossacks, amongst others.

They armed themselves. New batches of weaponry were being carried through the cordon. The situation deteriorated rapidly and reserves of arms within the White House were now more than sufficient. In addition, there was a good supply of provisions. The 'peaceful' plan was clearly not working. Some deputies were arriving at the White House, whilst others were leaving it forever, but by now none of it was of great importance. The White House as such was quickly turning into a hotbed of political tension that emanated a direct threat of armed conflict.

Meanwhile, up until October 3rd, the Kremlin was acting within the framework of the approved concept that Sergei Shakhrai, himself formerly a deputy, had formulated — 'impose no state of emergency, conduct no arrests of the former deputies, prevent bloodshed in Moscow and the provinces, and do not rise to the bait'. This formula can be shortened to just one word: wait.

Wait till the standoff would resolve itself, till the deputies would tire of sitting around in the White House, till they would get fed up with their own appeals, until they would realise that the new election was inevitable.

The idea seemed naive. Moreover, it was possibly this very passivity

---

* *Alexander Barkashov* was the leader of the Russian National Unity (RNU), an organisation preaching undisguised fascism and nationalism; Terekhov headed the radical Officer's Union; Albert Makashov was a retired general who has called repeatedly for overthrowing the new power; and Victor Anpilov was the leader of Working Russia. — *Author's comment.*

of approach that brought about the tragic developments. The two main protagonists both had their own logic. Both were involved in overthrowing GKChP in the August of 1991. The details of the putsch were all too fresh in their memory. The Kremlin was trying to avoid repeating the mistakes made by the GKChP. It was precisely the state of emergency, armed military vehicles and troops in the streets that provoked an outburst among the people. The Kremlin was doing its best to distance itself from the logic of a 'coup' as the only way to overcome the crisis and to avoid a civil war.

The White House had a different logic. It was exactly because of the intractable resistance and reliance on the 'living circle' of the White House defenders that the GKChP collapsed which meant acting in the same way as in 1991, or even taking a tougher line!

'The first blood was shed on Thursday evening, on September 23rd. Eight people in fatigues shot a militiaman dead and burst into the CIS United Armed Forces' headquarters situated in Leningradsky Prospekt. Following this, the attackers disarmed two security guards, seized their weapons and disappeared. An elderly lady standing by her window was accidentally killed by a stray bullet. Witnesses identified one of the attackers as Alexander Terekhov, chairman of the Officers' Union. Viktor Anpilov, leader of a militant left-wing movement Working Russia, who at the time of the attack was making a speech from the White House balcony told his audience that the Officers' Union was assaulting the headquarters... and called upon those present to join in the assault,' was the newspaper coverage of the first armed conflict in September.

Even before this tragic incident it was clear that the 'peaceful scenario' was not working so the question arose as to how to disarm the Supreme Soviet's supporters? The mayor of Moscow, Yuri Luzhkov, sent an ultimatum to Rutskoy, Khasbulatov, Achalov, Barannikov and Dunayev wherein he demanded that all firearms and ammunition be handed over to law enforcement bodies. Within the White House, the absence of water and electricity, was already creating siege conditions.

These sentiments were not only spreading among those within the parliamentary building but spilling over to the streets. Clashes with militia became more frequent yet the militia had received orders 'to prevent casualties and clashes' and carry no service weapons. Thus, with each new day they were growing more and more embittered as they felt impotent against the crowds. Yet blogs at the time showed this was not entirely one sided. 'October 1st. I witnessed mass beatings of Moscow citizens near the Pushkin monument. The operation aimed at intimidation of demonstrators was carried out by a Special Task Unit (OMON) from the Sofrinskaya Brigade of the Interior Ministry with some 25-30 troops. Their uniforms were black and brown in colour, with some green and beige insignia... Shame on Yerin and his henchmen!' (G. Malakhov, Professor of Historic Sciences). There were numerous other accounts of the same nature.

Those who during those days sided with the Supreme Soviet were far from a homogenous mass. Strange though it may seem but dyed-in-the-wool nationalism also worked as a unifying factor — ironically, since these were the people advocating the return to the multi-national USSR! It was during those days that the RNU leader, Barkashov, gave an interview where he was singing praises to Hitler and his guards from the RNU appeared with swastika on their armbands. It was during these days that General Makashov appealed from the White House balcony 'to hang all Judo-Masons.' There were numerous anti-Semitic rumours circulating. Such incidents were quite commonplace. The atmosphere was very different to that in 1991.

The mutinous crowds behaved differently too. The messages on the banners were different: the word 'kill' was ubiquitous. In 1991, the crowd was defending their stronghold — the White House. In 1993, the crowd was wild and charging the cordon around the White House.

On the 3rd, inevitably, the crowd scattered the militia cordon. Battered and disarmed, stripped of their batons and sometimes even their greatcoats, the militiamen ran for their lives.

It was all a long way from the concert on September 25th in Red Square. Then the National Orchestra of Russia performed a concert conducted by Mstislav Rostropovich featuring Prokofiev's suite, *Alexander Nevsky** and Tchaikovsky's *Eighteen-Twelve*** Overture in front of one

---

\* *Alexander Nevsky* (1220-1263) was the Prince of Novgorod and Grand Prince of Vladimir principalities during some of the most trying times in history. Commonly regarded as the key figure of medieval Rus, Alexander rose to his legendary status on account of his military victories over the German and Swedish invaders.

\*\* The war with Napoleon.

hundred thousand people gathered on the square. Yeltsin had showed up before the concert started and was greeted with an ovation. Rostropovich performed his concert that went down in history as an example of direct intervention of music into human affairs. He showed his support to the person he believed worth supporting and it is impossible to forget him as he was during those minutes. It was an astonishing and striking gesture of a citizen and a musician.

Now, however, the majority of people across the country were listening, minute by minute, to the events in the centre and simply waiting to see who would prove the stronger

Both the Kremlin and the White House tried to engage people of authority in the negotiations. Even the Russian Orthodox Church took part. Intense consultations were underway from September 29th, both in the White House and in St Daniel's monastery, between Patriarch Alexius II, Kirsan Iliumzhinov, a member of the Federation Council from Kalmykia, and Zorkin, Chairman of the Constitutional Court.

On the morning of September 30th constituent entities of the Russian Federation assembled in the Great Hall of the Constitutional Court. Sixty-eight out of 89 members were in attendance. The main condition for lifting the blockade around the White House was still the voluntary surrender of arms.

The delegates suggested to Chernomyrdin, "Let us, the constituent entities of the Russian Federation, go to the White House; if you issue us passes we shall see whether there really are missiles and whether they are really giving out submachine guns." Chernomyrdin issued four passes. Together with another four regional leaders — Potapov, Chairman of Buriatia's Supreme Soviet; Gustov, Chairman of the Leningrad Soviet; and two more heads of administrations — we set off towards the White House." They came back with the inventory of a small arsenal including, reputedly, a *Stinger* missile.

On the night between September 30th and October 1st, participants in the negotiations managed to agree on provisions of the peace protocol. On the

---

* *Square* of *Free Russia*. Anthology of testimonials regarding the events in September — October 1993

presidential side there was Head of Administration, Sergei Filatov, and from the side of the Supreme Soviet, deputies Abdulatipov and Sokolov, who were to have this protocol endorsed. It was apparently fairly convivial meeting.

Under this preliminary agreement, early in the morning of October 1st electricity was switched on in the building of the parliament. First Vice-Premier Oleg Soskovets and representatives of the White House signed in St Daniel's monastery an agreement concerning the gradual lifting of the blockade from the White House on condition of the complete disarmament of individuals with no right to carry or possess arms. On the night of October 2nd the blockade was relaxed.

However, the deputies of the Supreme Soviet rejected ratification of the agreements on the grounds that the negotiation commission had overstepped their authority. Later that morning, Khasbulatov called off his negotiators, branded the problem of weapons in the White House an 'artificial one' and refused to take part in any other negotiations until Decree No 1400 was rescinded saying, 'This regime is dead and there is no reason to continue any relations with it.' And again — 'Yeltsin's junta will be thrown out of the Kremlin.'

At this point, the crowd moved from its focal point in Smolenskaya Square towards the White House brushing away all cordons as the militia fled. The Mayor's Office, then situated in the former Comecon headquarters, some 200 metres from the White House, was by now under assault. The first shots were fired by both sides. The crowd burst into the building, beat up the guards and captured the head of Luzhkov's staff. Complete pandemonium raged around the White House, too. 'Victory, victory!' chanted the crowds.

From the balcony of the White House, General Makashov was urging the crowds to seize the Ostankino TV centre. Several scores of armed individuals got into cars seized from the militia whilst the rest of the crowd roamed towards the centre and along Prospekt Mira waving their flags and banners.

Moscow stopped in its tracks.

Where were the militia? Where was the OMON? Where was anybody? The White House militants were all over Moscow, armed, unhindered. No one was trying to stop them.

*The Echo of Moscow* was broadcasting some grim, portentous music — nothing else. Once every ten minutes presenters would cut in with recent updates but there was nothing to present. There was no official reaction, Makashov and Barkashov's supporters were en route towards the TV centre. On TV, they were showing football, Spartak versus Rotor, but the broadcast was cut short in the middle of the second half. The TV Centre at Ostankino was guarded by several dozen militiamen and about 30 members of the Special Task Force of the Interior Ministry's Vityaz (Knight) unit. To set the ball rolling, a truck carrying Makashov's troops suddenly accelerated and rammed into the glass doors of the building. This done, they fired a shot from the grenade thrower that killed one *Vityaz* soldier, one support staff member and one guard. There was a skirmish. The militants flooded onto the ground floor, fighting their way towards the first floor. One was carrying a video with a record of Rutskoy's intended TV address.

At the time I lived near the TV centre. It was impossible to work out what was going on inside the building — there were no programmes and no broadcasts. I heard the shots and came out onto the balcony and saw a convoy of armoured personnel carriers crawling along the street. There were several of them and they were making a slow and cautious progress.

In the rapidly descending darkness the armoured personnel carriers (APCs), still following Kremlin orders, positioned themselves to the left from the crowd. They fired several multiple-round bursts with tracer bullets trained above people's heads. Meanwhile, a battle was raging within the TV centre.

Someone in the crowd hurled a Molotov cocktail against the APC's side. What followed is what one might have expected. The vehicle's commander flew into a rage and barked an order that the crowd should be dispersed by firing salvos. As the crowds stampeded, people ducking under bushes and scrambling for refuge in the little park, the machine gunner was still firing bursts of shots into the darkness, eager for new targets. Some were killed, some wounded… Those unharmed dashed away or tried to give first aid. Soon Korolyov Street was echoing with sirens of ambulances.

Tracer bullets were reaching Argunovskaya Street.

At about eight in the evening Yeltsin set off to Moscow from Barvikha in a helicopter. It took him 20 minutes to get to the Kremlin and disembark in Ivanovskaya Square within the Kremlin, near to the cathedrals. He made his way into his office and asked to be put through to Defence Minister Grachev who was nearby, in the Defence Ministry in the Arbat. 'The troops are on their way,' he told Yeltsin.

In truth, the APCs of the Interior Ministry's Sofrinskaya Brigade, the ones that had killed several people and wounded several dozen near the TV centre and left after aborting the assault, were the only 'troops' who were fighting on the presidential side that night. Later that night the Russian television was back in service. The live broadcast was coming from the reserve studio in Yamskogo Polya Street.

On air were journalists, politicians and well-known TV presenters. Yegor Gaidar called upon Muscovites to make their way to the Moscow Soviet and several thousand responded to this appeal. They were arming themselves with whatever came to hand, Gaidar was there too. This was a necessary step since the perilously weakened power had to be aware that it represented and was protected by the common citizens, not just the professional army personnel; meanwhile the professionals also had to realise that when they carried out orders, at the critical moment the rank-and-file people would be on their side. Others who appeared on the TV, however, advised against such action

Yegor Gaidar, the First Vice-Premier of the Government, later wrote about that night:

'After the TV appeal we went to the Moscow Soviet. Not long ago there were only small voluntary patrols in front of its entrance now the square is filled with people all the way up to Pushkin Square and the *Moskva* Hotel. They were building barricades and fires. They are aware of what's going on in the city, they have just seen on TV the battle at Ostankino. They are castigating the authorities, democrats and probably me as well, for having failed to deal with the scoundrels without subjecting them to danger and tearing them away from their homes and families. They are right, of course. But they keep pitching up near the Moscow Soviet. Yes, they are ready to sort it all out afterwards: who is to blame, who did what or did it wrongly. But now they are coming, unarmed, to try and shield with their own bodies the future of the country and their children. They want to keep the opportunists out of power.

I speak before those assembled and tell them that militants have been thrown back from Ostankino. I appeal to them to stay where they are, not to dispel, start forming units and be ready, should the need arise, to support the forces loyal to the president.

The main entrance to the Moscow Soviet is shut. We pick our way towards it with difficulty, round the barricades. The building was only recently partially controlled by the opposition. A group of Moscow Soviet deputies tried to set up one of their centres here but by now the building has been cleared by Luzhkov's people. Luzhkov himself is cheerful, excited even.

I phone Chernomyrdin and describe the situation in the city centre. I ask him what he knows about the approaching troops. On the whole, the situation is vague and fraught but it feels that the opposition has started to lose its momentum. I make another speech by the Mossoviet and am whisked by car towards the Saviour's Tower* where another assembly point is situated. From the window of my car I can see that Moscow is so much transformed, it is so awake. Lots of people, fires ablaze in places, somebody sings, line-ups of volunteer brigades. Having come together, people are now aware of their might, they have a new confidence.

People had assembled by the Saviour's Tower in Red Square on their own initiative. The mood is anxious; the organisation poor. A military man comes up to me and introducers himself as a retired colonel. He is asking for instructions. The ranks are much closer-knit by the Mossoviet, so this is probably our most vulnerable spot.'

Shamil Tarpishchev, the Presidential advisor on sports, recollects that time.

'When in the Kremlin, we made our way at once to Barsukov's ** office. As soon as we stepped in Yeltsin calls, "What is going on there?" Barsukov reported, "Don't worry, everything is OK here. Everything's in order. We shall find out more and get back to you." Ten minutes later Yeltsin called again, "I am going by helicopter, will be with you shortly." His helicopter landed within the Kremlin, the three of us *** met him. It so happened that I started acting as a kind of a liaison officer in Korzhakov's reception:

---

\* Of the Kremlin.

\*\* Head of the State Security Service. — *Author's comment.*

\*\*\* Tarpishchev, Korzhakov and Barsukov. — *Author's comment.*

## TEN BLANKS (1993)

I manned the phones and there was a mad swirl of people around me. They made me put on a bulletproof vest. I came out to the Vasilievsky Spusk, listened to some of the speeches. Everybody was enormously worked up. Five minutes later I couldn't recall a word of what I had heard. A deputy was speaking before me, long-winded and muddled. So I grabbed the initiative, "Why are you here? Let half of you go to the White House and the other half— to Tverskaya Street." And they all left.'

Meanwhile, much quieter and more deliberate speeches were being made in front of the White House. 'There was a lively discussion of what to do with Yeltsin when he was caught. Someone suggested that he should be publicly hung by the neck — but not in Red Square, too much honour for the likes of him. The others were in agreement, "Let's hang him! But before that, we shall put him in a cage, like a snake, and take him across liberated Russia to scare people with the sight of him."' (Leon Aron). This wasn't just idle talk. The order on Yeltsin's execution by firing squad had been issued long before this night.

At that point Yeltsin was on the premises of the Defence Ministry, in Grachev's office, among the generals. There was only one question: when would the troops make it to Moscow? The generals were silent. This was another crisis, another moment of an ordeal but he knew that he could not leave the office until he prevailed and they issued the order.

Finally Yeltsin uttered the words that up until this moment no one had dared utter: the White House must be taken by storm.

The generals pricked up their ears.

It wasn't them who put forward the idea and that was important.

Yeltsin started making towards the door and Grachev asked him, embarrassed, 'Boris Nikolayevich, will you give the order in writing? Without your order on paper...'

'I shall have it delivered,' said Yeltsin grimly and closed the door behind him.

The military operation started at 7:30.

One thousand three hundred troops of the Kantemirovskaya, Tamanskaya, Tulskaya and Ryazanskaya Divisions, along with armoured vehicle formations, entered Moscow. APCs broke the line of barricades near the White House. By this time, there was no living circle. The White House started shooting back. The shots were ringing out — booming, then muffled. Lieutenant General Kulikov was urging the White House defenders to surrender.

Negotiations drew a blank.

Ten T-72 tanks crawled onto the Novoarbatsky Bridge.

A huge crowd of onlookers gathered around the White House.

No one was trying to dispel them. The rest were watching the live broadcast of the assault on TV. The commentary by a CNN correspondent was translated simultaneously while the agency was showing just one image all day long: the White House, tanks, the White House windows and then tiny figures of people storming the building.

Finally, that morning, the tanks fired at the White House 12 times: the famous 10 blanks and the two incendiary shells which didn't kill or wound anybody. However, the top floors of the White House caught fire. The flames, fumes and heavy smoke started escaping from the windows. The battle inside the White House and around it lasted several hours. The assault was to be lead by Alpha Group But, as in 1991, this unit did not wish 'to take part in politics'. Yeltsin spoke to Alpha's commander Karpukhin personally. But the unit refused to carry out even the orders issued by the Supreme Commander-in-Chief. So they were put on buses and taken up to the building to see for themselves. One of them was killed by a marksman's shot. Following this, Alpha made their way into the building in order to evacuate the people. This was the account as given by Alexander Korzhakov. An hour later it was all over.

Deputies started filing out of the White House. They were slowly making their way through the ranks of special task force and militia; they were searched and put on buses parked nearby. Among the very last ones were Khasbulatov and Rutskoy. Rutskoy was wearing trainers and a tracksuit, and carrying a big sports bag, his personal effects ready for prison… He forgot the bag by the exit, though, and someone was sent to fetch it for him. Everybody was waiting tensely till the wretched bag was recovered. Khasbulatov had nothing with him. He sported a white shirt and no tie. All deputies were casting alarmed glances around them. It had been some time since they were outside, in the fresh air. A man ran up to some deputy, gave him a push on the shoulder and then a clip around the ear. The militia drove this person off and took the deputy away. It took quite some time for all the White House occupants to get out and get on the buses.

However, many 'White House defenders' escaped through underground communications after which they scattered around nearby courtyards and rooftops so skirmishes continued for a long time. A TV crew recorded a piece of graffiti on the belfry of a nearby church, 'I killed six people and am very glad of it!'

Not a single deputy of the Supreme Soviet was killed or wounded during the attack on the building. Everybody was safely escorted out of the premises, although quite a few peaceful citizens, including teenagers, were caught in the crossfire and in skirmishes between soldiers, militiamen, militants and snipers. The toll of casualties as announced two days later ran to over 150 people.

Some other, much more terrifying statistics were also quoted: several thousand dead bodies in the White House — but it simply wasn't true. For several days running, grief-stricken relatives were identifying the bodies of casualties in Moscow mortuaries. Some were never formally identified since those were people, eager to fight, who came to Moscow without any documents. Still, there were only a handful of such cases. It was a grim and terrible victory.

On the morning of October 4th Yeltsin finally made his televised address which had been awaited all through the night. He mourned the losses and praised the people for their support and made a heart-felt call for national unity'.

As soon as the skirmishes around the White House ceased people went shopping. Everyone had been cooped up for several days and ignored the smell of war, the occasional bursts of fire and single shots that rang out, to get to the bakeries.

In essence, the real reason why Yeltsin was successful, somewhat against expectations, was that the country had refused to support the mutinous parliament. There were no strikes, rallies or mass manifestations. Official statements by leaders of local Soviets were only a formality: like everyone else, they were simply waiting the situation to play out. Not a single military unit or militia detachment came over to the Supreme Soviet's side, despite all efforts of the latter. The only exception was several individual soldiers who came to the White House. The threat of an open civil war against the new political system in Russia was over.

The country announced a period of mourning in memory of the victims — all of them, irrespective of which side they had been on, all those whose death had been an accident or not. A curfew was announced in Moscow for two weeks. During this time militia was busy 'mopping-up' the city and arresting all suspicious individuals without charge.

Newspapers were writing of Yeltsin's victory and that the price had been too high. The threat had been dispelled, yet Yeltsin had lost something forever. He lost a huge number of his supporters who believed that democratic revolutions in Russia could be bloodless and free of the armed conflict for power. These people lost their faith in the possibility of political struggle in Russia that would stay within a civilised peaceful context. The same faith that they had felt they had acquired after the events of 1991. Most of all, however, he lost his illusions of democracy and market economy entering Russia in accordance with his plan, peacefully and quietly, and in the shortest time possible.

Possibly, it was then that he first realised that his knowledge of the country had been incomplete, that he never fully appreciated the impact of the 70 years of the Soviet power and decades of political apathy. Probably, it was then that he finally saw how long and arduous the path into the common realm of civilisation was going to be. Boris Yeltsin saved the country from total carnage but innocent blood still had been shed. On December 12th, Russia ran the elections for the new parliament and the referendum on the new Constitution. The nation made its way to the polling booths again.

# 'We Believe in You...'
# (1994)

Things were clear at last. It was clear who was passing laws and in what way, who appointed the government and the supreme judicial bodies, which rights and freedoms were guaranteed by the new Constitution, who was the head of state, how this person was elected, in which cases he could be dismissed and what he was supposed to do. The new Fundamental Law approved at the referendum on December 12th provided sufficiently distinct definitions for the presidential and parliamentary remits.

Nearly all analysts and researches agree that 'Yeltsin's constitution is, to a large degree, modelled on the one formulated by de Gaulle and adopted under similar historic circumstances: the break-up of the French empire with its endless political crises, economic depression and overall consequences. The French president had also resorted to direct appeals to the nation and referendums in order to resolve political problems.

Yeltsin's Constitution and the political system he created started bearing economic and political fruit and ushered in the era of economic stability — similar to that which had happened in de Gaulle's France. However, France did not have the complication of a 'super power's complex', neither did they have a militaristic economy, and most of all — they didn't have 70 years of *Bolshevik* legacy or a total overhaul of the state ideology.

Almost immediately after the October events, by the end of the autumn of 1993, Yeltsin put forward three decrees: on the state flag, the state anthem and state symbols of the Russian Federation which the President justly believed the country must have. On the other hand, it was senseless, even cruel, to ask the nation which flag and which anthem they would prefer — now, at the time of a serious depression, when the nightmare of the last October was all too fresh in memory. Society was split with some hating the new power whilst others glowed with hope and optimism

As it turned out, the flag of the February revolution*, of democratic Russia — that is the state that had lasted for less than a year — has become a firm presence in our country, despite initial derision. It was a different story where it concerned the anthem. The selected majestic tune by Mikhail Glinka**, had no lyrics so the text for the new state anthem became a veritable bone of contention. This first national anthem lasted nine years and in 2002 yielded its place to the old tune by Alexandrov and the new lyrics composed by the author of the Soviet anthem — Sergey Mikhalkov. Finally, for the insignia, the double-headed eagle clasping the sceptre served as a reminder of history in its old days of monarchy. Thus, the eagle has also survived. Technically, these decrees were the first actions undertaken by Yeltsin to denote the new era but basically he was in new territory

He flatly refused to extend the duration of a curfew in Moscow although the situation in the capital wasn't quite back to normal yet (the 'curfew' and 'extraordinary powers' lasted only two weeks). He allowed the publication of communist papers where the newspaper *Day* was replaced by *Zavtra* (Tomorrow)). The very first post-putsch issue of *Zavtra* carried a huge portrait of Stalin on its front page whereas both *Pravda* and *Rossiya* changed neither their names nor their views. He cut down considerably the list of extremist organisations whose activities had been subject to a ban and all the more significant opposition parties, particularly the

---

* The February Revolution of 1917 was the first of two revolutions in Russia in 1917. Its immediate result was the abdication of Tsar Nicholas II, the end of the Romanov dynasty and of the Russian empire. The Tsar was replaced by a Provisional Government. It was an alliance between liberals and socialists who wanted political reform.

** *Mikhail Ivanovich Glinka* (1804-1857), was the first Russian composer to gain wide recognition within his own country and is often regarded as the father of Russian classical music.

communist party, took part in the elections forthwith. He had renounced the temptations of a dictatorship despite the allegations of the communists.

The idea of 'national conciliation and consent' was created by him and his advisors as the principal political enabling concept during 1994. The main barrier to economic reforms and to steering the country from an economic dead-end had been political strife during 1992-1993. Now, when the undeclared 'civil war' against private property had receded from the political arena and Moscow streets, he had a chance of being able to move forward.

However by December 1993 and during January-February of 1994 things became much less clear than they had seemed over the summer and autumn. To many, the results of the first elections to the new State Duma were a jolt. The famous phrase by a political commentator and writer Yuri Karyakin's — 'Russia, are you out of your mind?' was carried by many papers.

The democratic and centrists parties received about *one third* of the votes. The communists improved their situation considerably since they managed to benefit from voting results in one-candidate constituencies and their presence in the new parliament became impressive. But the main sensation was the victory scored by Zhirinovsky's party, the LDPR, with 23% of the vote. It seemed as if a sizeable number of people didn't want to vote for either democrats or communists and thus chose the 'third option'.

This 'third option' signalled danger. What did Zhirinovsky want? Quite simply that Russia should become a mono-ethnic state — 'Russia for Russians'. Russia should communicate with her neighbours and the entire global community only in the language of strength, Russia should seek global domination, Russia's enemy was the Western world, the Islamic world, the Asian world, in a word — naked nationalism. Zhirinovsky found a new vent for the social tension that had been accumulating within the society as a result of the disintegration of the Soviet Union and the 'shock therapy' administered by Gaidar. It amounted to a hatred for anything 'non-Russian', 'foreign', combined with 'Russia's enemies' laying siege on all sides, generally manifesting itself as xenophobia and nationalist aggression.

This revanchist ideology fell on fertile soil. Many Russians sincerely believed that a great country had been lost in 1991, that it was 'corrupt swindlers' that had come to power, that neither 'reds' nor 'democrats' were capable of leading the country out of the blind alley. Was 'conciliation and consent' really an option in a country where such a party could triumph at the election? In short, the new Russian parliament proved completely different to what the Presidential team had been envisaging on October 3rd.

The second most important event in 1994 was Gaidar's latest resignation that took place in January. He was completely disillusioned with the loss of the election and, with it, any hope ever becoming Premier but also he had the feeling that he was already being marginalised in the latter part of the previous administration.

For the Russian public this resignation was a complete surprise. Nothing had seemed to indicate such a development. The first financial sign of stabilisation had appeared in the last quarter of 1993 whilst Gaidar himself had behaved quite heroically during the October putsch. By now, he was an experienced politician, his party had seats in the Duma and he still had a serious economic programme in progress. However, it was also true that in January of 1994, Prime Minister Chernomyrdin announced his plan for a single fiscal and monetary union between Russia and Byelorussia along with new subsidies for the agro-industrial complex and financial allowances to enterprises in debt. Gaidar didn't agree with these decisions which could spur another round of inflation but, most of all, he didn't agree with the fact that he had been kept in the dark about those initiatives.

Yeltsin signed his letter of resignation rather promptly which made the main news at the beginning of 1994 when he came to realise that the epoch of Gaidar was over. Or to be more precise, what was really over was the hope of a *quick economic miracle*. The time for shock therapy was over. A reliable and stable 'heavyweight' such as the less divisive Chernomyrdin suited him much better under the particular circumstances.

By and large, it was impossible to appoint to the higher state posts in the new Russia people with roots in the old Soviet *nomenklatura*. Whether in economics, domestic or external policy, the problem was consistent. There was an entire class of seasoned professionals who had been through the school of Soviet academies and departments but now found themselves in the new situation: some adapted to the new system but the others couldn't and generally Yeltsin was simply forced to hunt for new people. These new people until quite recently had been working in their local towns and cities, occupying modest positions as heads of laboratories or chairs in some provincial universities, teachers or district authorities, and no idea what was in store for them.

The new convocation of the parliament, with LDPR and CPRF holding majority, revealed their hostility towards the President practically from the start. On 26 February 1994, Russia's Procurator's Office carried out the State Duma's resolution on the act of pardon. The people who had been directly responsible for the events of October 3rd and 4th, the putsch organisers who had almost caused the deaths of thousands of people, with potentially mass reprisals and a civil war, were now free to go.

Vyacheslav Kostikov, Yeltsin's press secretary at the time, recorded:

'It was a real shock for the President when the conspirators in the 1991 plot and the failed coup of October 1993 were released from prison. It was a meticulously calculated intrigue behind the President's back that had been implemented with undue rapidity. Diehard enemies of the President: Khasbulatov, Rutskoy, General Makashov, Dunayev ex-deputy of the Interior Minister, Konstantinov, the leader of the Front for National Rescue along with the communist extremist and Working Russia's leader Anpilov and the insurgents' leader, Barkashov. Seventy four people in all were set free. It was a direct challenge to Yeltsin.

Barkashov, the organiser of the assault on the state TV centre, left the prison on crutches. When asked by a journalist about what he was going to do now he answered, 'Same as I did before'. It felt like a conspiracy. The government stayed silent and distanced itself from the issue of pardon, as if it had nothing to do with them.

Boris Yeltsin's actions were somewhat contradictory. It was evident that he couldn't but be aware that the State Duma had opened the question of pardon. However, he seemed to be under the impression that the procedure was likely to be protracted and that the decision would be taken somewhere closer to spring.

The State Duma's resolution on the act of pardon was signed by the Chairman of the State Duma, Ivan Rybkin and it stated that the resolution should come into force at the moment of publication. Natalia Polezhayeva, Editor-in-Chief of *Rossiyskaya Gazeta*, reported subsequently that Rybkin personally called her on the phone and asked her to expedite the publication of the State Duma's resolution on the pardon.

On that day, Saturday, February 26th, Ruslan Khasbulatov was freed at 16:05 and the others shortly afterwards. The President, on the phone from his dacha in Barvikha, was trying, in vain, to put a stop on the execution of the parliamentary decision whilst Procurator, General Kazannik, made a public statement about his personal disagreement with the State Duma's decision — "The act of political pardon shall forever be an ignoble page in the history of Russian parliamentarianism". For all that, he maintained he was unable to carry out Yeltsin's demand to suspend the release.

Kostikov's memoir continues:

'On Monday February 28th the aides suggested that the President should urgently prepare a decree provisionally entitled "On Additional Measures in Support of the Constitutional System".

Having got his consent we were aware that the countdown was measured in hours and, keen to expedite the events, passed the draft to Korzhakov, the chief bodyguard who had the right to enter the President's office not via the reception but through the lounge. We were invited in and Boris Nikolayevich was at his desk, the final draft before him.

"Weak... Too turgid," he said. To be frank, we were astonished since the language of the draft was sufficiently tough and said as much.

"It should be even more severe," responded the President. The gist of his comments was that the situation should not be "fudged" and, instead, "those released on pardon must be re-arrested right away". The President was in very resolute mood. He pressed the button on his control and immediately started a conversation with Yerin, the Interior Minister, "You must make immediate arrests. You know whom I mean," said he not naming specific names.

We could hear Yeltsin's answers for the President did not consider it necessary to keep the conversation from us and the telephone was on speakerphone. Yerin replied that he was ready to carry out the order but he needed the official consent of the new Procurator General Ilyushenko who had just replaced the dismissed Procurator General Kazannik.

"You shall have it," said the President tersely and hung up.

I have no information on what happened after the President departed from the Kremlin. We were waiting all day for Yeltsin's decree to be implemented. But time was passing and there was no news. Later in the evening I called my friends at the *Interfax*\* and asked them, without revealing the reason for my curiosity, whether there was any news. There was not. Nothing happened the next morning either. Some brakes were applied somewhere and Yeltsin's order was either blocked or rescinded.' Yeltsin was stunned and enraged.

However, Yeltsin managed to control his rage. After weighing up all the pros and cons he realised that neither Rutskoy, nor Khasbulatov, or anyone else of this reactionary crew presented a 'public threat' within the new parliamentary framework, which subsequently proved to be the case. Many of those released completely drew back into the shadows whilst the others stayed in politics but had little further impact on Russian life.

This pent-up annoyance became obvious with one manifestation becoming something of an international incident. The former President of the United States, Richard Nixon, was visiting Moscow privately and decided to meet with the recently freed Rutskoy. Yeltsin stripped Nixon of the governmental car and all state security. Poor Nixon had to go to the airport as best he could in an embassy car, while only twenty years previously Muscovites had been flanking Leninsky Propekt and greeting him with waving flags and flowers! As a result, everyone had to apologise: the Kremlin Administration, the Foreign Ministry and even Bill Clinton, the new US President who had to make his obeisance and explain the antics of the Russian president back home. Yeltsin himself had no apologies to offer. In his eyes, Rutskoy was a criminal released from custody thanks to the State Duma's rash and thoughtless actions thus, for the first time, his annoyance erupted in public.

At the end of February in 1994 Yeltsin suddenly suggested to Naina that they should go on holiday to Sochi, a resort on the Black Sea. A holiday in chilly weather, in early spring, out of the blue, amid turbulent political developments — the commentators were astounded. Some read it as 'a confirmation of the fact that Yeltsin had never recovered from the events in October of 1993'. Others insisted that it was typical of him to flee Moscow after a political storm and lapse into depression and inactivity when the time was actually ripe for active measures. Some merely speculated about the state of his health.

---

\* News agency.

As Yeltsin was swimming in the cold Black Sea an anonymous document started its rounds in Moscow, being passed from hand to hand. Originally, it carried the title 'Version No 1', then it appeared as an edited 'Version No 2'. Its authors were never identified but they were asserting that in spring or summer of 1994 a group of highly-placed statesmen 'intended to attempt to remove Yeltsin from power'. Allegedly, this group had already been in touch with the enforcement ministers: Grachev, Yerin and Stepashin. The signal for action was supposed to come in the form of an appearance on the TV Channel One of a 'well-known public figure' and the pretext was going to be the 'President's worsening state of health and his physical incapacity to rule the country'.

The document was distributed to the radio station *The Echo of Moscow*, the presidential press service and offices of central newspapers, and turned out to have been faxed through from a false number. The document, however, was a complete forgery for it listed completely incompatible individuals as 'conspirators' including the head of the Army's General Staff and the Speaker of the Council of the Federation. It goes without saying that all alleged 'conspirators' immediately disavowed their involvement, branded the document 'a phoney' and demanded an official investigation. The scandal was so serious that *Izvestia*'s Editor-in-Chief phoned Yeltsin in Sochi for his reaction. In the same telephone interview to *Izvestia*, when answering a question about health he said, 'I see no doctors, take no medical treatment... I am working... In a word, there is no sign of disease...'.

Yeltsin himself described his state in his *President's Journal* that came out in spring of 1994:

'I had to go through it all: exhausting bouts of depression, bleak thoughts at night, insomnia, headaches and despair at the sight of filthy, impoverished Moscow... the baggage from the decisions made, the anguish caused by those who had been near but betrayed me in the time of need as well as those who either didn't help or displayed no endurance.'

In short, the holiday in Sochi brought no improvements.

A man who used to devour official papers like an automaton, remember hundreds of figures and memorise whole pages of text was now returning analytical memos to his assistants without any comments. We were happy, they recollected, when we would spot at least a pencil tick in the top

## 'WE BELIEVE IN YOU...' (1994)

corner, for it meant that he at least paid some attention to it. More and more frequently Yeltsin was throwing his schedule into disarray, cancelling meetings or pushing them back and leaving the Kremlin for Zavidovo or Barvikha where he would spend several days at a time. A particular agony was caused by protocol events, for example, the delivery of credentials by foreign ambassadors. During the ceremony he would have to stand for an hour or an hour and a half which always ended up in excruciating pains in his leg.

His aides commented that the most immediate task for the president upon his return from vacation was to persuade or force the opposition to sign the Treaty on National Reconciliation but often he was poorly and absent from the Kremlin. The president suffered from pains in his legs and, during an attack, not only walking but sitting was painful. More and more frequently, pre-scheduled meetings had to be cancelled and adversaries were using every such occasion to claim that the president disabled.

In April of that year the assistants would write their first letter to Yeltsin whereby they expressed their concern over 'the loss of speed' and suggested measures to rectify the situation: to meet such and such, put forward such an initiative and speak on TV. This suddenly flaccid, silent and withheld Yeltsin was an increasing worry for his entire team.

Even at the end of the preceding year, 1993, Yeltsin was due for a meeting with representatives of the intelligentsia in the Kremlin. His secretary was by the door, waiting anxiously for the President to finally put in an appearance. He went on to record, 'This time, his walk was slower than usual and he was dragging his leg. "You have no heart, Vyacheslav Vasilievich*," said Yeltsin. "You have no pity for your President." When Kostikov assured the President didn't have to say anything in the meeting the President suddenly came to a halt and turned round to face Kostikov. "Don't you understand?" he said in a steely voice, "today I find it hard even to be sitting down."'

The Treaty on National Conciliation was signed on 28 April 1994. This important and solemn occasion was held in St George's Hall in the Kremlin. Some of those who put their signature to the text were

---

\* Kostikov.

irreconcilable enemies, for example Gaidar and Zhirinovsky. His assistants say that 'it was one of those days when he was genuinely nervous.' Would it really be feasible at last to reach a stage when it would be possible to carry out unhurried reforms and lead Russia out of a crisis?

As Yeltsin put it on 28 April 1994:

'Nearly eight decades ago our country sustained a terrible tragedy. Russia was plunged into the abyss of civil war... The bloody boundary ran between the 'whites' and the 'reds', our own and aliens, making everyone an enemy of everyone else. This murderous spate must be stopped. Our fathers and forefathers failed to do it. It is down to us to achieve this goal. We must do it so that we could hand over a peaceful Russia to our children...'

However, the Treaty was met by Russian society with much less enthusiasm than he had expected. The leader of Russian communists, Ziuganov, and the leader of Yabloko, Yavlinsky refused to sign the text and the democratic intelligentsia were critical of the price that the President was prepared to pay. Yet the situation did shift. The period of blatant standoffs gave way to a series of backstage deals, with bargains and compromises. Yet, it was much better than a prospective civil war.

The communists put forward several unacceptable conditions: give up privatisation, stop reforms, remove reformers from the government particularly Chubais and reinstate state ownership in priority sectors.

Yeltsin's assistants write, 'Since there was no pro-Presidential majority in the Duma... the executive authorities were forced to resort to unorthodox moves for pushing their decisions through. Practically, it boiled down to various forms of bribery — handing out privileges and preferences to commercial companies behind the various factions. Clearly, the more this was happening, the higher was the price of the deputies' "services".'

In the summer of 1994 Yeltsin eventually came to a conclusion that the dream of a political contract, a political truce in society with the concerted effort of all parties and movements was, for the time being, unrealistic. They had no shared platform. Yeltsin's press secretary, Vyacheslav Kostikov, would later write,

'In their desire to save Yeltsin from the hail of criticism on the economic front, members of the Presidential Council were quite insistent in their recommendations that he should distance himself from the actions of the government, particularly in view of the more unpopular economic measures being unavoidably on the way. The president heeded their advice, withdrew from managing the economy directly.

However, he had matured in the thick of economic activities. As a former secretary of the CPSU *Obkom*, responsible for a huge industrialised region, economic management was what he was used to. So now, at the age of 63, having given up the heavy economic backpack to Chernomyrdin and, seemingly, having freed the time and energy for the national strategy, he found himself without an internal pivot.

Meanwhile, Moscow was shell-shocked by all recent developments and regarded the phrase 'reconciliation and consent', ironically. Nothing was further from the daily life. The first half of 1994 was the time of the collapse of 'financial pyramids', the most notorious being the *MMM* scheme — the brainchild of Mavrodi brothers. The *MMM* was not the only one — it was simply the biggest and the most popular. The idea was simple: after buying *MMM* shares, the so-called *Mavrodiks, one* could sell them at a higher price virtually two or three months later. Unfortunately, there was no economic basis for these shares. The pyramid was self-propagating so it was clear that one day it was bound to collapse and leave investors empty-handed. When this inevitably happened the crowd laid siege to the *MMM*'s headquarters in Varshavskoye Schosse and blocked all entrances. It was a non-stop 24/7 rally. Tens of thousands of people kept constant vigil near the building, their mood being nothing short of hysterical.

A traffic policeman on the beat tried to stop the crowd but was pushed aside but not until after he had fired a shot. Following this the investors were dispersed by the OMON troops.

It is easy to understand the anger of these people: many of them had sold their flats or borrowed huge sums of money to invest in the *MMM*'s shares. Some enterprises in Moscow even paid their wages not in roubles but with *Mavrodiks*. Ironically, Mavrodi himself was convinced that by the end of 1994 he would convert *Mavrodiks* (bearing his portraits) into a 'stable payment instrument'. The multi-coloured *Mavrodiks*, bright pieces of paper that devalued with lightning speed were, in effect, a parody of vouchers issued by the state in the course of voucher privatisation.

These state vouchers came into existence on 1 July 1992 when President Yeltsin had announced the launch of a programme of voucher privatisation. Millions of TV viewers had been greeted by the sight of the head of the State Property Management Committee, Anatoly Chubais, pointer in hand, trying to explain, with graphs and diagrams, how the state enterprises were to be transformed into the private ownership. This historic occasion could be said to mark the starting point of the collapse of national industry with the suspension of production in many enterprises. In reality, the industrial crisis had started several years previously when the state subsidies were discontinued, state orders cancelled and economic ties between regions and republics severed as the centralised planned economy of the 'socialist' countries crumbled. Reasons for this belonged to both political and economic spheres. In reality, the Soviet economy had ceased performing back in 1989-1991.

The Soviet state itself fell apart and without it the Soviet economy couldn't survive. In the final days of the Soviet Union, under Ryzhkov, there emerged the so-called 'concept of a complete cycle of economic management' whereby, by the end of Gorbachev's era, the head of an enterprise could take complete charge of the key assets of his enterprise as he saw fit. As a result, by the very end of 1991, the 'spontaneous privatisation' was in full swing. Most commonly, there were two patterns applied for privatising the state property. In the first case, the assets of a state company were simply reregistered as a constituent part of a newly created Joint Stock Company. The second case presupposed the state property was privatised through an ingenious transaction of a "lease with an option to purchase"'. (*Privatisation: Russian style*).

Anatoly Chubais quoted a classic case of this spontaneous privatisation by top managers of the Research and Production Corporation (NPO) *Energy*. The charter capital of this joint stock company registered the manufacturing facilities of the huge plant and the 'intellectual property of a comrade Petrov' as being of equal value thereby giving the said Petrov, ownership. Chubais went on to recount that, 'it is practically impossible to reverse a deal like this, for the newly-created joint stock companies are immediately incorporated into new joint stock companies where they are valued and re-valued all anew... It is a foolproof scheme for absolutely boundless realms of embezzlement.'

Privatisation by 'directors' was gaining momentum. Politically, these 'red directors' spoke against Gaidar's reforms and advocated restoration of state orders and the planned economy. But in reality, they were interested in delaying the law on denationalisation for as long as possible. In the absence of such a law their hands were free.

Chubais went on to ask, whose interests were served by this spontaneous privatisation in 1992? The acquisition of assets was, in effect, being commandeered by the Party management, regional authorities and labour unions. The state received nothing: the interests of the treasury were simply not brought into the equation. And the workers? They had no part in these processes. The wonderful phrase, a "workers collective", served only to disguise a deal from which the bosses alone stood to profit.

Since spontaneous privatisation was going ahead full blast, it was impossible to procrastinate any longer on launching a managed, legitimate privatisation. The state had to curb the process. It had a responsibility to provide the majority of citizens with their share of property and give them a chance. How and when it should be done became the subject for heated debates.

The Directorial lobby were insisting that it was necessary to wait till the price reform stabilised inflation which would enable them to fill the market with goods and the state budget with real money. In essence, it meant delaying privatisation indefinitely, and possibly — forever. Chubais rejected this. The scope of, what was effectively, uncontrollable theft was expanding and the authorities, although aware of the need to interfere, were unclear on how to go about it.

Chubais and his team tried to analyse privatisation patterns in the former socialist countries. 'We examined, for example, the experience of privatisation in Poland. Over there, they started selling off assets at cash auctions. However, a lack of foreign and internal investment reduced the speed of sales* to a snail's pace and brought relatively little money into the budget. In the space of the first two years... they only managed to sell controlling blocks of thirty-two large and medium-sized companies and all it gave to the budget was 160 million dollars.' The main point of this example was not even the amount of money but 'the snail's pace' of

---

* Of controlling blocks of shares. — *Author's comment.*

privatisation. What Chubais wanted was to use privatisation for turning each citizen of Russia, even the poorest one, into an owner.

They considered another model, that of the Czechs.

'Over there at least, each citizen could receive privatisation vouchers and freely participate in an auction. However, we couldn't copy this model in its entirety either, since Czechoslovakia is a small country where, instead of many voucher auctions, they ran just one where they offered assets of all their companies.'

Eventually it was decided to marry the Czech model with the experience of nascent 'directors" capitalism. They decided to take account of the fact that entering a full-frontal conflict with the corps of directors would be a huge political risk for Russia. Directors should have some privileges but the majority of the population should not be forgotten, either. Chubais's fundamental idea had been that each Russian citizen should take part in the privatisation! It was a nice idea but a major stumbling block was the lack of 'live' money in the country at that stage.

A simple example: in 1994, the Norilsk Nickel was for sale at approximately 200 million dollars. At today's values, it was an ostensibly ludicrous low sum. However, even to raise even this amount cost Potanin's management group a lot of effort and when his company came to inspect the enterprise and saw the state it was the new owners told the Government to keep the money but take back your company! Three years later, in 1997, Svyazinvest* was sold at an open auction already for 1,875 million dollars. Within those three years there had finally appeared owners with money but this day had not yet dawned in 1992. Even if foreign companies had been allowed to take part without any prejudice, it still offered no solution. Back then, in the early nineties, foreigners acted with great caution, reluctant to invest in Russian industry — the French, for example, refused to buy Sibneft in 1997. Besides, the political risk of selling nearly all of the national economy into foreign hands looked too great.

Finally, the following plan was put forward. All citizens, including children, were offered privatisation vouchers with a nominal value of 10,000 roubles but available at 25 roubles each. Each citizen had a right to sell his vouchers

---

\* Company providing communications services.

without any limitations, take part in voucher auctions where vouchers were replaced with shares of privatised companies and invest them in investment voucher funds. Employees of the privatised companies had an additional right of using their vouchers for buying shares in their enterprise through a private subscription. This prescribed that 25% of preference shares (without a right to vote) was to be distributed among the employees free of charge. In addition, members of the work collective had a right to buy another 10% of ordinary (voting) stock — for cash but at a 30% discount. The managers remained with 5% available to them although not at a discounted price. Under this scheme, employees of the company received 51% of voting shares, that is, a controlling interest. The shares were bought by individual workers and not in the name of the 'entire collective' which meant that they could then be sold on. It was a compromise with the directorial lobby but it was a compromise that suited the government, particularly Chubais and Yeltsin, since it seemed workable and it meant private property was emerging in Russia.

'In response to unremitting pressure the directors lobby there appeared the third scenario for privatisation whereby managers of middle-sized companies were given the right to buy 40% shares for very low prices although the political cost of excluding large companies from this scenario was high. The argument against this was that if thousands of directors overnight turned into multi-millionaires it would incite people's wrath."*

A peculiarity of privatisation done the Russian way emerged in that the 'red directors' clawed out unthinkable and unprecedented privileges, so much so, that Chubais, in his book on the history of privatisation, contemplates whether it the price wasn't too high?

Inevitably the conclusion was that had there been no compromises there would have been no privatisation. Never the less, railroads, the aerospace industry, the fuel complex, enterprises of public health and education and most defence companies were excluded from the overall privatisation programme but even this concession cost Chubais dearly when he was pushing it through the Supreme Soviet The first stage — the

---

* The so-called 'basic' option for privatisation used at the majority of Russian companies was a compromise between the government and the faction of Russian communists. It is worth mentioning that in Khasbulatov's parliament communists were fighting tooth and nail in favour of the 'directorial' option. — *Author's comment.*

voucher privatisation — was earmarked for completion in 1994 but another crisis was on the way. The voucher market value plummeted. A voucher became worth about 3.5 thousand roubles whilst its starting price had been 10 thousand. Most companies were in no hurry to take part. Everyone was hoping that it will all go away and there was still a good deal of hostility. However, by the summer the situation had changed. Regional bureaucrats became frightened of being blamed for rejecting the programme and a list of companies to be privatised was finally drawn up. By July 1st those companies had been sold.

So how did the general public dispose of their vouchers? Twenty-five percent went into investment funds which, sociologists later worked out, were favoured by the intelligentsia. Another 25% were quickly sold, largely by those who were sceptical of privatisation plans, and these vouchers fell into the hands of large companies and enterprises. The remaining 50% were invested by members of work collectives into their own companies. All in all, 95-96% of the vouchers issued were used. Chubais called it a 'very good result'.

Nevertheless, things didn't go smoothly despite the classic example given by Alfred Koch: 'In the course of the voucher privatisation, ordinary workers of Norilsk Nickel would receive about 300 shares of their company through private subscription. If they managed to sell those shares at the peak of demand (at 16-17 dollars per share) each would profited by about 5,000 dollars, which was the price of the *Volga* car that Chubais had promised to TV viewers on 1 July 1992 and which was held against him many times subsequently. As a rule, however, shares were sold for much lower prices since the people didn't understand how to manage them properly.

Oleg Deripaska, now one of the richest people in Russia, told me during an interview that he used to stand by the gatehouse of the Sayany aluminium plant with a sandwich board — 'I'm buying vouchers'. And the employees were happy to sell. Soon, Oleg became one of the plant's owners with a gift for management, after which he extricated the plant and then the entire sector, out of the crisis.

As a result, the assets were accumulated by those who understood ownership. Vouchers were invested anywhere but into the workers own factory and such shares were sold instantly for the first price offered and, consequently, people were handing over the management of their facilities into the buyers hands without a murmur. The 51%, originally assigned to workers' collectives, subsequently grew in price enormously. In the next decade a voucher which could have been exchanged for Gazprom* shares by the end of 2008 was worth several tens of thousands dollars.

Chubais calls creation of the so-called 'voucher investment funds' a major mistake of privatisation. He says, '… the main blunder in privatisation was that it was never explained that there was no such thing as a 'quick buck' in privatisation! Chubais goes on to explain that 'pyramids' — companies that were promising unrealistically high returns (the notorious *MMM* among them) — ended up outside the state's remit. No one was responsible for them — neither the Ministry of Finance nor the State Property Management Committee yet this was precisely where a lot of vouchers landed eventually. The state managed to terminate their activities only in 1994 and, as a result, lots of ordinary people lost their chance to take part in the process and their hard-earned money evaporated.

The stable way of life, with all its reference points was rapidly vanishing. It was impossible to conceive of the commercial streak penetrating all spheres of life and that one now had to pay for things that had been considered free by definition. Doctors, paramedic, teachers were all demanding cash in hand. The majority of people simply had no way to earn additional money. As the customary ways of existence, the state support and the state guarantees were disappearing a 'new Russian criminality' swept over Russia in the wake of the slump.

An analytical memo on the social problems appeared on Yeltsin's desk in the first half of the following year, 1995, which said, for example, from a regional interview, 'People are gripped predominantly with feelings of powerlessness and isolation. Everyone deceives them: bureaucrats and militia alike. There is no protection anywhere…. the fear is of destitution.

A huge part of his workload in 1994 was foreign visits. Yeltsin, however, had troubles adjusting to any protocol, especially that of diplomacy. During the Russian-American summit of that year, US President Clinton and

---

* Open Joint Stock Company Gazprom is the largest extractor of natural gas in the world and the largest Russian company.

President Yeltsin, both in high spirits, came out to meet the journalists. Yeltsin had had a glass of white wine at breakfast; he was ebullient, 'gesticulated a lot and joked incessantly'. Clinton was trying to behave as if it was all as should be to the point where he burst out laughing and Clinton's infectious laugh extended for a full four minutes. It was suggested that Clinton was laughing 'artificially' trying to save the day.

The next day, on the way back from New York, the Russian President's plane landed in Shannon airport in Ireland. A 40-minute meeting with the Irish Prime Minister had been scheduled but Yeltsin never got out of the plane. Instead, an hour later, there emerged a sheepish Vice-Premier Oleg Soskovets.

After the episode, the press, equally in Russia, widely portrayed Yeltsin as 'being legless with drink' in what has become an apocryphal incident.

Naina Yeltsin, however, tells a different story. She says that Yeltsin had fainted in the toilet and that together with Korzhakov, the chief bodyguard, they quickly pulled him onto the bed, after which the doctor was summoned, installed a drip, and gave him injections. It could possibly have been a heart attack or a small stroke. However, the official justification was rather less convincing, it was maintained that he had merely he overslept — since Yeltsin didn't like to reveal his weaknesses.

However, the President's health would become the primary of political scrutiny for quite some time. Indeed, Yeltsin's assistants were in a constant flurry over the state of the President's health, his harmful habits and his psychological state. The episode in Berlin thus became the catalyst.

On 31 August 1994, Yeltsin, along with Chancellor of Germany Helmut Kohl, was attending the ceremonial parade on occasion of the withdrawal of Soviet troops from Germany. The beginning of the visit presented no problems. As was his wont, on board the plane bound for Berlin, Yeltsin was reading memos and briefing papers prepared by his aides, getting ready for the visit. The schedule was very tight — a series of protocol events. Only on August 30th did his working calendar register a 'free evening'. This free evening was spent in the company of the Defence Minister, Pavel Grachev, with whom their personal chat ran into the night but finally Yeltsin found himself unable to sleep, insomnia had set in. Come the morning, Berlin was in the grip of a heat wave and to relax and calm down Yeltsin had some beer. He started his scheduled appointments, yet right away something unscheduled happened. As Yeltsin was laying the flowers at the monument of the warrior-liberator in the Treptower Park a crowd carrying placards assembled across the road from the monument. Yeltsin disregarded his security and set off towards these people whose placards with their less than friendly messages. They were chanting anti-Russian slogans. The 'clash' with the picket was brief but something really got under Yeltsin's skin. On hearing the opening chords of the police band blasting out *Kalinka-malinka*\*, Yeltsin came up to the conductor and took his baton. This impromptu performance by Yeltsin didn't go unnoticed by either the Russian or the world media. The image of Yeltsin conducting the orchestra became iconic and is now inseparably associated with Yeltsin for all time.

The verdict of the Russian democratic press was by far more severe than the comments in the West. For example, *Izvestia* was writing that 'the President is not a private person and does not only represent himself with his tastes and preferences. Thus, every public appearance of his, every word he utters, each movement he makes tells not only about him personally but about us, too, about the political level and cultural standards in the new Russia.'

As exemplified above, one subject that kept cropping up was that of the first Russian President's 'harmful habits'. The style in the Party and *Komsomol* bodies was identical: he who didn't drink was not one of us. It was essential to be able to drink a lot but to keep control. It was well-known which vodka Yeltsin preferred, how he also liked cognac. Never the less, despite the stories, it is worth adding one point. Yeltsin was taking sleeping pills and some long-term medications for his heart, to regulate blood pressure and, probably, painkillers (as a result of his back injury). This being the case, of course he should have abstained from alcohol even in small doses. But he always tried to defy his age, he couldn't acknowledge diseases and didn't believe that his body could fail. Essentially, before his heart surgery Yeltsin had unswervingly believed his health to be sound as a bell.

In fact that Yeltsin's health was rapidly deteriorating. Of course, there were some forewarnings, untoward interjections, unprepared statements

---

\* Russian folk song, one of the best known ones internationally.

and agenda disruptions. But during those years (1994-1996) the president's workload was overwhelming. Yeltsin's team were well aware of the problem, a worry that increased during 1994. They felt that the President was not only losing his political initiative (although his ratings were still high), but his energy and abilities were also on the wane.

Upon return to Moscow all Yeltsin's aides decided to present the position in writing. Yeltsin's chief assistant, Viktor Iliushin, eventually agreed to give the letter, signed by them all, to Yeltsin during a flight to Sochi on September 4th. The response was instantaneous: 'What's this junk you slipped me? What bloody nonsense is it? Some assistants you are...' He hurled the letter back at Iliushin. 'Why have you done it, Viktor Vasilievich?' said Naina, 'What was that you gave him? What is going to happen now?' 'It was necessary, Naina Iosifovna,' replied the dejected Iliushin.

However, in Sochi the president was surprisingly calm, no conflicts, nothing; he simply didn't speak to them and kept his own counsel. Eventually, Yeltsin did refer to this speaking to Lyudmila Pikhoya, head of his speechwriters' group, some half a year later, in the winter of 1995. 'Why did you do it?' he asked. 'Why didn't you speak to me personally?'

Some retribution for the staff followed but one person among the signatories to the letter stands apart: Alexander Korzhakov. Technically, Korzhakov was employed by a private security company and held no official posts in Yeltsin's team between 1988 and 1990 and during various political battles. Yeltsin was often getting around Moscow in Korzhakov's *Niva*\* and was a frequent visitor to his dacha outside Moscow. During the crises of 1991 and 1993 this support became even more important.

As a bodyguard, he was invaluable but limited in such a powerful position and the first thing missing, most notably, was an awareness of the boundaries of his authority. Korzhakov never made a secret of his broad interpretation of the word 'security'. He would report on the other assistants and use his influence to interfere in the affairs of the Presidential Administration, the relations between Yeltsin and Chernomyrdin and even

---

\* A Russian car make.

international politics in terms of visit preparations and schedules. Through his special status he became of head of the 'enforcement bloc' in Yeltsin's circle and was gradually becoming an independent figure working his way towards the levers of power. He managed to talk Yeltsin into placing 'his' person in the State Property Management Committee and arranged a special decree whereby the National Sports Fund benefited from trade in spirits and cigarettes since he had his agent there, too.

By the first half of 1995, the list of Korzhakov's people, that is his friends or protégés, was already quite extensive. On it, there were the Procurator General Ilyushenko, Vice-Premier Soskovets, head of the State Security Service and later — the Federal Seciruty Service Barsukov, along with the Vice-Premier and subsequently Head of Administration Nikolai Yegorov. Korzhakov was even trying to appoint 'his own' Chairman of the Russian TV service. Within the framework of this disingenuous but very effective strategy, the September demarche of the main players in Yeltsin's near circle played right into the hands of the 'decent and loyal' bodyguard.

The year was becoming increasingly difficult. On 11 October, 'Black Tuesday', the rouble collapsed. The rouble had lost 27% of its value in a day, consequently a real threat of an economic crisis emerged. The President called the situation 'an attempted financial coup'. Bankers were blaming the developments on the inactivity of the Central Bank of Russia and the Government whilst State functionaries were pointing the finger at commercial banks. President Yeltsin promptly fired the "sagacious banker," Gerashchenko, the Central Bank's Chairman.

One version of the story was that, whilst Gaidar was championing strict financial stabilisation in 1992, the Central Bank's boss — answerable only to the Supreme Soviet — turned on the money-printing machinery full blast. Gerashchenko was also providing huge 'technical credit' to CIS countries.

The vast amounts of 'free' money that had appeared by the late eighties and early nineties wasn't secured against anything, this, combined with the impossibility of buying anything with people's savings, had dictated the logic of Gaidar's reform. It was of course perfectly clear even before

Gaidar's times that this money supply should be cut down. But the decisive action was continually being deferred.

In the beginning of the nineties, Boris Yeltsin spent nearly all his political capital supporting Gaidar's reforms yet they didn't seem to have brought about the desirable result.

When prices are set free, the economy always faces a threat of hyperinflation. a result it is very hard to satisfy the demand and arrest the prices, consequently, In addition, the resistance to reform within the state and the elites at the time was considerable; the gigantic planned economy was reluctant to obey the laws of stabilisation.

The commentator Yevgeny Yasin writes: 'Prices were liberalised and for the first 3-4 months Gaidar's team held the money in a very tight grip. However, the companies that were used to state subsidies and could not understand what to do next and hung on for another month or two but, it was impossible to survive so they had to close down. In essence, this was the source of the initial conflict between the government and Yeltsin on the one hand, and the parliament and the Supreme Soviet — on the other. Hence it was Viktor Vasilievich Gerashchenko who did put a stop to all of this when arrived as the head of the Central Bank. They started printing money — a lot of money.

This was a powerful political blow to Gaidar's government. The genie was let out of the bottle. By 1992, inflation amounted to 2,600%! In 1993 it was 930% annually. The first signs of financial stabilisation appeared only after January-April, 1993 when Gaidar's tight grip was still tangible, essentially by the summer of 1993 when the new national currency, the Russian rouble, appeared and the CIS countries were forced to withdraw from the so-called 'Rouble zone'.

Yasin continues, 'the price (for some reduction in inflation) was the biggest slump in production during the entire nineties. By early 1994, the volume of production fell by about 20%. Again, some concessions were made notably for planting in agriculture so more new money was issued until the day of reckoning came on 11 October 1994'

Even so, the biggest and by far the most grievous trial of 1994 still lay ahead.

# Journey into the Whirlwind
# (1995)

On 10 December 1994 the Kremlin was busy sending out Presidential greetings on the occasion of the forthcoming Constitution Day. 'According to his status,' Yeltsin's aides recollect, 'President of the Chechen Republic was on the official circulation list. In the whirl of activity, no one noticed it. Yeltsin's letter of congratulations was practically on its way to the mutinous general when a bewildered state communications officer stepped into the speechwriters' office and asked what method of delivery he should use in communicating with Grozny*.' This vignette was another illustration of indecisiveness and disorder dominating the relations between Moscow and Grozny after 1991. A military operation was underway in the Caucasus which, essentially, meant war.

'In November 1990 "The First National Congress of the Chechen People" (NCCP) took place in Grozny**. From the outset, this body was preparing the ground for ethnic cleansing,' wrote Yeltsin's assistants. 'Starting from the summer of 1991, the NCCP was taking practical steps in order to seize

---

* Capital city of Chechnya.

** It was subsequently renamed into the National Congress of the Chechen People (NCCP). — *Author's comment.*

power and got particularly active after the August putsch. On August 28th-29th, NCCP's forces blocked the town centre and seized the Council of Ministers' headquarters, the radio and TV centres and the airport.' Moscow responded promptly and sent down its delegation whose brief (as formulated by Yeltsin and Khasbulatov — himself a prominent member of the Chechen diaspora) to come to an arrangement with the local elite and stop disorder and bloodshed.

They failed to do so. On September 6th, an assault was launched against the House of Government while the Supreme Soviet of the Checheno-Ingush Republic* (still in existence at the time) was in session. Deputies who showed resistance were attacked. Chairman of the municipal Soviet, 60-year old Vitaly Kutsenko, smashed a window and tried to leap out. But the window was high up, the impact was on his head and he died in hospital several days later. Twenty people were rushed into the accident-and-emergency.

This was the beginning of an independent Chechnya.

Meanwhile, to Yeltsin, these developments in Grozny looked most contradictory: according to one interpretation, Doku Zavgayev, the head of the republic, 'was like a spider that had ensnared the entire republic in his web, placed his thugs everywhere and was desperately clinging to power. Perhaps, it makes sense to remove him by Gorbachev's decree?' Another version suggested: 'in the beginning of September of 1991, an anti-constitutional coup has been mounted in the republic… The republic has thus been plunged into a profound political crisis the consequences of which will be undoubtedly catastrophic.'

Sergei Filatov, a member of the Supreme Soviet wrote at the time:

'The day after this carnage, Khasbulatov, Acting Chairman of the RSFSR Supreme Soviet, sent this telegram to Grozny: "Dear compatriots, I was pleased to learn that the Chairman of the republic's Supreme Soviet has resigned and that, finally, a favourable political situation has emerged…" Khasbulatov virtually seethed with a ferocious hatred for Zavgayev, and found the latter's independence infuriating; so much so

---

* A former autonomous republic within the Union of Soviet Socialist Republics on northern slopes of Caucasus Mountains. Split into republics of Chechnya and Ingushetia within Russia in 1992.

that, allegedly, Khasbulatov once lost it completely and started screaming down the phone, urging Zavgayev's execution by a firing squad. However, not much love was lost on the other side, either. Zavgayev once let it slip: "When all of this is over and the situation in my native land is back to normal I shall ensure that only one person will go to jail — Khasbulatov. He is a diehard criminal!"'

Thus, two communiqués with contrary accounts of events in Chechnya ended up on Yeltsin's desk. He made a note on the second document addressed to First Vice-Premier Burbulis: 'Do we really have a profound understanding of the processes in the Checheno-Ingush Republic?' Soon, however, this republic ceased to exist as an entity within Russia. On 27 October 1991, elections into the Chechen parliament took place and the 'Congress of the Chechen People' drew borders between Chechnya, Ingushetia and Russia.

Whatever the motivations of those who rose in Grozny, the federal authorities saw the situation as mutiny and sedition, and to make matters worse, this mutiny involved arms. On October 19th, Yeltsin forwarded to Grozny an ultimatum wherein he demanded that within three days all seized buildings and premises should be vacated and arms handed over to the internal security agencies whilst unlawful paramilitary groups should be disbanded. If only he knew how many more similar ultimatums he would have to sign! On 6 November 1991, the President of Russia imposed a state of emergency in the Checheno-Ingush Republic.

At the time, the Russian KGB was headed by Viktor Ivanenko who later told the journalist Leonid Mlechin that when the rioters had captured the KGB headquarters in Grozny, he gave an order to 'burn all the files' and tried to telephone Yeltsin in Sochi but 'failed to be put through'. In his interview, Ivanenko expressed indignation that 'the head of security services could not get in touch with the president when things like that were underway in the country!' So what did he want to tell Yeltsin? '... Our choice was between applying force and trying to come to an arrangement with Dudayev.'

In reality, there was no choice...

Later, in his memo to Yeltsin Ivanenko would say, 'A considerable proportion of the population, primarily ethnic Chechens, support the dissolution of the Checheno-Ingush Supreme Soviet. Given the situation, the crisis can only be overcome by political means, since the use of force will only serve to escalate violence and push up the number of casualties while discrediting the policy pursued by the RSFSR and its leadership.'

This is what Sergei Filatov writes about the situation in his book.

'Before night fell, Khasbulatov arrived at the White House and together we went downstairs to meet Rutskoy who undertook control over the arrangements for the state of emergency in Grozny. We waited until it was 5 A.M. but around 5 or a little earlier it became clear that the internal troops that were supposed to play a major role hadn't moved — due to the order given by Barannikov, then the USSR Minister of the Interior, on Gorbachev's instructions. I believe that if Gorbachev had chosen a different tactic the events in Chechnya would have unfolded in a much less dramatic way, for each transgression against the law had to be punished. The decision on the issue was postponed until 14:00. Consequently, as instructed by Khasbulatov, at 14:00 I entered Rutskoy's office where all the insomniacs were already assembled. Rutskoy presented his plan for dealing with the problem. That was when I saw Rutskoy with new eyes: I realised that this person was overpowered by ambitions and emotions. At this instant he was ruthless — he suggested that the defiant republic should be encircled by the army and subjected to carpet bombing. I revolted against such a ruthless option and asked to move the discussion to the Supreme Soviet's session, for they were authorised to either endorse or bin the decree on the state of emergency. The problem was, the decree appeared on the eve of a holiday and the parliament was in recess. Clearly, no state of emergency could be organised, the preparations were disrupted, everyone was hoping the other would do it and consequently nothing got done.'

Yeltsin understood the developments in Chechnya perfectly well. However, he understood something else too: an escalation of military conflict now, in November of 1991, three months after the August putsch, was impossible. The configuration of power had not been completely worked out yet. It was necessary to arrest the knock-on effect of a civil war but Yeltsin was not prepared to resolve civil conflicts through the use of force.

Chairman Khasbulatov went to Grozny to set up a new body: the Supreme Provisional Council, with another prominent Chechen, Lecha

Magomedov, head of Russia's State Committee on Prices, practically a minister, at its head. Unfortunately, the path towards a political resolution had already been blocked by General Dzhokhar Dudayev.

It is curious to work out why the Chechens chose him as their leader. After all, like many other prominent Chechens, Air Force General Dudayev had never lived in Chechnya and only returned in 1991. His wife was Russian, and his entire career had been spent in garrisons in Ukraine, Siberia and the Baltics. Besides, highly-placed Chechens included not only Khasbulatov (second person in the country) but also two ministers, several deputy ministers, academicians, entrepreneurs and prominent CEOs. So why did it have to be Dudayev?

Most likely, Chechnya was fiercely proud of its only army general and sang in triumph when he had made the rank. The Ossetians had their own generals and well-known military heroes, but not the Chechens. And so he was invited to Grozny as a main contender for leadership. Chechens being a warrior people, military valour was placed above all else.

Everyone in the Kremlin, too, thought that it was completely logical for Dudayev to become the Chechen leader: he was charismatic, with stars on his epaulets* and extremely handsome into the bargain. And thus *Krasnaya Zvezda*** interviewed Dudayev in the autumn of 1991 and published the latter's comments:

'Yes, I often was given difficult postings but I always turned them around and made them exemplary. I was the best divisional commander. The army gave me a lot, practically everything. But my people's attitude towards the army is very negative, primarily because our young men are ruined there. They are born warriors. They cannot eat pig's lard, for example, not because it is fatty but because the young mountain dwellers have a particular physique. Yet in the army they are made to eat it, and made to clean up someone else's shit. As of today, the republic has formed its own national guards — sixty-two thousand-strong, with a territorial army of about three hundred thousand. We have embarked on the process of developing a legal basis for our armed forces and an entire defence system. Any armed intervention by Russia into Chechen affairs will start

---

* General's insignia in the Soviet army.

** *Red Star*, country's principal army newspaper.

a new Caucasian war. It will be atrocious. We have been taught in the last three hundred years how to survive. What's more, not as individuals but as one nation. The other Caucasian people will not stay idle either... Yes, it will be a war without rules and rest assured that we have no intention of waging it on our territory. We shall transfer this war back to where it came from.'

Dudayev, of course, was saying all of this back in 1991, when the Soviet Union still existed and the Russian leadership was making its first tentative steps towards untying the Chechen knot. Dudayev, however, already offered a ready-made concept, he had it all worked out: extreme nationalism and fanaticism.

On 2 November 1991 the Congress of People's Deputies of Russia declared the Chechen elections illegal, but already in 1992 the same congress accepted abolition of the Checheno-Ingush Republic and formation of two new entities: Chechnya and Ingushetia (another Soviet general — Aushev — became Ingush president). Thus, the republic was *de facto* recognised within the 1938 boundaries. Meanwhile events there were getting ever more dramatic.

In 1992, the Russian troops (garrisons of the Soviet army formerly deployed over there) were pulled out of Chechnya. By agreement with the Chechen side, most arsenals of weapons had been left behind. Yegor Gaidar, Acting Premier at the time, was among the signatories of this document and regarded it as a tragic inevitability since the residents of the military settlements — women, children and the elderly — remained hostages to the Chechen side.

As troops were withdrawing from Chechnya and the division of military armaments were negotiated, another serous conflict broke out in the Northern Caucasus — between the Ossetians and the Ingushes.

As Yegor Gaidar writes in his book:

'I remember well how it all started. For the first time in several months I decided to have a lie-in on Sunday, and not go to work. Early in the morning the phone went off. There were large-scale riots along the border between Ingushetia and Ossetia. The armaments of an interior ministry troop battalion had been hijacked. A battle was raging. The Security Ministry had spectacularly missed all signs of an explosive situation brewing there. We learnt about it all as a *fait accompli*. And now we were facing a realistic threat of a new Karabakh with long-lasting hostilities — this time within Russia.

With the president away on a tour of the country I got in touch with the General Staff and asked for the urgent deployment of paratroopers... and that the military should provide full cover from the air. I then instructed Georgy Khizha* to fly urgently to Vladikavkaz** and manage the on-site government task unit, sending along Sergei Shoygu***, who had proved himself during peace-keeping operations in South Ossetia, Georgia and Moldova, as backup. Having set things in motion, I went to the airport to meet Boris Nikolayevich and update him on the events.****

'... The first thing I did was go to Nazran*****. I was transported by the internal troops' APC but, even so, the spectacle was not for the squeamish. Around me were traces of a real battle, a lot of destruction and houses in the Prigorodny District on fire. Easy to guess, it was mostly Ingush homes. Ruslan Aushev met me on the border with Ingushetia. He said that I should not go any further by APC — I would become a target. So I climbed into his car, he was driving. The central square in Nazran was chock-a-block with refugees, thousands of desolate people that had fallen prey to the politicians that had played that simplest and the most dangerous card of radical nationalism. En route, Aushev was trying to find out what I thought about the real players behind this blood-soaked mayhem. Unfortunately, I couldn't help him, since reports from the Security Ministry were still confirming their utter helplessness. Then — negotiations with the Ingush leaders and a delegation from Chechnya, headed by Yaragui Mamadayev, who had arrived into Nazran to prevent the conflict from spreading over onto the Chechen territory. Then — some heart-rending conversation with the people in the square. At least it helped

---

\* Vice-Premier in the Gaidar's government. —*Author's comment*.

\*\* *Vladikavkaz* is the capital city of the Republic of North Ossetia -Alania in southern Russia.

\*\*\* Chairman of the Committee for Emergency Situations. —*Author's comment*.

\*\*\*\* Yeltsin authorised Gaidar to resolve the Ossetian-Ingush conflict, vested powers in him. —*Author's comment*.

\*\*\*\*\* *Nazran* is a town in the Republic of Ingushetia, Russia. It served as the republic's capital in 1991-2000.

to achieve this: the Ingushes were no longer certain that the Russians had made up their mind in advance as to the rights and wrongs in the conflict.'

As the Interior troops and paratroopers were making their way into the Prigorodny District to pull the adversaries apart, the Russian leadership were also considering an option of resolving the Chechen problem in one fell swoop: say, capture Grozny and remove Dudayev from power. After all, there was a state of emergency in Ingushetia, things could be spread around a bit. On second thoughts, the idea was discarded as 'spreading things thinner' was not the answer.

Separatism in a rebellious region would be a terrible headache even for a stable political system yet Russia was in the process of transformation: it didn't even have yet its own Constitution, no laws applicable to this situation, no new federal treaty. New international relations were only starting to take shape.

The conflict between the President and the Supreme Soviet, as well as all other political events of 1991-1993, suggested that in relation to Chechnya it was wise to play a waiting game. The Russian authorities were not ready for a full-scale conflict — not morally, not organisationally and not ideologically.

But in Chechnya it was a different story: the nation was unanimous in their support of Dudayev — they believed he had given the Chechens their independence.

In May-June of 1993, Dudayev did away with his parliament and dispersed the Constitutional Court. 'In his fight against his own opposition, Dudayev vested his security agencies with practically unlimited powers. Political opponents were being buried in mass graves in the Korpinsky Cemetery in Grozny's suburbs. The new ruler of Chechnya outlawed all opposition parties (Daimokh and Marsho) and their publications, imposed draconian censorship over all mass media. Live TV broadcasts were banned, and censorship extended to culture, particularly theatre' (*Yeltsin's Epoch*). The famous picture gallery of Grozny was pillaged, educational institutions and federal bodies closed down and Sharia law imposed — in a word, the new regime was introducing Islamic fundamentalism on an ever-increasing scale.

Still, the Chechen authorities were seeking a formal contact with

Moscow trying to endorse, albeit temporarily, the delineation of powers. Chechnya, for example, sent its 'ambassador' to Moscow; what's more, his letter of credence was composed with due ceremony, according to strictest diplomatic requirements:

'With a view to strengthening bilateral relations between the Chechen Republic and the Russian Federation, instilling into them confidentiality and sincerity and in pursuit of enhanced cooperation and reanimation of constructive and creative aspects in the Russo-Chechen relations... the Government of the Chechen Republic has accredited Mr Apazov, Soltmurat Neserhoyevich, and hereby requests you to extend your benevolence towards him and place faith in everything that he will have the honour of expounding to you...'

A Victorian English gentleman would not have put it more elegantly.

They didn't draw a line at that but sent to Moscow a 'Foreign Minister' and a representative delegation for negotiations. Yeltsin wrote to the Russian Foreign Ministry: 'Judging by the report, the negotiations would be useful. I would ask you to carry on. But our position should provide a basis for the operation of all federal bodies... I believe the Foreign Ministry should define this line... B. Yeltsin.'

Deputy Foreign Minister Adamishin replied to the President: 'Appointing a Foreign Ministry coordinator at the negotiations with Chechnya would mean that the Russian side recognises the republic as having the status of a foreign state.' In other words, leave the Foreign Ministry out of this, Boris Nikolayevich!

The desultory talks with Chechnya produced no results, although the Russian side involved some key politicians and prepared a draft Treaty on Separation of Jurisdictions. Dzhokhar Dudayev himself was very active, too. Unlike his ministers and advisors, his way of expressing himself was neither high-flown, nor verbose. He spoke a no-nonsense language:

'Boris Nikolayevich,

I have decided to address you with this missive since I find the situation between the Chechen Republic and Russia to be far from normal... As a first step, we could embark on the road to compromise: on the one hand, by recognising the right of the Chechen Republic, independently, to identify its own export quotas (for oil) and provide licensing. On the other — the

Chechen Republic will consent to pay Russia transit duty on the basis of mutually agreed rates…'

Dudayev sent this letter to Yeltsin back in July of 1992 and Yeltsin addressed to Gaidar: 'I ask you to consider Dudayev's proposals and draft our response.'

Meanwhile, Russian departments and institutions continued treating Chechnya as a Russian territory, and pensions, benefits, decrees and instructions were duly sent across. It wasn't quite clear who was receiving it all since federal organs no longer operated in Chechnya. At times, it led to some absurd situations. One of the State Property Management Committee's bosses, Alexander Kazakov, narrates:

'I shall never forget my business trip to Chechnya. I was carrying the Russian President's letter addressed to General Dudayev, with a proposal to run a voucher privatisation scheme within their territory. Since at the time there were no hotels there — I stayed overnight with the boss of the public amenities department of Ingushetia. The next day Dudayev and I managed to get in touch by telephone. A vehicle with a submachine gunner was sent to fetch and deliver to his residence.

I was received with deliberate coldness and was kept waiting for over an hour. Presently I got to my feet and, having dropped a sufficiently rude remark about the general, made my way out of the room. They caught up with me in the corridor and took me to see Dudayev. Since any initiative from Moscow left him seething, he had already replied to Yeltsin's missive saying that the population of Chechnya would never take part in voucher privatisation. I tried to explain to him that the Chechens should not be stripped of what belonged to them by law, and that the citizens of the republic could still take part in privatisation on the territory of, say, Ingushetia. There was a fleeting moment when I even thought that he agreed with me but the talks came to nothing. However, the Chechens did take part in privatisation but they received their vouchers but in Ingushetia.'

Judging by the 'diplomatic correspondence' and attempts to have the Foreign Ministry involved, Yeltsin himself wasn't sure who in the Russian top echelons should deal with this problem — the Government or his Administration? But given the stand-off with the Supreme Soviet, the dire situation in the economy and the new Constitution still not approved, in effect the power in the country was split.

Sergei Filatov is convinced that Dudayev was seeking contacts with Yeltsin for an understandable reason: his prestige started dwindling sharply, for whatever anyone's take on it, there was no state. 'People started arming themselves, nearly all schools were converted into army barracks and migration was colossal. Dudayev had to demonstrate that Moscow reckoned with him. For Dudayev, to sit down to the negotiating table with Yeltsin would have meant that Russia recognized the legitimacy of his power. It would have been, of course, a different story if the person to meet Yeltsin would be General Dzhokhar Dudayev, the Chechen leader.'

But Dudayev and his retinue just weren't having any of it.

Chechnya became the metastasis of the global sickness that affected Russia's entire political organism, the sickness that started developing right after the break-up of the Union. For example, in the early nineties, a desperate struggle broke out over the independence of Tatarstan, and a movement in favour of creating the 'Far-Eastern republic' emerged in the Maritime Territory. Such a republic had existed during and shortly after the civil war (1920-1922), and before the Soviet Union was created it had been an independent state. Then again, in 1993, on the initiative of the Sverdlovsk Oblast Council, the Sverdlovsk Oblast ran a referendum on establishing the 'Urals Republic'. Only the President's intervention in the autumn of 1993 helped prevent this extremely dangerous political manoeuvre of the Urals elite.

Separatism was spreading like wildfire.

The Kremlin, however, was constantly procrastinating and treading cautiously. No one knew how to fix this troublesome area, how to arrest the process, which glue to use and where to apply it.

Chechnya became the first self-proclaimed republic which ran its elections in spite of Moscow and came into being without a single agreement with Russia, not even a legal document on its status and delineation of authority. The Chechen regime created its illegal army and supplied it with Russian weapons, seized by blackmail and threats. They had introduced their own currency, and traded in practically stolen oil. Their leader kept threatening Russia while regularly providing asylum to terrorists and hostage- takers. In May of 1994, Chechen gangs had three times hijacked commuter buses bound for Mineralnye Vody*, demanded ransom and a helicopter to fly them back to Chechnya. Twice their demands were met, but the third time the command was to free the hostages and this operation left five Russians dead. Passenger trains crossing Chechnya were regularly robbed and there were many cases involving counterfeit financial documents that enabled Chechen producers, through deceit or blackmail, to take huge sums in cash out of Russia. Ethnic cleansing and deportation of ethnic Russians continued to the extent that, according to statistics, 147 thousand people fled Chechnya** in 1992-1994 alone. Still, main question was this: what was to be done with this process in principle?

By 1994, Moscow was aware that realistically-speaking, the choice lay between a military operation or lengthy talks. So, after the events of October 3rd and 4th, having elected a new parliament and adopted a new Constitution, Russia realised that the issue of territorial integrity could not be pushed back any longer. But before sitting down to the table of negotiations Russia had to identify the negotiation partner. War-mongering Dudayev did not fit the bill — it had to be a new leader.

This new approach made sense since in 1994 Dudayev's power started melting away. The Chechen opposition seized the area in the Terek River basin and entered into contact with Moscow-based Chechens. They all agreed that Dudayev's power was hanging in the balance! The event that finally made a monumental impact on the course of the Russian history was ostensibly humdrum. In the summer of 1994, prominent Chechens of Moscow assembled in the Peking Hotel and decided that they would support the opposition. Few people paid attention to this at the time, perhaps only the hotel commissionaire noticed that so many people of the Chechen diaspora gathered in one place. This consolidated opinion of the 'Chechen dignitaries' must have tipped the balance of the Administration's attitude.

A little later Moscow decided to recognize the Provisional Council of the Chechen Republic, the chief figure in Dudayev's opposition, Umar

---

\* Mineralnye Vody (*mineral waters*) is a town in Stavropol Territory, Russia.

\*\* This figure is at odds with the one quoted by Sergei Filatov (300 thousand), the real number will have to be established by future historians. — *Author's comment.*

Avturkhanov, at its head. He was head of the Nadterechny District Administration and an ex-militiaman. Moscow delegated its representative to this body.

Finally and most importantly, the Presidential Administration now favoured the idea of launching an attack on Grozny in order to displace Dudayev by the hands of the opposition that now openly supported Moscow. In an interview, a Kremlin spokesman put in thus: 'The idea was — one Chechnya, two systems. The Chechen Republic would stay but the three northern districts would be receiving humanitarian assistance such as the building of hospitals and kindergartens, and pensions would be paid. People should decide what they liked better: to do without in the independent Chechnya or be affluent within the federation.'

However, the opposition leaders themselves knew perfectly well that these beautiful plans were totally unrealistic: in Chechnya, one could only win by force. That is why they turned to the Moscow emissaries with a request: arm us and we shall take Grozny. Besides, how was one supposed to go about ensuring security of those three 'northern districts' against intervention? There was only one way: by overthrowing Dudayev.

In the beginning the idea was to draw a line at providing military advisors. Then the opposition asked for tanks and helicopters.

Sergei Filatov's recalls:

'In Chechnya, the desire was brewing to settle accounts with Dudayev by their own efforts, primarily with the hands of those who had been victimised by the regime. The opposition forces were headed by Gantamirov and Labazanov. Either to settle some internal score or *pour encourager les autres*, Dudayev made an attempt to capture Labazanov in Grozny. About three hundred people were killed in the process and the severed heads of Labazanov's relatives were thrown into a public square. After this massacre I doubted strongly that it was possible for Yeltsin and Dudayev to meet. My doubts were confirmed when I met Boris Nikolayevich. Dudayev himself had burned his bridges to negotiations with Russia's President.

'About the same time, opposition forces, led by Avturkhanov, came into action too. The head of the Nadterechny District Administration had been defying Dudayev's power from the very start, so much so that Dudayev's representatives never once made it into his district. The opposition were all for holding presidential elections not in 1995, as decreed by Dudayev, but in

1994. At their congress, the opposition formed a Provisional Council and appealed to the President of Russia to provide help in restoring normality in Nadterechny District and other areas where Dudayev's influence had been lost.

'It was suggested that I should meet with Avturkhanov. ... I was reminded... that Avturkhanov's opposition dictated no terms to the Russian authorities. Just the opposite, unlike other opposition leaders, they confirmed their adherence to the Constitution of the Russian Federation. I agreed to this meeting. Avturkhanov and I met in Moscow in June of 1994... and I agreed to pass the message from the National Congress of the Chechen people to the President. It was a request to the federal authorities to recognise the Provisional Council, help bring the life in the republic back to normal and reinstate the social security of its residents. Boris Nikolayevich instructed the Government of the Russian Federation to provide assistance to the Provisional Council in preparing and holding elections in Chechnya. I was secretly hoping that the President would make me responsible for the oversight of this matter but no such instruction was made.'

Thus, Yeltsin supported the opposition plans.

On 17 November 1994 anti-Dudayev opposition crushed one of Dudayev's posts in Bratsky village. On November 25th, under the cover of the evening darkness, at 21:10 the opposition launched an attack on Grozny. The offensive by Labazanov's and Gantamirov's units was supported by Russian helicopters which shelled Dudayev's military bases on the Tersky Ridge and in the northern suburbs of Grozny. Following a rocket airstrike, armoured columns set off towards Grozny.

At 7 A.M. on November 26th, six tanks broke through to the presidential palace. The opposition troops had seized the city centre, the 'state security' headquarters and 'the interior ministry'. The presidential palace was empty but for security guards. Pieces of paper were floating in the breeze and the windows had been left wide open. Dudayev and his guards fled, leaving Labazanov's unit to celebrate victory by firing in the air. 'By 16:30 the fighting in the Chechen capital city was practically over. In his TV address to the citizens of the republic, Avturkhanov announced that the power in the republic had been transferred to the Provisional Council. In the absence of real resistance, Avturkhanov's forces got carried away and were ready for celebrating a seemingly easy triumph,' historians would write later.

The triumph, however, was short-lived. As the assault stopped, Dudayev's grenade-throwers set about methodically destroying the tanks while from the rooftops, marksmen were executing the tank crews leaping out of their blazing machines. Infantry back-up for the tanks was completely insufficient and consequently Gantamirov's and Lavazanov's troops were scattered and destroyed. Worst of all, many Russian military personnel — excluding helicopter crews, of course — were killed, wounded or captured. Dudayev's troops captured 150 people, out of which about 70 were Russian.

It was a catastrophe.

The Chechens were covering the heads of the dead with white towels. These chilling white towels were scattered all over the streets of Grozny. At the same time recorded interviews with imprisoned Russian soldiers and officers were shown on TV. All in all, it proved possible to recapture some of the original 40 tanks, but it didn't save the situation. Commanding officers and tank crews had been hired by the Federal Counter-Intelligence Service on the basis of individual contracts for a 'secret mission in the line of service duty'. Their military record cards had been left with counter-intelligence officers, thus they carried no IDs. In their regular places of service they were not kept on file and the army supreme commanders supposedly knew nothing of this operation although it is hard to credit. The Chechen authorities warned that the 70 Russian soldiers and officers taken prisoner would be executed unless the Russian leadership admitted to the fact that they had been fighting on the opposition side.

This day, November 26th, was the date when Russia crossed the threshold beyond which a political process was no longer an option. Having believed the anti-Dudayev opposition, Russia found itself dragged into a regular war.

Yeltsin was holding one conference after another, Chechnya being on the agenda of every single one. The Administration was working out whether they should redeploy new Russian troops in support of the opposition or start talking to Dudayev? The first attempt to do so had failed, so the emergency plan had to be approved by all three security ministers. Interior Minister Yerin was against the instant escalation in hostilities. Defence Minister Grachev had his doubts, too: what if it leads to more unjustified casualties? There was no consensus among them.

The way Sergey Filatov remembers it: '... A draft decree on the state of emergency in Chechnya was prepared. What was required was to bring in internal troops and help the Provisional Council keep its power in Grozny. I think it was the then Interior Minister, Yerin, who put the brakes on this process. He told the President that the developments in Chechnya had to be properly verified and that for several days we should just follow the events.

'The President hadn't signed the decree... eagerly awaited by all agencies. When I informed Grachev about it..., his voice fell and he asked to be sent, if only on his own, to Chechnya. He felt responsible for his people and kept repeating, "How shall I ever look them in the eye?" Then, several days later, the Security Council decided to send in the troops... It is a shame that the political line of abstaining from force in Chechnya became distorted. Dudayev was alone; he had practically no support of either his own people or the expatriate Chechen community. At the same time everyone abroad, including the Chechens themselves, were insisting that the troops should never be brought in. Thus, the nature of war altered dramatically: it was now the question of national liberation and Dudayev was acquiring the status of a hero. A warning to Dudayev was issued on the eve of the invasion in the form of an ultimatum to lay down arms. Then the operation started.'

True, Dudayev was gradually losing control over the Chechen territory and his power was being compromised by internal conflict. But a civil war between the chiefs of various *teips* and clans, into which they had successfully lured the Russian security agencies, suddenly acquired the character of a war with Russia, and the warring Chechens immediately united against the common enemy.

Yuri Baturin, presidential aide on national security, recalls that on November 29th Yeltsin summoned him and asked for his opinion. Baturin honestly answered that he could see no military solution to the problem. A political plan was needed. A negotiator should be appointed to arrange a swap of prisoners. A military option required improved coordination between enforcement agencies which should take at least a month. Besides, a war would cost the budget trillions of roubles. 'Yeltsin,' continues Baturin, 'gave me a long examining glance and said, "I have called the meeting of the Security Council to discuss Chechnya. You shouldn't attend."'

Those who planned and approved the assault on Grozny by the opposition forces were, primarily, Head of Administration Sergei Filatov and director of the Federal Counterintelligence Service (FSK) Sergei Stepashin — both formerly deputies of a democratic persuasion, and in terms of their outlook and experience, both rather closer to being 'doves'. The resulting picture was truly odd: democratic 'doves' were all for an immediate solution through the use of force while the military 'hawks', the enforcement agencies, were finding refuge in silence and biding time.

In 1994 there really was another way forward: an economic blockade, isolation of Dudayev's regime and help to Nadterechny District. It is a shame it wasn't explored.

Thus, seventy Russian soldiers ended up in captivity. The murderous carnage in Chechnya and the fear of chaos were prodding the Kremlin to take decisive measures and adopt a clear stance. By the end of November 1994, it became evident that half-measures didn't work.

On November 29th, Yeltsin appealed to all parties in the armed conflict and demanded that within 48 hours hostilities should be stopped, arms laid down, armed units disbanded and all prisoners and those forcibly detained set free.

'Should this demand be not met within the time allocated, the state shall apply all resources at its disposal on the territory of the Chechen Republic in order to put a stop to the bloodshed, protect the life, rights and freedoms of the citizens of Russia and restore constitutional legitimacy, law and order, and peace within the Chechen Republic.'

It sounded like the President had made up his mind and war was now unavoidable. Yet those close to Yeltsin still harboured some illusions.

Presidential aide Georgy Satarov was saying later to Leonid Mlechin, a journalist, 'I know that there were several actions plans developed simultaneously. The ones with which I was familiar rather made sense. They didn't envisage a full-scale war. So when we learned that the army had gone in we were shocked. I submitted a letter of resignation but my colleagues stopped me, "You leave, he leaves... Who will remain to advise the President?"'

The plan that Satarov refers to presupposed deployment of the troops along the Terek River, establishing control over the three districts in the north, and a sanitary cordon around the rebellious Chechnya. This was a painstakingly slow plan while, at the time, it felt like there was a shortcut alternative.

The President started routine preparations for a military operation: Nikolai Yegorov (Minister for Ethnic Affairs) became a permanent Presidential representative in Chechnya while and Sergei Gryzunov (at the time, head of *Roskompechat*, the Russian National Press Committee) — head of the Provisional Information Bureau.

On December 5th, Grachev, Yerin and Stepashin flew to Mozdok* where Grachev personally handed over Yeltsin's ultimatum to Dudayev: lay down arms and disband the army, otherwise it's war.

The 'Information Bureau' kicked off its existence with live coverage of the personal meeting between Grachev and Dudayev. TV programme *Vesti* showed the hut used as a venue, followed by unique footage where Grachev and Dudayev were still together, all smiles. Then — the interview. Dudayev naturally said nothing on camera, only Grachev spoke.

'We retired to a room next door, just the two of us. I told him directly, "Dzhokhar, this is your last chance, let's talk like one army man to another. Let us resolve it all in such a way that the Afghan experience would not be repeated and there would be no bloodshed in Chechnya. Do you really think, Dzhokhar, that you can wage a war against us? I'll smash you in any case."

He asked, "Will you really open hostilities?"

"Yes, the decision has been made to prepare for a real war. Before it's too late it is necessary to admit the illegality of the decisions taken and reject the use of force."

---

* *Mozdok* is a town and the administrative centre of the appropriate district of the Republic of North Ossetia in southern Russia.

He then declared that he could not accept it.

I asked him, "Why can't you?" And he blurted out, "I am not my own person. They will simply never let me go. There will be others and they will proceed to carry out the decision that we have already taken." So I said to him, "Then it is war." And he answered, "War it is."'

However, on December 6th, as the two generals had their meeting in a tiny hovel on Grozny's outskirts, the plan for a military campaign was only starting to take shape. The troops were on the moved, redeployed, but there was no clarity as to who would take part in the main thrust. Preparations were sped through.

Once, in *Ogonyok*, I read the diaries of a Soviet tank officer who had taken part in the Soviet invasion of Czechoslovakia in 1968. He said that training — briefings, drills, exercises and advancing towards the border — had started half a year prior to the actual start of campaign. Although the Soviet generals were confident that the Czech army would never retaliate by direct warfare they were still preparing thoroughly and meticulously.

The final decision on starting the military campaign against the Chechen Republic was passed by the Security Council. Among its members were Boris Yeltsin, Viktor Chernomyrdin (Chairman of the Government), Pavel Grachev (Defence Minister), Yuri Kalmykov (Minister of Justice), Andrei Kozyrev (Foreign Minister), Yevgeny Primakov (director of the Foreign Intelligence Service), and the others. Everybody was in favour. The only person who voted against was Minister of Justice Kalmykov, a native of the Caucasus, who was soon made to retire.

Yeltsin issued three decrees on Chechnya within three days, one of which, of December 11th — 'On Measures to Ensure Legality, Law and Order, and Public Safety within the Chechen Republic' — was classified as top secret. On the same day the President addressed the citizens of Russia, 'Our purpose,' said Yeltsin, 'is to find a political solution TO the problem associated with one constituent entity within the Russian Federation — that of the Republic of Chechnya, and to protect its residents against armed extremism. Peaceful negotiations and free will of the Chechen people have been encroached upon by the looming danger of a full-scale civil war.'

All official authorities — from the State Duma to the Government — were swept up in a maelstrom of activity: setting up commissions, appointing extraordinary representatives and plenipotentiaries, creating 'working groups' and so on.

But the military circles were in a state of discord, not just acute but worse of all — public, some of the top bosses — Chief of General Staff General Kolesnikov, Commander-in-Chief of the ground troops Semenov, and head of the Federal Border Service Nikolayev — scathing about the imminent hostilities. However, when the final decision was endorsed the General Staff did send down several hundreds of their military advisors, although according to General Troshev, who had been involved in the assault on Grozny, those advisors were creating all kinds of pointless fuss.

However, the top commanders en masse were carrying on annoyed by and at odds with each other: the campaign was not ready by the specified deadlines, the plan wasn't detailed enough. All stakes were placed on a quick success.

In those days a lot depended on Pavel Grachev but he kept switching his stance. For example (and later he would be constantly reminded of it) he famously proclaimed that Grozny could be taken by a single airborne regiment. As an Afghan veteran with a firsthand experience of a hellish war he could only have said it in a state of tremendous agitation, after his tête-a-tête with Dudayev.

But sometimes his behaviour was really difficult to explain. For example, at one of the early sessions of the Security Council on the issue of Chechnya, Yeltsin asked Grachev about how much time he would need to prepare. Grachev answered, three days. A stunned Chernomyrdin told Grachev, 'Pavel Sergeyevich, go for ten days at least.' Grachev looked doubtful. 'OK, a week.' But on December 18th, at the joint session of the Cabinet of Ministers and the Security Council, when asked this question again a gloomy Grachev answered, 'Half a year.' He must have believed himself to be a hostage of the situation.

General Gennady Troshev writes about Grachev: 'The way I see it, Pavel Sergeyevich's was completely disillusioned about a successful completion of the war, along with many other serious and fundamental things.

Back in the days of conferences and briefings in Mozdok and Grozny, I noticed the discrepancy between Grachev's attitude, and his words and deeds. For example, he never went into details of our tactical plans. He would listen to you, give a nod, ask a couple of insubstantial questions and finish it off with some slogan like "Kill the gangsters!" or "Take care of your people!" or "Don't skimp on decorations for soldiers!" and the like.

... Grachev was a pro who had climbed every rung of the career ladder and cracked down on mujahedeen in Afghanistan, unlike most of us who hadn't tasted much of real combat. We were, therefore, expecting that he would come up with some striking decisions, off-beat moves and, most of all, offer constructive criticism.

Unfortunately, it felt like he had stashed his Afghan experiences in a museum's storeroom, and there was no spark in him, no flare… he was lukewarm, even detached.'

But Grachev must have had other reasons to be 'burnt out': political, as well as ideological and moral ones. Most probably he was overwhelmed by a sheer enormity of responsibility that he now had to shoulder. He worked out quickly that the operation had been poorly planned and doomed to end in a bloody failure.

Already on December 12th, the *next* day after the war was declared officially, the casualty returns from the Defence Ministry registered:

– Killed: 7, out of which 2 officers;
– Wounded: 13, out of which 6 officers;
– Captured: 17;
– Lost: 1 tank, 1 MPC, 22 vehicles.

The troops had barely set off towards Grozny when the fierce resistance was already showing what lay in store for the Russian army. Dagestan and Ingushetia were outraged, too, so the army's progress was full of danger. The troops had no time for a so-called 'operational coordination', hardware was breaking and the deployment was hasty. Nevertheless, until 1 January 1995 there still was hope that Dudayev's supporters, at the sight of this formidable force making progress towards Chechnya, would come to their senses, sit down to the table of negotiations and offer some alternative options.

On December 10th, Yeltsin checked into the Kremlin hospital. Doctors insisted on immediate surgery on his ventricular septum needed to increase the flow of oxygen to his heart. Yeltsin agreed but the time was ill-chosen. On December 17th, three days before his discharge Yeltsin convened a meeting of the Security Council right there, in the hospital. All those attending had to wear white hospital coats.

The Security Council emphasised that the deadline for a voluntary surrender of arms and the promise of amnesty expired on the night between December 17th and 18th. Yeltsin authorised Yegorov and Stepashin to invite Dudayev to Mozdok 'to identify procedures for the surrender of arms and military hardware'. 'There will be no more sessions of the Council on this issue, and I do not intend to make any addresses on this account,' he said in conclusion. Did he hope that Dudayev, being a career officer, would realise the horror of using modern weaponry and at the last minute get cold feet? But Dudayev never came to Mozdok, although he sent Yeltsin a telegram expressing his readiness to receive the Russian delegation in Grozny.

'Carry out the Security Council's decision in full,' Yeltsin told Grachev.

A protracted telegram exchange gave Dudayev some breathing space, although on the radio he kept urging his compatriots 'to purify our land from this filth', 'drench the bastards' route in blood' and 'shift the frontline to Moscow, to the Kremlin'. Having once more confirmed that Dudayev was expected for negotiations in Mozdok Yeltsin instructed his staff to stop replying to Dudayev's messages.

Chairman of the Government Viktor Chernomyrdin expressed his readiness to meet Dudayev without delay but the decision on negotiations kept being postponed. On December 29th, when an assault on Grozny looked unavoidable, Dudayev responded, at last, with a panic-stricken telegram: 'I declare and confirm my readiness for personally heading negotiations with the Russian side at the level of Chernomyrdin full stop delegations have been formed for negotiations at any other level full stop...'

Dudayev wanted a meeting with Yeltsin badly, he dreamt of it: be it in the Kremlin, in Grozny, abroad, anywhere. Some of the presidential advisors, for example Emil Pain, recommended to Yeltsin in their memos that 'the level of negotiations should not be lowered' and he should meet Dudayev in person.

But it never happened. Yeltsin was proceeding from the assumption that Dudayev's concern was not peace but, eventually, independent status of his republic. He wanted legitimacy since his state wasn't recognised by

## JOURNEY INTO THE WHIRLWIND (1995)

anyone, so he had to show the entire world who was calling the shots. He never made it to Mozdok for those disarmament talks.

At the end of December the troops finally made it to Grozny and started preparing for a siege. They had to build shelters and dug-outs, entrench themselves, deliver provisions, store munitions — all this while sustaining daily losses. Meanwhile Yeltsin found himself in the crossfire of fierce public criticism. The outrage of journalists, deputies and political commentators knew no bounds. Many were keen to finish this war as soon as possible.

General Troshev recalled at the time:

'31 December 1994 was the start of the operation to capture Grozny. Some generals believed that the idea to do it on the date of a public holiday came from the Defence Minister's inner circle where, allegedly, they wanted to give their boss a birthday present* by capturing the city. I am not sure whether this is true or not but it is a fact that the operation was rushed and not supported by proper estimates of the hostile forces and deployments. There hadn't even been time to devise a code name for the operation.

'From the operational data on the armed units defending the city it was calculated that a storm would have required at least 50-60 thousand men. These calculations had been tested by time and history. Yet in Grozny, as of January 3rd, we had no more than 5 thousand men while the insurgents had twice as many!

'Radio communication between assault units was practically paralysed by chaos on air. Units had practically no coordination of movement and most tank and APC mechanics and drivers were inexperienced. Preparation fire rendered several roads chosen for attack impassable with rubble. Mixed columns (vehicles and armour material) stretched out along the streets with no space for manoeuvre. As a result, those in the buildings were firing at the infantry and operational hardware at point-blank range. Commanders, from battalions down, had no maps of Grozny, hence the frequent "route slip-ups" and loss of bearings, and if there was a map it would be dating back to before 1980...

---

* Pavel Grachev was born on January 1st.

'In essence, militants just waited till the armoured vehicles appeared in the city and then applied the classical tactics, same as mujahedeen in Afghanistan had done: they would kill the first and the last vehicles in a column and then target the other vehicles, effectively trapped, with intense fire... Tanks and MPCs broke into the city centre but without cover by grenadiers most of them were destroyed by anti-tank grenade launchers. The element of surprise was wasted and catastrophe ensued. Only North and North-East units made it into the city but they were fighting against overwhelming odds.'

An inter-service team of about 300 fighting men, writes Troshev, got lost in the city and stumbled across the railway station. They took it and for more than 24 hours were fighting off attacks of Dudayev's men who had encircled it. The unit commander, Colonel Ivan Savin, decided to break out and was killed, but some of his men survived, although more than 70 men were killed in action. In the early days of January this episode received the most TV coverage, some terrible statistics were quoted: 300 casualties, 500... People were furious at the mediocrity and haste in planning the campaign.

And consequently, the very nature of this war, unwanted by anyone, became clear. Within the first three months, the Russian troops had lost about 14,000 men. Informational support for the campaign was as poorly thought out as the military aspect. Russian and foreign journalists alike were reporting directly from the streets but the Kremlin propaganda had no coherent line or an intelligible plan. The country was simultaneously hit by depression and hysteria.

Demands to withdraw the troops immediately were coming from all sides. It was probably the only war in the XX century that got covered in the absence of any censorship whatsoever.

The real size of a political catastrophe was slowly becoming clear. A plenipotentiary presidential envoy for human rights, Sergey Kovalyov, returned from Grozny in the beginning of January. In response to Kovalyov's numerous interviews where he was calling upon the authorities to stop this war and quoting numerous transgressions against human rights in Chechnya, Yeltsin publicly retorted that those rights had been violated for over three years, ever since Dzhokhar Dudayev came to power. Kovalyov responded with a new appeal to Yeltsin:

'The President of Russia may be displeased with my mission but for my part I am also displeased with the President. It is time that the bloodshed among civilians was stopped. The President is the guarantor of human rights, there is a provision in the Constitution about this... I may only answer in kind. For some reason, for over three years the President has been silent and then sent in the bombers... Let him explain whose decision it was to bomb the city. If he is President he should be in the know and should take measures to prevent deaths among non-combatants. He has been completely correct in saying the right to life is a fundamental right*.'

Kovalyov prepared a voluminous report and officially applied for an audience with Yeltsin after which he called a press conference. Yeltsin himself writes:

'I remember the effort that the meeting with Sergei Kovalyov cost me. From the very first days of the campaign he took the separatists' side and then came over to Moscow to tell me about the destruction and casualties in Grozny. I was virtually torn apart by inner contradictions. Here in front of me was seated a decent person, a democrat, a human rights activist, a plenipotentiary for human rights. How should I bring home to him the message that the statehood of Russia and its very life were at stake? He wouldn't heed my arguments.

'Those were very dark days when my assistants perceived every military TV broadcast as treason. Had we then decided to use emergency measures and curtail the freedom of speech, the schism would have been imminent.'

Yeltsin listened to Kovalyov's report in silence, gloomily, thanked the latter coldly and bid him farewell. However, Kovalyov's stance was completely intractable and irreconcilable. He had visited Dudayev's camp and was using their data, often unverified.

Many Russian generals and Yeltsin's inner circle alike were demanding Kovalyov's immediate return, even by force, termination of his employment as a presidential envoy and even his arrest. Yeltsin did, however, respect Kovalyov's bravery and that much was clear to all.

---

* Yeltsin had been saying that for three years that the most fundamental right — the right to life — had been violated in Chechnya. — *Author's comment.*

Meanwhile, the polemics were raging not only in mass media — debates were fierce within his team in the Kremlin too.

Presidential aide Satarov was telling Yeltsin that he may lose support of the democratic press, top military figures would be increasingly viewed with resentment, a schism in the parliament and the government would cause a chain of resignations and finally, he may lose the next presidential elections...

And this is the memo of the presidential think tank forwarded to Yeltsin at approximately the same time by head of Presidential Security Service, Alexander Korzhakov. All things considered, this memo looks more like denunciation:

'... The Presidential advisor Satarov has distanced himself from the President's standpoint on the expediency of bringing troops into Chechnya... He has also pointed out that, in his view, actions at all levels of the state apparatus have been characterised by a total lack of harmonisation. Satarov also has commented that if this is a standard practice for the state bodies' operation it would bring about, sooner or later, the collapse of the regime existing in Russia.

'The above* proves that the members of the think tank totally disagree with the President's political views in respect of the Chechen problem and that, on the contrary, their opinion coincides with that of both parliamentary and non-parliamentary opposition. Taking into account the fact that Kovalyov is also a member of the think tank... the thought suggests itself that members of the body have been selected for making mutually encouraging noises and saying yes to one another.

'It is also curious to point out that, with the exception of Lobov and Filatov, practically nobody has mentioned the violations of human rights by Dudayev's forces and the criminalisation of the republic where the arms trade and the drug industry are thriving. Neither has it been mentioned that Chechnya is an unalienable part of the Russian Federation...

'... What is required, first of all, is the urgent replacement of several members of the Presidential Council...'

---

* Korzhakov quotes statements made by other think tank members: Volkogonov, Pain, Karyakin, Gozman, Masarsky and Yasin — all of whom were also sharply critical of Yeltsin and his stance on Chechnya. — *Author's comment.*

'Yeltsin celebrated the New Year modestly. From January 1st to 3rd he kept himself to himself, not receiving even Korzhakov and Barsukov, only reading updates on Chechnya. But what the assistants did record was the change of his attitude.

On January 4th, Yeltsin convened in the Kremlin a briefing on Chechnya. He asked many difficult questions:

What had been the purpose and the underlying idea of the Grozny operation? They had entered the city — now what? What was the army's objective? Why had the operations in the city been carried out without the support of the Interior Ministry troops?

Why were these young unseasoned soldiers involved in combat? Had they been trained to fight in an urban area?

What had been the reasons for using tanks and armoured vehicles in the streets?

Why hadn't southern approaches, along with other routes suitable for militants, been blocked?

When could control be established over the key facilities in the city? Was it possible in principle?

What was the real toll: on our side and, also, amongst the militants and civilians?

Why were the oilfields on fire?

As for Dudayev: was he in his bunker or had he fled? If he was on the run why hadn't he been arrested?

He was scathing in his criticism but believed that the army should learn the lesson, even from this horrendous experience.

From this point onwards, he was in the clutches of two profoundly opposite options: either dismiss quite a few army and public leaders, freeze the hostilities, stop the war and distance himself from his own decision; or impose a state of emergency, curtail freedom of speech and effectively delegate some of his authorities to brass hats and chiefs of security agencies.

But in the end he did neither.

Yeltsin 'shielded with his own body' the top echelons of the Russian army ensnared by their own internal contradictions. He assumed complete responsibility and channelled all his dwindling political recourses into his support of the army. He repeatedly emphasised when speaking on TV: he alone was responsible for the consequences of the war in Chechnya.

In response to criticisms over the army's equipment, where instead of using high-precision weapons of a new generation it had to rely on bombings and missile attacks which caused devastation and killed lots of civilians. Running counter to any logic of warfare, Yeltsin repeatedly promised that bombings and the use of air power 'would be discontinued' after such and such date (after January 1st, for example).

Still, the President was reluctant to admit defeat by withdrawing the troops instantly (at least back to the Terek River) — a demand put forward by democrats, human right activists and international agencies. Having sustained such human losses in tiny Chechnya the Russian army simply could not withdraw. This seemingly simple theorem, in practice, had no solution. The defeat of the Russian army in Chechnya in the beginning of 1995 portended not a lesser but a bigger political catastrophe for Russia. Besides, much as the generals were wary in the beginning, it was extremely dangerous to kick them out of action after the war had started.

Thus Yeltsin moved into spring — between the rock of civil displeasure and the hard place of a military mutiny. The problem was that had he admitted at the beginning of 1995 that the army was not ready for combat duty, pulled the troops out and thus confirmed, *de facto*, Chechnya's self-proclaimed status the generals would have accused him of 'betrayal' and claimed that he had stolen their when he suddenly gave an order to stop military action and the air raids.

Thus he tried to accommodate both ideas: to minimise losses among civilians and to pursue war to its logical conclusion. Meanwhile the Russian army was coming to understand what a dangerous enemy they had to deal with. Dudayev's 'army of savages' that was supposed to scatter at the sight of the formidable Russian military might with its planes and tanks, in reality turned out to be a well-trained and prepared army of saboteurs in receipt of serious help from outside. To start with, it simply did not occur to Russian TV viewers what was meant by the reports of 'Arabs' whose bodies were found among the dead. The Russian army was fighting Islamic fundamentalism that was fanning the flame of this extremely useful war with finances, weapons, intelligence, 'military advisors' and propaganda.

## JOURNEY INTO THE WHIRLWIND (1995)

This was the first advent of the 'war of civilisations' that would become a much talked-about subject in future and that would manifest itself again in Afghanistan, New York, London and Madrid.

Meanwhile by springtime there were the first successes. General Troshev recollects:

'... In the course of February, Grozny was finally hemmed in from all sides... By April, the militants had been dislodged towards the foothills of the Greater Caucasian Mountain Range. In April, the group under command was ready for action in the mountains. However, we needed some breathing space. Some urgent problems had accumulated over several months of practically incessant combat, for example we had to repair damaged vehicles, carry out maintenance work and replenish supplies. People were tired out... Besides, according to the overall plan of the Chechen campaign, various political measures were envisaged for execution at various stages of combat: negotiations and the like... Our side was strictly adhering to all moratoriums (of which there had been several in the first Chechen war) while the enemy was contentedly transgressing them...

'Anyway, in spring of 1995 we still hoped that Dudayev's army could be driven into surrendering their arms and stopping resistance. I was also involved in negotiations; I was among the first top commanders to meet Maskhadov[\*]. On 26 April 1995, when President Yeltsin signed the decree "On Additional Measures for Normalising the Situation in the Chechen Republic", we realised that the moratorium was a purely political measure: the country was getting ready to mark the 50th anniversary of the victory in the Great Patriotic War[\*\*\*] and numerous foreign delegations were due to attend the festivities.'

... Russia was getting ready to celebrate the 50th Victory Day against the background of the Chechen campaign. A huge Victory Memorial was

---

[\*] *Aslan (Khalid) Maskhadov* (1951-2005) was a leader of the Chechen separatist movement and the third President of the Chechen Republic of Ichkeria.

[\*\*] Unfortunately, these negations led to nothing. — *Author's comment.*

[\*\*\*] The name assumed in history of the Soviet Union and Russia for the part of WWII (1941-1945) when the Soviet Union was involved in fighting fascism.

under construction in Moscow on the Poklonnaya Hill. War veterans were expected to take part in the grandiose parade and there were to be concerts and functions, in a word — a great festival.

Despite fears that the world leaders would not attend it because of Chechnya, the celebration did take place. Yeltsin was standing on the rostrum together with the other G8 leaders: Clinton, Mitterrand, and Kohl (apart from them, top leaders and heads of diplomatic missions had arrived from dozens of countries from all over the world). Respect paid to Russia, the Victory and the Russian people was particularly important at this stage.

It felt very bizarre to celebrate the Great Victory in those awful days. We were remembering Stalingrad and Kursk while the battle was raging in Grozny and the broadcasts were eerily reminiscent of the war-time footage: soldiers in helmets, powder fumes and deafening cannonades. Small nations defend themselves sometimes cruelly, sometimes inadequately or desperately. They do not fight, they cling on to life; they have no choice. Sometimes it is possible to resolve those conflicts militarily, sometimes not. Iraq, Vietnam, Algiers and Afghanistan — they all had their own tragedy and their own historical truth. The 'correct peace' can only be established through a compromise with local elites and can take decades to achieve.

In June of 1995 a new leader appeared on the Chechen scene — Shamil Basayev\*. He was the one who made good the erstwhile Chechen promise 'to transport the war to the Russian territory'. It was during these days that the militants launched their first terrorist operation in Russia.

'At 11:30 on June 14th, traffic police at Checkpoint No 1 located, on the 104th kilometre of the Georgievsk-Kaspiysk motorway, a convoy of three *KAMAZ* lorries and a *Lada* with militia insignia — a crudely painted navy line and a beacon. The convoy was heading towards the town of Budennovsk. All passengers in the *Lada* were wearing militia uniforms, looked Slavic and spoke without an accent. None of the vehicles had licence plates and traffic police ordered the convoy to stop. A man stuck

---

\* *Shamil Basayev* (1965-2006) was a Chechen militant Islamist and a leader of the Chechen rebel movement.

his head out of the "escort *Lada*" and snapped, "This convoy is exempt from inspection, it is carrying 'Cargo No 200!" (dead bodies of the Russian soldiers)'. (*Yeltsin's Epoch*).

The militiamen made the convoy turn and directed it towards the Budennovsk Interior Department. This is when the tragedy started to unfold. Militants in the lorries and the *Lada* first captured the municipal militia headquarters and then seized the buildings of the Administration, the children's centre, the fire station and finally — the district hospital. By that time they had already taken 400-500 people hostage. The hospital counted 450 medical staff and about as many patients, including some women on the maternity ward. The total number of hostages reached 1,400. Seven patients who turned out to be servicemen were executed on the spot. Several militiamen were killed during the initial attack, and six militants died too.

On the night of June 14th and 15th, militants demanded over the phone that the military action in Chechnya be stopped. This demand was voiced by Shamil Basayev who introduced himself as the guerrilla unit commander. Negotiations started...

That was the beginning of the lengthy and torturous Budennovsk epic. 'At 8:20 on June 15th, because the press had failed to appear in the hospital at the appointed time, five people were executed on Basayev's orders...

Chernomyrdin interrupted his vacation and returned to Moscow. From this moment onwards, on instructions from the President, he would be the main negotiator from the Kremlin side. Prime Minister proved to be a gifted negotiator — but he had no sway over the actions of security forces, and this weakened his position considerably.

Yeltsin had left, as scheduled, for the G8 meeting in Halifax, Canada, on June 15th. However, before his departure it had been decided that if the militants shot more hostages the thing to do would be to go 'tough'. Later this raised the question of why he hadn't sacrificed the international negotiations in order to negotiate with Basayev *himself*. I believe that to appoint a cautious and experienced Chernomyrdin, with his penchant for compromises, was the best move. Harsh and intractable Yeltsin was just unimaginable in this role. Besides, he thought that this meeting with the world leaders could be used as a chance to explain Russia's approach to Chechnya.

At 4:50 on June 17th, there was an attempt to attack the hospital premises. The first storm lasted four hours. The ground floor was captured but a fire started on the first floor, so the terrorists ensconced themselves on the second. The assault didn't only fail but led to huge losses. Among the hostages, 120 were killed and 80 wounded — some by 'friendly fire' and some executing by terrorists who were punishing everyone who resisted and refused to form the 'human shield'. Three Alpha and seven interior troopers were killed, too…

Everyone wanted to know who ordered the assault Yeltsin gave a clarification from Halifax: 'Yerin and I made this decision prior to my departure but we wanted a day or a day and a half to prepare so as not to make a mess of it.'

But the intent 'not to make a mess of it' didn't work. Yet once more, he assumed all the responsibility and covered up for the generals. However, in Budennovsk, his confidence in security forces was finally exhausted. At 14:00 there was the second assault that lasted only 55 minutes, after which Basayev asked for a ceasefire to let out 120 women. The footage of scared exhausted women in hospital gowns, running away from the hospital, made headlines the world over.

When the smoke lifted it became clear that after all one had to talk to the militants. As a result, Basayev's demands were partially met and an order was issued to discontinue the action and start negotiations in Chechnya.

Chechnya welcomed Basayev as a hero and the long-awaited negotiations on 'the withdrawal of troops' finally kicked off. Yeltsin, back from Halifax, presided over the Security Council's session on June 29th where he dismissed head of the Stavropol Territory Administration Kuznetsov, Interior Minister Yerin, FSB director Stepashin, and Vice-Premier Yegorov. The President didn't sign letters of resignation submitted by Defence Minister Grachev and Security Council secretary Lobov.

Despite everything, Budennovsk became an important turning point in the history of the first Chechen war. Prior to all this, Dudayev's government had had some feeble chances of justifying their actions and gaining international recognition — now they had none. In Budennovsk the spectre of the future nightmare first took shape: human trafficking, severed heads, stone pits where people would be kept for weeks, months and years in their own excrement, and hostage-taking. Up until Budennovsk we had had no experience of a war where pregnant women and children took part. The 'victory' in Budennovsk became a prologue to the defeat of the Islamic fundamentalists in Chechnya. The world recoiled from them.

However, apart from Chechnya the country had to deal with some other pressing issues — primarily, a new parliamentary election. In September of 1995, Yeltsin's Administration embarked on an urgent preparation of the election campaign. The Kremlin decided that its interest were to be represented by two parties at once (political commentators were making knowing faces, 'It would mean introducing the civilised bi-partite system'). The parties were to be from the 'right-centre' and the 'left-centre'. The former (Our Home — Russia) was to be headed by Viktor Chernomyrdin and the latter — the party of social-democrats — by Ivan Rybkin, the State Duma's Speaker.

However, it didn't work. The 'party of bureaucrats' — as Chernomyrdin's OHR was nicknamed right away — despite its powerful administrative resources and the fact that many heads of administrations, major industrialists and mayors hastily joined its ranks — came only third in the election and indeed got fewer votes than Gaidar's Russia's Choice in 1993. Only four electoral associations made it into the Duma — the very same who had been leading from the very start: CPRF that gained 22.3% votes (some 15 million people voted for it); LDPR — 11.18% (7.7 million); Our Home — Russia — 10.13% (just over 7 million); and Yabloko — 6.89% (4.8 million).

This was the greatest triumph of the communists in all years of their existence in the new Russia.

Yeltsin viewed the parliamentary election as a test for Chernomyrdin as a successor. It is easy to imagine this situation: Our Home — Russia would get 30-35% of votes, receive the majority of seats and Yeltsin would turn down the second term with an easy heart. Unfortunately, the election results delivered Chernomyrdin a crushing blow and the question of 'Who?' became even more acute. Yeltsin's poll ratings fell from 20% in the beginning of the year (it was still at 30% early in 1994) to three percent at the year's end.

In the second half of 1995, Yeltsin Boris Nikolayevich survived two heart attacks, one after another — referred to in the official press as 'coronary heart disease'. 'The first heart attack', writes a journalist Oleg Moroz, 'is believed to have happened on the night between July 10th and 11th.' A paramedic on duty discovered Yeltsin on the floor in the bathroom and the President was rushed into the Kremlin hospital. This was the result of all the events over the recent years. Yeltsin had never followed medical advice and continued from stress to stress, from one combat to another.'

However, Yeltsin discharged himself before the course of treatment was finished. The stay in hospital was followed by visits to France and the USA. After this, Yeltsin went to Sochi to recover. 'Recovery' didn't happen.

The second heart attack occurred on October 26th. The first spasms caught up with him in the steam room in a bath but he still believed himself indestructible. The board of Kremlin doctors stated, on October 27th, that the 'blood supply to his cardiac muscles remained unstable' although there were no signs of heart failure. This time the doctors were implacable: he was to spend an entire month (November) in a hospital, probably for the first time ever. He used this time to think about a successor — everybody was more or less sure it would not be him — given his health and the burden of a war in Chechnya.

The Kremlin was awaiting Yeltsin's decision: under the circumstances they simply didn't dare push him towards the second term in office. Yeltsin kept silent and offered no comment.

But Yeltsin's heart infarction made him face up to the question in earnest: he had to decide whether he should or shouldn't stand again and whether Chernomyrdin was ready to become his successor.

Should there be a presidential election in 1996, and if so, what would it all mean — given that his health was so undermined and the war in Chechnya was still raging on?

# 'With Him, We Feel Safe'
## (January-July of 1996)

In 1995, the Kremlin Administration carried out a nationwide survey of people's attitudes towards the President's policy. 'It revealed,' write Yeltsin's assistants, 'a wide range of negative perceptions: "old", "ill", "doesn't deliver on his own promises", "doesn't ensure enforcement of laws and decrees" and "has harmful habits". The residual positive response was piecemeal: "gave us freedom", "experienced", "with him, we feel safe", etc.'

This 'feeling safe' felt particularly counterintuitive in the aftermath of October 1993, the trauma of the reforms and the Chechen war.

To start with, the approaching New Year did not bode well with him. In December of 1995 Yeltsin had another heart attack which sent him constantly shuttling between the Kremlin hospital, a health resort in Barvikha and the Kremlin. On New Year's Eve he traditionally assembled his closest colleagues in his office. They cracked open a bottle of champagne and filled their glasses. Yeltsin looked at them, a touch of irony on his face: 'Champagne for you, a substitute for me!' he said wistfully.

At the end of 1995 the Central Election Committee finalised the results of the Duma election and it turned out that communists had scored an important victory. True, they didn't receive the so-called 'qualifying' majority which would have given them an automatic veto or a right to initiate impeachment, but what they did get was quite sufficient for filling most key Parliament jobs with their members. Yeltsin's assistants recollect that for the next four years the State Duma became a 'well-appointed and comfortable headquarters of the communist party'. Their leader Gennady Ziuganov topped the list of candidates in the presidential elections.

The war in Chechnya, too, was a source of all kinds of terrible surprises.

On December 9th, a party of militants commanded by Dudayev's son-in-law — a former *Komsomol* functionary Salman Raduyev — made an assault on the Dagestani town of Kizliar. First they tried to attack a military airfield and destroy helicopters but then changed their route and captured a hospital, a maternity ward and a school. They drove several thousand people, at gunpoint, into the hospital building. Several dozen they shot. The nightmare of Budennovsk was repeating itself.

En route, Raduyev's group encountered 'several thousand Russian troops' and got through quite a few road blocks and militia cordons — all of which proved totally ineffective (the fact later confirmed by the events in the Moscow theatre and Beslan). The war had spread to within Russia and it was simply not feasible to put in tight border controls between localities and provinces.

At the time the FSB's boss was Mikhail Barsukov — a person who came from a particular background. Previously he had been in charge of the Kremlin security and therefore calling him a security professional would have meant stretching the point.

In the Dagestan nightmare, the service under his command positively failed to impress. Initially, it all looked like a re-enactment of the Budennovsk script: Prime Minister Chernomyrdin and the Dagestani leaders opened negotiations with the terrorists, guaranteed them an unimpeded withdrawal to the Chechen border and made buses available. Together with the hostages (as in Budennovsk, about 150 people), representatives of the authorities, deputies and two journalists got on the buses and the convoy set off on its agreed route.

... At which point, the Russian helicopters opened fire. The buses made an emergency U-turn and made for the village of Pervomaiskoye, near the Chechen border. The terrorists and the hostages were encircled by the army, militia and the FSB. Moscow clearly had had a change of heart and now wanted to detain the terrorists — whatever the cost. It caused an outrage in Dagestan. Several thousand local residents approached the village in an attempt to break the blockade and prevent bloodshed but were stopped by the troops. Meanwhile the terrorists herded locals together at gunpoint and lined them up in a human shield.

Then the charge started. Artillery was shelling the village and the helicopters were targeting it with rockets. Finally, the special task force came in and the village was raised to the ground. Scores of hostages and non-combatants died alongside the militants, but Raduyev and some of his men managed to break through the siege and escape to Chechnya.

Although it was the security agencies that persuaded Yeltsin to agree to the use of force, although the idea was to punish the hostage-takers and thwart their plans, although Yeltsin said, 'We have provoked a new tragedy by our past decisions (those taken in Budennovsk)', the operation was clearly botched, lots of hostages died, the village got reduced to rubble and the chief gangster escaped unscathed. The country gasped when FSB General Mikhailov stated, bluntly, in his TV interview that the destiny of the hostages had been determined from the very start.

Most astonishing, however, was that Yeltsin, yet again, assumed the entire responsibility for these events and stayed firm in his support for the *Siloviki*. Perhaps it was just an attempt to prevent panic from escalating beyond control.

But it did feel that confidence in the President as a democratic leader had now been exhausted.

Then there came another moment of truth. Yeltsin writes in his book *Presidential Marathon*, '... There I was, buffeted by every wind and draught, all but keeling over in those powerful gusts: my strong constitution had let me down; "closest friends" had already found a replacement for me — just like a pack, surreptitiously and gradually, would select a new leader; and finally, those I had always relied on, the moral leaders of the nation, had turned their backs on me. As for the people — they could not forgive either the "shock therapy" or the ignominy of Budennovsk and Grozny. It looked like everything had been lost.

At this moment, however, it suddenly felt like the road to Damascus: if I stand, I'll win — no doubt about it, despite the forecasts, the ratings and political isolation. But should I stand? Maybe it's time to retire from the political scene?

But in doing so I would facilitate the advent of communists to power and this thought seemed preposterous...

By the end of December I had made my choice...'

The Kremlin assistants knew perfectly well that Yeltsin had no intention of giving in and retiring from politics, that is was against his nature. However, they thought it wise, for the time being, to keep quiet.

Back in 1994, no election laws were yet in place. The election in 1993 was held in the context of a dire political crisis that unfolded immediately after the October insurgence. The election was prepared in less than two months so as not to delay it unnecessarily: firstly, to prove Yeltsin's democratic intentions, and secondly, to provide a podium for political forces and thus prevent them from going underground. As a result, the first Duma was elected only for two years.

Now was the time to decide on procedures for running the campaign, to adopt a law and identify the timeline. The Parliament and President spent the entire year of 1994 fine-tuning the law that was effectively to regulate the life of all Russian political institutions. The Chechen war was already in progress and several parliamentary factions had initiated the impeachment procedure (that is, they made an interpellation to the Constitutional Court to establish whether the President's actions in Chechnya were compatible with the Constitution). An open debate broke out: *is it really worth running any elections at all* — be it for the Presidency or the Duma, in 1995 and 1996? Wouldn't it be better to wait for two years?

Delaying the elections had many advantages. The deputies could stay for two more years, strengthen their position and their networks and enhance an illusion of political stability. Political commentators, too, were insisting that, basically, Russia was tired of elections. Many sentient analysts were also in favour of a delay, especially in view of the war in Chechnya.

For example, Gennady Burbulis, former Secretary of State and the then head of the Strategy Foundation, wrote, 'The President should agree to option "plus two"* without an election but then should not stand in 1998. Today, it is the most constructive scenario for all of us. The President himself would be interested in seeing what choice of leaders may crop up. Whereas now, as soon as Chernomyrdin sticks his head above the parapet and somewhat improves his ratings, a scenario is instantly designed on how to make sure that Viktor Stepanovich gets his comeuppance, sticks to his control buttons in the gas sector and stops passing himself off as a politician of national calibre… There will be four additional years and there will be no point for Yeltsin to trip up his competitors…'

Whether or not Burbulis was right about Yeltsin's desire 'to trip up' his competitors he did put forward one valid argument: the head of state must be elected — in effect, for the first time ever, democratically — in a situation of stability and in the presence of a 'choice of leaders', so that people could really have a *choice*.

But when all is said and done, any delay of elections, for whatever reason, could have destroyed forever the nascent democratic culture in Russia. Any postponement could have become a permanent and convenient tool for keeping power. In other words, it was a threat to the very legitimacy of the state.

Despite all political advantages and dividends, Yeltsin managed to sense this danger and resist it. He refused to delay the parliamentary (and hence, presidential) elections. After the crisis of 1993, it was impossible for him to transgress the Constitution born of such ordeals and agony. He was awaiting the results of the 1995 parliamentary elections with intense anticipation. Would Chernomyrdin and his party score a convincing victory and get a majority of seats? Would he become his successor in the presidential race? However, there was little comfort in the election results.

… To start with, Naina Iosifovna pleaded with him not to stand again. She believed that it was as good as committing suicide. However, after the parliamentary elections in December, those conversations within the Yeltsin family stopped. 'He never sought our advice when taking this or that decision,' Naina Iosifovna tells me. 'The only exceptions were in 1987

---

* Which is to say, delaying the elections by two years, until 1998. — *Author's comment*.

and in 1996. We would often get together in the living room, he in his armchair and all of us around him, and he would contemplate out loud: who is likely to stand? Who can beat Ziuganov? It looked like there wasn't anyone — it had to be him. Gradually, we came over to this view, too...'

There was, of course, the issue of his loneliness — not in private life, not as as a human being. But why, then, these notes of despair in his confession — '"the closest friends" had already found a replacement — like a pack, surreptitiously and gradually, selects its new leader; and finally, those I always relied on, the moral leaders of the nation, have turned their backs on me.' Whom did he have in mind?

In the beginning of January Yeltsin fired Anatoly Chubais, what's more, for a very bizarre reason — 'insufficient standards of performance'... Truth be told, if anything, it was just the opposite. Within the government, Chubais was responsible for the financial complex and had acquired enough enemies in his quest to squeeze taxes out of raw materials monopolies and demand timely payment of interest on international debts in order to raise creditors' confidence in Russia. Despite the resistance of the Supreme Soviet, Chubais managed to complete the first stage of privatisation. For the first time in the new Russian history, the reserves of gold started growing, although they still amounted to only 12 billion dollars.

Yet privatisation was still under fire from all sides. Yeltsin was convinced that the failure of Chernomyrdin's party at the parliamentary election had something to do with the 'chief privatiser', since Chubais had become extremely unpopular. In a fit of anger, Yeltsin blurted out that Chubais must have cost the NDR\* at least ten percent of votes.

Chubais' retirement proved to be the last straw for those whom Yeltsin called 'the moral leaders of the nation'. Although ideas of democracy and market economy, then as now, were not popular in the Russian society, these people were in the foreground and their claims for moral leadership were completely justified.

On behalf of the political council of his party, Yegor Gaidar appealed to

---

\* Our Home — Russia.

Yeltsin not to stand for office. 'If the incumbent president stands for second term in office the communists will thus receive the best gift imaginable,' he said. His reasons included the assault of Pervomaiskoye and a range of personnel replacements, in particular the removal of Anatoly Chubais and Sergei Filatov. On the same day Gaidar forwarded to Yeltsin a letter of resignation from the Presidential Council, quoting his disagreement with some of the President's recent steps. Gaidar's example was followed by Sergei Kovalyov, the economic writer Otto Latsis and a famous lawyer Sergei Alekseev who all left the Presidential Council.

Democrats got busy trying to find 'a candidate from the democratic side'. Gaidar urgently flew to Nizhny Novgorod to try and talk the Oblast Governor Boris Nemtsov into standing for presidency, but an hour of intense discussions yielded no result. A disappointed Gaidar gave an interview where he kept insisting that Nemtsov's chances of success were very good since he was the only young Russian leader who shared democratic values and was 'not to blame for a thing'.

Gaidar tried, yet again, to come to an agreement with Yavlinsky, so that the DVR and Yabloko joined forces with some other democratic parties and supported Yavlinsky. Yavlinsky didn't agree. Gaidar's colleagues were suggesting that he should put himself down as this very 'one candidate'. He had the good sense to decline.

The only person in the DVR's political council who dissented and obstinately insisted — to the accompaniment of indignant cries from Sergei Kovalyov and other democrats — that Yeltsin shouldn't be written off was Anatoly Chubais. The very same Chubais that Yeltsin had just kicked out of the government.

... Democrats were sincerely convinced that his nomination would be 'the worst possible present to democracy' and the dream gift to the communists, revanchists and out-and-out fascists.

St Petersburg democrats, on their own initiative, ran a meeting of the 'group of voters' in support of nominating Viktor Chernomyrdin for president. Yes, it should have been anybody at all as long as it was not Yeltsin.

Thus, the Russian democrats found themselves in a fix. They were thrashing around and could not make up their mind: Gorbachev, Chernomyrdin,

Yavlinsky, Nemtsov, Gaidar... In the worst case scenario they could boycott the elections. Feverish panic-stricken statements, actions, talks... In a word, the 'moral leaders of the nation' ended up in a state of complete consternation.

Nonetheless, apart from Yeltsin there simply wasn't a realistic candidate that could be a counter-balance to the communists in the presidential campaign. That is why the uncertainty that descended on the democratic camp was perfectly understandable.

At the end of December, Yeltsin announced to his family his final decision to try for second term.

On January 15th it was announced that a campaign office was to be created and initially managed by First Prime Minister Oleg Soskovets. The news stunned the democrats and the communists alike. Since Yeltsin made no official statement, the office found itself in a somewhat awkward position. 'Is this Yeltsin's office?' journalists were asking bluntly. 'No, we support the electoral process as such,' Soskovets replied with a broad smile. The Duma tried to summon Soskovets to a session so that he could explain why the First Vice-Premier was going to 'support the electoral process as such' instead of attending to his direct duties? Soskovets never showed up, hiding behind vague missives. But what could he say? Yeltsin kept his obstinate silence.

Meanwhile the team already got to work. To win an election, it was necessary to know where the votes would be coming from. In January of 1996 Yeltsin had 3% (in answer to the sociologists' question — 'Who would you vote for if the election took place today?'). The leader of the Russian communists Ziuganov had 26-28%. So Yeltsin had to work out who were those people that he had to attract over to his side. The analysis prompted that the electorate would vote not so much for him as against the communists.

Sociologists, experts and his assistants were all saying that whilst the polls showed that Ziuganov's ratings were sky-high the same polls revealed that a large number of those polled (from one third to a half) were undecided.

Back in 1996, the most active and socially aware were those who hated the Soviet way of life because of its plethora of humiliating and degrading bans. To be temporarily unemployed, eating into one's last resources but being able 'to read whatever one wanted' and 'listen to the music of your choice' and total absence of ideological control were perceived as a principal and fundamental achievement. True, this typically 20-40-year-old voter of Yeltsin's hardly ever was a person of business; he or she could fastidiously distance themselves from flea markets but they were determined to keep their options open: perhaps, go into business 'when things got normal'. More often than not they had no money for foreign travel but were certain that, eventually, they would save enough to go to Turkey, India or elsewhere. In a word, this generation, born in 1950-1960, was on the one hand sufficiently young and on the other — remembered the Soviet power all too well.

Besides, starting from 1996 the economic situation had been slowly rectifying itself, and so there was already enough people earning enough to be able to afford cars, flats, PCs, expensive white goods (still perceived as miraculous). Of course, in the nineties 'winners' were much less numerous than 'losers' — those who had lost employment, customary social support and traditional values. Some were hectically trying to find a new way forward. Even so, paradoxically, they weren't too eager to return to the old system, or to be more precise, they didn't believe it was possible.

Ziuganov's base consisted of the much older voters, more often than not those from deprived social strata or regions: pensioners, villagers, menial workers who in the nineties found themselves out of regular and socially-protected employment. In this sense, Ziuganov's party was pursuing a noble mission as protectors of the most wretched and dispossessed, 'the robbed ones'. It is a different story that Ziuganov was deceiving them by promising a miraculous and speedy revival of social justice. This was a loyal and reliable electorate but there was a drawback — it couldn't grow.

That is why the presidential campaign of 1996, probably unlike any other in the history of global democracy, focused not on specific social programmes, not the issues of economics or politics — be it internal or external, but the question of *values*.

These are the dry statistics that underpinned the strategy implemented by Yeltsin's team:

'While "rigidly" anti-Yeltsin and mostly pro-communist electorate ranged from 29% ("I never did support Boris Yeltsin and I do not now") to 42% ("Under no circumstances shall I support Yeltsin"), in the autumn of 1995 54% of those polled declared that "they do not consider the communist system acceptable for Russia". When the nation-wide sociological survey in January of 1996 asked whether people agreed to the communist regime being reinstated, 39% answered in the affirmative and 61% in the negative.'

'In January of 1996, the survey asked a question of what would be better — to fill the shops with a lot of expensive goods or with few cheap ones available at the state-controlled prices. The former option was preferred by 59% and the latter by 41%. These results held a mirror to the respondents' own position: 36% stated that "it was impossible to bear our miserable existence any longer" and 57% answered that "life was hard but bearable". Yeltsin's position was particularly strong among the young Russians. Numerous surveys revealed that Russians aged between 20 and 44 years of age (38% of the country's population) were rejecting communism irrespective of how the question was phrased.' (Leon Aron).

Results of the parliamentary election were also taken into account. True, the communist party had won but the overall picture, including the votes given to the parties that hadn't made the 5% threshold, looked as follows: 21 million votes were given to pro-reformist democratic parties (including those in opposition, such as Yabloko and DVR); 11 million — to the parties on whose electorate Ziuganov could count only in a small measure, say, a third.

Such was the first stage of Yeltsin's analysis. The second stage was assessment of the chief competitor, the communist leader Ziuganov — his potential, his reserves. In this sense the situation in 1996 was worrisome.

In January of 1996 choosing either Yeltsin or Ziuganov felt like a very bad option. Moreover, the scales were slowly tipping towards Ziuganov. The logic was simple: Yeltsin was unelectable. Could one vote for Ziuganov *in principle*? Turned out one could.

Andrei Siniavsky, a writer, put it this way:

'There would be no tragedy in France if Chirac didn't get re-elected. Similarly, there would be no tragedy in America if Clinton didn't get his second term. Why is it always a tragedy in Russia? If not Yeltsin, it's a tragedy.'

Or as Yakov Krotov, a priest, expressed himself:

'No, excuse me... I do not accept the concept of a "lesser evil". I do not want to be in evil's company, even if it is a small one. Besides, it is somewhat subjective to assess Yeltsin as a "lesser evil". For the family of a Chechen killed in 1996 Yeltsin is the biggest evil. And in any case, it is bizarre to turn the lesser evil into a motto for fighting the bigger one. It is as if instead of celebrating Easter one would celebrate Lenin's birthday under the slogan "Come on, at least it's not Hitler*!"'

After his hour of triumph in the parliamentary election the media flung their doors wide open for Ziuganov was set about building not simply an image of 'a warrior for the rights of the downtrodden' but the image of a warrior with integrity.

In his capacity of Persona Number One in the Russian political establishment, Gennady Ziuganov** was invited to the Davos World Economic Forum. He was received with avid interest (the forum opened on February 1st). Everybody cared about the future of Russia. A 'Russian day' was planned in advance as the focus of the agenda. The first event was Ziuganov's press conference. The turnout was impressive; the audience was listening with bated breath and taking notes.

'It is essential to identify an adequate ratio between state ownership and the property in private hands, on condition that everybody abides by laws, pays taxes in good time and that the economic system functions in such a way that it is beneficial to work instead of stealing or drinking,' Ziuganov was saying.

'The state control is imperative in the key sectors of economy but if our party comes to power the large-scale nationalisation of property is out of the question. We realise that if tomorrow something gets taken from somebody by force, the day after tomorrow the entire country — from Murmansk to Vladivostok — will take up arms. Those privatised enterprises that perform well and observe labour laws will have every opportunity to carry on. Only those companies will be in danger that are destroying and embezzling

---

\* All three occasions may take place in April: the Orthodox Easter shifts from end of March to May, Lenin was born on April 22nd and Hitler — on April 20th.

\*\* Ziuganov.

production assets. As in any country, this should be dealt with by competent authorities and in strict accordance to law,' Ziuganov promised.

'People in our country, investors among them, fear that things may go to pieces and the country gets destabilised. That is why our point of view, which is on record, is that the entire production complex must be normalised without any commotion or a civil war. The CPSU was not a party but a system of managing the country whereas CPRF is a fully fledged political entity which, unlike its predecessor, advocates a mixed economy and political plurality. The CPRF has rejected atheism and is open for dialogue with any political forces,' Ziuganov was insisting.

Following this speech Ziuganov was invited to various breakfast meetings and lunches, his interviews were in great demand. Many ladies, Russian and non-Russian alike, made this mental note when watching him on TV: Ziuganov suddenly blossomed; he cut a presentable figure and suddenly was dressing well.

At this point, Anatoly Chubais put in an appearance. He was somewhat late and, generally speaking, came to Davos as a private individual since a month earlier he had been dismissed from the government. However, on seeing Ziuganov among, as Chubais put it, 'his own friends' — owners of major companies with whom he had been negotiating for years, and on registering that they were drinking in every word uttered by the leader of Russian communists, Anatoly Borisovich flew into a rage.

On February 5th, Chubais called his own press conference in Davos. He asked his audience to compare what Ziuganov was telling his foreign partners with what he had been saying in Russia, thus contrasting a Ziuganov for export and a Ziuganov for internal consumption. He simply pulled out a brochure — Ziuganov's electoral programme, and started reading out entire chapters*.

---

* Back then, in 1996, the matter in hand was 'establishing the power of workers' and 'revision of the privatisation results'. Few things changed in the CPRF programme since. In 2008, the CPRF immediate programme envisages 'establishing the power of workers and people's patriotic forces'; nationalisation of Russia's natural resources and strategically important sectors of economy with subsequent use of the profit generated by these sectors in the interests of all citizens; return of state financial reserves from foreign banks back into Russia with their subsequent use for economic and social development; revision of laws 'exacerbating the workers' material well-being and providing for pilfering of the country's natural resources'. — *Author's comment*.

## 'WITH HIM, WE FEEL SAFE' (JANUARY-JULY OF 1996)

The audience gasped.

Strictly speaking, a genuine communist should not lie, at least not so blatantly. Although Lenin, to gain tactical points — at least during a civil war– allowed deception, bribery, sabotage and terror. Ziuganov tripped up because he started a game on someone else's field and his punishment was severe. The point, of course, was not that 'Chubais exposed Ziuganov before the West' — Ziuganov didn't really care as this trip to Davos was not a matter of principle, just a tactical move.

But Chubais' spontaneous outrage proved a wake-up call for that part of Yeltsin's electorate — the intelligentsia, the democrats and the young — who had hereto been in a kind of a stupor. There in Davos some ten or fifteen individuals represented Russian business, and what they saw helped them make up their mind.

Their delegate was Boris Berezovsky. He approached Chubais with an incredible offer: Chubais himself should manage Yeltsin's campaign and 'win the election' — such was the wish of all major Russian entrepreneurs.

To start with, Chubais was reserved. However, negotiations with Yeltsin's advisors had already started via Yeltsin's daughter Tatyana who, in turn, spoke to her father. Yeltsin proposed that he and Chubais should meet, for the first time after the latter's dismissal in mid-February. What Yeltsin offered Chubais was straightforward: to treat the election campaign as a technological process, to make it streamlined and efficient. Chubais found the idea feasible and convincing, and so he accepted.

So how did Yeltsin's younger daughter Tatyana become involved? This is the story in her own words:

'The offer was totally unexpected. Firstly, I had just given birth to my son Gleb and, understandably, had my hands full. Secondly, I had never been attracted to politics. Like with any other métier, it required professionalism and serious training. But Dad said that on his team he needed a person who would act as a kind of an unbiased observer and update him 24/7. He asked for my help, "There simply isn't anyone else".

I was often asking myself: if not Dad, then who? Plus, I wasn't just thinking about it, I was saying it out loud, too.' However, in the beginning Tatyana rejected her father's offer flatly.

Valentin Yumashev, Yeltsin's literary assistant, quoted an international precedent. Jacques Chirac's daughter, Claude Chirac, joined her father's election team and became his official image advisor. Days were passing by and it became impossible to procrastinate any longer. After all, was she not as good as Chirac's daughter? Most importantly, she was not going to meddle in politics — simply help her father.

To start with, team members took this 'appointment' with indifference, even condescension. Korzhakov believed the scheme to be a 'daughter's treat', a president's whim. By force of habit, he perceived Tanya simply as a family member, a child that should be protected and could be patronised. Later, she was recalling the meetings in February of 1996 as a kind of a 'bad dream'. 'No one there was prepared to discuss things analytically or plan long-term strategies while discussions were sluggish and more or less for the sake of "ticking the boxes". It was a lot about making a nice report and no progress. I was horrified,' she said later.

Tatyana's assessment is corroborated by a letter that Yeltsin received from his assistants:
'Dear Boris Nikolayevich,
We address you because of our deep concern over the course of your electoral campaign. According to analysts' observations, with which we agree, the campaign's problems stem from the personality and performance by Oleg Soskovets.
It is clear that he is not a specialist in the sphere of public politics and election technologies, and this has become apparent from the very start.
... The office has not even started operating yet. He cannot deal with people of a different mindset to his, even if they are good for the campaign. His influence over the regional leaders is nothing more than brutal... abuse of administrative power, which doesn't simply compromise the President but alienates his possible allies. He applies the same methods, and with the same results, when dealing with governmental agencies, mass media, commercial and banking circles. The most bizarre is that Mr Soskovets has not been able to resolve even the most important issue: to mobilise financial resources needed for the campaign.
In consequence, more than a month has been wasted... Two rumours

are making rounds: that the President has been "sold down the river" by communists and now traitors are stonewalling his campaign, and that poor organisation (or, to be precise, failure) of the campaign will drag the President into a situation wherein he will be forced to either cancel the elections or override their results'.

Tatiana then decided that the Russian businessmen's idea — to incorporate new blood into the team — had both potential and operational advantages.

On February 15th Yeltsin made an official announcement in Sverdlovsk (soon to become Yekaterinburg) that he was going to stand for office. He suddenly felt a sharp desire to communicate with people spontaneously, in the midst of a crowd.

As an unpleasant consequence of his street improvisations in the cold, he very nearly lost his voice — he could hardly hear himself on the podium.

The President's pivotal idea of his platform that day was: it was impossible for the country to return to its communist past. 'To live through so much, to realise so much,' he was saying in this hoarse voice of his, 'to be on the threshold of a civilised life and then to slide back — this would be our common defeat and disgrace. Can I not take part in the presidential elections, given the situation? I have asked myself this question more than once but for as long as the threat of a clash between the "reds" and the "whites" persists, my duty as a human being, a citizen and a politician who had initiated the reforms is to ensure consolidation of all the positive elements in the society, to prevent possible perturbations and to avert a civil war. Despite insistent appeals for me to retire with dignity, my withdrawal from the election would be irresponsible and wrong. The cause to which I have given all my strength must be brought to a fruitful completion. I am sure I shall be able to steer the country through the troubled times. Which is why I have decided to stand for the office of President of Russia and announce this decision of mine here, in the hall that is dear to me, in my native city — to you, my fellow Sverdlovsk residents, to all citizens of Russia and to the attention of the entire world...

'I am often reminded of a promise I made long ago to put my head on the railway track. But I would like to jog your memory and say that I did abide by my promise when in April of 1993 I insisted on a referendum and presented my destiny to the voters. But the point of the current election is not just my destiny. All of Russia will find itself on the railway track, and we must do our best so that we, Russians, and our country would not perish under the red wheels of the past.

'We are stronger than those who over the years have been putting a spoke in our wheel, impeding our progress towards a great and free Russia, towards a decent life for all Russians. We are stronger than our disappointments and doubts. We are tired but we are all together and we shall win!

'Do you remember those huge queues for bread and sugar in 1991?' he was asking his audience. 'Do you remember how people were waiting even through the night, keeping themselves warm by the fires? It's not there anymore. Shops have plenty of stocks and your children and grandchildren will never know what shortages or food coupons were all about. What has caused this cornucopia? It has been a result of price liberalisation introduced in 1992! Hyperinflation has been curbed, the state treasury holds considerable gold reserves, and the rouble is now stable.'

Russians, Yeltsin went on to say in that speech, now had the most valuable right: the right to choose. A free election was the only way to restore the state, the only way to gradually get rid of temporisers and corrupt bosses. Free elections had been introduced for all time. He was talking about freedom of speech, freedom of faith, freedom to travel abroad, freedom from ideological shackles.

Yeltsin delivered this simple message and his audience understood him perfectly: if the communist candidate won at the election, the situation in the country would become explosive.

Back in Davos, following Ziuganov's presentation, journalists were asking Russian entrepreneurs whether one had to fear the return of the communists to power.

One phrase of Ziuganov's, with which he was hoping to pacify the West: 'We realise that if tomorrow something will be taken from somebody by force, the day after tomorrow the entire country — from Murmansk to Vladivostok — will turn to arms', was duly noted. In principle, everyone agreed. But the way the communists intended to set about returning privatised property to the nation was described clearly and in detail by a deputy from the communist faction, the lawyer Yuri Ivanov. Here it is as reported by *Izvestia*:

'By that time Ivanov and his like-minded associates had identified a number of "major" enterprises that they would nationalise as a matter of priority as soon as they came to power. The list had about 200 entities. Commercial banks would also be nationalised unconditionally, at least 90% of those, since they presented a "national threat".

What would be the procedure for nationalisation? It was of course possible to go through arbitration courts and prove the "illegal nature" of privatisation, but this, in the opinion of communists, was too slow and too much trouble. One can, Ivanov was saying, employ a "fast track procedure" — through "commissions vested with special powers". The procedure itself, as per Ivanov, was to be as follows: "I would develop it within a month with a small group. It would be a procedure to be used by the commission, not judicial bodies."' (Oleg Moroz).

Nationalisation, according to Ivanov and Ziuganov, was not at all a peaceful and legal procedure. To call a spade a spade, it was expropriation of property. Of course, Ziuganov's main argument in the dialogue with the West was that the erstwhile CPSU 'had not been a party but a system of power' whereas the new CPRF was a normal parliamentary party. True, Ziuganov's party did have seats in the parliament, voted on laws, approved budgets — albeit unrealistic inflationary ones. But this was not the point. Every party had a platform of ideology. In their platform the communists managed to marry socialism and nationalism, plus the imperial idea and what's more — of the most radical kind.

Characteristically, Ziuganov was saying at the time:

'Starting from XIX century, the worldview, culture and ideology in the Western world have been increasingly affected by Jewish expansion whose influence is growing not by the day, but by the hour. As "its own market" develops, the Jewish diaspora that traditionally has controlled the continent's financial life transforms into a kind of a holder of the "controlling block" of shares of the entire Western civilisation's economic system. The themes of being "the elect", of being "pre-destined from above" to manage the world, of their own pre-eminence — intrinsically inherent in Judaic religious faith — are now beginning to produce a considerable impact on the Western consciousness. At the same time, development of the Islamic civilisation is practically frozen and presents no serious threat to Western domination whiles the other world cultures prove incapable of withstanding the military, economic and ideological expansion of the West. In view of this, the Slavic civilisation personified by the Russian empire grows in significance in its capacity of the last seat of resistance to Western hegemony.' (Gennady Ziuganov, *Beyond the Horizon*).

Ziuganov again:

'In my village, only two people were arrested in 1937, and it turned out — with good reason.' In other words, this notorious GULAG did do some good.

It wasn't just that in 1996 Ziuganov advocated extremely nationalistic views and was attracting people of similar ilk: all those scholarly 'ideas', when circulated among impoverished and embittered masses, could really spark pogroms and arsons similar to those in 1905 or 1918-1920.

His entire programme was predicated not on construction but hatred.

That is why Russia's leading entrepreneurs had a lot to discuss with Yeltsin. Ziuganov gave them determination and courage. The meeting took place on March 19th.

'... I met the bosses of major banking and media groups: Gusinsky, Khodorkovsky, Potanin, Berezovsky, Friedman, et al. — all well-known names in business... It was my first meeting with business people of such standing. The initiative to meet came from their side, and to start with, I was holding back. I realised that they had no other option but to support me and imagined that they would probably talk about financing my election campaign. Yet they embarked on a totally different topic: "Boris Nikolayevich, the way things are done in your office under Soskovets almost certainly means failure. It is precisely for this reason that some businessmen go to Ziuganov and try and make a deal while others are packing their suitcases. We have no one to make a deal with. The communists will hang us from the lampposts. If the situation is not reversed radically, in a month it will be too late." I expected nothing as tough, of course,' Yeltsin writes in his *Presidential Marathon*.

'Someone had to alert the President to this bitter truth: he isn't popular anymore. Who should it be? Chubais perched his briefcase on the elegantly laid table, opened it and pulled the papers out. "Boris Nikolayevich," he started, undaunted, "the situation is far from simple. Your rating is five percent!" President glimpsed at the papers and flung them aside. "What utter nonsense!" Then he enunciated slowly, curbing his ire, "Anatoly Borisovich, it is necessary to work out who prepared these ratings. I believe they are wrong." He emphasised the last word — "wrong". Now it was Chubais' turn to blush. A long pause hung in midair. Then Gusinsky chipped in, "Boris Nikolayevich, everything your people are telling you is a lie." Yeltsin turned and eyed Gusinsky keenly. "And how do you know what my people are telling me?" "Boris Nikolayevich," answered Gusinsky, "I see it in how you behave. They are supplying you with incorrect data." Another long pause... Still, the conversation, although desultory, continued. The bankers suggested that Chubais should be put in charge of the electoral campaign. They left, having exchanged handshakes with Yeltsin, but without a clear view of how the meeting had finished.' (David Hoffman, *The Oligarchs: Wealth and Power in the New Russia*).

At this point the so-called oligarchs (whom no one called that at the time, the term was introduced in 1997 by a furious Boris Nemtsov, a convinced liberal) did offer serious assistance to Yeltsin's election campaign, not just financial but mainly organisational and intellectual. In those days Russian business could attract talented specialists in all spheres: lawyers, sociologists and political analysts. They did want to know, however, how Yeltsin's election headquarters would manage this assistance. Would these resources be wasted? In other words, who was the boss in this team, who was making decisions? Most of individuals from this community he met for the first time ever: as a rule, they all rather shunned publicity and interviews. However, he understood where they were coming from: they could not imagine a normal life under Ziuganov. But did he perceive the *danger* associated with all of this?

'Of course he didn't,' Tatyana is answering my question, 'Dad never gave a thought to what problems he may face in future. He was completely confident of his own strength.'

'Why?'

'I don't know — he just was. That was the person he was. Yet those same businessmen could have simultaneously approached Chernomyrdin — to bargain with him, lay down their own terms, this really could have happened. But apparently, it was no use bargaining with Dad. Besides, one should not forget even with this attitude, some of them were in concurrent talks with the communists. They worked with them in the Duma, lobbied for certain laws, and were considering what would happen if Dad lost. So the whole thing was far from straightforward.'

Yeltsin was not taken aback by the notorious 'Point 5"* characterising most of those present. He never had any problems on that score. History proved that he was right here, for today most prominent Russian businessmen display a vast variety of ethnicity — Russians are in the majority but there are also Tatars, Jews, Georgians, Azerbaijanis and natives of various Central Asian republics. He was, however, disconcerted by the desperate and panic-stricken tonality of their conversation.

Moreover, right after this meeting with the country's top businessmen, he reshuffled his election team. He appointed his aide Viktor Iliushin coordinator of all subdivisions. Within the team, he set up the Analytical Group — a kind of a 'think tank' — and placed Chubais at its head. The 'think tank' also included Georgy Satarov, Sergei Shakhrai, Tatyana Dyachenko, Igor Malashenko, Vasily Shakhnovsky, Alexander Oslon, Vyacheslav Nikonov and Sergei Zverev — all of them specialists in various fields: a lawyer, an information specialist, a sociologist, a political strategist and an analyst — experts, bright people capable of helping Yeltsin win the election. In effect, it was a crisis management unit that eventually played the first fiddle in Yeltsin's election strategy. The election campaign council was also created — with Yeltsin in the chair. The council was expected to convene weekly and that was how it was initially, but after a while the President took to discussing progress of the campaign only with the kernel of his analytical group.

Yeltsin met major businessmen and created the Analytical Group only on March 19th — thus, it had taken him quite some time to swing into action. What provided final impetus?

On 15 March 1996, Russia's State Duma denounced the Belovezha Accords and issued a special decree proclaiming them illegal. In effect, it was a

---

* In the Soviet days, all identity forms required for providing personal data listed ethnic origin under Point 5. Routinely, 'problems with Point 5' was a euphemism for being a Jew.

constitutional coup, albeit for the time being only *de jure*. Yeltsin made a fighting response in which he stated:

'Whatever motivated the recent resolution, it wouldn't hurt its initiators to consider its consequences for Russia and the Commonwealth of Independent States... Such an attempt may be seen as an attempt by the Duma to abolish our statehood which I have guaranteed to the citizens of Russia, peoples of the Commonwealth of Independent States and the global community. The Russian Federation shall maintain its status and adhere to all treaties it signed.'

His assistants later wrote:

'On the morning of Sunday, March 17th, Yeltsin's secretaries made numerous telephone calls summoning President's aides, speechwriters, some ministers and other dignitaries. At noon, <they> assembled round the conference table in the President's office. President explained the task — to prepare a legal framework and the text of an appeal on the subject of dissolving the State Duma, banning the CPRF and deferring the presidential election. Those present responded negatively but Yeltsin was intractable. Instructions given, he bundled the assembly off, out of his office.'

Having conferred among themselves, Yeltsin's assistants set about composing a memo insisting that it was a very bad idea to dissolve the Duma; the Duma was deliberately provoking the President to use force which the provinces would never understand, thus the hard-line scenario would only lead to a total loss of political face. On the other hand, banning the CPRF and cancelling the election could be an option. When Iliushin reported all this and explained that the draft decree was not ready Yeltsin, yet again, told them 'to get down to work immediately!'

Interior Minister Kulikov, head of presidential security Korzhakov, and the FSB boss Barsukov were waiting in Yeltsin's reception. They saw the downcast presidential assistants filing out of Yeltsin's office and Kulikov realised what was going on. As he recounted later in his book:

'I could see Yeltsin was worked up. He shook my hand and without preliminaries explained, "I have decided to dissolve the State Duma. They are fighting above their weight and I have no intention of tolerating it any longer. We should ban the communist party and defer the elections." "I need two years," he was repeating this phrase as a mantra. "... You will receive the decree in the afternoon."'

Kulikov's first reaction was that of an old army hand used to obeying commands unquestioningly: '"Boris Nikolayevich", I said, "You are President and the Supreme Commander-in-Chief, you can make such decisions. We must obey. I shall issue all the relevant orders right away."'

'But with your permission,' said the minister to President, 'I would like to think it over and present my detailed considerations later on, by 17:00.'

Upon his return to his ministry, Kulikov assembled the board, informed them of the President's decision and ordered 'to prepare the allocation of resources.'

'Something was telling me,' recollects Kulikov, 'that somebody was really winding the President up. The excessive agitation of Oleg Soskovets and Alexander Korzhakov made me think. They acted as if the President's decision was unexpected but laid it on a bit too thick. As such it was understandable, Soskovets had messed up the initial stage of the election campaign, plus his team was incapable of taking Yeltsin to victory. Korzhakov, who, as it transpired later, was virtually viewing Soskovets as a future President, was complicit in all this. This entire situation was devised, effectively, as a means of preparing the route for these people's rise to power. They were provoking and manipulating Yeltsin and, at some stage, he succumbed to their ministrations and adopted this "strategy" of his.'

On his own initiative, Kulikov invited Procurator General and Chairman of the Constitutional Court to Yeltsin's reception. They met at 17:00. A grim scene ensued:

'The President was glum, his face livid, cold... I reported briefly, "Boris Nikolayevich, we are following your instruction, allocations are underway. But we," I pointed at Yuri Skuratov and Vladimir Tumanov, "consider it a mistake." I suggested that my colleagues should explain and they, basically, seconded my words.

'The President didn't like it one bit that all three of us came along. It was as if I had suborned the others to revolt. He said to me reproachfully, "But you told me nothing of this in the morning." I replied, "Boris Nikolayevich, there was nothing to tell you in the morning, that's why I asked to be seen at 17:00. Our conclusion now is that this shouldn't be done and I'm ready to explain why." I started with saying that there was still time before the election, so it was still possible to improve the ratings. Nevertheless, the biggest danger was a possible social explosion in the country whilst we had no resources to control the situation and none could be made available — our resources were in Chechnya, employed in the war. I went on to say that it would be much easier for us just to click our heels and then put the blame on the President but we decided to make our fears known.

'Yeltsin interrupted, "Minister, you displease me profoundly! There will be a decree. Go and carry it out."'

Soon Kulikov learned that the people who were supposed to prepare the decree were also opposed to it. On his way out he dropped into Iliushin's office and asked, 'Are you busy preparing the decree?' The Interior Minister's glance above his glasses was, as per usual, unemotional and sharp-eyed.

'Kulikov', Yeltsin's assistants testify, 'had with him his memo — with arguments and objections. He showed it to the assistants. They showed their own memo. The texts turned out to be very similar, down to some definitions. Parting, they agreed to act in unison.

'At 19:30, along came Chubais, "Guys, he who writes the decree is responsible for the consequences, irrespective of whether it has been signed. All that's left is to put in the letter of resignation. This decree is the President's political death warrant." The assistants showed him the memo with their objections at which Chubais mimed the President's reaction as if tearing it up and throwing it away.

'By 22:30, the memo (not the decree) was ready. Among other things, it said, "The decree hasn't been prepared since there are no legal grounds for it. Besides, the decree as a response to the Duma's resolution is ill-matched to the potential danger. If such a decree were adopted, the threat of a civil war would loom large."

'At 22:50, Iliushin called the President's dacha to arrange the delivery of the memo. Yeltsin refused to speak to him. It was decided that Iliushin should wait until the morning. The President arrived at the Kremlin at 5:45. At 5:50 Iliushin made his way into his office and placed the memo of the desk. Yeltsin asked, "Who signed it?"

Iliushin listed the signatories.

Yeltsin stayed in his office since a briefing with chiefs of the enforcement agencies was to start at 6:00. In 15 minutes' time the briefing opened.'

Round the table in the President's office were: Yeltsin, Chernomyrdin, Kulikov, Barsukov, and across the table — Soskovets, Iliushin, Korzhakov and Yegorov. Also invited were the bosses of Moscow militia.

The previous day, Barsukov and Korzhakov had agreed with Yeltsin a plan whereby by the evening of March 17th the premises of the State Duma should be occupied by the OMON and the Chief Security Department. All the staff and deputies who were on the premises at this time were ordered out. However, staunch resistance of nearly everybody who was to carry out his instructions made Yeltsin suspend the plan. He was hesitating.

To return to Kulikov's memoirs:

'We entered the office where the President was even gloomier than the day before. He didn't greet anyone. When we were seated I asked, "Boris Nikolayevich, may I present my report?" "No, take your seat, I don't want to start with you." Thus he signalled immediately that his attitude towards me was negative. "I want to listen to the Muscovites…" Meanwhile, Korzhakov slid into his hand a piece of paper with names and patronymics of the Moscow generals[*]. Yeltsin scanned it and raised the head of the Moscow Oblast GUVD, "Please, Alexander Nikolayevich, your report on the progress of preparations." The latter updated us on what had been done, "According to the target set by the minister, we have run an assessment of forces and resources and have taken control of several facilities, 16,000 people are deployed but we need at least another 13,000."

'The President feigned satisfaction, "So, the Moscow Oblast performs well — unlike the Interior Ministry!"

'I expected that the President would now turn the sheet of paper face down on his desk[**] and sign the decree on my dismissal. After a pregnant pause, the President said (I thought he was forcing himself), "True, they must be disbanded. I need these two years. The decree is ready for signing. We shall probably be resolving the problem in a stage-by-stage fashion…

---

[*] Those were two Interior Minister's namesakes: head of Moscow's Main Interior Department (GUVD) General-Colonel of the Militia Nikolai Kulikov and his colleague from the Moscow Oblast General-Colonel of the Militia Alexander Kulikov. — *Author's comment.*

[**] Kulikov believed that the decree on his dismissal was already prepared. — *Author's comment.*

For now, the premises of the State Duma and the communist party stay vacant. Go. Wait for my command."

'When Yeltsin said all this I realised that now nothing terrible would happen. The President had found enough courage to master himself, his own temper. He realised that the enterprise could have a tragic ending, that he was being used. I had no doubts that "Wait for my command" was simply a weak echo of a thunderstorm that had already passed us by.'

Yeltsin's own recollections of those two days are illuminating:

'... Frankly speaking, at the time I thought that what was needed were tough decisive measures. It was clear that a war of nerves had already started. We would waste time in all those election games and then what?

'I must confess I have always been inclined to use straightforward solutions. I always thought that to cut a Gordian knot was easier than spending years untangling it. At some stage, when comparing the two strategies put forward by two teams whose approaches to the situation were completely disparate\*, I felt that I didn't have to wait till the election results transpired in June, I had to act now!

'I made up my mind and told my staff, "Get the documents ready!" What followed was a complicated legal task. Several decrees were prepared, for example, a decree on banning the communist party, the dissolution of the Duma and delaying the presidential election. These formulae were like a verdict: I had failed to curb the crisis acting within the framework of the current Constitution.

'At 6 A.M. a closed session took place which was attended by Chernomyrdin, Soskovets, the enforcement ministers and Head of Administration Nikolai Yegorov. I presented the plan...

'Unexpectedly, Anatoly Kulikov, Minister of the Interior, spoke out strongly against those plans. "The communist party," he said, "controls local legislative authorities in half of Russia's regions."

'Chernomyrdin took the same attitude and announced that he didn't see the need to make such abrupt and irreversible moves.

'However, most participants in this morning session favoured my idea of delaying the election. "Boris Nikolayevich," I was told, "after all, you do

---

\* An important admission, do pay attention. — *Author's comment.*

not refuse to hold elections, you simply defer them by two years, so it's impossible to accuse you of violating the principles of democracy... This is probably a good time, your ratings are on the rise, and everyone will follow your lead."

'Finally I said, "All clear, the majority are in favour. The conference is adjourned. Go, I'll think it all over myself."

'When on my own, I came to the conclusion that it all should be resolved within 24 hours but again, I had this cold feeling inside me — I had to make this decision myself and be personally responsible for it.

'While I was in my office, Tanya called Chubais and asked him to come to the Kremlin. "Dad, you must listen to a different opinion — you simply must", she said. And I suddenly realised, it was true, it was a must.'

Yeltsin goes on to give a brief summary of his conversation with Chubais:

'"Boris Nikolayevich," he said, "it is not 1993 now. The peculiarity of the current moment is in the fact that now those going beyond the scope of the Constitution will burn first. It is an insane idea to crack down on communists in this fashion. The communist ideology is in people's heads, you will not attach new heads by a presidential decree. When we have built a normal, strong and rich country, only then will it spell the end to communism. You mustn't cancel the elections."

... We spent about an hour talking — I was objecting, I was raising my voice, finally I was practically yelling, which I almost never do. And yet I cancelled my decision. I am still grateful to fate, to Anatoly Borisovich and Tanya for this alternative voice that sounded at the right moment.'

The logic of those who mounted a desperate resistance to his prior decision and who deserve credit for their courage and a principled stand was, essentially, that it was too dangerous so they were basically trying to scare Yeltsin.

Chubais was talking about something else. He was saying that Yeltsin would definitely win the election if he wanted to, that 'when we have built a normal, strong and rich country, only then will it spell the end to communism.' His arguments for how dangerous it was to cancel the election were different. You could not build democracy in a country where elections were cancelled, deferred or rearranged depending on the political situation.

Chubais must have also told Yeltsin some other blunt truths. Without naming Korzhakov personally, he must have showed Yeltsin who was prodding him to cancel the elections. Thus, the dilemma became inevitable; he had to choose between those who didn't believe in his ability to win and those who did. Clearly he chose the latter. It must have suddenly dawned on him that a new Russia he was talking about so often in his speeches, for so many years and in various situations, this new Russia already existed. It had already become a tangible, *peaceful reality*, emerging through the smoke of his political and, unfortunately, military battles. And this new Russia demanded that he should play according to the rules that he himself introduced.

One cannot understand the essence of the relationship between Yeltsin and Korzhakov through referring to simplified patterns: 'master — servant' or 'tsar — *éminence grise*'. History is full of similar examples but this particular case had its own paradigm. Based on the American precedent, Korzhakov set up, within the Kremlin, a new entity — by transforming the former Ninth Department of the KGB, the service for ensuring security of the highest administrative officials, into an independent (and much more powerful) Presidential Security Service (SBP). Like any special service, it had its own analytical department in which, on their chief's instructions, Korzhakov's visionaries were profiling an ideal president-tsar. This is a brief quote from one of their extremely convoluted and bureaucratic memos:

'...Point 11. Thus we reach this conclusion. The image of the <Presidential> Code: the tradition of Harmony in Russia is above the tradition of Legality and the Code of Russian presidency is superior to the Law on President.'

In other words, a democratic president in Russia should be like an absolute sovereign, it's the only way. However, it did raise the issue of a code and moral taboos for those next to people in power who, at times, could be almost in too close a proximity.

It was true that Korzhakov, who was constantly by Yeltsin's side and proved his personal loyalty repeatedly, had a thorough understanding of his nature, habits, reactions, behavioural traits and the subtlest nuances of communication, and thus, had a colossal influence over the entire political milieu around the president.

Korzhakov was physically incapable of staying in his boss's shadow and with time, the roles were somewhat reversed. It was a very complicated process, largely spontaneous but perfectly traceable. Aware of that fact that the President's health problems were gradually making him retreat from the sphere of public politics, starting from 1994 Korzhakov set about, step by step, creating, in the shadow of the presidential establishment, a duplicate entity, his own corporation of power. His plans were unashamedly grandiose and embraced everything: economics, security, internal and foreign policies.

'In the summer of 1995, President's closest circle with Korzhakov at its head was having confidential discussions as to whether the treasury should be detached from the Ministry of Finance and merged with the State Repository for Precious Metals, the State Property Management Committee and other departments, thus concentrating the management of financial flows and transactions with that of property, and becoming practically independent of Government's control. This monster was to be managed by a functionary of the first Vice-Premier's rank who would report directly to President. That was supposed to help finance electoral victory. All the requisite documents and resolutions were prepared but when the President sought his assistants' advice, they were strongly against it. As a result, he rejected this dangerous idea and never returned to it later.' (*Yeltsin's Epoch*).

Another idea was to snatch control over raw materials from the head of the government. On 30 November 1994, Korzhakov sent a letter to Prime Minister Chernomyrdin whereby he asserted: '... the national economy will never be strengthened at the expense of foreign investments in the sector of raw materials... To grant a so-called "non-discriminatory" access to oil pipelines would mean nothing else but curtailment of freedom of export policy pursued by the Russian Fuel & Energy Complex (TEK) and imposition of financial agreements beneficial to the EBRD but not beneficial to Russia.'

The final paragraph of the letter spelled out the main point: Korzhakov 'deemed it advisable' to suggest that the Chairman of the Government should instruct First Vice-Premier Oleg Soskovets to set up a commission to run an 'expert valuation' of these seditious steps taken by the former Minister of Economic Affairs and aimed at the attraction of foreign investment.

'Who then is running the country: Yeltsin, Chernomyrdin or General Korzhakov?' *Izvestia* was asking at the time.

Still, this was only a warm-up, a flexing of the muscle. Korzhakov progress in the sphere of security was to the extent that ever since the former Kremlin's commandant Barsukov left the Kremlin to head the KGB, the latter started reporting to Korzhakov, thus practically merging the two services. After the war started in Chechnya, Defence Minister Grachev was depressed and broken-down, and the Foreign Minister Andrei Kozyrev, whom Korzhakov couldn't stand, was fired at the beginning of 1996. The only 'security baron' who remained outside the scope of his influence was Interior Minister Kulikov which was ultimately proven by the developments in 1996.

An important role in the corporation meticulously erected by Korzhakov was played by Oleg Soskovets, formerly Minister of Metallurgy in the Soviet government under Gorbachev. It is believed (or at least asserted in many books on that epoch) that Korzhakov considered him the most likely candidate to replace Yeltsin.

In reality, by the beginning of 1996, Korzhakov's sphere of influence had spread so far as to include some ministers, head of the Kremlin Administration Yegorov, industrialists and businessmen, but most importantly — middle management. Elections in 1996 were a real irritation to this group. It wasn't exactly that they feared that Yeltsin would lose — all common-sense people feared it. What they didn't need was a Yeltsin who was popular again, who would communicate with journalists and speak to the people. Such Yeltsin would ruin the group's plans and these plans, as we have seen, were far-reaching.

Yet Korzhakov was extremely cautious and therefore unlikely to have told Yeltsin that he didn't believe in his victory. It must have happened for the first time on March 18th, at the historic briefing that opened at 6 A.M. When the Duma had denounced the Belovezha Accords, Korzhakov's group saw it as their chance. They knew that such a chance should not be wasted. They could predict Yeltsin's reaction in advance — any serious specialist on strategy could foresee that he would demand hard-line measures.

It is not by chance that General Kulikov mentioned about Soskovets and Korzhakov's state of 'extreme agitation' on the day when the decision on the hard-line scenario was taken.

However, nothing revealed Korzhakov's intentions and strategy at this point. That said, there do exist documents that reflect the truth more or less completely. One such document is actually quoted in his book by Alexander Korzhakov himself. He writes that after his unexpected vacation in February, the Prime Minister Viktor Chernomyrdin started actively seeking to meet with him. Korzhakov agreed to a meeting only after February 15th, the date of the official registration of Presidential candidates. Chernomyrdin, says Korzhakov, had 'on the sly' collected over a million signatures and this enraged Alexander Vasilievich Korzhakov.

*Chernomyrdin.* I have another question. Who needs to be constantly setting me and the boss against one another?

*Korzhakov.* In what sense?

*Chernomyrdin.* In any sense. Maybe even, push us aside. I am seen as an enemy. I don't give a damn, of course, but it has always been emanating from the Administration… I told Iliushin that I cannot work out where it stems from.

*Korzhakov.* Iliushin never meddles in such things.

*Chernomyrdin.* The only thing he confirmed was that he saw it all… But someone keeps trying.

*Korzhakov.* Say, you go on a business trip and meanwhile, your people get together over an evening and propose toasts to the health of President Chernomyrdin, not our President… Besides, they are large as life about it.

*Chernomyrdin.* Is that true?

*Korzhakov.* Yes.

*Chernomyrdin.* Those who are by my side?

*Korzhakov.* Yes, the very same… Your entourage damages you a lot.

*Chernomyrdin.* All I can say is this: I cannot vouchsafe for anyone now, this is not my way… to go and betray someone just like that. I am disgusted. At my age — I don't need it. I am really at the end of my tether. My job is not easy.

*Korzhakov.* Of course.

*Chernomyrdin.* And I should turn and start the double game?

*Korzhakov.* In theory you have no time but this game is played on your behalf.

*Chernomyrdin.* It flashes through my mind that I should give an interview that I am not going to stand.

*Korzhakov.* Viktor Stepanovich, who was it that came up with the idea that you should stand at all? After all, under the Constitution, should anything happen to the President you replace him anyway. You could have easily brushed them all aside: "I cannot when President is alive, and if anything happens to him I shall step in whatever!"

*Chernomyrdin.* They were trying to talk me into it even now, sort of "Go ahead!" But I said "No, I shouldn't, we need Yeltsin today in order to keep this country together… Not Chernomyrdin, not anyone else."…

*Korzhakov.* I think the election must be cancelled. The thing is that Yeltsin will win with a small majority; he'll get 51-52 percent of votes. The opposition will start yelling at once, "It's been rigged!" They may even go on a rampage.

*Chernomyrdin.* Indeed?

*Korzhakov.* Surely. We have seen it all already in October and Yeltsin losing must be prevented at all costs. The initiative on the deferral of the election must come from the communists. I told them, "Look here, guys, joking apart — we shall not give up power!"… I told him openly, "… You have seen that we mean business when the Duma was seized on Sunday the 17th. So we shall not yield. Let us instead come to an agreement. Maybe we shall divide some portfolios." The main thing is that the boss will be against it* but we can bring him round.'

It is hard to imagine that the head of presidential security dared invite the Prime Minister for a conversation being aware in advance that he would be recording it on a dictaphone. It is equally difficult to imagine that the head of presidential security may talk *in this fashion* to the second person in the country. What was his real agenda? On the eve of March 17th Korzhakov

---

* Cancelling the election. — *Author's comment.*

was actively trying to force Chernomyrdin out of Yeltsin's inner circle and was busy assembling damaging evidence.

Korzhakov did exactly the same in December by squeezing Anatoly Chubais out of the government, and in the beginning of the Chechen war — by setting Yeltsin at loggerheads with democrats and members of the government beyond his, Korzhakov's, control, such as Chubais, Shokhin, and Chairman of the Central Bank Dubinin. In effect, this was his intention toward anyone who could independently influence Yeltsin.

Why spend so much time describing these backstage tussles of the election campaign? The point is that there is a myth alleging that the election in 1996 was 'not fairly' won. Each side has its own axe to grind: the communists are accusing the presidential team of falsifications; Korzhakov accuses Chubais and Co. of turning Yeltsin into a 'puppet'; the American group of political advisors who in the process of the campaign ended up surplus to requirement later claimed to have been 'the authors of the victory' (there is even a film on this subject); and finally, contemporary opponents of Yeltsin's epoch insisted that 'democracy was nowhere to be seen' and but for the oligarchs' money he would never have won.

So how did it happen in reality?

Yeltsin's decision to join the presidential marathon immediately after the three heart attacks, at the height of the unpopular Chechen war, after Budennovsk and Pervomaiskoye, with the lowest poll ratings among his contemporary politicians, was among the most significant of his life. It seemed insane.

Everything that followed after January of 1996 was only a consequence of this one *personal decision*: the new team around him, the forthcoming removal of Korzhakov's 'group', the emergence in the political arena of a new Russian business elite, the end of the Chechen war, the entire dynamics of the political life — all this was aligned and spun into being by that very first step.

As soon as Yeltsin made his decision and 'woke up', his ratings immediately started going up. On March 19th when the President was receiving the leading entrepreneurs in the Kremlin his ratings reached 15% — not the three or five that it had been in January. These are the precise figures:

*December of 1995 — 2%.*
*30 January 1996 — 5.4%*
*February 25th — 11%*
*March 17th — 15%.*
*March 31st — 18%.*
*April 21st — 21%.*
*May 12th — Yeltsin topped the list.*

Thus, already by April, Yeltsin's ratings had somewhat exceeded those of Ziuganov's. It wasn't a miracle but a grassroots response predicted by sociologists back in January of 1996. Yeltsin had his own electorate — a huge and passive mass of people who had not taken part in the December election of 1995, who initially couldn't make up their mind and who were avoiding a clear decision.

Yeltsins' election campaign started with identifying his political allies. Although the democrats unequivocally distanced themselves from Yeltsin, he sent Gaidar a letter:

'Yegor Timurovich,' the letter said, 'destiny brought us together in a most crucial and dangerous moment for our country. To a great degree, it was your courage that helped launch the economic reform and political transformations. Whatever they say now, I stay loyal to this course.

I know that it isn't personal gain that motivates your active involvement in politics. I hope very much that when dealing with extremely complicated political problems of the current year your cornerstone, like before, will be not emotions but the interests of Russia and that in the most dramatic moments you will display a clear strategic vision.' Yeltsin thus left the door open.

His second step was to identify a strategic ally at the election: the one who would come in third and would be able to give Yeltsin his votes in the second round.

On 24 January 1996 Yeltsin's representatives met Yavlinsky.

This is how it is remembered by Yeltsin's assistants.

'Boris Yeltsin's representative let it be known that the conversation was taking place at his own initiative... The reasons given were the worry over the overall political situation at the election; that Yavlinsky had no chance of winning (he didn't object); the President's chances were better (Yavlinsky offered no comment which was amazing since Yeltsin's ratings at the time were lower than his own) and that they both faced the danger of communists coming to power (Yavlinsky was totally supportive, he saw no future for himself after the victory of communists).

At the conclusion of the negotiations... the President's representatives had a signed decree on appointing Yavlinsky's First Vice-Premier. It only took his consent to send the text immediately to press. But the consent was never given...'

This story had a follow-up. On the eve of the first round, Yeltsin met Yavlinsky in person. Yet again they talked about the Grigory Alexeyevich* joining the presidential team and being appointed First Vice-Premier in charge of the economy. Yavlinsky again refused determinedly. He wanted to continue his fight for the post of the president. Yeltsin made a pause and then completed the conversation, "You know, Grigory Alexeyevich, in your place I would do the same."

The vacancy of the 'strategic partner' remained unfilled. 'Then the main attention switched over to Lebed. It all looked simpler here and when the General consented he received help that took shape of some sizeable media and organisational resources. It didn't take long to manifest itself in General Lebed's improved ratings...'

In 1996 Lebed had turned 46: a paratrooper, an officer with practical combat experience, formerly Commander-in-Chief of the Tula Division of Air Landing Troops, and a veteran of Afghanistan. Then there was the Trans-Dniester conflict** when Lebed, commander of the Fourteenth Army, was frequently present on TV. After that he disappeared from the

---

* Yavlinsky.

** The War of Trans-Dniester was a limited conflict that broke out in November 1990 at Dubăsari (*Dubossary*) between pro-Trans-Dniester forces, including the Trans-Dniester Republican Guard, militia and Cossack units, and supported by elements of the Russian Fourteenth Army, and pro-Moldovan forces, including Moldovan troops and police.

media's eye but suddenly re-emerged during the 1995 Duma election. Everyone forgot that he had been initially brought into politics by the communists. Lebed was supported by big business, both financially and in terms of media coverage.

Generally speaking, for many Russian businessmen the election in 1996 became a kind of a testing ground. Up until that point they had never played any part in politics. However, in 1996 it dawned on them that if they stayed aside they could lose everything. It wasn't only about supporting Yeltsin's candidature for presidency; each important businessman was playing his own game: Gusinsky supported Yavlinsky; Alfa-Capital Group* placed their bet on Lebed, etc. Lebed thus became this third force with whom the presidential team decided to cooperate.

Everything that Yeltsin's team was doing in those — pre-election — months boiled down to classic electoral tactics. An electoral campaign dictates its own laws; one must indentify one's strengths and one's adversary's weaknesses. So there is no wheel to re-invent, it is just a question of hard work and usual promises. These are only several of Presidential Decrees that came out in spring of 1996:

'On Increasing Allowances to Undergraduate and Post-Graduate Students of State-Owned Educational Establishments';

'On Additional Measures to Develop Mortgage Lending', etc.

Not to mention, constitutional guarantees of a citizen's title to land, measures to step up combat against terrorism, a housing programme *Own Your Home*, measures to strengthen state support for science and higher educational establishments and 'The Programme to Regulate the Crisis in the Chechen Republic'.

Of special importance was Decree No 66 'On Measures to Ensure Timely Payment of Salaries, Pensions and Other Benefits from the State Budget All Levels' and the Decree released in February, 'On Some Additional Measures to Ensure Timeliness of Paying Salaries to Public Sector Employees'.

By issuing all those decrees, Yeltsin was trying to pay off old debts

---

* Alfa Capital was founded in 1996. It is a part of Alfa Group, one of Russia's largest privately-owned financial-industry conglomerates with significant presence in key sectors of the Russian economy.

and patch up holes. These were populist measures and some of them were simply impossible to implement as there was no money in the treasury. However, this was at least a gesture.

The situation with salaries, however, was hopelessly bad and the war in Chechnya made a huge hole in the budget. The President had started a lengthy war with regional authorities that had not been paying salaries for months and was personally controlling developments at daily briefings. He appointed a special aide — Mr Livshits — to deal with the issues that, theoretically, were in the government's brief.

'Each boss was threatened instant dismissal for siphoning off the budget resources. More so, *pour encourager les autres*, President did fire several federal functionaries and demanded a daily briefing… It was an exhausting procedure: the President was nervous, arriving into the Kremlin earlier and earlier each day. Once Livshits reported at 7 A.M. and inadvertently caused President embarrassment. The aide was complaining that he had to link up with almost every district centre, and a particular nuisance was some bloody village of Butka in Sverdlovsk Oblast. "There's nothing bloody about it," President took umbrage: "I was born there."

… Operation *Salary* did have one rather good spin-off. Not only did people start receiving their money but the overall discipline of executing orders and instructions improved too. Procurators came to life and state agencies in charge of safeguarding social rights became more active. *Rostrudinspektsia*\* alone reimbursed the general public with about 1.5 trillion roubles' worth of salaries.' (*Yeltsin's Epoch*).

However, this was but a first step. For the first time ever in Russia an election was treated as a strategic process. No one before had ever been tried to measure the effect of pre-election decisions and addresses.

The image of an 'awakened lion' started bringing results. Practically every time that Yeltsin would appear on TV — be it a trip to some region, a TV address or an interview — it would bring a tangible increase in ratings. This was because 'Yeltsin's niche' in the sphere of expectations, hopes and worries had been basically vacant. It could only be occupied by him. His sudden rejuvenation revealed a genuine long-awaited need for someone who would offer guarantees of a peaceful future.

---

\* The State Labour Inspectorate.

## 'WITH HIM, WE FEEL SAFE' (JANUARY-JULY OF 1996)

Alexander Oslon, a sociologist, briefly defines which suggestions of the 'think tank' were conceptually new: 'In 1996, for three months President Yeltsin rejected the role of Person Number One (all this given his temper), became just a "candidate" in sync with his analytical group.'

Yeltsin was used to speaking in front of the people but now each regional trip that he made had been preceded by comprehensive sociological research that would highlight the most serious local grievances, commonest expectations and overall attitudes — and Yeltsin didn't simply speak off the cuff but was taking the 'think tank's' recommendations on board too.

Having said all this, the hardest of all was to change his personal attitude, for now Yeltsin was obliged to speak to the people not as the President but as a *presidential candidate*.

... Just as in 1989-1991, during his first election campaign, he was face to face with an exhausted ailing country that was asking him a variety of questions, eager to look him in the eye.

He was overcome with this new type of meetings. 'Over the recent years, Dad got used to more "protocol"-type events, he had been accompanied everywhere by his guards and they kept people at bay for reasons of security. After one such meeting Dad ordered that the cordon be removed, he wanted to see people at close range, at the distance of an outstretched hand. He was incredibly excited by this, he liked it a lot. On the other hand, it was an enormous physical input. I kept asking myself whether he would survive this campaign, for the rate was simply insane: city after city, region after region. And every time before a meeting he had to study documents, then make several presentations, work out local circumstances, resolve specific local problems,' Tatyana Yeltsin recollects.

Alexander Oslon's memoirs continue:

'Nowadays it is hard to imagine the people's astonishment when in his very first pre-election public speech Yeltsin suddenly got onto the subject of women, pensioners, children, mass impoverishment, etc. Moreover, he used simple human words, free from bureaucratic speak, and his tonality was that of compassion. Of even greater effect was his official electoral advertising campaign, with its famous mottos of "Chose with your heart!"

and "I believe! I love! I hope!"' It was so much in contrast with his image since 1993, that of someone harsh and even cruel, that it started eroding this perception — and that was what the "think tank" was after.'

It isn't easy to calculate how many trips he made in those several months: 'In April, May and June Yeltsin visited 26 regions, travelled across Russia from the North Polar Circle to the Caucasian Mountains, and from the Baltic Sea to the Sea of Okhotsk, having visited Belgorod, Astrakhan, Ufa and Perm**. In the last week of the campaign he laid the foundation stone of the Christ the Redeemer Cathedral in Kaliningrad, and the next day, having covered eight time zones, was urging voters in Khabarovsk to preserve their feeling of solidarity, hope and trust. Within one day, June 11th, he spoke in Khanty-Mansiysk... where the grass was timidly peeping through the tundra, and in Novocherkassk, 2,400 kilometres to the south, where watermelons and big, dark, juicy sour cherries were about to hit the market stalls.' (Leon Aron).

In the Novosibirsk metro an curious occurrence took place: as he descended down to the platform suddenly a woman came up to him and told him softly that the Bible prohibits the sale of land. Upon his return to Moscow he instructed his assistants to look into it. They set about researching the 'reference source' (that is the Bible) and then wrote to their boss. 'Dear Boris Nikolayevich, there are no direct instructions in the Bible on the subject of a ban of sales and purchases of land. Theologians of various persuasions believe that the statement of the woman in Novosibirsk is sectarianism. On the contrary, the New Testament contains direct evidence of transactions with land. This is the precise quote:

The Acts of Apostles (Chapters 4 and 5).

"... For neither was there among them any who lacked, for as many as were owners of lands or houses, sold them and brought the proceeds of the things that were sold, and laid them at the apostles' feet, and distribution was made to each, according as anyone had need..."' (*Yeltsin's Epoch*).

---

\* The slogan was making a reference to 1 Corinthians (13:13) of the New Testament: 'And now abideth faith, hope, charity, these three; but the greatest of these *is* charity.' (King James's Bible).

\*\* And the list is far from exhaustive. — *Author's comment*.

## 'WITH HIM, WE FEEL SAFE' (JANUARY-JULY OF 1996)

Yes, the welcome he enjoyed varied. In some places groups of people were carrying placards 'Put Yeltsin's Gang in the Dock!' But the communist electorate didn't worry him: he would place wreaths at War Memorials in front of irate war veterans; he would descend into mines, drop into deprived shops in the suburbs, and gradually people would start approaching him and asking questions. There were no cases of a real boycott, no one would recoil, storm out or heckle.

There were lots of requests.

They asked for help in affairs — big and small, and in any crowd 'there would necessarily be those who came not out of curiosity but in order to complain of being persecuted or simply to ask for something'. Assistants used to keep a pad handy wherein they would enter 'supplicant petitions'. An entire group was busy processing such requests and notes.

At times there were incidents that proved memorable to all those present. In the village of Ateptsevo, near Moscow, Yeltsin was supposed to perform, under the close scrutiny of TV cameras, a number of ceremonial deeds: issue greetings to newlyweds, visit a worker's family and have some tea (Yeltsin ushered his entourage out), visit a shop and a school — but suddenly there was this strange pause. The date was May 7th* and a jovial war veteran had been waiting for Yeltsin on his tiny dacha plot, two shots of vodka in his hands. He had been dreaming of sharing a toast with Yeltsin. Assistants had received strict instructions from the medics: no vodka whatsoever! So they rushed to the old man with admonishments and remonstrations. 'Come on, fellas, I shall bring some out for you too,' exclaimed the veteran, eager to placate them. But Yeltsin led him, arm-in-arm, vodka and all, to the rear side of his plot, where they spent quite some time 'in the kitchen garden'. The content of this conversation between two people, advanced in years, was never recorded and, in essence, no one ever learned what they had been talking about — it might have been of historical significance... Yet it stayed a secret. Nevertheless, through his response to this elderly veteran Yeltsin was persuading the whole country that there was hope and that it was not long to wait till 'the full recovery'.

---

* Two days before the date when Russia celebrates the Victory Day (May 9th) — on occasion of victory in the Great Patriotic War (Russian part of the Second World War).

415

During this time Boris Nikolayevich lost 9 kilograms whilst radiating energy and strength. It had been a long while since he last travelled without Naina Iosifovna. She only joined him a few times. 'Mum was very popular, yet the "think tank" decided that she should not be constantly by his side so as not to vex people. In many cities she had her own programme,' Tatyana recollections are helped by her elder sister Yelena who was helping her mother.

As for Tatyana, she took part in all trips that Yeltsin made as a member of his election campaign: an active coordinator with speedy reactions. She took in the minutest details and kept an eye on how recommendations were executed. Very quickly it became clear that in terms of perseverance and firmness she was her father's daughter. At the time it attracted everybody's attention since such an approach was highly unorthodox for our country.

We should give his family their due. Not one of them succumbed to the natural temptation of constantly flashing across TV screens, taking some high post or using their influence to further a private agenda.

Naina Iosifovna and the President's daughters gave very few interviews to journalists but I happened to be talking to Tatyana in the summer of 2000, after the election: 'Tanya, the public need for female politicians is huge. Don't you want to head some newspaper or a TV company or, say, take part in some elections, at least in the future? Maybe our country will finally have a woman as a president?'

Her answer was terse, 'If the country needs a woman as a president it is possible to start looking. But I personally will have nothing to do with it. I don't want to go into politics — ever.'

Yeltsin was participating in this campaign physically on his last legs, a resuscitation specialist constantly by his side. Yeltsin would often slink away so that a doctor could check his blood pressure, give a pill or administer an injection. 'For the election game, Yeltsin put his own health on the line and possibly risked his life,' his press secretary Kostikov wrote subsequently.

'I feared the election greatly,' Naina Iosifovna was saying, 'but as we were talking in December 1995 he kept asking: tell me, who? Chernomyrdin? Yavlinsky? I knew that his life was at stake but at the same time I realised that he couldn't lose. For him, it was impossible. That was just the way he was.'

## 'WITH HIM, WE FEEL SAFE' (JANUARY-JULY OF 1996)

On his trips Yeltsin was accompanied not only by his family and aides but also the most popular rock musicians. For some of them it was additional income, but some viewed it as their civic duty. The young that normally hate politics and ignore elections heard, at these concerts, clear and sensible arguments in words understandable to all. 'I have already experienced the communist regime and don't want to do it again,' said Andrei Makarevich*. 'Come along on June 16th and cast your votes, so that Mashina Vremeni could continue to play.' Alisa, Tsvety, Nautilus**– all of them represented the generation that had grown up in a situation of protest, the context of fighting bans and bureaucratic censorship. Yeltsin's main message — the fight for freedom — resonated with their personal ideology.

In Volgograd, Boris Nikolayevich climbed the stage before the rock concert. Tens of thousands had gathered in the square. He made a short speech and when they roared in delight he broke into a dance. It became a classic entry in his iconography: an awkward older man danced the twist with a young singer.

'We were pleading with Dad not to do it,' Tanya was telling me. 'We nearly held him by his arms but he was unstoppable. The sight of a huge young audience at the rock concert sent him into wild raptures.' Although far from everybody responded to this vignette with a smile, it became unquestionably clear: with him, we had nothing to fear. He never promised an easy life but the 'hard life' that he did promise was predictable and more understandable than what the communists had up their sleeve.

Week after week, the tone used by leading Russian media was also changing. A harsh, critical and often aggressive tonality in the beginning of Yeltsin's campaign was giving way to unquestionable support.

'We may as well admit it, society has gone through a civil war, albeit of a "cold" variety,' the boss of the ORT's*** sociological department would write

---

* Andrey Makarevich (b. 1953) is a Soviet and Russian rock musician, founder of the Russia's oldest still active rock band *Mashina Vremeni* (Time Machine). For about a decade they played in the underground.

** Popular Russian rock groups.

*** Russian Public Television; Channel One — the official TV channel.

several days after the election. 'True, under the circumstances, the television was not impartial. It was biased in favour of democracy, in favour of survival of the mass media as an outlet for public opinion. It would have been nicer for us simply to inform the public and appeal to common sense and intellect. This will become possible when we are to choose between social and economic programmes, not between a bad freedom and a good prison.'

It was quite a phenomenon in the 1996 election: top managers of the electronic media, newspapers and magazines were supporting Yeltsin with such sincerity and passion that it was well in excess of the 'think tank's' expectations.

All this notwithstanding, there was a time bomb on Yeltsin's path towards a victory in public politics: Chechnya. Back in March Yeltsin announced that he had 'seven plans for overcoming the crisis' although which one was the best and which path he was going to choose remained unclear. The plethora of plans and the routinely broken moratoria on hostilities were no use, the war in Chechnya was raging on, with no apparent way out of the crisis until the end of April in 1996 when two circumstances suddenly intervened in the previously irresolvable situation. At the end of April news agencies reported that Dzhokhar Dudayev was dead. A *Niva* car carrying the Chechen leader on his way from a hide-away to a location for holding negotiations by radiotelephone was hit by a self-targeting Russian missile. There came a moment when several months of preparation by the Russian special services proved more efficient than all the guerrilla-type security employed by Dudayev's bodyguards.

This event turned out to be a turning point in the entire war.

The Russian and global media took a long time believing the news but Dudayev's funeral and the official mourning were evidence enough. Thus, the principal obstacle was removed from the path of negotiations. The remaining Chechen leaders — Zelimkhan Yandarbiyev and Aslan Maskhadov — were potential negotiators that suited the Kremlin much better. They didn't have a chip on the shoulder like Dudayev and therefore could be more flexible. A kind of a moral barrier for contact at the highest level was now lifted.

The second conducive circumstance was General Alexander Lebed's position. The determination to 'stop the senseless war' became the mainstay of his election programme. The long-awaited mediator entered Russian politics, a person of repute, influence and unquestionable moral authority.

He came into politics and started scoring political points right away. In this he was helped by his saturnine appearance of a special force commando speaking in this extra-low bass. He was doing his utmost to acquire the reputation of an all-Russian peacemaker, a military man who could teach a lesson to all those civilian politicians on how to dampen down local conflicts. It was Lebed's pet project — to stop the war in Chechnya despite the attitude of the high brass and, unquestionably, the army had a lot of respect for him. Although the Russian army was reluctant, and with good reason, to withdraw from Chechnya in defeat, Lebed's appearance on the political arena meant that Yeltsin acquired a powerful ally for his peace strategy.

Several days after Dudayev's death, there was an attempt on Zelimkhan Yandarbiyev's life (he was Acting President of Chechnya). Suddenly there was a vacuum of power and various militant groups were clearly eager to fill it. Moscow realised that it must make haste with the negotiations ot the conflict between warlords could become uncontrollable. Thus Yeltsin gave immediate instructions to prepare a meeting with the Chechen representatives. The first question was: where should they be received? Yeltsin set off on a tour of the Kremlin.

'The choice fell on one of the oblong halls with a big table. It had three doors: one opposite the table's head, leading into the President's quarters; and two on the side. The President gave orders to keep one of the doors shut and place an armed and uniformed guard by each of the other two.'

The Chechen delegation was supposed to enter by the side door and take their seats along the table on the left from the President's chair, after which members of the federal delegation were to enter the hall: Prime Minister Viktor Chernomyrdin, chairman of Chechnya's Provisional Council Doku Zavgayev and the Secretary of the Security Council Oleg Lobov who were supposed to sit on the opposite side. Further to that, the President was to make an appearance through his door, make a short speech of general welcome and then ask everyone to take their seats. That was the plan.

Meanwhile, Moscow followed closely updates from Chechnya on the progress of Yandarbiyev's delegation. To enhance the convoy's security their route was changed several times. The delegation was stopped at check points. Finally, they made it to where Ingush President Aushev's private jet was already waiting for them. The Chechen delegation wanted to take 120 militants along to Moscow. However, a short discussion was enough to persuade Yandarbiyev and his people to change for the plane sent by Russia's President. Apart from the official delegation, this charter flight took on board 17 armed people

Vnukovo-2 airport was teeming with OMON and plain-clothed security agents. The Minister of Justice, Sergey Stepashin, and an OSCE* representative, Tim Guldemann, came to meet the Chechens. It had to be decided who would go to the Kremlin. The Chechens insisted that it would be five official delegation members, while the others stayed onboard and waited till the agreement was signed.

A cortege of ten vehicles made it to the Kremlin in 15 minutes. 'When the Chechens entered the empty negotiations hall and the protocol service started escorting them to their seats, a small fracas ensued. The Chechens were displeased with the seating plan: Yandarbiyev wanted to sit vis-à-vis the President, not Doku Zavgayev. The President was to be seated at the head of the table. Since the Chechen delegation was late, Yeltsin, Chernomyrdin and the others entered all together — whereas according to the initial plan, the President was supposed to be the last to come in. Immediately, Yeltsin invited everyone to take their seats. The Chechens declared that they refused to take the seats allocated to them and were ready to leave the negotiations. At which point the President gave a sharp order, 'Shut the door and let no one out!" (*Yeltsin's Epoch*).

The guards obeyed the order at once and the arduous negotiations took off.

On the evening of May 27th, after two hours of negotiations, Chernomyrdin and Yandarbiyev signed the agreement on a complete termination of hostilities as of midnight of June 1st. But Yeltsin had a surprise up his sleeve. On the morning of that day, before the negotiations got off the

---

* Organisation for Security and Cooperation in Europe.

ground, the President announced, 'Tomorrow I shall fly to Chechnya!' This is how the episode was described by Boris Nemtsov whom Yeltsin took along as a governor who had collected, within his oblast, a million of signatures urging a stop to the war.

'The trip promised to be hard and tense. Militants were threatening to kill Yeltsin and made many other promises. When at Vnukovo-2, the then FSB boss Barsukov pulled out a red folder containing strictly confidential documents. One of them was an FSB report: "Agent with a code name 'In-law' informs us that at the time of Russia's President Boris Yeltsin's presence in the village of Znamenskoye an attempt on his life will be carried out by Basayev's band who plan to use a Stinger missile. We recommend that the trip be cancelled."

Barsukov said to me, "Yeltsin likes you, tell him not to go. You must persuade him to stay in Moscow." At one minute to nine Yeltsin was taken to the gangway, and the departure was scheduled for nine. He got out. We were standing there: Korzhakov and me. Behind our backs was the plane packed with Special Task Force and Alpha troops.

"What's up?" Yeltsin asked.

"Boris Nikolayevich, Alexander Vasilievich* and Mikhail Ivanovich** believe that we shouldn't go. There is a dispatch from their agent," said I and handed over the sheet of paper to the President. Yeltsin read it and declared, "Boris Yefimovich***, get onboard and you, cowards, stay behind."'

'Yandarbiyev and members of his delegation learned about Yeltsin's trip to Chechnya from the evening news on TV. In essence, they had spent that entire day at a luxurious dacha near Moscow in the role of hostages,' Yeltsin's assistants recollect. On May 28th, at 11:00, the presidential plane landed in Mozdok. The President and his entourage were moved to helicopters. 'The choppers were aligned overhead in a circle. They would land and soar up right away. In this merry-go-round it was impossible to work out which one of them was being used by Yeltsin. Finally, they all came to the ground.'

---

\* Korzhakov.

\*\* Barsukov.

\*\*\* Nemtsov.

After that a helicopter took Yeltsin to Grozny, to the location of the 205th Motorised Infantry Brigade. General Troshev remembered Yeltsin's words there, 'The war is over. You have won. You have triumphed over Dudayev's rebel regime.'

'But we, the army men,' Troshev goes on to say in his memoir, 'were aware that this was an exclusively opportunistic statement made with one purpose only — to attract the votes. Most of us by then had come to realise a simple truth: our peacemaking efforts were taken by our adversary to be a sign of weakness, therefore, the problem needed a radical solution.' Yet Yeltsin hoped that once the war was over Chechnya could be lured into the Russian orbit by purely economic measures.

The first Chechen war was petering out...

Ziuganov, like Yeltsin, was touring the country tirelessly. Wherever he arrived, he would be given, by the gangway or the train carriage, a traditional 'bread and salt' welcome by the local 'functionaries', typically communist deputies or representatives of local authorities. Two weeks before the elections, only 49 out of 80 regional bosses had expressed their support for Yeltsin. The 'red belt' regions and rural communities supported Ziuganov practically without exception, and local administration heads, factory managers and *kolkhoz* chairmen made no secret of their joy over the return of the Soviet power. Thus, in Volgograd Oblast, out of all its constituent districts only one out of thirty openly approved of Yeltsin.

The communists had formidable resources, primarily organisational ones. Once their party was reinstalled they re-established 20 thousand primary cells. Nearly half a million people were paying membership dues. Hard to say how many more were sympathetic to their cause. Guided by the strict precepts of the party discipline, for the duration of the electoral campaign they all became active canvassers. The local press, as a rule, was also in the communist hands. A local paper is often the only accessible channel of information in the countryside and according to sociological surveys a quarter of the Russian population read nothing else. With such a powerful resource at their disposal, Ziuganov's people refused to buy expensive TV time and only used free allocation of the time on air to which they were entitled under the election law. Still, all central channels gave Ziuganov coverage on their own initiative.

A central concept of Ziuganov's election platform was an appeal to the sentiment of national humiliation that dominated public opinion. The majority of the country's population dreamed of the revival of a superpower that would show the West its proper place. That was Ziuganov's trump card — along with promises of a return of equal starting opportunities and social fairness. Rallies in support of communists were becoming ever more active, numerous, ubiquitous and vehement.

Meanwhile, a bitter fight was still going on in the background between those who believed in Yeltsin's victory and those who didn't — in other words, those who were looking for options of a compromise and a deal with the communists, now that the use of force had been decidedly rejected in March. Those in favour of a compromise made these arguments: supposing Yeltsin made it into the second round (in April and May, all independent sociologists were already talking about this possibility with confidence) and the votes were split down the middle between Yeltsin and Ziuganov, then, 'The communists would lead the people onto the streets' and a social conflict would be inevitable.

Strange though it may seem, the first person to raise the subject was Sergey Filatov, chairman of the public movement of support to the president and the former head of the Kremlin Administration. He insisted that 'there should be no war between the "reds" and the "whites"' and all voters should be taken into account. 'We are one people, whatever our political views and preferences.' Accordingly, he believed, there should be no winners at the election so as 'not to suppress dissent'. Unexpectedly, in April this peacekeeping appeal met with the support of 'leading entrepreneurs'.

Their address came out on April 27th under the title 'To Break the Deadlock'. The text had been signed the biggest names in the Russian business: president of LogoVAZ\* Boris Berezovsky, chairman of the board of directors of the Most Group\*\*\* Vladimir Gusinsky, president of

---

\* Based on the historic allocation of symbolic colours during the civil war that broke out after the communists first came to power in 1917: 'reds' are communists (because of the colour of their flag) and 'whites' are monarchists and liberals.

\*\* LogoVAZ, the USSR's first capitalist car dealership.

\*\*\* A media holding.

Rosprom\* Leonid Nevzlin, president of the *ONEKSIMbank* Vladimir Potanin, chairman of the board of directors of the Alfa Group Mikhail Friedman, chairman of the board of directors of the *Menatep* bank Mikhail Khodorkovsky and others.

'Our society is split,' the text was saying, 'and the gap is getting wider with each day. This cleft dividing us into "reds" and "whites", our own and aliens, runs through the heart of Russia... The forces behind politicians' backs are biding their time. They will charge forward the very next day after either party's victory. This will happen with fatal inevitability and despite the will of individuals. Ultimately, the results of the vote in June will practically provide a minority — whichever one it will turn out to be, "red" or "white" — with a mandate to implement the rules of life categorically unacceptable to a huge proportion of the population. Eventually it will be not a triumph of somebody's truth but the spirit of violence and sedition. The mutual antagonism of the political forces is so powerful that either one of them can only establish its dominance by way of pushing Russia towards a civil war and disintegration.'

It is curious that the same people (Berezovsky, Gusinsky and the others) who in March came along to the Kremlin to meet with Yeltsin and all but demand that he should step up his election campaign, a month later changed their tune and started talking about an impasse and the need for a compromise. So what did they offer?

'At this dramatic point we, the entrepreneurs of Russia, urge all people of intellect, the military, representatives of legislative and executive branches of power, of law-enforcement agencies and mass media, all those wielding the real power and on whom Russia's destiny is reliant to join forces for identifying a political compromise that can avert bitter conflicts endangering Russia's main interests and its very statehood. Russian politicians must be compelled to agree to profound reciprocal concessions, strategic political agreements that should be endorsed legally...'

But the initiative died before it took off — neither of the two main contenders wanted a compromise: Yeltsin was propelled by the momentum of his campaign and Ziuganov believed that the victory was his anyway..

---

\* Federal Agency on Industry.

On the night between June 19th and 20th the final results of the first round were announced. They were as follows: Yeltsin received 35.28%; Ziuganov — 32.03% whilst amongst the rest, Lebed had 14.52%; Yavlinsky — 7.34% and Zhirinovsky — 5.7%. None of the other received over 1%. The turnout of voters was sufficiently high with over 70% of those who had a right to vote coming to the ballot boxes on June 16th.

For Yeltsin, it was the first round that had the most significance. The democratically-minded votes could have been split by Yavlinsky, Lebed and Fyodorov who were all diverting the votes of Yeltsin's potential supporters. 'Making it into the second round,' writes sociologist Alexander Oslon, member of the Analytical Group, 'was already a miracle.' Yeltsin's advantage over Ziuganov in the first count was 2-3% — a minuscule lead.

So the outcome of the second round scheduled for July 2nd was a cause for worry amongst analysts, journalists and common people alike. July 2nd was already high summer, the time for vacations in offices and universities, the time for seasonal agricultural work carried out by a considerable number of urban dwellers*, which meant that the turnout would drop, thus increasing Ziuganov's chances since his electorate — mostly older people and rural residents — did not depend on the seasonal factor..' On the other hand, 'it became clear that the results of the second round would largely be shaped by participation of students and middle-aged voters.' (Mr Oslon). The chances were still practically equal.

Against all expectations, at the time of the first round there were no incidents over counting of votes, no pressure on the election commission, and no rallies or demonstrations. The 'electoral purity' was safeguarded by a huge number of Russian and foreign journalists. The communists behaved with equal civility. They had practically no complaints after the votes had been counted. Complaints came later, several years afterwards. For as long as there was a chance to win, Ziuganov's team kept quiet.

Immediately after the first round was over Yeltsin appealed to those who had voted for Lebed, Yavlinsky and Fyodorov. He urged them to give

---

* Most people in Russia have their summer houses, dachas, used by many as allotments.

their votes 'to a single democratic candidate', that is the president. It was indicative that he crossed everyone else, including Zhirinovsky, off the list — despite the latter's attempts, before the first round, to ingratiate himself to Yeltsin, blackmail him and get into the government on the crest of the election wave.

Hard negotiations with Lebed were underway. The votes were analysed: what could the price be for Lebed's votes? Yeltsin appointed Lebed Secretary of the Security Council, dismissed Defence Minister Pavel Grachev and reassigned the duties of coordinating *Silovikis* (formerly performed by his assistant Baturin) to the new SC secretary — all these were Lebed's terms. Equally, Yeltsin was trying to turn Yavlinsky into an ally and offered him a post in the government but to no avail.

In a nutshell, Yeltsin's script for victory was being implemented, although it was not a landslide but a hard-won victory 'on points'.

However, on that night when the votes were still counted, a totally unexpected event took place. In the evening of June 19th, two individuals were apprehended at the entrance to the White House: Arkady Yevstafiev and Sergey Lisovsky were stopped by the Presidential Security Service and the White House guards. Lisovsky was carrying a box — but not 'the one used for a Xerox' (as was reported later) but the *one used for the Xerox paper*.

This smallish box, as transpired from the interview transcript, contained 'densely packed stacks of money in foreign currency', about half a million dollars. Yevstafiev belonged to the Financial Services Department of the president's election team and reported directly to Chubais. Lisovsky, a musical producer and an advertiser, was responsible for advertising campaigns 'Vote or Lose' and 'Yeltsin — Our President"*. These involved major rock and pop stars while both individuals themselves were prominent figures too. The detainees were kept in the guards' room for about 10 hours (they had been apprehended at 17:00) and set free in the small hours. An emergency news release came out on the NTV Channel about 2 A.M. The presenter, Yevgeny Kiselyov, his voice trembling with emotion, announced that a coup was in the making, its purpose sabotage of the second round of elections. 'A moment ago,' he was saying, 'when this emergency broadcast

---

\* A TV social advertising campaign in support of Yeltsin's candidacy.

was already on air I was told that FSB Director General Barsukov, in his telephone conversation with an executive of Boris Yeltsin's election team, confirmed the fact of Lisovsky and Yevstafiev's detention.

'The subversive nature of this measure is crystal-clear and is a logical follow-up to the well-known stand taken by the generals in the security agencies who advocated curtailment of democracy and cancellation of presidential elections. This attitude was made public by General Korzhakov in his notable interview, broadcast in Russia and abroad in the beginning of May. It indicated that the country was likely to be on the threshold of a political catastrophe.'

Which Korzhakov's interview did he refer to? Was any of this true?

In his interview to London's *Observer* right after the May Day communist rally, Korzhakov was unequivocally insisting on the need to put off the presidential elections in Russia — to prevent unrest which was unavoidable, whatever the outcome. According to Korzhakov, should Boris Yeltsin win, the radical opposition would not accept the election results, proclaim the election rigged and take to the streets. However, should Ziuganov come first the same people would prevent him from pursuing a moderate policy, which, again, promised nothing but dramatic conflicts. In this interview, Korzhakov went on to say that his point of view was shared by 'many influential people'. Somewhat later he provided some clarifications to *Interfax:* 'Today one cannot but hope that the presidential election anywhere in Russia will take a civilised form.' There are 'entire territories where a civilised expression of the people's will is not yet possible.'

'The society is being split, whole families are split: some support Yeltsin and some support Ziuganov. This segregation of minds is dangerous.'

Yeltsin's comment on May 6th was: 'I do believe in the wisdom of Russian voters, that is why the election shall take place within the timeframe stipulated by the Constitution.' He then added, 'I told Korzhakov not to meddle in politics and refrain from such statements in future.'

Yeltsin's warning had no effect.

Subsequent events were the first ever attempt in Russian history to kick up a political scandal on the basis of an election — a kind of a Russian Watergate. However, this scandal proved to be both pettier and more complicated than its American precedent. Neither side, either before or after the election, managed to prove that the other was going against the law, falsifying results or intriguing in some other way. Neither the presidential side (after the events of March 17th-18th) nor the communists made any attempts to circumvent the elections, go beyond the Constitution or break the law (as was the case in America in 1972) — by, for example, resorting to bugging the phones, blackmail, threats, attempted murders and the like.

And so Korzhakov's team had only this last reserve: a high-profile scandal with criminal overtones. Thus, the paradox: the decision to sabotage the elections was taken not by the two contestants (quite the opposite, both were stubbornly sure of victory) but by a third party! A scenario of this kind was our Russian know-how, our home-made Watergate.

Judging by some details, in their initial interview with the detainees, officers from the FSB and the Presidential Security Service were not particularly interested in the money — what was it for or from what source. Instead, they were trying to intimidate and, according to Yevstafiev and Lisovsky, dig up dirt on other individuals, primarily, Chubais and Chernomyrdin: your criminal gang has been exposed, we've been keeping tabs on you, and it's useless to deny anything! Yevstafiev remembered one phrase particularly: 'as for the president, he will win whatever, but it will not be thanks to those who got in on the act but the "true patriots".'

Then again, shortly before the first round Korzhakov forwarded Yeltsin a memo whereby he was warning his boss of 'a possible exposure of certain sources of financing* and allocation of financial resources' and of the 'danger that originals or copies of certain documents may fall into the hands of the competition or unfriendly mass media'. Therefore he was asking President to hand over 'all financial documentation and electronic copies' to the Presidential Security Service 'for safe-keeping'. 'With a heavy sigh,' Korzhakov writes, 'Yeltsin made me personally responsible for keeping control over all financial activities of the campaign.' It is true — on the memo Yeltsin inscribed 'Transfer everything'.

However, Yeltsin's assistants point out in their book:

---

\* Of the election campaign. — *Author's comment.*

'The piquancy of the situation was in the fact that it was none other than Korzhakov who was overseeing all transfers and was responsible for their safety. His deputy Rogozin kept an eye on all transactions. ... <Thus,> if they viewed cash changing hands as a transgression they were in a position to stop it all much earlier.' Thus, for the duration of the election campaign Korzhakov stood in control of financial flows. So why was this particular moment chosen for a 'special operation'?

Korzhakov had prepared meticulously, thought things through, tracked everyone down and selected fall-guys. Detention of Yevstafiev and Lisovsky was part of the plan. Luckily, the document that Korzhakov himself had carefully preserved and made publics sheds light on his intentions. After his defeat and ignominious resignation, two days later, still in the heat of the fight, Korzhakov wrote Yeltsin a letter which said, in part:

'... I hope you realise how ruinous and dangerous for you is to take to your heart a person hated by the entire country — Anatoly Chubais. People not well-versed in the intricacies of the market economy still understand perfectly well that it is Chubais who has ruined them by changing money into worthless vouchers; it is Chubais who has promised them flats by the year 2000 and *Volga* cars against each voucher purchased; it is Chubais who has declared the arrival of economic stability in the country where over 40 million people live below the poverty line. Everyone knows that this person bears the brunt of responsibility for the Russian plants and factories now being in foreign hands, Russian subsoil and raw materials sold for a song, unprofitable contracts signed on terms of enslavement and the country ending up in bondage to the International Monetary Fund...

'Alongside Chubais, the multinational corporations are angling for power; they have already enmeshed this country economically but as yet have no real political power. These forces are placing their bet not on you but on the obedient and controllable people. Proof of this is in numerous reports stemming from the White House Administration and Washington. The main object of multinational strategy is to render you unfit for action and compel you to abdicate from power, descending to any means, wriggling their way even into your family's confidence. The first step has already been taken: a staged provocation has led to the main security agencies of Russia being demoralised and Russia's security being thus endangered.

'In consequence, you have abandoned those who were there for you, who protected you against scoundrels selling their Motherland piecemeal... Besides, Chubais is already trying to make you announce your successor and will have no peace until you have given over power to someone chosen for Russia by the multinational corporations...

'I am ready to help you out in this time of need. We have resources, we have professional analysts at our disposal to help you win the campaign and ensure your victory in the second round. One soldier doesn't make a battle — do understand this and let us help you. We are ready to provide, in the shortest time possible, an urgent action plan to remove Chubais from your election team and instigate against him and his henchmen *a whole range of criminal proceedings*\*...'

The 'Xerox box' was only the first step — a tool to launch the plan, and a 'whole range' of stage-managed criminal cases would have followed without delay. The list of 'targets' had undoubtedly been long since prepared and mostly included 'think tank' members.

Quite probably, Korzhakov didn't doubt Yeltsin's victory but this victory should be masterminded by 'real patriots', not 'traitors of their Motherland'. He had been preparing for this moment — and the people who were providing real help to Yeltsin in his election campaign were to be transformed overnight into 'embezzlers', and 'agents of transnational forces' and 'the global backstage' (his terminology here is almost identical to that used by Ziuganov). Korzhakov knew his boss's nature, knew that he never intervened in criminal cases and operation of security agencies (for example, in 1994 when the conspirators were about to be pardoned Yeltsin did want to intervene but stopped short in good time).

Did Korzhakov realise that the hostage of this situation would be Yeltsin himself? Clearly, by instigating proceedings against his election team (Chernomyrdin, Iliushin and others) he was targeting Yeltsin as well and turning him into a puppet. Such risks could only be taken for a very good reason.

---

\* Italisised by the author.

In his book about the 1996 elections, Oleg Moroz quotes a fragment of his conversation with Anatoly Chubais:

"'No, I don't think he wanted to derail the second round,' says Anatoly Borisovich. 'That wasn't it. But it was clear that he was heading towards a political fiasco and we were in a situation of a head-on collision. By detaining Yevstafiev and Lisovsky he was hoping to tilt the situation in his favour: to demonstrate to the president that only he and his team were reliable while everyone else working for the election was either a conman or a thief.'

"What could Korzhakov have lost had he not taken the step that proved fatal? Yeltsin would have remained President, he, Korzhakov, would have remained his senior bodyguard so where's the loss?"

"He had no intention of remaining a bodyguard... He saw himself as the second person in the state, the one ruling Mother Russia. That was exactly his fear: that after his victory, Yeltsin would have made him a bodyguard, nothing more...'" The stakes were too high.

Korzhakov's idea ('the staff coup') was rather simple: having arrested Yevstafiev and Lisovsky, he could convince Yeltsin, without much ado, to remove Chubais. No one would want to 'wash the dirty linen in public' and elucidate 'internal squabbles' in the election team. Following this, he could do away with the 'think tank' members one by one.

As events were unfolding that night the 'think tank' members held an emergency meeting. Everyone feared that the first arrest would be closely followed by another one, and another one. Mercifully, it didn't happen. Frightened by the NTV news update, officers interrogating Lisovsky and Yevstafiev changed their tune. They filed a receipt in the case folder: it was hand-written, obviously in great haste, but still, it was a document. They offered tea and coffee and, finally, let them free.

Tanya stayed in the office until 5 A.M. — going home that night was a very bad idea.

In trying to work out what was going on Naina Iosifovna called Barsukov and Korzhakov:

'In the beginning, Barsukov tried to be polite and reassure me. Korzhakov didn't come to the phone at all. I spoke to Barsukov twice and thought that he was in a state of inebriation. I was amazed. But he kept insisting that he hadn't had any updates. I thought maybe he was at some function, and so called the third time, trying to get Korzhakov. Again, he didn't answer. So I said, "What are you doing, you, the head of such a service, and at the most crucial moment of the entire campaign? How do you mean — you are not up-to-date?" "You are interfering with my work!" Barsukov snapped and hung up.'

As it happened, that night a lot depended on Naina Iosifovna. 'Shortly before the first round,' Naina Iosifovna narrates, 'Boris Nikolayevich flew to Khabarovsk to meet his voters. I came along and while Boris Nikolayevich attended some venue Korzhakov asked me for a word in private. I was stunned when he started talking about the need to dismiss Chernomyrdin, the sooner the better, and that it was imperative to persuade Boris Nikolayevich of this need.

'He was accusing him of various abuses, of playing his own game (it wasn't his first attempt, either, he had already showed Boris Nikolayevich some papers earlier). Presently I asked, so who should replace him? And here he said something that gave me a chill: "It should be Soskovets", and started ardently extolling his virtues. This is where I got it, their entire plan. The ultimate purpose was to eliminate Boris Nikolayevich physically. The first stage — make Soskovets Premier. The second — there is no need for Boris Nikolayevich, since in case of his death Soskovets becomes the First Person.

'Death, disease, an aggravated heart attack — after all, Korzhakov had control over everything. Knowing Boris Nikolayevich's habits, he was at all times by his side, so he could have easily provoked an attack on a tennis court, in a swimming pool, you name it. Korzhakov concealed from us the doctors' opinion on the catastrophic state of Boris Nikolayevich's heart. He knew how bad things were and told us nothing, never showed us the papers. Why? So, after the conversation in Khabarovsk by June I was prepared; I knew what sort of people they were.'

Before 3 A.M. Naina Iosifovna woke up Boris Nikolayevich.

'What's all the hoo-ha about?' he was disgruntled.

Having been briefed, he called Korzhakov straight away: 'What's going on?' – and appointed an audience for the morning. At this point the fate of Alexander Korzhakov's group was irrevocably sealed. Next morning in the Kremlin Yeltsin met with Korzhakov, then Chernomyrdin, then Chubais. He called his senior aide Iliushin and asked him to prepare papers on termination of employment: Korzhakov, Barsukov and Vice-Premier Soskovets were removed from their posts and both generals — discharged from the army. Yeltsin gave his reasons in his usual terse and abrupt style — 'They have been taking a lot but giving little back'.

Those watching the TV broadcast remembered yet another phrase of Yeltsin's — grammatically clumsy but very clear in its message: 'First those generals, you know what I mean? Now these ones too...' and he gave a wave of his hand, annoyed. He signed those orders on the morning of June 20th.

At his press conference, held in a highly tense atmosphere — the 'think tank' leader was practically shaking — Anatoly Chubais uttered a phrase, rather counterintuitive in this controversial context: 'Today, the final nail has been driven in the coffin of communism...'

Seemingly, to call Korzhakov and Barsukov communists would have been going too far. Yet Chubais did have a point. Korzhakov's plan, some of which he confessed to Yeltsin in a fit of openness — about 'a whole range of criminal proceedings', could really have reversed the course of history.

There is, however, one question that still demands an answer. What was that money taken out of the White House, what happened to it afterwards and why, come to think of it, was there so much of it in that box?

The answer is quite obvious.

Elections mean money. Big time elections mean big time money. It is the same the world over, even in the well-established democracies with well established election laws. This is what Yeltsin's assistants have to say on the subject:

'The discrepancy between provisions of the Law on Elections stipulating the upper threshold of the election campaign expenses and the real costs was consistently creating a need to settle in "black cash". It was practised by everyone — this is exactly why competing sides never accused each other of it. It is self-evident that the same applied to Yeltsin's team.'

Says Arkady Yevstafiev (one of the two detainees):

'It was impossible to channel budget money into the election campaign even logistically. However, commercial banks that had been backing our campaign could keep their money with the Ministry of Finance and lend it against security. That was precisely what had happened prior to the first round: it transpired that the money was catastrophically short. Chubais kicked up quite a fuss and demanded to mobilise all resources, hence the haste. The Procurator Office's interrogators who worked on this case identified no *corpus delicti* in our actions, since no party had been affected.'

… Meanwhile the second round was drawing close and, seemingly, the worst for Yeltsin was over. But then there was yet another dramatic development. On June 26th, several days before the second round 'I came back from work to the dacha at about 17:00. The day had been exhausting. I made several steps along the hall, sat down in an arm-chair — to rest up before going upstairs to change. Suddenly I had this weird sensation — as if I have been picked up by someone big and strong, under my armpits, and carried somewhere. There was no pain yet, only this deadly fear: a second ago I was here but now am elsewhere…

And then — this excruciating pain\*, huge, overpowering. Thank God, there was a doctor on duty. He grasped instantly what was happening and started administering the right medications — virtually immediately. They laid me down right here, in the same room, transferred me to a bed and connected to necessary equipment. My women made an awful fuss, they were so frightened. I must have cut a… ghastly figure. I kept thinking, "My God, why am I so unlucky? You can count the days before the second round!" The next day it took all my willpower to sit up and I kept repeating, "Why, why now?"'

… It was an absolute emergency.

In theory, Yeltsin was supposed to rest in bed — standard practice in cases of cardiac infarction. He should have gone to hospital but in reality it was impossible. If a presidential candidate had disappeared from TV screens on the eve of the second round it would have been the end of everything achieved so far.

---

\* It was another heart attack. — *Author's comment*.

Those who by force of circumstance now had to make decisions, namely Anatoly Chubais, Tatyana Dyachenko, Valentin Yumashev and Viktor Iliushin, met on June 27th to discuss the situation. The consensus was to do all it takes to prevent rumours of Yeltsin's condition from splashing across newspaper pages and TV screens. The meeting between Yeltsin and Lebed was scheduled for the *very next* day, June 28th, so it was impossible to cancel it.

'... My bed was moved to the sitting room, hastily fitted out as a kind of a study. The cameraman (one of ours, of course, from the Kremlin) was clever with the shots and excluded anything extraneous, especially the grand piano... and, of course, the bed. They threw some cover over the medical equipment. Naina was only pleading, "Borya! Don't get up! Stay seated in the armchair! You mustn't!" But I bit on the bullet and willed myself out of the armchair to greet the visitor.' (*Presidential Marathon*)

Meanwhile the team were trying to explain Yeltsin's absence by 'a common cold' but according to Chubais, each such day was pushing ratings down by 'by 1.5-2%'. The countdown was in days. Mercifully, the second round was not far off. As Yeltsin comments himself in his book, a heart attack a month earlier, at the height of the election campaign, would have been much worse.

But there were two more trials ahead, two mandatory TV appearances: a meeting with Chernomyrdin and casting his own ballot on July 3rd. A number of other events had to be cancelled: say, on June 30th Yeltsin couldn't attend the All-Russian agricultural conference. It cost him votes but there was no other way.

The assistants recalled the process of recording the President's TV appeal before the second round:

'The text was cut down and simplified as much as possible. But even this was not the point. The very procedure was considerably altered, too. Normally, the President used to get into the studio several minutes before everything was completely ready. If Yeltsin was in good spirits he would wisecrack, chat to the crew and then do the recording. After some more exchanges and often a commemorative snapshot, he would take his leave.

But his appeal before the second round was a completely different story. You could have cut the tension with a knife. At a given time all those involved in preparations were commanded to leave the room. A bit later they were invited back. A deadly pale Yeltsin was sitting very still in an armchair facing the camera. There was an order to go ahead. By the skin of his teeth, President enunciated a brief appeal to the citizens of the country and urged everyone to come to ballot boxes. Then Chernomyrdin entered the room and sat down near Yeltsin, the camera momentarily changed the angle and shot the President's meeting with his Prime Minister. After it was over all those present were asked to retire. The TV crew, depressed with what they had seen, were told to pack their equipment.'

And the last trial was the vote itself. On that day, cameras all over the country are traditionally trained on the polling stations. The main story as always was the candidates voting themselves.

In Yeltsin's case:

'Naina was insisting,' he recollected, 'that a ballot box be delivered to my home. "It is in the law!" she was saying, close to tears. "Yes, it is legal but I want to vote with everyone else." "So what do you suggest?" I called Tanya and we discussed all options. The first one was to vote at my Moscow address. It was rejected practically outright: a long corridor, a staircase, a long walk along the street. I was doggedly determined but even I realised it was not possible. The second option: the health resort in Barvikha, next door to our place. It had its own polling station, everyone voted right there, it would be nice and legal. Press could also be invited.

But I had my doubts, "What sort of voting is it, surrounded by sick people?"

"Dad, the journalists will come in smaller numbers but do believe me, there will there: major TV channels, informational agencies, the lot!" Tanya was reassuring.'

… It looked like the only realistic way of going about it.

Voting in a health resort and not in a regular polling station was almost an open admission of Yeltsin being poorly. Still, he was answering questions and smiling.

During the night between July 3rd and 4th the Central Election Committee totalled the election results.

## 'WITH HIM, WE FEEL SAFE' (JANUARY–JULY OF 1996)

The official results, as of 11 p.m.: Yeltsin — 52%; Ziuganov — 41%. By midnight, Yeltsin had 52.3%; Ziuganov — 41.1%. By one in the morning the split was 53.9% versus 39.7%. However, Ziuganov was ahead in the 'red belt' — in Lipetsk, Kurgan, Stavropol. Still, the overall vote was in Yeltsin's favour. By 5:30 in the morning he had 53.9% and Ziuganov — 40.2% and at 8 a.m.: 53.55% against 40.55% in President's favour.

The official announcement of the second round's results came on July 9th. Yeltsin received 53.82%, more than ten million votes more than his contender who got 40.31%.

'The election of July 3rd had been sufficiently well organised — as regards performance of commissions or the provision of the required documentation,' announced Valentin Kuptsov, a major player within the CPRF. 'Some isolated cases of violations could not have any serious consequences.'

Ziuganov himself didn't look depressed. All his pronouncements of 'his victory having been hijacked' appeared nearly a year later — when it became profitable. But on the day in question he was full of philosophical thoughtfulness: 'Over 40 percent of voters gave their votes to the Popular Patriotic Bloc and thus its public significance has been confirmed... A bi-partite system now exists in the country: the Popular Patriotic Bloc championing ideals of legality and fairness and the party in power that has no clear-cut political structure.'

The elections got a high rating from international observers of whom there had been quite a few. They deemed the election 'free, unbiased and fair'. In the course of the second round, they had detected no 'rigging or falsifications.'

Everyone in Russia and abroad knew that in the second round Yeltsin won with such a wide margin at the expense of those who had voted for Lebed and Yavlinsky, and that meant several million people. For all of that Yeltsin's advantage was impressive. Counted not in percentage terms but in votes it meant about ten million people.

At this point we might digress and consider just this one question: why did the country select him?

A person who was unwell, a target for most severe criticism, the author of probably the most unpopular reforms in the XX century, with all his notorious antics and eccentricities, whose mere name was and still is often pronounced with hatred? What sort of latent interior force made Russia vote that day not for the cheerful healthy Ziuganov who had been promising a land flowing with milk and honey, not for the super-macho Lebed, nor the 'bright cookie' Yavlinsky, nor the vociferous Zhirinovsky, nor the 'honest and decent' Gorbachev who had only scraped together one percent of votes?

The answer was predictable: with him, we felt safe.

Yeltsin was receiving messages of greetings in his hospital bed, gazing at the whitewashed ceiling of his ward, and the unfathomable deathly tension was gradually ebbing away. There still were some torturous moments ahead — his inauguration and the presidential oath taken when his legs barely supported him. Ahead were the days full of routine strain and effort.

From July 3rd medics started insisting on an operation — a coronary artery bypass surgery. They didn't conceal from him that it was far from straightforward and there was some risk attached. A certain percentage of patients do not survive the bypass. On the other hand, it was so well honed technologically and a standard practice elsewhere in the world, so the risk was minimal. Having given it some thought he made up his mind and, moreover, it made no sense to keep withholding the truth about the state of his health. The battle had been won. On September 5th he addressed the nation and said, among other things, this: he wanted this surgery since it may bring about a *full recovery*.

The doctors had promised him…

# The Second Term
# (1996-1999)

The first decisive conversation with his doctors took place already on 3 July 1996.

'And if I don't agree to it?' Yeltsin still had his doubts.

The doctors' reply was firm: 'The state of your health shall steadily deteriorate. Your efficiency at work shall be inevitably going down. We cannot be sure whether you will survive for a year or three, possibly less.'

... On 9 August 1996 he took the oath in the Kremlin Palace. He was enunciating the words, his hand on the Constitution. The ceremony was cut down to 25 minutes, yet Yeltsin had trouble coping, everyone in the audience could see that clearly. You could glean a lot even by watching the TV coverage of the event. After the inauguration he kept to the dacha in Zavidovo, preparing for surgery.

But rest brought no relief, on the contrary — his haemoglobin plummeted. He described his state in this way. 'I am getting weaker each day, I feel no hunger, no thirst. All I want is to stay in bed. I called my doctors, "Is this it? Is this the end?" "No, Boris Nikolayevich," they answered, "it cannot be. It's all going according to plan."'

The decision to have it done in Russia wasn't an obvious one either. Many Russian cardiologists admitted it openly: the technology in the West was better, it would be safer it were performed some place abroad.

But he was adamant: only in Russia. However, the legendary American cardiac surgeon Michael E. DeBakey was invited over; he flew in and acted as a consultant to our specialists.

He was sent for coronarography — an intrusive procedure whereby some iodine-based liquid is administered into the heart through a catheter to check the efficiency of the cardiac valves. The test revealed that the blood flow was impeded and vessels blocked. Whilst previously the purpose of the operation had been to rehabilitate normal cardiac output, the examination showed that urgent surgery was needed to save his life.

Nevertheless he carried on working: met with Premier Chernomyrdin and discussed the new cabinet, appointed a new Head of Administration — Anatoly Chubais, yet the appointed date was bearing down on him. Sooner or later this top state secret would have to be released into the public domain.

The doctors' verdict left President Yeltsin face to face not only with psychological and personal problems but some political complications as well.

He had to withdraw from his office yet again, disappear from the Kremlin (and TV screens) for a rather lengthy period of time: a month, two, possibly three... Asked about the time needed for a full recovery, the doctors were distinctly vague.

It was not easy to convince the President that it was wrong and dangerous to keep the fact of his operation secret. His new press secretary Sergey Yastrzhembsky wrote him a letter which said, 'It is not a private matter of the Yeltsin family'. He spoke for the entire new administration who was convinced that the surgery should be announced.

At long last, he was ready to give an interview to the television channel RTR. He was seated in the conservatory, dressed in his home clothes... He addressed the country and explained, in very plain language, what was about to take place. He had been reluctant to talk about it before but the Russians had to know the truth: he was keen to raise his work efficiency; he wanted to be able to operate *normally*. Yeltsin emphasised especially that the surgery would take place here, in Russia. And this simple message was unexpectedly heart-rending.

The autumn of 1996 was a time of calm and peaceful fatality.

November 5th.

In the grey of pre-dawn hours, several black jeeps made a U-turn through the snow and drizzle and pulled into the entrance to the cardiological centre. The press was invited to arrive at noon to be briefed on the results of the surgery.

Earlier that morning Yeltsin entered the hospital reception, Naina Iosifovna by his side. He was greeted by a crowd of people in green scrubs, their faces tense, even pale.

He tried to ease the tension with a joke. It came out somewhat macabre: 'You got your knives on you already?'

But a not-too-funny joke still helped to cheer up the medics. They, too, broke into smiles.

'The surgery started at eight in the morning,' writes Yeltsin in *Presidential Marathon*. 'It was finished by two p.m. It turned out that not four but five bypasses were needed — new blood vessels implanted into the heart and taken out of my own legs. The heart started up as soon as I was disconnected from the machine.' The surgeons were reluctant to dwell upon the course of the operation but from what Yeltsin says himself, it transpires that the surgery was far from straightforward.

Two decrees had been prepared in advance: on the transfer of all presidential powers to Viktor Chernomyrdin (including the so-called 'nuclear button') and on the return of those to the President. As soon as Yeltsin came round he immediately signed the second decree.

Still, how was he coping? The question was a concern not only to the Russians. Yeltsin's pulse and the rhythm of his cardiac muscle were of great interest to the whole world.

'... Already on November 7th I was put in an armchair. And the following day I started walking — supported by nurses and doctors. I walked around my bed for about 5 minutes. The ribcage was in agony: during the operation it had been sawn apart and then pulled together with iron clamps. The cut-up legs hurt too. The weakness was incredible. But all this notwithstanding — a huge feeling of freedom, lightness and joy: I am breathing! My heart does not ache!

On November 8th, despite doctors' remonstrance, I discharged myself from the special recovery ward and left for the Kremlin hospital…

On November 22nd I moved to Barvikha. I was rushing the doctors, harassing them: when? When? When? They thought I could return to the Kremlin after the New Year… Doctor Belenkov, very sensitive to my moods, asked, "Boris Nikolayevich, do not force our hand, nothing good will come out of it! Take it easy."

On December 4th I moved from the health resort to my dacha in Gorky — basically, back home. My family noticed that I had changed. "How do you mean, changed?" I was asking. "Grandad, you are so kindly now …" granddaughter Masha giggled. "So I used to be nasty?" "No, it's just that now you notice everyone around you. You look at things, you respond to everything in this different way."

I knew it myself that the operation had changed me from within…

On December 9th a helicopter took me to Zavidovo for the final recovery. Helmut Kohl paid me a visit there. In essence, it was not a diplomatic mission. Helmut simply wanted to see how I was doing and so he just popped over…

On December 23rd I returned to the Kremlin, thus having beaten the speediest schedule put together by the physicians. Everyone noticed that I had lost a lot of weight and got very light on my feet. True enough — I was not walking but flying. My speech got faster. I didn't recognise myself in the mirror…

Meanwhile the New Year was unexpectedly upon us. I felt like seeing… the people in the streets: what they were doing, how they were getting ready for the festive season…

"Why not pop into a shop to buy some toys for my grandchildren?" I thought. On my way back home from work I dropped into "Aist" (Stork) in Kutuzovsky Prospekt and was immediately surrounded by sales assistants. It had been ages since I was in a toy store.

I bought this huge children's car for Gleb — I adore big presents…

On December 31st we went to the Yuletide show — that was our private nickname for the festive occasion in the Kremlin usually organised by Yuri Luzhkov.

... Within the very first seconds in the Big Kremlin Palace I was full of those new and unfamiliar sentiments. After a long time away I was physically aware of thousands of attentive eyes watching me. Turns out your sensitivity is greatly altered by an operation. It was as if my skin had grown thinner — I had expected nothing of the kind.

... And several days after the New Year I went to the sauna. I was trying to convince myself: that's enough. Enough of the sick ward, I am a normal person. I go to work, I drink champagne, I go to the sauna. I came along, took my clothes off. And the sauna hadn't been properly heated yet.

On January 7th I was hospitalised in the Kremlin hospital. Doctors suspected pneumonia.' (*Presidential Marathon*).

After 7 January 1997 recurring bouts of chronic pneumonia would become a fixture.

However, let us go back by several months.

The interval between the first round of the elections and Yeltsin's heart surgery was time enough for a serious episode to have taken place in the politics of Russia: a meteoric rise and an equally speedy downfall of General Alexander Lebed.

The armistice signed in May with the Chechen delegation in the Kremlin, as is often the case, was soon curtailed. Neither Russian generals nor the Chechens had any intention of admitting defeat.

In August the insurgents secretly infiltrated Grozny with a plan to encircle and destroy the Russian task group in the city. Lebed went over to Chechnya for a series of urgent meetings with Aslan Maskhadov, the leader of Chechen separatists.

Yeltsin's aides quote in their book the verbatim records of these negotiations.

'*Maskhadov*. Both in Russia and in Chechnya the attitude towards this war is that it is the politicians who fight, etc. I think everyone is bored with this war.

*Lebed*. Precisely.

*Maskhadov*. The Russian state means territorial integrity, grand statehood. Chechnya means sovereignty, independence, and so on. I think the people don't give a damn about any of this: statehood and their territorial integrity.

*Lebed*. I agree.

*Maskhadov*. So let's be realistic politicians who don't go into all this: what is to ensue, which government and so on. The purpose today is to finish this war.'

True to the agreements reached prior to the second round Yeltsin vested Lebed (the new Secretary of the Security Council) with special authority for conducting peaceful negotiations.

On August 14th Lebed met with Yeltsin in the Kremlin and the latter signed the Decree 'On Additional Measures to Regulate the Crisis in the Chechen Republic'. Lebed was now entirely in charge.

On August 16th Lebed told a press conference that the Russian troops were sustaining unjustifiably high losses in Chechnya: during the period from August 6th to 15th, there had been 247 killed; 1,020 wounded; 120 were missing in action.

The figures were, indeed, horrific. He summed it all up thus: 'The state, if it is a real state, cannot afford to merely simulate tireless efforts.'

A condition for Lebed and Yeltsin's alliance before the second round was to replace Defence Minister Grachev with General Igor Rodionov. But Lebed went further: discharged several Deputy Defence Ministers on the pretext of a 'military coup' allegedly brewing in the ministry. He was clearly after total control over the security agencies. General Rodionov who had acquired his notorious reputation during the events in Tbilisi in 1989 saw Lebed's advent to power as a complete *carte blanche*. The first thing that the new Defence Minister did was take down the President's portrait from the wall in his office and replace it with the emblem of Russia. A very meaningful gesture: I don't take my orders from Yeltsin...

Having dealt with Grachev Lebed's new target was another of Yeltsin's 'enforcers' — Interior Minister Kulikov. Their stand-off was so uncompromised and public spates so vehement that one or the other clearly had to go.

It was self-evident that if Lebed stayed in control over the enforcement agencies (especially after Yeltsin's surgery) the situation would become unpredictable. 'Leaving him in the Kremlin... was dangerous,' Yeltsin was economical with words.

The events were developing rapidly: on August 17th General Pulikovsky (Commander of the troops in Chechnya) signed the order on termination of hostilities; but on August 19th he publicly demanded that insurgents should pull out of Grozny. Civilians started leaving the city. The huge Chechen army was, in essence, blocked. The Russian army could have won but at what cost?

When talking about the state 'simulating tireless efforts' Lebed sort of had a point: in 1996, the country simply lacked the resources and, primarily, the high moral ground for either a comprehensive victory or continued warfare.

On August 22nd Lebed made Pulikovsky sign the document on disengagement of parties to the conflict, and on the 30th he signed the so-called Khasavyurt Accords (the full official name was 'Fundamental Principles of Determining the Mutual Relations between the Russian Federation and the Chechen Republic'.

This event is still subject to extremely conflicting appraisals. On the one hand, this 'peace' brought no peace, only ensured a breathing space between the first and the second wars in Chechnya. It solved no problems, created no basis for long-term negotiations or a step-by-step withdrawal of troops and delineation of power, as had been envisaged in the beginning, And although Moscow recognised the election of a new Chechen president, entered into official relations with the republic and in 1997 Maskhadov — in his tall astrakhan hat — paid several visits to the Kremlin, this was nothing more than a respite. The treaty was too rushed and politicised and therefore not prepared.

On the other hand, by that stage the Russian society was so tired of this unpopular war that the Khasavyurt Accords caused no serious protests; the troops were being pulled out quietly, without too much fuss.

But here is an interesting detail.

Journalist Leonid Mlechin, referring to a high source within the Kremlin administration, writes that Alexander Lebed 'upon his return by air from signing the documents with the Chechens was still agitated. I* started asking what would happen next. Among other things he said, "We must train some killers." "Whatever for?" "But we cannot deal with those people — Yandarbiyev, Maskhadov. We'll have to find a solution." I am not a novice in politics but I shuddered.'

The Chechen peace was Lebed's important political victory: the peace was so badly wanted that the signing of the accords caused nothing but profound relief. On the other hand, the general sincerely believed that Yeltsin was so gravely ill that his, Lebed's, ascent to power ahead of schedule was a matter if not of several weeks, then several months. And that was his big mistake.

In Russia's modern history Lebed cuts both a tragic and a comical figure. To start with, a whole group of political advisors (Boris Berezovsky among them) were seriously taking him for a new president of Russia. But his very first weeks in the Kremlin showed that Lebed not only didn't have the faintest idea of how the power structure worked and how a delicate balance was struck between legislative and executive branches, between the Administration and the government, but he had no desire to learn either. It wasn't a coincidence that he promptly dismissed the security to which he was entitled by his post and brought his own people into the Kremlin: the so-called 'Lebed's landing troops', that is to say an elite special force unit that reported to him alone. It wasn't by chance, either, that Lebed never commented on actions undertaken by the government and the President in excessively diplomatic terms. One is hard put to recall anyone using more populist language on Russian TV — in this respect Lebed outdid even the early Zhirinovsky. Having spotted that he was being followed (on orders from Interior Minister Kulikov, fearful of Lebed's direct threats) Lebed ordered militiamen in plain clothes 'face down on the asphalt'. A skirmish in the centre of Moscow was narrowly averted.

Still, in a way he was a tragic figure. This is what Yeltsin writes about him: 'I felt how restless this highly unusual person was, how he craved

---

* The source. — *Author's comment.*

certainty, clarity and perspicuity of his earlier days — and how uneasy he felt since in his new life there was none. I didn't just feel it, I was sympathetic. Journalists sensed this good feeling and hurried along to name Lebed as my successor.' (*Presidential Marathon*).

And then — briefly and to the point: 'He could never, of course, be a successor'. Yeltsin had grasped the logic of the new Security Council's Secretary's behaviour and in placing a bar on his activities was calm and unemotional: first, he stopped receiving him, then answering his telephone calls. Lebed tried to go visit him in Gorky but Yeltsin refused to see him.

The President set up a new state body: the Defence Council — thus stripping Lebed of some of his most important powers. And subsequently, when Lebed's public hysterics reached their crescendo, he simply ordered him to resign.

Yeltsin is the subject of many stereotypes and myths. One of such consistent stereotypes is that his deteriorating health during his second term in office became the main factor in Russian politics. Periods of huge enthusiasm displayed by a thinner and luminous Yeltsin would give place to grim TV images shot in 1998-1999: puffiness, sluggish reactions and the careful gait of an elderly person.

... So what was really going on?

By 1997 the new country, Russia, having started from a blank page no longer looked like a pure intellectual construct, an empty carcass. It had developed new laws, acquired the world status, political institutions and even history — short but dramatic.

It proved possible to overcome the crisis of the duality of power. The economic abyss of the nineties was now a thing of the past — with its empty shop counters, a non-existent banking system, a slump in the production of oil and depleted gold reserves; gone were the hyperinflation and the plummeting production volumes: slowly but surely the country was getting out of a dead end. It had proved possible to somewhat mitigate the Chechen crisis, if only temporarily. It had proved hard but possible to win the elections. All his main enemies had lost — completely and comprehensively.

Ostensibly, now was the time to complete the economic, social, military and legal reforms; to make the country's economy a market economy and to render society open.

But one enemy of his was still there — the one that no amount of political effort could overcome.

Its name was the Russian mentality. It is probably ill-suited to call it 'Russian' — Russia is a multi-ethnic state. On the other hand, everywhere in the world we are called Russians, whatever our real ethnicity. Thus, a correction: it was the mentality of citizens in our country. It was our mentality — shared by bureaucrats and militia, farmers and builders, intellectuals and everybody else.

A national mentality is a sum of many components.

It includes national pride — all counties have it, big or small. It includes national complexes, national grievances, temperaments and habits, suspicion of and even animosity towards neighbours, rivals, foreigners or migrants, in a word — aliens. It is a global phenomenon, there is nothing specifically Russian there.

But there are things that can only be defined by us, the people who live in this country of ours. These features are dormant, but for all of this perhaps all the more strong and defining. In Russia, for example, a lot of people still worship Stalin, believe that his rule was 'the most suitable'. This is understandable since the harsh structure of governance has remained practically unchanged for centuries. But within this structure, as a kind of subconscious response, concealed and profound, has always lurked the anarchy of the Russian ways. The state itself, having long since usurped the power of the church, gave rise to this anarchic confusion of concepts, values and *moral* norms. So when this state collapsed, the reverse side of this rigid hierarchy of values started seeping through:

The inherent inability to observe any bans.

The inability to follow rules.

The ignorance of laws.

The dislike towards and a lack of respect for our own state — up to the point that this state starts retaliating though a mechanism of self-defence, and even resort to repressions.

We also have this lack of respect for somebody else's property and the right of others to hold their own views, to stand on a different platform.

We share this inability to resolve disagreements in a civilised way.

It all started, as we remember, while the economy was still operating under the norms imposed by the Council of the People's Commissars in the thirties. Then followed the breakdown of everything else: the state and social morals.

The bigger part of the political elite started ardently advocating the idea of a 'strong state'. Yeltsin was facing a formidable task: to build a whole new system of values and rules, moreover, not only in the economic sphere. Such rules were absent in business, and management, and in press.

But what happens to law and order when they are not upheld — for whatever reason? What is the mechanism of social consensus in this case?

Some tacit agreements come into force — certain spontaneous rules of engagement, at times running completely counter to the formal, legal and pronounced ones.

That, too, is a form of order, albeit a shadow one. It is not reflected in the Criminal Code and has nothing to do with rational thinking, contract and social norms ostensibly accepted but *superficial* morals.

When young Yeltsin became a boss and demanded that his staff were punctual and stuck to the point in their work reports, when he didn't tolerate lateness and any deviation from hierarchy (which earned him the reputation of crassness and cruelty) — in effect, he demanded compliance with the written, formal rules of the game. He repudiated double moral standards.

He rejected the 'unwritten laws', spinelessly or deliberately accepted by most, this dark force of common practices, tacit social norms and customs that have no name, lie low but rule supreme.

... When in Sverdlovsk and Moscow Yeltsin combated inefficiency in deploying the workforce, theft in the retail system and idleness of his subordinates — he was up against the musty customs and hackneyed popular traits.

Incidentally, today his business style of the Soviet period (construction trust, *Obkom* and Moscow *Gorkom*) would have looked matter-of-fact and natural. He would have been on the same wavelength as today's managers — terse and to-the-point people whose fault tolerance is low and who value results above the process. Yeltsin was among the first 'efficient managers' of the Western type in our country.

In spring of 1997 the government received two new figures — both First Vice-Premiers.

One of them — Anatoly Chubais — had worked in the government before.

The second person was Boris Nemtsov, formerly Governor of Nizhny Novgorod.

It is known that Nemtsov had been vehemently against moving to Moscow. He was a popular governor and a convinced democrat: a young and bright up-and-coming politician. With good reason, Nemtsov believed that his time for 'the major start' had not come yet, that he needed to gain some more political capital and, most importantly, find the right moment. Had this been the case he could have been a serious contender at the presidential elections in 2000.

We recall that in the beginning of 1996 Yegor Gaidar came down to Nizhny Novgorod to try and convince Nemtsov to stand as a 'single democratic candidate' for presidency. Some unrelenting pressure had been applied but Nemtsov had the good sense to say no.

Yeltsin's closest associates — Anatoly Chubais, Tatyana Dyachenko and Valentin Yumashev — believed that the decision couldn't be pushed back anymore. The time was running out: the presidential decree on forming a new government had been already prepared and even dated, but Nemtsov still hadn't given his consent: was completely against giving up his post of a governor. Thus, Tanya got into a car and the following morning was in Nemtsov's office in Nizhny Novgorod. It meant that the offer to work for the government came from Yeltsin himself. In such a case it was difficult to say no.

Even before, Nemtsov had enjoyed a special relationship with the president: it had been warm, confiding and lightly peppered with irony. So now, in Moscow, he saw himself not as a new Vice-Premier but as a person possibly groomed for a special role.

This is how he himself describes those events:

'In 1997, President Yeltsin invited me to become the new Vice-Premier. I came to Moscow and took up residence at a dacha in Arkhangelskoye. No permanent accommodation was forthcoming and I felt in Moscow as if I were on a long-term business trip... Boris Nikolayevich asked me about my living conditions and social status several times. He was adamant that a Vice-Premier cannot be a person without registered domicile. With his decree\*, he allocated me a flat at this address: 19, Sadovo-Kudrinskaya Street.

'... My Moscow residence permit was an even more incredible story. About a month after my appointment Yeltsin asked whether I had been registered. Astonishingly, my daily problems were now under the patronage of the president of Russia. Thus, Boris Nikolayevich instructed his daughter to find a school for Zhanna\*\*, and Tatyana Dyachenko helped us find School No 20 at the Patriarch's Ponds. Yeltsin was interested in every tiny detail of my life. Well, I came to Moscow at the age of 37 and no place to call my own...

'But as for the residence permit,' Nemtsov continues his tale, 'Yeltsin told me once, "You see, for as long as you have no residence permit you cannot be insured, neither your daughter nor your wife can come to see a GP. Should militia check your documents, they even might extradite you from the city, place in a slammer. Such is life, so you must register at your place of domicile at once."

'I wrote a letter to Mayor Luzhkov with a request to provide me with the residence permit. A month went by, two, three... No answer from Yuri Mikhailovich\*\*\*. I was embarrassed to telephone the Mayor directly...

'Once I came along to see the president over some report... We had our talk, all went well, so we had some tea and started chatting about life. All of a sudden he asked, "Have you registered?" I answered, "No." He burst out, "This is sheer lawlessness! What sort of a country is this where the First Vice-Premier is a tramp!" Right there and then he picked up the phone and asked to be put through to Luzhkov.

'Several seconds later I heard the phrase that I will always remember:

---

\* To be more precise, it was an instruction. — *Author's comment.*

\*\* Nemtsov's daughter. — *Author's comment.*

\*\*\* Luzhkov.

"Yuri Mikhailovich, your behaviour is way too petty!" And he rang off. The next morning, at nine o'clock I had the Moscow Mayor's mandate on my desk at work, whereby Luzhkov was authorising the registration of citizen Nemtsov in the capital of our Motherland.'

On having learned who had been Yeltsin's visitor Luzhkov got the picture straight away.

The episode with the residence permit is just a tiny detail that goes to confirm that Yeltsin was truly forming a new team. It was *his* government. At the time, a generation of 40-year-olds came to work in the White House: Mayor of Samara Oleg Sysuyev, Maxim Boiko and many others. Yeltsin's approach towards all of them was forward thinking: he expected them to be working in the government for a long time.

Their concerted effort was to be aimed not only at shifting the situation in the economy — Yeltsin was setting a more global task: that of strengthening the role of the state and it seemed that the result was at hand.

By 1997, the overall economic situation had shown signs of real progress. The slump of production had been arrested, national currency was stabilised. And, most importantly, the country's middle class was emerging — slowly but surely. A personal car, a new flat, a private school and a holiday abroad were no longer luxury affordable only to the *nouveau riche*. These were small businessmen, middle-ranking managers, public servants — the 'white collars' whose humble incomes had been steadily growing. However, the structure of their income deviated from standards existing anywhere else in the world.

'By using the consumption data,' writes Leon Aron, for example, 'a more reliable source than the records on income, experts could see that the per capita income and living standards were 50-100% higher than those reported to the tax authorities… In 1997, the number of families owning a car[*] were 31 out 100 — a gigantic leap for the country where seven years previously[**] only 18 families out of 100 were car owners…'

---

[*] This is a very important figure. — *Author's comment*.

[**] That is, in 1990. — *Author's comment*.

Let us digress a little and pause for thought. How much was a second-hand car in 1997 — a foreign make as a rule? Let us assume that on average it was between 2 and 10 thousand dollars. We remember that in 1997 already one third of Russian families were car owners! And those weren't only old *Moskviches* and *Volgas* — but also *Volvos, Toyotas, Peugeots,* etc.

At the same time, practically all those people had saved for a car not through long-term economising (fat chance of any long-term saving in those years) but by earning more in the preceding two or three years. But in the official balances and declarations the same people were showing their income as being practically on the breadline (in 1997, 112 dollars of monthly takings was the official annual per capita average). The money in envelopes, the 'grey economy' that avoided taxation was feeding, clothing and building Russia.

This was particularly true of Moscow, St Petersburg and other major cities.

Growing consumption found its expression not only in figures. A lot of it was visible to the naked eye. 'The cities registering growth saw their life restored virtually before your very eyes, a fact that could be confirmed by any visitor who still remembered the Soviet times. Gone were the queues and crowds of downcast poorly-clad folk trudging along the cracked pavements in search of fruit, sausage or cottage cheese, carry-alls, cases or string bags in hand. Instead, clean and colourful window displays sprung up everywhere... and there appeared carefree people in bright garments, strolling along and munching on a pie or a sandwich purchased right there, in the street.' This is a somewhat naive (to our taste) description given by Yeltsin's American biographer Aron.

But a pie or a sandwich purchased 'right there, in the street', a comprehensibly new system of commerce, the housing market, the mass acquisitions of dacha plots, a different system of entertainment, total computerisation, and many other things bore witness to the fact that the official statistics failed to reflect some very important truths.

It is simply not possible that a person who lives from hand to mouth (namely, on a monthly income of 100-300 dollars as declared officially) would be able to take his family on a foreign journey, or buy a desktop, not to mention a car. Meanwhile, every ninth Russian (from 16 to 20 million people) made foreign trips in 1997 — on business or for pleasure.

453

Such a person would not be able to build a dacha, top up his or her wardrobe in which to walk down the street and quietly munch on a pie. It was an economic impossibility.

So how did it all come to pass?

'The share of official earnings was only 40 percent. Wages in private companies and shops were 2.5 or 3 times higher than figures shown in tax returns. According to the Russian authorities, unaccounted earnings in 1996 amounted to 250 trillion roubles (46 billion dollars) or one tenth of the country's GDP.' (Leon Aron).

And yet another figure — simple but significant: in the summer of 1997 Moscow registered a baby boom. The number of newly-born babies leapt by 35% in comparison to the preceding year — the first such increase since 1991.

A new life was taking root.

Nonetheless, this new life had one fatal flaw: people kept concealing their real incomes, if they had them, from the state.

'From 50 to 70 percent of trade transactions* were carried out in cash to avoid accountability. Ninety percent of the entire private sector output, sales and profits were kept from the authorities. A Russian family was calculated to lower its income by an average of 40%... On the whole, the country's economy exceeded the official statistics by 50-100%.'

The sad thing was not in the fact that small economic players were hushing up their incomes really sad were the reasons that explained it all. The mere thought of voluntary tax discipline felt insane. It had never been necessary in the 70 years of Soviet power: the state had always collected its taxes itself.

Russian citizens were understandably reluctant to reveal their real budgets to avoid being targeted by corrupt officials, protection racket or tax inspectors capable of torture to death any individual or company in breach of the established rules of the game. This deeply-rooted resistance is there even today. It is not by chance that Russia has the lowest income tax rate in the world — 13%, in an attempt to get matters off the ground. But even now, ten years hence, when the economic climate is favourable

---

* In the country. — *Author's comment.*

## THE SECOND TERM (1996-1999)

and the law enforcement agencies exert additional pressure, according to some researchers one third of Russian salaries are paid in envelopes.

This was certainly the situation in 1997. It was the same picture not only in the lower echelons but in the middle and higher circles, too.

The 'middle-ranking echelon' included the class of the so-called 'red directors' — former Soviet managers who came to own factories, plants, construction associations and so on. Making full use of the voucher privatisation they bought out their own employees and found their feet within the Russian economy (and often an experience of underhand dealings).

'Forced to act at their own risk and peril most managers sought to derive income from "renting" their premises and using political connections, not from investing into productions and innovations. Their response to a gradual dwindling of subsidies and termination of state contracts was not to restructure, design new products and identify new markets but to curtail production, dismantle and sell equipment, indulge in extravagance and reckless borrowing, delay tax payments and run up huge debts,' writes Leon Aron. One can put it even more bluntly: new owners, born out of the former Soviet functionaries, turned into 'fat cats' and put all their efforts into maintaining a *status quo* that would allow them generate giant incomes and siphon off the profits due to the government and their own staff. Some honest operators and people balancing on the edge of common sense didn't change the overall picture that couldn't fit into any normal plan of economic renaissance.

It is probably worth reminding that 1995 was the year when the second stage of privatisation commenced: sales of major state companies dealing in natural resources. Oil and metallurgical giants were going into private hands. The purpose was simple: to attract investments into the sector that was defining the economic climate in the country.

In the absence of such investment, it was impossible to arrest the slump in those sectors. Besides, following the collapse of the Soviet planned economy and the entire economic system these giants were in dire need of a new and modern system of management. This is what led to the creation of Lukoil, Sibneft, Sedanko, Tomskneft, Novolipetsky

Metallurgical Integrated Works, Nizhnetagilsky Metallurgical Integrated Works, Norilsky Nickel and many other much smaller companies.

It was a deliberate state policy: to replenish the budget, to make the enterprises more efficient. But in 1997 it was practically impossible to sell those companies for their real value. For example, the story with Norilsky Nickel: Potanin's company paid over 200 million dollars to get the controlling block of shares of this industrial giant. But when confronted with its problems — those of social, financial and production kind, they lost heart and even tried to give the facility back to the state.

Sibneft was negotiating the sale of a large block of shares to a French oil company, for 650 million dollars. However, after a lengthy negotiation — it was already after the election in 1997 — the French pulled out of the deal: the investment risk was too high. No one wants to remember those stories, all that stays in memory is that our companies were sold off dirt cheap. Now they are worth tens of billions but in mid-nineties their market value was completely different. In addition, the global crisis, yet again, has pushed their value down by an order of magnitude.

When Yeltsin was removing Chubais from the government in 1995, the latter was accused, among other things, of those very voucher auctions.

But this is the opinion of a prominent Russian economist Mikhail Deliagin: 'It is worth reminding that Chubais was and still is the only Russian politician who tried to exercise the right of the state as the owner of those shares, through actions and not just talk. He was trying to make sure that those state-owned enterprises were at least paying their taxes and that they refrained from directly sabotaging the tax policy. It was Chubais' management of the federal block of shares in 1995 that in the course of the voucher privatisation practically saved the country from bankruptcy and allowed it to somehow pay its debts.'

Mikhail Deliagin believes that impinging, in the course of the voucher privatisation, on the interests of some commercial entities (not indulging their vested interests) was one of the reasons for Chubais' dismissal.

Nonetheless, being sold 'for a song' allowed the metallurgical and the oil industries to overcome the crisis. The only target that the new owners could realistically pursue during the initial years was to strive to break even and invest greatly into improvement and modernisation of production, often with negligible profitability or even at a loss. Throughout the nineties, prices for metals, coal and, finally, oil stayed low. For instance, here are the figures for oil: $19 per barrel in 1993; $13.6 in 1998. But gradually, thanks to private investment, the slump in the output was brought under control. Growth followed: 40 and then 60 million tonnes of oil per annum. The sector started generating profits for the treasury and turned into a source of hard currency.

Still, the emergence of truly big economic players in Russia didn't solve the problem — the economy remained 'grey' in colour. The Duma, where communists ruled the roost, passed no requisite legislation (the Tax Code was approved only in 2001). Presidential decrees used as a basis for economic relations were *a priori* weaker than laws. A legal loophole thus emerged which everybody was only too happy to exploit.

The country's progress towards relative stabilisation (after the succession of economic crises in 1993-1994), as remembered by Anatoly Chubais, started as early as the second half of 1995. And although in the beginning of yet another grim year for Russia (the war broke out in Chechnya) things were still hanging in the balance, by its end the government had managed to ensure a certain 'compaction of the money supply', in other words — to slow down the money-printing machine and bring the inflation down to an acceptable rate... The price of this stabilisation was high: public spending was dwindling, cash in circulation was short, industrial production was still declining. Later on came the so-called 'electoral-economic cycle' (the term introduced by American economists in the sixties). It meant that the state got generous with its spending and, accordingly, printed more money for such was a requirement of the political process.

Following his election victory Yeltsin formed the new government and then retired for several months from the task of dealing with major problems. First, there were preparations for his cardiac surgery, then the operation itself and the subsequent recovery. Consequently, the president only returned to the Kremlin in December.

By this time, however, it had become clear that Chernomyrdin's new government, approved in the summer of 1996, was turning out to be weak and compromised, bound as it was by agreements and promises made in the course of the election campaign. The new Vice-Premiers were unprepared to usher in serious economic reforms whilst poorly thought-out and unrealistic budgets, political crises and the overall lack of stability in the country served to exacerbate the chaos in the economic policy. At this point, in December of 1996, Yeltsin decided he needed to completely revamp the government.

The new cabinet faced an obvious task: to render economic relations in the country clear and transparent. Without this, they justly thought, market mechanisms would never kick in. Yeltsin, therefore, set two deadlines for the 'old-new' government: to clear the backlog on pensions by June 31st and on salaries by 31 December 1997. Structural reforms in the economy proved a harder nut to crack. Chubais recollects that, for the first time since 1991, both key Vice-Premier posts were filled by reform-minded politicians. Traditionally, one senior deputy was responsible for the financial policy, that is macroeconomics, and the other was in charge of the 'tangible sector' which means industry. Boris Nemtsov was overseeing this very 'tangible' sector, including the so-called state monopolies. In 1997 the President prepared a decree on structural changes in 'natural monopolies'. It was based on the reform that had been carried out earlier in the coal industry — Chubais recollects that the reform enabled them to shut down many loss-making or unsafe mines which helped bring down horrific statistics of miners' mortality rates several-fold. The gist of the reform was in splitting the sector (for example, Russian railways from the power industry) into producer and service companies.

Yet it wasn't the payment of pensions and salaries, nor the structural changes in the economy that proved a stumbling block for the new government. The new cabinet set about executing a seemingly simple task of increasing the revenue base for the budget, making major companies pay their taxes on time, imposing rigorous financial discipline while simultaneously cutting down unnecessary costs, curtailing unjustified benefits in order to finally launch transparent privatisation. Yegor Gaidar insists that back in 1997 it provided grounds for tackling the strategic objectives pursued by the country: to increase industrial production and create conditions for investment in the Russian economy. Thus the All-Russian Extraordinary Commission for Tax and Duties Collection was set up.

## THE SECOND TERM (1996-1999)

As an example of the issues, in those years everybody was entitled to social support without reference to a family's income. For some families the subsidies were very useful while for others they were a pure formality. The government was eager to target benefits and allowances to specific recipients; protect those who needed this protection and increase the tax burden of those whose income was above average. Another blow to the 'grey economy' was delivered by making declaration of incomes mandatory for all functionaries — be they employed by central or local agencies. This started an enduring process in the Russian system. When Yeltsin first published his income in the press it caused shock. It was completely unorthodox at the time. By the time of Putin's presidency, Ministers and staff of the Presidential Administration started regularly publishing their incomes whilst under President Medvedev they already had to provide tax returns for the members of their families. But Yeltsin made the first step.

A real step towards genuine federalism was the transparent separation of the revenue due to the federal and local budgets. When the budget of a region was formed on the basis of a taxable base understandable by all, it did away with another chance for abuse. The overall result was that the government managed to curb inflation in as much as it stabilised around a tolerable rate of 13% — but most importantly, an influx of investments into the country's economy had started. The index of the Russian stock exchange *tripled* within the first half of the year and grew to 570 points. This record was only broken in the beginning of the following decade (in 2003-2004) and was explained by peak oil prices that had soared exponentially. Foreign trust in securities was also growing. It was symbolic that, based on the results of that year, journalists of *Euromoney* named Anatoly Chubais the 'best Minister of Finance in Europe'.

Privatisation was also beginning to generate revenue. In the third quarter of 1997 the consolidated budget received the unprecedented revenue of 7.8 trillion roubles. Finally, the year 1997 was the year when Russia's GDP started rising which it continued to do, barring a hiccough in 1998, until 2008. The market mechanisms were finally operating. For Chubais, and his team, who had suffered guilt and blame for the break-up of the country, to see the GDP rise from, the first inkling of 0.4% to a respectable 1.6% in 1997 was a huge relief.

Never the less, a further issue became clear with respect to whether the government could be absolutely independent and self-sufficient in making its decisions, independent primarily from big Russian businesses that by then had already emerged. 'Who is the master in this country — us or them?' was the question the Young Reformers were asking themselves. An illustrative episode was the attack launched by the young Vice-Premier Nemtsov on the trust deed of Gazprom's that could have secured its boss, Rem Viakhirev, 40% of its shares at knock-down prices. This is how Nemtsov himself remembers it all. The Government refused the privatisation of the gas monopoly and prevented Viakhirev from buying company shares for next-to-nothing through a trust deed. Yeltsin took Viakhirev by the hand, lead him to the Vice-Premier and said quietly, 'Nemtsov is right. The trust deed must be torn up. This is burglary of Russia. If you fail to comply, expect problems.'

Nemtsov had also attempted to develop and submit to the State Duma an anti- corruption bill. The backbone of this law would have been a ban on entrepreneurial activities of functionaries in high office. He quoted the example of the Moscow Mayor, Yuri Luzhkov's family as an example since his wife, Yelena, was said to be worth billions. However, this was not to be. It took another 11 years before the State Duma finally passed this law in 2008.

A key spark to this conflagration was the auction of Svyazinvest which had been expanded from a joint stock company into a powerful state monopoly in control of all communications, including satellite, mobile, long-distance and local services. Twenty-five percent were put up for sale. The earlier voucher auctions had given way under this government to open auctions where whole entities or blocks of shares in the enterprise were auctioned to the highest bidder. These so-called 'open' auctions were designed to top up the budget with live money and that is what they did. They were also used as a tool to achieve a significant rise in the capitalisation of Russian enterprises.

When the envelopes of the Suvazinvest bid were opened in the presence of both parties the winner offered $1.875 billion versus $1.710 billion offered by the other party. The winner was a consortium headed by Vladimir Potanin and his ONEKSIMbank whilst the unsuccessful group was lead by the Spanish company Telefonica which had been brought to the table by Vladimir Gusinsky and Mikhail Friedman. At the time, Mikhail Friedman who was representing the unsuccessful party lodged no complaints regarding the procedure of running the auction. Indeed, it's hard to imagine what complaints could have been registered when Friedman himself, in full possession of his faculties, had entered the figure '1710' while his competitor merely scribbled '1875'? Never the less, afterwards an immense fuss was kicked up by Gusinsky and Berezovsky. Curiously, whilst Gusinsky had at least brought Telefonica to the table, it was hard to imagine what Berezovsky had to do with this deal

Vladimir Gusinsky, with his intentions of acquiring Svyazinvest, had been making preparations for two years. He did a lot of groundwork with the military and the Federal Agency for Governmental Communications as owners of 'closed' frequencies. He assembled financial resources. But in the blink of an eye all bets were off.

This developed into a media war.

Chubais and Nemtsov announced that they would cleanse Russia of the oligarchs. Berezovsky and Gusinsky retaliated through their media outlets which made slanderous, unsubstantiated claims about the conduct of leading politicians. Using their media resources, the 'oligarchs' led a campaign against the government. The war of words was raging on. But there could be no winners here. Yeltsin was watching the warring parties in annoyance and wanted to be sure the government was as pure as they were insisting that businesses should be. There were incessant claims that government policy was incompetent, poorly thought-out, fraught with contradictions, unprofessional and wrong. The evidence for this was not only the Svyazinvest deal but the entire policy of privatisation in the recent years and all actions undertaken by the Young Reformers' government.

Why was the Svyazinvest auction so important? Basically, it was the point Yeltsin lost the support of Russian business. 'I believe,' says Valentin Yumashev, head of the Kremlin Administration at the time, 'that the Svyazinvest episode, however bizarre it sounds, was of key importance for the history of Russia at the end of the nineties. But for that incident everything could have been different. Most likely, there would have been no default. No crisis in 1999. The whole country's development could have taken a different turn. Business and leadership made a huge mistake.'

Here, it is worth digressing to consider the figure of Boris Berezovsky who keeps appearing at various points and is present in the Svyazinvest drama.

What sort of a person was he? What was his relation to President Yeltsin? Is it true that Berezovsky was the 'Kremlin Godfather', that he used to kick open the door to the President's office?

'Of course, this is complete rubbish and idle talk,' says Valentin Yumashev. 'Boris Nikolayevich met Berezovsky in his office at best three times. He couldn't quite get the measure of him, he felt no affinity. That's why he didn't like him much.' Yet Berezovsky became an important presence on the presidential team. How did that happen?

Nicknamed BAB* in the press, Berezovsky first set foot in the Kremlin during the preparation of the decree on ways of supporting the ailing AvtoVAZ** in 1994. Back then, the relations between authorities and entrepreneurs were in their infancy. On the whole, Russian business had remained apolitical. However, Gaidar's retirement had created something of an intellectual void that needed to be filled. A group of Russian businessmen, including Friedman, Gusinsky, Berezovsky, and Khodorkovsky amongst others, actively engaged in a dialogue and presented some new ideas to those in power. Development of entrepreneurship and the economy on the whole required legal underpinning and these business representatives brought along some ideas on taxation, pension reform, reform of the Public Health and housing sectors as well as other areas particularly the banking system which was only in an embryonic state at that point. The dialogue between those in power and those in business started largely thanks to Berezovsky. Besides, he was always insisting, plausibly, that his purpose was not business, not the money, but the proper development of the country.

---

* *Boris Abramovich Berezovsky*. A lot of confusion exists in the Western world about Berezovsky's patronymic and his original partner's surname — Roman Abramovich. In the case of the letter it virtually means 'the son of Abram' and is stressed on the second syllable. The reader must have noticed, by now, that using both the name and the patronymic corresponds to the Russian form of polite address. As for Roman Abramovich — the surname is stressed on the third syllable.

** *AvtoVAZ* is the Russian automobile manufacturer, formerly — VAZ (Volga Automobile Plant situated in Togliatti), Its cars are known to the world under the trade name of *Lada*.

Among the first important ideas that the group brought along to the Kremlin in 1994 was the proposal on the new, *public* TV. At odds with the radical changes in the country's economic system, new Russia's TV had continued to be a profoundly Soviet entity. All channels were indistinguishable and really seen as a state service. Berezovsky, together with Oleg Boiko, Peter Aven, and Alexander Smolensky maintained that it was necessary to create a TV in the public sector. He suggested that a pool of businessmen should be set up and entrusted with financing the First Channel where there would be no single owner. In January of 1995 this public TV was started in the form of the ORT channel but then one of the directors was murdered and some suspicion descended on Berezovsky however unlikely this was in reality. There was some friction between Berezovsky and the government over the replacement director.

Despite irregular funding and conflict amongst the backers, Berezovsky and the team that had come to work for the channel still managed to make quality TV for ORT, making it the only channel that could at that point compete successfully with the first private channel — NTV owned by Vladimir Gusinsky. Still, ORT's debts continued stockpiling and Berezovsky was continually asking the Kremlin for a bail-out.

Berezovsky then came up with a scheme that he maintained would solve the problem with ORT financing once and for all. Berezovsky had won the voucher auction of Sibneft, paid over a hundred million dollars to the state and, together with Roman Abramovich, became the owner of this oil company. Sibneft was to cover the debts of ORT. This oil company was at the very bottom of the voucher auction plan; all the bigger companies with higher production output figures had all been already privatised and passed into other hands — Lukoil, Sidanko, TNK, Surgutneftegas — all these companies produced much more oil. For example, Lukoil was extracting 40 million tonnes per annum while Sibneft was only producing 15. It is still not clear how Berezovsky gained access to voucher auctions without help. A number of possibilities have been put forward, including Yeltsin himself although it is unlikely Berezovsky had sufficient access to him at this time.

In 1996, Boris Abramovich took part in Yeltsin's election campaign in the capacity of an analyst, expert and advisor although formally he never joined Chubais' group. 'He practically never showed up for the group's meetings,

I remember him there virtually only a couple of times,' Tatyana Yeltsin recollects. Yet it seems clear that attracting Lebed as Yeltsin's ally after the first round of the election and his subsequent appointment of himself to the post of the Secretary of the Security Council, was Berezovsky's idea. After the election, Berezovsky's political activity reached its apogee. He saw Lebed as a bright political star and even accompanied him in 1996 to Chechnya. Pragmatic Lebed also thought Berezovsky useful.

On the appointment of Berezovsky to be a government advisor, Yeltsin himself explained it in his book very simply that he decided it was better to have Berezovsky on his side than on someone else's. Appointing Berezovsky to an official post caused bitter conflict in the Kremlin Administration.

Generally, however, Berezovsky, if he considered it advisable, had little trouble switching from one political player for another. Until 1996 he had been in an active relationship with Korzhakov but then they became sworn enemies. He had been Chubais' associate and then arranged his character assassination on the ORT. Or, for example, he had been friends with his closest partner Roman Abramovich for years and then didn't just part company but started litigation proceedings against him in the British court. That was one of his characteristics.

Tatyana Yumasheva, Yeltsin's daughter refers to her relations and those of the other political figures with Berezovsky in her blog referring to the events of 1996.

'At that point the strife between Korzhakov and Chubais reached a crescendo. And I was trying to somehow reconcile the two adversaries. Berezovsky called me up in the *President Hotel* and asked to come along to the LogoVAZ office. I told him I was busy, but that he himself should come over. He insisted that it was very important, Boris Fyodorov wanted to meet me and he could only do it there. I thought it was the former Finance Minister so couldn't quite see why he wouldn't meet in the election team headquarters. So I went to LogoVAZ. I asked Valentin Yumashev to keep me company. Off we went. It transpired that it was a different Boris Fyodorov who wanted to meet me: president of the National Sports Fund. I knew Boris — he was a friend of Tarpishchev's. We took our seats and then spent an hour going over how dreadful Korzhakov was, how he was trying to extort money from the business, how he was setting the president up, etc. I said my goodbyes. On the way we discussed it all with

Valentin and decided that we wouldn't tell a soul about any of it. We had quite enough of a conflict between Korzhakov and Soskovets on the one side and Iliushin, Chubais and the analytical group on the other. And then a couple of days later, the recording of this conversation appeared in *Moskovsky Komsomolets*. The article was huge, its author, Alexander Minkin, was commenting on the recording. To tell the truth, I wasn't named in the article — my cues were ascribed to a certain *woman*. But only an idiot wouldn't see who could be told things about Korzhakov and about Yeltsin being set up. After that incident I realised that I could never again trust Berezovsky.'

When Berezovsky took up his new post there was quite a lot of ado in press and especially in the Duma. He was travelling to Chechnya to negotiating the release of hostages. His major idea at the time, despite the fact that Chechnya's status had not been agreed, was that Russia must bind Chechnya in economically. Money must be allocated to the restoration of destroyed infrastructure; jobs had to be created, pensions paid. At this point, ORT started showing him as the Security Council's Deputy Secretary and Berezovsky turned into a public figure with each business trip of his to Chechnya getting coverage on the channel whereas previously, no one had known him. He was actively involved in organising the presidential elections in Chechnya, as a result of which, Aslan Maskhadov became President.

After the Svyazinvest debacle, it was through ORT that the formidable attack on the team of the Young Reformers was mounted entirely masterminded by Boris Berezovsky.

Valentin Yumashev in an interview was clear on the issue.

'By this time Russian business had both feet firmly on the ground with each group already having its own powerful media resources. In addition, everyone had their connections within the power structures and the law enforcement system. All of this was brought to bear on the task of destroying their perceived enemies. Gusinsky and Berezovsky, on their channels, were saying how bad for Russia were those terrible businessmen, Potanin and Prokhorov, and even worse — those helping them — Chubais, Nemtsov and Koch. *Izvestia, Komsomolskaya Pravda* and the Russian TV Channel were joining in. Nemtsov and Chubais decided that this merry-go-round could only be stopped by removing Berezovsky from the post of Security Council's Deputy Secretary. It was naive. I was telling them that by dismissing Berezovsky you would only untie his hands. Naturally enough, that's just what happened. Immediately after his discharge he released into the media materials from a criminal case instigated by Interior Minister Kulikov. Kulikov couldn't stand Chubais and his team in the government which Berezovsky knew only too well. That is what gave rise to the notorious investigation of fees, the 'book case', which culminated in resignation of the majority of Chubais' team'. The scandal was in connection with fees paid to Anatoly Chubais and his co-authors for their book on privatisation for which they had received 450 thousand Dollars as an advance in a completely open and legitimate fashion but the media savaged them over it.

Having quickly recovered after his dismissal, Berezovsky deployed all his talents and powers of persuasion into landing himself another high post. Several weeks prior to the CIS Moscow summit he went round the capital cities of the former Soviet republics, met their presidents and convinced them of the need to support his nomination to the post of the CIS Executive Secretary. Yeltsin himself describes the incident, 'When we met in Moscow, in the Hall of Saint Catherine, to my complete astonishment President of Ukraine Leonid Kuchma, no less, suggested that Boris Berezovsky should be made CIS Executive Secretary'. A little later, the President summoned to his recreation room the Chairman of the Government Sergey Kirienko and the Head of his Administration Yumashev. Both were categorically opposed to such an appointment. President Yeltsin's daughter Tatyana recollected, 'When I learnt about it I was horrified. I was completely against it, went over to Dad and started virtually pleading with him not to do it. But he answered that CIS presidents offered the candidature themselves, he couldn't say no to them, he sounded vexed talking to me. Dad always paid a great deal of attention to the stand taken by CIS leaders. Just at that moment Shevchenko entered the office and brought along Berezovsky. So now it was in his presence that I continued to stick to my guns saying that Boris Abramovich must not be appointed, the country wouldn't understand it. Dad told me sharply, "You may go."'

Having spoken to Berezovsky Yeltsin made up his mind. Half an hour later Boris Berezovsky was unanimously appointed executive secretary of the CIS.

Subsequently, Berezovsky put a lot of effort into convincing all and sundry that appointing Putin was his project. For example, three days before the vote on the new President was to take place in March of 2000 he gave a big interview to *Vedomosti* newspaper wherein he spared no detail in explaining what a close relationship he enjoyed with the candidate for presidency. However, Putin never was 'Berezovsky's project'. Moreover, Berezovsky was among the last to learn that such an option was a possibility. Nonetheless, it was Berezovsky who brought the good news to Putin in August of 1999 when the latter was on holiday. Berezovsky was trying to be the first in everything. Putin's response was terse: 'when I am told by the president I shall be ready to discuss this topic'.

On 15 September 1997 business representatives assembled in the Kremlin to hear Yeltsin's appeal to them 'to try and get along'. Then silence fell. Mikhail Friedman who had been at that meeting would later tell Timothy Colton, Yeltsin's biographer, 'We didn't get it, not one of us. We left that meeting nonplussed.' Yeltsin was reluctant to set the rules himself. He believed that these people should have enough of a sense of responsibility to be able to answer for their actions. It turned out they didn't — the information war continued. Somewhat later Yeltsin would tell Nemtsov, 'I am fed up with having to defend you'.

During all the excoriating criticism received personally, by Yeltsin and his government he was never tempted to suppress the media. The President never forgot that he had come to power on the crest of *glasnost*, defending freedom of speech as a fundamental value. Out of principle, he could not afford to gag journalists, even when they were telling blatant lies at the instigation of their paymasters. He believed that contracted lies were a lesser evil for the country than the state censorship

Beyond the fallout from the Svyazinvest incident Yeltsin proposed to have a national referendum on the issue of interring Lenin's body. Opinion polls showed that, on this score, society was split right down the middle: half were in favour and half — against it. The administration convinced him to 'let the sleeping dogs lie', especially in the face of public opinion. Practically half the country wanted to keep Lenin's mummy in the mausoleum thus preserving the sacred Soviet site — the shrine of the 'state's founder'. Yeltsin himself, though, insisted that Lenin was not the founder but the destroyer of the state.

Between May and July Yeltsin signed several documents that in his view were supposed to put a full stop to many raw and insoluble problems in the post-Soviet world. On May 12th he signed the formal peace treaty with Chechnya's president-elect Aslan Maskhadov. Moscow, recognised legitimacy of a free election in Chechnya and initially Maskhadov suited Moscow — he seemed the most 'moderate' out of the Chechen leaders. Soon, however, this moderation evaporated. Maskhadov's influence started dwindling; he was losing control over the situation in the republic, with real power shifting towards the radical, Basayev. However, Yeltsin was certain that the peaceful solution to the Chechen problem was irreversible, that there would be no return to hostilities.

Afterwards a peace treaty was signed between Ossetia and Ingushetia thus defusing the bloody stand-off around the Prigorodny District that had emerged in 1992. Moldova's President Luchinsky and President of the Trans-Dniester republic Smirnov signed a memorandum in Moscow whereby Moldova confirmed sovereignty of the disputed area. In August, subsequent to a two-week's consultation in the Kremlin, President Ardzinba of Abkhazia paid a first visit, since the Georgia-Abkhaz war of 1992-1994, to Tbilisi and met with Edward Shevardnadze. In July, once again in the Kremlin, representatives from Tajikistan and the Islamic opposition signed a peace protocol. Thus, many years of a large-scale civil war in Tajikistan came to an end.

The hardest but probably the most important document was the agreement on peace and cooperation with Ukraine, signed on May 31st by Yeltsin and Kuchma. The negotiations on dividing the Black Sea Fleet had been going on for several years. Ukraine's stance was intractable — they didn't want any Russian military bases on their territory as was the case in other CIS republics: Kazakhstan, Belarus and Georgia. Yet a compromise was reached.

At the Commonwealth summit in 1997 Yeltsin was tough, for the first time ever, when addressing leaders of the former union republics. The Commonwealth, Yeltsin was saying, was a mutual arrangement but that Russia was not about to sacrifice its national interests. At that summit Yeltsin outlined a new stage in the relations between Russian and the CIS: a move towards clear limits and rules of partnership and mutual co-existence.

## THE SECOND TERM (1996-1999)

At the most critical moment of the break-up of the Soviet Union and the Soviet economy Yeltsin had done everything to mitigate the impacts on the former Soviet citizens. Up until 1993, the Soviet Rouble had still been in circulation around the entire ex-Soviet territory. This single currency spelt a huge inflationary burden on the Russian economy which had already been operating under conditions of an unprecedented crisis through large credits for developing CIS economies. However, during President Yeltsin's second term this task underwent a transformation. The CIS had already been in existence for five years. It was time to move on. The countries characterised by dissimilar living standards, disparate outlooks, differing ideas about their place in the world pursued different agendas within the CIS. Within the CIS there emerged, for example, a regional organisation with a lesser degree of economic and military interaction — GUUAM: Georgia, Ukraine, Uzbekistan, Azerbaijan and Moldova.

In bilateral interactions, Yeltsin's relations with Alexander Lukashenko, the leader of Belarus were highly controversial, each for their own reasons, but both Russia and Belarus had always been interested in creating a union state. For Russia it was rather a question of defence and politics but for Belarus it was economic. In the beginning of 1997, yet another attempt was made to formalise these relations and sign a union treaty. This treaty was largely put forward by Belarus but did include provisions for a role of Lukashenko in Russian affairs so was rejected at the last minute by Yeltsin.

In general, however, over this period, for all the nationalistic rhetoric in some quarters, Russia was surrounded by countries dependent on it and being part of the zone of its influence. Yeltsin was seeking to keep a unified economic area within the CIS countries — similar to the European Union: with a shared defence system, unified customs and a free labour market.

A highly significant, symbolic step undertaken by Yeltsin in 1998 was the interment of the royal remains of the last tsar and his family in St Petersburg. The remains of the tsars' family were discovered in a mine near Yekaterinburg. The execution took place in 1918, so there followed a painstaking expert examination. Presently, forensic experts issued their verdict: yes, it was them.

Yeltsin and his wife, Naina, flew to St Petersburg on the anniversary of the execution. In his own account Yeltsin emphasised that it was a family event, not a state funeral. The Romanov descendents each threw a handful of earth* into the grave and the dry thud as the earth hit the coffins Yeltsin found quite emotional.

The Russian Orthodox Church had not recognised the conclusions arrived at by the state commission on the identity of the remains and the ceremony of burying the remains was prudently truncated and the names of the deceased, as Yeltsin remembered, were never enunciated. That was why the interment of the royal family remains, despite 52 descendents of the House of Romanovs assembling in St Petersburg, was not granted the status of a state event. Yeltsin himself decided to attend only at the last moment. Nevertheless, it was a special day for Yeltsin himself. The Ipatiev House**, the distressing monument in Yekaterinburg that had been pulled down on his orders, had always been weighing heavily on his conscience. The press, too, were tireless in reminding him of this transgression, even if he had been forced into it. Even now, however, the country is still not ready to express the feelings of repentance for those events. The last tsar is still considered not a victim but a perpetrator. The national take on history is still largely Soviet, the one born in the days of the revolution.

Back in 1997 this mentality was forced to go through yet another important test. Several years had been spent in persistent negotiations and finally Yeltsin signed the Founding Act on Mutual Relations, Cooperation and Security between Russia and NATO. When speaking on Russian TV Yeltsin himself commented the fact:

'The NATO plans of eastern expansion… present a danger to Russia's security. How should we have reacted? Any schism (between Russia and the West) endangers everyone and that is why we have chosen negotiations. The task was to reduce the negative consequences of the North-Atlantic Alliance to a minimum and prevent a new split in Europe. By signing the document between Russia and NATO the leaders of seventeen countries have confirmed that we shall have a new peaceful Europe not fragmented into blocs. We all need this including Russia.'

---

* At the end of an Orthodox funeral, the closest to the one deceased throw a handful of earth into the grave.

** The Ipatiev House was a building in Yekaterinburg formerly owned by the engineer Ipatiev where the former Emperor Nicholas II of Russia, his family and members of his household were executed following the *Bolshevik* revolution. Coincidentally, its name is identical with that of the Ipatiev Monastery in Kostroma, from where the Romanovs came to the throne in 1613.

## THE SECOND TERM (1996-1999)

Although this has been much criticised, the fact was that the Russian economy at the time was weak. The new democratic Russia was only starting to shape its relations with the global community but, most importantly, a conflict with the West was not in the country's interests. Realistically, other sovereign states, albeit recently part of the Soviet Union, could not be prevented from joining the alliance voluntarily. The year 1997 had a very specific significance for Russian citizens.

The status of a military gendarme of Europe had been lost long before 1997. When Yeltsin was 'inspecting the parade' in Berlin in 1994 as the Soviet troops were pulling out, he had a very clear view of what was to follow. It is a serious mistake to consider Yeltsin a politician who had given in to pressure. His real objective was to change Russia's mentality in order to become a *peaceful* state, a member of greater Europe. He justly believed that democratic Russia couldn't be in a perpetual military stand-off with the rest of the world *viz a vis* the Soviet Union. This had simply to be ruled out.

This indeed put the President into conflict with the Defence Minister Igor Rodionov in 1997. It culminated in their last exchange at the Defence Ministry's board meeting[*] to consider changes in deployment of airborne forces. Yeltsin appeared in the conference hall; he appeared cold, austere and unapproachable. He greeted the members and gave the floor to the minister.

"You have fifteen minutes to present your report."

"Fifteen minutes is absolutely insufficient," replied the minister.

"Fifteen minutes," repeated President.

"...In which case I refuse to make a presentation," the minister spoke resolutely.

"Chief of General Staff, you are welcome to take the floor," Yeltsin was addressing Samsonov.

"I refuse too."

"Igor Dmitrievich Sergeyev[**]."

Sergeyev rose to his feet and, believing that it was his turn to report, headed to the table where President was seated. "Wait a minute," Yeltsin stopped him. "Enter upon the duties of the Defence Minister."

---

[*] On the military reform. — *Author's comment.*

[**] Commander-in-Chief of the Strategic Missile Forces. — *Author's comment.*

"Yes Sir!" Sergeyev responded succinctly.

The President turned towards the Security Council's secretary seated to his left and uttered just one word: "decrees"* (*Yeltsin's Epoch*)

In the same year of 1997 Yeltsin attended the G-8 summit in Denver, Colorado. It was the first time that Russia was recognised as a rightful member of the world leaders' club. He took part in all meetings of the G8 without exception, including — for the first time ever — the closed sessions on financial regulation.

Western politicians were sufficiently appreciative of Yeltsin's role in the international relations of that era, the nineties for a number of reasons. To start with, he averted the further disintegration of the country and kept the country from a civil war. The very intensity of Yeltsin's schedule of meeting with Western leaders was, of course, without precedent. In his epoch, Russia, for them, stopped being *alien* — something to be wary of and Yeltsin was someone they could do business with.

Yet probably his main achievement in international relations was that, under Yeltsin, Russia stopped being a closed country for its own citizens. Millions of people started travelling abroad on the basis of simplified visa procedures without the humiliating ideological control and supervision. Usually, what is mentioned in this connection is the huge emigration from Russia but there was a reverse side: a huge migration into Russia — from Europe, USA and Israel. Many Westerners would be coming on business and then stay for years or even decades. The situation in the country changed, and one could not only live there but earn one's living too and people started returning.

'Where are you spending this summer's vacation?' 'By the sea.' In the nineties, for many Russians this meant Turkey, Tunisia, Egypt or Greece. This trend — to see the world, to spend your vacations abroad lasted for the entire decade. Just as it had been prior to 1917, the concept of studying and working abroad was there once more without being harassed by special services.

By the end of 1997, Yeltsin was convinced that the 'second economic offensive' must be brought to fruition, although the situation within and

---

\* On discharging one and appointing another. — *Author's comment.*

around the government continued to be exacerbated by strife. The initial plan of the Chubais-Nemtsov objectives, the 'Government's twelve top priorities', was also stalling. The Land Code wasn't passed as the Duma excluded the provision on selling land into private ownership and the Tax Code was rejected. The housing reform was also delayed indefinitely. Most importantly, as Yeltsin was fully aware — the Government itself was split. The 'ideal' construct of a mature Premier Chernomyrdin and his two younger reform-minded deputies vested with special powers was clearly not working. The change had to be much more decisive.

On March 23rd Yeltsin met with Chernomyrdin and announced to him that the Government was dissolved. The Premier was greatly shocked as was the Duma and the entire country.

The new appointee as Premier was a 35-year-old ex-banker, Sergey Kirienko who had been heading a commercial bank in Nizhny Novgorod and, under Nemtsov, became first Deputy Minister and then Minister for the Fuel and Energy Complex. He was new in Moscow and had no connections with any major banks or financial and industrial groups which, for Yeltsin, was important. Which begs the question — why not Nemtsov himself? Throughout 1997, at all the most important governmental events, he was constantly by Yeltsin's side. Yeltsin liked him as a person and trusted him. After Chernomyrdin's departure Yeltsin also fired Chubais although Nemtsov remained in the government.

So why was it, then, that the Prime Minister's post was to be filled by another, relatively unknown younger man? Yeltsin's plan in relation to Kirienko's nomination was extremely simple: it would be to direct an unswerving economic break-through. This 'technocratic government' would have the means to impose order on the economy within the time left before the presidential elections and would do its utmost to stamp out corruption. In effect, Kirienko's appointment was an attempt to bring Gaidar's reform back to life in the new context and to see it through to the end. Only continuing on this route, first embarked upon in 1992, did he see the ultimate result of transformation being concluded. The economy had to be rendered open and efficient with no monopolies, state intervention, or bureaucratic and military interference.

Finally, the success of the reform would untie his hands for resolving the paramount question: identifying his successor, a young political leader that would come to the lead the country in 2000. During Chernomyrdin's premiership, each trip around the country or abroad, each public speech after January of 1998 was already part of his election campaign of 2000. Yeltsin was not happy about this as he didn't see Chernomyrdin as President — a fact he admitted in his book whilst, at the same time, expressing his profound appreciation of his personal qualities of decency, loyalty and a huge experience as a manager. Chernomyrdin had been with him through all the most difficult years — from 1992 to 1997, however, to Yeltsin, Chernomyrdin was from the *old cohort of leaders*. He would be promoted as if by right and this was not the way forward.

In addition, by the beginning of 1998, Nemtsov himself was steeped in controversy. This became ever more acute after the incident on Channel One when during TV debates LDPR leader Zhirinovsky and Nemtsov threw a glass of orange juice into each other's face. This put him in the same class as Zhirinovsky. Besides, in Yeltsin's estimation Nemtsov was above all a political figure. In 1998, Yeltsin wanted the government to be headed by an economist, a pragmatist who would bring things to completion, who would do the impossible and then leave before the election, before the decisive contest.

So at the end of March Yeltsin introduced the new Prime Minister to the State Duma. Twice, the Duma torpedoed this nomination which it saw as absurd after which Yeltsin issued a stern and unequivocal warning that he would act in accordance to the Constitution and, should the Duma reject the premier suggested by him for the third time, he would have no qualms about dissolving it and announcing an early election. Kirienko made it at the third time of asking.

In early 1998, the new Government headed by Kirienko didn't just have to continue pushing through the already ongoing reforms but engage with the paramount task of leading the country out of the dead end of internal debt. Elsewhere, financial crisis was already ravaging stock exchanges. Ultimately, it resulted in Russia in the disastrous debt default of 1998. Former Finance Minister Alexander Livshits, provides an account in the co-authored *Yeltsin's Epoch*:

"'Black Monday" in 1998 was brought about by the same factors as "Black Tuesday" in 1994: bad budgetary decisions and the reforms stuck mid-way. The tax revenues had been poor for years. There had been a fear of cutting back the costs and the deficit was covered with loans, primarily from the internal financial market, borrowing that got so out of hand that, in the end, there was nothing to pay back the old debts with. There was an impact of too many foreigners present in the market, for example whilst in 1996 their share in the market of GKOs-OFZs* accounted for 16%, by the beginning of 1998 it had risen to 28%. This meant an increased dependency on the global financial system. As soon as the Asian financial markets collapsed investors started withdrawing capital from anywhere where a threat of default loomed large, Russia included.'

The internal debt in the USA is measured in astronomical sums whilst in Russia, with its weak and unstable economy, the internal debt presented the only way to conquer the budget deficit. The state had to spend too much (on social programmes, the housing sector, the needs of defence) while it was receiving too little in tax revenues. The country that had no habit and, hence, no desire to pay tax, with half of its economy being in the 'shadow' sector resulting in the need to run up an internal debt. The plan of replenishing the budget at the expense of internal borrowing was, generally speaking, not a bad one. It was developed with a view to foreign investors buying shares in Russian companies, entering the securities market and, finally, the investments growing at the expense of other sources such as sales of land, major state companies and — ultimately — economic growth. Unfortunately, apart from a gamble with 'short-term' securities no other investment came into Russia and all of this was against the background of a catastrophic oil prices which sank to 13 dollars a barrel. The foreigners, with nearly 30% of the debt, started getting rid of their GKOs and demanding urgent payment of interest.

With the budget held up in the Duma, tax not even on the agenda, privatisation plans going hay-wire and foreigners not interested in buying unsold assets in Russia, the budget fell for short of the planned 5 trillion 'old' roubles.'

Against this background what instruction did Yeltsin give to his new Premier? Journalist, Leonid Mlechin recounts:

---

* GKO and OFZ are abbreviations for (Russian) Gosudarstvennoye Kaznacheiskie Obligatsii, Государственные Казначейские Облигации, 'Short-Term State Treasury Bills' and (Russian) Obligatsyi Federal'novo Zaima, Облигации Федерального Займа, 'Federal Loan Obligations', respectively.

'Kirienko told me that on March 23rd, the day of his appointment, the President asked,

"Are you aware of the developments in the country?"

"I am," Kirienko replied. "We are heading towards a debt crisis. Unless some urgent measures are taken the consequences may be grim."

"Do you believe it is possible to overcome this crisis?"

"It is. But it would require the toughest measures."

"Go and do it, Sergey Vladilenovich."

Kirienko deemed it necessary to lay down just one condition.

"Boris Nikolayevich, I do not do politics and have no desire to go into any of it." Yeltsin gave an approving nod. "Good, don't! The previous government's major mistake was barging into politics too much whereas the government should occupy itself with managing the economy. Work on the economic programme and leave politics to me…"'

However, in truth, the President had failed to take onboard the sheer scope of the emerging crisis. Yes, Kirienko was in constant consultation with Russia's best economists and they had been supplying him with 'valuable advice'. But that was not enough. What was required was some decisive but cautious measures — skilful fine-tuning. Quite simply, in the spring of 1998 the new government didn't have enough time to accumulate the necessary political and organisational momentum. The time they had just proved too short. Suggestions from abroad included floating the rouble to avoid crashes such as were happening in Mexico and Thailand where the authorities were holding the fort to the bitter end, spending all their currency reserves but still failing to save their currencies. 'We didn't heed this advice,' Livshits concludes. Even so, floatation would have immediately made millions of people destitute. Their incomes would have been wiped out as ultimately happened in September of 1998. The question is whether Kirienko's government could have survived it but most likely, not.

To add to all these worries, Russia was gripped by industrial actions amongst which the most symbolic in 1998 were miners' strikes in spring and autumn and pickets built by teachers and doctors outside the White House. The TV channels were covering the strikes extensively, 'meals on wheels' were constantly delivered to their midst and leaders of the Duma's major factions (Ziuganov, Zhirinovsky and others) addressed them. All this resembled a siege of the government with the strikers being supported not only by the communists but figures from other camps — for example, Moscow Mayor, Yuri Luzhkov.

During the governmental crisis in the autumn of 1998, rumours were going rounds in Moscow that Berezovsky was insisting on entrusting the government to Lebed — 'a weaker politician would simply not cope'. At the time, already Krasnoyarsk governor, Lebed indeed put in an unexpected presence in Moscow and 'offered himself as saviour of the Motherland on two TV channels at once — whether on his own or someone else's initiative.' (Leonid Mlechin). It was quite a common view then that Russia needed a politician of just this type — a retired general, a 'defender of the poor' and the sheer embodiment of strength — to succeed Yeltsin at that point in history. It was believed such a person alone would know how to reconcile voters to the current political system and democratic institutions and finally, only a leader like this would know how to complete the economic transformation. His powerful charisma could be a shield against the disgruntled electorate. Eventually, of course, Vladimir Putin established the political peace between the 'left' and 'right' of the electorate along a market-orientated, political and civil course.

Yeltsin was often called, in jest 'Tsar Boris'. However, this tsar had more in common with a much earlier historic era when there had existed, prior to the emergence of imperial power structures, a certain popular right, a *'veche'* whereby citizens had a right to vote. He had been striving to bring order into life through a public contract. The will of a tsar alone had not sufficed. This want of a public contract, of a fair play endorsed, not from above, but a *consensus* had been corroded over time yet it hadn't disappeared completely. Yeltsin managed to awaken civil instincts in the society emerging from the Soviet experience and moreover — did it at a time of tectonic change.

During the summer of 1998, overcoming pain and fatigue, Yeltsin toured the country using every opportunity, every meeting with journalists to announce that the crisis was resolvable, the critical point was behind us and the exchange rate mechanism would not be removed. Through June and July he still believed in the young, bright and well-educated economists of the post-Chubais and post-Nemtsov call-up — until the financial tornado struck. After several days of being closeted in his office with a group of experts in feverish attempts to find a way out of the crisis,

Kirienko, ashen-faced from lack of sleep, announced on 17 August 1998: *we are defaulting*. Simultaneously, the Government made a decision to broaden the currency exchange margin at which point, the price of a dollar starts to take-off stratospherically: 10, 12, 18, 20 roubles for one dollar, almost hour by hour.

The 1998 default sent into a turmoil not only investors but everyone. The collapse of the national currency precipitated the collapse of all banking transactions and payments — all business life. Basically, all financial doors in Moscow slammed shut at once, leading to many-hour-long, sometimes, overnight queues in front of bank entrances, shops closed for stock re-evaluation and cessation of the exchange — in a word, everything that in any way at all related to money. Things that were happening in the country in the last days of August and throughout September could hardly be described only in economic terms. It was a panic comparable to 1990 and 1991 that forced people to get ready for a 'hungry winter' by buying up cheap staples: cereals, sugar, potatoes and canned meat. During those sunny but cool days, farmers' markets were teaming with crowds with no one knowing for how many months ahead there would be no salaries, for how long deposits in commercial banks would be frozen. There was only one thought: how to make sure that children would not starve?

Many private companies also closed down and numerous banks declared themselves bankrupt. Newspapers were full of the direst commentaries, with claims that the country had been living beyond its means, the nascent affluence was a fiction and that now a great depression was on its way. The depression, however, never came, mainly because the default announced by Kirienko's government was a belated but an adequate measure. The weakening of the Rouble proved beneficial for many enterprises, since their output suddenly became competitive. However, the positive consequences of the default would emerge only several months later and would be inherited by the succeeding Government. As for the government of Young Reformers, they resigned to much acrimony and derision. Together with Kirienko, Nemtsov also left the government although Yeltsin did suggest that he should stay.

The next day, Yeltsin spoke to the public on TV where he tried to explain to the people the reason for the crisis emphasising that it was a global development, not a purely Russian one. He was calling upon people to keep calm and maintain order, after which he went on to announce that Viktor Chernomyrdin would be Acting Premier and explained his motives for choosing him with the words, 'The country now needs those who are habitually called political heavyweights...' This about face was probably due to Yeltsin underestimating the significance of the financial crisis in 1998. After all, since 1991, Russia had experienced quite a few similar crises and this one appeared to be within the typical limits. This perception had been confirmed by all leading economists and he believed, largely with good reason, that the economic situation in 1998 was considerably better than, say, in 1992 or 1994.

He thought that too much was being made of the crisis and that it wasn't representative of the overall positive tendencies. He reckoned that the efforts of a 'new-old' Premier who would manage to stabilise the situation within several months after which it would prove possible to bring back into the government those who would be carrying out those badly needed reforms.

When in September Yeltsin first presented Chernomyrdin's candidature to the Duma it became clear that the deputies were out for a fight. The Duma was like a cauldron, with the communists declaring themselves ready to set up a coalition government representing various factions, albeit principally the communists. Most importantly, however, the deputies' resoluteness was very much in tune with the public sentiment, of the many for whom access to household budgets and savings were suspended, and with no indication as to exactly when the banks would unblock their accounts.

Of this period, Leonid Mlechin says:

'Chernomyrdin gladly accepted Yeltsin's offer but on his own terms. He would receive considerably broader authority while President would agree to limit his own power. He had to get the Duma's support and undertook to give the opposition what it had been after for many years, the President's renunciation of his omnipotence. His view was that he would meet the opposition's most cherished demands through a constitutional reform with redistribution of powers to the Duma's and the Government's advantage. Chernomyrdin suggested that principal Duma factions should prepare a political agreement with the view that, if the President signs it, the Duma would automatically endorse Chernomyrdin."

Finally, a political agreement between Yeltsin and Chernomyrdin was conceived after two unsuccessful votes in the Duma where, supported by Yeltsin, the Government, administration and the Duma's Council worked together to find a way out of the impasse. The Duma didn't want to be dissolved and the Kremlin was doing its utmost to have Chernomyrdin approved. Under the political agreement, Yeltsin guaranteed to the Duma that Chernomyrdin would not be replaced until the election in 2000. Chernomyrdin was conducting the tense negotiations with the Duma factions while promising whatever he could, down to individual posts in government. When all the leaders of the various factions were ready to put their signatures on the document all of a sudden something unforeseen happened. Before the third vote the communists unexpectedly changed their tack. With or without an agreement, Chernomyrdin didn't suit them anymore. It transpired later that this happened after Ziuganov's people had spoken to Moscow Mayor, Yuri Luzhkov. Luzhkov attempted to undermine Chernomyrdin's appointment because he deemed himself the only realistic nomination to the Premier's post.

The political ambitions of the mayor of Moscow had taken a long time coming to mature. Although in the early nineties Yuri Luzhkov could take a stand on political matters and make statements on the issues but, on the

---

\* Oleg Moroz tells it differently. 'The main objective of a political agreement as seen by the Duma was elucidated by the Speaker of the lower chamber, Seleznev. "The essence is that President must guarantee that the coalition government would not be tampered with constantly; that the Prime Minister would have every authority to rule the cabinet and would identify its composition himself." Seleznev also added that he and his colleagues intended to address the president and urge him to introduce the requisite amendments into the Constitution himself.

'... In the end, it seemingly proved possible to prepare a draft agreement without a demand to alter the Constitution, although it was intimated that the "process of revising the Fundamental Law should be launched". There was also a demand to introduce changes into some other legislation. This draft looked acceptable to all. However, at the eleventh hour, before taking a Duma's vote on Chernomyrdin's candidacy, communists announced that their faction was refusing to sign and would vote against President's nomination. Since this faction had 135 seats it wasn't yet definite that the results of the vote would be negative (it required at least 226 votes to approve a Premier). Taking, however, into account the mood in other factions and groups of deputies, this result was more than probable.'

whole, he was quite happy within his role of the huge metropolis's master. Against the common troubled background, Moscow was the only region in the country going through an economic boom and the Moscow government made sure that all financial flows in the capital city were managed, one way or another, from Mayor's Office. To manage the city's complex economy took a lot of effort and, in the early years, Luzhkov was taking his cue from Yeltsin. He was perfectly aware that his situation was totally dependent on what sort of president was incumbent. However, as Luzhkov's connections with other regions grew and his financial influence increased, it became increasingly clear that the role of a large-scale manager — that of a governor or mayor — would not sate his appetites. Starting from 1996, Luzhkov's close ties with the Menatep bank and with Gusinsky, who was actively involved in political lobbying and the promotion of 'his own' politicians, had added spice to the whole story. They wanted to see the mayor in the White House and in the Kremlin, whilst Yeltsin failed to visualise him in either place. It seemed to him that the mayor's working methods did not fit big politics although they never once had an open conversation on the subject. The mayor, however, showed his hand abruptly and controversially when he derailed the vote on Chernomyrdin.

Yeltsin loathed pressure and never made decisions under duress since this would be a violation of the entire political structure of his presidential republic and the basics of the constitutional form of government. And here was Luzhkov pressurising him. There was only one thing to do: put Chernomyrdin forward for the third time and, in case of a failure, dissolve the Duma and run a new election or come up with an alternative nomination. All of a sudden, Luzhkov found supporters within the Kremlin Administration. These turned out to be Yeltsin's press secretary, Sergey Yastrzhembsky, and the Security Council's Secretary, Andrei Kokoshin. A rift was emerging within the administration so Yeltsin invited Yumashev, Yastrzhembsky and Kokoshin over to his Gorky residence and heard them out: all 'pros' and 'cons' of Luzhkov's candidature. Then he dismissed them all without a word. Sometime later he calmly confirmed that he just couldn't see Luzhkov as a Prime Minister.

Valentin Yumashev recollects:

'His main problem was whether to dissolve the Duma. Basically, within himself he was ready to do it. All the conferences in the Kremlin between the first and the second rounds of voting to which I would invite my closest associates — presidential aides and my deputies — were on precisely this issue. Are we ready for the dissolution of the Duma? What should the subsequent scenario be? What shall we have in the new Duma? And so on. Alexander Voloshin, by the way, in those conferences was resolutely in favour of the third round with Chernomyrdin. He believed that the Duma would take a fright and he would make it. Even if the deputies failed him, however, and we had a new election, with the support of the key elites and the TV we would achieve a decent result in the new Duma. My view was that the Duma should not be dissolved. We couldn't afford the risk, given the severe financial crisis, strikes and the political crisis related to the dismissal of the government. I updated Boris Nikolayevich on this range of views. The final decision was his.'

Meanwhile the Duma was debating the topic heatedly. Yabloko's leader Grigory Yavlinsky took everyone by surprise by suggesting Yevgeny Primakov, the Foreign Minister, with a comment both unexpected and to the point: Primakov was a compromise that suited everybody. Chernomyrdin hoped there would be the third vote. His logic was akin to Voloshin's: 'They won't have the guts to see the Duma dissolved, nothing to worry about!'

Head of Administration Valentin Yumashev was awaiting Yeltsin's decision. He had already spoken to Primakov (long before Yavlinsky's proposal), trying to work out whether he would accept the offer in case of a voting fiasco.

Primakov replied with a categorical refusal: 'I am not a public figure. I want to make it to my retirement without fuss, and leave, together with Boris Nikolayevich, in 2000.' When he learnt about this, Chernomyrdin suggested to Yeltsin a new scenario: to offer to the two additional names, two First Vice-Premiers — Masliukov and Primakov. 'We are a troika,' he was saying. 'We are a powerful troika. We shall be supported.'

Only hours before the submission of the President's official letter to the Duma, Yeltsin invited over Chernomyrdin, Masliukov and Primakov and insistently proposed the nomination of Yuri Masliukov — a member of the communist faction, an economist and the final boss of the Soviet

*Gosplan*. But Yeltsin's daughter Tatyana and Vladimir Shevchenko, Chief of Presidential Protocol and an old friend of Primakov's, made one final attempt to convince him.

Primakov himself described the events:

'On the way out of the President's office I bumped into several people anxiously waiting for me: Head of Administration Yumashev, Chief of Protocol and Boris Nikolayevich's daughter, Dyachenko. I made a helpless gesture and said I couldn't agree. So Volodya Shevchenko, my pal of many years, virtually hit the ceiling. I never saw him so exercised. "You're only thinking about yourself! Don't you realise what we are facing here? August 17th has caused the economy to cave in. The government is no more. The Duma is about to be dissolved. The president may physically collapse at any point. Don't you have a sense of responsibility?"

I countered with a question, "But why me?"

"Because today the Duma and everyone else are happy with only your candidature and because you can do it." After my spontaneous consent they all started hugging me. Someone rushed over to tell the president.'

'Dad had no qualms about dissolving the Duma,' Tatyana comments. 'Unlike his Head of Administration he didn't consider this a crisis. And he never offered premiership to Masliukov since the latter represented communists. He didn't and couldn't do it.'

The candidature of the new Premier was approved by the Duma at the first attempt and with an overwhelming majority. Thus began his short time in office, the time of 'Primakov's stabilisation' which, nevertheless, produced a significant impact on the subsequent course of events.

But let us have a closer look at the situation that Yeltsin found himself in that autumn, in 1998. What were his gains and failures?

The 'coalition government' advocated by the communists had finally been formed. Apart from Masliukov it included another communist: Mr Kulik, a Vice –Premier overseeing agricultural matters. However, the head of government was not a communist but Yeltsin's Foreign Minister. Thus, Yeltsin avoided the risk and didn't dissolve the Duma, having resolutely brushed away Luzhkov's claims to premiership and, thus, to future presidency. So, overall, against all expectations Yeltsin was victorious yet again: he emerged unscathed from the crisis brought about by the default and the insurgent Duma.

But what did he lose?

Primarily, he lost the initiative. The election was getting near while the post of Prime Minister was held by a temporary figure — a compromise-ridden Primakov who had been practically *imposed* upon him. Yeltsin also lost Chernomyrdin, 'his very own' reliable Premier whose candidature he was already considering as his successor at the presidential election in 2000.

However, to start with, Yeltsin had no serious grounds to worry on account of either the coalition government or Primakov's performance. The cabinet of ministers where Yuri Masliukov played the lead acted cautiously, advisedly and avoided abrupt manoeuvres. Significantly, from the very start, Primakov invited Sergey Kirienko as a Vice-Premier. Primakov must have known that Kirienko would refuse but it was his way to signal adherence to the government's line in the economy.

Yevgeny Maksimovich Primakov had worked with Yeltsin for a very long time — from 1991. In the days of the August putsch, the two prominent 'Gorbachevites' — Primakov and Volsky made a timely statement denouncing the GKChP. In the autumn of 1991, when replacing Gorbachev's team, Yeltsin invited Yevgeny Maksimovich to head the Foreign Intelligence Service.

Career intelligence officers approved of this nomination (Yeltsin didn't just appoint him — he put his offer to a vote at the FIS board meeting). While not a professional in this sphere, Yevgeny Maksimovich was nevertheless well versed in the 'job specifics'– thanks to his extensive travels around the Arab world on critical confidential missions — similarly to any *Pravda* foreign correspondent. This is how Primakov describes it himself in his book:

'Having worked for *Pravda* for three years I was appointed the paper's correspondent in the Middle East and posted in Cairo. Pravda being the organ of the CPSU's Central Committee, I was regularly carrying out important missions on behalf of the Central Committee and the Politburo. Some of those would be kept in the Special File for which very few people had clearance. As a rule the KGB would be responsible for security and communications.'

The intelligence community must have appreciated something else: Primakov was very calm and composed, ready to find a compromise. Having succeeded, in 1995, Andrei Kozyrev as Foreign Minister Primakov yet again showed himself in the best light possible — thanks to his professionalism and *sangfroid*.

He was the type Yeltsin understood perfectly well: a Soviet manager well-versed in the rules of the game and ready to stick to them unfailingly. Besides, Primakov personal reputation was irreproachable: honest, not inclined to scheming, capable of turning on the charm and very bright.

'Primakov's secret was his ability to deliver speeches where everyone could hear what he or she wanted. The liberally-minded got promises of reforms and freedoms. Communists revelled at the state regulation and control... He would hold forth on a subject of the need for drastic measures and immediately point out that it didn't mean a state of emergency. He would promise "a sharp turn towards democracy, reforms of the society, creation of a mixed economy and political plurality" and say something like: "We cannot move forward in a belief that the free market debauchery will provide all the answers."'(Leonid Mlechin's biography of Primakov's)

Primakov was perfectly aware of the role his government within the new political structure. The Duma was supportive of *any* of his initiatives. So the government that was initially thrusting towards 'state regulation' unexpectedly turned out to be quite liberal. 'One could see how respectfully Ziuganov was shaking his hand,' writes Leonid Mlechin. 'The communists couldn't afford to have Primakov's government removed by their refusal to vote for the budget. Yet it was the toughest budget in all recent years. First of all, it provided for dramatic cutbacks on social spending. The Minister for Economic Affairs... told the deputies bluntly, "The envisaged rise in inflation and the size of the federal budget revenue in 1999 would prevent us from ensuring stabilisation of living standards at the previous year's level."' In plain Russian it meant that the government was urging us to 'tighten belts' and make economies. This appeal was taken onboard.

Still, the most acute stage of the crisis was over. From 1999 onwards, the Russian economy had been displaying a tendency towards steady growth. Primakov was reaping the benefits of financial stabilisation for which Kirienko and Nemtsov had paid with their resignation. However, the cabinet's stayed 'reserved and moderate' too (by the way, many of Kirienko's ministers kept their jobs).

Initially, Primakov was very cautious towards Yeltsin. He kept talking about 'leaving simultaneously, in 2000', of fishing together when retired. He talked about health, his own included — like Yeltsin, Primakov was advanced in years and suffered from a range of complaints, including pains in his back and legs.

However, it only took two or three months for the political situation to start escalating. The alarm bells first rang when Viktor Iliukhin, a communist deputy, submitted a bill 'on the state of health of the President of the Russian Federation, Boris Nikolayevich Yeltsin'. Iliukhin had tried it several times before and even suggested that a state commission should examine Yeltsin and make him resign on medical grounds. But in the beginning of 1999, under Primakov, the communists spread their wings and felt empowered. One could see that deputies started thinking that the President didn't wield full authority and was only living out his last months in office. General Makashov, also a communist deputy in the State Duma, made several anti-Semitic statements. His vitriolic diatribes about 'Yids' in the Kremlin and on TV incited no protest in the Duma, the other way round — his colleagues rushed to his defence. New FSB director, Vladimir Putin, publicly denounced 'any forms of extremism'. But the passions were flaring up.

Yeltsin responded with a decree dismissing Valentin Yumashev (who stayed on as his advisor) and appointing General of the Frontier Service, Nikolai Bordiuzha Head of Administration. Thus the latter came to wear two hats, since he was also the Security Council's Secretary. In his book Yeltsin admitted that this appointment was symbolic: he wanted the deputies to realise that he was in control of the situation and ready to take any constitutional measures for preserving political stability.

Power and increased popularity revealed traits of Primakov's character that Yeltsin hadn't noticed before — or had been reluctant to notice. It transpired that this elderly calm person, psychologically and personally close to Yeltsin who had been with him through the toughest years as head of intelligence and Foreign Minister proved to be a total stranger in terms of *mentality*, in a way, his complete antithesis. Key posts in the government were immediately filled with representatives of the special services and former KGB officers. As soon as Primakov came to power Russian business found itself under pressure. He was constantly harping on to Yeltsin about 'an impossibility of such mass media': he would turn up for his meetings with the President fully armed, with carefully prepared files containing quotes most uncomplimentary towards to the government. 'In the beginning, Dad would be surprised and say, "Yevgeny Maksimovich, don't you pay attention, look how much flak I have to put up with. Later, he wasn't surprised anymore,' says Tatyana.

Primakov's public statements were holding a mirror to the complexity of the political process. He was often aggressive and repeatedly doffed his hat to communists. The economic and political climate started changing stealthily and a disagreeable chill crept in. When the Duma approved the act of pardon, Primakov told a government session that penitentiary facilities could now handle those who had committed economic crimes. This phrase was picked up by all TV channels as breaking news and the Russian businessmen took these words seriously.

Yeltsin also took it all in. The 'File' that Primakov had been bringing along to their meetings contained not only newspaper clippings but also the compromising materials on businessmen and those in power. Eager to keep everyone 'under his thumb', he wanted control over the FSB and because of that was always complaining to Yeltsin of Vladimir Putin, demanding the latter's immediate dismissal. It is said that their relations got off on the wrong foot from the start since Putin refused to bug conversations of politicians and businessmen — contrary to new Premier's wishes. The matter primarily concerned Grigory Yavlinsky who was openly accusing several cabinet members of corruption thus making Primakov fly off his handle.

Primakov retaliated by accusing Putin of bringing too many of 'his own' people from St Petersburg to the FSB leadership. Putin brought along his entire board in an attempt to show Primakov that only two deputies out of ten were new. Later on, the Prime Minister confronted Putin over bugging his own conversation and putting a tail on his movements. In addition, he was constantly trying to drag the President into his complicated relations with the FSB's young director.

This long-standing conflict couldn't but give way to some serious considerations. Why was the Premier, whose brief before everything was to manage economy, getting so involved with the security agencies? Why did he try to exercise control over the FSB, the Ministry of the Interior and the Procurator's Office?

Yeltsin wrote afterwards, 'Some bizarre criminal charges were pressed, and innocent people were arrested. When questioning businessmen and searching their premises, some security service staff didn't deem it necessary to hide how keen they were to avenge the past years. There was a real threat of the country splitting in two over the main issue: the issue of economic reforms.'

Primakov's ardent supporter Leonid Mlechin comment on the above with dismay: 'It is strange to read it today. An onslaught on the freedom of speech, the security services taking vengeance, criminal investigation of prominent industrialists, arrests and searches — rather similar to what was happening after Primakov's resignation when Yeltsin's successor Vladimir Putin became President.'

There is no contradiction here. Under President Yeltsin not a single Premier — be it Chernomyrdin, Primakov or Putin — could change the political climate in the new country. Primakov could have believed that his was the only way for setting the country to rights: through reprisals and pressure on the media, through intimidating and bringing everyone who disagreed or resisted to their knees. President Yeltsin could have been aware that this policy resonated with the 'soul of the people' and that any new leader would try to resort to this recourse. But *under him*, he was telling himself, that was not going to happen. No way.

Yeltsin — and it is highly important to underscore — was perfectly aware of the limits of his competence. Like a builder he knew which section of the project was his and where his duties started and finished.

'Primakov's stabilisation', as Yeltsin called theses months in his book, in reality — an attempt to take an alternative political course, manifested itself only in episodes, isolated impromptu events and muted internal conflicts. Practically none of it came to public notice. But Yeltsin managed to identify the tendency and this tendency was not at all to his liking. Yeltsin saw 'Primakov's stabilisation' as an accidental return to the past. For

## THE SECOND TERM (1996-1999)

all that, the President never once criticised his Premier's actions publically and kept meeting him weekly, inside and outside Russia. And they did have enough subjects to dwell on.

In March of 1999, as NATO started bombing Belgrade, Primakov's plane made a U-turn over the Atlantic Ocean. It was a famous diplomatic gesture: Primakov cancelled his visit to the USA right there, despite being airborne. Yeltsin was in agreement with this tough stand. He was enraged and insulted at the Americans' course of action. Records of his telephone conversation with Clinton reflect the entire range of those emotions. As Yeltsin himself writes in his book:

'I told Bill that it was inadmissible to have hundreds and thousands die because of just one person\*, to allow his words and actions provoke us. We should work to make sure that he was among some other people, so that he would find it impossible to carry on in the same vein... For the sake of our future relations and the future security in Europe, I ask that you countermand this attack. We could meet somewhere and identify tactics of fighting Milošević personally... It is unclear who will come after you and me and will have to deal with reducing strategic nuclear weapons. It is known, however, what we ourselves should be doing — bringing those stockpiles further and further down.'

The war in Yugoslavia deleted many years of the Russian diplomatic efforts in the region. It obliterated international law.

They were as one with Primakov on that score.

To digress a little: over all these years Yeltsin, his deteriorating health notwithstanding, continued his unprecedentedly intensive communication with Western leaders. It was during these years that Russia formalised its diplomatic relations with the North Atlantic Alliance, became member of the Parliamentfry Assembly of the Council of Europe the and other European bodies. It was the most important result of Yeltsin's diplomacy during his second term.

In 1999, relations between Russia and the West were aggravated not only because of the Yugoslavian crisis but over the second Chechen campaign too. In November of that year at the OSCE summit in Istanbul,

---

\* Milošević. — *Author's comment.*

Yeltsin had to withstand the formidable pressure from France and Germany, his permanent partners in negotiations. This is how he describes it himself:

'I was ruthless in editing the first draft that had been prepared for me*. I inserted the toughest and most forceful language possible. The text would come back all smoothed out and sleek. The Foreign Office feared a blunt confrontation with Western partners. Having read one more option, I called Voloshin up in the middle of the night: "Are you poking fun at me, Alexander Stalievich?"

… Once more, I entered my hand-written comment in the text: *"No one has any right to criticise us over Chechnya."* and passed it on to Igor Ivanov** for revision. Somewhat later they came back and started insisting that that wasn't the way to go about things. And I was forced to read it just like that, with my hand-written insertions. Clinton sensed… that I would take a tough stance and entered through the "wrong" door, not the one prescribed by the protocol, and crossed the entire hall, some one hundred metres, saying hello to everyone, smiling and generally giving to understand who was master.

I showed him the watch, "Running late, Bill!"

… I felt it physically: the huge audience was as if strewn with shards of mistrust and incomprehension. Chirac and Schröder's faces were grim. They clearly hadn't expected such tension.'

An account of the same events has been given by his aides:

'First, the President pounced at Russia's critics: 'You have no right to criticise Russia over Chechnya!' In addition, he was deliberately uppish with Jacque Chirac and Gerhard Schröder and contrary to previous protocol arrangements gave them only 10 minutes. Afterwards he simply went and departed for Moscow, having left Foreign Minister Igor Ivanov with OSCE leaders to work at definitions. Three weeks later, on December 10th, during his visit to the People's Republic of China the President resolutely reminded his "buddy Bill" that Russia was still in full possession of a complete nuclear arsenal.' (*Yeltsin's Epoch*).

---

\* His speech at the summit. — *Author's comment.*

\*\* The Foreign Minister at the time. — *Author's comment.*

However, despite the Yugoslavian crisis, in March-April of 1999 his relations with the Premier revealed a serious crack. At one of the meetings (it was taking place in a hospital which serves to emphasis its importance) Primakov started nervously talking about the President's near circle setting the President against him, meanwhile he harboured no political ambition, merely asking the President to confirm his authority until the year 2000. Yeltsin replied calmly: all agreements hold, you and I work quietly and step down when my term in office expires.

Primakov asked if he could invite a TV crew, so that Yeltsin could repeat those words publically. Yeltsin did as he was asked and confirmed, before the TV cameras urgently rushed over from Ostankino, that he had no intention to change the government. But Primakov still didn't believe him. His next step was to prepare a draft document and push it through the Duma, thus endorsing the mutual obligations between the President and the parliament: essentially, that the President was not to dissolve the government and the Duma was not to fire the President until the year 2000.

Primakov's explained his demand (publically and then in writing) of an additional guarantee of inviolability 'until the year 2000' thus: he got wise to the intrigues behind his back, he sensed Yeltsin's mounting irritation. He did it out of the sense of responsibility for the government although, in reality, the reason was different. Oral guarantees that Primakov's government would continue peacefully until 2000 were given by the President back in September 1998 when convincing Yevgeny Maksimovich to take up the post. At the same time it was also mentioned that President Yeltsin and Primakov would jointly look for a presidential candidate, a prominent young politician, who would stand for office. It was also clear that this new politician may sit, prior to election, in the Prime Minister's chair, and so sooner or later Primakov would be replaced. In the beginning, Yevgeny Maksimovich did start looking and discussing options, at one point he was considering Sergey Stepashin, some other names. But eventually, his attitude changed: he saw *no one* in this role and set about trying to highjack power. Yeltsin wouldn't have it.

The political structure formed by spring of 1999 around the Prime Minister could no longer stay neutral: it was plunged into a bitter conflict between legislators and the presidential office. The State Duma hurriedly launched the impeachment procedure in an attempt to snatch the power from the incumbent President and pass it over to the Premier. The episode with Procurator General Skuratov that took place in the spring of 1999 gave Yeltsin reasons to fear a new crisis.

Skuratov had always seemed like an honest, well-mannered and mild man, so Yeltsin's attitude to him, to start with, was neutral. Very soon, however, this 'gentle person' started showing an unprecedented political bias as was illustrated by the so-called 'Sobchak case'. During his election campaign in St Petersburg, Mayor Sobchak's adversaries invented a criminal case against him — on trumped up charges to do with repairs in his flat. After Sobchak lost the election, the Procurator General's office escalated the case into a veritable witch hunt. As a rule, Yeltsin never meddled into operation of courts or the Procurator's Office. In his view it was like carrying out legacy of the communist system. Under communists, he would say, there was a 'telephone law*'; we should not stoop so low.

Meanwhile Skuratov closely supervised cases that promised him political dividends. However absurd the charges against Lisovsky and Yevstafiev, he was in no hurry to close the 'Xerox box case'. The money allocated to artists involved in the election campaign, legally speaking, was completely transparent, there were no wronged parties but people were still summoned for questioning and kept under surveillance. It suited the Procurator General just fine.

However, in the spring of 1999 the Procurator General, a high-profile fighter against corruption, organised crime and mafia suddenly appeared before the public eye in a totally new light. Or — to be more precise — he appeared completely naked.

A fly-on-the-wall video camera had been installed in a rented flat where Skuratov was enjoying himself in the company of prostitutes. Most likely, one of Skuratov's 'friends' decided to use the oldest trick in the book — a classic case of blackmail. Should the Procurator refuse to play ball, the compromising video would come in very handy. Why someone decided to pull the rug from under Skuratov or what was it that he had

---

\* Meaning — a telephone call from high-up official could tip the balance of any such investigation.

THE SECOND TERM (1996-1999)

refused to do (or not to do) remained unknown. Whatever the motives, the cassette ended up in the Kremlin and Skuratov was forced to resign 'for reasons of health'. He sent Yeltsin this letter:

'Esteemed Boris Nikolayevich, the heavy workload has recently started taking its toll: headaches, pains in the cardiac area, etc. In view of this, I would ask you to table a motion on releasing me from my current position of the RF Procurator General at the Council of the Federation. I would be grateful for a job with a lesser scope of responsibilities. Yuri Skuratov. 01.02.99.'

Yeltsin was told that Skuratov was quite poorly and about to be admitted to the Kremlin Hospital. Yeltsin asked to prepare documents on releasing him from his post. At this stage he certainly knew nothing about the tape. Meanwhile, a 'support group' of sorts formed around Skuratov and started urging him to fight back in order to keep his elevated position: the most active being members of the financial group Menatep (a major shareholder in Yukos). During that period, Menatep wielded a lot of influence within the Council of the Federation — to the extent that Menatep's premises served as a venue for a kind of the 'senators' club'. At the same time, Menatep was hand in glove with Luzhkov and one of their key players had been working for years as chief of Moscow government's administration.

The situation had instantly escalated and got a lot of publicity. The alignment of interested parties was as follows: Skuratov in need of support and Luzhkov with a powerful political base in the Council of the Federation, so the Procurator General's conflict with the President played right into Luzhkov's hands (it the Council of the Federation that appointed or dismissed a procurator general). An ample scope for backstage negotiations was thus created: a voting stance in exchange for some perks or concessions from the centre. At the same time, each governor had his own 'topic', his own reason to haggle with the Kremlin. And finally, Menatep, too, was eager to have a 'controlling block of shares' in either removing or appointing the procurator general.

What followed — to use the official cliché — were 'active consultations'. Before the first vote, Head of Administration Bordiuzha sanctioned the broadcast of the compromising tape on Russian TV (at night). However, this failed to impress members of the supreme chamber, and the senators voted against Skuratov's discharge. The grand auction was thus started.

Half a year before the events described above, in the autumn of 1998, Skuratov had received a call from the Swiss Attorney General Carla Del Ponte. She informed him of an audit that had been run on financial statements of a Swiss engineering group Mabetex. The audit had revealed accounts related to Yeltsin's family members. Significantly, Skuratov didn't utter a word about this to either Yeltsin or head of his administration. He pushed the documents deep into his personal draw for a possible use later and first mentioned the 'Mabetex case' right there, in the Council of the Federation. He dropped the name as part of his pledge to fight corruption in the higher echelons of power.

Thus, after the first vote at the Council of the Federation Bordiuzha told Yeltsin about the sleazy tape on Skuratov's pastimes. The next meeting took place in the Central Kremlin Hospital and was attended by three parties (apart from Yeltsin): Skuratov, Prime Minister Primakov and head of the FSB Putin. Skuratov was depressed, pleaded to be allowed to keep his post and promised 'full cooperation'. Yeltsin was firm, 'I shall not work with you!' (This is how Yeltsin remembers the episode in his book). Primakov also asked the procurator to resign. Putin as the FSB boss unemotionally reported on the official forensic results: the tape was genuine, not a falsification. Yeltsin handed Skuratov a pen and paper and said, 'Write your letter of resignation!' Skuratov wrote the second letter. The Council of the Federation received a new presidential submission on Procurator General's dismissal but Skuratov unexpectedly showed up at the session with a request to stay. His dismissal got a minority of votes and so the Kremlin lost the second round too.

'Yevgeny Maksimovich Primakov was seemingly in favour of Skuratov's resignation,' Tatyana Yeltsin recollects, 'but I remember how in one of our conversations he suddenly told me, "Tanya, why are you digging in your heels over this Skuratov? If he stayed he would be in our pocket." I was stunned with this logic.'

Meanwhile the crisis was escalating. After the second vote in the Council of the Federation, Alexander Voloshin, the incumbent head of the Presidential Administration — suggested a compromise: those in favour of Skuratov should stop their support of him and guarantee that he would resign, whilst the new Procurator General must be approved of by both conflicting parties. Such a mutually acceptable candidate was found (Moscow procurator Ponomaryov) and ostensibly the crisis was over.

However, all of a sudden, Menatep put forward some new conditions. The President was to sign a letter on promoting Ponomaryov's nomination *prior* to the vote on Skuratov. Only in such a case would they guarantee the latter's resignation.

Yeltsin gave orders to stop all negotiations with Skuratov's representatives.

In relation to 'Mabetex case' (let me remind you that Skuratov first announced its existence at the Council of the Federation, during the first vote), criminal proceedings were instigated against Procurator General himself.* Yuri Skuratov was temporarily suspended from office and an Acting Procurator General was brought in.

Skuratov took active part in discrediting Yeltsin and his family in the summer of 1999 and even tried to stand for presidency in 2000 where he collected 0.43% of votes, but on the whole he was slowly drifting into public oblivion. He had nothing else to produce apart from the notorious 'Mabetex case'.

'So what was this "Mabetex case" all about?' I ask of Valentin Yumashev.

'It was simply a case of self-defence. Skuratov was trying to present things in such a way that the tape would be seen as a frame-up needed to drop the investigation of Yeltsin's family. In reality he launched no investigation. The case was properly looked into after his retirement when Tanya and Lena were summoned to the Procurator's Office for questioning. The records of those interviews exist, all filed in the case materials.'

'So what transpired? What were the investigators' conclusions?'

'The Procurator's Office spent a long time trying to work out how, why and when those ill-fated credit cards came into existence (the total amount drawn from them over three years was 70 thousand dollars). In the end it turned out that the money had been drawn from a personal

---

* The case materials revealed that the Presidential Chancellery had ordered a dozen of expensive suits for Yuri Skuratov.

account, Boris Nikolayevich's fee for his memoirs, that's all. The case was investigated and closed.'

As for Primakov's eventual resignation nearly all those who tried to explain it later preceded from the assumption that it was President's response to the crisis — allegedly, Yeltsin decided to strengthen his position and keep his power. However, had Yeltsin really needed *guarantees* of a quiet existence in the Kremlin until the year 2000 he would have clasped at the draft political contract suggested by Primakov. Moreover, the core of Primakov's effort was to fix, secure and somewhat 'freeze' the political situation. Small sacrifices, little trade-offs and compromises — that was the gist of what he was offering by way of a new course, yet this was exactly what was sitting so wrongly with Yeltsin — this new climate where the very concept of the country's development would alter.

Meanwhile the developments were accelerating. On 9 April 1999 Yeltsin made a public announcement: 'Do not believe the rumours that I want to dismiss Primakov, disband the government and so on. All this is idle talk and gossip. This is not what is happening and it won't happen. I believe that at this last stage, at this phase, Primakov is useful, afterwards we'll see. It is a different story that the government must be strengthened. This question is, indeed, on the agenda.'

Primakov answered several hours later revealing his pique on TV:

'I would like to use this opportunity to address, once again, those who create this anti-government fuss: calm down, I have no ambitions or desire to stand for presidency, I do not cling to my position of Prime Minister, all the more so since the timeline for my performance has been identified — today I am useful and then we'll see...' It was their first public 'skirmish'. A thunderstorm was brewing.

Yeltsin's next step was to appoint Sergey Stepashin, Minister of the Interior, to become First Vice-Premier. Stepashin was the only person in the government who used '*ty*' speaking to Primakov, they were on excellent terms. Several days later, at a session held on April 27th, Yeltsin suddenly came to a halt, frowned and said, 'Your seating is all wrong. Stepashin is the First Deputy. Kindly swap places.'

## THE SECOND TERM (1996-1999)

On May 12th when Primakov came along to the Kremlin with his routine report Yeltsin delivered a message that the former had been expecting for some time: 'You have fulfilled your role. Now you probably have to resign. Please make my task easier, write the letter and quote any reason you like.' He didn't want a row. He was grateful to Primakov but was experiencing some dismay and unease. There was nothing personal in this decision — he felt profound respect for Primakov, he was simply carrying out his own plan.

Primakov asked the President no questions, certain that he had been 'toppled' by the mischief-makers and intrigue. 'During those weeks,' writes Leonid Mlechin, 'Primakov had it tough. He was struck down with an acute attack of sciatica and needed an operation, but he kept his spirits.' So his response was grim and tense: 'No, I won't do it. I have no desire to make it easy for anyone. You have every constitutional authority to sign the respective decree. But I would like to warn you, Boris Nikolayevich, that you are making a huge mistake. It is not about me, it is about the cabinet of ministers that works well. The country has overcome the crisis. The people believe in the government and its policy. It is a mistake to replace the government.'

Yeltsin was reluctant to part with Primakov on this sour note. For some reason he asked whether Primakov had a car and how he would make it home. Primakov sullenly replied that he would take a taxi. At which point Yeltsin suddenly felt poorly, pushed a button and the doctors rushed into the office. As soon as the president felt better and the medics had left he got to his feet, gave Primakov a hug and said, 'Let us still be friends.' That is how Yevgeny Maksimovich remembered this episode.

Yeltsin himself recollected this resignation somewhat differently:

'I looked at Yevgeny Maksimovich one more time. What a shame. What a terrible shame. It was the most dignified resignation I had ever seen. Also the most courageous.'

The Dumas' communist faction had foreseen such developments and was rushing the impeachment procedure seeking to remove the president from power by constitutional means. It should have started days later but Yeltsin's decision was unexpected: to dismiss Primakov not after the vote but before. The step looked illogical. On learning about this unceremonious treatment of the popular premier the Duma would hit the ceiling. But it turned out differently.

The communists failed to get enough votes for a formal impeachment and suffered yet another defeat to Yeltsin. The deputies didn't want to exacerbate the situation yet again and Sergei Stepashin became Premier at the first attempt. He was spared the painful experience of a failed vote that Chernomyrdin and Kirienko both had to go through. As it transpired, Stepashin's premiership was short-lived — only three months. It would be reasonable to ask — why?

... In this connection, in an interview to *Time* weekly Vladimir Putin said that his first conversation with Yeltsin had taken place as early as autumn of 1998 although no one had known about it.

'When had it been decided that Putin was the main candidate for Prime Minister? When had their first conversation taken place and how and when had Yeltsin made this decision?' I ask of Valentin Yumashev.

'Most likely, during 1997-1998, the president must have had such preliminary chats with several people. Among them — I am only guessing here — must have been First Vice-Premier Boris Nemtsov, the former Minister of Justice in Gaidar's government, president of the Chuvash Republic Nikolai Fyodorov, certainly — Viktor Chernomyrdin. By spring of 1999 Yeltsin included Sergei Stepashin in this list too (at the time he was Minister of the Interior) and Minister of Railways, Nikolai Aksenenko. There may have been others. Yeltsin was trying to assess his interlocutors' reactions; it was as if he was trying to feel their pulse, have the measure of them. Naturally, every one of them was asked to keep their conversation strictly confidential.'

Stepashin's appointment was this 'long pause' for which Yeltsin was famous. It preceded his final move. In his book Yeltsin explains that it would have been wrong and dangerous to announce Putin as his successor over a year before the election. The economic situation in the country was difficult and the premier had to shoulder the burden of unpopular decisions which is why it was important to show your hand only at the last moment.

There were, however, other reasons. By dismissing Primakov Yeltsin had been taking risks already. He was understandably apprehensive lest

## THE SECOND TERM (1996-1999)

Putin's appointment should send unwanted tremors and cause a conflict within special services. He feared that the State Duma, being aware of his troubled relations with Primakov, would not vote for him. On the other hand, Stepashin's relations with Primakov were close and warm. So this also influenced Yeltsin's decision. Opinions within the presidential team were divided. Anatoly Chubais for example, was in favour of Stepashin whilst Yumashev was against. After a long reflection Voloshin was also inclined to be supportive.

Having heard all arguments Yeltsin made his decision. He submitted Stepashin's candidature to the Duma. To the amazement of the sceptics, the deputies approved his nomination relatively painlessly. So, although Vladimir Putin remained the main candidate, Sergei Stepashin now had a realistic chance to amend this pre-election set up. His post gave him sufficient grounds for laying claims to leadership.

However, Sergei Stepashin started wasting his potential rather rapidly. From the very first steps, he entered into a stand-off with First Vice-Premier Nikolai Aksenenko. He decided that Aksenenko had his sights on his post and was rather nervous when Boris Nikolayevich would sometimes invite Aksenenko to their meetings. However Yeltsin had been doing the same years before when he would invite — to the Kremlin or his residence in Gorky-9 — Chernomyrdin together with Nemtsov and Chubais. He treated the government as one team. Nevertheless, Stepashin was put out by it.

The conflict between the premier and his senior deputy turned the atmosphere within the government sour; the consequence was a paralysis of will, and a vacuum of decisions. By the end of July a vexed Yeltsin realised that it was time to move. He couldn't procrastinate with Putin's appointment any longer. Once more, Sergei Stepashin's resignation was painful for Yeltsin. He liked Sergei Vadimovich, they had come through a lot together, particularly as after the Budennovsk disaster in 1995 when Stepashin had resigned he didn't sink into obscurity, along with the other *Siloviki*. He carried on, first working for a government department, then as Minister for Justice and finally as Interior Minister. Yet now, at the pinnacle of his career, Yeltsin had to part with him.

Yeltsin asked Vladimir Putin, the future Premier, and First Vice-Premier Nikolai Aksenenko to come over, too, and be present at the decisive conversation with Stepashin. The conversation proved difficult and uncomfortable. Sergei Stepashin took his resignation even harder than his predecessor. Having already retired, he kept blaming Aksenenko for such a turn of events and felt slighted by Yeltsin's aides who, in his view, had prompted the president's decision. In fact, no one could 'prompt' Yeltsin into anything. His 'prompt' and 'impact' had come from elsewhere: sober pragmatism and Yeltsin's famous *gut feeling* that had always been guiding his actions in the moments of crisis.

This 'delayed' appointment was taking place against the background of some dramatic events of the summer of 1999 as the pace of events progressively quickened.

After Primakov left and Stepashin first came to office a new media war was gaining momentum as a witch hunt was mounted against the president and his family.

The subject of the 'Family' first appeared in 1998 — as a kind of target practice. Huge hoardings had been erected along Moscow thoroughfares, on them — the message: 'The Family loves Roma. Roma loves the Family.' The newspaper *Moskovsky Komsomolets* hurried to provide the key, in case someone had been a little slow on the uptake: *Roma* meant Roman Abramovich, the owner of Sibneft. The friendship between Valentin Yumashev, Tatyana Dyachenko and Abramovich was first mentioned by Alexander Korzhakov in his controversial book that came out in 1997.

Why had the topic of the 'Family' been selected — rather than something else? After all, a variety of other themes had already been road-tested by the communists: economic depression in the early nineties; devastation caused by default; the deplorable state of events in public health and the social sphere, in the army and science, and if nothing else — the state of Yeltsin's health including his proverbial alcoholism.

The answer is evident — it was the most *striking* subject, a reflection of the times. Entrepreneurship in the new Russia was teeming with close relatives (wives, children, brothers and sisters) of regional leaders and mayors of small towns, since no legal ban on 'profiteering from family connections' had existed at the time. Moreover, it was practically impossible to impose a ban like this when many other countries do not have it either. It is a different story that legislation in these cases is much more detailed in an attempt to prevent corruption and emergence of monopolies. It's no coincidence that European states are frequently shaken by scandals caused by mere 'trifles' from the Russian point of view: expensive gifts, business trips sponsored by the wrong party or unreasonably high personal expenses of functionaries. It is not only a fear of going beyond the law that is a regulator of social relations; there it is also the mechanism of public opinion, an independent press and the centuries-old ethical traditions.

The Russian independent press in the nineties was very actively closing in on 'high-placed bosses launching their relatives in business'. The Russians knew perfectly well of Yuri Luzhkov's family getting rich, or the riches accumulated by Samara's governor Titov. Many other governors and mayors were in the frame too.

It was hard for a common person to believe that the Russian president and his family *do not follow suit*, do not behave in this way, so common in Russia. The seeds fell on fertile soil and the first salvo rang out in May of 1999. NTV's programme *Itogi* (Outcomes) offered detailed explanations of who was distributing the financial flows, who was in charge of what within this murky structure that had virtually enslaved the politics and economy in Russia: Yumashev, Dyachenko, Voloshin, Berezovsky, Abramovich, Mamut and, finally, President Yeltsin himself, the Godfather of the criminal syndicate. Tatyana, Yeltsin's daughter, became a fixture in the *Kukly*\* (Puppets) show. Whilst previously the show's main themes had mostly been political battles, now it was the 'Family' and its influence.

The next stage in exposing the 'Family' was a dedicated 45-minute-long broadcast about a dacha in Nikolina Gora\*\*, allegedly owned by Yeltsin's daughter; followed by a programme on the 'Family's' assets abroad: villas in Germany, castles in France, houses in England. The 'Mabetex case' was dug up again, along with bank accounts in the West, embezzlement of the IMF tranche in 1998 and 'underhand dealings' with the GKOs. The term 'the Family's purse' became ubiquitous. This tag was being slapped now on Abramovich, now on Mamut, and then on Berezovsky.

The second fashionable theme was usurpation of power: Yeltsin was being isolated (his health came to the fore yet again), it was impossible to

---

\* A show similar to *Spitting Images*.

\*\* Nicholas' Hill, prime real estate nearby Moscow.

break through to see him since the 'Family' had erected tall barriers, his dependence on others while making decisions — all of this is, even now, cropping up in one book or another.

The pretexts were easy to find. Media holdings belonging to Gusinsky were bursting with articles on the subject, with *Segodnia* (Today) daily and *Itogi* (Grand Total) weekly firmly on the case and closely followed by their TV counterparts. TV audiences, of course, had no way of knowing that it was the same people carrying out the same orders. However, by now it was of little consequence: the main thing was that the theme had lifted off.

Moscow's municipal media, city channel sponsored by Luzhkov among them, were keeping pace with NTV. Luzhkov couldn't forgive Yeltsin his failed attempt to become Premier in 1998. The hurt still rankled. At the high point of this character assassination campaign, the Moscow Mayor announced publically that the president must refute charges of theft *in court*. The saddest thing was that this public persecution was primarily instigated by the channel on NTV, ostensibly the most 'democratic' and liberal network that announced objectivity to be their mission statement, and the *truth* — their main achievement and banner. In addition, Yeltsin's adversaries knew perfectly well that the president would not press charges against the media: it was his age-long unbreakable principle. It all looked like a win-win situation.

'I have never been close to Gusinsky,' Valentin Yumashev tells me, 'but I did know NTV director Igor Malashenko well, we were friends, he had been actively involved in the elections in 1996. In July of 1996 Malashenko was the leading candidate for becoming Head the Administration, right after the election. Igor then turned it down and the post went to Chubais. This is just to show how open and trusting my attitude towards him was. When it was debated who would replace Kirienko after the crisis in August and the President asked me for my opinion, I asked him to receive me together with Malashenko. I told him that the question was so complex that it baffled straightforward assessment and it would be better to have several opinions. We then spent over an hour discussing the most sensitive issues, the 'pros' and 'cons' of each candidate. I trusted Igor implicitly and knew that he would not leak any information he had received that meeting. Then a mere year later all this hogwash started coming from NTV. I met Malashenko and asked him, "Igor, you do know

## THE SECOND TERM (1996-1999)

Tanya, Boris Nikolayevich and his family. You know that they are pure as snow, how can you lie through your teeth, every day, on air?"'

'And what did he reply?'

'He said, "Yes, I know. But these are team rules and I cannot do a thing. You have already lost, you do not control the situation, you are off-course politically, you are doomed. That is why the media campaign will go ahead."'

By the end of this campaign (which smoothly petered out on the NTV channels by March of 2000, right after the completion of the presidential election) the readers, viewers and listeners came away with a very clear feeling: that the 'Family' owned everything, practically, the entire country. They were in possession of the atomic industry, non-ferrous metallurgy, civil aviation, oil production, entire companies, wells, fields and so on.

But now, years later, a logical question suggests itself. Where is all this that, allegedly, once belonged to them?

Tatyana Yumasheva, Yeltsin's daughter provided the answer in her blog:

'There is this well-publicised lie that as long as I was working for the Kremlin I had been putting together an estate worth tens of millions (hundreds of millions or billions — depending on acuteness of a writer's schizophrenia). I repeat: it is a lie. Still, I will try to put a full stop in this discussion. How? It's simple: by going through each lie and each piece of gossip. I suggest that we use the simplest tool — *glasnost*. Do you remember this old word that sprang up in the eighties?

Now the charges against me — allegedly, during my years in the Kremlin I was rendering services to various businessmen who, as a pay-back, gave me shares in companies they owned. Next: I was paid not only in shares but was given villas, houses, flats, mansions, residencies and other real estate: in Moscow, in the country and abroad — in England, France, Austria, Germany, Italy and other European countries. Also mentioned have been presents of cars, beautiful and expensive — but this is already a trifle, a cherry on the cake.

I have never owned shares in any companies: be it Sibneft, Gazprom, Lukoil, Aeroflot, ORT, Svyazinvest, Rusal or Nornickel — not one of them. I suggest that you add the names of every company created or privatised — in the nineties or since. It is easy to verify this information. Nearly all companies have changed hands, they are owned by new names that, understandably, have no duty to pay me (although the old ones owed me nothing, either). It is easy to access the register and check that I am telling the truth.

There were scores of publications about my palatial residence at Nikolina Gora. The first articles appeared in 1998 and by the end of 1999 there was a tsunami of such accounts. Some commentators are still asking me about this house. This is what I propose and I'd like to be specific here: journalists who were describing the riches belonging to me at Nikolina Gora were working for the NTV and the TVT Channels, newspapers *Segodnia* (by now extinct), *Versia*, *Top Secret* and some others. You can all make your way to that house, knock on the door and ask the owners when they moved in and how long they have been there. Moreover, one can approach, on behalf of any publication, local authorities and verify with whom that house and the land plot are registered and receive the information on the owners. It can be done by anybody. But I can predict what you will find. Neither I, nor anyone of my relatives has ever had anything to do with that house.

What about France, the Côte d'Azure? From time to time various villas, chalets, houses and the like are brought to people's attention. I stated in my interview to the magazine *Medved* (Bear) — I have nothing. I also added that any person who finds any property that belongs to me anywhere in the world may keep it.'

The paradox is in the fact that when Yeltsin was President he would routinely dismiss those suspected of pursuing a personal agenda. At times he was unfair but he believed it to be a very serious argument: if there is controversy this person must leave. That is why he kept Luzhkov from entering the major power structures and parted with Korzhakov and his team — such examples are numerous. But it was lining his personal pockets — a charge hurled at him by those who were far from being angels themselves — that is so unjust.

The theme of the 'Family' was mooted from another angle too.

It was said and intimated in writing that when very poorly, Yeltsin was only accessible to several individuals and that it was those individuals, the narrow circle, that in effect was in command of everything, who could push through any decision, get any document signed.

Valery Semenchenko, chief of presidential secretariat in Yeltsin's times, recounts:

'The procedure for submitting documents to the president and receiving them afterwards had always been in place, of course, but at the point when Korzhakov was getting documents signed by Yeltsin, under Chubais as Head of Administration, this procedure was made considerably tighter. President Yeltsin would not be able to sign anything that had not been given approval by the government and enforcement agencies, amongst others. Any document could only get to him from me, carrying all the necessary signatures and satisfying all formal requirements. Not a single sheet of paper could bypass my folder. No one could get Yeltsin to sign anything without having collected all the requisite signatures first.'

'It is alluded to in press that in his final years the President had very few meetings, access to him was impeded and one could get an audience only through Tatyana, his daughter. Is it true?' I asked.

'It was impossible for purely technical reasons. An aide-de-camp on duty was responsible for updating the President of all telephone calls received by the special communications terminal. In other words, any minister, general, high-placed functionary with a special communications phone on his desk could place a call to him at any time, and the officer on standby would report. He would do it without fail; otherwise it would have been a breach of duty. Moreover, a rather large group of people had a direct line to the president, that is to say, a telephone directly connected to Boris Nikolayevich's desk unit — the Prime Minister, ministers of enforcement agencies, all his aides — and they were using this facility constantly. As for Yeltsin's working schedule, it was always very intense wherever he was, be it in the Kremlin, at home or in hospital. As a rule, once or twice a week he would meet Prime Minister, Head of Administration and his aides. He was constantly in communication with Vice-Premiers, deputy administration heads and all the enforcement ministers. A large pile of documents would end up on his desk daily in a rather thick folder, each of which he had to read and enter his opinion or signature.'

I ask Valentin Yumashev once more, 'They say and write that during the last years it was a "collective Yeltsin" — the President delegated his principal functions to a narrow circle of advisors and that they, or rather you, were making decisions instead of him while Yeltsin would only agree to what you said.'

Yumashev responded, 'Yeltsin never made his decisions without first sounding several people out. Examples abound in memoirs and the published documents. For example, in March of 1996 when dissolution of the Duma was at stake which included the date for elections, Yeltsin sought the opinions of his aides and the *Siloviki* — Korzhakov, Barsukov, Interior Minister Kulikov and Chubais, and only after that he came to his own conclusion. Or, say, Berezovsky's appointment to and dismissal from the post of Security Council's Secretary (by the way, on both scores my view was different to that of Yeltsin's). Or take the post-default situation when the Duma wouldn't endorse Viktor Chernomyrdin as Premier. Luzhkov's candidature split the administration right down the middle, so on Boris Nikolayevich's request I brought Sergei Yastrzhembsky and Andrei Kokoshin to Gorky-9, so that he could listen to them directly and not be briefed through a memo or by me. I was opposed to appointing Sergei Stepashin Prime Minister after Primakov (I thought Putin should be appointed there and then). But Boris Nikolayevich would get everyone's views and then make up his own mind. In other words, if I am one of the prominent "Family" members Boris Nikolayevich often did exactly the opposite to what I advised.'

In his book, *Presidential Marathon*, Yeltsin wrote the chapter on Putin's appointment with a somewhat tongue-in-cheek heading 'Yeltsin Looses His Marbles' –echoing the public reaction to a new Prime Minister. Everyone was puzzled at what fault could the President have found with an easy-going and amiable Stepashin. Not only did the opposition, still seething over Primakov's dismissal, not know what to make of it — friends were at a loss too. Anatoly Chubais saw it as his duty to warn the President of conceptual mistakes, trying to prove that Putin wouldn't do and Stepashin was the best option. Stepashin, too, was hurt when he told to resign and made two attempts to make the President change his mind.

The statistics showed that during his time in office Yeltsin fired five premiers and over thirty Vice-Premiers. What was he trying to achieve? In his book, Yeltsin gives this explanation: the time was moving too fast, the priorities flashing by with kaleidoscopic speed. Besides, he adds, thanks to their work in the government, new politicians were emerging on the political arena, they were making a name for themselves and following their resignation were filling a political vacuum inherent in a new democracy. With few exceptions, this was true. Even Alexander Rutskoy came out of Lefortovo and became governor, not to mention Lebed and others. It was clear evidence that in the great scheme of things Yeltsin was not vindictive. He had no doubts when deciding on yet another dismissal for he knew that if those people would prove their integrity and usefulness they would return.

In this case, however, the implication behind this new appointment was different. President Yeltsin believed that Russia's future was at stake. He was right of course. It is a different story whether he saw it correctly and managed to guess its course adequately.

Vladimir Putin was approved by the Duma as Acting Premier with unexpected ease, already in the first round. His future looked vague, though. Yeltsin's adversaries felt elated. They didn't take Putin seriously — he was hardly known, with negligible poll ratings of just 2%. At this point, Yeltsin and his family were being hunted down with an increasing frenzy.

And then came a moment when Russia froze in shock. The second Chechen war broke out. Initially, in the summer of 1999, no one made too much of the Chechen militants' incursion into Dagestan but soon after a full-scale military operation followed — with none other but Putin in command. Then, in September, there were explosions in Moscow, which sent shivers through the country. These were spine-chilling events: physically — since the houses blown up in the dead of the night buried hundreds of peacefully sleeping people under the rubble, but psychologically — it was a shock, too. Suddenly, fear reigned.

In all my life I do not recall when I was so frightened of living in Moscow...
In September of 1999 Muscovites were afraid of going out of their homes, letting the children go to school, getting around in the city. It

was hugely similar— in terms of its psychological impact — to the New York tragedy that occurred two years later. Residents were forming neighbourhood watch schemes, spending the sleepless wandering around their houses, torches in hand. Militia was inundated with tip-offs on 'suspicious individuals' as people were staring fixedly out of their windows into the pitch dark of the night...

The first Chechen war caused a public outrage. The second was approved by the majority of the population and practically all political elites.

But not right away.

It is forgotten now, but sociological surveys initially showed that the idea of the second Chechen war was *extremely unpopular*. It was believed that the army was ill-prepared and the political risk was too high. The first positive response came with the first triumphs of the Russian army.

'The Presidential Administration considered that the consequences of yet another Chechen operation would be unpredictable and the risk unjustifiably high. I personally suggested to Putin that the full-scale operation should be delayed till at least after the election,' said Valentin Yumashev in our conversation. 'Putin responded, "We may never make it to the election." He was convinced that the answer should be tit for tat, otherwise the fear would destabilise the country. I felt that getting bogged down in Chechnya for the second time was insanely risky. But Boris Nikolayevich supported Putin right away.'

For the first time in his entire presidency Yeltsin delegated coordination of the security ministries to a new Prime Minister. At the time, no one could predict that the war in Chechnya, with its thousands of casualties on both sides, with horrible TV images broadcast morning and night — just as in 1995, would prove, bizarrely, to be Putin's launch pad in politics. Putin's own view was that he was a hostage of circumstances, so he envisaged that once his duty was done he would be sent into retirement.

Meanwhile, he called for to the state to mobilise its armed force. Here was a Prime Minister who managed all the enforcement agencies in a businesslike and level-headed manner. Also, he spoke the language of the courtyard, the street, a food queue, and the country went wild over his famous 'we shall wipe them out in the privy'. In a nutshell, Putin injected into the political mentality the idea of indomitable *force*, the force used as the last and decisive argument to overcome a crisis. People wanted the Kremlin to be occupied by a victor, a protector. The new readiness to fight the Chechen lawlessness quickly extrapolated to a readiness to fight any lawlessness as such. Putin's behaviour signalled these messages: to punish, to chastise, to install order, to set up rigid barriers, to demand unquestionable submission to the will of the state. Within several months Putin's poll ratings grew phenomenally.

There is a plethora of theories, guesses and ideas as to why Yeltsin chose Putin. The President's closest aides suggested him among other candidates, but the final decision was unquestionably Yeltsin's.

So what prompted his choice?

Unlike the scenes during Chernomyrdin, Primakov and Stepashin's resignation, when Yeltsin could see how those politicians latched on to the idea of future power, Putin amazed him with his self-control.

To him — like the entire country — Yeltsin's offer was a shock. He couldn't really believe that he would be raised to such a high post. Both presidents describe that situation in their books and recollect their dialogues practically verbatim. But even the exact recollection of words still does not explain the subtext.

Putin simply didn't see himself as a public politician, a future president. He was trying to make Yeltsin understand. The heavy burden of becoming the first person in the country was a totally unexpected turn of events in Putin's estimation — yet it was impossible to refuse. There was, of course, the fact that Putin, although an FSB director and a career KGB officer to start with, had worked for a long time for Anatoly Sobchak's administrations and later for the administration in the Kremlin. He was, therefore, perfectly cognizant of the nitty-gritty of politics in the Kremlin and generally was at home there. First and foremost, however, Yeltsin had Vladimir Putin down as a firm democrat and a zealous support of market economy which, without doubt, for Yeltsin was the decisive argument.

Meanwhile Russian troops had occupied the Chechen territory along the Terek River, blockaded Grozny and started pushing the militants into the foothills. Initially, the war looked competent, reasonable and unquestionably efficient. The end seemed in sight.

There, have, of course been a number of conspiracy theories concerning Putin's advent to power. The perennial one, at home and abroad, maintains that the intervention of militants into Dagestan and the explosions in Moscow and Volgodonsk had been a deliberate scenario. There are some vague 'testimonials' about the Kremlin representatives having met with the Chechen emissaries in the spring of 1999. There are some fragmented and perfunctorily dated records of Berezovsky' telephone conversations with leaders of the Chechen separatists. There are also some partial evidence on the FSB having allegedly been in the know about the terrorist acts in preparation. The general premise seems very tendentious.

A government that has started a war which sooner or later becomes unpopular is always accused of being the one who has provoked the war in the first place. This is ABC of politics. Moreover, during the initial years of the 'independent Ichkeria"'s' existence, separatist leaders were making money engaging in the unsophisticated criminal business. However, starting from 1999, they turned to setting up terrorist acts within Russia. Proof to this is in subsequent developments such as the Dubrovka[**], Tushino[***], Beslan[****] and Avtozavodskaya Metro blasts[*****]. All these acts had been planned meticulously and reveal the same hand. The fact that the war

---

[*] The Chechen's word for denoting the name of their republic: Chechnya.

[**] The Moscow theatre hostage crisis, also known as the 2002 *Nord-Ost* siege, was the seizure of the crowded Dubrovka Theater on 23 October 2002 by some 40 to 50 armed Chechens who claimed allegiance to the Islamist militant separatist movement in Chechnya. They took 850 hostages and demanded the withdrawal of Russian forces from Chechnya and an end to the Second Chechen War.

[***] 5 July 2003 — According to the official version, 20-year-old Chechen woman Zulikhan Elikhadzhiyeva blew herself up outside a rock festival at the Tushino airfield near Moscow; her bomb did not detonate as expected.

[****] 1-3 September 2004 — A group of armed, mostly Ingush and Chechen, Islamic terrorists took more than 1,100 people (including 777 children) hostage at School Number One in the town of Beslan, North Ossetia. Some of the adult hostages were killed. On the third day, Russian security forces stormed the building. At least 334 hostages, including 186 children, died, hundreds more were injured and many were reported missing.

[*****] The Moscow Metro bombing occurred on 6 February 2004 when a male suicide bomber killed 41 people near Avtozavodskaya Metro station (on the Zamoskvoretskaya Line) in Moscow. Up to 120 people were injured in the incident, some of the more common injuries being broken bones and smoke inhalation.

## THE SECOND TERM (1996-1999)

in Chechnya proved to be new Russian President's first step towards an unprecedented popularity could not initially been predicted.

Meanwhile, the parliamentary elections earmarked for December of 1999 were drawing close. By now, the media attacks on Yeltsin were no longer backed by the communists. In the autumn of 1999, Luzhkov and Primakov joined ranks openly, whilst NTV's owner, Gusinsky decided to support this political tandem. Primakov's political gravitas and Luzhkov's organisational and financial capacity were now channelled into setting up a party of 'disgruntled governors'. This party was called Otechestvo (Fatherland) which, come the election in December of 1999, took a new course — a course against Yeltsin. Yeltsin and all his policies provided the principal target. Despite the number of governors in the party dwindling after each new statement of Putin's, it still wielded force. Together with the communists Otechestvo stood a chance of finally getting an absolute majority in the parliament and legally seizing power in the country in the run-up to the presidential election.

Yeltsin's administration actively set about creating yet another party — Yedinstvo (Unity). As soon as the new prime minister expressed his support for this new entity its rating immediately soared. Yedinstvo (together with SPS, the party of democrats headed up by Sergei Kirienko) received a sufficient number of seats in the parliament to prevent Otechetsvo and the communists from gaining a majority. It was an important victory. Moreover, a year and a half after the election Yedinstvo and Otechastvo announced that they were merging — which is how Yedinaya Rossia (One Russia) came into being.

Vladimir Putin's election team came to be led by a young St Petersburg lawyer Dmitry Medvedev. Few could foresee the role that would be played in the history of Russia by of this unassuming well-mannered young man who seemed to shun publicity. Yeltsin was following the election progress closely. He was witnessing what had looked totally unrealistic only several months earlier: the presidential party was winning while Primakov, Luzhkov and the communists were lagging far behind. These were moments of encouragement for him but, ultimately, the triumph gave way to major doubts.

Yeltsin didn't want to leave prematurely. His view of the election in 2000 was that at the appointed time he would leave, having handed over his authorities to the president elect, in full adherence to the law and the Constitution. It would all go according to plan. However, the political situation decreed something else. Putin was at the peak of his popularity as Prime Minster, but what if there were surprise developments in the Chechen war? What was to happen in the new parliament? Which dangerous corners were lying in wait in the next few months? What if he, the incumbent president, would be in the way of a newly elected one? Yeltsin however became certain that Putin would be President. Yeltsin consequently spent several days in agonised reflection, received no advisors, and devised a plan for an early election. In addition, the parliamentary election and Putin's debut coinciding with the milestone date in history — the dawning of the new millennium — Yeltsin had always been the person for the big and striking gesture. The new era in Russia would come to the chime of the Kremlin clock -

… It would be really dramatic.

He decided to keep this decision to himself until he reluctantly include those who needed to know about his New Year farewell to the nation, these being: Putin, Voloshin, Yumashev and his daughter Tanya.

On December 31st Yeltsin came to the Kremlin for the last time. His heart was heavy but he was hiding his emotions. He was trying to keep himself together. In the morning he recorded his address. He met with Patriarch Alexis II who came along to offer him seasonal greetings. He summoned to his office all his staff, aides, advisors, speechwriters, secretaries and aides-de-champ, clinked glasses with everyone and gave everybody a personal goodbye.

He noticed tears in many eyes.

He was overwhelmed with the most powerful emotions: here, in this office, he lived through so much as God forbid anybody else would have to.

He then gave Putin his pen with which he had been signing decrees.

There would be no speeches, no live coverage, no packed audiences. There would be no show.

'Take care of Russia,' he said to Putin.

Yeltsin stepped out of the entrance into the frosty air of the New Years Eve — the scene of many events in his life. He climbed into the car and left for Gorki-9. He went home.

This is what the country heard on that day.

'Dear citizens of Russia!

The magical date in our history will arrive shortly. The year 2000 is approaching; it will mark a new century and a new millennium. We have all tried it for size. As children and later, when we grew up, we used to envisage how old we would be in 2000, how old our Mum would be, and our children. It once felt that this singular New Year was so far ahead…

Dear friends! My dears!

It is my last time today to offer you my New Year greeting. But this is not all. Today is the last time that I am addressing you as President of Russia.

I have made up my mind.

I have been pondering over it long and hard. Today, on the last day of the outgoing century, I am retiring. I have heard it said many times: Yeltsin would cling to power by hook or by crook, will never give it up. It is a lie.

This is not the point. I have always been saying that I would not digress from the Constitution by one iota, that the Duma elections must be held within the timeframe stipulated by the Constitution. And this is what has happened. It was also my desire that the presidential election would be held on schedule — in June of 2000. It was important for Russia. We are setting the momentous precedent of a civilised handover of power — from one President of Russia to a newly elected one.

However, I have made a different decision. I am leaving. I am leaving ahead of the due time.

I have realised that I must do it. Russia must enter the new millennium with new politicians, new faces, with new, bright, strong and energetic people.

And we, those who have been in power for many years now, we must leave. Having seen how much hope and trust has been invested by people in voting for the new generation of Duma politicians I have realised that I have done the most important duty of my life. Russia, now, will never turn the clock back. Russia will only be moving forward now.

And I mustn't impede this natural course of events. Why hold on to power for another half a year when the country has a strong person worthy of presidency and the one on whom practically every Russian is pinning his or her hopes for the future? Why should I hold him back? Why wait another half a year? No, that's not my style! It's not in my nature!

Today, on this incredibly important day for me, I would like to say something very personal, more personal than usual. I want to ask your forgiveness.

I ask your forgiveness because many of our dreams have not come true and many things that seemed easy have turned out to be torturously hard. I am asking forgiveness for having not justified the hopes of those who believed that we would be able, in one thrust, in one fell swoop, to leap from the grey and stagnant totalitarian past into the bright and rich civilised future. I believed in it myself. It felt it would only take one surge.

One surge has proved insufficient. In a way, it turns out I have been too naive. Some problems have been simply too hard. We have been cutting our way through mistakes and failures. Many people had been profoundly shaken in those hard times.

But I want you to know something. I have never said it before and it is important for me that I say it today. The pain of each one of you was resonating in me, in my heart...

I am leaving. I have done all I could. I am being succeeded by a new generation, the generation of those who would be able to do more and better.'

Next Boris Yeltsin announced that under the Constitution, Vladimir Vladimirovich Putin was to be Acting President and that the early presidential election would take place in three months' time.

He wished everyone happiness and peace. He offered his New Year greetings.

And then he left.

# Six Peaceful Years

In 2000, immediately after his resignation, Yeltsin visited Israel. He went to Bethlehem and Jerusalem, as he explains in his book, to attend festivities on the occasion of the 2000th anniversary of Christianity. 'At the airport I asked a member of the welcoming party, "And what about the star, has it risen yet?" Bashfully, he replied that the visibility was poor because of the rain. I simply had to see that star over Bethlehem. After all, the start of a new millennium since Christ's birth marked my second birth too.'

The new page in his life was not completely free of drama. Early in 2001 Yeltsin succumbed to a serious bout of pneumonia. In effect, he was at death's door and had to be connected to the ventilator, for which purpose an artificial coma was induced. Chancellor Helmut Kohl, who paid him a visit at that time said, 'It looks like I would have to visit Russia again, shortly, and on a very sombre mission.' Kohl was wrong — Yeltsin pulled through and survived. By the summer of 2000 his recovery, though slow, was complete. Yeltsin even resumed playing tennis.

In the autumn of 2007 when I arrived in Barvikha to interview Naina Yeltsin I asked to be taken to Yeltsin's library, his favourite room after retirement. There is yet another myth about Yeltsin — allegedly, he was an ignoramus. But in the years of his presidency he had to read scores, even hundreds of documents, complex texts full of specialised terminology. Luckily, Yeltsin could read in pages and had a photographic memory (his daughter Lena takes after him in this respect).

'Come along, I'll show you something,' said Naina Iosifovna. 'He brought it from Sverdlovsk.' I looked over and there, on the shelf, cheek by jowl sat the familiar 200 volumes of the World Classics Library*, all well-thumbed and tattered. I couldn't believe my eyes: Yeltsin had read everything! There was a shelf with war memoirs, with books on history, art and psychology. He also read fiction, for example decided to read the complete works of Haruki Murakami, but having read two of his titles said that he got it all, thank you, no more. He ordered Tanya to choose some contemporary Russian authors and she would bring him 20-30 books a week.

He was making up for wasted opportunities after years in a most punishing job. He was enjoying this new life of his so much and hated it when Naina Iosifovna had to leave his side. The family tried to reason with him: come on, Mum also wants to go somewhere, go out sometimes. He grumbled, 'So what... she finds it more interesting than my company?' But he didn't like to stay at home either, loved theatre and the company of friends. They were inseparable with Naina Iosifovna, especially on travels, of which he was a great enthusiast. Trips were planned well in advance. In January he and his assistant of many years — Vladimir Shevchenko — would sit down together and make monthly allocations. Afterwards, he demanded unswerving adherence to 'the plan', as had been his wont during the years in the Kremlin. Normally, he made three or four foreign trips a year.

Having retired, Russia's first president had no intention of becoming a hermit. Yet, his 'public debuts' were heavily mixed with anxiety: how would they greet him in his new capacity? On 7 January 2000 the first Russian president, together with Naina Iosifovna, attended the ceremony of the Triumph Awards**. The audience got to their feet and gave him a standing ovation. Yeltsin was deeply moved.

He believed that he shouldn't just retreat into his private life, sever all ties with those he had worked with him through the years. Among the first of

---

* A famous series first initiated by Maxim Gorky in 1918.

** An important prize in the Russian Federation awarded for the best works in literature and arts.

such appointments was a meeting with the Kremlin pool: journalists and media reporters who had been accompanying him on the trips within and outside Russia. All those present remembered his jokes and warm parting words, although in the past many of them had been less than friendly in their writing. With the help of his trusted assistant Shevchenko, Yeltsin introduced an iron routine of meetings and contacts: President Putin, Head of Administration Voloshin, Yeltsin's *Siloviki*, heads of the CIS countries and Yeltsin's G8 colleagues — Clinton, Kohl and Chirac.

He made three visits to France — to attend Roland Garros, the world's premier clay court tennis tournament, and the Davis Cup final that was won by the Russian team. After the decisive match he rushed down to the court to hug 'our boys'. Watching sports on TV was Yeltsin's second passion — after reading. Once after a night-time programme he was getting ready for bed. The lights were dimmed; he didn't notice a step, fell and fractured the neck of his femur — a serious injury at this age. This happened in the autumn of 2006 in Italy, and although the surgery was successful he was left with persistent pains in that leg.

During those years Yeltsin travelled twice to Italy, visited Ireland and Greece, Norway and Jordan. He also spent some vacations in the Crimea as a guest of the Ukrainian President Kuchma, visited the presidents of Kazakhstan and Kirgizia, travelled a lot around the country and was by no means a stranger in his native Yekaterinburg where he would visit the major annual international volleyball tournament bearing his name. In a word, he lived a full life. And though from time to time he would be grumpy: 'I cannot go on like this, I need to be doing something!', he never returned to public life.

Putin was a politician whom he had led into the Kremlin by the hand and so Yeltsin believed himself responsible for all his actions, which is why he could express any criticism and his point of view only in private, and in no other way and why he was inaccessible to journalists, took no part in international conferences, conducted no lectures and did not write any more books.

And this is probably what gave rise to the last myth around Yeltsin — about 'special arrangements' between Yeltsin and Putin. Hundreds if not thousands of articles and books have been published on the nature of those arrangements. On the other hand, it is understandable since Yeltsin's silence was in a way mysterious. But Yeltsin realised better than anybody that no arrangements would make sense: a new president must make his own way and one shouldn't hold him to any commitments.

The decree on presidential retirement had nothing to do with some special guarantees or arrangements. This decree simply came to fill the vacuum for which the preceding Duma was to blame. The new Duma of 2000 made a law that applies to all presidents of Russia who resign or retire. In a legal sense it is a summary of similar laws that exist elsewhere. Yeltsin's Decree on the retired President of the USSR, Gorbachev, had been based on the same precepts but since it concerned the president of a vanished country it couldn't form the legal base for legislators.

The provisions of this law deal with simple things, the daily 'details' that appear in such cases. Where should the former president live? What method of transport should he use and at whose cost? In case he is entitled to personal security (if only as a repository of a lot of classified information) — what shape should it take, out of where should it be financed? Should the incumbent president wish to make an urgent call to the former one — who must ensure the availability of this urgent and timely communication?

These provisions have been borrowed from international practice, none of it came into being solely because of President Yeltsin. Incidentally, contrary to public belief, provisions do not apply to members of the president's family.

During those last six years Yeltsin loved his domesticity, although he was an unusual stay-at-home person. The house where he lived is a huge residence with hectares of an adjacent park around it. One can go for long walks there, especially if one had company. But the family, steadily growing over the years, was the focus of those years. In 2001 Tanya married Valentin Yumashev and they had a daughter together, Masha. Thus, Yeltsin had six grandchildren: Katya, Borya, Masha, Gleb, Vanya and another Masha, the little one. His granddaughters Katya and the older Masha, born in 1979 and 1981 respectively, gave him four great-grandchildren. Yeltsin loved splashing around with his brood in a swimming pool, and go on long walks. For him, these six years were by no means boring. By the end of his life God granted him peace.

At the end of April he went to the Kremlin hospital for some scheduled procedures. He felt better and was even going to return home. On the morning of the day when Naina Iosifovna was getting ready to go and collect him from the hospital she received a call from the hospital telling her that he was very ill. Ignoring doctors' arguments, in the morning he suddenly hustled to get up, swung out of bed abruptly and passed out.
This is the official communiqué on his death:
'The first President of Russia died from 'the progressive cardio-vascular multisystem failure, i.e. dysfunction of all internal organs caused by the cardio-vascular disease'. He passed away on Monday, 23 April 2007, at 15:45 at the Central clinical hospital.'

# Epilogue

On 24 April 2007, at about five in the evening I came out of the foyer of the Kropotkinskaya Metro Station. A queue was winding along the embankment: people lined up in front of the Cathedral of Christ the Saviour to bid farewell to Boris Yeltsin. Later I learned that people had been reserving a place at three in the morning, sometimes by entire families. There were young faces, people of my age — let's call them middle-aged — and, of course, lots of older people too.

I had envisaged something like a funereal Hyde Park — passionate political debates and pronouncements incited by the personality of the deceased but it wasn't like that at all. People were sad and calm, taking stock of each other as if trying to see who came along and why, their faces strangely familiar, as if some images from the old photographs, newsreels of the late eighties and early nineties, with their rallies, the Vasilievsky Spusk and the White House. There was no frenzied commotion, no hysteria. It took me some time to understand my own emotions.

… Like everybody else I made my way towards the cathedral's gate, went through the metal detector erected by the militia, caught sight of the vaulted ceiling covered with paintings, and heard the words of prayer officiated by priests.

I could see the president's family, seated on chairs around the coffin. Mourners were many and varied — presidents, former and incumbent, artists, actors, writers, just friends. It was a family event. The most out-of-place thing was the guard of honour: the old Soviet tradition whereby big

# EPILOGUE

bosses, replacing each other in accordance with their rank, stand guard, red armbands in place, and affect dolour. This waft of officialdom was unpleasant.

The farewell to the first president was said in the church. This was the first such occasion in the atheistic and profoundly Soviet XX century. The last Russian tsar to have been given the church burial was Alexander III. It happened in 1883. Yeltsin was lying in state, his body barely visible under flowers. I gazed across the gilded barrier at his pale motionless face.

'Please, do not linger,' the guard spoke softly but firmly.

On the way back, by the metro, I finally heard what I had been expecting: a heated argument between two elderly members of intelligentsia.

'Under him, there was freedom!' explained the first.

'There was hunger!' retorted the other.

The first one thought it over and answered firmly, 'You know, there has always been hunger but never freedom.'

Yes, it was a revisited monologue from Dostoyevsky's 'Grand Inquisitor'. I looked closer at those two old men. And suddenly I worked out my feelings and could finally give a name to the sentiment of the queue — its tacit, reserved and quiet concentration.

The queue wasn't formed of millions, stampeding and sobbing like it was at Stalin's funeral, certain that the world had collapsed but tens of thousands of reasonable, clear-headed and strong people, his voters. It was essential for us, those in the queue, to work out: what are we grateful to him for?

The spring evening was chilly, fragrant and light. By the cathedral I bumped into my friend, a news photographer Yuri Feklistov. We dropped into some tiny restaurant in Ostozhenka Street, to drink to Boris Nikolayevich's memory. Yuri smiled as he remembered photographing an excited Yeltsin, hot from a game on the tennis court, or the White House in 1991, when Rostropovich suddenly appeared there. He was the author of this famous image: a beaming Rostropovich, cradling a submachine gun as if it were a cello, and a hefty guy, asleep on his shoulder.

Stepping out of the bar into the darkness I suddenly realised: it was the end of that era.

When Yeltsin died it was as if a heavy pause hung over the country for several hours. Everyone was in a state of shock. Just then President Putin was meeting with the President of Turkmenistan and the accredited journalists were saying later that on learning about Yeltsin's death he couldn't control his emotion. On 24 April 2007 *Kommersant* daily wrote that 'President Putin was preparing a statement on the occasion of the demise of the first president of Russia. The text was composed by him personally, he corrected the draft several times. In his TV address to the nation he announced that April 25th would be the day of national mourning:

'... Today I am offering my deepest and most sincere condolences to Naina Iosifovna, the family and those close to Boris Nikolayevich. It is our grief, too. We will do our best to ensure that the memory of Boris Nikolayevich, his noble designs, his words "Take care of Russia" will remain our moral and political benchmark... Gone is the person who started a new epoch. A new democratic Russia has been born.'

Only after that did the mass media recover. Thank God, this warmth, as if on cue, was not hypocritical, merely initiated from above. It was sincere, but to substantiate this sincerity, it took some other voices speaking in contrast to the rest.

Some of Yeltsin's principal enemies were castigating him even on those days. Strangely enough but it was them who put an important question before everyone watching their TVs: had he been a *great historical figure* or a destroyer?

Leon Aaron, his American biographer, sums this up: 'There are few comparisons in modern history: either a country is not sufficiently large and important, or the scope and profundity of crisis is not as huge, or there hasn't been one single person that has played such an absolutely pivotal role. Against those criteria, only two very tall men may be seen as Yeltsin's predecessors*. They were against not only an abrupt breakdown of the state's integrity and viability across the entire country's territory but also a catastrophic disruption of the popular consensus over national objectives and ways of their attainment, as well as rights and duties of citizens. To call

---

\* Abraham Lincoln and Charles de Gaulle. — *Autours comment.*

someone a great man means to admit that he... made a deliberate step and progressed significantly beyond the scope of ordinary human abilities...'

Yeltsin did make this step, no doubt about it. However, this was the American perception of Yeltsin, a global view if you will. How about the Russian view?

*Vladimir Putin*: 'Having become president on the will of the millions he changed the face of power, destroyed the impenetrable wall between the society and the state and served his people loyally and courageously... At times he deliberately attracted fire to himself, assumed personal responsibility for the tough but necessary decisions, boldly shouldering the hardest roles when creating key democratic institutions.'

*Anatoly Chubais*: 'More than once I have caught myself thinking that we wouldn't have been able to do a thing had... his career not spanned the posts of a construction companies' boss, the First Secretary of the Sverdlovsk *Obkom* and then of Moscow *Gorkom*. He would have lost a huge portion of his base and, accordingly, we would have been doomed. In other words, Yeltsin's personality was bringing together people of different worlds, languages, mentalities and values. One thousand years of our history are rich in dramatic events but few of them have been equally profound and cataclysmic... This was the stroke of luck for Russia — that Boris Nikolayevich turned out to be not only a big personality comparable to the greatest names in Russian history, he turned out to be equal to the scope of change.'

*Yegor Gaidar*: 'One shouldn't have him down as a professional historian or a professional economist, but what this country is all about and how complex it is he, to put it bluntly, understood better than most. He didn't welcome violence and always tried to eschew it. In the grand scheme of things he managed to do this. He did avert a full-scale civil war like the one in 1917-1918 although to avert violence completely was probably not possible at the time...'

*Eldar Riazanov*: 'His honesty, naivety and absolute integrity, so unusual in a statesman, were delightful. He could be sly but it was so artless and, of course, Boris Nikolayevich was uncommonly charismatic. He simply had this gift.'

On the anniversary of his death, a TV channel showed the documentary about Yeltsin shot by Alexander Sokurov, probably the best film about him — which ends thus: Yeltsin leaves for Moscow, in his office car, along a common country road. He passes by forests, meadows, country houses — our normal landscape, to the accompaniment of the heart-rending symphonic music. Sokurov's lens lingers on Yeltsin's car as if he wants to tell him something, to pass on some hidden sentiment. The film was made at a very troubled moment when it was not clear what was to happen to Yeltsin or to us. *Yeltsin's journey* is enigmatic but this journey was formidable and must never be forgotten.

On the day of his resignation and his final speech, on 31 December 1999, I received a telephone call from my university friend Lena, a rather bright lady. She asked me what I was making of it all. I said that the old man did all right. 'You reckon?' she answered. 'As for me, without him, I am suddenly uneasy. Aren't you?'

Some were full of dread in Yeltsin's time. Some were uneasy when he left. We are all different. I have written this book so that we all try and pause for thought: about him and about us.

And about Russia, of course.

# Photographs

Boris Yeltsin at the Soviet-US Conference on Trade and Economic Cooperation.
Moscow, 4 December 1991.

Photo: Alexander Chumichev / ITAR-TASS Russia News Agency

Boris Yeltsin at the Security Council meeting.
Moscow, 8 March 1996.

Photo: Alexander Chumichev / ITAR-TASS Russia News Agency

Boris Yeltsin addresses his election campaign rally and the audience at the concert in his support. *Vasilievsky Spusk, Moscow, 12 June 1996.*

Photo: *Alexei Sazonov, author's archive*

Boris Yeltsin speaks at his election campaign rally, before a concert at the Vasilievsky Spusk. Moscow, 12 June 1996.

Photo: *Alexei Sazonov, author's archive*

Borsi Yeltsin. 1996.
Photo: *Archives of the Boris Yeltsin Presidential Centre*

Nikolai and Klaudia Yeltsins. The village of Butka, Sverdlovsk Oblast.
Photo: *Family album*

The house where Boris Yeltsin was born. *Butka in the 1960s.*
Photo: *Family album*

The house where Boris Yeltsin borne, taken in 1994.

Photo: *Anatoly Semekhin / ITAR-TASS Russian News Agency*

Naina Yeltsin. 1950s.

Photo: *Family album*

Boris Yeltsin and his books. 1959.

Photo: *Family album*

Boris Yeltsin as a coach of the Urals Polytechnic women's volleyball team. A knockout tournament — the RSFSR National Volleyball Championship. Kurgan, July of 1952.

Photo: *Family album*

DSK's personnel at the May Day demonstration. 1960s.

Photo: *Family album*

First Secretary of the Sverdlovsk Obkom Boris Yeltsin at a meeting with the studenst. The Youth Centre, Sverdlovsk, 1982.

Photo: *Archives of the Boris Yeltsin Presidential Centre*

Yakov Ryabov, First Secretary of the CPSU Sverdlovsk *Obkom*, and Boris Yeltsin, Member of the Obkom, at a *subbotnik* (voluntary community work). Early 1970s.

Photo: *Archives of the Boris Yeltsin Presidential Centre*

First Secretary of the Sverdlovsk Obkom and Boris Yeltsin on manoeuvres with the Urals Military Command. 1978.

Photo: *Archives of the Boris Yeltsin Presidential Centre*

First Secretary of the Sverdlovsk Obkom Boris Yeltsin on a tour of inspection to assess preparedness of the oblast's farms for the upcoming sowing campaign. Artemovsky Disrict. 12 May 1979.

Photo: *Archives of the Boris Yeltsin Presidential Centre*

In December of 1985 Boris Yeltsin was appointed First Secretary of the Moscow Party's *Gorkom*.

Photo: *Yuri Lizunov, Alexander Chumichev / ITAR-TASS Russia News Agency*

Following his speech at the October plenary of the CPSU in 1987 Boris Yeltsin was removed from the post of the CPSU Politburo's candidate member and stripped of duties of the Moscow party cell's first secretary. Pictured: Boris Yeltsin, Jurmala, 1988.

Photo: *Sergei Kivrin / Author's archive*

Boris Yeltsin at a rally in support of Gdlyan and Ivanov. Moscow. 20 May 1989.
Photo: *Victor Koshevoi / ITAR-TASS Russia News Agency*

Boris Yeltsin at a rally in Mezhdurechensk, 18 August 1990.
Photo: *Valentin Kuzmin, Valery Zufarov, Anatoly Kuziarin / ITAR-TASS Russia News Agency*

Boris Yeltsin at the miners' rally, Prokopievsk, 30 April 1990.
Photo: *Dmitry Sokolov, Anatoly Kuziarin / ITAR-TASS Russia News Agency*

Boris Yeltsin, in front of the RSFSR's House of the Soviets reads out the appeal 'To Citizens of Russia'. Moscow, 19 August 1991.

Photo: *Valentin Kuzmin, Alexander Chumichev*

Boris Yeltsin sworn-in as the President of the RSFSR. 10 July 1991.

Photo: *Dmitry Donskoy / Archives of the Boris Yeltsin Presidential Centre*

Boris Yeltsin and his mother. Late 1980s.
Photo: *Vladislav Vetlugin / Archives of the Boris Yeltsin Presidential Centre*

Boris Yeltsin, June 1997.
Photo: *Archives of the Boris Yeltsin Presidential Centre*

President of Russia Boris Yeltsin and Elizabeth II, Queen of the United Kingdom, in the foyer of the Moscow's Bolshoi Theatre. 18 October 1994.

Photo: *Dmitry Donskoy / Archives of the Boris Yeltsin Presidential Centre*

President Yeltsin and Elizabeth II, Queen of the United Kingdom,
with spouses, before the official lunch on board the Royal Yacht Brittania.
St. Petersburg, 20 October 1084.

Photo: *Alexander Chumichev / ITAR-TASS Russia News Agency*

The NATO-Russia summit. A meeting between President of Russia, Boris Yeltsin and President of the United States, Bill Clinton. Paris, France. 26 September 1997.

Photo: *Alexander Chumichev, Alexander Sentsov / ITAR-TASS Russia News Agency*

At the G-8 summit, with the US President Bill Clinton.
Birmingham, UK. 17 May 1998.

Photo: *Alexander Chumichev, Alexander Sentsov / ITAR-TASS Russia News Agency*

President of the United Stated Bill Clinton, President of the Russian Federation Boris Yeltsin and President of the Ukraine Leonid Kravchuk (left to right) at the tripartite meeting. Moscow, 14 January 1994.

Photo: *Alexander Chumichev, Alexander Sentsov / ITAR-TASS Russia News Agency*

President of the Russian Federation Boris Yeltsin (on the left) and Prime Minister of Japan Ryutaro Hashimoto are about to set off on a boat trip down the Yenisei River. The Pine Residence near Krasnoyarsk became the venue for the first informal meeting between the leaders of the two countries.
Krasnoyarsk Territory, 1 November 1997.

Photo: *Alexander Chumichev / ITAR-TASS Russia News Agency*

London. Prime Minister of the United Kingdom John Major is leading the official delegation at Boris Yeltsin's departure at the airport. 26 September 1994.

Photo: *Alexander Chumichev / ITAR-TASS Russia News Agency*

President of Russia Boris Yeltsin and President of the United States Bill Clinton (left to right) at their joint press conference. Naples, 25 July 1994.

Photo: *Alexander Sentsov, Alexander Chumichev / ITAR-TASS Russia News Agency*

The 1996 Nucelar Security Summit. Jean Chrétien, Bill Clinton, Jaqcues Chirac, Lamberto Dini and other summit participants, at the gala performance in the Kremlin. Moscow, April 1996.

Photo: *Dmitry Donskoy / Archives of the Boris Yeltsin Presidential Centre*

President Yeltsin talking to Yekaterinburg residents. June 14, 1996.

Photo: *Alexander Chumichev / ITAR-TASS Russia News Agency*

President Yeltsin chatting to the Second World War veterans.
Heroes' Sqaure, Krasnodar, 16 April 1996.

Photo: *Alexander Chumichev / ITAR-TASS Russia News Agency*

Boris Yeltsin among his think tank (Analytical Group) members.
From left to right: Georgy Satarov, Sergei Shakhrai, Vasily Shakhnovsky,
Yeltsin's daughter Tatyana, Boris Yeltsin, Anatoly Chubais, Victor Iliushin,
Igor Zverev, Igor Malashenko. June 4, 1996.

Photo: *Dmitry Donskoy/ Archives of the Boris Yeltsin Presidential Centre*

In his office (study if at home). Moscow, 28 May 1998.

Photo: *Alexander Chumichev / Archives of the Press and Information Office of the Presidential Administration of Russia*

In his office (study if at home). Moscow, 1998.

Photo: *Archives of the Press and Information Office of the Presidential Administration of Russia*

President of the Russian Federation Boris Yeltsin. December 25, 1996.

Photo: *Alexander Chumichev / ITAR-TASS Russia News Agency*

A business meeting between Boris Yeltsin and Chairman of the Russian Federal Government, Victor Chernomyrdin. Central Kremlin Hospital, Moscow, September 29, 1996.

Photo: *ITAR-TASS Russia News Agency*

Boris Yeltsin presenting a gift of a pen to Vladimir Putin. December 31, 1999.

Photo: *Alexander Chumichev, Alexander Sentsov / ITAR-TASS Russia News Agency*

Boris Yeltsin on vacation. The Volga Crag health spa.
Samara Oblast, 5 August 1997.

Photo: Alexander Chumichev, Alexander Sentsov / ITAR-TASS Russia News Agency

# Timeline of
# Boris Nikolayevich Yeltsin's Life

| | |
|---|---|
| 1931 | Born on 1 February 1931 in the village of Butka, in Talitsky District of Sverdlovsk Oblast in the family of Nikolai and Klavdia Yeltsins |
| 1950 | Enters Urals Polytechnic (UPI) to study industrial and civil engineering |
| 1955 | Graduates from the institute and works for *Uraltyazhtrubstroi* complex of enterprises mastering various trades |
| 1956 | Marries Anastasia (Naina) Guirina, fellow UPI student |
| 1957 | Becomes foreman of the *Yuzhgorstroi*. His first daughter Yelena is born |
| 1960 | His second daughter, Tatyana, is born |
| 1961 | Joins the Communist Party of the Soviet Union (CPSU) |
| 1966 | Becomes director (top manager) of the DSK |
| 1968 | Is appointed head of the Sverdlovsk CPSU *Obkom*'s construction department |
| 1976 | First Secretary of the Sverdlovsk *Obkom* of the CPSU |
| 1985 | Is appointed head of the CPSU Centrals Committee's Construction Department, then CC CPSU Secretary for Construction, First Secretary of the Moscow *Gorkom* |
| 1986 | Is elected alternative member of the Politburo of the CC CPSU |
| 1987 | Presentation at the October plenary of the CC CPSU, dismissed as the *Gorkom*'s First Secretary at the Moscow *Gorkom* plenary |

1988   Is appointed First Deputy Chairman at the USSR *Gosstroi*, dismissed from the post of Politburo alternative member, elected delegate to the XIX All-Union Party Conference

1989   Elected deputy of First All-Union Congress of People's Deputies, at the Congress joins the Inter-Regional Group of Deputies

1990   Is elected deputy to the First Congress of the RSFSR People's Deputies where is elected Chairman of the RSFSR Supreme Soviet, resigns from the Communist Party

Is elected President of the RSFSR

1991   On *August* 19th-21st heads resistance to the putsch (GKChP); *December*, together with Ukraine's President Kuchma and Chairman of the Byelorussian Supreme Shushkevich signs Belovezha Accords whereby the USSR cesses to exist as a 'geopolitical reality'

1992   Heads up the new government of Russia, launches an economic reform later referred to as 'shock therapy' (on 1 January 1992 prices set free; transition to market economy)

1993   Signs Decree No 1400 whereby the Congress and the Supreme Soviet of the People's Deputies of Russia are pronounced dissolved; new parliamentary election and a referendum on the new Constitution of Russia; issues an order on suppressing the insurgence of the Supreme Soviet's supporters by military force; signs a decree on the new Russian Federation's symbols of power (anthem, emblem and flag)

1994   In *December*, a military operation is launched in Chechnya

1996   Is re-elected President of the Russian Federation

1998/1999   A dire financial crisis in the country brings about a crisis in politics and a sequence of Prime Minister's resignations (Chernomyrdin, Kirienko, Primakov and Stepashin)

1999   A new war in Chechnya. On 31 December 1999 Boris Yeltsin announces his early resignation and a handover of power to Vladimir Putin

2007   On April 23rd the first President of Russia Boris Nikolayevich Yeltsin dies. Is buried at the Novodevichie Cemetery in Moscow

# Bibliography

Aron, L., *Yeltsin: A Revolutionary Life* (New York: St. Martin's, 2000)

Boiko, M., Vasiliev, D., Yevstafiev, A., Kazakov, A., Koch, A., Mostovoi, P. and Chubais, A., *Privatizatsia Po-Russki* [Privatization: Russian Style] (Moscow: Vagrius, 1999)

Boldin, V., *Krushenie Pedestala: shtrikhi k portretu M.S. Gorbacheva* [A Smashed Pedestal: Brush-Strokes on Mikhail Gorbachev's Portrait] (Moscow: Respiblika, 1995)

Chernyaev, A., *Shest Let S Gorbachevym* [Six Years with Gorbachev] (Moscow: Progress, 1993);

Available in English as: Anatoly S. Chernyaev, *My Six Years with Gorbachev*, trans. and ed. R. D. English and E. Tucker (University Park: Pennsylvania State University Press, 2000)

Doktorov, B.Z., Oslon, A.A. and Petrenko, E.S., *Epokha Yeltina. Mnenia Rossiyan. Sociologicheskiye Ocherki* [Yeltsin's Epoch. Opinions Held by Russians. Sociological Essays] (Moscow: 2002)

*Epokha Yeltsina: Ocherki Politicheskoy Istorii* [Yeltsin's Epoch: Essays on Political History] (Moscow: Vagrius, 2001)

Filatov, S., *Sovershenno Nesecretno* [Strictly Non- Confidential] (Moscow: Vagrius, 2000)

Gaidar, Ye., *Guibel Imperii* [Collapse of an Empire], (Moscow: 2006)

Available in English as: Gaidar, Ye., *Collapse of an Empire*, trans. A. W. Bouis (Brookings Institute Press, 2008)

Gorbachev, M., *Soyuz Mozhno Bylo Sokhranit* [The Union Could Have Been Saved] (Moscow: AST, 2007)

Available in English as: Gorbachev, M. S., *On My Country and the World*, trans. G. Shriver, (Columbia University Press, 2000)

Gorbachev, M., *Zhizn I Reformy* [Life and Reforms] (Moscow: Novosti, 1995)

Available in English as: Gorbachev, M., *Memoirs* (New-York, Maryland: Doubleday, 1996)

Grachev, A., *Gorbachev: Chelovek Kotory Khotel kak Luchshe* [Gorbachev: A Man Who Meant Well] (Moscow: Vagrius, 2002)

Available in English as: Grachev. A. S., *Gorbachev's Gamble: Soviet Foreign Policy and the End of the Cold War* (Polity, 2008)

Iz Istorii Sozdaniya Konstitutsiyi Rossiyskoi Federatsiyi [From the History of Creating the Constitution of the Russian Federation] (Moscow: 2007)

Khinstein, A., *Yeltsin. Kreml. Istoria Bolezni* [Yeltsin. Kremlin. Clinical Records] (Moscow: Olma, 2006)

Korotich, V., *Ot Pervogo Litsa* [First Person Narrative] (Moscow: AST, 2000)

Korzhakov, A., *Boris Yeltsin: Ot Rassveta Do Zakata* [Boris Yeltsin: From Dawn till Dusk] (Moscow: Interbruk, 1997)

Kostikov, V., *Roman S Prezidentom* [An Affair with the President] (Moscow: Vagrius, 1997)

Lebed, A., *Spektakl Nazyvalsia Putch* [This Show Was Called Putsch] (Tiraspol: 1993)

Levandovsky, A.A., Shchetinov, Yu.A. and Mironenko, S.V., *Istoria Rossiyi: XX — Nachalo XXI Veka. Uchebnik dla 11 klassa obshcheobrazovatelnykh uchrezhdeniy.* [History of Russia: XX — Early XXI Century. Textbook for 11th Form of the Institutions for General Education] (Moscow: 2007)

Ligachev, Ye., *Predosterezheniye* [Warning] (Moscow: Pravda International, 1999)

Maniukhin, V., *Pryzhok Nazad. O Yeltsine I Drugikh* [A Leap Backwards. On Yeltsin and the others] (Yekaterinburg: Pakrus, 2002)

Mlechin, L., *Kreml. Prezidenty Rossiyi. Strategiya Vlasti ot B. N. Yeltsina do V.V. Putina* [Kremlin. Presidents of Russia. The Strategy of Power from Boris Yeltsin to Vladimir Putin] (Moscow: Tsentrpoligraph, 2003)

Mlechin, L., *Yevgeny Primakov. Istoria Odnoi Kariyery* [Yevgeny Primakov. History of a Carrier] (Moscow: Tsentrpoligraph2007)

Moroz, O., *Tak Kto Zhe Rasstrelial Parliament?* [So Who Shot the Parliament Down?] (Moscow: Olimp, 2007)

Nemtsov, B., *Ispoved Buntaria* [Confession of a Nonconformist] (Moscow: Partisan, 2007)

Pikhoya, R., *Moskva. Kreml. Vlast* [Moscow. Kremlin. Power] (Moscow: Rus-Olimp, Astrel, AST, 2007)

## BIBLIOGRAPHY

Primakov, Ye., *Minnoye Pole Politiki* [The Minefield of Politics] (Moscow: Molodaya Gvardia, 2007)

Ryabov, Ya., *Moi XX Vek. Zapiski Byvshego Sekretaria TsK KPSS* [My XX Century. Notes of a Former CC CPSU Secretary] (Moscow: Russiy Biographicheskiy Institut, 2000)

Shakhnazarov, G., *S Vozhdiami I Bez Nikh* [With and Without Headmen] (Moscow: Vagrius, 2001)

Sobchak, A., *Khozhdeniye Vo Vlast* [The Journey into Power] (Moscow: Novosti, 1991)

Sukhanov, L., *Tri Goda S Yeltsinym. Zapiski Pervogo Pomoshnika* [Three Years with Yeltsin. Notes of a Senior Aide] (Riga: Vaga, 1992)

Tarpishchev, Sh., *Pervyi Set* [The First Set] (Moscow: Vremia, 2008)

Troshev, G., *Moya Voina, Chechenskiy Dnevnik Okopnogo General.* [My War. The Chechen Diaries of a General from the Trenches] (Moscow: Vagrius, 2004)

*V Politburo TsK KPSS... (Po Zapisiam Anatolyia Cherniayeva, Vadima Medvedeva, Georgia Shakhnazarova)* [At the Politburo of the CC CPSU... (As recorded by Anatoly Cherniayev, Vadim Medvedev and Georgy Shakhnazarov)] (Moscow: The Gorbachev Foundation, 2006)

Vorotnikov, V., *A Bylo Eto Tak... Zapiski Byvshego Chlena Politburo* [And This Is How It Happened: Journal of a Former Politburo Member] (Moscow: Sovet Veteranov Knigoizdaniya, 1995)

Yakovlev, A., *Sumerki* [Twilight] (Moscow: Materik, 2003)

Yeltsin, B., *Ispoved ne Zadannuyu Temu.* [Confessions on a Chosen Topic] (Moscow: Ogonyok 1990)

Available in English as: Against the Grain: An Autobiography, trans. Michel Glenny (New-York: Summit, 1990)

*Yeltsin, B., Zapiski Presidenta* [President's Journal] (Moscow: Ogonyok, 1994)

Available in English as: Yeltsin, B., *The Struggle for Russia,* trans. C. A. Fitzpatrick (New-York, Random House, 1994)

*Yeltsin, B., Presidnetskiy Marafon* [The Presidential Marathon] (Moscow: AST, 2000)

Available in English as: Yeltsin, B., Midnight Diaries, trans. trans. C. A. Fitzpatrick (New York, Public Affairs, 2000)

*Yemelyanov, A., Gorbachev-Yeltsin: 500 Dnei Politicheskogo Protivostoyaniya* [Gorbachev-Yeltsin: 500 Days of a Political Stand-Off], in: Dobrokhotov, L.N., (ed.), Gorbachev-Yeltsin: 500 Dnei Politicheskogo Protivostoyania [Gorbachev-Yeltsin: 500 Days of a Political Stand-off] (Moscow: Terra, 1997)

DEAR READER,

thank you for purchasing this book.

We at Glagoslav Publications are glad to welcome you, and hope that you find our books to be a source of knowledge and inspiration.

We want to show the beauty and depth of the Slavic region to everyone looking to expand their horizon and learn something new about different cultures, different people, and we believe that with this book we have managed to do just that.

Now that you've got to know us, we want to get to know you. We value communication with our readers and want to hear from you! We offer several options:

- Join our Book Club on Goodreads, Library Thing and Shelfari, and receive special offers and information about our giveaways;

- Share your opinion about our books on Amazon, Barnes & Noble, Waterstones and other bookstores;

- Join us on Facebook and Twitter for updates on our publications and news about our authors;

- Visit our site www.glagoslav.com to check out our Catalogue and subscribe to our Newsletter.

Glagoslav Publications is getting ready to release a new collection and planning some interesting surprises — stay with us to find out!

Glagoslav Publications<br>
Office 36, 88-90 Hatton Garden<br>
EC1N 8PN London, UK<br>
Tel: + 44 (0) 20 32 86 99 82<br>
Email: contact@glagoslav.com

# Glagoslav Publications Catalogue

- *The Time of Women* by Elena Chizhova
- *Sin* by Zakhar Prilepin
- *Hardly Ever Otherwise* by Maria Matios
- *The Lost Button* by Irene Rozdobudko
- *Khatyn* by Ales Adamovich
- *Christened with Crosses* by Eduard Kochergin
- *The Vital Needs of the Dead* by Igor Sakhnovsky
- *METRO 2033* (Dutch Edition) by Dmitry Glukhovsky
- *METRO 2034* (Dutch Edition) by Dmitry Glukhovsky
- *A Poet and Bin Laden* by Hamid Ismailov
- *A Russian Story* by Eugenia Kononenko
- *Kobzar* by Taras Shevchenko
- *White Shanghai* by Elvira Baryakina
- *The Stone Bridge* by Alexander Terekhov
- *King Stakh's Wild Hunt* by Uladzimir Karatkevich
- *Depeche Mode* by Serhii Zhadan
- *Wolf Messing - The True Story of Russia`s Greatest Psychic* by Tatiana Lungin
- *Herstories*, An Anthology of New Ukrainian Women Prose Writers
- *Watching The Russians* (Dutch Edition) by Maria Konyukova
- *A Book Without Photographs* by Sergei Shargunov
- *The Grand Slam and Other Stories* (Dutch Edition) by Leonid Andreev
- *The Battle of the Sexes Russian Style* by Nadezhda Ptushkina
- *Down Among The Fishes* by Natalka Babina
- *disUNITY* by Anatoly Kudryavitsky
- *Sankya* by Zakhar Prilepin
- *Andrei Tarkovsky - A Life on the Cross* by Lyudmila Boyadzhieva
- *Solar Plexus* by Rustam Ibragimbekov
- *Don't Call me a Victim!* by Dina Yafasova
- *Tsarina Alexandra's Diary* (Dutch)

More coming soon...

www.ingramcontent.com/pod-product-compliance
Lightning Source LLC
Chambersburg PA
CBHW020036120526
44589CB00032B/355